THE OPEN LEARNING FOUNDATION

An Active Learning Approach

Business Economics

THE
OPEN
LEARNING
FOUNDATION

An Active Learning Approach

BUSINESS ECONOMICS

E.W. Orchard, John Glen, James Eden

BLACKWELL
Business

Copyright © Open Learning Foundation Enterprises Ltd, 1997

First published 1997

Blackwell Publishers Ltd
108 Cowley Road
Oxford OX4 1JF
UK

Blackwell Publishers Inc
350 Main Street
Malden, Massachusetts 02148
USA

British Library Cataloguing in Publication Data

A CIP catalogue record for this book is available from
the British Library

Library of Congress Cataloging-in-Publication Data

Library of Congress data has been applied for.

The ISBN for this title is 0–631–20179–3

Typeset in 10 on 12pt Times New Roman

Printed in Great Britain by T. J. International Ltd.

This book is printed on acid-free paper

Acknowledgments

For the Open Learning Foundation

Martin Gibson, *Series Editor*

Maurice Bennington, *Open Learning Editor*

David Royle, *Copy Editor*

David Forrest (University of Salford), *Reviewer*

Leslie Mapp, *Director of Programmes*

Stephen Moulds, (DSM Partnership), *Production Manager*

Tim Gutteridge, *Publishing Manager*

Rachel Spungin, *Programmes Assistant*

The Foundation would also like to thank Kathleen Farren and Lynda Kerley for their assistance in producing this text.

Copyright acknowledgments

CONTENTS

Unit 5   The Theory of Distribution   237

Unit 6   Introduction to the Macroeconomy   277

Unit 7 National Income Determination 333

Unit 8   The Role of Money and the Financial System

Unit 9   National Income Determination and Aggregate Supply

GUIDE FOR STUDENTS

Course introduction

Welcome to Business Economics. The objectives of this guide are:

- to give you an outline of the subject of business economics;
- to explain why it is necessary for you to study business economics as part of your degree;
- to describe the nature of the material on which this workbook is based;
- to outline the programme which you will be following;
- to offer some practice hints and advice on how to study business economics using the open learning approach; and
- to point out some of the advantages to you of studying business economics by the method used in this book.

What is business economics?

Economics is concerned with the study of scarcity and the consequences of scarcity. Individuals, households, businesses and nations all experience some level of scarcity, in that they do not possess all the resources to satisfy all their wants and needs. Decisions have to be made to balance those scarce resources in order to improve what can be achieved with them. Individuals have to decide how to spend their income, household budgets have to be managed, business need to deploy their resources in order to ensure their profitability and governments need to consider the best possible balance of spending to meet the needs of competing groups within society. Economics is concerned with how these decision are made, with how the resources of a nation or a business are allocated and utilised in the production of goods and services, and with how the rewards of these activities are distributed.

Within this text we are particularly concerned with how the analytical tools and concepts of economics can be used in order to create an understanding of business behaviour.

In the first part of the text we focus in particular on what economists term the "microeconomics environment". Here we are concerned with behaviour of the individual firm and to understand this we will need to consider the relationship between the business and its market. We will explore the ways in which demand and supply conditions operate and interact and how this influences such factors as, for instance, the price of goods and services and decisions about the quantities that will be produced.

In the second part of the emphasis shifts to the "macroeconomic environment", the term used to refer to the study of the economy as a whole. In particular we will be concerned with understanding the ways in which governments attempt to influence economic activity by for instance altering the conditions which affect supply and demand for goods and services, by adjusting the supply of money, changing the tax structure and so on. Prevailing economic conditions clearly have an impact on business as do expectations about future economic conditions. The emphasis in this text is upon the interaction of business and the economy, with factors such as inflation, economic growth and unemployment being considered in terms of their relevance to business.

Why study business economics?

Economics is a vital part of the business studies curriculum and it is one of the key disciplines contributing to our understanding of the business environment and business decision making. Prevailing economic conditions, including for example the rate of inflation, the level of unemployment or the government's taxation policies all impose constraints (or in some cases create opportunities) for business. Likewise more rational business decisions will be possible if managers understand factors affecting demand for their products, can operate with some level of certainty about foreign exchange rates and set prices at levels which will improve profitability. All of these issues will be explored within Business Economics.

The text provides you with the analytical tools and concepts you need to understand these issues. It assumes no previous knowledge of economics and therefore combines the objectives of an introduction to economics text with those of a more applied text. By working carefully through the activities you will acquire a strong grounding in the foundations of the subject together with an understanding of how they can be applied to analyse business issues and problems.

Business makes considerable use of professional economists especially in an advisory capacity on issues such as economic forecasting, investment appraisal and pricing strategies. But more significantly it can be argued that all those employed in making business decisions should have a grasp of economics in order to contribute to sound commercial practice.

Economics does not in general provide answers to the complexities of economic problems. But it can help in analysing those problems more systematically. Indeed economics provides a useful general grounding in problem solving and the analysis of complex situations which will prove valuable in understanding business problems more generally.

Economics cannot of course claim to provide a complete understanding of business behaviour. The constraints on business are not only economic in nature and economic objectives are not the only factors which motivate the entrepreneur. It is therefore important to consider the ideas in Business Economics alongside the other explanations of business activity that you will encounter elsewhere in your course.

What is in this workbook?

The core of the workbook are 10 study units by authors who are experienced in teaching on such courses. These were written specifically for undergraduate business students by authors who are experienced in teaching on such courses. The content has been revised as a result of the comments of tutors and students who have worked through the material.

The units are particularly useful to students, like you, who may be following a course where an "open learning" approach is being adopted. The features which make it particularly suitable for open learning include:

- very careful sequencing of the material so that there is a clear and logical progression.
- a step by step approach so that you will be able to understand each new point thoroughly before proceeding to the next one.
- a very clear layout with relatively short headed sections and paragraphs.
- many worked examples, particularly in the computational areas, with an emphasis on understanding rather than on computation.
- lots of opportunities for you to check that you understand what you have just read using the large number of "activities" and "self-assessment questions" which are interspersed through the units, to which solutions are provided at the back of the relevant unit.
- plenty of opportunities for you to test your progress through end-of-unit exercises to which solutions are provided.

Students on more conventional courses will also find that the material is a useful supplement to other text books which may not use these open learning features.

Reader

At the back of the book there is a Reader, which is a collection of journal articles and extracts from texts. This allows you the opportunity of wider reading but in a way which ensures that your reading is relevant and closely integrated with the material covered in the units. Particular features of the Reader are:-

- a significant number of journal articles and extracts from texts, each dealing with a significant issue in business economics.
- relevant material, some of which will deal with topical issues.
- fairly short articles and extracts.
- articles and extracts written in clear, non-technical language.
- material particularly relevant to business studies students.

Using the workbook

You will probably find it most effective to work through the units in sequence. You should begin by noting the points which the unit outlines identify as the crucial aspects of the material. This will put the contents of the units into context and guide you through them.

Each unit is interspersed with a number of "activities" and "self-assessment questions". There are "additional exercises" at the end of each unit. All of these are intended to be attempted by you as they arise and completed before you move on. The suggested solutions to each activity are given immediately following the relevant activity. The solutions to the self-assessment questions and additional exercises are given at the end of the relevant unit.

The activities are intended to be a combination of a check that you are following the unit and understanding it, on the one hand, and a way of making you learning a more active experience for you, on the other. By working through the activities you can effectively divide your study time between that necessary to taking on new ideas and that which is necessary to reinforce those ideas.

The self-assessment questions are intended to give you the opportunity to see whether you have really grasped the content of the unit. The additional exercises are intended to give you further practice and the opportunity to reinforce your knowledge and understanding. Avoid the temptation to skip through the exercises, they are there to assist you develop your knowledge and understanding and your confidence with the material.

Typically, the activities will only take you a few minutes to deal with. By contrast, the assessment questions and additional exercises may quite easily take 20 minutes or more to complete. It is important that you discipline yourself to complete each activity, self-assessment question or exercise before you refer to the solution provided. If you get stuck part way through a question you should try to get help from the solution only on the point causing you difficulty and then continue to complete the question before referring to the solution again.

You should read the items in the Reader when recommended.

Avoid rote learning

In respect of each topic in the workbook, it is important that you thoroughly understand what you are doing and why you are doing it. It you are clear on the underlying logic you will find it unnecessary to learn up a list of rules to be followed.

This will mean that preparation for tests and for final examinations will be easier for you. It will also mean that you will be fairly comfortable in dealing with unfamiliar problems. This is an important point since dealing with problems which require the application of principles and techniques which you have learned, but which are of a type which you have not specifically encountered before, will most probably be a feature of your assessment.

By working through the exercises, by reflecting on the ideas and their implications, by attempting to relate them to your wider understanding of business you will develop a far deeper understanding than if you simply attempt to commit the material to memory.

Set aside time for your study of Business Economics

It is necessary for you to spend an amount of time during each study period in mastering the material concerned. The flexibility which the open learning system allows should not lead you to overlook this fact. Clearly at the start of the study period you will not know how long it will take to do the necessary work. It is sensible therefore, to make a start on the work at an early stage in the study period. Try to discipline yourself to set particular times in the week to study Business Economics, though not necessary the same time each week.

Experiment with different ways of studying the material until you find one which best suits you. Try skimming each unit to gain a broad grasp of the ideas covered before you go through it in any detail. Alternatively try reading the unit objectives and the summaries before you settle down to study the unit in any depth. Try to find the most suitable time to study, when your concentration is at its highest and interruptions are at a minimum and do set aside enough time to complete all the activities-they are a crucial part of the learning process.

UNIT 1
AN INTRODUCTION TO ECONOMICS

Introduction

Every day you face a variety of problems of an economic nature, and so have to take decisions about the use of resources in your possession, such as money and time. Examples of such problems include: whether to replace your car now or next year, save or spend, how much to spend on the National Lottery this week, how much to pay off your Visa statement, and so on. Not only do you face such problems, we all do, and our parents before us, and so on, all the way back through history. Just reflect on the economic problems faced by your ancestors 2000 years ago: they may have had fewer problems to face, but just think of the penalties for getting the solutions wrong – starvation and death. As a result of these economic problems we spend a lot of our time, more than we realise, making decisions which have implications for those resources at our disposal.

In short, we are all performers on an economic stage, hence the term *homo economicus*, or economic man (and woman). Even though we all perform on this stage every day of our lives, few of us seem to realise it. We earn our income, then dispose of it, without thinking how we spent that income the way we did over the last year.

Furthermore, we all make decisions every day which have economic repercussions for ourselves and others. If we buy that car, it will affect others in some way, for example nobody else can have it, unless we give it to them, or they steal it from us. When a business closes down there are implications for its employees and the local community. Tax changes affect how much we have in our pockets and so the amount of money we can spend in shops: this will affect how many people are employed in shops. Changes in interest rates, the prices of goods, and so on affect us all in various ways. As a result, we all need some understanding of economics and with this knowledge we could make better informed decisions and so make fewer mistakes, or none at all. We could use our resources more efficiently, even increase those resources available to us. We could spend less time regretting past decisions. Though regrets are useless, we all have plenty of them, don't we? In the busy times in which we live, as time passes us by even more quickly, we all need to use our resources better.

Now that we have looked at why economics can be useful – helping us to make more informed decisions about how we use our resources – we need to define what economics is. Accordingly, this unit will consist of two sections.

In Section 1 we will be looking at what constitutes the heart of the subject matter of economics, the economic problem of **scarcity**: why it arises and what are its implications, especially the need to allocate scarce resources to produce goods and services people want to buy. Because there are different ways of allocating resources we have different types of economy, all of which have to find answers to seven general economic questions. Our attention will focus mainly on one type of economy – the market economy and its basic unit, the market. After this we'll look at the two branches of economics, microeconomics and macroeconomics, and, finally, at the distinction between positive and normative statements.

In Section 2 the concept of the **Production Possibility Boundary** will be introduced and applied to help you better understand and consolidate some of the basic concepts and distinctions covered in Section 1. Section 2 will also introduce you to the way economists represent information using graphs.

Please note that there is no Unit Review Activity for Unit 1 but a Unit Review Activity is included at the end of Unit 2 covering the content of both Units 1 and 2.

Objectives

By the end of the unit you should be able to:

- explain the nature and causes of the fundamental economic problem of scarcity
- outline the problems arising from scarcity
- list the implications of scarcity
- classify economies into market, command, and mixed economies
- distinguish between positive and normative statements
- distinguish between microeconomics and macroeconomics
- explain the difference between resources being fully employed and efficiently employed
- outline the benefits of economic growth.

SECTION ONE

The Content of Economics

Introduction

In Section 1 we will consider the economic problem of **scarcity:** why it arises and what are its implications. We will examine different types of economy and the seven general economic questions each has to find answers to. We will focus mainly on one type of economy – the market economy and its basic unit, the market. We will go on to discuss the two branches of economics, microeconomics and macroeconomics. Finally we will examine the distinction between positive and normative statements.

1.1 Defining economics

When we begin a study of something new to us we normally begin with an expectation of quickly determining what it is that we are about to start studying. So you may have approached this first unit with a question something like, 'what is economics?' We then expect to see the question answered concisely. Here we will have to disappoint you, as we cannot express in a concise form a definition of economics which is adequate for the purpose. Attempting to define subject matter concisely and adequately is not a problem peculiar to economics. Consider mathematics or history. How would you define them? As a result of the problems of defining something like economics, there are numerous definitions, each tending to reflect a different viewpoint.

To give you an appreciation of how difficult it is to define economics we will briefly look at five definitions, each of which has been put forward by a major economist over the last two centuries.

First, we have the definition by Adam Smith (1723–1790), generally held to be the founder of modern Economics. Smith saw economics as:

'...an inquiry into the nature and causes of the wealth of nations.'

(From A. Smith, *An Enquiry into the Nature and Causes of the Wealth of Nations*, 1776.)

In the nineteenth century John Stuart Mill (1806 –73) described economics as,

'...the practical science of the production and distribution of wealth'.

(From J. S. Mill, *The Principles of Political Economy*, 1848.)

Both of these definitions focus on the material aspect of the subject, or wealth.

In 1890 the late-Victorian economist, Alfred Marshall, saw economics as being quite comprehensive in its coverage:

'Economics is the study of mankind in the everyday business of life'.

(From A. Marshall, *The Principles of Economics*, 1890.)

Lionel Robbins (1898 – 1984) saw economics as:

'... the science which studies human behaviour as the relationship between ends and scarce means which have alternative uses'.

(From L. Robbins, *An Essay on the Nature and Significance of Economic Science*, 1932.)

Rather grandly, John Maynard Keynes (1883-1946), arguably the most famous of Britain's economists, saw economics as being involved with social improvement, practitioners of economics being:

'... trustees of the possibility of civilisation'.

(From J. F. Harrod, *The Life of John Maynard Keynes*, Macmillan, 1951.)

We will come across Adam Smith and J.M. Keynes in later units.

As you look at these definitions it is possible to see differences. Consider the key words in the definitions: production and distribution, wealth, science, and human behaviour. Each definition tends to emphasise different aspects of the subject matter of economics.

If we look at the *Penguin Dictionary of Economics* (1972 edition) we see economics defined as,

'The study of the production, distribution and consumption of wealth in human society'.

The dictionary then suggests that: 'This one (definition) is as good as any', and 'Economists have never been wholly satisfied with any definition of this subject'. We think you may now agree with the latter statement. You may wish to have a look at the latest edition of the dictionary.

Though defining economics is problematic and there's no agreement on a definition, it is possible to identify the subject matter. Here we could accept the invitation of the *Penguin Dictionary of Economics*:

'The reader will gain a good notion of the scope of Economics by examining the coverage of this dictionary. ...This dictionary contains over 1600 entries.' Fortunately, you will not have to familiarise yourself with all of them.

We will now move on from the problem of defining economics concisely to look in more detail at what economists consider to be the core of its subject matter: the fundamental economic problem of **scarcity**.

1.2 The fundamental economic problem: scarcity

WANTS

Economics is concerned with scarcity and the problems which arise from it. To appreciate this we need to look first at the concept of **wants** and how they are satisfied.

People, individually and as part of a social grouping, (e.g. a family, club, community) have wants. These consist firstly of our demand for goods and services, such as food, drink and shelter, needed to satisfy our physiological needs so that we can survive. Secondly, wants consist of our desires for long and healthy lives, security, contentment, knowledge, fame, and so forth: wants are not limited to just material possessions. Economics deals with material possessions, rather than non-material wants or possessions, such as security and contentment.

The amount of resources owned by an individual varies from person to person. Consider for a moment the extent to which the wants of a person with very limited resources are satisfied, for example a homeless person, or somebody in one of the very poor parts of the Third World. Then consider the extent to which wealthy individuals with substantial resources are able to satisfy their wants. In short, you can't always get what you want, and what you get depends on the resources at your disposal. Also, most of us would like more (there will always be some who are satisfied with very little, or who don't want any more).

What we have said about people is also generally true of business organisations and governments. These also have wants to be satisfied – the wants of the individuals comprising them – and only limited resources to satisfy them.

So, people, businesses and governments (these three groups are called **economic agents**) all face a similar problem: how to satisfy their many wants from limited resources. As economic agents form the basic components of an economy, we have the fundamental economic problem faced by all countries' economies, whatever their size, that of scarcity. Scarcity is a fact of life, something faced by all of us numerous times every day. If there were enough resources – a true world of plenty – we could have everything we wanted.

ACTIVITY 1

How is the problem of scarcity similar for:

(a) Robinson Crusoe

(b) the central government of a country

(c) British Petroleum

(d) Yourself?

They all have limited resources, e.g. a budget, with which to satisfy their numerous wants.

RESOURCES

Having looked at wants and seen how they are satisfied – by the using up (this is called **consumption**) of commodities – we now need to consider where these commodities come from. Most of them have to be produced in some way: fished from the sea, manufactured, extracted, distilled, and so forth. In order to produce commodities, ingredients have to be used. These ingredients are called **raw materials** (or **inputs**) and in the production of commodities they are used up, or consumed. So when you consume something it is the final stage in a sequence of activities which began with the milking of a cow, the sale of that milk, and so on, until you purchased it. Here you may have noticed the words sale, and purchased, indicating that each stage in the sequence of activities also has a monetary aspect – for every purchase there is a sale. So we have a sequence of economic activities, involving the using up of resources and the exchange of commodities for money. (Commodities may be exchanged for other commodities as well – this is called **barter**.)

Economists are very interested in this sequence of economic activities, which involves production, distribution, and consumption:

- **production** involves the using up of resources, or raw materials
- **distribution** involves getting commodities to end-users (or consumers)
- **consumption** involves the using up of commodities to satisfy wants.

All these activities take place within an economy, so that the wants of economic agents can be satisfied – the extent to which they are satisfied being dependant on the resources available to each individual, firm, or government. In brief, an economy is a very complex type of organisation wherein a series of activities take place, the purpose of which is to satisfy the wants of economic agents to an extent limited by the availability of resources.

The **resources**, called **factors of production**, needed to produce commodities are traditionally grouped into four, the names of which reflect economists' earlier pre-occupation with agricultural activities. The four groups of factors of production are:

- labour
- capital
- land
- entrepreneurs.

We will now look at each of these.

Labour
Workers, managers, supervisors and other individuals are needed to make things, organise the productive and distributive processes, etc., that is, manual and mental effort are required. We call this labour.

Capital
Secondly, labour has to be combined with machinery, tools, forklift trucks, and other types of man-made equipment, called **capital**. This is sometimes called **real capital**, as opposed to **money capital** or **financial assets**, such as your money deposits in a bank. Real capital is used to assist labour in the processes of production. Increasingly in a variety of industries the amount of labour which has to be combined with capital to produce a commodity has fallen, for example, as in the case of the motor vehicle industry.

Land

Once we have labour and capital, raw materials are needed, and these begin their existence by being extracted from the seas, the land surface – from the soil, or from forests, or from below the land surface (natural gas, oil), or from the air. Fish, timber, crude oil, sand, iron ore, and so forth occur naturally, and are sometimes called the 'free gifts' of nature. Such free gifts form the third group of resources, called **land**.

Entrepreneurs (or risk-takers)

Finally, labour, capital and land have to be combined by somebody. Undertaking this function of combining resources to produce and/or distribute commodities to consumers can be very expensive and involve the individual(s) concerned taking substantial financial risks. In return for taking the risks, these individuals may make a lot of money, that is, they get the financial benefits from taking the risks. They may, on the other hand, incur all the losses and so lose all their money. These risk-takers are called **entrepreneurs**. Examples of such individuals are people like Richard Branson, Terence Conran, Alan Sugar, Anita Roddick and Freddie Laker. Can you add to this list? When we talk about entrepreneurs we tend to think of famous people like those just mentioned. We should not forget that entrepreneurs can be found running the local paper shop, the local Chinese take-away, and all the market stalls.

Remember that these resources at any point in time are only available in finite amounts: there is only so much crude oil, labour, and capital available to oil producers. Similarly, with iron ore, fish, limestone, timber, and all the other raw materials. Now try Activity 2.

ACTIVITY 2

1 To which type of factor of production do each of the following belong? Indicate your answer to the right of each factor.

(a) a tractor

(b) a police car

(c) a fax machine

(d) a computer

(e) a warehouse

(f) office furniture

(g) soil

(h) Tiny Rowlands

(i) sea water.

2 What do they all have in common?

---

1 (a), (b), (c), (d), (e) and (f) are all forms of capital

(g)   land, e.g. nursery-gardens use soil

(h)   entrepreneur (Lonhro)

(i)   land, e.g. production of sea-salt.

2 They are all limited in the amount available at the present time.

It may be useful at this point to summarise the key points of our discussion so far.

1 We all have wants, and wants for the community (be it local, regional, national, global) are unlimited: infinite.

2 The satisfaction of wants requires the using up of resources (factors of production) which are limited in supply: finite.

3 Somehow those limited resources have to be allocated to satisfy wants, but which ones? How are resources to be allocated?

4 Economics is the study of how those resources are allocated amongst those competing wants, i.e. the fundamental economic problem of scarcity.

1.3 The implications of scarcity

We will now go on to explore two issues arising from the problem of scarcity: the implications of scarcity and the social institutions which have evolved in response to scarcity – different types of economy.

Economic scarcity means that all economic agents have to make choices. For instance, you have only a limited budget, and so have to take economic decisions such as: 'I have enough money for changing my car or going on holiday. I can't have both. So I'll have to change my car, and go without the holiday until next year, by which time my finances will have improved'. Similarly, if you spend everything you can't save – but you may do a bit of both, and by saving you can't have as expensive a car as you would have had if you had decided to save nothing at all.

Individuals have to make decisions about what to buy, and so by inference, what not to buy. Suppose you want A and B, but you can only afford one: if A is chosen, then B has to be given up. In short, scarcity implies choice. In selecting A rather than B, B had to be given up. B is known as the **opportunity cost** of A. Everything has an opportunity cost: what's the opportunity cost of your current studies? Just think of all the time (and money) you'll devote to your studies, when you could have spent those resources on socialising, shopping, doing paid work – foregone earnings are an important element of the opportunity cost of undertaking further and higher education.

In the example above the opportunity cost of A was B: B is assumed to be the next best alternative to A, and so A is what had to be sacrificed, for A. Governments also face the problem of scarcity and so have to choose. Try Activity 3.

ACTIVITY 3

Suppose a government has £40 million which is enough to build a new motorway, or two hospitals. The government has a choice: the motorway or two hospitals. Suppose it selects the motorway. What's the opportunity cost of the motorway? Explain your answer fully in the space provided below.

The opportunity cost of the new motorway is two hospitals. Remember that the economist's term for the cost of something expressed in terms of what has to be given up, or foregone, is called the opportunity cost.

When an individual has to choose one commodity from many, they may be placed in some order of preference. For example, if there are 10 books you would like to buy, but you can't afford them all, you might put them in order of importance (or preference) and buy only those at the top of your list. We should add here that priorities change with changing circumstances. For example, if your exam results show that you are really gifted in one subject and rather weak in another, you might alter the ranking of the textbooks.

Economists are not concerned with how commodities are prioritised by economic agents. We only need to be aware that prioritisation does take place.

ACTIVITY 4

Consider how your priorities with respect to the items you'll be purchasing have changed now that you are a student. List some of the differences you expect will take place as your priorities have changed.

Based on your experience as students, you may:

spend less on clothes, eating out, entertainment

eat more baked beans

spend more on coffee, paper, books, pens

take fewer holidays abroad

watch less TV.

To sum up: as our circumstances change so do our priorities i.e., the way we rank commodities is not permanently fixed.

In economics it is assumed that economic agents act rationally, seeking to maximise or minimise something (this is called **optimising**). For example, individuals attempt to maximise utility, where **utility** represents well-being, or satisfaction. Commodities are wanted because they provide utility, not just for their own sake. As a result, individuals will prefer commodities which provide a high degree of utility to those which provide little or no utility. This results in individuals ranking their preferences for commodities, as we have just seen, to produce a scale of preferences. We should add here that economists are not concerned with the moral or ethical issues relating to scales of preferences.

1.4 Types of economy

Economies differ from country to country as a result of differences in the way decisions about the allocation of resources is determined, and who owns the country's resources.

At one extreme we have the **command economy** where decisions about the allocation of resources is determined by the command of the state – hence the term *command* economy. Here economic decision making is said to be centralised. The country's resources are mostly, if not all, owned by the state and the state-owned sector (called **the public sector**) is responsible for producing most, if not all, of the country's goods and services.

At the other extreme is the **market economy** where decisions about the allocation of resources is decentralised to millions of private individuals and businesses. Here most of the resources are owned by private individuals, and most of the country's goods and services are produced by businesses which are privately owned, called **the private sector**. In a market economy the role of the government is limited to providing those services needed to ensure that law and order is preserved and the country is defended against external attack. In between these two extremes are **mixed economies**, which vary from those with large public sectors and small private sectors to those with small public sectors and large private sectors.

We will now look at the different types of economy:

- the command economy
- the market economy
- the mixed economy.

With the latter we must remember that economies of this type have a publicly-owned sector (state-owned) and a private sector (privately-owned), and the relative importance of each, in terms of its contribution to the country's production of goods and services, varies from country to country.

THE COMMAND ECONOMY

In a command economy decisions about production, distribution and consumption are taken by some organisation created by the government: the state plans, then directs, or commands, how resources will be allocated in production. In effect the state determines how resources will be allocated using a very complex system of economic planning, which attempts to co-ordinate economic decisions and sets output targets. Whereas decisions about the allocation of resources is highly decentralised in a market economy, in a command economy economic decisions are highly centralised, being taken by a relatively small group of state officials, as in the former USSR (Gosplan was the name given to this committee of officials, who undertook the central planning of the USSR) and its satellite states. We should note that in some command economies economic decisions were decentralised to the regions, as in the former Yugoslavia. Even so, the degree of centralised decision-taking there was still very high when compared to that found in any market economy.

In command economies the state owns the means of production and distribution, so the public sector is very large, and the private sector, where resources are owned privately, is extremely limited in terms of its contribution to the country's output of goods and services.

Command economies need to be continually planned, and this requires a vast amount of data to be collected and interpreted so that targets can be set, or revised. This results in economic decision-taking being very slow and inefficient. Meanwhile, time passes, resulting in shortages, poor quality, long waiting lists, unwanted commodities, a lack of incentives, and corruption.

By the early 1980s, about one-third of the world's population lived in states with command economies – the list of such states was quite extensive. In 1985 Mikhail Gorbachev became the general-secretary of the Communist Party of the Soviet Union. Concerned at the inefficiency of the economy of the USSR, he attempted to revitalise it by means of increased control. However, after two years of this increased control Gorbachev was convinced that radical economic reforms were needed to restructure the economy (*Perestroika*) along western market-economy lines. After this events moved very quickly, so that by the mid-1990s there are only a few command economies left, for example, Cuba and China, and of these China, along with many countries in Central and Eastern Europe, is undergoing rapid economic reform. At varying rates the former command economies of the USSR, Central and Eastern Europe, and beyond, are moving towards the market economy, incurring many economic and political changes during the transition, for example, high levels of unemployment for the first time.

These changes have involved:

- a reduction in the size of the public sector. Industries previously owned by the state (i.e. in the public sector) are now being sold off to private individuals and overseas companies. This process of selling-off state-owned resources is called **privatisation**.

- de-regulation of business. In command economies the government controlled economic activity using numerous rules and regulations – red tape – which made it very difficult, if not impossible, for people to set up their own businesses. These rules and regulations are now being removed to allow people to set up their own businesses. The removal of such rules and regulations is called **deregulation**.

These two changes have resulted in rapidly developing private sectors in the former command economies and to private individuals now owning resources (i.e. to a new property-owning class).

To this trend we must add that countries which have followed the middle way, with roughly equally-sized public and private sectors (in terms of their contributions to their countries' outputs of goods and services) have also seen their public sectors reduced over the last 10 to 20 years. This has been a result of western governments like those in the UK, USA, Japan and France adopting policies to improve the operation of their markets in order to ensure that economic agents are better able to respond to signals emanating from the markets. These policies are called **supply-side policies**.

THE MARKET ECONOMY

Here all the millions of economic agents, acting independently of each other and pursuing their own self-interests, buy and sell goods and services in markets. Individuals sell their labour for income and use this income to buy commodities in pursuit of their own interests – to maximise utility. Firms engage workers in order to produce commodities which are then sold. In this case firms are also motivated by their self-interest, for example, to maximise profits. All these transactions involve decisions by buyers and sellers, and it is these decisions which determine how resources are allocated in a market economy. In the market economy economic agents enter into transactions of their own free choice: the parties to a transaction are not coerced in any way. These transactions which constitute **trade** take place in personal face-to-face transactions as we see in high-street shops and car-boot sales, or over the telephone, or by telex, or e-mail, or through a third party – an agent, as with the estate agents in the housing market. Whatever the type of contact between buyers and sellers, the process of exchange between them constitutes **a market**. The process of exchange may involve goods and services being provided in exchange for money, or for another good or service, i.e. by barter.

In the market economy goods and services (from here onwards we'll use the term **commodities** rather than goods and services in order to *economise* on our use of words!) are allocated to economic agents on the basis of their having money to pay for them, that is according to **the ability-to-pay principle**. Provided the market economy is working properly there is just enough of each commodity supplied by firms (i.e. sellers) as is required by buyers of the commodity at each price. Shortages and surpluses tend to be temporary occurrences. Further, the commodities available change over time as a result of new fashions, changes in technology, and so on. So it would seem as if there is something, or some mechanism co-ordinating the operation of the market economy. In the *Wealth of Nations*, first published in 1776, Adam Smith compared this co-ordinating mechanism to an *invisible hand*, a simile for the price mechanism, whereby changes in the prices of commodities lead to resources being allocated. (We will examine this fully in Unit 2, but here we can briefly indicate how the price mechanism, operates in a market economy.)

A market economy consists of numerous markets, in each of which changes in price act like a signal to effect changes in the behaviour of economic agents and subsequently, to changes in the allocation of scarce resources amongst the commodities being produced. (We need to add here that all economic agents are assumed to have information about the prices of different commodities, and this information is available free of charge.) Let us consider first the effects of a rise in price.

Suppose buyers increase the amount of a commodity they wish to purchase, a shortage of the commodity will appear and its price will rise. In response to the increase in price, firms will produce more of the commodity and new firms producing the commodity may appear (as a result of entrepreneurs seeing this commodity as a good opportunity from which to make more money). In short, more resources will be allocated to the production of this commodity. These extra resources will be allocated to the commodity by firms, increasing the amount available, in response to the rising price.

In the case of a reduction in the sales of a commodity, a surplus will appear and so firms will reduce the amount of it they produce, or stop producing the commodity. So there will be a reduction in the resources used to produce this commodity. Perhaps the firms which produced the commodity which fell in price may move into the production of a commodity which is rising in price. In these ways resources are constantly being re-allocated within the market economy in response to price changes.

Thus in a market, price acts like a signal communicating information to economic agents which will lead to changes in the amount of a commodity buyers want to buy and the amount sellers want to sell. These changes will then initiate a sequence of activities which will produce a new situation – a new allocation of resources.

To summarise: in a market economy, despite resources being allocated in a decentralised way through the decisions of economic agents, it is co-ordinated by the operation of the price mechanism: the tendency for prices to change in response to shortages/surpluses and so lead to, or signal, a re-allocation of resources.

The perfect market

In order to appreciate how resources are allocated in a market economy we will focus in Unit 2 on its basic unit – the market – where independent economic agents, in pursuing their self-interest, determine the allocation of resources. However, in order to lay the foundations for Unit 2 we can spend some time here on the concept of the perfect market.

The term **perfect market** refers to an ideal type of market used by economists to help explore how markets operate. In reality it is doubtful whether any markets can be described as perfect: they fail to meet all the conditions for being called a perfect market. Nonetheless, economists believe that if markets met more of the conditions listed below, economies would operate more efficiently. In any case, by exploring what would happen under a given set of ideal conditions, we can better understand what happens in the real world.

In exploring the operation of a perfect market (say for commodity X) a number of assumptions are made by economists. These assumptions (or conditions) which have to be met for a market to be perfect are as follows (look at each one carefully and reflect on how realistic it is):

- in the market for X there are many buyers who pursue their own self-interest and act independently of any other buyer.

- there are many sellers who pursue their own self-interest and act independently of any other seller.

- buyers and sellers are **price-takers**: because the amount bought by any one buyer is such a small proportion of the total amount bought, and the amount sold by any one seller is such a small proportion of the total amount sold, buyers and sellers are unable as individual buyers and sellers to affect the price of a commodity, i.e. they are price-takers. (We will return to this when we look at perfect competition in Unit 3.)

- units of the commodity sold by different sellers are homogenous, that is identical to each other.

- there is freedom of entry and exit: buyers and sellers are free to enter or leave the market, i.e. there are no financial costs involved in entering/leaving the market.

- information is freely available in the market about the price of the commodity.

   (This allows us to interpret prices as being like signals, price changes leading to changes in the behaviour of economic agents, e.g. a fall in price will lead buyers to purchase more of the commodity.)

As a result of these assumptions:

- A market will respond quickly to changes in what buyers want to buy (this is called **demand**) and what sellers want to sell (this is called **supply**).

- Changes in the price of a commodity lead to changes in the amount of a commodity buyers want to purchase and sellers want to sell, i.e. to a change in how scarce resources are allocated to the production of different commodities.

We will explore these two important points very carefully in Unit 2. Now try Activity 5.

ACTIVITY 5

Which of the following markets are not perfect? Briefly explain your answer:

1 the telecommunications industry in the UK

2 the UK foreign exchange market

3 the UK market for Rolls-Royce shares

4 the world market for uncut diamonds

5 the world market for crude oil.

1,4,5, for example because for each there are only a few sellers (suppliers) of the commodity; potential suppliers would not be free to enter the industries, i.e. there would be formidable obstacles to overcome, e.g. setting-up costs, resistance from existing suppliers.

2 and 3 are good examples of markets which are nearly perfect – there are many buyers and sellers. Current prices are freely obtainable, etc. However, there are financial costs involved in entering the market for foreign exchange/Rolls-Royce shares – a small charge has to be paid when buying/selling these commodities. For example, when you bought your foreign exchange before going on holiday last time, you may have had to pay a commission of so much per £100, usually 1-2%. These changes are also called **transaction costs**.

THE MIXED ECONOMY

So far we have tended to look at economic systems as extremes, at one end of an economic spectrum, or continuum, we have the command economy and at the other end the market economy. This view of extremes or opposites can be shown simply, as in Figure 1 below:

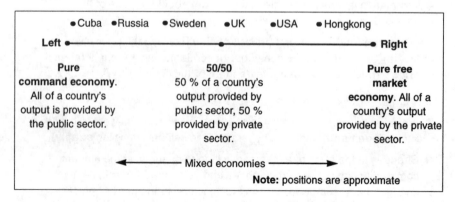

Figure 1: Types of economy

In reality, it's unlikely that there have ever been examples of economies corresponding to the pure extremes. For example, the market economy of the UK in Adam Smith's time (the late eighteenth century) had a small public sector and both sectors owned productive resources at the same time. So decisions about the allocation of resources were determined partly by the state and partly by independent individuals and firms pursuing their own self-interest in the market-place. An economy with both a public sector and a private sector is called a mixed economy: Figure 1 indicates their great variety in terms of the relative importance of the two sectors.

To summarise: we are currently witnessing the shifting of many economies from the left and the middle of the economic spectrum towards the right. This reflects the perceived economic superiority of the decentralised market economy (based on the market and the private ownership of resources) over the centralised command economy (based on state direction and state ownership of resources).

Economists are very interested in how the market economy works and how resources are allocated. Unit 2 will focus on how markets function and why they sometimes don't function properly. Whatever the type of economy, an economy exists because of the fundamental economic problem of scarcity and, as a result, the need to allocate resources. Now try Activity 6, which tests your understanding of the types of economy just discussed.

ACTIVITY 6

Complete the following sentences:

1 In economic theory there are ___ extreme types of economy.

2 At one extreme is the command economy, where decisions about the allocation of resources are taken by _____   ___ and resources are owned by _____.

3 In a market economy, decisions about the allocation of resources is _____ i.e. by the independent actions of many individuals pursuing their own _____.

4 A public sector is where _____.

5 A private sector is where _____.

6 A mixed economy contains elements from both command and _____ economies.

1 two

2 state officials (or something close, e.g. civil servants, state committees)
   ...the state

3 decentralised...self-interest

4 economic activities, such as production, are undertaken by state-owned
   businesses

5 economic activities are undertaken by privately owned businesses, (e.g.
   Marks and Spencer, C & A, Ford, etc.)

6 market.

1.5 The general economic questions

The fundamental economic problem of scarcity gives rise to seven general or basic questions answers to which have to be provided by all types of economy. These questions are summarised as follows.

1 WHAT TO PRODUCE?

As we've seen, the wants of a country's inhabitants are extremely large and have to be satisfied by the consumption of commodities. So the first question to be answered by any economic system must necessarily be: which commodities? Having decided what's to be produced resources are then allocated to the production of those commodities. For example, in the former command economies the state determined that military commodities were the priority and the planning authorities allocated resources to the production of military equipment. The opportunity cost of such production was reflected in a chronic shortage of consumer goods, such as cars, TVs and fridges, because few resources were allocated to their production.

2 HOW MUCH OF EACH COMMODITY TO PRODUCE?

Having decided to produce a particular set of commodities, decisions about how much of each commodity to produce have to be taken. If it's decided to produce commodities A, B, C, rather than X, Y, Z, then X, Y, Z have to be given up. Also one has to remember that more of A implies less of the other commodities, B, C,...Here, we may re-call the concept of opportunity cost.

3 HOW IS THE OUTPUT OF COMMODITIES TO BE SHARED OUT?

Once commodities are produced they have to be shared out among economic agents. In a market economy commodities are shared out on the basis of the ability to pay principle, with those who have more in terms of income and wealth being able to obtain more than those with less income and wealth. By contrast, in command economies, individuals work for the common good according to their ability and expected to be rewarded according to their needs, regardless of their position, i.e. on the basis of the **according-to-need principle**.

Finally, in a mixed economy, we have the distribution of national output determined partly by the ability-to-pay principle in relation to private sector output, and partly by the according to need principle in the public sector. This latter principle led to many public sector commodities being freely available to all in the UK and elsewhere, such as education and health services. However, in recent years this free availability has been replaced with the introduction of charges for many publicly-provided commodities, such as dental care, eye tests, school milk, spectacles, and so forth. However, low-income groups are exempt from the ability-to-pay principle.

How a country's output of commodities is determined has long been of interest to economists. In fact, economics developed out of political economy, which concerned itself with explaining the distribution of wealth amongst the different classes of society. Remember Mill's definition earlier, '...the distribution of wealth'? Issues relating to the distribution of income and wealth remain a source of much debate in economics.

4 HOW ARE COMMODITIES TO BE PRODUCED?

Because there is, generally, more than one way to produce a commodity, decisions have to be made about how each type of commodity is to be produced. This question concerns methods of production. It may be possible, for example, to produce a commodity X by means of a method which employs a lot of labour and only a small amount of capital (**labour-intensive**), or a lot of capital and only a minimum of labour (**capital-intensive**), or some intermediate combination of labour and capital. In the case of the manufacture of motor vehicles the method of production has changed over time from being labour-intensive to a capital-intensive method based on robotics and computer systems. In determining which method is to be used firms seek to find the one which is the most efficient, producing at the lowest cost per unit (we will return to this in Unit 3).

5 ARE RESOURCES BEING EFFICIENTLY EMPLOYED?

Given that resources are scarce it is vital that they are used in the best possible way, that is efficiently. Supply-side policies are aimed at improving the efficiency with which resources are allocated to the production of commodities in both the public and private sectors: in Section 2 of this unit we will look at the distinction between resources being efficiently employed and fully employed. For now we can say that resources are efficiently and fully employed if it is not possible to increase the output of one commodity without reducing the output of some other commodity. If it is possible to produce more commodities and resources are fully employed then resources are inefficiently employed – resources are being wasted. In a world of scarcity it is important that resources are efficiently employed.

6 ARE RESOURCES FULLY EMPLOYED?

Here the focus is on whether resources are fully employed as opposed to being efficiently employed. In short, if resources are not fully employed they are said to be **unemployed**. Unemployment represents economic waste. The term unemployment refers to all the four factors of production, though we tend to associate it only with labour. Given that resources are scarce, economists are interested in what can cause resources to be unemployed.

7 IS THE ECONOMY GROWING?

Most of us have hopes about the future, especially that we'll be better off and enjoy a higher standard of living. To satisfy these expectations it's vital that an economy's capacity to produce commodities increases over time.

Questions 1 to 5 are examined in that part of economics called **microeconomics**, and issues relating to questions 6 and 7 are explored in **macroeconomics**.

In Section 2 we will use the concept of the Production Possibility Boundary to explore some of these questions further.

To summarise: we listed above the seven general economic questions relating to the use of a country's resources. Even so, other questions of interest to economists remain, such as: 'Is the exchange rate the correct one?, 'Is the value of money being reduced by inflation?', and so on. Such questions are seen as being of a more specific nature.

1.6 The distinction between microeconomics and macroeconomics

Economics is divided into two fairly distinct compartments: microeconomics and macroeconomics.

Microeconomics is concerned with the workings and failings of the market system and the price mechanism. Thus it examines the determination of prices, the forces leading to price changes, the consequences of price changes, the inter-relationships between markets, and market failure – why some commodities are underproduced (or not produced) and others over-produced, that is, why there are shortages and surpluses. Examples of microeconomic questions are: what determines the price of Premier League footballers? What's the effect of a minimum wage? What's the effect of an increase in the rate of VAT on a particular sector of the economy? Essentially, microeconomics focuses on the components or parts of the market economy.

Key concepts are: **markets, price, equilibrium and disequilibrium**.

Macroeconomics focuses on the whole, or aggregate view, and so is concerned with totals or aggregates – consumption, investment, government expenditure, savings, taxation, imports and exports. Macroeconomics seeks to explain the causes and effects of increases and decreases in the aggregates. It also attempts to identify the conditions making for a stable economy. Macroeconomic questions include: what caused the recession of the early 1990s? What are the consequences of a single European currency? What are the effects of an increase in interest rates on the savings rate, consumption, investment and the balance of payments? What are the effects of an increase in the rate of VAT on the economy?

Key concepts are: **the circular flow of income, leakages (withdrawals), injections, aggregate demand, aggregate supply, equilibrium, disequilibrium, and economic growth**.

Please note: Units 2, 3, 4, 5 will be concerned with the subject matter of microeconomics;

Units 6 to 10 will be concerned with macroeconomics.

Now try Activity 7 to test your understanding of the terms microeconomics and macroeconomics.

ACTIVITY 7

Which of the following questions or topics are microeconomic-based; which are macroeconomic-based?

1 Why do doctors get paid less than Premier League footballers?

2 What would be the effect on the price of cannabis if it was legalised?

3 The effects of a rise in interest rates on the level of spending by consumers in the economy.

4 A reduction in the basic rate of income tax from 20p in the £, to 18p in the £.

5 Causes of the Great Depression from 1929 onwards.

6 The price of a share in ICI.

7 The effects on house prices if the government abolished tax relief on mortgages.

8 Why is Britain now one of the poorest countries, relatively speaking, in the European Union?

9 Membership of the European Union on UK trade with Europe.

10 Auction prices.

1, 2, 4, 6, 7, and 10 are microeconomic-based; 3, 5, 8, 9 are macroeconomic-based.

1.7 Positive and normative statements

In studying economics it is important to appreciate the differences between positive and normative statements. (This can be quite a complex subject. Here we will only focus on the main issues.)

Consider the following statements:

- William Shakespeare was alive in the sixteenth century.
- Today it is raining.
- Tomorrow it will be Saturday.

These are examples of **positive statements** and concern what was/what is/what will be the case. Whether they are correct or not can be tested by appealing to the facts: positive statements are said to be *testable*. For example, we can test the statement that 'it is raining today' i.e. it is a positive statement. Disagreements about positive statements can also be resolved by appealing to the facts: if both parties to the dispute stand outside in the rain they should be able to agree that, if it is raining, then it is raining. However, if it is not raining the positive statement can be shown to be wrong – it is *refutable*.

Now consider the following statements:

- Euthanasia should be legalised.
- Cigarette smoking ought to be banned.
- Economics must be studied from the age of eight.

These statements are concerned with what ought to be the case. They are called **normative statements** and are based on value judgements about what is desirable, or undesirable. If a person says that cigarette smoking should be banned then a view about what is desirable has been expressed. This viewpoint reflects the holder's value system about what is acceptable/unacceptable. (A person's value system, or code of morality, arises from several factors, for example, religious upbringing, experiences through life, parental influences, etc.) Another person may strongly disagree and argue that smoking should not be banned. Here the disagreement cannot be resolved by the disagreeing parties appealing to the facts, and so it is not possible to show that either view is wrong: *normative statements are not testable*. As a result, disagreement over normative statements have to be resolved by other means, such as conciliation, the courts, fighting, intimidation and diplomacy. Economics is concerned with positive issues, which can be expressed in the form of positive statements such as:

- an increase in the price of a commodity will reduce the amount of it which is purchased
- the imposition of a minimum wage will reduce the number of people employed
- ice-cream sales are higher in summer than winter.

Disputes about these issues can be resolved by an appeal to the facts. In their analysis of such issues economists endeavour to follow a value-free method of enquiry. There is now general agreement that it is impossible for economists to always be completely value-free, or objective, after all economists are human beings and their perceptions of any economic issue are bound to be affected by their value-systems and emotions. Nonetheless, economists are still able to explore economic issues with a high degree of objectivity, i.e. maintain a disinterested approach to their subject. Economics being concerned with developing and testing positive statements against factual evidence is largely a positive subject. (Even so an important branch of economics is concerned with normative questions – welfare economics.) You may recall that the seven general questions outlined earlier were all expressed in positive terms. Now try Activity 8.

ACTIVITY 8

Which of the following statements are positive?

1 Adam Smith lived between 1723–1790.

2 VAT is inflationary.

3 Violence on TV has to be banned.

4 Abortion should be made illegal.

5 All the homeless should be re-housed immediately.

Only statements 1 and 2 are positive. The others are normative, indicating views about what should be: no violence on TV, no abortion, no homelessness. They reflect opinions based on what people consider to be right/acceptable or wrong/unacceptable.

Now try Activity 9, which summarises the key points relating to the distinction between positive and normative statements.

ACTIVITY 9

Complete the two sentences as appropriate with the following key words: free, laden, subjective, objective, correct.

1 Positive statements are value _____ and_____.

2 Positive statements are not always _____.

3 Normative statements are value- _____ and _____.

1 _____ free _____ and objective.

2 _____ correct. Positive statements can be wrong (i.e. they could be refuted), e.g. J. M. Keynes lived between 1883 and 1956 is not correct, because he died in 1946.

3 ____ laden _____ subjective.

Summary

In this section we began by looking at a number of definitions of economics. We went on to look at why scarcity arises, its implications, and the need for some means of allocating resources to produce commodities to satisfy wants. We considered the different types of economy which arise from different methods of allocation, in theory, two extreme types of economy: command (centralised decision making about the allocation of resources), and market (decentralised) economies. We found that, in reality, economies have elements from both extremes: economies are said to be mixed as a result. Then we saw how all economies have to answer seven general questions in allocating resources.

The section ended by looking at two sets of important distinctions: between microeconomics/macroeconomics and between positive and normative statements. In short, we have covered several concepts/distinctions which are of fundamental importance to an understanding of what constitutes the subject matter of economics. In Section 2 we will explore some of the concepts/distinctions further by employing a new concept: the **production possibility boundary**.

SECTION TWO

The Production Possibility Boundary and its Implications

Introduction

In this section we will use some of the subject matter covered in Section 1 by using the concept of the production possibility boundary. This will consolidate some of what we have covered, help to clarify some of the issues and extend our discussions. It will help you to answer questions like:

- Is it possible for a country to produce more goods and services?
- What is the difference between the statement that resources are fully employed and the statement that resources are efficiently employed?
- How do you graphically represent a re-allocation of resources from one sector of the economy to another, e.g. following privatisation?
- Is a country making the best use of its scarce resources?
- What are the benefits of economic growth?

2.1 The production possibility boundary (PPB)

ASSUMPTIONS

The **production possibility boundary** is also referred to variously as the **production possibility frontier**, or the **transformation curve**. It represents the boundary between combinations of public sector output and private sector output which are just attainable or attainable and combinations of output from the two sectors which are not attainable. We'll use PPB, the abbreviated form for the production possibility boundary.

We saw earlier that economies are mixed, consisting of a public sector (the state owns the resources) and a private sector (resources owned by private individuals). We can show how economies vary in their mix of sectors by examining the PPB for an imaginary economy.

To do this we need to make some assumptions:

- the economy consists of two sectors, one public, the other private
- the country's resources are fully employed
- the country's resources are efficiently employed
- resources can move easily from one sector to the other
- the economy is not growing over time: it is stationary.

USING GRAPHS – THE BASICS

The basic features of graphs are as follows:

- A graph has a vertical side (called the 0y axis) and a horizontal side (called the 0x axis). The two sides meet at the origin.

- The axes measure values, the size of which increases with distance, to the right and upwards, starting from the value of zero at the origin.

- Each point has a unique two number reference called its co-ordinates: the first number represents its position on the 0x axis, the second number represents its position on the 0y axis. For example, suppose we have a point such as A with the co-ordinates (3,4) this means it will be located 3 units along the 0x axis and four units up the 0y axis.

- The units can be expressed in single values, in tens, hundreds, etc. and can refer to any unit of measurement, such as inches, metres, tonnes, litres, etc.

These basic features are shown in Figure 2.

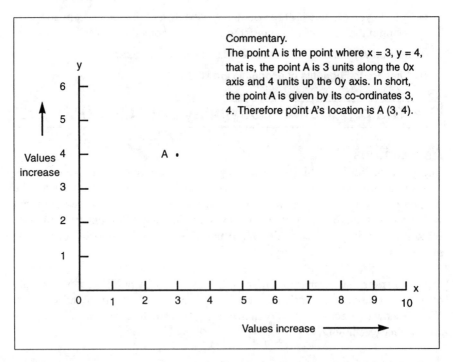

Figure 2: The basic features of a graph

ACTIVITY 10

Redraw the set of axes that we have just been referring to on a separate sheet of graph paper and plot these additional points: B(3,3), C(7,3), D(0,1), E(1,2), F(4,3).

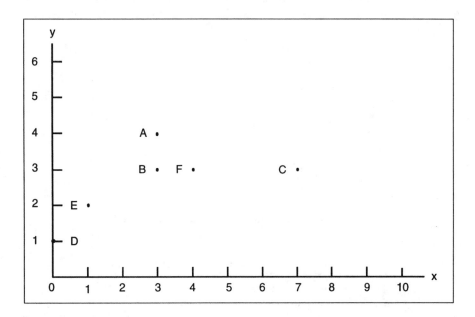

You should note how important the order of the two numbers is by looking at A and F where the numbers are the same but the order is different, so their locations are different. We adopt the convention that the first number in a set of co-ordinates refers to the horizontal axis and the second to the vertical axis so that A(3,4) is the point where x=3, y=4, whereas the point F (4,3) is the point where x=4 and y=3.

So we now have a system of identifying points by their co-ordinates and for plotting points using their co-ordinates. This represents the basis of drawing graphs.

With graphs the points are joined by a suitable line to produce a curve, examples of which include the production possibility boundary and the market demand curve, etc. (as we'll see in Unit 2 and other later units).

GRAPHICAL REPRESENTATION OF THE PPB

Given the five assumptions noted earlier and what we have just said about graphs we can now represent the total output of a country by means of a point on a graph with the location of the point varying according to the mix of the economy between the two sectors. To see this we'll take an imaginary economy with two sectors and vary the sector-mix to see how the combinations of output from the two sectors change. We will represent these different sector-mixes on a graph which uses the 0y axis to represent the public sector and the 0x axis to represent the private sector.

Suppose for a moment that our economy is a pure (or extreme) command economy with all resources owned by the state (i.e. there is no private sector). Total output could be shown by the point A on the 0y axis in Figure 3, representing a combination of ya from the public sector and xa from the private sector (=0).

Now suppose that our economy is a pure market system with no government intervention and all resources owned by private individuals (on the extreme right of Figure 1). Total output could be shown by the point B on the 0x axis in Figure 3, representing a combination of xb from the private sector and yb from the public sector (=0).

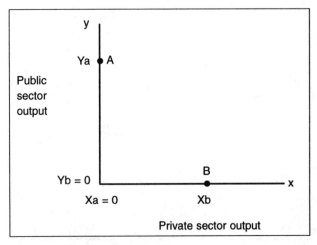

Figure 3: Output under command and pure market economies

Here A represents a combination of ya, (public sector output) and xa (zero output from the private sector). B represents a combination of yb (public sector output =0) and xb from the private sector.

Let us now turn to the mixed economy. Suppose our economy now has a large public sector relative to the private sector), with a total output of C, as in Figure 4 below.

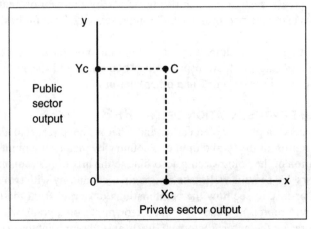

Figure 4: A mixed economy with a large public sector

C now represents a combination of output of yc from the public sector and output of xc from the private sector.

By contrast, if our economy has a large private sector and a relatively small public sector we could represent total output by D in Figure 5.

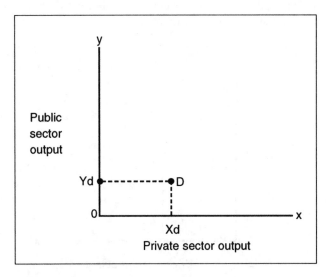

Figure 5: A mixed economy with a large private sector

Here D represents the combination of output yd from the public sector and output xd from the private sector.

When we put all this together we have four combinations of output, shown by the points A, B, C and D in Figure 6.

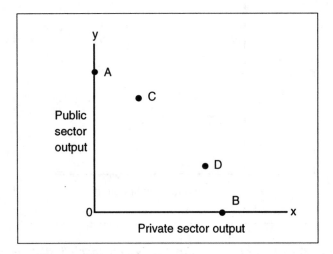

Figure 6: Different economies

Suppose we had also examined our economy at four other public/private sector mixes and found that the total outputs at each mix was E, F, G and H. When we plot these along with A, B, C and D we would have eight points as shown in Figure 7. When we join up these points we would have a PPB for our economy, with each point on the PPB representing different combinations of output from the two sectors. For example, the point E represents an output from the public sector of ye and an output from the private sector of xe.

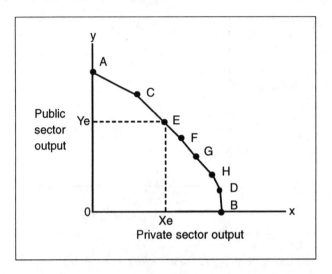

Figure 7: The production possibility boundary

THE PPB

Look at Figure 8 for a moment.

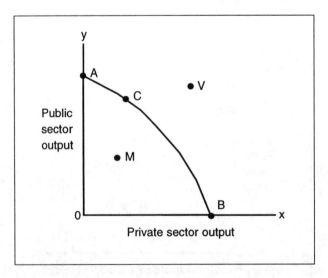

Figure 8: The PPB as the boundary between attainable/just attainable and non-attainable combinations of output from two sectors

The PPB thus represents the boundary between combinations of public sector output and private sector output which are just attainable (represented by points, such as A, B, C.... H) or attainable (represented by points to the left of the PPB, or below it, for example M), and combinations of output from the two sectors which are not attainable (represented by points to the right of the PPB, or above it, for example V). Given our five assumptions earlier, our economy can only be represented by a point on the PPB, for example C.

In Figures 7 and 8 you can see that we have drawn the PPB as sloping downwards (i.e. has a negative slope) and is concave to the origin. Now you might ask two questions here. First, why does the PPB slope downwards? Secondly, why have we drawn the PPB as a curve and not a straight line? The PPB slopes downwards because in an economy where resources are fully and efficiently employed, it is only possible to increase the output of one sector by reducing the output from the other sector, i.e. there is an opportunity cost of a sector producing more. However, because resources vary in their efficiency at producing different commodities, it will be necessary to transfer increasing amounts of resources from one sector to the other in order to achieve equal increases in output, and so the PPB is concave to the origin: this is the phenomenon of **increasing opportunity cost**. Though the explanation for this is quite complex, we can still provide you with an intuitive explanation of the phenomenon.

Consider Figure 9 carefully for a moment.

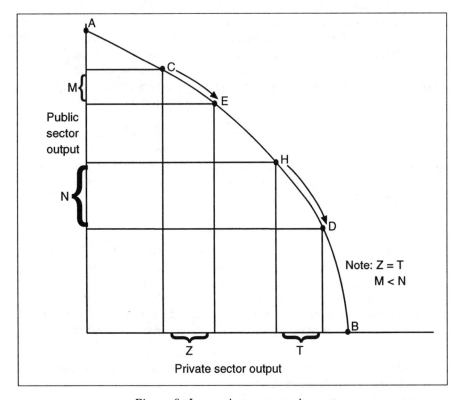

Figure 9: Increasing opportunity cost

The economy consists of two sectors: a public sector producing defence goods such as tanks, and a private sector producing food. Let's assume that workers vary in their abilities to make things: some workers are better able (i.e. produce more) to make defence goods such as tanks, than private sector commodities such as food; others are better at making food. (Remember here that we all differ in our abilities to do/make things e.g. some of us are good at gardening and hopeless at car maintenance, others are good at photography/do-it-yourself, but have no idea with gardening, etc.)

Suppose that an economy is at the point C on its PPB. To increase private sector output by a given amount (say by an amount represented by z) would require (say) 1,000 workers being transferred from the public sector to the private sector. Suppose that these workers are more productive making private sector commodities (for example food), and less productive at making public sector commodities (for example, tanks): the loss of the 1,000 workers to the public sector may only reduce public sector output by an amount equal to m, but increase private sector output by z.

In order to achieve a further increase in private sector output equal in size to z, it will be necessary for more than 1,000 workers to move to (i.e. be reallocated in) the private sector. For example, if the economy is at point H, the amount t (=z) can only be achieved by, say, 5,000 workers moving to the private sector because these workers are a lot less productive at making private sector commodities than the workers who transferred earlier to the private sector. So it will now take a lot more workers to transfer from the public sector to produce a given increase in food. Conversely, these workers were the best people at the making of tanks, so their loss to the public sector will result in a dramatic fall in the output of the public sector, as shown by n, which is larger than the earlier reduction in public sector output represented by m. Thus, to produce an extra amount of private sector output t (=z) now requires a reduction in public sector output of n (n is greater than m).

In short, the opportunity cost of having increasing amounts of private sector output is ever-increasing reductions in the amounts produced by the public sector. So much for a movement down the PPB. A movement upwards along the PPB would result in increasing (equal) amounts of public sector output and ever-increasing reductions in the output of the private sector.

It may be useful to summarise our discussions so far.

1 If an economy's total output is represented by a point on the PPB, it is only possible to have more output from one sector by decreasing the output from the other sector. This would require a re-allocation of resources from one sector to the other. Thus an increase in output from one sector has an opportunity cost measured by the amount of the reduction from the other sector: this is reflected in the negative slope of the PPB.

2 The shape of the PPB (i.e. concave slope) reflects the phenomenon of increasing opportunity cost, which arises because resources are not equally productive in all economic activities.

ACTIVITY 11

In the space below show:

1 what you think the PPB would look like if resources were equally productive in all their uses

2 the PPB for an economy which experiences decreasing opportunity cost.

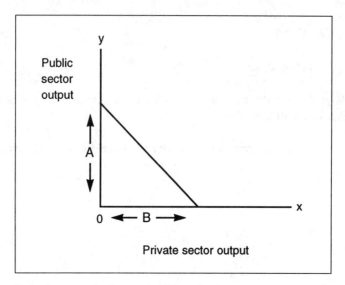

1 Here there is a constant opportunity cost as resources are equally efficient at providing public sector and private sector commodities.

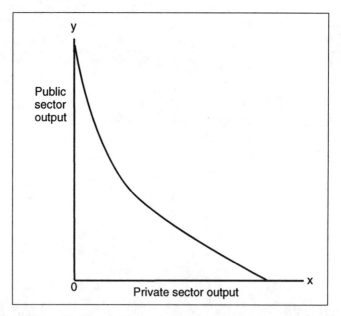

2 Here increases in output from one sector result in ever-decreasing reductions in the amount of the other sector's output that have to be given up. The PPB in this case would be convex to the origin.

REALLOCATING RESOURCES

Suppose our economy is producing x_p private sector output and y_p public sector output, and this is represented by point P on the PPB. Is it possible to have more private sector output?

Consider Figure 10 for a moment.

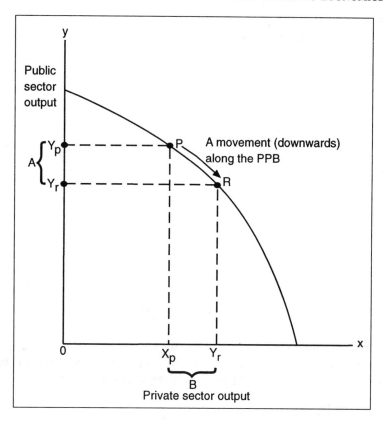

Figure 10: Resource reallocation

If the economy is at P, it will only be possible to increase private-sector output by reducing public-sector output, i.e. by reallocating resources. For example, to have the combination represented by the point R, public sector output will have to be reduced by A = $y_p y_r$, the opportunity cost of the increased private sector, B = $x_p x_r$, (i.e the increase in the scale of the private sector) is A, the public sector output foregone. A reallocation of resources and, accordingly, a change in the relative importance of the two sectors, is represented by a movement along the PPB. For example, a movement down the PPB represents a reallocation of resources in favour of the private sector.

ACTIVITY 12

'In wartime the relative importance of the public sector increases'. Show this graphically.

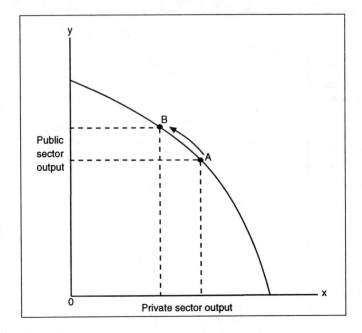

Resources are reallocated over time, either by the state commanding/directing that resources will shift from one sector to another (e.g. in wartime resources move to the public sector in response to government demands like conscription).

INSIDE THE PPB

Consider Figure 11 for a moment.

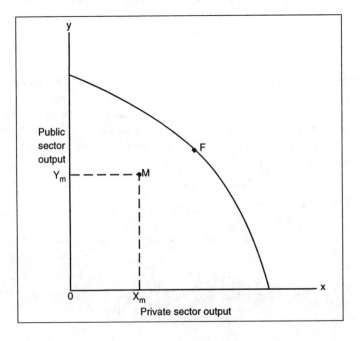

Figure 11: Inside the PPB

Is it possible for an economic system to be operating inside its PPB, for example at M? The answer is no if we retain our assumptions that resources are fully employed and efficiently employed. If we relax either, or both, of these assumptions together, then an economy can operate to the left of its PPB, for example at a point like M in Figure 11. When the economy is operating to the left of the PPB, resources are being wasted: at a point like M, the combination y_m private sector output, and x_m public sector output is produced – output from both sectors could be increased.

Suppose the government wishes to move the economy to its PPB, for example to a point like F, it would have to ask first, why is the economy at M? Economists could offer three explanations – resources are not fully employed, resources are not efficiently employed, and a combination of resources not being fully and efficiently employed. Our government would then ask what can be done to shift the economy to its PPB as represented by a point such as F. Three solutions could be offered, each one reflecting the suggested explanation of why the economy is at M.

1 If the explanation is that resources are not being fully employed (i.e. unemployment) our economists would advise the government to reflate the economy, for example by reducing interest rates (monetary policy) and/or reducing tax rates (fiscal policy) in order to get people to spend more money. These are called **demand-side policies**.

2 If the explanation is that resources are not being efficiently employed our economists would advise the government to adopt policies to improve the efficiency with which resources are employed. These are called **supply-side policies**. Economists (and others) have identified numerous causes of economic inefficiency, for example powerful trade unions, weak management, poor education and training, divisive class system, inefficient public sector, excessive government regulation. As a result, supply-side policies consist of a variety of measures to improve the workings of the market economy and reduce the scale of the public sector (for example by privatisation), tax cuts, initiatives to increase training and retraining, deregulation, etc. and so shift the economy towards its PPB.

3 If the economy is at M because resources are unemployed, and those employed are not efficiently employed, our economist could recommend a mix of policies: reflationary monetary and fiscal policies, combined with supply-side policies.

ECONOMIC GROWTH

If we restore our assumptions that resources are fully and efficiently employed, but relax our assumption that the economy is stationary, output will increase as the economy's productive capacity grows over time. So by means of economic growth it will be possible to have more output from both sectors. This is shown in Figure 12.

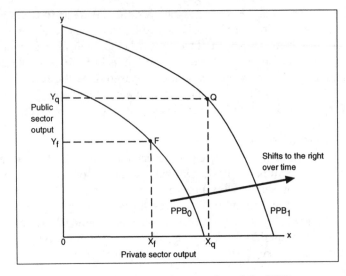

Figure 12: Economic growth and the PPB

As a result of economic growth the PPB has shifted to the right from PPB_0 to PPB_1. Initially the combination of output from the two sectors was F. After the PPB shifted to PPB_1, the combination Q is now obtainable, so that public sector output has increased by $y_f y_q$ and private sector output has increased by $x_f x_q$. The attractiveness of economic growth is that it allows the amounts produced by both sectors to increase.

ACTIVITY 13

In our example above it was assumed that the two sectors both grew at the same rate, say 3% per year. Sketch a graph to show the effect of the public sector growing more slowly than the private sector over several years.

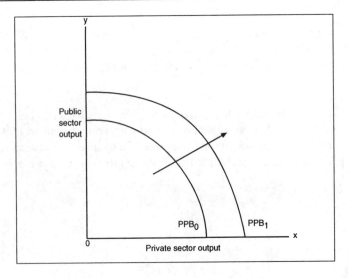

The PPB has shifted to the right to PPB_1, which represents larger combinations of output than those represented by PPB_0.

Summary

In this section we discussed the concept of the production possibility boundary and used graphs to illustrate how economies vary in their mix of sectors.

We discovered that a movement along a PPB is due to resources being transferred over time, from one sector to another (a reallocation of resources), whereas economic growth causes a shift of the PPB outwards to the right over time.

In a stationary economy with resources fully and efficiently employed, it is only possible to increase the output of one sector by reducing output in the other sector, i.e. by re-allocating resources. This is represented by a movement along the PPB: it is impossible to increase output from both sectors. If resources are not fully and efficiently employed, it is possible to increase output from one or both sectors by an appropriate combination of demand-side and supply-side policies. This is shown by a shift of the economy from a point inside the PPB to a point on the PPB, representing a full and efficient allocation of resources.

In a growing economy with resources fully and efficiently employed, it is possible to increase output from one or both sectors, without having to reduce output in one of the two sectors. Economic growth is represented by the PPB shifting to the right over time.

We established that the PPB concept can be used to help clarify and represent many issues in economics, for example the distinction between resources being fully and efficiently employed; economic growth; opportunity cost; the phenomenon of increasing opportunity cost and the re-allocation of resources.

Unit Summary

In Section 1 of this unit we began our study of economics by considering the problem of scarcity and its implications, especially how resources have to be allocated amongst competing wants. We noted that resources can be allocated by the state, or by economic agents pursuing their own self-interest, or by a combination of the two i.e. by the mixed economy. All economies have to provide answers to seven general questions, which we listed and discussed.

We established that the study of economics is divided into microeconomics and macroeconomics and looked at the distinction between positive and normative statements, and its significance for economists.

In Section 2 we employed the production possibility boundary (PPB) concept to consolidate some of what we covered in Section 1 and to extend our discussion of basic economic issues. We were also able to take the opportunity to introduce the basics of employing graphs.

We will now be moving on to Unit 2, *The Theory of Allocation* – how markets work (i.e. allocate resources) and why they may not work so well, or at all.

Recommended Reading

Begg, D, (1994) *Economics,* Chapter 1, McGraw-Hill, 4th edn

Eichner, A S, *et al* (1983) W*hy Economics is not yet a Science*, See introduction, esssays 1,3, and 8, Macmillian.

Friedman, M, *Essays in Postve Economics*, See essay 'The Method of Positive Economics', p.3–43.

Hayek, FA, (1945) *The Price System as a Mechanism for Using Knowledge,* (Originally published under the title, 'The Use of Knowledge in Society') American Economic Review. Vol 35, No 4. September 1945, p.519–30.

Katouzian, H, (1980) *Ideology and Method in Economics*, Macmillian.

Knight, F H, *The Economic Organisation,* See 'Social Economic Organisation' p.3–30.

Lispsey, R G and Chrystal, K A, (1995) Chapter 1, 2 and 3, Oxford University Press, 8th edn

Parkin, M and King, D, (1995) *Economics,* Chapter 1, and 3, Addison-Wesley, 2nd edn

Popper, K, (1934) *The Logic of Scientific Discovery,* (Translated into English 1959), Basic Books, New York.

Robbins, L, (1932) *The Nature and Significance of Economic Science,*

Sloman, J, (1994) *Economics,* Chapter 1, Harvester-Wheatsteaf, 2nd edn

Smith, A, *The Wealth of Nations,* Penguin Classics (Covers books I–III only)

UNIT 2
THE
ELEMENTARY
THEORY OF
ALLOCATION

Introduction

The price of a commodity often bears little relationship to the cost of producing it, or to the value of a commodity. For example, water is more essential than wine, but is still cheaper than wine in the UK. Again, consider diamonds: these command high prices but are hardly essential for our existence. You may have noticed that sometimes the price of a commodity may rise sharply at certain times of the year, for example flowers near Mother's Day. Also, the prices of certain commodities such as crude oil (and so petrol) are very responsive to events overseas, like the outbreak of a war, or a revolution. When there is a higher than average incidence of frost in Brazil, the price of coffee soars.

So what determines the price at which a commodity is sold? This unit will help you to understand how prices of commodities are determined, why prices change, and the consequences of a price change for a supplier – their income and profit.

This unit is divided into three sections:

- Section 1 looks at how markets work: how prices are determined, why the price of a commodity can change, and the consequences of a change in price for the way resources are allocated to the production of different commodities.

- Section 2 is concerned with the concept of elasticity: the measuring, or quantifying, of the responsiveness to a change in price, or income, of the amount people buy of a commodity. For example, if the price of compact discs (CDs) falls by 50%, what will happen to sales of CDs? Will the amount increase sharply, say by more than 50%, or hardly at all? Also, we'll look briefly at the effect of price changes on the amounts producers are willing and able to supply. Some of the ways in which the different measures of elasticity can be used in the business world will be described.

- Finally, in Section 3 we'll look briefly at market failure: what it is and how a government may respond to it. For example, suppose a producer is damaging the local environment by emitting noxious gases, what can the government do in order to reduce the producer's environmentally-damaging activities? We'll see that one course of action would be to tax the producer, but how effective this would be will depend on how responsive sales of the commodity are to the rise in its price following the imposition of the tax.

Objectives

By the end of the unit you should be able to:

● explain the meanings of demand and supply and show why demand and supply change

● show how demand and supply interact to determine the price of a commodity and how changes in demand and supply affect the price of a commodity

● distinguish between equilibrium and disequilibrium

● explain and apply the concept of elasticity

● interpret the values of different measures of elasticity

● explain the meaning of market failure

● list some of the different ways a government could remedy market failure.

SECTION ONE

The Market and the Market Economy

Introduction

In this section we will consider how markets work and look specifically at the concepts of demand, supply and price. We will see how prices are determined and why the price of a commodity can change. We will examine the consequences of a change in price for the way resources are allocated to the production of different commodities.

We need to recall, briefly, that a market economy consists of numerous buyers and sellers trading with each other in numerous types of market: there are markets in goods, services, labour, foreign currencies, money, rented accommodation, and so forth. In this section we will look at a market, the market for commodity X. What we learn about this market can be applied to any market because commodity X can be anything from a kilogram of potatoes to a degree qualification.

To understand how a market operates, and so the market economy we need to proceed in three stages, the order of which is as follows:

- demand
- supply
- price.

1.1 Demand

The quantity demanded of a commodity is the total amount all the buyers are willing and able to purchase at a particular price, over some period of time, such as a week, or a month.

In order to understand the concept of **demand** we need to begin with a typical individual, who we'll call consumer A, and look at how much of a particular commodity A will be willing and able to buy per week. We'll refer to this commodity as commodity X, or just X. In short, we'll be looking at the individual demand for X. Once we have looked at the individual demand for X, we'll go on to look at the market demand for X: how much of X will all the buyers in a market be willing and able to buy per week?

When considering demand we must not forget that in a market the demand for a commodity arises from the decisions of numerous buyers who act independently of everybody else. Buyers are assumed to pursue their own self-interest - to be as well-off as their income allows, or as an economist would say maximise their utility, where utility means well-being, or satisfaction.

INDIVIDUAL DEMAND

Imagine asking a consumer A, 'How much X would you buy in a week at 40p a can'? A may reply: '10 units'. Suppose we had said 60p, we could reasonably expect A to indicate less than 10 units, say 5; and if the price was only 30p? (20p? 10p?), A may have said 20 units (30 units, 35 units). We can use a table to express this information about how much of X our consumer A buys at different prices. Table 1 shows such a table: it represents the individual demand schedule for consumer A. The middle column (quantity demanded per week) represents the amount A wants to buy of X each week at different prices. (Remember we are using imaginary data for what we believe to be a typical consumer.)

Price (p)	Quantity demanded per week	Point on graph
10	35	a
20	30	b
30	20	c
40	10	d
60	5	e

Table 1: The individual demand schedule (consumer A)

Using the vertical or 0y axis to represent price, and the horizontal or 0x axis to represent the quantity demanded per week we can plot this data to derive an individual demand curve for A, as shown in Figure 1. Note that the points a, b, c, d, e represent the rows shown in Table 1, i.e. the quantity demanded per week at various prices.

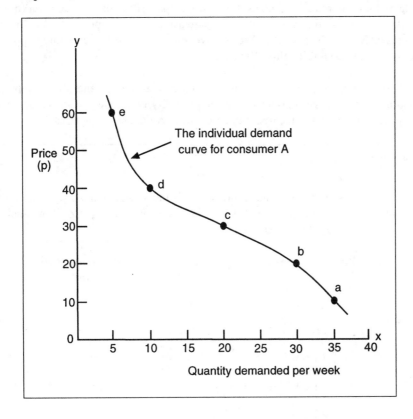

Figure 1: The individual demand curve (consumer A)

The shape of an individual demand curve will vary from consumer to consumer, reflecting differences in how much consumers like a commodity. Some curves slope downwards gently, others steeply. Though they are usually drawn curved, they can also be represented by a straight line. In nearly all cases individual demand curves slope downwards from left to right. (As we are only looking at the elementary theory of allocation we don't have to worry about demand curves which slope upwards. However, you are free to look into this if you so wish. So for our purposes here we'll only look at demand curves which slope downwards.)

From Table 1 and Figure 1 we can see that A will buy less of X when it is expensive (price is high). This raises an important question: why does A buy less X at higher prices and more X at lower prices? We can offer a brief explanation here.

Suppose there are other commodities besides X, and some of these are similar to X (that is they are substitutes for X) and their prices do not change as the price of X increases. When the price of X increases it becomes relatively more expensive, and so consumers may switch to cheaper substitutes for X, so the amount of X wanted decreases. Let us take a simple example. Suppose that X is a tin of cola called X–Cola which has a very close substitute, M-Cola, and both types of cola cost 40p a can. Suppose also that A buys five tins of each type of cola each week (A likes them equally). If the price of X-Cola increases to 50p, A will want to buy less X-Cola and buy more of M-Cola as it is now cheaper. If the price of X-Cola rose to £1, A may stop buying it as it is now too expensive. So as the price of a commodity increases, X will buy less of it. We'll leave you to consider what would happen if the price of X-Cola fell below 40p a can.

In short, if the price of a commodity increases (decreases) and all other prices remain the same, the amount of that commodity consumers want to buy will decrease (increase), i.e. the quantity demanded will decrease (increase).

ACTIVITY 1

Use the following table (which represents A's individual demand schedule for another commodity, Z) to plot A's individual demand curve for Z. How much of Z will be bought at (1) £0.85 and (2) £1.35?

Price per metre^2 (£)	Quantity demanded per month
0.5	200
0.75	175
1.00	150
1.25	125
1.50	100

1   At £0.85 A will buy 165m² per month.

2   At £1.35 A will buy 115m² per month.

Note: in the example considered here A's demand curve for Z was a straight line demand curve, hence you were able to calculate your answers for (1) and (2) accurately. Just to make sure you got the graph correct here it is:

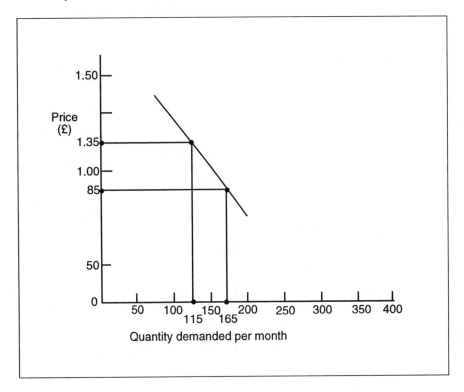

DEPENDENT AND INDEPENDENT VARIABLES

We have seen that changes in the price of X lead to changes in the quantity demanded of X by individual A, that is there is a relationship between the price of X and quantity demanded of X. Here price and quantity demanded are called **variables**, since their values can vary: they are not fixed or constant.

There are two types of variable: **dependent** and **independent**. In our example quantity demanded per week is a dependent variable because the amount of X our consumer wishes to buy depends on the price of X. By contrast, the price of X does not depend on the quantity demanded by A for its value: price is an independent variable. A change in the value of an independent variable will cause a change in the value of a dependent variable. We need to add that though many variables are related to each other, we can't always be certain which is the dependent variable and which is, or are, the independent variable/variables. We appreciate that all this seems rather technical, but it is necessary and we will use the terms relationship, dependent and independent variables quite soon! To help you grasp the basics try Activity 2

ACTIVITY 2

For each of the following pairs, state whether there is a relationship (yes/no), and indicate which variable is the dependent variable:

1 weight, height of people

2 age, weight of people

3 petrol consumed by a car and, miles driven in that car

4 salesperson's bonus, amount sold by salesperson.

Relationship (Yes/no)	Dependent variable
1	
2	
3	
4	

1   Yes. Weight (generally, weight increases with height).

2   Yes. Weight (generally, weight increases with age).

Important: here you may note that the value of a dependent variable can be determined by more than one independent variable. Here weight would seem to be determined by both height and age. (In reality this is true).

3   Yes. Petrol consumed.

4   Yes. Salesperson's bonus.

To summarise: when one variable, Y, changes in response to changes in another variable, we say that there is a **relationship** between the two variables. This can be expressed in another way. We can say that Y is a **function** of X. In symbols this is written as a function like this:

$Y = f(X)$.

Here:

Y represents the dependent variable (e.g. quantity demanded)

= f stands for 'is a function of', or 'is related to', or 'depends on'

(X) represents the independent variable (e.g. price).

If Y is a function of several independent variables, such as (X,Z,A,B,C) we will have the following function:

$Y = f(X,Z,A,B,C)$.

Now try the following activity.

ACTIVITY 3

In people, weight, height and age are related. From the list below choose the correct expression, or expressions.

1 age = f (height, weight)

2 height = f (age)

3 weight = f (height, age)

4 weight = f (height)

5 height = f (weight)

---

1   You chose: age = f (height, weight). Incorrect: this expression says that age is a dependent variable. (It says that people can change their age by putting on weight or height.) Go back to the question and choose another answer.

2   You chose: height = f (age). Correct: this expression says that height is a dependent variable and is related to age. As children grow older they do grow taller, and as adults grow older they often shrink a little (or quite a lot).

3   You chose: weight = f (height, age). Correct: this expression says that weight depends on, or is related to height and age.

4   You chose: weight = f (height). Correct: weight is related to height. As people get taller they get heavier, and on average tall people are heavier than shorter ones.

5   You chose: height = f (weight). Correct: height is related to weight. As people get taller they get heavier.

As we have seen the relationship between a dependent variable and an independent variable can be shown graphically (as in Figure 1) where the individual demand curve showed the relationship between price and the quantity demanded, *other things being equal* (the significance of these last four words will be examined soon).

One final point is necessary here. You should be able to recall that the two variables price and quantity demanded move in opposite directions to each other. For example, a rise in the price of X led to a fall in the quantity demanded of X. This type of relationship is called an inverse relationship: a change in an independent variable causes a change in the dependent variable, but in the opposite direction. So, the individual demand curve represents the inverse relationship between the price of X and the quantity demanded of X. As a result of the inverse relationship between price and the quantity demanded, the individual demand curve has a negative slope (that is, it slopes downwards from left to right, as we saw earlier in Figure 1).

INDIVIDUAL DEMAND CONDITIONS

We now need to look at the other factors which determine how much of X our consumer will want to buy. These other factors or determinants, are called **demand conditions**, and include:

1   the prices of other commodities

2   how much income A has available to spend

3   A's tastes

4   fashion

5   health considerations

6   marketing activities

7   other factors.

We will now briefly look at each of these demand conditions.

1   The prices of other commodities

As the prices of other commodities change, the amount X our consumer would like to buy may change. Some examples may be useful here.

Let's take two commodities which are substitutes for each other, for example beef and lamb. Suppose the price of the two types of meat is £5 per kilogram and the price of beef increases sharply so that it becomes more expensive. If A considers that beef and lamb are substitutes for each other, A will buy less beef and more lamb. So the amount of beef bought will decrease, and the amount of lamb bought by A will increase because A switches from the more expensive meat, beef, to the relatively cheaper lamb. So a rise in the price of a commodity will increase purchases of its substitutes. This you should recall is what happened when we looked at the effect of an increase in the price of one type of cola on the purchases of a substitute.

You should appreciate that what constitutes a substitute for a commodity is a matter of personal choice. Would you consider tea to be a substitute for coffee? They may be substitutes for consumer A, but for me there is no substitute for coffee. Would you consider Typhoo and Tetley tea-bags to be substitutes?

Now let's take two commodities which complement each other, such as turkey and cranberry sauce. Here an increase in the price of turkey would lead to a decrease in the quantity of turkey demanded, because our consumer would switch to a cheaper substitute, such as chicken. Because A buys less turkey the amount of cranberry sauce bought would decrease. Similarly, with fish and chips a sharp rise in the price of fish could reduce the amount of chips bought by A. So an increase (decrease) in the price of a commodity will reduce (increase) purchases of its complements.

ACTIVITY 4

Suppose that early frosts destroyed much of the coffee crop.

Explain what you think would probably happen to:

1   the price of coffee

2   sales of tea

3   sales of Coffeemate. (Coffeemate is a coffee whitener or milk substitute for use only in coffee but not in tea.)

---

1   As coffee becomes scarce we would expect the price of coffee to increase.

2   Since tea is a substitute for coffee, sales of tea would also tend to rise as people switched from coffee to tea.

3   Since Coffeemate is a complement of coffee, and less coffee will be drunk, we would expect sales of Coffeemate to fall.

2   Income
If the income of A increases, for example because A has just acquired a better paid job, then A may buy more of X. In this case X is called a **normal good** (the term also applies to services), and the relationship between income and the amount of X bought by A is a positive one: the increase in income led to an increase in the amount of X wanted by A. However, if the increase led to a decrease in the amount

of X wanted by A, X is said to be an **inferior good** (nothing to do with quality). Examples of inferior goods include public transport, tripe, potatoes, mild beer, and holidays at English seaside resorts. Normal goods include wine, lager, white meat, pasta, foreign holidays.

3 Tastes

These refer to long-term or long-standing desires for a commodity. For a variety of reasons we develop tastes for particular commodities and these tend to remain fixed over several years.

4 Fashions

What is fashionable may exert a strong influence on the sales of certain commodities, but only for a short time, for example a few months. As fashions change quickly so sales may rise sharply and collapse just as quickly.

5 Health considerations

When individuals learn that something may damage their health (for example, certain oral contraceptives, red meat, butter, asbestos), sales may fall. Favourable publicity may increase sales of some commodities such as leisure equipment and health foods. However, we should note that an increase in sales of some commodities may be due to more than one factor. For example, increased sales of leisure commodities by individuals may also reflect the fact that they are now better off (more income).

6 Marketing activities

These can be very effective in creating a demand for a new commodity, stimulating purchases of existing commodities, and getting an individual to switch to a substitute commodity provided by a competitor. Also, they can be effective in building up loyalty to a commodity (this is called **brand loyalty**), so reducing the chance of an individual like A switching to a substitute because it is better or cheaper, or for some other reason.

7 Other factors

Several other factors may affect how much of X our consumer will want to buy. These are likely to be less important than the first six demand conditions so we'll put these together and call them the **residual factors**.

THE INDIVIDUAL DEMAND FUNCTION

All these factors which determine an individual's demand for a commodity can be summarised in the form of an individual demand function like that shown here:

$$Q^d_x = f(P_x, P_s,..., P_{sm}, P_{c1},...,P_{cn}, Y,T,F,H,M,R).$$

Here:

Q^d_x represents the amount of X wanted, or quantity demanded, by the individual A

= f, as you'll recall means is a 'function of', 'or related to', or 'depends on'

P_x represents the price of the commodity X

$P_{s1},...,P_{sm}$ represents the prices of the m substitutes for X

$P_{c1},...,P_{cn}$ represents the prices of the n complements of X

Y represents the income of A

T,F,H represents tastes (T), fashion (F), health (H)

M represents marketing activities.

R represents all the less important factors which may affect the amount of X our consumer wishes to buy, or the residual factors, hence the use of R.

Don't be put off by the look or length of the individual demand function. You should remember that it merely summarises something from the real world: that the quantity demanded of a commodity by an individual is determined by its price and several other factors, such as how much money the individual has and various other demand conditions.

ACTIVITY 5

Look at the expression $Q^d_m = f(P_m,Y,T,F,R)$.

1 Q^d_m is what type of variable?

2 All the factors inside the bracket are called _____ variables.

3 What does the expression tell you about commodity m's substitutes and complements?

---

1   a dependent variable

2   independent

3   if the expression is correct, it would appear that commodity m has no substitutes and no complements.

THE DISTINCTION BETWEEN A MOVEMENT ALONG AN INDIVIDUAL DEMAND CURVE AND A SHIFT OF THE INDIVIDUAL DEMAND CURVE

We have seen that the quantity demanded of a commodity is determined by its price (this is called its own price) and several other factors called demand conditions. We will now examine how changes in the price of a commodity and the demand conditions affect the quantity of demanded by our consumer A.

First, we'll look at the effects of changes in the price of X. A change in the price of a commodity will lead to a movement along the demand curve. (In the third part of this section – on price – we'll look at why the price of a commodity can change. For now we only need to accept that the price of a commodity can change.) For example, if the price of X increases, A will want to buy less of it. This is shown by a movement (upwards) along the demand curve from A to B in Figure 2 indicating that the quantity demanded has fallen from q_0 to q_1 in response to a rise in the price of X from p_0 to p_1.

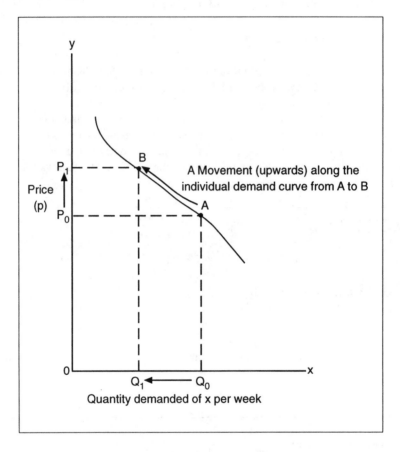

*Figure 2: A **decrease** in the quantity demanded*

Here we may recall that when we examined the effect of a change in price earlier, we assumed that everything else stayed the same. This assumption is called *ceteris paribus* which is the Latin for 'other things being equal'. (This assumption is needed so we can examine the effects of a change in an independent variable on a dependent variable, for example the effect of a change in price on the quantity demanded of commodity X.) In short, other things being equal, a rise in the price of X will lead to a fall in the quantity demanded of X by A.

What happens if the price of X is reduced? Other things being equal, a fall in price of X will lead to more of it being demanded by A. This is shown by a (downwards) movement along the demand curve from A to B in Figure 3 , indicating that the quantity demanded has risen from q_0 to q_1 as a result of the price of X falling from p_0 to p_1.

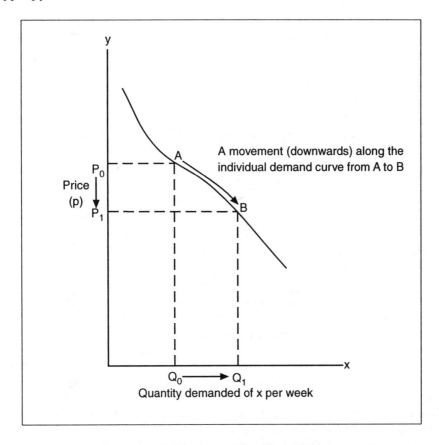

*Figure 3: An **increase** in the quantity demanded*

To summarise: a decrease in price will lead to an increase in the quantity demanded. This is shown by a (downwards) movement along the individual demand curve.

Now let's look at what happens if one of the demand conditions changes. If we return to our example where A got a new job and a rise in income, we saw that A may want to buy more of X, (i.e. X is a normal good). How can we show the increase in the amount of X our consumer wishes to buy following the increase in income?

All other things being equal (that is none of the other demand conditions change, and the price of X does not change), with an increase in income A will buy more X at the current price and at any other price. The effect of the increase in income is illustrated in Figure 4: the demand curve shifts to the right, from d_0 to d_1, indicating that A will want to buy more of X at each price. This is called an **increase in demand**.

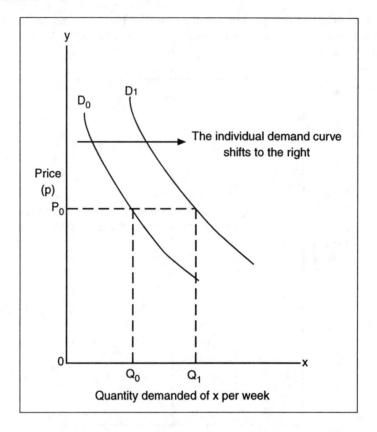

*Figure 4: An **increase** in demand – more is demanded at each price.*

Before getting the new job and the higher salary A was only willing and able to purchase q_0 of X at the price p_0. With the new higher salary A will now be willing and able to buy q_1 of X at the price p_0. The increase in income has increased the quantity demanded by $q_0 q_1$. Similarly, at any other price the quantity demanded of X by A will increase, because of the increase in A's income.

Here we have seen how an increase in income will cause the demand curve to shift to the right, indicating that more of a commodity is bought at each price. We now need to look at a shift of the demand curve to the left.

Suppose that a substitute for X becomes cheaper than X. Other things being equal, A may switch from X to the cheaper substitute and so the quantity demanded of X will fall. Figure 5 illustrates the effect of the fall in the price of the substitute on the quantity demanded of X by our individual A. The demand curve for X shifts to the left from d_0 to d_1, indicating that less of the commodity is demanded at each price because of the fall in the price of a substitute for commodity X.

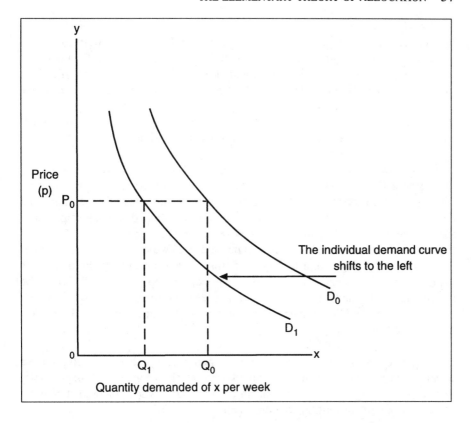

*Figure 5: A **decrease** in demand-less is demanded at each price*

Before the decrease in the price of the substitute the quantity of X demanded by A at the price p_0 was q_0. After the fall in the price of the substitute A will now only buy q_1 of X at the price p_0. The decrease in the price of the substitute has reduced the quantity demanded by q_1 q_0. Similarly, at any other price the quantity of X demanded by A will be reduced.

A brief summary of individual demand may prove useful at this point.

1   Other things being equal, a change in the price of X will lead to a change in the quantity of X demanded at that price. This is shown by a movement along the demand curve. (See Figures 2 and 3.)

2   Other things being equal, a change in any of the demand conditions will lead to a change in demand: the quantity demanded at each price will change. This is shown by a shift of the demand curve. (See Figures 4 and 5.)

3   The individual demand curve illustrates the inverse relationship between the quantity demanded of a commodity and its price, other things being equal. The points on the individual demand curve represent the rows of the individual demand schedule. (Did you remember this? If you had forgotten, go back to Table 1 and Figure 1.)

MARKET DEMAND

We have looked in detail at the individual demand for a commodity: how the amount of a commodity demanded by an individual will vary with the commodity's own price, and how changes in income and the other demand conditions will affect the amount of a commodity demanded by a consumer. Now we need to extend our examination of demand by looking at consumers as a whole, or in the aggregate, to derive the market demand for commodity X. Again, in our discussions here we will assume only the price of X changes, other things being equal.

Let us begin with consumer B, to see how much of X consumer B would buy at each of the prices noted earlier. Suppose the responses were 40 (10p), 35 (20p), 25 (30p), 20 (40p), and 15 (60p). From this information we could construct the individual demand schedule for consumer B, and B's individual demand curve, just as we did for consumer A earlier. If we repeated these exercises for consumers C, D and all the other consumers in the market for commodity X we could derive the market demand schedule by summing together (that is, adding up) all the quantities demanded by each consumer at a particular price, say 50p. This would give us the total or market demand for X at 50p. If we also have information on how much each consumer would buy at another price, say 20p, we would know what the market demand for X is at 20p.

If we repeated this process of summation, or summing together, for each price we would derive a market demand schedule like the one shown in Table 2. In principle, this process of summation across consumers is the same whether a market consists of two consumers, or millions of consumers.

Price (p)	Quantity demanded (millions) per week	Point on graph
10	500	a
20	400	b
30	300	c
40	200	d
60	100	e

Table 2: The market demand schedule (all consumers)

If we plot the information contained in the market demand schedule we derive the market demand curve, like that shown in Figure 6.

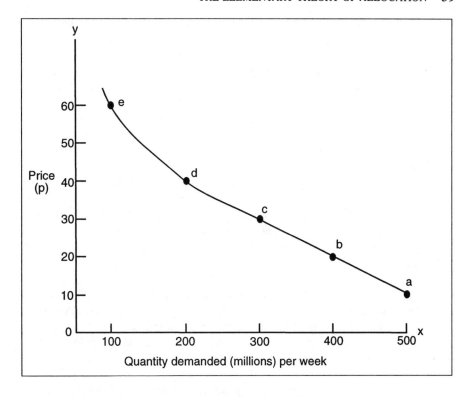

Figure 6: The market demand curve

As with the individual demand curve, the market demand curve slopes downwards, reflecting the inverse relationship between changes in the quantity demanded of a commodity and changes in its price, other things being equal. Now try Activity 6.

ACTIVITY 6

1 Explain in your own words what a market demand curve represents.

2 Complete the following sentence by selecting the correct ending from those supplied below.

A demand curve will have a negative slope (i.e. downward sloping) when

(a) the quantity demanded falls as the price increases **OR**

(b) the quantity demanded rises as the price increases.

---

1   The market demand curve represents the relationship between the price of the commodity and the quantity demanded by all the consumers in the market for that commodity. Usually the curve has a negative (or downward) slope,

indicating that as the price increases (decreases) the quantity demanded decreases (increases).

2   (a) is correct. A market demand curve is drawn with price on the 0y axis and quantity demanded per unit of time (e.g. a week, or month) on the 0x axis. In the general case where the quantity demanded increases (decreases) as the price is reduced (increased), the graph representing the market demand curve will slope downwards from the left to the right, that is have a negative slope.

MARKET DEMAND CONDITIONS

When we looked at the individual demand for a commodity we looked at seven factors which can affect how much of a commodity an individual wants to buy: these factors we called demand conditions. When we look at market demand we need to add two extra factors to our list of demand conditions, changes in which will cause the market demand curve to shift, to the left or the right, reflecting a change in demand.

These two extra factors are: the size of the population, and how the total income of a country is distributed amongst the population. Regarding the former demand condition, the larger the population the larger the number of consumers for a commodity. For example, the demand for compact discs will be higher in a country with 60 million people than in a country with only 50,000.

To see how the total income of all the consumers in a market affects the quantity demanded of a commodity, suppose that we have two countries with roughly equal populations and total income. In one country (M) there are some very rich people and most people are very poor – income is very unevenly distributed in this country. Here the rich will buy very expensive items such as luxury cars, big houses with swimming pools, etc.; and the poor will spend their money on basic foodstuffs (for example, potatoes, bread) and rented accommodation. In the other country (N) income is evenly distributed across the population: consumers' incomes are average or close to the average. Here consumers will buy better food, cars, property, enjoy better holidays (in the other country only the rich may be able to afford holidays) and so forth. In short, how the total income of a country is distributed amongst its population will affect the size of different markets, for example in country M the market for Rolls-Royce cars may be bigger than the market for Rolls-Royce cars in country N, whilst country N has a bigger market for home-ownership (people buying their own homes).

THE MARKET DEMAND FUNCTION

With these two extra demand conditions we are now in a position to write out the market demand function which summarises the factors which determine the quantity of a commodity demanded by all the consumers in the market for that commodity. Though the market demand function looks quite daunting, you should remember that it is only a means of summarising one aspect of the complex real world: what factors determine how much of a commodity people would like to buy.

ACTIVITY 7

Using what you have learnt about the individual demand function and the two additional market demand conditions, see if you can complete the market demand function for commodity X:

$$Q^d_x = f(P_x, P_{s1},...,P_{sm}, P_{c1},...,P_{cn}, \underline{\hspace{5cm}}).$$

...Y, Y_d, T, F, H, M, P, R)

Y_d (or something similar) represents the distribution of income across the population. P represents the population and should precede R which represents all the other less important or residual factors.

You should be aware of the following:

1   Q^d_x stands for the amount of X wanted or demanded in the market by all the consumers in that market (consumers A, B, C, etc.).

2   The demand conditions which we discussed in our examination of individual demand now apply also to the market demand for a commodity. For example, income now refers to the income of all the consumers in the market.

THE DISTINCTION BETWEEN A MOVEMENT ALONG A MARKET DEMAND CURVE AND A SHIFT OF THE MARKET DEMAND CURVE

All that we said earlier about movements along the individual demand curve and shifts of the individual demand curve apply to the market demand curve. The main points are summarised below:

1   A change in the price of a commodity, other things being equal, will lead to a change in the quantity demanded of that commodity in the opposite direction to the price changes. (This reflects the negative slope of the market demand curve.) The change in price will be represented by a movement along the demand curve.

This inverse relationship between the quantity demanded of a commodity and its price constitutes the **law of demand**.

2   A change in any of the demand conditions, other things being equal, will lead to a change in demand: the quantity demanded at each price will change. This is shown by a shift of the demand curve to the right (an increase in demand) or to the left (a decrease in demand).

To help clarify the distinction between a movement along/shift of the market demand curve try Activity 8.

ACTIVITY 8

The straight line market demand curve for commodity J below shows that at
the point A 100,000 units are demanded each week at a price of 75p per unit.

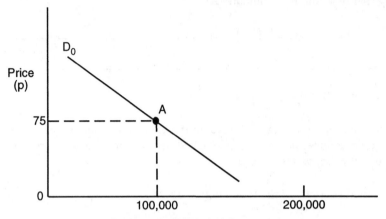

Quantity demanded of J per week

Suppose: (1) the price of a substitute for J is increased and this leads to a 50%
increase in the demand for J, then (2) the producers of J increase its price by
a third.

How much of J will be demanded at the new price? (You can assume that the
50% increase in the demand for J led to a parallel shift of the demand curve).

Use the space below to work out your answer.

(**Hint**: to work out the answer begin by drawing the new demand curve for J.)

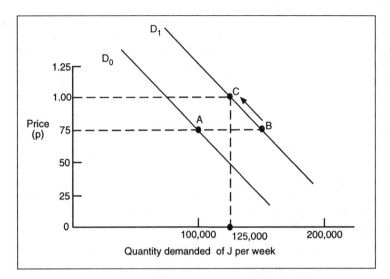

Quantity demanded of J per week

Quantity of J demanded = 125,000 units per week. **Explanation:** the increase in the price of the substitute increased the quantity demanded of J by 50% to 150,000 units at 75p (the demand curve shifted to the right from d_0 to d_1). Then the producers increased the price of J to £1.00 (an increase of one-third from the original price of 75p), causing a fall in the quantity demanded of J to 125,000 units: this was represented by a movement (upwards) along the new demand curve (d_1) from B to C. If you got the correct answer, well done. If you were not successful try again using the explanation to see where you made your mistake (or got lost?).

In this activity you used the elementary theory of demand to analyse the effects of a change in a commodity's price and a demand condition on the quantity of a commodity demanded in a market, taking one change at a time and assuming other things being equal at each stage.

Having examined demand we will now go on to look at the other side of a market, the supply side – stage 2. This will be a shorter stage because a lot of the terminology and concepts we'll need to use here have already been introduced under demand. From here onwards when we use the term 'demand' we'll mean **market demand**, not individual demand.

1.2 Supply

The quantity supplied of a commodity is the total amount all the suppliers (for example, sellers, firms) are willing and able to sell at a particular price, over some period of time, such as a week, or month.

Instead of the term producer we'll be using the term firm: a firm can be any type of business organisation in the private sector, or the public sector, which purchases inputs (raw materials, etc., i.e. factors of production) and converts them into outputs (for example, by manufacturing processes) which it sells in order to make a profit (the difference between the costs of producing an output and the money it receives from selling that output). Here we will be assuming that firms exist to make profits which are as large as possible. This is called profit maximisation. (Remember that we assumed utility maximisation in the case of individual consumers.) In reality, though firms exist for a variety of reasons, the desire to make profits is a very powerful motivation for many businesses.

In our discussion of supply we'll only be looking at market supply: part of Unit 3 will be concerned with an individual firm's supply – **individual supply**.

THE MARKET SUPPLY CURVE

If we continue our assumption of other things being equal, as we must, we can examine the relationship between the price of a commodity and the amount firms are able and willing to sell.

Suppose we have information on how much firms are willing and able to make available for sale at a number of different prices each week. We could construct the market supply schedule like the one shown in Table 3 for commodity X.

Price (p)	Quantity supplied (millilons) per week
10	100
20	150
30	300
40	350
60	400

Table 3: The market supply schedule

If we graph this information we will have the market supply curve for commodity X as shown in Figure 7. Please remember that we have used imaginary data here. Nonetheless, it portrays what is typical of the real world.

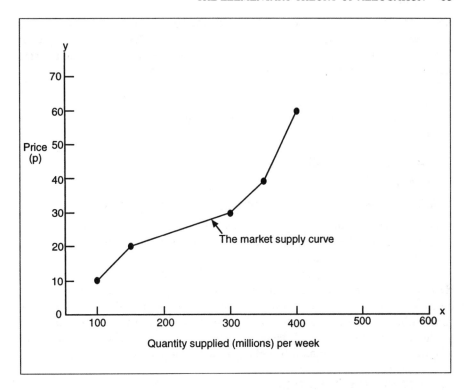

Figure 7: The market supply curve

Here you can see that the supply curve slopes upwards from left to right, so it has a positive slope: an increase in price will increase the amount firms are able and willing to produce, or the quantity supplied; a decrease in price will reduce the quantity supplied. This relationship whereby an increase (decrease) in price, other things being equal, leads to an increase (decrease) in the quantity supplied constitutes the **law of supply**.

Why there is a positive relationship between price and the quantity supplied will be examined in Unit 3. Even so, a brief explanation may be useful at this point.

Other things being equal, as the amount of a commodity X produced by a firm increases, so will the cost of providing an extra unit: the higher the output the higher the cost of producing an extra unit, for example, because suppliers have to pay overtime wage-rates. For example, it may cost £2,000 to produce 1,000 units, and then an extra £4 to produce an extra unit, i.e. it costs £1,004 to produce 1,001 units. Let's suppose that the price of the commodity is £3 per unit. At this price the firm will not consider it worthwhile providing the extra unit, because the money received by the firm from selling the extra unit would not cover the costs of producing it. By producing the extra unit the firm would be £1 worse off than if it had not produced and sold the extra unit.

Now suppose that the price of the commodity increased to £5. If the firm produced the extra unit and sold it, the firm would be £1 better off than if it had not produced and sold the extra unit: its profit will have increased by £1. In short, the rise in price prompted the firm to increase its output by one unit. If we repeated our example for even higher prices and other firms, we have the same result: an increase in price leads to an increase in the amount firms are willing to produce.

Also, as price increases and firms already producing the commodity make bigger profit, other firms not yet producing the commodity will be attracted to its production.

Thus the quantity of the commodity produced will increase as its price increases for two reasons:

- firms already producing the commodity produce more of it, and
- provided there are no major problems in being able to produce the commodity, other firms will begin producing it, attracted by the opportunities to make profit.

Here we can see how an increase in price, by providing opportunities to make extra profit, can act like a signal to firms to expand the production of a commodity. By contrast, a fall in price leads to a reduction in profit, so firms reduce or cease production. In Unit 3 you will see in more detail how firms make decisions about whether to produce a commodity and how much of it to produce.

MARKET SUPPLY CONDITIONS

We can now look at the factors which determine how much of a commodity firms wish to produce at any given price. These other factors, or determinants, are called **supply conditions**, and include:

1 the prices of inputs.

2 technology

3 the objective(s) of firms

4 other factors.

We will now look briefly at each of these supply conditions.

1 The prices of inputs

Other things being equal, the higher the price of any input used by firms to produce a commodity, the lower the profit from making that commodity, and so less will be supplied at any given price – there will be a decrease in supply.

By contrast, the lower the price of an input, other things being equal, the more profitable is the production of a commodity, and the higher the amount firms will produce and offer for sale at any given price – there will be an increase in supply.

2 Technology

Over time technology advances and this can help reduce the costs of producing a commodity, other things being equal, thereby increasing profits and so the amount of a commodity available to consumers at any given price – there will be a change in supply.

3 The objective(s) of firms

As mentioned earlier, we are assuming that firms seek to maximise their profit: if opportunities exist for firms to make more profit, the amount produced will increase. If the price of a commodity falls, profit will fall and so the amount of a commodity produced will decrease. If firms adopt some other objective such as to maximise market share, other things being equal, this could affect the amount produced at any given price – there will be a change in supply.

4 Other factors

Several other factors can affect the amount firms are willing and able to supply at any given price, other things being equal: natural disasters (earthquakes, frost, hurricanes, major flooding), political factors (wars, revolutions, sanctions), excise taxes and subsidies, environmental concerns (increasingly important in affecting the behaviour of firms, and in questioning the acceptability of the profit-maximisation objective of most firms), and so forth.

The market supply function

All these factors which determine the supply of a commodity can be summarised in the form of a supply function like that shown here:

$$Q^s_x = f\ (P_x,\ P_{i1},...,P_{in},T,G,H).$$

Here:

Q^s_x represents the amount of X firms are able and willing to supply, or the quantity supplied

$=f$, as you should recall means is a function of, or depends on

P_x represents the price of the commodity X

$P_{i1},...,P_{in}$ represents the prices of the n inputs i purchased by the firms to produce the quantity supplied of X

T represents technology

G represents the objective (or goal) of firms supplying the commodity X.

H represents all the other less important factors which affect the quantity supplied of the commodity: they are the residual factors.

As we said when we were looking at the individual and market demand functions, don't be put off by the supply function, it merely summarises some aspect of the real world: that the quantity of a commodity firms supply is determined by its price and several other factors (i.e. the supply conditions). Now try Activity 9.

ACTIVITY 9

1 Q^s_x is what type of variable?

2 All the factors inside the bracket are called _____ variables.

---

1   a dependent variable

2   independent.

THE DISTINCTION BETWEEN A MOVEMENT ALONG A MARKET SUPPLY CURVE AND A SHIFT OF THE MARKET SUPPLY CURVE

We have seen that the amount of a commodity firms wish to supply is determined by its price and several other factors. We now need to look at the effects of changes in the price of X and the supply conditions on the quantity of X supplied.

First, we'll look at the effects of changes in the price of X. A change in the price of a commodity will lead to a movement along the supply curve.

For example, if the price of X increases, firms will want to provide more of it – we have seen a little earlier why this is so. (If you have forgotten please go back to our discussion of the market supply curve.) This is shown by an (upwards) movement along the supply curve from A to B in Figure 8 indicating that the quantity supplied has increased from q_0 to q_1, other things being equal.

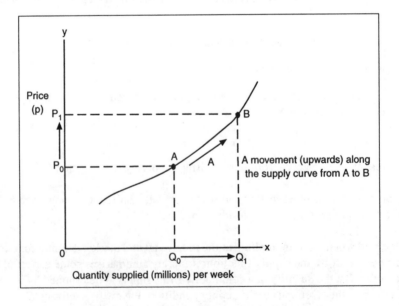

*Figure 8: An **increase** in the quantity supplied*

ACTIVITY 10

Show diagrammatically what happens to the quantity supplied following a fall in price. (**Hints**: begin by drawing the axes, supply curve; work on the curve the points corresponding to the original price and subsequent price; and indicate on the axes the original price/quantity supplied and demanded, subsequent price/quantity supplied and demanded.)

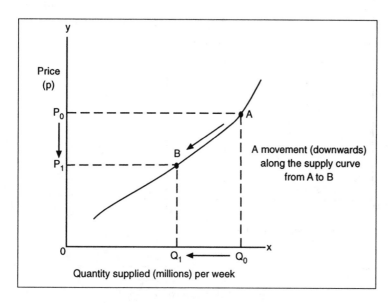

*A **decrease** in the quantity supplied*

As the price fell from p_0 to p_1, the quantity supplied was reduced from q_0 to q_1, other things being equal. This movement is represented by a (downwards) movement along the supply curve from A to B in the diagram above.

To summarise: a change in price will lead to a change in the quantity supplied. This is shown by a movement along the supply curve.

Now let's look at what happens if one of the supply conditions changes. Suppose, other things being equal, firms use a lot of electricity to produce X and the price of electricity increases by 10%. As we noted earlier, when we looked at supply conditions this will reduce the profitability of firms (because its production costs have increased) and so reduce the amount they are prepared to produce and offer for sale at any given price. In short, there will be a decrease in supply: this change will be represented by a shift of the supply curve to the left.

In Figure 9 the increase in the price of electricity has had the effect of shifting the supply curve, S_0 to the left, to S_1 indicating that firms are supplying less at each price. For example, at the price of p_0 per unit, q_0 was supplied. Following the increase in the price of electricity only q_1 is now being supplied. There has been a reduction in the quantity supplied at the price p_0 of q_0q_1 – decrease in supply. Similarly, for any other price.

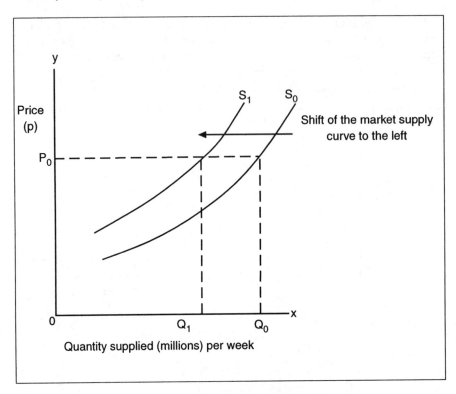

*Figure 9: A **decrease** in supply*

Let us take another example to show the effect of a technological breakthrough in the production of commodity X. As we noted earlier this will reduce the cost of producing a commodity and so increase firms' profits. This will lead to an increase in the quantity supplied at any given price: there will be an increase in supply, which is represented by a shift of the supply curve to the right.

In Figure 10 the new technology has had the effect of shifting the supply curve S_0 to the right to S_1 indicating that firms are supplying more at each price. For example, at the price p_0 per unit, q_0 was supplied. With the new technology q_1 will be supplied at the price p_0. There has been an increase in the quantity supplied at the price p_0 of q_0q_1 – an increase in supply. Similarly, for any other price.

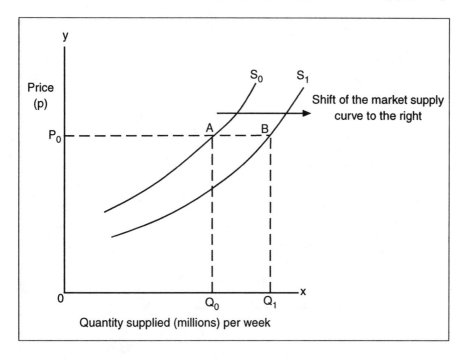

*Figure 10: An **increase** in supply*

Now attempt Activity 11.

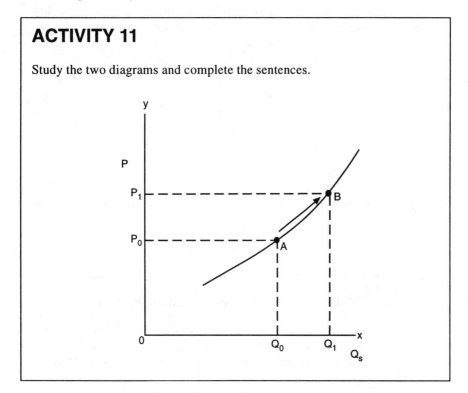

ACTIVITY 11

Study the two diagrams and complete the sentences.

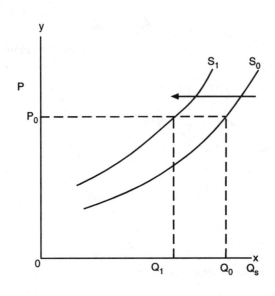

1 The movement along the supply curve from A to B represents _____ due to an increase in the ____ of the commodity.

2 The shift of the supply curve to the left represents _____. The quantity supplied at the price P_0 after the shift of the supply curve is now _____.

3 Suggest four reasons for the shift of the supply curve from S_0 to S_1.

1   ...an increase in the quantity supplied...price

2   ...a decrease in supply...q_1 .

3   Our answers included:

   (a) A rise in the cost of labour (e.g. the wage-rate of workers employed by firms producing the commodity has increased).

   (b) A rise in the price of raw materials.

   (c) A change in the objective of firms producing the commodity.

   (d) A strike of workers involved in the production of the commodity.

   (e) New legislation (e.g. a reduction in the length of the working week) which increased the costs of employing workers: the effect will be similar to increasing the wages/salaries of workers employed in making the commodity.

A brief summary of supply may prove useful at this point.

1   Other things being equal, a change in the price of X will lead to a change in the quantity of X supplied at that price. This is shown by a movement along the market supply curve. (See Figure 8 and Activity 10.)

2   Other things being equal, a change in any of the supply conditions will lead to a change in supply: the quantity supplied at each price will change. This is shown by a shift of the market supply curve. (See Figures 9 and 10.)

3   The market supply curve illustrates the positive relationship between the quantity supplied of a commodity and its price, other things being equal. The points on the supply curve represent the rows (i.e. price – quantity supplied combinations) of the supply schedule.

Finally, remember that we have only focused on the concept of **market supply**. In Unit 3 you will be looking at the concept of **individual supply** in some detail.

To ensure you have the basics now try Activity 12.

ACTIVITY 12

1   In your own words explain what the market supply curve represents.

2   Complete the following sentences by selecting the appropriate ending supplied below:

(a) A supply curve will have a positive slope (i.e. upward sloping) when _____

(i) the quantity supplied falls as the price increases.

(ii) the quantity supplied increases as the price rises.

(b) When a supply curve shifts to the right there will be _____.

(i) an increase in the quantity supplied at a given price.

(ii) a decrease in the quantity supplied at a given price.

---

1   A supply curve represents the relationship between the price of a commodity and the quantity supplied per unit of time, such as a week, or a month, other things being equal. (Something similar to this answer is acceptable).

2   A (ii)   is correct. The quantity supplied increases as the price rises.

B (i)   is correct. When a supply curve shifts to the right there will be an increase in the quantity supplied at a given price.

Finally, let's try applying what we've learnt about supply in Activity 13, to a real example, the world supply of crude oil.

ACTIVITY 13

Show graphically (on a separate sheet of graph paper) the effects of the following on the world supply curve of crude oil. For each provide a brief explanation for your answer. Take each case individually – remember, other things being equal!

Assume the current price of crude oil is $30 per barrel. (In this example the horizontal axis will need to measure the quantity supplied per day.)

1 UN sanctions against a major oil producer being lifted

2 the discovery of new oil fields in the Scottish Highlands

3 a major earthquake in Saudi Arabia

4 improvements in the deep-sea oil extraction techniques

5 a rise in the price of crude oil

6 global warming

7 the major oil companies becoming more 'environmentally aware'

8 a global recession.

To help you get started we'll do the first one for you.

1   Lifting UN sanctions against an oil producing country would represent a change in the supply conditions affecting the supply of crude oil (if you have forgotten, see market supply conditions, other factors, discussed earlier) and an increase in the quantity supplied of crude oil at $30. We would show this by the supply curve shifting to the right, representing an increase in supply. This is shown diagrammatically below.

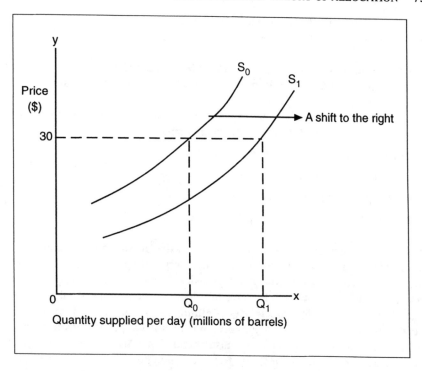

The world supply curve for crude oil

Lifting the UN sanctions would increase the quantity of oil supplied at $30 from Q_0 barrels to Q_1 barrels per day: this is represented by the supply curve shifting to the right from S_0 to S_1.

2 Possibly no change. For environmental reasons these oil fields might not be exploited and so there would be no increase in supply (i.e. the supply curve would not shift to the right). However, if the oil fields are exploited then there would be an increase in supply (i.e. the supply curve would shift to the right).

3 Shift to the left (decrease in supply). Saudi Arabia is the world's largest oil producer.

4 Shift to the right. Would reduce production costs, increase oil producers' profitability, so increase the quantity being supplied at $30 (or at any other price).

5 Note carefully: this would lead to a movement upwards along the supply curve: the supply curve would not shift.

6 This would affect the demand for oil, rather than the supply. So no change.

7 Oil producers may reduce, or close down oil production in environmentally sensitive areas. So less would be supplied at $30 (or at any other price).

8   Would affect the world demand for crude oil; it would be unlikely to affect the world supply curve for crude oil. So no change.

These are our answers – others are possible. Some reflection on our suggested answers should give you a fair indication of whether your answers are correct.

We are now in a position to examine price. This will involve us in using all that we have learnt about demand and supply so far, especially:

- the market demand and supply curves
- demand and supply conditions
- changes in the quantity demanded/demand
- changes in the quantity supplied/supply.

If you are quite happy that you now have the basics of demand and supply we can proceed to our third stage in developing an understanding of how markets work. If you are not happy, then go through the basics of demand and supply again very carefully. In the next stage – price – we'll be looking at questions like the following: Why do prices fall? How are shortages eliminated? What happens if there is an increase in the demand for a commodity? What could happen if a government tries to fix prices? In the real world, economists spend a lot of their time finding answers to such questions, on behalf of, for example, governments and business organisations.

1.3 Price

We have now reached the critical stage of our study of the elementary theory of allocation. Here we will bring together what we have learnt about **market demand** (from here onwards **demand**) and **market supply** (from here onwards **supply**) to see how:

- the demand for a commodity and the supply of a commodity together determine the market price;
- a change in demand and supply conditions will lead to a change in price;
- a change in price will lead to a change in the allocation of resources to the production of commodities.

But first, let's be clear what we mean by the term **price**.

The price of a commodity represents the amount of money consumers have to pay to acquire one unit of the commodity: it also represents the amount of money a firm will accept when selling one unit of the commodity it provides. For example, if the price of a commodity X is £50 per tonne a consumer will have to pay £50 to buy 1 tonne of it, and the firm would receive £50 per tonne for it.

THE DETERMINATION OF PRICE

Let's now bring together in a single table, Table 4, the data representing the market demand schedule (Table 2) and the market supply schedule (Table 3) for commodity X, which we examined earlier.

Price (p)	Quantity demanded (millions) per week	Quantity supplied (millions) per week
10	500	100
20	400	150
30	300	300
40	200	350
60	100	400

Table 4: Demand and supply schedules for commodity X

This data is represented in Figure 11 by the demand curve and the supply curve.

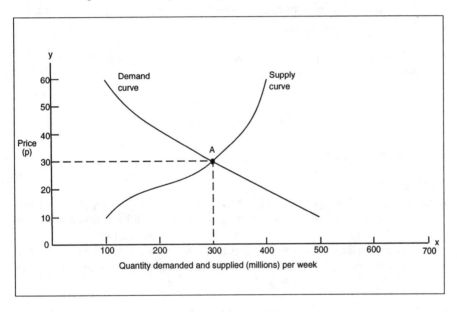

Figure 11: The determination of price

Here you can see that at the point A the demand and supply curves intersect, or cross each other. A corresponds to the 30p (price) – 300 (quantity demanded, or q_d) combination on the demand schedule, and the 30p (price) – 300 quantity (quantity supplied, or q_s) combination on the supply schedule. In short, at a price of 30p, q_d = q_s = 300 units per week: what consumers want to buy (300 units per week) is equal to the amount firms want to sell (300 units per week). For any pair of curves, provided the demand curve slopes downwards for its entire length and the supply curve slopes upwards for its entire length, there will be only one price at which the quantity demanded will be equal to the quantity supplied. The price at which the quantities demanded and supplied are equal to each other is called the **equilibrium**

price. The amount bought and sold at the equilibrium price is called the **equilibrium quantity**. At this price the market for a commodity will be cleared, so there is neither a **shortage** (some consumers did not get all that they wanted) nor a **surplus** (consumers did not buy all of the amount supplied by firms): the market is in **equilibrium**.

At prices above the equilibrium price, the quantity supplied is greater than the quantity demanded. For example, at 60p, the quantity demanded is 100 million units and the quantity supplied is 400 million units: there is a surplus i.e. an excess supply of 300 million units. At any price below the equilibrium, there will be a shortage, i.e. an excess demand. Provided that none of the demand or supply conditions change, the price will remain at 30p and the market will be in equilibrium.

ACTIVITY 14

Using the information in Table 4 complete the following sentences.

1   At a price of 10p, quantity _____ is more than quantity _____ , i.e. there is
    a _____ or excess _____ of _____ units.

2   At a price of 40p, quantity demanded _____ quantity supplied, i.e.
    there is a _____ or excess _____ of _____ units.

---

1   demanded....supplied...shortage...demand...400.

2   is less than...surplus...supply...150.

DISEQUILIBRIUM
If any one of the demand conditions change, or any one of the supply conditions change, the market will no longer be in equilibrium: it will be in **disequilibrium**. In reality, demand and supply conditions are changing all the time so markets are rarely in equilibrium. So market equilibrium refers to a state of balance towards which markets are tending to be driven by consumers and firms pursuing their self-interest.

In order to see how a market will respond to a change in any one of the demand conditions or supply conditions, let us assume that the market for X is initially in equilibrium. Suppose there is an increase in consumers' income and X is a normal good (that is one in which sales increase as incomes increase). What will happen? Study Figure 12 carefully.

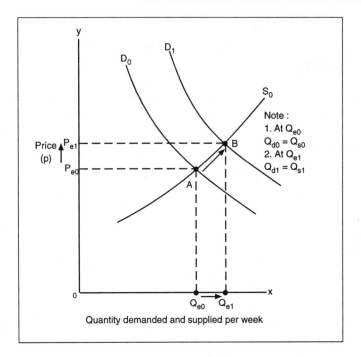

Figure 12: The effects of an increase in demand

In Figure 12 the market is initially in equilibrium of the price p_{e0} and the equilibrium quantity is q_{e0} (where the quantity demanded, q_{d0} is equal to the quantity supplied q_{s0}).

The increase in income will result in an increase in demand which is represented by the demand curve for X shifting to the right from d_0 to d_1. The equilibrium price will rise from p_{e0} to p_{e1}, and the quantities demand and supplied will increase to q_{e1} where the new higher quantity demanded (q_{d1}) will be equal to the new higher quantity supplied (q_{s1}).

So, an increase in income will lead to an increase in price. This increase in price will lead to an increase in the quantity supplied, equal to the increase in the quantity demanded. Thus equilibrium will be restored in the market.

COMPARATIVE STATIC ANALYSIS

This type of economic analysis in which we compare the situation after some change with the initial situation is called **comparative static analysis**.

Having looked at the effects of an increase in demand we need briefly to look at each of the following:

- a decrease in demand
- an increase in supply
- a decrease in supply
- an increase in demand and an increase in supply.

Now work carefully through Activity 15.

ACTIVITY 15

Using comparative static analysis show the effects of the following on the market for commodity X. Use the space provided for the answers.

1 A decrease in demand

2 An increase in supply

3 A decrease in supply

4 An increase in demand and an increase in supply

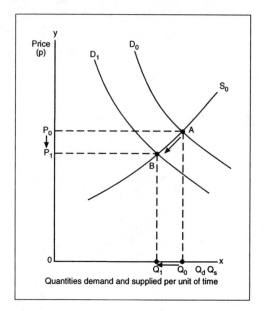

1   Fall in equilibrium price from P_0 to P_1 and a fall in the equilibrium quantity (from Q_0 to Q_1).

2   A movement (downwards) along the supply curve from A to B.

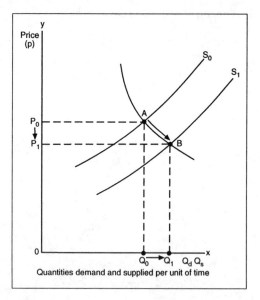

1   Fall in equilibrium price from P_0 to P_1 and a rise in the equilibrium quantity (from Q_0 to Q_1).

2   A movement (downwards) along the demand curve from A to B.

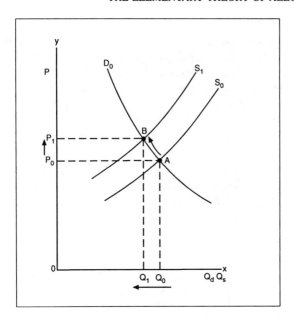

1   Rise in equilibrium price (from P_0 to P_1) and a fall in the equilibrium quantity (from Q_0 to Q_1).

2   A movement (upwards) along the demand curve from A to B.

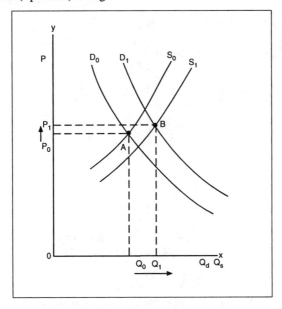

Both curves unit shift to the right. Effects equilibrium price, equilibrium quantity will depend on how much the curves shift relative to each other. So there is a range of possible answers . Our answer is just one possibility from this range of possible answers.

DYNAMIC ANALYSIS

Having seen how comparative static analysis can be used to show the effects of a change in demand and supply conditions on the equilibrium price and equilibrium quantity, we need to briefly mention **dynamic analysis**. This is concerned with analysing the stages a market will proceed through in order to eliminate disequilibrium (i.e. a surplus or a shortage) and so restore market equilibrium. For example, suppose that the market for X is in equilibrium and one of the demand conditions changes. How will equilibrium be restored?

We can represent the initial equilibrium in Figure 13 by the point A where the demand curve (d_0) and the supply curve (s_0) intersect. At A the equilibrium price is p_{e0} and the equilibrium quantity is q_{e0} (where $q_{d0} = q_{s0}$).

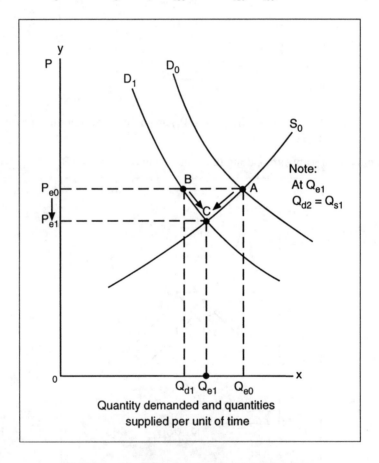

Figure 13: The restoration of equilibrium

Now suppose that the price of a complement for X increases. The demand curve for X will shift to the left to d_1, resulting in a surplus of X (=AB) at the equilibrium price p_{e0}, because buyers now only want to buy q_{d1} at that price, but firms want to sell q_{s0}. In order to reduce the surplus firms will have to reduce the price of X. As the price of X is reduced, the quantity demanded will increase from q_{d1} to q_{d2} (i.e. there will be a movement downwards along the demand curve d_1 from B to C because commodity X is now cheaper) and the quantity supplied will decrease from q_{s0} to q_{s1} (i.e. there will be a movement downwards along the supply curve from A to C because the price of X is lower and so less profitable). Eventually, a new market equilibrium will be reached at the lower price of p_{e1} and equilibrium quantity q_{e1} ($q_{d2} = q_{s1}$).

So, an increase in the price of a complement to X led to a surplus of X, producing a fall in the price of X. Subsequently, this led to firms reducing the quantity supplied and to consumers increasing the quantity of X demanded.

Now try Activity 16, taking care to locate the surplus or shortage arising from each of the various changes specified.

ACTIVITY 16

Using dynamic analysis, show how equilibrium will be restored in the market for X following:

1 a rise in the price of a substitute for X

2 improved technology employed in the production of X

3 an increase in the price of raw material used in the production of X

Use separate sheets of paper for this.

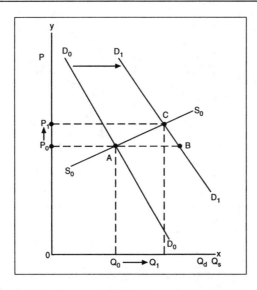

Increase in demand

Demand curve shifts to the right: shortage produced (= AB) at price P_0, price will rise to P_1, increasing quantity supplied, reducing the quantity demanded. Eventually, new equilibrium, C, produced at P_1 with equilibrium quantity = Q_1

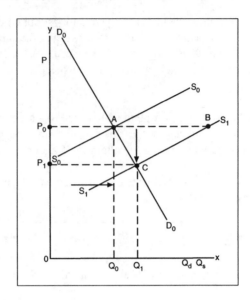

Increase in supply

Supply curve shifts to the right: surplus produced (=AB) at price P_0, price will fall to P_1, increasing quantity demanded, reducing the quantity supplied. Eventually, new equilibrium, C, produced at P_1 with equilibrium quantity = Q_1

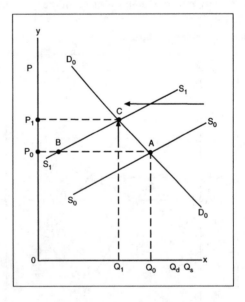

Reduction in supply

Supply curve shifts to the left: shortage produced (=AB) at price P_0, price will rise to P_1, increasing the quantity supplied, reducing the quantity demanded. Eventually, new equilibrium, C, produced at P_1 with equilibrium quantity = Q_1

Summary

In this section we looked at how the market operates, and hence the market economy, in three stages: demand, supply and price. We saw how the market price of a commodity is determined and how changes in demand and supply conditions (by leading to changes in prices) affect the allocation of resources. For example, we noted how changes in income lead, over time, to the expansion of industries involved in the production of normal goods and the decline of industries producing inferior goods. We also examined the effects of changes in the prices of substitutes and complements for a commodity on the demand for that commodity.

An understanding of how a market functions is very useful and helps economists analyse and explain all sorts of issues in economic life.

Before we move on to Section 2 *Elasticity*, answer the short questions in Activity 17. (No guessing! Carefully think out the correct answers.)

ACTIVITY 17

1 Label the curves to show the causes of an increase in price.

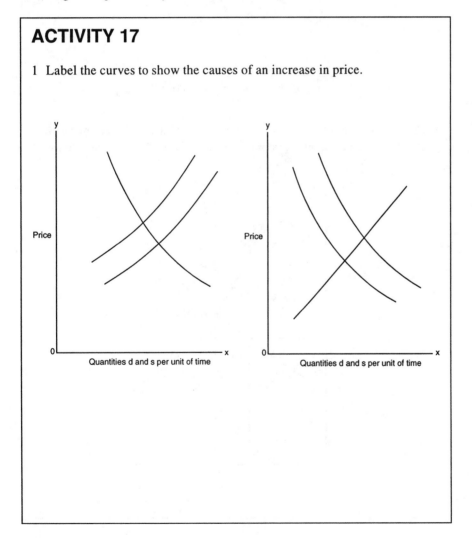

2 The diagram below could be used to represent an inferior good. True or false (delete wrong answer)?

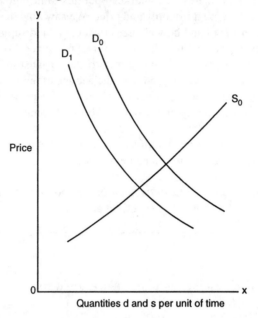

Quantities d and s per unit of time

3 The diagram below represents the effect of a rise in the price of a commodity on the quantity supplied. True or false (delete wrong answer)?

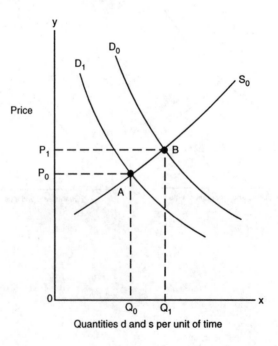

Quantities d and s per unit of time

4 In the diagram below, is the surplus AB, or DC, or BC, or AD, or AC? Or somewhere else?

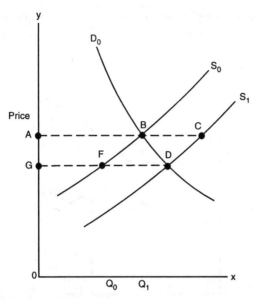

5 Complete the following sentence.

When we analyse the effect of a change in a demand or supply condition on the market equilibrium, we assume._____

1

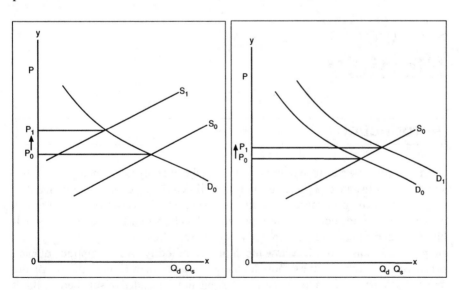

2   True. As income increases, quantity demanded of the commodity at each price is reduced: there has been a fall in demand.

3   True. The increase in demand led to an increase in price, causing the quantity supplied to increase i.e., there was a movement along the supply curve from A to B.

4   BC. The shift of the supply curve to the right increased the quantity supplied at the original price, producing a surplus of BC, or q_0q_1 at the price p_0.

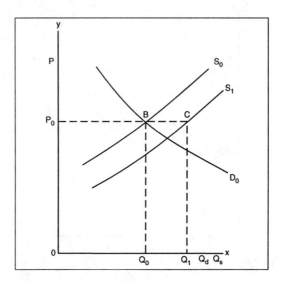

5   ...other things being equal, or *ceteris paribus*. (You must not forget this assumption.)

SECTION TWO

Elasticity

Introduction

We have seen how a change in price will affect the quantity demanded and quantity supplied. For instance, an increase in price will lead to a decrease in the quantity demanded, or to an increase in the quantity supplied. Also, we have seen how a change in any of the demand conditions will affect how much of a commodity will be demanded at each price. Similarly, we've seen how a change in any of the supply conditions will affect how much of a commodity will be supplied at each price. But, though we know how a change in price or a change in any of the demand or supply conditions will affect the quantity demanded or supplied we don't know by how much. For example, suppose the price of crude oil increases by 10% how much will it reduce the amount of oil demanded? By how much will it increase the quantity supplied?

In this section we will discuss the concept of **elasticity**: the measuring or quantifying of the responsiveness to a change in price, or income, of the amount people buy of a commodity. Economists use different measures of elasticity to get some idea of how much the quantity demanded or supplied of a commodity will change in response to a price change, or any of the demand/supply conditions.

Let us take an example. Suppose we have two commodities, A and B, and their prices increase by 10%. If the amount of A consumers buy fell by 5%, we can say that A is not very responsive to a change in price: the quantity demanded is said to be **inelastic**. If, on the other hand, the amount of B consumers buy fell by 50%, we can say that B is very responsive to a change in price: the quantity demanded is said to be **very elastic**. This measure of the responsiveness of the quantity demanded to a change in price is called the **price elasticity of demand**.

Other measures of responsiveness include:

- the **income elasticity of demand** which measures the effect of a given change in income on the quantity demanded
- the **cross-elasticity of demand** which measures the effect of a given change in the price of a substitute or complement on the quantity demanded of another commodity
- the **price elasticity of supply** which measures the effect of a given change on the quantity supplied.

Before we look at these three measures of elasticity we will examine the price elasticity of demand in more detail.

2.1 Price elasticity of demand (PED)

WHAT IS THE PRICE ELASTICITY OF DEMAND?

The price elasticity of demand (PED) is a measure of the responsiveness of the quantity demanded of a commodity to a change in the price of that commodity.

To see how the PED is measured we will take another example involving two commodities, A and B, the market demand schedules of which are presented in Table 5. Look at the two demand schedules: which would you say is the more responsive to the price increase?

COMMODITY A		COMMODITY B	
Price (p)	Quantity demanded (millions) per week	Price (£)	Quantity demanded (000 metres^2) per day
50	1000	200	50
55	950	220	25

Table 5: Market demand schedules for commodities A and B

In the case of A, a 10% increase in price (5/50 × 100 = 10%) led to a reduction in the quantity demanded of 5% (50/1000 × 100 = 5%).

In the case of B, a 10% increase in price (20/200 x 100 = 10%) led to a reduction in the quantity demanded of 50% (25/50 × 100 = 50%).

So, for a given increase in prices of 10%, the quantities demanded of A and B fell by 5% and 50% respectively. Thus B is more responsive to a price change than A. This responsiveness can be expressed numerically using the PED formula:

$$\text{PED} = (-) \frac{\text{Percentage change in quantity demanded of A}}{\text{Percentage change in price of A}} = \frac{\% \, \Delta \text{QdA}}{\% \, \Delta \text{PA}}$$

Note: here Δ means change in. (Δ is the Greek letter delta).
    Qd represents prime
    P represents prime
    Therefore ΔQd means change in the quantity demanded, and
    ΔP means change in price

If we use this formula we can calculate the PEDs for A and B, or any other commodity. Now try Activity 18.

ACTIVITY 18

1 Using the data in Table 5 calculate the PEDs for commodities A and B following the increases shown in their prices.

Using the data in the table below (the market demand schedule for commodity C), calculate the PED following a rise in the price of commodity C from £1,000 to £1,200.

Price (£)	Quantity demanded per week (millions of tonnes)
1000	6
1200	4.8

1   PED of commodity A = $\dfrac{-5\%}{+10\%}$ = –0.5

    PED of commodity B = $\dfrac{-50\%}{+10\%}$ = –5.0

2   PED of commodity C = $\dfrac{-20\%}{+20\%}$ = –1.0

The increase in price of 20% led to an equal (i.e. 20%) reduction in the quantity demanded.

You should note carefully the following points:

1   PED (and elasticity value generally) is expressed in decimal form, for example –0.5 not (– $1/2$), or a half. They are not expressed as percentages!

2   It is possible to compare PEDs and other elasticity values of different commodities whether the non-price units are expressed in terms of weight, tonnage, length, etc., and whether the units of currency are expressed in p, £, or $, etc. This allowed us to make comparisons between the responsiveness of the three commodities to changes in their prices, despite A being in millions of units, B being in square metres, and C being in tonnes.

3   If you calculated the three PEDs carefully you should have found a negative sign before each of them, reflecting the negative relationship between the price and the quantity demanded of the commodity, or the negative slopes of the individual demand curve and the market demand curve. Following convention, from now on we'll drop the negative sign in our discussions of PED.

4   When calculating elasticities, the dependent variable (for example, quantity demanded) is always the numerator; and the independent variable (for example, price, income) is always the denominator.

5   For PED the Greek letters η, or ε are often used. We'll use PED as it's easier to remember.

From your calculations you should have found that the PED of A was 0.5, that for B was 5.0, and that for C was 1.0. What's the significance of these values?

ELASTIC AND INELASTIC DEMAND

If the PED is less than 1.0 (<1) the quantity demanded of the commodity is said to be **'price-inelastic'**. Here a 1% change in price will lead to a less than equal (<1%) change in the quantity demanded. Thus commodity A is price-inelastic (PED of A =0.5).

If the PED is equal to 1.0, the quantity demanded is said to be **'unit price-elastic'**. Here a 1% change in price will lead to an equal percentage change in the quantity demand. Thus commodity C is unit price-elastic (PED of C = 1.0).

If the PED is more than 1.0 (>1), the quantity demanded is said to be **'price-elastic'**. Here a 1% change in price will lead to a more than equal (>1%) change in the quantity demanded. Thus commodity B is price-elastic (PED of B = 5.0).

Now try Activity 19.

ACTIVITY 19

The makers of SARB cement sell 2,000 tonnes a week. A 15% increase in the price reduces the quantity demanded by 100 tonnes.

1 Calculate the PED for cement.

2 Are sales of cement price-elastic, price-inelastic, or unit price-elastic?

1

$$PED = \frac{\dfrac{-200}{2000} \times 100}{+5\%} = \frac{\dfrac{-1}{10} \times 100}{+5\%} = \frac{-10\%}{+5\%} = -2.0$$

NB Don't forget: we can ignore the minus sign before 2.

2   Sales of cement are price-elastic, as the PED is greater than 1.

In theory the PED of a commodity can vary from 0 (zero) to infinity (this is shown by the sign ∞). So we have:

1   If PED = 0, Qd is perfectly inelastic.

2   If PED <1, but >0, Qd is inelastic.

3   If PED = 1, Qd is unit elastic.

4   If PED >1, Qd is elastic.

5   If PED = ∞Qd is perfectly elastic.

Important: except in three cases, the price elasticity of demand varies along a demand curve. The three cases where the PED does not change (i.e. is constant), unit elastic demand, perfectly inelastic demand and perfectly elastic demand, are illustrated in Figures 14–16.

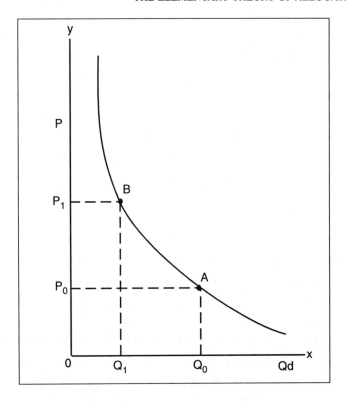

Figure 14: Unit elastic demand curve

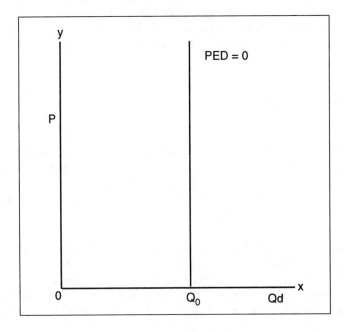

Figure 15: Unit elastic demand

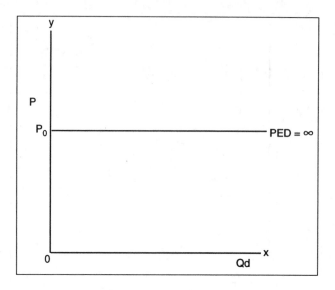

Figure 16: Perfectly elastic demand

You will come across the perfectly elastic demand curve when examining perfect competition in Unit 4.

POINT PRICE ELASTICITY OF DEMAND

If you have difficulty with this sub-section, don't worry too much, just try to grasp the basics. Throughout our discussion so far we have been using the arc PED concept, which uses discrete changes in price and quantity demanded, i.e. measures PED between two points on a demand curve. However, in order to calculate the PED accurately, it has to be calculated at a point on the demand curve, using the point PED formula:

$$\text{Point PED} = (-)\frac{\Delta q/q}{\Delta p/p} = \frac{\Delta q}{\Delta p}\cdot\frac{p}{q}$$

Here p/q is the price divided by the quantity at that price (point), and $\Delta q/\Delta p$ is the inverse of the slope of the demand curve in the case of a straight-line demand curve. In the case of a non-linear (or curved) demand curve $\Delta q/\Delta p$ is the inverse of the slope of the tangent to the demand curve at the price (point) under consideration. In short, **arc elasticity** is an approximation to the PED.

The point PED can be used to show that the PED of a straight-line demand curve varies along its length, except in the three cases where the price elasticity of demand was equal to 1, or 0, or ∞ (see Figures 14–16). In short, except for the three cases just mentioned, we can only refer to the elasticity of a part of the demand curve, not to the complete curve. Figure 17 shows how the PED for a commodity varies along the length of the demand curve.

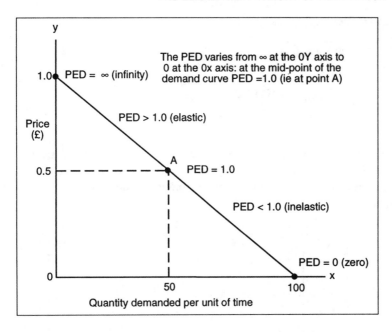

Figure 17: A demand curve of variable elasticity

To pursue the discussion of point PED further you'll need a knowledge of differential calculus. Assuming that you haven't, you may be pleased to know that we won't pursue this matter any further.

PED AND TOTAL REVENUE

We now need to look at the relationship between the PED and the total revenue a firm obtains from selling its commodity. The total revenue a firm receives over time depends on how much it sells, or the quantity demanded of what it produces times the price per unit. Put simply, total revenue (TR) represents quantity sold (Q) times ($\times$) the price (P) of each unit sold: $TR = Q \times P$. At this point try Activity 20.

ACTIVITY 20

Answer each of the following questions.

1 A firm sells 500 units per week at a price of 50p per unit, what will be its total revenue?

2 If the price increases to 60p, and the quantity falls to 350 units per week:

(a) what will be the firm's total revenue now?

(b) is the firm's commodity price-elastic?

---

1   £250.00 per week.

2   (a) £210.00 per week; (b) Yes

$$\left(\text{PED} = 1.5. \quad \text{PED} = \frac{\%\Delta Qd}{\%\Delta p} = \frac{33\%}{20\%} = 1.65 \right)$$

How much a firm can sell of its output at each price can be represented by a curve like that shown in Figure 18. (This type of curve is known as the demand curve of an individual firm. This and its related industry demand curve will be fully examined in Unit 4.)

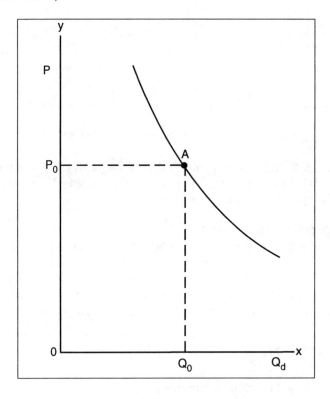

Figure 18: A firm's total revenue

Each point on the curve represents how much of the firm can sell at each price. The area under the curve at each point represents a firm's total revenue from selling its output at that price. For example, at the price p_0 the firm can sell q_0 units, producing a total revenue represented by the rectangular shaded area $p_0 A q_0 0$.

ACTIVITY 21

Study the diagram below. What is the firm's total revenue if the price of its commodity is P_1?

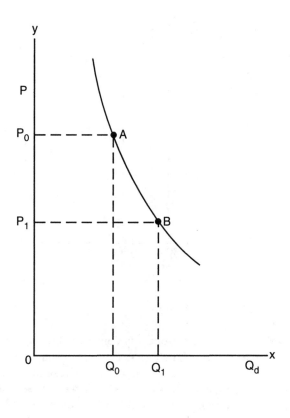

$P_1 Bq_1 0$ (= the area under the curve at point B)

We are now in a position to see how different values of the PED affect a firm's total revenue following a change in price. Look at Figure 19 carefully for a moment. The PED for this commodity following a price increase from £10 to £11 is 2.0 (the quantity demanded is elastic).

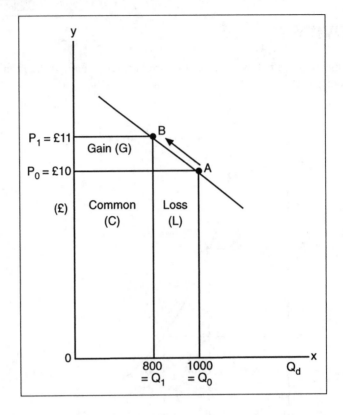

Figure 19: The effect on a firm's total revenue, PED > 1.0

The increase in price will reduce the quantity demanded by 200 units, so revenue will fall by $200 \times £10$ (= £2000 = Loss = (L)). However, each of the 800 units sold will now bring the firm an extra £1 each, so they will produce an extra £800 (= GAIN = (G)). If we subtract the loss from the gain, we can see that the effect of the 10% increase in price will be to reduce total revenue by £1200 (= £800 − £2000 = − £1200, where the minus sign indicates a net loss of revenue as a result of the price increase).

At the price p_0 total revenue (TR) = p_0Aq_00 = (C) + (L)

$$= £10 \times 1,000 = £10,000.$$

At the price p_1 total revenue (TR) = p_1Bq_10 = (C) + (G)

$$= £11 \times 800 = £8,800.$$

As a result of the price increase, total revenue has fallen by £1,200, because the loss (L) in revenue resulting from the 20% reduction in the quantity demanded (= 200 × £10 = £2,000) was greater than the gain (G) in revenue resulting from the 10% increase in the price (= 800 × £1 = £800). **Conclusion:** provided the PED > 1.0 (i.e. elastic) a price increase will reduce a firm's total revenue.

ACTIVITY 22

Suppose a 10% decrease in price from £10 (p_0) to £9 (p_1) increases the quantity demanded from 1,000 units per week to 1,200 units.

1 Calculate the PED of the commodity.

2 Is the quantity demanded of the commodity price-elastic?

3 What's the effect on total revenue of the price reduction?

4 What conclusion can you draw?

5 What advice would you give the firm on how to increase its total revenue?

---

1   20%/10% = 2

2   elastic (> 1.0)

3   at p_0, TR = 1,000 × £10 = £10,000; at p_1, TR = 1, 200 × £9 = £10,800. So TR has risen by £800.

4   **Conclusion:** provided the PED > 1.0 (i.e. elastic), a price reduction will increase a firm's total revenue.

5   To increase total revenue the firm needs to reduce its price (the increase in revenue from the 20% increase in sales would offset the loss arising from the 10% reduction in the price of each unit sold).

Now let us turn to the effects of price changes on the total revenue of a firm when the demand for its commodity is price-inelastic. In order to do this very carefully work through Activity 23 which follows.

ACTIVITY 23

Using the information contained in the table below complete each of the following sentences.

Price (£)	Quantity demanded per week (millions of metres^2)
40	50
50	45

---

1 (a) If the price increases from £40 to £50, PED = ____.

(b) Total revenue will _____ by _____ .

(c) The conclusion here is that if PED < 1.0, an _____ in price will _____ total revenue.

2 (a) If the price is reduced from £50 to £40, PED = _____.

(b) Total revenue will ____ by ___.

(c) The conclusion here is that if PED < 1.0, a _____ in price will _____ total revenue.

---

1 (a) PED = 0.40 (PED = 10%/25% = 0.40).

(b) ...increase... £250.

At £40, TR = 40 × 50 = £2,000; at £50, TR = 50 × 45 = £2,250; so, TR increases by £250.

(c) ...increase ...increase

2 (a) PED = 0.55 (PED = 11%/20% = 0.55.

(b) ...fall...£250.

At £50, TR = 50 × 45 = £2,250; at £40, TR = 40 × 50 = £2,000; so, TR decreased by £250.

(c) ...decrease ... reduce.

Here is a brief summary of the relationship between the PED for a firm's commodity and the firm's total revenue in which P↑ represents an increase in price (P), P↓ represents a reduction in price and ⟶ means results in, or leads to. TR represents total revenue.

1 (a) If PED > 1.0, P↑⟶TR ↓ (Figure 19).

(b) If PED > 1.0, P↓⟶TR ↑(Activity 22).

2 (a) If PED < 1.0, P↑⟶TR ↑ (Activity 23 Question 1).

(b) If PED < 1.0, P↓ ⟶ TR↓(Activity 23 Question 2).

You should now be able to appreciate why estimates of the price elasticity of demand are important to a firm when it is considering whether to change its price. Just to make sure try Activity 24.

ACTIVITY 24

A firm produces two types of commodity: commodity A and commodity B. Suppose it knows that the PED for commodity A is 2.0 and that for B is 0.5. The firm is considering a 10% increase in the price of both commodities. It asks you for your advice. What would you advise?

(Something like the following would be acceptable). Other things being equal, I would advise the firm to reduce the price of commodity A (demand is price-elastic and this price reduction would increase the firm's total revenue), and increase the price of B (demand is price-inelastic and this price increase would increase the firm's total revenue). Such a course of action would increase total revenue more than just increasing both prices by 10%.

DETEMINANTS OF THE PED

The main factors determining the PED for a commodity may be summarised as follows.

● **The number of substitutes available.**

Other things being equal, the more substitutes there are for a commodity the higher will be the PED for that commodity. When there is no close substitute for a commodity the PED will be close to 0, for example, insulin. Similarly the demand for petrol is price-inelastic because there are few substitutes for petrol.

● **Whether a commodity is habit forming or not.**

If a commodity has habit-forming properties demand for it will tend to be highly inelastic, for example, tobacco. Hence the Chancellor's regular tax increases on tobacco, beer, spirits. However if prices increase sharply then demand may become price-elastic.

● **The proportion of income spent on a commodity.**

The smaller the proportion of income spent on purchases of a commodity the more likely that the demand for it will be price-inelastic. Hence the low PEDs for commodities like salt and disposable lighters, provided that prices remain low in relation to income.

● **Whether the commodity is a necessity or a luxury.**

Generally speaking, commodities which are necessities have a lower PED (< 1) than commodities which are seen as luxuries (> 1). However, whether a commodity is a luxury or a necessity varies between individuals, and over time. Thus what is a luxury to one generation becomes a necessity to the next. Also when an individual's circumstances change. For example, through redundancy, what was once perceived to be a necessity may be seen as a luxury and so possession becomes optional rather than essential.

● **Marketing activities**

Successful marketing activities build up brand loyalty to a commodity, thus reducing its price-elasticity. For example, Coca Cola and Nescafe both have low PEDs (<1).

● **The time factor**

Buyers adjust only slowly to price increases, because the search for acceptable alternatives takes time.

Finally, we should realise that the PED for a commodity may be the result of one or more of these factors. For example, salt has a PED of less than 1.

ACTIVITY 25

Explain why salt has a PED of less than 1.

An acceptable answer would be something along the following lines: salt has a PED of less than 1.0 because its price is low in relation to average income; there are few, if any, substitutes for salt; salt is seen by many people as a necessity when cooking and eating food.

Having examined the PED in some detail we can now turn to look at the other types of elasticity: income-elasticity of demand, cross-elasticity of demand, and price-elasticity of supply.

2.2 The income elasticity of demand (YED)

WHAT IS THE INCOME ELASTICITY OF DEMAND?

This is a measure of the responsiveness of the quantity demanded to changes in income. The formula for the income elasticity of demand (YED, where Y stands for income) is:

$$YED = (\pm)\frac{\text{percentage change in the quantity demanded of A}}{\text{percentage change in income}} = (\pm)\frac{\%\Delta QdA}{\%\Delta Y}$$

(**Note:** ± means the YED can have a positive or negative value).

Here income is *per capita* income, or the country's total income divided by its population. As the value of the YED can vary from + ∞ (plus infinity) to −∞ (negative infinity) we have to include the sign with the value of the YED.

If a commodity has a YED which is greater than 0 (zero), that is positive in value, then the quantity demanded of that commodity will increase as income increases: the commodity is said to be a normal good. Over time the quantities demanded of these commodities will increase, for example leisure services.

If the quantity demanded of a commodity falls as income increases the commodity is said to be an inferior good: the YED will be less than 0, or negative. (We saw the terms normal good and inferior good earlier when we looked at the factors affecting the individual demand for a commodity.)

Figure 20 shows the relationships between the quantities demanded of three different types of commodity and changes in income.

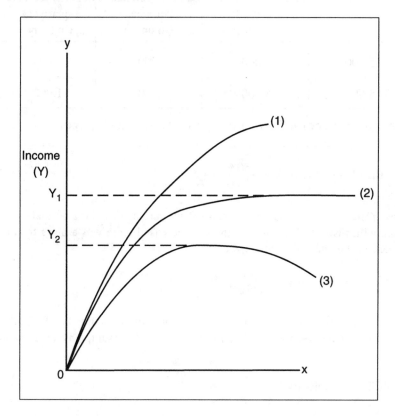

Figure 20: Different income elasticities of demand

The curve (1) for commodity X represents a commodity for which the demand increases as income increases: X is a normal good.

The curve (2) for commodity Y represents a commodity for which the demand increases as income rises. Eventually, further increases in income do not lead to any further increases in the demand for X. So commodity Y was a normal good until income reached Y_1.

The curve (3) for commodity Z represents a commodity for which the demand increases as income rises. Eventually, further increases in income beyond Y_2 lead to a reduction in the demand for Z, so Z becomes an inferior good. Now try Activity 26.

ACTIVITY 26

Using the information in the table below, calculate the YEDs for commodities A, B and C. Which of the three commodities is an inferior good?

Income (£)	Commodity A quantity demanded per week, (in tonnes)	Commodity B quantity demanded per week (in units)	Commodity C quantity demanded per week (in tonnes)
5,000	2,000	5,000	2,000
5,500	3,000	5,000	1,900

Here you must be careful with your plus (+) and minus (−) signs.

1   YED of commodity A = $\dfrac{+50\%}{+10\%} = +5.0$

As the YED is positive and greater than 1.0, we can say that C is a normal good and elastic with respect to income: as income increased there was a more than equal increase in the quantity demanded of A.

2   YED of commodity B = $\dfrac{0\%}{+10\%} = 0$

Here a change in income does not affect the quantity demanded of B at all, B is neither a normal good nor an inferior good. (A possible example is the demand for salt.)

3   YED of commodity C = $\dfrac{-5\%}{+10\%} = -0.5$

As the YED is negative and less than −1.0, we can say that A is an inferior good and inelastic with respect to income: as income increased, there was a less than equal fall in the quantity demanded of C.

EXPANDING AND CONTRACTING INDUSTRIES

In the real world commodities which have high positive YEDs are found in expanding (**sunrise**) industries, such as the tourism, leisure, fast-food and do-it-yourself industries. By contrast, the demand for some commodities decreases as income increases, such as porridge, bus journeys and the services of chimney sweeps. Industries involved in the provision of such commodities are called **sunset industries** and contract over time. With economic growth and the steady rise in income there will always be expanding and contracting industries. To be successful in a market economy (i.e. make profit and survive) a firm will need to produce a commodity (or commodities) the demand for which is increasing over time because consumers are spending more of their increased income on it (or them).

2.3 Cross-elasticity of demand (CED)

WHAT IS THE CROSS ELASTICITY OF DEMAND?

This is a measure of the responsiveness of the quantity demanded of a commodity to a change in the price of some other commodity – a substitute, or a complement. The formula for the cross-elasticity of demand (CED), where C stands for cross, is:

$$CED_{MN} = (\pm)\frac{\text{Percentage change in quantity demand of M}}{\text{Percentage change in the price of N}} = (\pm)\frac{\%\Delta QdM}{\%\Delta P_N}$$

Here as the commodity N can be a substitute for M, or a complement to M, the value of the CED can be positive (in the case of substitutes), or negative (in the case of complements), hence $\pm$, and so we have to be careful when calculating cross elasticities of demand to include the correct sign with the elasticity value. Thus CED = +3.0 indicates that a 1% rise in price of commodity N will increase the demand for M by 3%: N and M are substitutes. In the case of CED = –3.0, a 1% rise in the price of N will reduce the demand for M by 3%: N and M are complements $(P_n\uparrow, Q_dN\downarrow, Q_dM\uparrow)$.

A knowledge of CEDs can be useful to a firm as it will help the firm to predict how much a change in the price of its commodity may affect the quantity demanded of a substitute produced by a competing firm. Also, a knowledge of CEDs can help a firm estimate the effect on the quantity demanded of its commodity following a change in the price of a competitor's commodity (i.e. a substitute). Now try Activity 27.

ACTIVITY 27

Suppose we have two firms A and B producing a similar type of car (a standard family saloon) for about the same price. Suppose that firm A is concerned about falling sales, and decides to reduce the price of its car by 10%. Given that the CED between the two firm's cars is +3.0, calculate the effect on the number of cars sold by firm B. (Assume that the time-period concerned here is one year).

The number of cars sold by B would fall by 30%.

Here CED $= \dfrac{\% \, \Delta QdB}{\% \Delta P_A}$, and the $\% \, \Delta P_A$ is negative because the price of A was

reduced by 10%. (ie $\% \, \Delta P_A = -10\%$) We want to know the value of $\% \, \Delta QdB$.

As we have $+3 = \dfrac{\% \, \Delta QdB}{-10\%}$, then $\% \, \Delta QdB = -30\%$ therefore, sales of B would fall
by 30%.

The price of A's model is reduced by 10%, so the quantity demanded of A's cars will increase as car buyers switch to A's model (as it is now relatively cheaper than previously). B would find its sales falling by 30% over the year (ie we have $-\%\Delta QdB = 30\%$).

Finally, for completeness we'll briefly look at the price elasticity of supply.

2.4 Price elasticity of supply (PES)

WHAT IS THE PRICE ELASTICITY OF SUPPLY?

This is a measure of the responsiveness of the quantity supplied of a commodity to a change in its price. The formula for the price elasticity of supply is:

$$\text{PES} = \frac{\text{Percentage change in quantity supplied of A}}{\text{Percentage change in the price of commodity A}} = \frac{\% \Delta Q_s A}{\% \, \Delta PA}$$

ACTIVITY 28

Draw a supply curve for a commodity which has a PES = 0.

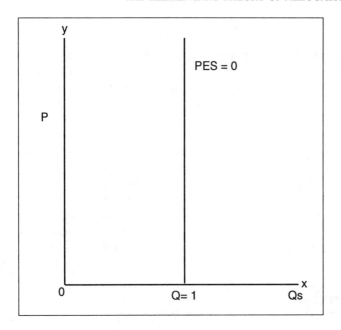

TIME AND THE PRICE ELASTICITY OF SUPPLY

One of the main factors determining the PES is time. Other things being equal, the longer the time that passes following a change in the price of a commodity, the higher the value of its PES. For example, currently the PES may be low, say below 1.0 (i.e. inelastic) because firms are unable to increase their production quickly: firms have to recruit and train extra workers, new machinery has to be ordered, made, transported and installed, premises may have to be expanded, and so forth – all of this takes time. In short, the quantity supplied of a commodity following an increase in its price will grow with time, and the value of the PES will therefore be greater the longer the time period over which the responsiveness of supply is measured. In Units 3 and 4 we'll be examining how firms vary the amount of a commodity they produce over time in response to changes in the prices of their commodities.

Now try Activity 29.

ACTIVITY 29

Consider a rice producer in Egypt and a whisky distiller in Scotland – both are firms! Assume rice and whisky prices increase by 10%.

1 Which of the two would be able to increase the output of their commodity more quickly?

2 Which of the two would have the higher PES, measured over three months?

The answer to both is the rice grower.

1   Suppose the rice producer grows maize as well as rice and is able to produce four crops of each a year. By growing less maize and more rice, the rice producer could produce more rice in a matter of a few months. In the case of the whisky-producer because the distillation process takes many years, it will not be possible to produce more whisky for several years.

2   After one year the rice producer may have been able to double the amount of rice produced, so the PES measured over three months would be 10.0 (100%/10%): the quantity supplied of rice is very price-elastic. In the case of whisky there would have been no increase in the quantity supplied as it was not possible to increase output, so the PES for whisky would be zero (0%/10% = 0): the quantity supplied of whisky is perfectly price-inelastic – the supply curve would be vertical, like the one you saw in Activity 28.

Summary

In this section we examined four different measures of elasticity – the price elasticity of demand(PED), income elasticity of demand (YED), cross-elasticity of demand (CED) and the price elasticity of supply (PES) – and some of their applications. We should add that elasticity has several other applications in microeconomics and macroeconomics: examples include the responsiveness of the demand for bank credit to changes in interest rates, and the responsiveness of the demand from overseas for commodities produced in the UK (i.e. exports) to changes in exchange rates.

We observed that no matter what elasticity measure is being used, it will express the responsiveness of a dependent variable to a change in an independent variable, in the form of an unambiguous numerical value, in whatever units the variables are expressed. We also discovered that, in whatever context an elasticity measure is employed, the term elastic has the same meaning: an elasticity value of more than 1.0 signifies that a change in an independent variable will lead to a more than equal (or proportionate) change in the dependent variable.

Similarly, for the term inelastic: an elasticity value of less than 1.0 signifies that a change in the independent variable will lead to a less than equal (or proportionate) change in the dependent variable.

SECTION THREE

Market Failure

Introduction

The economic case for the market economy is based on the proposition that it will lead to an optimal allocation of resources. When resources are allocated optimally they are said to be efficiently allocated, so that it is not possible to produce more of one commodity without reducing output elsewhere. An optimal or **efficient allocation** of resources can be represented by a point on the production possibility boundary (PPB).

However, for a variety of reasons a market economy may be prevented from achieving an optimal allocation of resources. In such a situation we have **market failure**, which we will discuss in this section. We will discuss what it is and how a government may respond to it.

Market failure does not mean that resources are unallocated: it means that resources are not allocated optimally, so that they could be reallocated and the output of at least one commodity could be increased without reducing the production of any other commodity. This is market failure in the allocative efficiency (or, just efficiency) sense. However, it is also argued by economists, politicians and others that markets also fail in an ethical sense: a market economy may lead to an optimal allocation of resources (i.e. there is allocative efficiency) but produce a distribution of wealth and income which is not equitable, so certain groups are disadvantaged, such as the low-paid, single-parent families, the homeless, and the unemployed. Market failure in both senses provides a rationale for government intervention in the workings of the economy, and so to the abandonment of a laissez-faire approach, in other words, to the abandonment of a free market approach. Our discussion of market failure will focus mainly on the efficiency aspect. We can note here that a policy which is designed to improve efficiency may lead to income (and wealth) becoming even more inequitably distributed.

Explanations for market failure can be quite complex. Nonetheless, a few of the major types of market failure will be noted, to be followed by an outline of some of the measures governments employ to offset market failure which leads to economic inefficiency and/or social injustice.

3.1 Types of market failure

Here we will look at three types of market failure: those due to externalities, public goods and monopoly power.

EXTERNAL COSTS AND BENEFITS

In the market economy economic agents are assumed to pursue their own self-interest and so do not take into account the effects of their behaviour on others. For example, if a firm dumps all its toxic chemical waste in a river, the **private cost** of its operations (production, and discharge of waste) may be £X million. However, there will be costs incurred by others who use the river, such as the owners of trout farms and swimmers, who may have to relocate their activities at some cost somewhere else as the river is no longer safe. These relocation costs are called **external costs** because they are borne by parties *external* to the activities of the chemical firm. If we add together the value of all the private costs and the external costs we have the **social costs** of the firm's activities which measures the cost to the community of the resources the firm uses – the raw materials, labour, etc. and the river (the private cost of which was zero).

When there is a difference or divergence between the social cost (to the community) and the private cost (to the firm) of producing a commodity, there tends to be a more than socially desirable amount of resources allocated to it, and the opportunity cost to the community is too high. So, there may be a case for reducing the scale of such an activity, for example, by indirect taxation, or stopping it altogether. As the government, or some government agency, may be the only organisation capable of taking action to deal with such an activity, there is a rationale for government intervention in the workings of the market economy. The case for government regulation of many types of economic activity reflects a concern to reduce their harmful effects, commonly known as pollution, for example noise, smoke, eyesores, etc. The effect of this type of market failure can be seen in Figure 21.

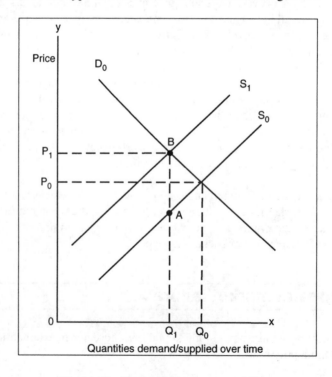

Figure 21: Market failure-external costs

Here the supply curve s_0 represents the market supply curve as determined by private costs. The effect of an external cost is for the supply curve (s_1) to be above the supply curve (s_0) as determined by just private costs. Thus the supply curve (s_1) as affected by external costs will intersect the demand curve at q_1 a lower output than q_0. The vertical distance between the two supply curves (AB) represents the external cost of the activity. Thus an activity which has a significant external cost will result in the production of a commodity being less than it would have been if resources were allocated efficiently. In short, in the presence of external costs, production is not efficient and resources are not allocated optimally. Action by the government (for example, a pollution tax) to reduce the external cost would result in the supply curve (s_1) shifting towards s_0 where external costs would be zero, and so social cost would be equal to private cost at the higher output q_0, the optimal output determined by market prices in the absence of any market failure (i.e. external costs). In short, social cost would now be equal to private cost.

Conversely, some types of activity result in a substantial benefit to the community (an **external benefit**), in addition to the private benefit enjoyed by the individual economic agent which undertook, or is undertaking the activity. Activities which generate a **social benefit** (private benefit plus external benefit) tend to have a less than socially desirable amount of resources allocated to them. As a result, the government may take action (for example, tax allowances, subsidies, grants) to encourage, or stimulate such activities so more resources are allocated to them. Examples include the provision by the state of education and health services, subsidising the arts, and public housing.

So by taking action to reduce/eliminate those activities which give rise to external costs, and encouraging those activities which give rise to external benefits, a government may decide to achieve an allocation of resources closer to that which would have been achieved in the absence of external costs and benefits. An alternative term for external costs and benefits is **externalities**.

Note: the discussion of externalities applies to both production and consumption activities which generate significant external costs and benefits. You may have noticed that though externalities may exist (a positive issue), the decision to deal with them is a normative issue and is undertaken by governments acting in the public interest.

PUBLIC GOODS

A **private good** X (good here can apply to services) exists where consumption of X by one individual prevents others from enjoying X. X is said to be **rivalrous in consumption:** once consumed by an individual, nobody else can consume it. Also, it is possible for an individual to exclude others from the benefits of X by the means of devices such as fences, locks, doors, safes, etc. So private goods are also **excludable in consumption.** At the other extreme to a private good X is a **public good** Y. Here, if one individual consumes it, so does everybody else, and nobody can be excluded from the benefits of an individual's consumption of Y. Thus public goods are said to be **non-rivalrous and non-excludable in consumption.**

In the case of a public good all but the first consumer are said to be **free-riders**. Hence public goods are also called **collective consumption goods**. Put differently, public goods generate major external benefits. In such cases no single individual will purchase a public good: why should I purchase a public good so everybody else gets the benefits free of charge and I can't get any money from anybody? As a result, because nobody will purchase the commodity, there is no effective demand for it, though there is a potential demand, and so the commodity will not be provided in the market. There is market failure. If such a good is felt to be socially desirable, then (so the argument goes) the government, or a government agency, such as a state department, should provide it and extract payment for it through the tax system. The classic case of a public good is defence (a service!). Other examples are debatable. Nonetheless, the following have been advanced: the courts (non-excludable?), the police (non-excludable?), street lighting, the prison service, lighthouses, harbours, dams, the Thames flood barrier, and so on. Others? One should note that commodities with public-good characteristics are increasingly being provided by private-sector organisations, but regulated by government bodies, for example prisons and the Home Office in the UK.

MONOPOLY POWER

Where a firm, or group of firms acting together, has control over the production and/or distribution of a commodity, it is said to have **monopoly power** and so the ability to restrict output to a level below that which would have been the case in the absence of monopoly power. By restricting output the monopoly will be able to charge a higher price for its commodity than if the commodity had been provided by numerous independent firms all competing with each other in conditions of perfect competition. (Monopoly and perfect competition will be examined in Unit 4.)

The existence of monopoly provides another argument for government intervention: to restrict monopoly power, encourage competition, and so increase availability of commodities and at lower prices. Hence the existence of legislation to control monopoly and abuse, such as price-fixing agreements.

3.2 Types of government intervention

Government may intervene in the workings of the economy at the microeconomic level and at the macroeconomic level. Here we will only be looking at the former to identify the different types of intervention. We should recall that government intervention may be motivated by a desire to improve the efficiency of the market economy so that the allocation of resources is closer to, or at the optimum, or to redress some of the inequities in the distribution of income and wealth. We will ignore the political reason(s) for intervention (a major study area in economics), and just accept that governments do intervene, thus leaving us free to concentrate on some economic aspects of intervention. With the collapse of the command economies, the debate is no longer about which is better, command economies, or free market economies, but about what constitutes the optimal public/private sector mix or, how much intervention is optimal?

Having decided to intervene (for whatever reason(s)), governments use legislation (laws, rules, regulations) to change the legal framework in which the market economy operates. As a result, governments are able to encourage the production of some commodities, or undertake their production in the public sector (for example, public goods). On the other hand, governments also seek to control or regulate some activities, and in a few cases prohibit them.

Governments provide subsidies, grants, and tax allowances to encourage production and consumption activities they think are socially desirable. To discourage socially undesirable activities a government can use legislation to make some practices illegal (for example monopoly power, tax evasion), or prescribe minimum standards (for example minimum wages) non-adherence to which may result in prosecution. Regulatory bodies are increasingly being established to set and monitor standards, examples are numerous and include OFWAT (the water-regulating body) and OFGAS (the gas-regulating body). Can you identify any other regulatory bodies? Taxation provides another means of reducing undesirable activities.

To provide some insight into the effects of intervention from a microeconomic viewpoint we'll look briefly at two types of intervention: price regulations, and the imposition of a tax on the sales of a commodity. We need to note here that what we say about government intervention applies also to its agencies, and to external supranational bodies (for example the European Commission in Brussels) to which national governments surrender some of their sovereignty (economic, legal, political) in the wider interests of a group of largely independent nation-states, such as those comprising the European Union (EU).

3.3 Price regulation (floors and ceilings)

For a variety of reasons associated with considerations of equity or fairness, governments override the price mechanism and set prices, either by specifying a maximum price, or a minimum price. Remembering that price can also refer to wage rates, interest rates, exchange rates, and rents, the discussion which follows can be applied to a number of different markets, such as the foreign exchange markets, capital markets, labour markets, etc.

Suppose that a government is concerned about the plight of low-income groups and in response to demands from various pressure groups decides to introduce legislation to set a national minimum hourly wage-rate, or floor, the payment of rates below which is illegal. What will be the effect on the level of employment? Look at Figure 22 carefully for a moment.

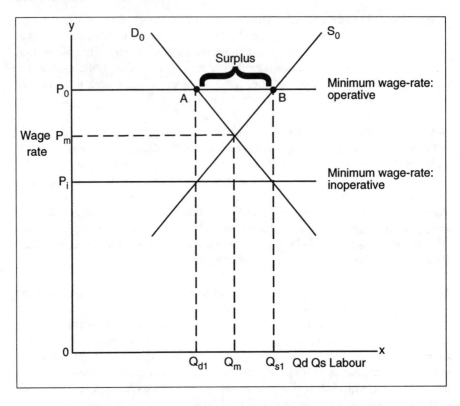

Figure 22: The effect of a minimum hourly wage rate

Suppose the free labour market hourly wage rate is p_m. At this level, the labour market is in equilibrium: there is just sufficient labour being provided to satisfy the demand for labour at that wage rate. Suppose now that the government imposes a minimum wage rate p_i. This will not be operative, or effective, as the market wage rate is above it. However, if the rate is fixed at p_0 (i.e. above the market wage rate), the minimum wage rate will be operative and the wage rate in the labour market will be forced to rise to p_0. This will increase the amount of labour supplied (individuals who were not prepared to work at p_m will now enter the labour market at this rate), and reduce the quantity demanded (firms will require less labour as it is now more expensive and so may increase the amount of capital employed, or increase labour productivity in some way). The result will be an excess supply or surplus of labour at the new minimum wage rate, or unemployment (= AB, or $q_{s1} > q_{d1}$).

In the case of maximum price legislation which sets a maximum price, or **ceiling**, for a commodity, above which it is illegal to sell, a shortage will result. Now look at Figure 23 carefully.

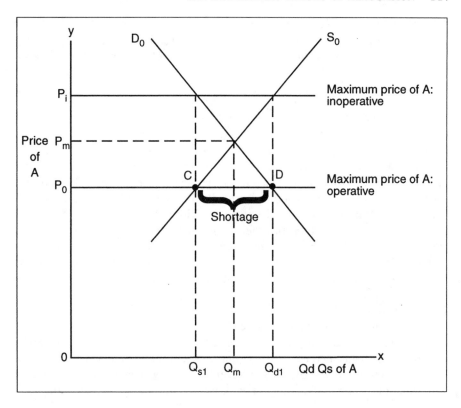

Figure 23: The effect of a maximum price

Suppose the market for A is in equilibrium at p_m, with the quantity demanded equal to the quantity supplied, so there is neither a shortage nor a surplus, the market is cleared. Suppose the government imposed a maximum price for A of p_i (above p_m). The maximum price will have no effect: it's inoperative because the market price is below it. However, if the maximum price is set below the market price, say at p_0, the quantity supplied will decrease and the quantity demanded will increase. The result of the operative or effective maximum price will be to create a shortage of the commodity (= CD, or $q_{s1} < q_{d1}$).

The imposition of legislation to set prices above or below prevailing prices, or prices that would have prevailed, in the market may be thus to create market disequilibria, which can't be eliminated by the operation of the price mechanism (recall what we learnt in Section 1), because its operation has been suspended by the government setting prices. As a result, alternative methods of sharing out the commodities which are in excess demand (or short supply) appear: queues (first-come, first-served principle), availability on alternative days, sellers' preferences (selling to long-standing and loyal customers only), payment-in-kind, black markets, and the introduction by the government of some form of official rationing.

Similarly, minimum price legislation may create surpluses which have to be purchased by the government at the official price, stored, and eventually disposed of in some way. So price regulation can lead to a misallocation of resources. There may be overproduction or underproduction and resources are diverted into the black economy, criminal activities and extra policing. In short, intervention may lead to scarce resources being wasted, or to an allocation of resources which is not optimal.

Other examples of price regulation include: the activities of OPEC in setting minimum oil prices; controls on the price of rented property (rents); mechanisms to regulate exchange rates, such as the Exchange Rate Mechanism; the Common Agricultural Policy (hence the butter mountains, wine lakes, etc.); prices and incomes policies. In the former command economies of the USSR, etc., prices for many commodities were fixed at very low levels and this helped to produce chronic shortages, a queue culture, and the eventual collapse of the USSR, as we saw in Section 1 of Unit 1. Today, in a number of Third World countries prices are sometimes also set too low. In order to provide adequate food supplies food production has to be subsidised, but this helps to produce government budget deficits. To eliminate these deficits efforts are made to raise prices. However, such efforts can produce severe political unrest, even revolution.

Through the survey of price regulation you should now be able to appreciate the fact that intervention can have significant resource costs, and raises issues of economic efficiency (waste) and equity/social justice (high prices on black markets favour the rich, rent controls can create housing shortages and increase homelessness etc.). Even so, you need to remember that intervention largely stems from efforts to deal with situations when markets are not working well, are failing, or have failed.

3.4 Taxes and subsidies

Taxes

A government can seek to affect the allocation of resources by means of the tax system, using taxes to reduce the production of some commodities (for example those generating external costs), and subsidies to increase the production of others (for example those generating external benefits). We will focus on the use of taxes to affect production and consumption.

Taxes are divided into two groups: **direct taxes**, which mainly affect incomes, and **indirect taxes**, which affect spending because they are levied on purchases of commodities. There are two types of indirect or expenditure taxes: **ad valorem (by value) taxes** such as VAT, and **specific taxes** such as excise taxes levied as so much per unit. We'll only look at the latter here: how a specific tax will affect the quantities demanded and supplied of a commodity which has significant external costs. (You will recall that governments aim to reduce those activities which generate significant external costs in order to achieve an allocation of resources closer to the optimum. Note that existence of activities which give rise to externalities does not necessarily lead to action by the government – it may decide not to do anything.)

To see how a specific tax will affect a commodity which generates significant external costs we can use a lot of what we have learnt so far in this unit. We will assume that the firms producing the commodity under discussion must pay the tax (on every unit it produces) to the government's tax authorities, and then recoup as much of the tax, as possible, from the consumers. Now study Figure 24 carefully.

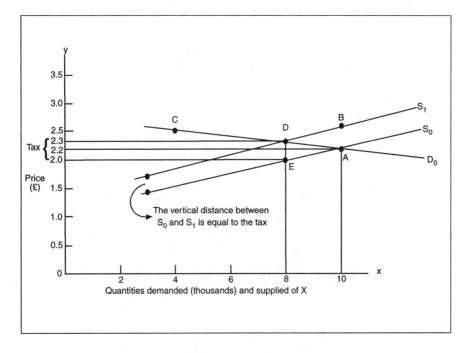

Figure 24: The effects of a specific tax

Suppose that before the tax of 30p per unit of X was introduced the market for commodity X was in equilibrium: the demand curve (d_0) and the supply curve (s_0) intersect at A. The equilibrium price is £2.20 per unit and the equilibrium quantity is 10,000 units.

In response to concerns expressed about the harmful effects of producing and consuming X, the government decides to introduce a tax of 30p per unit on X. What will happen to the quantities demanded and supplied of X?

Firms producing X before the tax was introduced produced and sold 10,000 units per week at a price of £2.20: that is, firms were prepared to provide 10,000 units at £2.20. When the tax is introduced firms still wanted £2.20 plus the tax (i.e. £2.50) for producing 10,000 units per week: we have a new price/quantity supplied combination shown by point B. This would apply equally to all the other quantities which firms could provide: there would be a series of points like B, each one indicating a new price (including tax) – quantity supplied combination. When these points are joined up we have the new supply curve s_1, which is above and to the left of the original (pre-tax) supply curve s_0. In short, the 30p per unit tax has led to a reduction in supply as shown by the supply curve shifting upwards. If firms charged the original price plus the tax, there would be an excess supply, or surplus of the commodity, indicated by CB.

In such circumstances, as we have seen earlier, firms will reduce their price to eliminate the surplus. Eventually, a new (equilibrium) price would emerge: at £2.30 the market is in equilibrium and the equilibrium quantity is now only 8,000 units per week (2,000 less than previously): this is shown by point D.

We can now see that the price which has to be paid by a consumer for a unit of X is not the original price plus 30p (i.e. £2.50), but £2.30. However, at the price of £2.30 firms will only receive £2.00 per unit (£2.30 less the tax). In short, the effect of a 30p unit tax is to increase the price of X to consumers by 10p, from £2.20 to £2.30 (so reducing the quantity demanded from 10,000 units to 8,000), and reduce the amount firms receive by 20p from £2.20 to £2.00 (so reducing the quantity supplied from 10,000 to 8,000 units). Put differently, we say that the **burden** or **incidence** of the tax is borne by consumers (10p) and firms (20p). Here we may note that a specific tax, in reducing what firms receive from each unit sold, has an effect similar to an increase in costs – a reduction in profitability and, as a result, a reduction in the quantity supplied.

The effects of introducing the specific tax may be summarised thus:

- A reduction in the quantity demanded of X of 2,000 units as a result of the rise in price from £2.20 to £2.30. This is represented by the (upwards) movement along the demand curve from A to D.

- A reduction in the quantity supplied by X of 2,000 units. Because each unit now brings firms 20p per unit less than previously, and to firms this is equivalent to a fall in the price of X of 20p, firms will reduce the amount of X they're prepared to produce and offer for sale at £2.00. This is represented by a (downwards) movement along the supply curve S_0 from A (10,000 units offered for sale at £2.20) to E (8,000 units offered for sale at £2.00).

- A shift of the supply curve upwards by the amount of the tax.

ELASTICITY AND SPECIFIC TAXES

In our discussion of the effects of imposing specific tax on commodity X we saw that the burden or incidence of the tax was divided between firms and consumers. The determinants of this division are the PEDs and PESs for X. The relationships between these elasticities and the division of the tax burden between firms and consumers is an interesting one. To give you some appreciation of these relationships try Activity 30.

ACTIVITY 30

Use demand and supply curves to work out who carries the main burden of a new unit tax of £1 per unit when:

1 demand is perfectly price inelastic, and

2 demand is perfectly price elastic.

We've drawn in the supply curves to start you off.

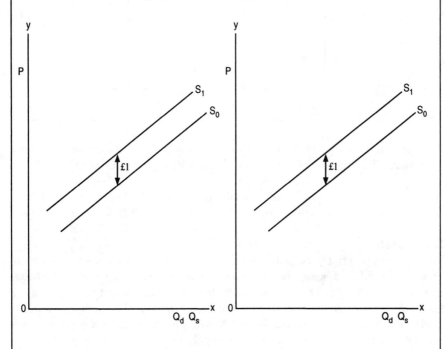

1 PED = 0

2 PED = ∞

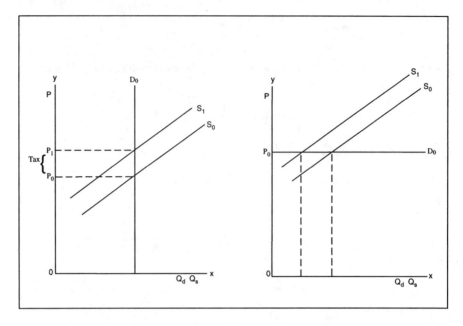

1   The whole of the tax is borne by the consumer. (The lower the PED for a commodity the more will a firm be able to pass on or shift the tax.)

2   The whole of the tax is borne by the producer. (The higher the PED for a commodity the less will a firm be able to pass on or shift the tax.)

SUBSIDIES

Finally, we can briefly note that subsidies may be paid by the government to producers (and to consumers) to encourage activities which have significant external benefits, or are socially desirable, but which in a market economy have a less than an optimal amount of resources allocated to them. For example, a subsidy paid to the producer of a commodity of X will reduce production costs, increase profitability and so increase supply: the supply curve will shift upwards by the amount of the subsidy, reducing the price and thereby increasing the quantity demanded. In short, more resources will be allocated to the production of X and the consumption of X will increase.

A brief summary may be useful at this point. By an appropriate mix of indirect taxes and subsidies, a government could attempt to achieve an allocation of resources which is closer to the optimum, by reducing the scale of socially undesirable activities (to which resources are overallocated), and by increasing those activities felt to be socially desirable (to which resources are underallocated). However, designing an ideal combination of taxes and subsidies which could maximise allocative efficiency would ignore other microeconomic reasons for taxation, such as the reduction of social inequality by progressive taxation. It would also ignore the macroeconomic reasons for taxation. Designing an optimal tax/subsidy combination is quite a daunting challenge.

3.5 A final note

In any discussion of market failure, it is very easy to inadvertently express normative statements, for example about what is socially desirable/undesirable. As always, economists must be careful to keep to the facts and to positive issues. By now you should be able to appreciate that this is not so easy.

Summary

In this section we looked at market failure and three types of failure in particular: the concepts of external costs and benefits (externalities), public goods and monopoly power. We also considered ways in which governments may attempt to remedy such situations by means of legislation and the use of taxes and subsidies.

Review Activity for Units 1 and 2

This activity is aimed at helping you consolidate much of the material covered in Units 1 and 2, especially the role of government in the market economy and the merits of the market economy.

Read Resource item 1.1 carefully, then answer the twelve questions which follow as fully as you can drawing freely from the material of the article.

Please note that some of the material you use to answer the twelve questions may be used more than once.

Generally, we will be using the term 'market capitalism' (or 'capitalism'), instead of 'market economy', 'market system', and so forth. In practice all these terms mean much the same thing.

Being able to comprehend and analyse articles like this will:

● help you with your learning as you progress through your course, and

● help you to prepare your assignments and projects.

Note: The article was written by N, Lawson (now Lord Lawson), Chancellor of the Exchequer 1983–89.

THE TWELVE QUESTIONS

1   What role(s) may be assigned to government under capitalism?

2   Identify any challenges facing capitalism at the present time. How could capitalism respond to these challenges?

3   What evidence is provided for the view that 'capitalism has appeared to be in the ascendent and socialism in retreat'?

4   Account for the 'unrivalled practical success of market capitalism'.

5   Why does capitalism still have its critics?

6   What are the features of capitalism?

7   To whom does N, Lawson assign the responsibility for the view that capitalism is based on the pursuit of self-interest?

8   How are Christianity's reservations about capitalism overcome?

9   Outline the arguments put forward against reducing inequality.

10 What can't capitalism do?

11 On the basis of the arguments set forth in this article, would you argee with each of the following statements?

   (a) '...would be the height of folly to doubt the legitimacy of market capitalism in the world in which we live...'

   (b) '...market capitalism's undoubted superiority in the world of practical achievement' wins 'the day'

   (c) 'Market capitalism...has...scored on every front..., it has proved itself to be a more favourable environment for economic growth than any other the world has known.'

   (d) 'There is nothing particularly surprising about the unrivalled practical success of market capitalism'.

12 Suggest a different title for N, Lawson's article.

Unit Summary

In Section 1 we began with the study of the market, in order to see how the price of a commodity is determined, why prices change and the implications of price changes for the allocation of resources amongst the production of different commodities. We looked in detail at the key concepts of demand, supply and price and showed how they interact. We distinguished between market equilibrium and disequilibrium

In Section 2 we explained and applied the concept of elasticity, which is concerned with quantifying the effects of changes in prices and demand/supply conditions. We examined four types of elasticity measurement in some detail, together with their related terminologies.

In Section 3 we looked at market failure: what it is, why it happens and how a government may respond to it. We paid special attention to the concepts of externalities, public goods and monopoly power, and how governments may attempt to remedy different interpretations of market failure (allocative efficiency, social justice/equity) by means of legislation (price regulation) and the use of taxes and subsidies.

You should now have another look at the objectives at the beginning of this unit and use them as a checklist for your own understanding of the subject matter of this unit.

Recommended Reading

Beggs, D, (1994), *Economics*, chapters 2, 4 and 5, McGraw-Hill, 4th edn.

Coase, R, (1960), 'The Problem of Social Cost', *Journal of Law and Economics,* October, 1960, p.1–44.

Lipsey, RG and Chrystal, KA, (1995), Chapters 4, 5, 6, 22, 23 and 24, Oxford University Press, 8th edn.

Parkin, M and King, D, (1995), *Economics*, Chapters 4, 5 and 6 , Addison-Wesley, 2nd edn.

Samuelson, P, (1954), 'The Pure Theory of Public Expenditure', *Review of Economics and Statistics,* Vol 36. 1954, p.387–9.

Answers to Unit Review Activity for Units 1 and 2

Our answers are as comprehensive as we can make them. If you have noted something that we have missed, well done! If your answers are a lot shorter, or less comprehensive than ours it is possible that you have not fully comprehended the article, and you should read it through again more carefully and slowly. After this, attempt the questions again.

Please note that our answers are based on the information in the article, so the answers are not exhaustive. Most probably you will have longer answers than ours as you will also draw on what you have read and learnt elsewhere. Do not worry about this, we would encourage you to read widely and apply what you have learnt to the questions.

1   Role(s) of government in market capitalism
- the provision of a system of social security;
- to create the legal and institutional framework for:

   (a)   market capitalism to thrive,

   (b)   achieving price stability,

   (c)   encouraging the freedom to create, and so

   (d)   ensuring (economic) growth (ie shifting the Production Possibility Boundary to the right).

2   Challenge(s) facing market capitalism

One challenge is that provided by the existence of the 'underclass'. Capitalism must respond to this by endeavouring to minimise its size.

Another challenge concerns: how can the problem of the existence of the underclass be solved without undermining capitalism? To respond to this challenge the government will need to create a 'well-designed social security net' to catch those who are severely disadvantaged by market capitalism.

3   Evidence for the ascendancy of market capitalism
- collapse of communism and the command economy in Central and Eastern Europe (CEE);
- leaders of CEE countries are 'the most passionate supporters of the capitalist market economy today...';
- recent events in China (are of interest);
- British Labour Party has reconsidered its... 'hostility to the market economy';
- much of the developing world has adopted market capitalism.

4   Reasons for the success of market capitalism

Reasons for the success of capitalism include:
- it allows individuals to give their best in a climate of freedom subject to the constraints of law and order;
- rational decisions about the allocation of resources are made possible as a result of price changes in a market economy signalling the need for resources to be re-allocated;
- its 'merits', which include:

(a)   proven ability to improve living standards/eliminate large-scale poverty;

(b)   unique harmony with political virtues of freedom and democracy, so that freedom is maximised and, therefore, creativity – necessary for growth ;

(c)   gives greater freedom than other systems;

(d)   by means of the price mechanism in a world of finite resources we become less wasteful, eg in our use of energy;

(e)   scores on every front: freedom, opportunity, protection for the environment, living standards;

(f)   produces a 'more favourable environment for economic growth than any other the world has known'.

5   Objections to market capitalism

- 'sloppy thinking', so that capitalism is held to be the cause of all the problems about us;
- capitalism encourges the promotion of self-interest/selfishness/self-gratification;
- aggravates social inequalities, eg how income and wealth are distributed.

6   Features of market capitalism

- channels self-interest for the greater good with the minimum of government intervention; (ie the 'least interposition of government'.)
- the firm (a model of effective co-operation);
- the family (foundation of a stable society);
- family businesses (important in the early stages of economic development. Importance is 'insufficiently recognised');
- 'voluntarism' – economic transactions are freely undertaken because each side benefits;
- free markets;
- private property.

7   A Smith

Adam Smith (1727–1790) – 'An Enquiry into the Nature and Causes of the Wealth of Nations', 1776.

8   Christianity and market capitalism

- capitalism frees the essence of individuals as it allows individuals to 'create' and this produces growth which allows individuals to improve their position without disadvantaging others, ie 'economic change is not a zero-sum game.'

- the self-interest of capitalism does not result in complete selfishnesss, as the pursuit of self-interest is restricted by the legal framework.

9   Reducing inequality in market capitalism

Arguments against seeking to reduce inequality:

- requires increasing government intervention in the form of coercion (and so reduces freedom of the individual);
- increases inequality of distribution of power between governed and government, i.e. the power of government increases;
- those who work harder receive no more than those who work less, so there is no incentive to work hard. The link between reward and effort is fractured. In short, equality is self-defeating as it produces less effort. Not rewarding people for effort expended is itself inequitable;
- we all differ in our abilities to do things, be it as footballers, or singers, ie we are in the 'sight of God' unequal, and so can't be made equal;
- pursuing equality leads to people being treated differently, ie unequally, eg 98% tax rates for some, much lower rates for others;
- pursuing equality maximises discontent;
- arguments for equality are often based not on improving the lot of the less well-off, but on the claims for social justice ('an empty tautology') and natural justice (not possible);
- instead of proponents of equality being motivated by the desire to reduce inequality, they're motivated by envy, ignorance, or personal dislike of those who have been successful, ie those who have 'more'. (The argument for equality is based on the 'politics of envy');
- reducing inequality is confused with relieving poverty – a different argument altogether.

10   Limitations of market capitalism

Capitalism can't:

- ensure the elimination of poverty altogether (hence the need for social security to which governments, even in a capitalist system, are wedded).

11   Claims for market capitalism

Whether you accept each of these statements depends on **your own value judgements**. Perhaps you may agree with all of them, and I may disagree with all of them. If we have such a disagreement we may discuss our views and come to an agreement – either to share a common viewpoint (eg we both agree with all of them or disagree with all of them), or to disagree – we just can't agree.

NB (a) – (d) are **normative statements** reflecting the author's opinions.

The author recognises this when he writes, 'It is obvious that I write from a particular perspective, which may not be universally shared. Morality, in any case, is a field in which it is particularly easy for intelligent people to reach divergent conclusions.'

12   Some possible alternative titles are:
- 'A rejection of the moral critique of capitalism'.
- 'In praise of market capitalism'.
- 'The moral superiority of market capitalism'.
- 'Criticising the critics of market capitalism'.
- 'The case for market capitalism'.

UNIT 3
THE THEORY OF PRODUCTION

Introduction

In Unit 1 we saw that economics is about the production and distribution of goods and services. In this unit, we will look more closely at the process of converting the factors of production – land, labour and capital – into goods and services. In doing so we are interested in the economics of production: for example, whether a commodity could be produced more efficiently by altering the proportion of the factor inputs. Put in other words, we will be working towards answering the following type of question:

'Given a small market garden, would it be better for the management to increase the number of workers (at a specified wage) or should it purchase equipment (at a specified price) if it wishes to increase output and keep costs of production to a minimum?'

To equip you with the understanding needed to tackle this type of question, we will have to examine the theory of production.

Objectives

By the end of the unit you should be able to:

- Describe the relationship which exists between marginal, average and total product concepts.
- Describe the relationship which exists between marginal, average and total cost concepts.
- Describe and explain the law of diminishing returns.
- Explain how cost curves can be derived from a firm's production function.
- Explain the difference between short-run and long-run cost curves.

SECTION ONE

The Production Function

Introduction

In this section we will explain the relationship between factor inputs (labour and capital) and output. We will also examine the relationship between inputs and outputs in the short-run, long-run and very long-run.

1.1 A simple production function

In our study of the economics of production we will start simply, then gradually make our study more complex. To begin with you might find it useful to have in mind a small factory making wire baskets. The firm employs a small number of workers (less than 10) and a small quantity of machines (capital equipment), let us say 10 machines.

Let us assume that **output** (Q), of wire baskets, will depend upon the number of workers (L) and the amount of **capital** (K) (number of machines) which are employed in the production process. We can represent this assumption by the following expression:

$$Q = q(L, K) \qquad (1)$$

This expression is called a **functional relationship**. It states that output (Q) varies with **labour input** (L) and **capital input** (K). q represents the relationship between output Q and labour and capital inputs (K,L). In expression (1) above the exact nature of the relationship between labour and capital inputs is not specified, that is we have not said by how much labour and capital inputs need to increase if we wish to produce one more unit of output. We will now look at the relationship between changes in inputs (K,L) and resulting changes in the level of output Q.

1.2 Short-run and long-run production functions

In order to produce more output we must increase one or both of the factors of production, capital and/or labour. In the following discussion we will assume that firms cannot vary both these inputs with equal ease. We will argue that labour can be varied at much shorter notice than capital. In order to analyse the impact of differences in the speed with which inputs can be varied we analyse the firm's production decision in three separate time periods.

The **short run** is that period of time when some of the inputs into the production process cannot be varied; these inputs are referred to as **fixed factors of production**. In the following analysis we shall assume that capital input is fixed in the short run. Therefore, in the short run, if a firm wishes to increase output this can only be done by increasing the variable factor of production, which in our analysis will be labour.

To what does this correspond in real life? If a manufacturer wishes to increase output he can only do this in the short run by employing more labour since it takes time to obtain more machinery (capital).

Note that the short run is not the same period of time in all industries. For example, in the electricity supply industry it may take three to five years to put the necessary capital equipment in place to allow output to be increased (that is the time which it would take to build a new power station). In the motor industry a period of three to six months would allow for a new production line (track) to be put in place. The length of the short run is therefore determined by how long it takes for extra capital equipment to be manufactured and installed.

The **long run** is that period of time over which all factors of production are variable. But the long run is not a sufficiently extended period of time to allow for changes in the basic technology of production. Hence the long run may be defined as that period of time when all inputs into the production process are variable, technology held constant.

The **very long run** is concerned with that period of time when the technological possibilities open to the firm are changing. This ultimately results in improvements to the product which is being made and improvements in the processes of production, that is the way in which output is produced.

We have looked at the meaning of the short run, long run and very long run. To confirm that you have understood these ideas try the following activity.

ACTIVITY 1

The management of Jaguar Cars wishes to increase output and a number of suggestions have been made to the board of directors:

1 develop a new 'electrically powered' luxury car

2 operate a night shift as well as the existing day shift

3 install a new production line.

Advise the board as to which of the suggestions are feasible:

(a) in the short run

(b) in the long run

(c) in the very long run.

In the short run output could be increased by employing more labour and hence suggestion (2) to introduce a night shift would achieve the objective of increasing output in the short run. The introduction of a new production line (3) will only increase output in the long run since new capital equipment will have to be purchased and installed. In the very long run Jaguar may be able to increase output by introducing a new 'electrically powered' car (1). However, the production of such a car would mean that Jaguar would have to develop a new car based on a new electrically powered engine. Such technological development can only occur in the very long run.

REVIEW ACTIVITY 1

1 The short run can be defined as that period of time when

The long run can be defined as that period of time when

The very long run can be defined as that period of time when

Summary

In this section we began by explaining the relationship between factor inputs (labour and capital) and output. We went on to define, and distinguish between, the short run, the long run and the very long run, in terms of inputs to the production process.

SECTION TWO

The short run

Introduction

In Section 2 we will introduce and distinguish between the important concepts of marginal, average and total product; we will also examine the relationship between them. We will then introduce and illustrate the law of diminishing returns.

In the short run we are concerned with what happens to output and cost as more or less of the **variable factor** (labour) is combined with a given quantity of the **fixed factor** (capital). In the following analysis we use the simple production function outlined in (1) and assume that the supply of capital is fixed with 10 units of capital (10 machines) being available for production each day. The supply of labour can be varied between 0 and 10 workers per day.

2.1 Output and factor inputs

When studying Table 1 you may find it useful to think in terms of the wire basket firm mentioned in the introduction to this unit. Table 1 illustrates the output of wire baskets as we vary labour input from 0-10, keeping the input of capital equipment fixed at 10 machines.

(1) LABOUR	(2) CAPITAL	(3) TP	(4) APL	(5) MPL
0	10	0	0	
				15
1	10	15	15.00	
				20
2	10	35	17.50	
				25
3	10	60	20.00	
				30
4	10	90	22.50	
				50
5	10	140	28.00	
				45
6	10	185	30.83	
				25
7	10	210	30.00	
				20
8	10	230	28.75	
				15
9	10	245	27.22	
				10
10	10	255	25.50	

Table 1

In Table 1:

column (3), TP, is total product (output), of wire baskets

column (4), APL, is the average product of the variable factor labour

column (5), MPL, is the marginal product of the variable factor labour.

Some of these concepts introduced in Table 1 are new to you and are explained in the following paragraphs. It is vital that you can clearly distinguish between marginal, average and total product before you proceed. Time spent clarifying these concepts at this point will pay large returns throughout Units 3,4 and 5 where the concepts of marginal, average and total values are used in different contexts.

Columns (1) and (2): record the possible daily combinations of labour (L) and capital (K) which are available to the firm in question.

Column (3): indicates the **total product** (output) resulting from the various combinations of labour and capital. Therefore, in Table 1 we can see that, when 3 units of labour are combined with the fixed supply of capital, total product is 60 units of output. When 9 units of labour are employed, total product is 245 units of output.

Column (4): records the **average product** of labour, which is the amount of total product per unit of variable input, in our example labour input. The average product of labour is calculated by dividing total product by the number of units of labour employed to produce that level of total product, as in the expression:

$$APL = \frac{TP}{L} \quad (2)$$

For example, if four workers are employed when 90 units of output are produced, then each worker produces 90/4 or 22.5 units of output on average.

Column (5): records the **marginal product** of labour, which is the change in total product due to the employment of one extra unit of labour. For example, Table 1 shows that the employment of two units of labour results in 35 units of output being produced; the employment of a third unit of labour increases total product to 60 units of output. It is therefore the case that the employment of the third unit of labour has caused output to increase by 25 units. Hence the marginal product of the third unit of labour is 25 units of output, that is, the amount by which the employment of that unit of labour adds to total product.

We have seen that marginal product is the change in output for a change in one unit of labour. We can say this more formally, using mathematical notation, like this:

$$\text{marginal product} = \frac{\text{change in total product}}{\text{change in quantity of labour employed}}$$

$$MPL = \frac{\Delta TP}{\Delta L} \quad (3) \text{ here the delta } \Delta \text{ means 'a change in'}$$

or

$$MPL_n = TP_n - TP_n - 1. \quad (4)$$

In equation (4) above, if $n = 9$ then the marginal product of the ninth worker is equal to the total product of nine workers minus the total product of $(n-1)$ or eight workers. That is the marginal product of the ninth worker is equal to $(245 - 230) = 15$.

Note that marginal product values are recorded at the middle of the class internal to which they apply. This is because marginal product records a change in output.

Before proceeding you should attempt Activity 2. You can often learn a good deal from studying graphs: in this activity you will be asked to plot two curves on one set of axes, then describe what you have drawn.

ACTIVITY 2

In the axes drawn for you on the graph below the y axis measures the average product of labour (APL) and the marginal product of labour (MPL). The x axis represents labour input. Plot the average product of labour (APL) and the marginal product of labour (MPL) on the graph using the data in Table 1.

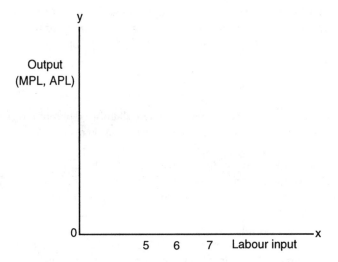

Study the curves you have drawn, then answer the questions and complete the sentences which follow.

1 Describe what happens to the marginal product of labour and the average product of labour as more labour is employed.

2 State the number of workers employed when the marginal product of labour
   (MPL) is equal to the average product of labour (APL).

3 The marginal product of labour (MPL) starts to decline when the ____ the
   worker is employed. But the average product of labour (APL) does not start
   to decline until when the _____the worker is employed.

4 The marginal product of labour (MPL) curve cuts the average product of
   labour (APL) curve when the average product of labour curve (APL) is at
   its _____ point.

5 When the average product of labour (APL) curve is increasing, the marginal
   product of labour (MPL) curve lies _____ the average product of labour
   curve.

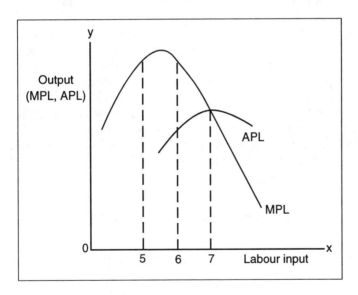

Note that in the diagram both the marginal product of labour (MPL) and the
average product of labour (APL) increase as more units of labour are combined with
the fixed capital supply (Question 1). Subsequently, however, both the marginal and
average product of labour start to diminish (fall). You should note that the marginal
product of labour (MPL) starts to diminish when the sixth worker is employed
(Question 2/3) whereas the average product of labour (APL) doesn't start to
diminish until the seventh worker is employed (Question 3). You should also note
that the marginal product of labour (MPL) cuts the average product of labour

(APL) curve at its highest point (Question 4). As long as the marginal product of labour (MPL) curve is 'above' the average product of labour (APL) curve then the average product of labour (APL) will be increasing (Question 5) .

2.2 The relationship between marginal and average product

As we stated above, the MPL starts to diminish when the sixth worker is employed; however the APL doesn't start to diminish until the seventh worker is employed. Also note that the MPL curve lies above the APL curve while the APL is increasing; only when the MPL curve cuts and goes below the APL curve will average product start to diminish.

The relationship between marginal and average values can be illustrated by the following simple example. If there are 10 students in a tutorial and they have an average age (mean) of 23 and an eleventh student enters the room aged 25 then the average age of the students in the tutorial will increase. Therefore because the age of the last student to enter the room (the marginal student!) is greater than the average then the average will increase. If the eleventh student to enter the room had been aged 20 then the average age of students would have fallen.

Returning to Table 1 note that MPL may be declining but, as long as it is greater than the APL, the APL is increasing. For example, Table 1 shows that the employment of the sixth worker results in a reduced MPL equal to 45 units of output, compared to a MPL of 50 when five workers are employed. But since this reduced value of the MPL exceeds the APL when five workers are employed the APL for six workers increases to 30.83 from a value of 28 units of output when five workers were employed. When the seventh worker is employed the MPL declines further to 25 units of output which is less than the APL for six workers and hence the APL starts to fall from 30.83 to 30 units of output.

To summarise:

if the MPL is *greater* than the average product of labour, then the average product of labour will be *increasing*;

if the MPL is *less* than the average product of labour, then the average product of labour will be *diminishing*.

2.3 The law of diminishing returns

We saw in the diagram in Activity 2 that after a period of rising productivity that both MPL and APL began to fall. What does this mean in practice? It means that at first, employing one worker increases output, employing a second worker produces a greater 'increase' in output than the employment of the first worker.

Employing a third worker produces a greater increase in output than employing the second worker and so on ... up to a point. Similarly, the average production per worker increases as more workers are employed. The average product of four workers is greater than the average product of three workers, which is greater than the average product of two workers. And so on up to a point.

After a particular number of workers have been employed the MPL begins to fall, and after employing still more workers, the APL begins to fall. Why should this be? Why should there be greater increases in production by employing three rather than two workers or four rather than three workers? Why is it that at first we get bigger jumps in production as more workers are employed? Activity 3 begins the process of answering these questions.

ACTIVITY 3

Think about the curiosity described above, and see if you can find a explanation for it. No right or wrong answers here, just write down an explanation which satisfies you.

That was a difficult activity, and it is quite likely that you will have come to a unique response. We will now look at the explanation economists offer.

We begin with a law which merely states that which we observed in the diagram in Activity 2.

The **law of diminishing returns** states that: if increasing quantities of a variable factor of production (in our example labour) are combined with given quantities of a fixed factor of production (in our example capital), the marginal product and hence the average product of the variable factor will eventually diminish.

In order to explain why this is so, consider Figure 1: to the left of the broken vertical line increased quantities of the variable factor (labour) ensure that the fixed factors (capital) are continually employed in a more efficient manner, resulting in increasing MPL.

Consider the practical implications of what has just been said: when one unit of labour is employed it must surely be the case that some of the 10 machines available will be underemployed. The addition of extra units of labour results in capital equipment being more fully employed and consequentially the MPL increases.

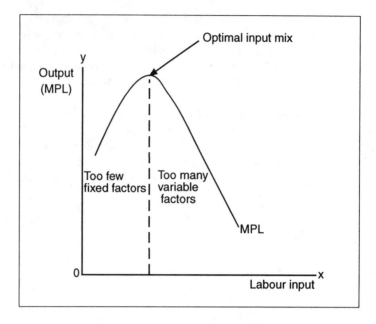

Figure 1: The law of diminishing returns

To the right of the hatched line there are too few machines (fixed factors) to fully employ the variable factors of production and therefore the marginal product of labour diminishes. (Too many cooks !) Now try Activity 4.

ACTIVITY 4

Explain why the law of diminishing returns can only apply in the short run. (**Hint:** Why do diminishing returns occur? How variable is a firm's input mix in the long run?)

In the short run there is at least one fixed factor of production which will ensure that diminishing returns are experienced. In the analysis outlined above diminishing returns occurred ultimately because there was not enough capital (machines) to fully employ increasing supplies of labour. However, in the long run all factors of production are variable and therefore the capital stock can be increased. This allows increased quantities of labour to be employed, with each extra unit of labour employed enjoying an increased MPL. These points are illustrated in Figure 2, which shows how an increase in the capital stock to 20 machines causes the MPL curve to shift upwards and to the right.

However, even with an increased capital stock diminishing returns will eventually occur, that is at some point the 20 machines will be insufficient to fully employ increased quantities of labour. Therefore it should be noted that the long run is merely a series of short runs

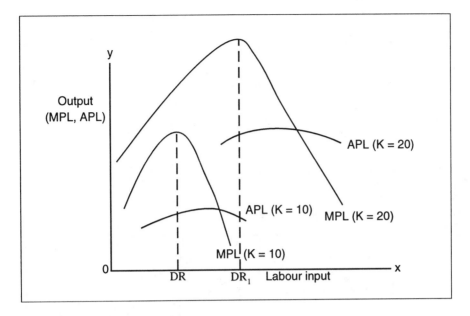

Figure 2: The effect of increased capital stock

DR shows the point at which MPL is maximised when K = 10. DR_1 shows the point at which MPL is maximised when K = 20. Figure 2 shows that with an increased capital stock (K) more units of the variable factor can be employed before diminishing returns are experienced. Note that it is only in the long run that the capital stock can be increased.

2.4 The relationship between total average and marginal product

Figure 3 depicts typical average marginal and total product curves and illustrates three important links between the marginal, average and total product curves.

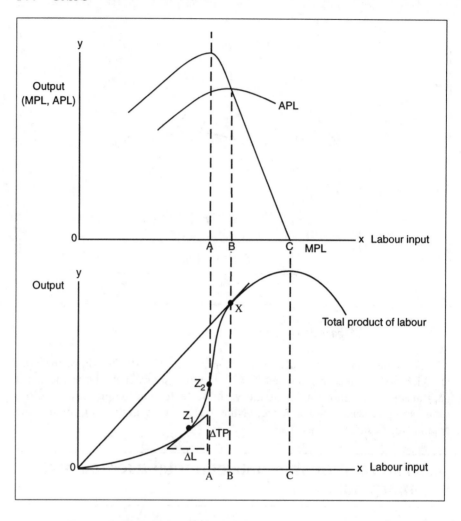

Figure 3: Typical average marginal and total product curves

First, the gradient (slope) of the total product curve, at a point, measures marginal product. Consider the tangent at point Z_1 on the total product curve, the gradient of the tangent is calculated from the increase in output and labour at Z_1 thus:

gradient of tangent at $(Z_1) = \dfrac{\Delta TP}{\Delta L} = MPL$, see equation (3)

Hence the gradient of the total product curve at point Z_1 gives the value of the marginal product of labour when 0A workers are employed.

Secondly, consider the significance of any straight line (chord) between the origin and any point on the total product curve. For example consider the straight line 0x, in Figure 3, the gradient of this line measures average product, since the gradient of 0x is calculated from total output and total labour between 0 and x, thus:

$$\text{gradient } 0x = \frac{xB}{0B} = \frac{TP}{L} = APL \text{ (see equation 2)}$$

Thirdly, total product is maximised when the slope of the marginal product curve is 0. This must be true, since as long as gradient of MPL > 0, then the employment of an extra worker must increase total product (output). Now try Activity 5.

ACTIVITY 5

Consider Figure 3 and explain the significance of points x and Z_2 on the total product curve in terms of the corresponding values of the marginal and average product of labour. This is a particularly difficult activity which requires a basic understanding of geometry. If you are able to, you may wish to discuss this activity with your colleagues and lecturers in a tutorial.

Point Z_2 is the point of tangency on the total product curve which has the steepest gradient and therefore is associated with the maximum value of the marginal product of labour.

The chord between the origin and 0x has the steepest gradient of all possible cords which could be drawn between the origin and points on the total product curve. Point x on the total product curve is therefore consistent with a maximum value of the average product of labour.

REVIEW ACTIVITY 2

1   In the table below TP is the total product of labour. MPL is the marginal product of labour and APL is the average product of labour. Fill in the missing values.

LABOUR INPUT	TPL	APL	MPL
0	0		
			?
1	10	?	
			15
2	?	12.5	
			?
3	36	?	
			8

4	?	11	
			?
5	50	?	

2   If we assume that the above figures are based on variable quantities of labour being combined with a fixed capital supply, use the data in the above table to illustrate the law of diminishing returns.

Summary

In this section we defined total product, average product and marginal product and explained the relationship between them. We introduced the law of diminishing returns and indicated that it exists only in the short run.

SECTION THREE

Costs of Production

Introduction

Our analysis thus far has examined the relationship between units of input (labour and capital) and the resulting units of output. In this section we will attach costs to the factor inputs and examine the relationship between an output and the cost of producing that output. In order to do this we need to employ a number of cost concepts: we will introduce the particular concepts of total cost, average total cost and marginal cost of production.

3.1 Total cost of production (TC)

The term is self-explanatory and simply means the total of all costs associated with producing any given level of production. **Total costs** can be divided into two constituent parts.

1   **Total fixed costs (TFC)**; these are costs which do not vary with the level of output. That is total fixed costs will be constant whether 100,000 units or 0 output is produced. For example a firm will have to pay rent on its premises whether or not it produces any output. You should note however, that in the long run all costs are variable, that is the notion of fixed costs only exists in the short run.

2   **Total variable costs (TVC)**; comprises all costs which increase as output increases. In the above example, since labour is the only variable input, then total variable costs will equal total wage costs.

Note that: $TC = TFC + TVC$ (5)

Therefore: $TC - TFC = TVC$ and $TC - TVC = TFC$.

3.2 Average total cost of production (ATC)

ATC is the total cost of producing any given level of output divided by the number of units produced, expressed as:

$$ATC = \frac{TC}{OUTPUT}   (6).$$

In the same way that total costs can be separated into its constituent parts (fixed and variable costs) so ATC can be sub-divided into **average fixed cost (AFC) and average variable cost (AVC),** where:

$$AFC = \frac{TFC}{OUTPUT}   (7)$$

and

$$AVC = \frac{TVC}{OUTPUT}   (8)$$

Therefore

$$ATC = AFC + AVC   (9)$$

You should note that equation (9) can be derived from equation (5) by, simply dividing both sides of the equation by output.

It follows from equation (9) that:

$$ATC - AFC = AVC   and   ATC - AVC = AFC.$$

ACTIVITY 6

1 Given equation (6) express:

    (a) output in terms of TC and ATC   Output = _____

    (b) TC in terms of ATC and output.   TC = _____

2 Given equation (7) express:

    (a) output in terms of TFC and AFC   Output = _____

    (b) TFC in terms of AFC and output.   TFC = _____

3 Given equation (8) express:

    (a) output in terms of TVC and AVC   Output = _____

    (b) TVC in terms of output and AVC.   TVC = _____

1    $\text{Output} = \dfrac{TC}{ATC}$ (6a)

    $TC = ATC \times \text{output}$ (6b)

2    $\text{Output} = \dfrac{TFC}{AFC}$ (7a)

    $TFC = AFC \times \text{output}$ (7b)

3    $\text{Output} = \dfrac{TVC}{AVC}$ (8a)

    $TVC = AVC \times \text{output}$ (8b)

3.3 Marginal cost of production (MC)

MC is the increase in total cost when output is increased by one unit.

$$MC = \frac{\Delta TC}{\Delta \text{OUTPUT}} \qquad (10)$$

Typically output is not increased in single units and hence the principle of marginal cost has to be applied to an increase in output of a given amount, that is output is increased in chunks. In such cases you are effectively calculating the average marginal cost of the chunk of extra output. This last point will be clarified at a later point in this unit. Now try Activity 7.

ACTIVITY 7

In the following table is an incomplete set of data from a firm showing the costs corresponding to various outputs. Calculate the missing values.

If you find this task difficult, try using hint 1. If you need more help use hint 2 and so on.

Hint 1: begin by calculating the total fixed cost for an output of 15.

Hint 2: complete the rest of the AFC column before going on.

Hint 3: if total fixed costs for an output of 15 is 150, what are the fixed costs for each other level of output?

OUTPUT	TC	ATC	AFC	AVC	MC
10	310	?	?	?	
					20
11	?	?	?	16.36	
					?
12	?	29	?	?	
					42
13	?	?	?	?	
					?
14	48	?	?	?	
					62
15	?	?	10?		

TC = total cost; ATC = average total cost; AFC = average fixed cost; AVC = average variable cost; MC = marginal cost. All figures are corrected to 2 decimal places.

OUTPUT	TC	ATC	AFC	AVC	MC
10					
11					
12					
13					
14					
15					

The key to solving the above matrix is centred on your understanding of the relationship between average fixed costs (AFC) and total fixed costs (TFC). (**Hint:** exactly what does an AFC = £10 , when output is 15, tell you about TFC?). The solution to this matrix can be found at the end of this unit.

REVIEW ACTIVITY 3

Complete the following definitions.

1 Total cost can be defined as:

2 Average total cost can be defined as:

3 Marginal cost can be defined as:

Summary

In this section we defined total cost, average total cost and marginal cost and explained the difference between fixed and variable costs.

SECTION FOUR
Short-run cost curves

Introduction

In Table 1 we examined the relationship between different combinations of labour and capital and the resulting levels of output. In this section we will show how output data can be converted into cost data. We will go on to look at the relationship between total cost and fixed cost and between average variable cost and average product of labour. We will then show how average total cost can be calculated by combining average variable cost and average fixed cost. Finally we will discuss the relationship between the marginal product of labour and marginal cost

4.1 Converting output data into cost data

By giving a cost to each unit of labour employed and each unit of capital employed we can construct a table which shows how much it costs to produce the different levels of output which are recorded in Table 1. In this simple example we assume that the only costs associated with producing output are the costs of labour and capital.

First, let us assume that labour costs are constant at £60 per employee per day and capital costs £15 per machine employed. Table 2 gives the costs associated with the output and input data presented in Table 1.

(1)	(2)	(3)	(4)	(5)	(6)	(7)	(8)	(9)	(10)
L	K	TP	TFC	TVC	TC	ATC	AFC	AVC	MC
0	10	0	150	0	150				
									4
1	10	15	150	60	210	14	10	4	
									3
2	10	35	150	120	270	7.71	4.28	3.43	
									2.4
3	10	60	150	180	330	5.5	2.5	3	
									2
4	10	90	150	240	390	4.33	1.66	2.66	

(1)	(2)	(3)	(4)	(5)	(6)	(7)	(8)	(9)	(10)
L	K	TP	TFC	TVC	TC	ATC	AFC	AVC	MC
									1.2
5	10	140	150	300	450	3.21	1.07	2.14	
									1.33
6	10	185	150	360	510	2.76	0.81	1.95	
									2.4
7	10	210	150	420	570	2.71	0.71	2	
									3
8	10	230	150	480	630	2.74	0.65	2.09	
									4
9	10	245	150	540	690	2.82	0.62	2.20	
									6
10	10	255	150	600	750	2.94	0.59	2.35	

Table 2

Before proceeding you should be sure that you understand how the figures in the above table have been calculated. Particular note should be paid to the calculation of marginal cost. The first value of marginal cost in Table 2 is 4. This has been calculated in the following way:

1   the relevant change in output is from 0 units to 15 units

2   the relevant change in total cost is 60 (from 150 to 210)

3   therefore, an increase in output of 15 has produced an increase in total cost of £60, hence 'on average' each unit of the extra 15 units of output has increased total cost by £4 and therefore marginal cost is £4.

We will now consider each of the cost concepts represented in Table 2.

4.2 Total cost and total fixed cost

Total cost (TC) (column 6) increases as output increases; note that when output is zero TC = TFC. This point is illustrated in Figure 4.

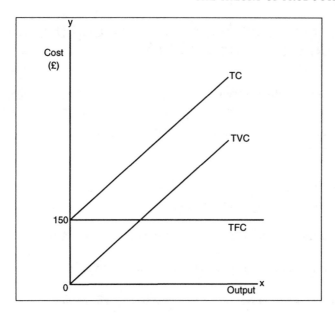

Figure 4: Total cost increases as output increases

Note that at each level of output the vertical distance between the TC curve and the TFC curve measures TVC.

Total fixed cost (TFC) (column 4): since TFC is constant at £150 for all levels of output, average fixed cost will decline as more output is produced. Figure 5 illustrates a typical average fixed cost (AFC) curve.

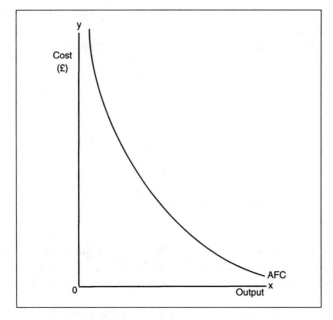

Figure 5: Typical average fixed cost curve

4.3 Average variable cost (AVC) and the average product of labour (APL)

In order to examine the relationship between APL and AVC please attempt Activity 8. Please remember that we can learn a lot by stating what may seem obvious.

ACTIVITY 8

Consider the following table and comment on the relationship between the average product of labour and average variable cost.

Hint 1: as more labour is employed what happens to the APL?

Hint 2: as more output is produced what happens to AVC?

LABOUR	TPL	APL	TVC	AVC
1	5	15	60	4
2	35	17.5	120	3.43
3	60	20	180	3
4	90	22.5	240	2.66
5	140	28	300	2.14
6	185	30.83	360	1.95
7	210	30	420	2
8	230	28.75	480	2.09
9	245	27.22	540	2.20
10	255	25.5	600	2.35

As the APL increases, so the AVC of production diminishes (convince yourself of this fact by studying columns 3 and 5 in the table above). Therefore, when the APL takes its maximum value (30.83) AVC takes its minimum value (1.95).

The relationship which has just been outlined on the basis of inspection can be expressed mathematically as follows:

$$AVC = \frac{TVC}{OUTPUT} \quad \text{(8 above)}$$

Note however that:

output = APL × labour input (L)

and

TVC = W (wage rate) × L.

Hence (8) can be rewritten in the following way

$$AVC = \frac{W \times L}{APL \times L}$$

hence

$$AVC = \frac{W}{APL} \quad (11).$$

Since the wage rate W is constant at £60 in the above example then it follows from (11), that AVC will take its minimum value when APL takes its maximum value. The relationship between AVC and APL is illustrated in Figure 6 below. Figure 6(a) shows that APL takes its maximum value when six workers are employed. You may wish to return to the table in Activity 8 to confirm this fact. Figure 6(b) shows that AVC takes its minimum value when 185 units of output are produced, again this is confirmed in the table in Activity 8.

This table shows that 6 workers need to be employed in order to produce 185 units of output and therefore as Figure 6 illustrates a minimum value of AVC will occur when the APL takes it minimum value.

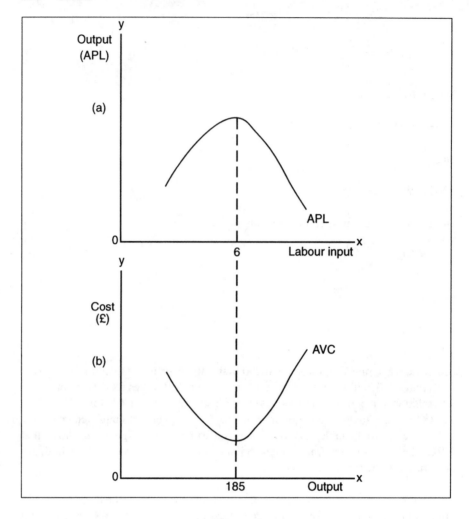

Figure 6

4.4 Combining average variable cost and average fixed cost to calculate average total cost

Returning to Table 2 and average total cost ATC (column 7): you can see that as output is expanded average total cost initially diminishes and then increases. Furthermore it should be noted (remembering that ATC = AVC + AFC), that when average variable cost starts to increase as output is expanded from 185 to 210 units that average total cost is still declining. The following calculation will illustrate why this is so:

output expands from 185 to 210 units

AFC is reduced by 0.1 (from 0.81 to 0.71)

AVC is increase by 0.05 (from 1.95 to 2)

ATC is reduced by 0.05 (from 2.75 to 2.71).

Effectively, the increase in AVC has been more than offset by the reduction in AFC and hence ATC falls.

ACTIVITY 9

Use the example which has been just been outlined above, and the data in Table 2, to explain, in terms of the changes in AFC and AVC, why ATC increases as output expands from 210 to 230 units.

---

output expands from 210 to 230 units

AFC is reduced by 0.06 (from 0.71 to 0.65)

AVC is increased by 0.09 (from 2 to 2.09)

hence ATC increases by 0.03 (from 2.71 to 2.74).

Figure 7 provides a geometric representation of the principle outlined numerically in Activity 9.

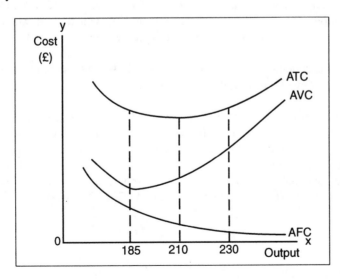

Figure 7: Average total cost, average variable cost and average fixed cost.

The reduction in average fixed costs over the range of output 185 to 210 units is sufficient to offset the increase in average variable cost over the same range of output and so average total cost continues to fall up to the point where 210 units of output are produced. However, over the range of output 210 to 230 units although average fixed cost continues to fall the increase in average variable cost is greater than the reduction in average fixed cost and so average total cost increases.

Figure 8 illustrates the geometric relationships which exist between the ATC, AVC and AFC curves.

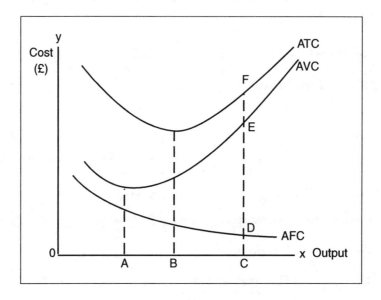

Figure 8

Firstly, note that as output increases the minimum value of AVC occurs at a lower level of output (OA) than the minimum value of ATC, which occurs at output level (OB). You may wish to confirm this point by reviewing Table 2.

Secondly, we should note that as output increases so AFCs continually diminish, due to the fact that total fixed costs are constant.

Thirdly, the vertical distance between the AVC curve and the ATC narrows as output increases. In order to explain why this is so recall that ATC = AVC + AFC, now consider output 0C in Figure 8. AFC is equal to the vertical distance CD and AVC are represented by the distance CE. Therefore distance cf which measures ATC must be equal to CD + CE. It should also be apparent that distance EF also represents average fixed cost (remember that AFC = ATC – AVC).

4.5 The marginal product of labour and marginal cost

The following discussion has a number of similarities with ideas discussed in Section 4.3. You should now procced by attempting Activity 10.

ACTIVITY 10

Consider the following table and comment on the relationship between the marginal product of labour and marginal cost.

Hint 1: as more labour is employed what happens to the MPL?

Hint 2: as more output is produced what happens to MC?

LABOUR	TPL	MPL	TC	MC
0	0		150	
		15		4
1	15		210	
		20		3
2	35		270	
		25		2.4
3	60		330	
		30		2
4	90		390	
		50		1.2
5	140		450	
		45		1.33
6	185		510	
		25		2.4
7	210		570	
		20		3
8	230		630	

LABOUR	TPL	MPL	TC	MC
		15		4
9	245		690	
		10		6
10	255		750	

You will no doubt note similarities between the relationship which was examined in Activity 7 and the relationship between the MPL and marginal costs of production. Namely, when the MPL takes its maximum value then the marginal cost of production is minimised. Let us recall equation (10):

$$MC = \frac{TC}{OUTPUT.}$$

In the example which has run through this unit changes in total cost are brought about by employing more of the variable factor of production, labour. The cost associated with employing more labour are wages (W), the extra output produced when one more unit of labour is employed is the marginal product of labour (MPL). Hence equation (10) can be rewritten as:

$$MC = \frac{W}{MPL} \quad (12).$$

Having examined the relationship between MPL and MC and reviewed Activity 8 you should now attempt Activity 11.

ACTIVITY 11

Given the information on the marginal and average product of labour contained in Table 1 and illustrated in the Figure on page 139, explain why:

1 The minimum value of marginal cost will occur at a lower level of output than the minimum value of average variable cost.

2 The marginal cost curve must cut the average variable cost curve at its lowest point.

1   Table 1 shows that the MPL is maximised when the fifth worker is employed and total product is 140 units. The average product of labour is maximised when the sixth worker is employed and total product is 185 units. Therefore, using our knowledge of the relationship between

(a)   MPL and MC, and

(b)   APL and AVC

we know that marginal cost will be minimised when output is 140 units and average variable cost will be minimised when output is 185 units.

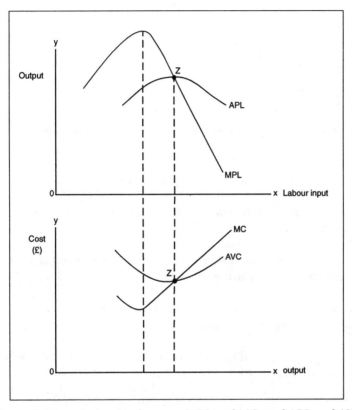

Figure 9: The relationship between MPL and MC, and APL and AVC

2   To answer the second question, consider Figure 9. At point z the MPL equals the APL and therefore, from equations (10) and (11), MC = AVC. Note that MPL = APL when APL is at its maximum value and hence MC = AVC when AVC are minimised.

4.6 Average total cost and marginal cost

Lastly in this section, we will look at the relationship between average total cost ATC and marginal cost MC. Three simple rules can be applied to describe the relationship between these two variables, which is illustrated in Figure 10.

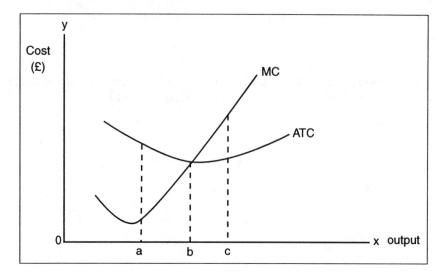

Figure 10: Marginal cost and average total cost

1   When marginal cost is less than average total cost, such as at output level (a) then average total cost will be falling.

2   When marginal cost equals average total cost, such as at output level (b), then average total costs will be minimised.

3   When marginal cost exceeds average total cost, such as at output level (c), then average total costs will be increasing.

As with the average variable cost curve, the marginal cost curve will cut the average total cost from below at the lowest point on the average total cost curve.

REVIEW ACTIVITY 4

1   When output is increasing if marginal cost is less than average cost then average cost will be _____

(a) increasing; (b) decreasing; (c) constant

2   Which of the following can be used to calculate average total cost?

(a) Average fixed cost – Average variable cost

(b) Total cost x Output

(c) Total cost/Output.

3 Draw a diagram which illustrates a typical average total cost and marginal cost curve. Comment on the point where the two curves cross.

4 Draw a diagram which illustrates typical average total cost and average variable cost curves. Comment on the relationship between the two curves.

5 Marginal cost can be defined as:

Summary

In this section we discovered how to calculate average, total and marginal cost when presented with data relating to output, factor inputs (capital and labour) and the cost of factors (wage rates and the cost of capital). We explained a number of cost-related relationships: between average variable cost (AVC) and average product of labour (APL), marginal cost (MC) and the marginal product of labour (MPL), average variable cost (AVC) and marginal cost, average total cost (ATC) and marginal cost, average total cost and average variable cost.

SECTION FIVE

Long-run cost curves

Introduction

So far we have been concerned with the short run where at least one of the factors of production is fixed in supply. In this section we will introduce long-run marginal and average costs. In the long run all factors of production are variable and hence the factor of production which was fixed in the short run can be varied. What happens when the supply of capital is changed? In Figure 3 we saw that when we increased the capital input K=10 to K=20 we increased both marginal and average product of labour.

5.1 Marginal and average cost in the long run

If the average and marginal product of labour can be increased in the long run then the associated marginal and average costs of production must fall. This point is illustrated in Figure 11.

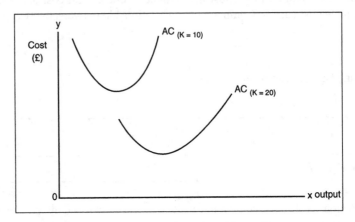

Figure 11: Changes in the scale of the industry and short run average cost

In the above example we would say that the scale of the industry has been increased because the supply of capital has been doubled. Strictly speaking, in order for the scale of an industry to be increased it is necessary that all factor inputs are increased by the same proportion. So, in the above example, both the input of capital and labour should be doubled, strictly speaking. The relationship between changes in the scale of a firm or industry and resulting changes in output is referred to as **'returns to scale'**.

- If inputs of factors of production are doubled and resulting output more than doubles then we refer to a situation of **increasing returns to scale.**

- If inputs of factors of production are doubled and resulting output doubles then we refer to a situation of **constant returns to scale.**

- If inputs of factors of production are doubled and resulting output increases by less than a factor of two then we refer to a situation of **diminishing returns to scale.**

Figure 11 shows what happens to the short-run average cost curve (AC) when the scale of the firm is changed, in this particular case the capital supply is increased from 10 to 20 units. Theoretically it should be possible to create a whole series of short-run average cost curves (SRACs) which correspond to different capital inputs. From this set of short-run average cost curves we derive the long-run average cost curve which illustrates the minimum average cost at which any output can be produced when all factor inputs are variable.

The long-run average cost curve (LRAC) or, envelope curve, is illustrated in Figure 12. The short-run average cost curves (SRACs) are also indicated.

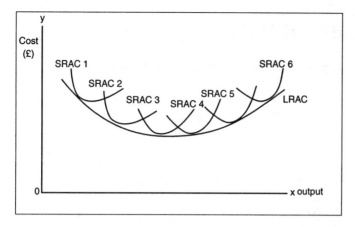

Figure 12

The long-run average cost curve (LRAC) can be split into three separate sections depending on whether or not average costs are declining, constant or increasing this point is illustrated in Figure 13.

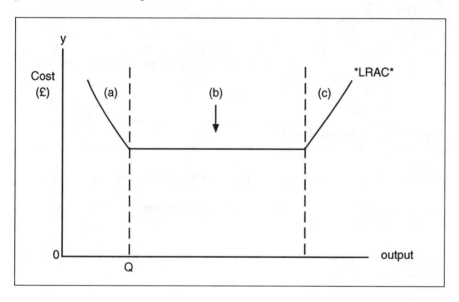

Figure 13: The long-run average cost curve

In section (a) of Figure 13 we say that economies of scale are being experienced as long-run average cost falls with increased output. In section (b) long-run average costs are constant. In section (c) diseconomies of scale are being experienced as increased output is associated with increased long-run average cost.

You can see that output 0Q defines minimum efficient scale since it is the minimum level of output that a firm must produce in order to experience minimum average cost.

REVIEW ACTIVITY 5

1   A change in the scale of a firm can be defined as

2   As the scale of an industry increases short run average costs fall, the industry is therefore experiencing _____

   (a) increasing returns to scale;

   (b) decreasing returns to scale;

   (c) constant return to scale.

Summary

In this section we explained what is meant by a change in the scale of a firm/industry. We also defined increasing returns to scale, constant returns to scale and diminishing returns to scale.

Unit Review Activity

In the axes which have been provided below draw the following three diagrams.

A diagram outlining the relationship between the marginal product of labour and the average product of labour.

A diagram outlining the relationship between average fixed cost, average variable cost and average total cost.

A diagram outlining the relationship between marginal cost and average total cost.

In all cases write a brief commentary on what you have drawn which explains the significance of where curves cross, the shape of curves and the distance between curves on the same diagram.

Diagram 1

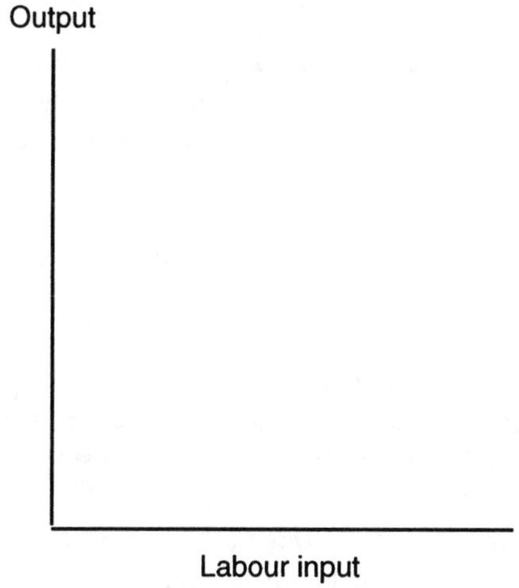

Output

Labour input

Diagram 2

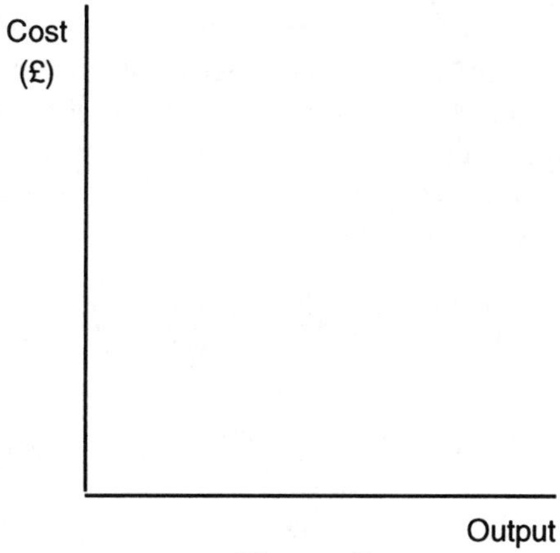

Cost
(£)

Output

Diagram 3

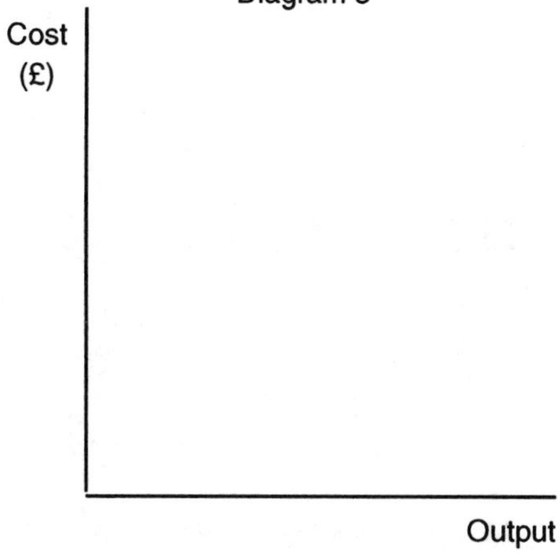

Cost
(£)

Output

| Unit Summary |

In this unit we followed up the coverage of the production and distribution of goods and services in Unit 1 by looking more closely at the process of converting the factors of production (land, labour and capital) into goods and services.

In Section 1 we explained the relationship between the factor inputs of labour and capital and output. We also defined the short run, long run and very long run in relation to the production function.

In Section 2 we introduced the important concepts of marginal, average and total product and examined the relationships and the distinctions between them. We then discussed and illustrated the law of diminishing returns.

In Section 3 we examined the relationship between an output and the cost of producing that output using a number of cost concepts: total cost, average total cost and marginal cost of production.

In Section 4 we looked at the relationship between different combinations of labour and capital and the resulting levels of output and showed how output data can be converted into cost data. We went on to examine the relationship between total cost and fixed cost and between average variable cost and average product of labour. We showed how average total cost can be calculated by combining average variable cost and average fixed cost. Finally we discussed the relationship between the marginal product of labour and marginal cost

In Section 5 we introduced long-run marginal and average costs.

Recommended Reading

Additional reading which deals with the material covered in this unit may be found in the following two books:

Parkin, M and King, D, (1995), *Economics*, Addison-Wesley, 2nd edn, pp. 243–64.

Sloman, J, (1995), *Economics*, Prentice Hall, 2nd edn, pp. 161–202.

Answers to Review Activities

Review Activity 1

1   ...some of the inputs into the production process cannot be varied.

2   ...all factors of production are variable.

3   ...the technological possibilities open to a firm are changing.

Review Activity 2

1

LABOUR INPUT	TPL	APL	MPL
0	0		
			10
1	10	10	
			15
2	25	12.5	
			11
3	36	12	
			8
4	44	11	
			6
5	50	10	

2   Initially, as more labour is employed (units one and two) MPL increases from 10–15, however, as further units of labour   are employed the MPL declines 11, 8, 6. It is this pattern of declining MPL which illustrates the law of diminishing returns.

Review Activity 3

1   ...the total of all costs associated with producing any given level of production.

2   ...the total cost of producing a specific level of output divided by the number of units of output produced.

3   ...the increase in total cost when output is increased by one unit.

Review Activity 4

1   ...decreasing.

2   (c)

3

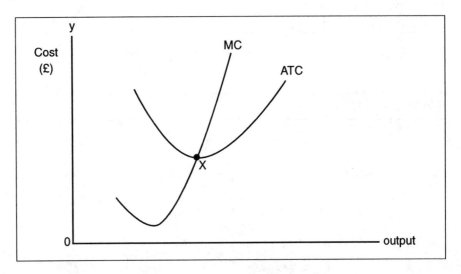

At point X the MC curve cuts the ATC curve from below and at the lowest point on the AT C curve.

4

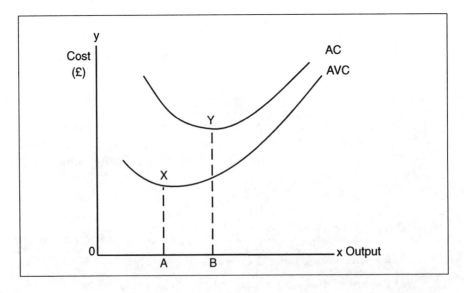

(i) the lowest point on the AVC curve will always be to the left of the lowest point on the ATC curve. That is, x is to the left of y.

(ii) As output increases, the gap between ATC and AVC becomes smaller. This is due to the fact that the difference between ATC and AVC is AFC and, as output increases, AFC becomes smaller.

5   The increase in total cost when output is increased by one unit.

Review Activity 5

1   ...a situation when all factor inputs are increased in the same proportion (by the same percentage).

2   (a)... increasing returns to scale.

Unit Review Activity

Diagram 1 (see activity 2)

In diagram 1 you should comment on the fact that marginal product of labour initially increases and then diminishes. (The law of diminishing returns). You should also note that the average product of labour does not fall until the marginal product of labour is less than the APL. It therefore follows that the MPL curve cuts the APL curve at its highest point.

Diagram 2 (see Figure 8)

First we should note that average fixed cost fall as output increases. Secondly the vertical gap between the AVC curve and the ATC curve at each level of output reflects AFC. Therefore as output increases this gap becomes smaller. You may also wish to look at the review activity for section four part 4! Which examines the relationship between the AVC curve and the AFC curve.

Diagram 3 (see Figure 10)

Here the important points to note are that as long as the marginal cost curve is below the average cost curve then average cost will be falling. Therefore it must be the case that the marginal cost curve cuts the average cost curve at its lowest point.

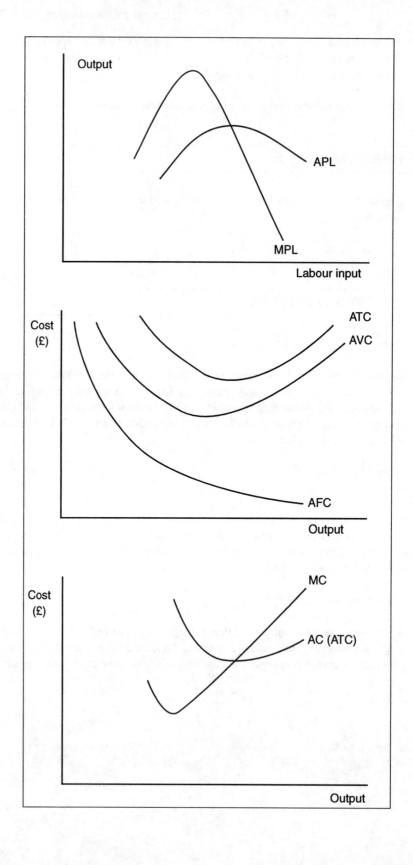

UNIT 4
MARKET STRUCTURES

Introduction

In the first part of this unit we will examine three different models of competition:

- perfect competition
- monopoly
- oligopoly.

The purpose of our analysis is to provide us with a range of predictions which suggest how firms may vary their price and output decisions under differing competitive conditions.

Two words of caution before we proceed: first, do not expect to be provided with an answer to the question 'which type of market is best?'. Our discussion will outline the costs and benefits of the three different models of competition. Secondly, this unit does not help you to explain the pricing and output decisions of a firm in any market you choose, since no real market perfectly fits any of our three models. However, you should expect to achieve an understanding of the ways in which the behaviour of firms will vary with the amount of competition faced in the market.

Objectives

By the end of the unit you should be able to:

- explain the theoretical models of perfect competition, monopoly and oligopoly and represent each of the models in diagram form
- develop an understanding of how firms develop price and output strategies in response to different levels of market competition
- develop an understanding of the level and sustainability of profits in markets where there is a lot of competition and in markets where there is little competition
- explain why firms collude, the benefits of collusion and what factors may cause collusion between firms to break down
- apply the theoretical knowledge you have developed to the issue of privatisation.

Section One

The Model of Perfect Competition

Introduction

In this section we make use of the idea of a **model**. While the term model may suggest a physical structure, models may be entirely symbolic. We can represent a model with a set of mathematical equations graph or a diagram. So what is the definition of a model? The word has many meanings, but the sense in which we use it is given by the following definition:

A model is a simplified representation or description of a complex system or entity.

Notice that a model is a simplified representation. It does not seek to explain all of the complexities of reality. The models which we will construct are intended to help us predict what will happen to variables such as output and price if the level of competition in a market changes.

The **model of perfect competition** examines the price and output decisions of firms who compete for sales soley on the basis of the price at which they are prepared to sell their output to consumers. Consumers are assumed to purchase output from that firm which charges the lowest price.

1.1 Assumptions about the model of perfect competition

The model of perfect competition is based on four critical assumptions which we will now examine.

1   Each firm in the industry produces a **homogeneous** product. This means that consumers can only distinguish between the output of different producers on the basis of the price. That is, the non-price characteristics of all goods in the market are identical, buyers are indifferent about from whom they purchase the good.

2   There are many buyers and sellers, none of whom is large in relation to total sales or purchases. The importance of this assumption is that no one buyer and seller is of a sufficient size to exert any independent influence on market price.

3   Buyers and sellers have perfect market knowledge of prices and product quality. This assumption implies that:

(a) buyers will always purchase output from the firm which is selling at the lowest price. There is a secondary assumption here that the buyer incurs no costs (transport, time) in purchasing from the producer who is selling at the lowest price.

(b) firms cannot gain a competitive advantage, even in the very short run, by cutting price in the belief that other players in the market will be unaware of their actions.

(c) perfect knowledge with regard to product quality implies that any improvements in product quality are disseminated throughout the market instantaneously.

4   The final assumption of the model is that firms have ease of entry into, and exit from, the market.

By this point you will realise that these assumptions are such that it is unlikely that any real market could be said to be perfectly competitive. There are, however, a number of markets which approximate very closely to the model which has just been outlined and examples would include some agricultural markets, foreign exchange markets and the stock market.

1.2 The perfectly competitive firm as a price

The above assumptions ensure that the individual firm operating in a perfectly competitive environment can have no influence on market price. The individual firm is said to be a **price taker**, that is, it must accept the market price which is determined by the industry's demand and supply conditions.

The individual firm is a price taker as a result of assumptions 1, 2 and 3 above. Since all goods sold in the market are homogeneous (assumption 1) the producer is unable to gain sales by attempting to sell a differentiated product. Assumption 2 states that no firm is large enough to exert an influence on market price by varying its own levels of output, since each individual firm is tiny in relation to the total size of the market. Lastly, assumption 3 ensures that buyers will only approach the producers who are selling at the market price. Any attempt to sell at a price above the existing market price would lead to sales falling to zero. Any attempt to sell at a price below the existing market price would be irrational since as we shall now see the model of perfect competition assumes that an individual producer can sell whatever output they wish to produce at the existing market price.

THE PERFECTLY COMPETITIVE FIRM'S DEMAND CURVE.

We have established that the individual firm is a price taker; so we must answer the question: 'what price is it that the perfectly competitive firm must take?' To answer this we must consider the conditions of supply and demand which exist in the market as a whole and of which the individual firm is a part.

Figure 1 (a) illustrates typical industry demand (D) and supply (S) curves which come together to produce an equilibrium price of £5 and an equilibrium quantity of 70,000 units of output. The individual firm, in the perfectly competitive industry, must accept the market price and faces an effectively unlimited demand (d) for its output at the market price (£5) (Figure 1(b)). At this point you should note the size of the individual firm relative to the size of the overall market. (**Hint:** look at the way in which the quantity axis has been graduated in each case.) Then try Activity 1.

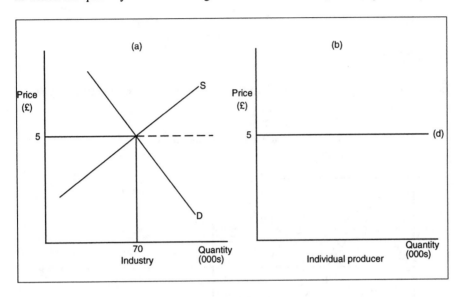

Figure 1: Typical demand and supply curves

ACTIVITY 1

From the following information on the industry demand and supply curves construct an individual firm's demand curve, assuming that the industry in question is perfectly competitive.

Demand curve $p = 50 - 1.5q$ where p is £/unit

Supply curve $p = 3.5q$ where q is 1000s of units

The individual firm will face a perfectly elastic demand curve at the price determined by the intersection of market supply and demand. Therefore, solving the market supply and demand schedules for equilibrium price and quantity gives an equilibrium price of £35 and a quantity of 10,000.

If p = 50 – 1.5q (demand)

and p = 3.5q (supply)

in equilibrium demand = supply, hence

3.5q = 50 – 1.5q

  5q = 50

   q = 10 (10,000 units)

If we substitute a value q = 10 into the supply or demand equation we get an equilibrium price of £35.

The market supply and demand schedules and the individual firm's schedule have been sketched in Figure 2.

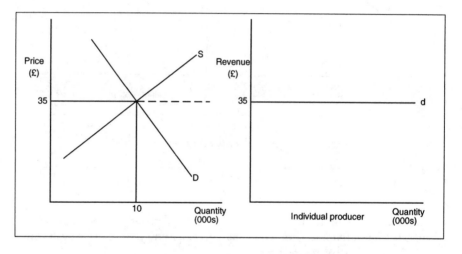

Figure 2: The market supply and demand schedules

1.3 What output will the individual firm produce?

Having determined the individual firm's demand curve (see (d) in Figure 2) we must now determine what level of output the individual firm will produce. In order to do this we use a number of cost and revenue concepts some of which were explained in Unit 3.

Firstly, we assume that the individual firm operating in the perfectly competitive market has the objective of maximising its profits. Therefore the firm will produce that level of output which maximises profits.

If this is the case then we will prove that the individual firm will continue to produce output until **marginal cost** (MC) is equal to **marginal revenue** (MR). That is, the firm will continue to produce output until the marginal cost of producing the last unit of output is equal to the increase in revenue (marginal revenue) from the sale of that last unit of output.

Before we proceed we should note that marginal revenue is the increase in total sales revenue when one extra unit of output is sold.

In order to prove the profit-maximising condition (MC=MR), which we stated above, we first need to derive a marginal revenue curve for the individual firm operating under perfectly competitive conditions. To do this look at Table 1. This table illustrates the typical price and output conditions faced by a perfectly competitive firm, that is selling price is constant at all level of output.

OUTPUT	PRICE	TOTAL REVENUE	MARGINAL REVENUE
1	£5	£5	
			£5
2	£5	£10	
			£5
3	£5	£15	
			£5
4	£5	£20	
			£5
5	£5	£25	
			£5
6	£5	£30	
			£5
7	£5	£35	

Table 1: Output and marginal revenue for the individual firm

In Table 1 we can see that, on the basis of the example data, at all levels of output (1,2,3....) marginal revenue is constant at (£5). The result, **constant marginal revenue**, is unique to firms operating under perfectly competitive conditions.

You should note that in this special case the individual firm's demand curve and marginal revenue curve are coincident (the same). Hence you will note that in Figure 3 and future diagrams we have labelled the individuals' demand curve d = MR or *visa-versa*. Figure 3 illustrates the profit-maximisation condition, you should note that the marginal cost curve cuts the marginal revenue curve at two points (A and B).

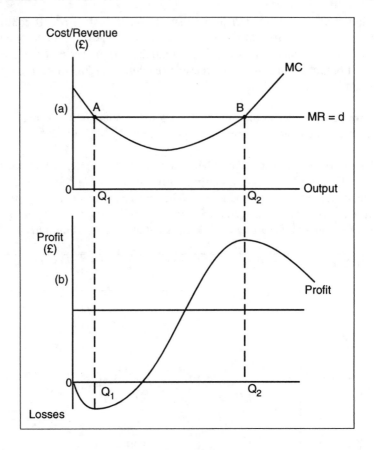

Figure 3: Profit maximisation

At point A the firm would produce output $(0q_1)$ and would in fact maximise their losses, as Figure 3 (b) shows. In order to explain this point consider the units of output $0q_1$, for each of those units with the exception of the last one (q_1) the marginal cost of production exceeds the marginal revenue from sales. Hence on every unit of output up to (q_1) the firm is making a loss. As the firm then produces beyond $(q1)$ successive units of output add more to revenue (MR) than they do to costs (MC) and profits start to accumulate. Profits will be maximised when output reaches $(0q_2)$, where the marginal cost curve cuts the marginal revenue curve at point B. Note that should the firm expand output beyond $(0q_2)$ then profits would start to decline since beyond (q_2) they would be producing units of output which added more to cost (MC) than they added to revenue (MR).

1.4 How much profit is made?

We have seen that in order to maximise profit the firm should produce a quantity of output at which marginal cost is equal to marginal revenue. Now we will find out how much profit is made when goods are produced in that quantity and sold at the market price. We must start by looking at the **average cost curve**.

1   The average cost curve which we will be using is the short run average cost
    curve which was derived in Unit 3.

2   The average cost curve accounts for all costs including profits. That is, average
    costs account for rent, wage, interest and *normal* profit payments. In this
    context **normal profits** are defined as that level of profit which is just sufficient
    to keep the entrepreneur engaged in his/her current activity. You may like to
    think of normal profit as the minimum return which entrepreneurs will accept
    for the risks which they have taken. Normal profit is treated as a cost because,
    just as wages have to be paid if production is to take place, so normal profit has
    to be earned if the entrepreneur is to find it worthwhile to organise production.

1.5 Short-run equilibrium for the perfectly competitive firm

Figure 4 illustrates short-run equilibrium for the individual firm operating in a
perfectly competitive market.

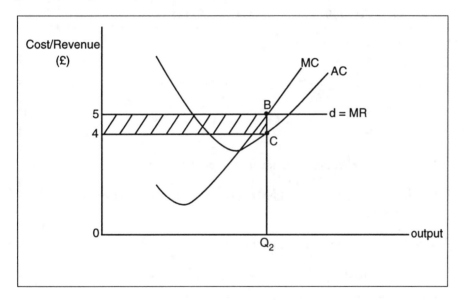

Figure 4: Short-run equilibrium

In Figure 4 the profit-maximising level of output ($0q_2$) is determined by point B
where MC=MR. At this level of output price (sometimes referred to as average
revenue) is £5. Average costs are £4, determined by point C on the average cost
curve. Note that for every unit of output ($0q_2$) which is sold price (average revenue)
(£5) exceeds average cost (£4). Therefore the entrepreneur is not only making a
normal level of profit which is already accounted for in average cost, but he/she is
also making an extra amount of profit equal to (BC) £1 on every unit of output
which is sold.

In Figure 4 **abnormal profits** are represented by the shaded area. This extra profit occurs when price exceeds average cost. Abnormal profits may be defined as profits over and above that necessary to induce entrepreneurs to remain engaged in their current activity (In some texts abnormal profits may be referred to as **economic** or **super-normal profits**). You should now attempt Activity 2

ACTIVITY 2

The following data represents the demand and supply conditions in a perfectly competitive industry:

Demand $pd = 200 - q$ where p is £/unit

Supply $ps = \dfrac{2q}{3}$ where q is 00s of units.

The following data represents the costs of an individual firm operating in the perfectly competitive industry:

OUTPUT (00s)	TOTAL COST (£000s)
5	25
6	29
7	36
8	44
9	54

1   At what price will the individual firm sell output?

2   What output will the individual firm described above produce if they wish to maximise profits?

3   Will the above firm be making losses or profits?

4   What will be the extent of losses or profits made by the above firm?

I have provided a full answer here: it may be that your answer is a lot shorter.

1   Output will be sold at a price which is determined by the market supply and demand curves. Specifically, price will be determined by the point where demand is equal to supply. Using the above demand and supply equations, we know that in equilibrium the value of price given by the demand equation will equal the value of price given by the supply equation.

That is: pd = ps

If this is the case, it must also be true that:

$$200 - q = \frac{2}{3} \, q.$$

Therefore adding q to both sides of the equation

$$200 = \frac{5}{3} \, q.$$

Multiplying both sides of the equation by $\frac{3}{5}$

$$120 = q.$$

Hence the equilibrium quantity in the market is 12,000 units.

If we then substitute this equilibrium value of output into either the supply or the demand equation we get:

pd = 200 – 120
pd = 80

or

$$ps = \frac{2}{3} (120)$$

ps = 80.

Therefore the individual firm will have to accept a market price of £80 per unit. This is illustrated in Figure 5.

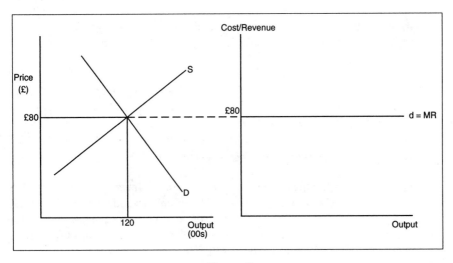

Figure 5

2   We know that the profit-maximising firm will produce at the point where MC
    = MR. In the above example the individual firm will have a MR of £80. (You
    may wish to revise the suggestion that marginal revenue is constant in a
    perfectly competitive market by looking at Table 1.)

Since we know that MR = £80 = price then the perfectly competitive firm, which
aims to maximise profits, will produce that level of output where MC = £80. In
order to work out what level of output has marginal costs of £80 we need to
consider the cost data given in Activity 2. From the total cost column we should be
able to create a marginal cost column. This is shown in the following table.

OUTPUT (OOs)	TOTAL COST (£000s)	MARGINAL COST (£)
5	25	
		40
6	29	
		70
7	36	
		80
8	44	
		100
9	54	

Marginal cost is calculated by dividing the change in total cost by the change in
output. (You may wish to return to equation 10 in Unit 3 if you are unsure about this
definition of marginal cost.) Hence when the output of the individual firm is
increased from 500 to 600 units total cost increases from £25,000 to £29,000.
Therefore marginal cost equals 4000/100 = 40.

From the above table we can see that when output is 800 units marginal cost is equal
to £80 and hence the profit maximising perfectly competitive firm will produce 800
units of output.

3/4 In order to determine whether profits or losses are being made when 800 units
    of output are being produced we must calculate the firm's average costs of
    production when output is 800 units. From equation (6) in Unit 3 we can see
    that average total cost is equal to total cost divided by output. Hence when 800
    units of output are produced average cost equals 44,000/800 = £55.

Therefore, if each unit of the 800 units of output costs, on average, £55 to produce
and sells for £80 then abnormal profits of £25 per unit are made. Therefore, total
abnormal profits are £25 × 800 = £20,000. Note that we cannot make a comment
on total profit since we have no information on the level of normal profits which
are already included in average costs.

1.6 Long-run equilibrium for the perfectly competitive firm

The existence of abnormal profit will also provide an incentive for new firms to enter the industry. Long-run equilibrium in a perfectly competitive industry relies critically on assumption 4 of the basic model, namely that firms are free to enter and exit the market. The existence of short-run abnormal profits as illustrated in Figure 4 will cause new firms to enter the market, this new entry will impact the model at both the industry and individual firm level. Figure 6 illustrates this.

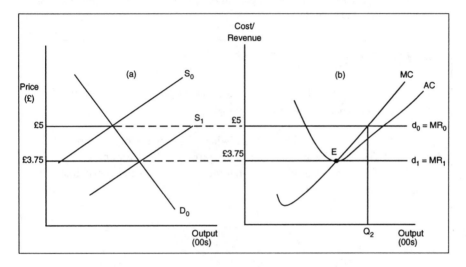

Figure 6: Long-run equilibrium and perfect competition

Figure 6 (a) shows the impact of new firm entry into the market at the industry level with the market supply curve shifting to the right (S_0) to (S_1). This occurs because the market supply curve is derived by adding up the supply curves of individual firms and if there are now more firms across which to aggregate, there will be a new supply curve positioned to the right of the original one. This causes market price to fall from £5 to £3.75.

Figure 6 (b) illustrates the impact of the fall in market price at the individual firm level. The individual firms demand and marginal revenue curves shift from d_0 $MR_0 = £5$ to $d_1 = MR_1 = £3.75$. If we then assume that both incumbent firms and new entrants operate under the same short-run cost conditions and that these are represented by the original cost curves MC and AC, then all firms in the industry will be in equilibrium at a point such as (E) in Figure 6 (b). Here price will equal average cost, firms will only be making normal profits and there will therefore be no incentive for new firms to enter the industry.

1.7 The marginal cost curve, short-run supply and the shutdown condition

Our discussion up to this point has been dominated by considerations of how to maximise profits. However, not all firms are profitable and the following discussion will examine what factors a loss-making perfectly competitive firm will take into consideration when deciding whether or not to cease trading, that is to shut down.

In order to carry out a discussion of the 'shut-down' decision we need to re-examine the role of the marginal cost curve in the perfectly competitive model. To start with, try Activity 3.

ACTIVITY 3

On the axes provided draw a marginal cost curve for an individual firm operating in a perfectly competitive industry.

Now try to explain, using the diagram, what will happen to the output of the individual firm as the market price of output falls. Remember that the individual firm is a price taker and that we assume that the individual firm wishes to maximise profits.

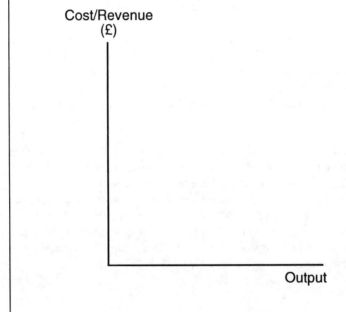

Figure 6 (b) illustrates the important role which the marginal cost curve plays, in the model, as an indicator of the firm's supply. Note that as the demand and marginal revenue curve moves in response to changes in market price, the marginal cost curve indicates what level of output the individual firm will produce.

This point is more clearly indicated in Figure 7, note that, as the d=MR curve shifts downwards, the profit-maximising level of output is determined by the intersection of MR_0, MR_1, and MR_2 respectively with the marginal cost. Therefore, the marginal cost curve is acting as the firm's supply curve, that is the marginal cost curve is indicating what output the firm will produce at different prices.

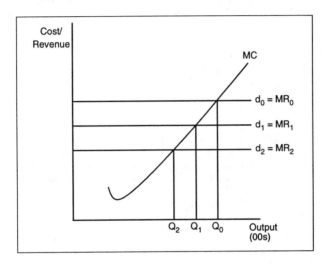

Figure 7: The marginal cost curve

SHUTDOWN

The above analysis has to be qualified in order to take account of the fact that there will be a point on the marginal cost curve below which the firm will not be willing to supply output. In order to develop this analysis we must now consider the conditions which would cause the firm to cease trading and shutdown. In the long run firms who have average costs of production which exceed the price which they can sell their output for will cease trading as they are making losses. This situation is illustrated in Figure 8 (a).

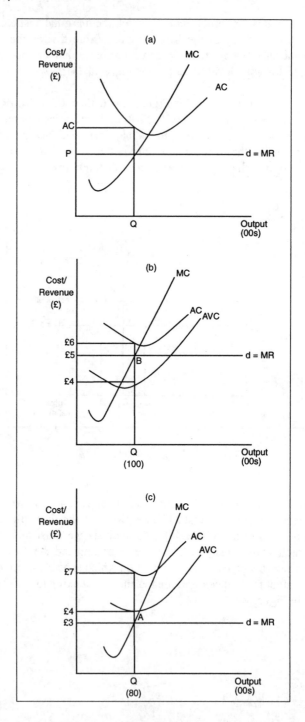

Figure 8: The shut down decision

In the short run, however, a firm will remain in business as long as price exceeds average *variable* cost. Consider Figure 8 (b), the profit-maximising firm will produce 100 units of output, determined by point (b) where MC=MR. For every unit sold the firm will receive a price of £5. In order to produce 100 units of output the firm incurs an average cost of £6, it is therefore obvious that if the firm were to continue to produce output it would make losses equal to £100.

Should the firm cease trading? The answer to this question is no. Firstly, we should note that we are dealing with a short-run situation, that is the firm will be incurring fixed costs which, should the firm cease trading, they would still be obliged to pay. Figure 8 (b) indicates that average fixed costs are £2 (AC-AVC=AFC) and therefore, as we are producing 100 units of output, total fixed costs are £200. Therefore if the firm continues to produce output it will make losses of £100 and if it shuts down it will make losses of £200. In the short run it would therefore be rational for the firm to remain in existence.

Figure 8 (c) illustrates the conditions which would cause a firm to cease trading. The profit-maximising level of output is 80 units determined by point (A) where MC=MR. Each of the 80 units of output can be sold for £3. However the cost of producing each unit of output is £7, hence total losses if the firm continues to produce output would be £320. If the firm were to shut down then it would incur costs equal to its total fixed costs which are £240(AFC=£3, output=80, therefore TFC= £240). It should therefore be obvious that in this case the firm would minimise its losses by ceasing to trade.

A close examination of Figures 8 (b) and 8 (c) illustrates that firms will continue to produce output in the short run as long as market price exceeds average variable cost. When price exceeds variable cost, revenue covers variable cost and makes a contribution towards fixed costs. If the firm were to cease trading it would make losses equal to its total fixed costs. Therefore the losses which the firm incurs by trading are less than total fixed costs and in the short run it is rationale to continue trading as long as price exceeds variable cost. Having established this general principle we can now state that the marginal cost curve will act as the individual firm's short-run supply curve but only that portion of it which is above the average variable cost curve, as illustrated in Figure 9.

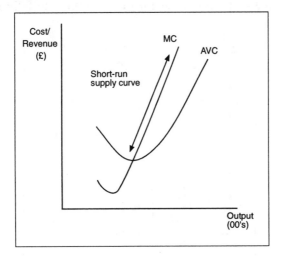

Figure 9: The short-run supply curve

Now see if you can apply what you've learnt in Activity 4.

ACTIVITY 4

Given the following information on three firms operating in a perfectly competitive industry, advise each firm whether in the short run it should:

(a) produce no output (shut down)

(b) maintain present output and sales

(c) increase output and sales

(d) decrease output and sales.

Firm	Price	Output	TC	TFC	TVC	AC	MC
1	5	1000	7000		5500		5
2	2	10000	9000				2
3	4	2000	7000		6000		5

(Note that in all cases marginal costs are increasing.)

In all cases P = MR, and hence if P does not equal MC then the firm is not producing the profit-maximising level of output. If P > MC then output should be expanded to reach the profit maximising level . If P < MC then output should be reduced. You may wish to consider Figure 10 in order to fully understand the above assertions.

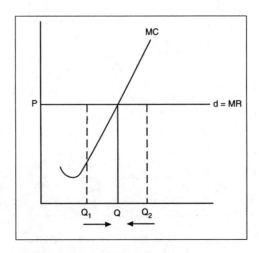

Figure 10: Profit maximisation and output

As Figure 10 shows, at output less than q, let us take q_1 as an example, p > MC. In such case the profit-maximising firm should expand output from q_1 to q. Conversely, when output is greater then q, let us take q_2 as an example P < MC. In this case output should be reduced from q_2 to q.

Once the profit-maximising level of output is reached then you should check if p > AC; if this is so the firm is making abnormal profits and everything is OK. If p < AC then you have to check if p > AVC (in some instances you may have to calculate AVC); if this is so the firm will continue to produce in the short run. If p < AVC then the firm should shut down.

Firm 1 is producing output at the profit-maximising point where MR (£5) = MC (£5). However, at this level of output AVC = £5.50 and therefore, since price is less than AVC, the firm should be advised to cease trading (the answer is (a)).

Firm 2 is producing at the point where MR (£2) = MC (£2). In this case the firm has average total costs of £0.9 (total cost/output) and a selling price of £2. Therefore, the firm is generating abnormal profit and should be advised to maintain its present output and sales (the answer is (b)).

Firm 3: in this case P < MC and therefore output should be reduced if the firm wishes to produce the profit-maximising level of output (the answer is (d)).

1.8 The market supply curve and perfect competition

Figure 9 illustrates the supply schedule for the individual firm in a perfectly competitive market. From this individual supply schedule it is now possible to show how the supply schedule for the whole industry is derived: by horizontally aggregating each producer's output at all prices. This is best illustrated by considering two producers (as in Figure 11), although you should appreciate that in actuality the described process would occur with many more producers.

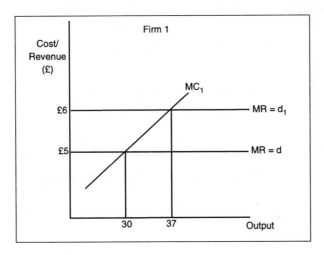

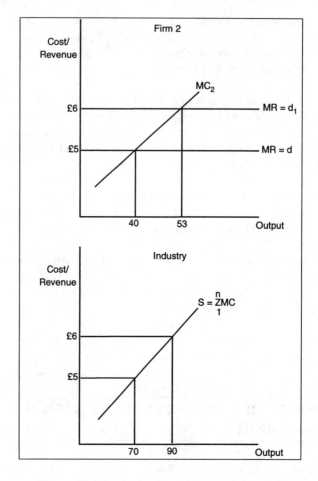

Figure 11: The derivation of the market supply

Figure 11 shows that at a price of £5 firm 1 will produce 30 units of output and firm 2 will produce 40 units of output. This results in an industry supply of 70 units of output at a price of £5. At a price of £6, firm 1 will produce 37 units of output and firm 2 will produce 53 units of output, resulting in an industry supply of 90 units of output. Therefore the upward-sloping industry supply curve is the summation of the individual firms' marginal cost curves.

1.9 Perfect competition and efficiency

There are two types of **efficiency** which need to be considered within the context of the perfectly competitive model. We will start by defining them.

1   **Technical efficiency:** this occurs when output is produced at minimum average cost.

2   **Allocative efficiency:** this occurs when the price at which output is sold is equal to marginal cost.

Figure 12 shows that the perfectly competitive firm will produce output up to the point where marginal revenue is equal to marginal cost is equal to £5. In this example, by producing 100 units of output the individual firm is being **allocatively efficient,** that is, from society's perspective the firm is devoting an optimal quantity of resources to the production of this good.

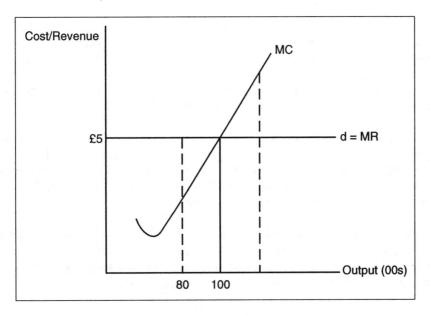

Figure 12: Allocative efficiency

In order to understand why this is so we must first consider three important assumptions which are being made.

1   The price that consumers are willing to pay for output is assumed to reflect the value or benefit that they get from consuming the particular good or service. That is to say price is acting as a proxy for utility. (You may wish to return to Unit 2 and revise the concept of **utility**.)

2   Marginal cost reflects the cost of producing an extra unit of output.

3   There are no **externalities** in production or consumption. Therefore private costs of production reflect the total cost to society of producing a good or service, and price reflects all benefits in consumption.

If these assumptions are valid, then, as Figure 12 suggests the firm should produce 100 units of output. If the firm produces less then 100 units, say 80 units, then the price received from selling the 80th unit of output exceeds the marginal cost of producing that unit. This means that the last individual buyer is getting more benefit from consuming the 80th unit of production than it is costing society to produce that unit of output. At this point you should remember that society's benefit from consuming a good or services is assumed to be indicated (measured) by the price which the person consuming it is willing to pay for that unit of output.

Where the marginal benefit to society from the consumption of a good is greater than the marginal cost to society of producing that good then another unit of output should be produced. In the above example this would be the 81st unit of output. As Figure 12 suggests, output, on the basis of the criterion developed above, should be increased until the 100th unit of output is produced.

What would happen if we were to produce the 101st unit of output? The MC of producing that unit of output would exceed the price at which the extra unit could be sold. Therefore, the benefit to society of that unit of output (the 101st) being consumed would be less then the cost of producing it. Therefore, that unit of output should not be produced and the resources which would have been employed producing it should be released and used elsewhere.

Hence producing 100 units of output is allocatively efficient, in the sense that it maximises society's welfare from the consumption of a good or service. If we were to allocate any more resources to the production of the good or service society's welfare must be reduced because we would be producing units of output which cost more to produce than their value when consumed.

If we now consider long-run equilibrium for the firm operating in a perfectly competitive industry (see Figure 6 (b)) we can see that simultaneously the firm achieves allocative and technical efficiency. That is to say, output is produced at minimum average cost and price is equal to marginal cost.

1.10 Reconsidering long-run equilibrium

The analysis thus far has resulted in a long-run equilibrium which ensures that price equals marginal cost and output is produced at minimum short-run average cost. This equilibrium will be stable only as long as no firm can alter their scale of production and produce at lower average cost. In order to understand this point, it is necessary to return to the analysis of short- and long-run average total cost.

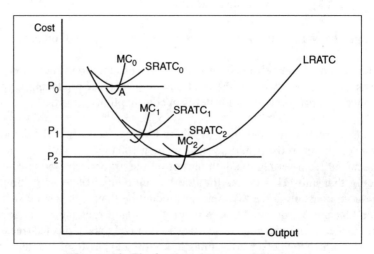

Figure 13: The long-run average cost curve

Consider Figure 13: if firms initially operate at a scale which is implied by ($SRATC_o$) in response to a market price (p_0), short-run equilibrium will occur at point (A) where(P_0)=MC=SRATC. However, as Figure 13 illustrates, by increasing their scale of production individual firms can operate at lower SRATC ($SRATC_1$ and $SRATC_2$), in doing so they will generate short run abnormal profits until other firms in the industry react and change their scale of production.

Therefore, long-run equilibrium in the market will only be attained when price (P_2)=LRATC=SRATC2=MC_2, and for it to exist in a perfectly competitive market output must be produced at minimum long-run average cost. Firms will only generate normal profits and therefore there will be no incentive for firms to enter the industry and those firms who are already engaged in production cannot earn short-run abnormal profits by varying the scale of production.

Note: in many textbooks SRATC will appear as SRAC (short-run average costs). In general, when a text refers to average cost the author will be referring to average *total* cost.

REVIEW ACTIVITY 1

1   Why do perfectly competitive firms engage in business activity?

2   Define: (a) normal profit; (b) abnormal profit.

3   Why will abnormal profits not exist in the long run in perfectly competitive industries?

4   Why do we need to assume that there are many buyers and sellers for a perfectly competitive market to exist.

5   Draw a diagram which illustrates a short-term equilibrium for an individual firm in a perfectly competitive market in which abnormal profits are being earned.

6   Draw a diagram which illustrates the position of the firm in question 5 in the long run.

Summary

In this section we described the assumptions which underpin the model of perfect competition. We explained how the assumptions of the perfectly competitive model ensure that the individual firm is a price taker. We went on to define normal and abnormal profit and to explain why abnormal profits will not exist in the long run in perfectly competitive markets. We also discussed the conditions under which a firm will stop trading. Finally, we introduced the concepts of technical and allocative efficiency with respect to the model of perfect competition.

SECTION TWO

Monopoly

Introduction

In this section we will deal with the concept of **monopoly**, which exists at the opposite end of the competitive spectrum to perfect competition. We will consider output and price under a monopoly, the profit a monopolist makes and the sources of monopoly power. Finally, we will evaluate monopoly and perfect competition and consider monopoly and price discrimination.

A monopoly exists when the output of an industry is produced by one firm. Alternative definitions of monopoly draw attention to consumers being faced with a single seller. This definition introduces the possibility of a monopoly situation existing with more than one producer, where producers form a selling cartel in order to gain monopoly power over the market. This latter definition of monopoly will be examined at a later point in this unit. In the first instance the analysis will assume that monopoly is consistent with a single producer.

2.1 Monopoly and revenue curves

The **monopolisation of output** means that, unlike the perfectly competitive firm, the monopolist can influence market price, the monopolist is not a price taker. As the only producer of output the demand curve which the individual monopolist faces is the industry demand curve. The industry demand curve is assumed to be normal, that is, downward sloping. When the demand curve is downward sloping marginal revenue will be less than price (average revenue), not equal to price as was the case with perfect competition. This point is illustrated by Table 2 and the associated Figure 14.

Note that when constructing the marginal revenue curve in Figure 14 values are plotted at the mid-point of class intervals. That is, as output increases from 1 to 2 units, (£7) the value of marginal revenue, is plotted against 1.5 units.

PRICE(£)	OUTPUT	TOTAL REVENUE (£)	MARGINAL REVENUE (£)
10	0	0	
			9
9	1	9	
			7
8	2	16	
			5
7	3	21	
			3
6	4	24	
			1
5	5	25	
			−1
4	6	24	
			−3
3	7	21	
			−5
2	8	16	
			−7
1	9	9	
			−9
0	10	0	

Table 2

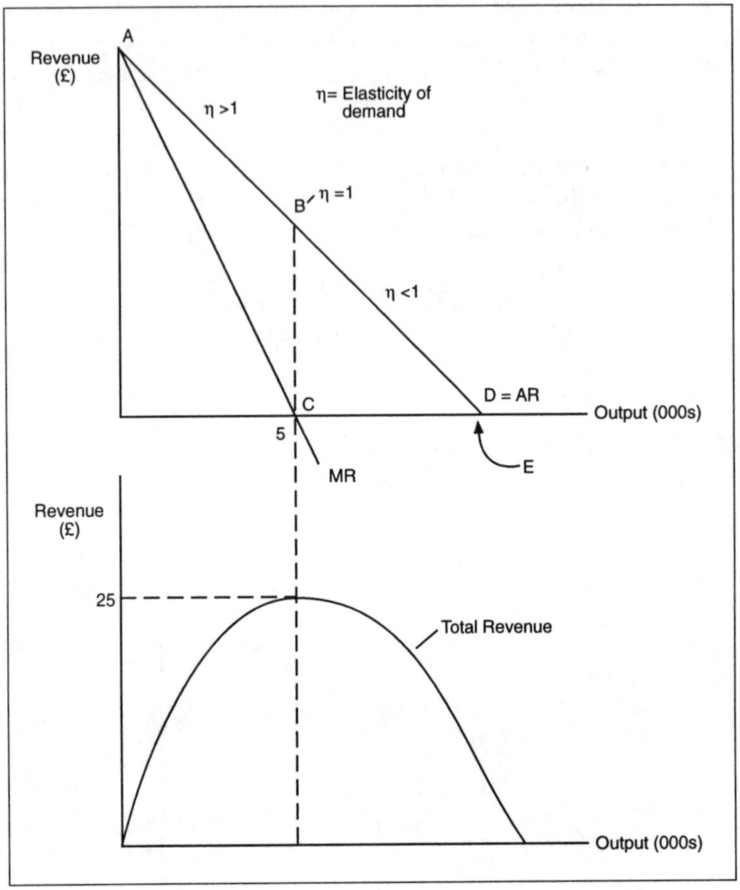

Figure 14: Elasticity of demand and revenue maximisation

You should note that the marginal revenue curve cuts the quantity axis at a distance which is half way between the origin and the point at which the demand curve cuts the quantity axis. You may wish to convince yourself of this fact by drawing the above marginal revenue and demand curves on a piece of graph paper. That is, distance OE = 2(distance OC). Note that, in order to draw the diagram correctly, you will have to plot marginal revenue values at the middle of the class interval as explained above.

Figure 14 can also be used to examine the relationship between marginal revenue, total revenue and values of elasticity of demand. In Unit 2 it was established that the value of elasticity of demand would vary along the length of a normal demand curve. A relationship between price changes, values of elasticity of demand and changes in total revenue was also established in unit 2. Namely:

1   If demand is elastic and price is reduced, then total revenue will increase.

2   If demand is inelastic and price is reduced, then total revenue will fall.

3   If the value of elasticity of demand is equal to one, any change in price will cause total revenue to remain constant.

Figure 14 shows that over the range AB, the demand curve is associated with positive values of marginal revenue range AC. Therefore reduction in price over the range (AB) of the demand curve is associated with increases in total revenue and accordingly demand elasticity is greater than 1. At the point where the marginal revenue curve cuts the quantity axis, a change in price results in no change in total revenue, marginal revenue is zero, therefore at point B on the demand curve elasticity is equal to 1. Over the range of the demand curve BE, reductions in price result in negative marginal revenue and therefore declining total revenue. Hence, as reductions in price are associated with falling total revenue, the value of elasticity of demand must be less than 1.

Having reviewed Section 2.1 you should now attempt Activity 5.

ACTIVITY 5

If a demand curve is described by the following equation $p = 100-2q$ derive an equation for the marginal revenue curve and draw a diagram of the demand and marginal revenue curves.

The analysis above has stated that the marginal revenue curve cuts the quantity axis at the mid-point between the origin and the point where the demand curve intersects the quantity axis. This is effectively the same as saying that the marginal revenue curve has a gradient which is twice that of the demand curve hence $MR = 100-4q$ (see Figure 15).

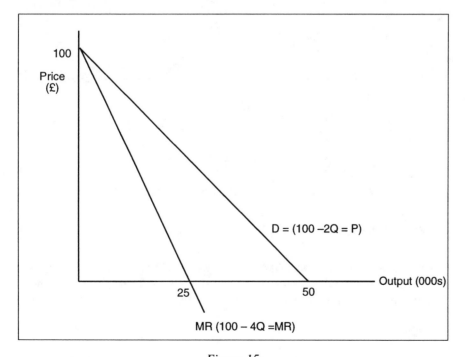

Figure 15:

2.2 Output and price under monopoly

As with the model of perfect competition, we assume that the monopolist is motivated by the desire to maximise profits. Therefore the monopolist will produce output up to the point where MC=MR. (At this point you may wish to revise the MC=MR condition for profit maximisation, if so please return to Figure 2 above.)

Figure 16 illustrates the basis of the profit-maximising monopolist's price and output decision. A standard marginal cost curve is superimposed on the marginal revenue and demand curves shown in Figure 14. The marginal cost and marginal revenue curves intersect at point A resulting in a profit-maximising output OB. The price at which this output is sold is then determined by point F on the demand curve, which results in a profit-maximising price of P*.

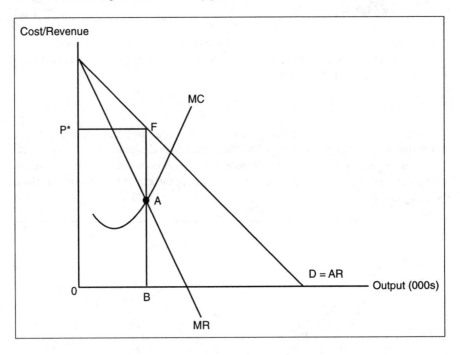

Figure 16: Monopoly and profit maximisation

You should review sections 2.1 and 2.2 and activity 5 before attempting activity 6

ACTIVITY 6

A profit-maximising theatre has a capacity of 3,000 and all seats are of an equal quality and therefore carry the same admission charge. The demand curve for each performance at the theatre is estimated by the equation:

$$p = 25 - 0.5q$$

where p is the price of a ticket in pounds and q is the quantity of tickets demanded in hundreds.

All costs associated with putting on a performance are fixed.

1 What ticket price would you recommend to the theatre management?

2 In order to pay for improvements to the theatre an Arts Council levy of £1 is to be charged on each customer. How will the levy impact on theatre attendances and ticket prices?

Hint 1: the theatre aims to maximise profits and therefore will always wish to charge a price which is consistent with MC=MR.

Hint 2: what is the value of MC, if all costs are fixed?

Hint 3: by equating MC and MR you will find the profit-maximising quantity of ticket sales.

Hint 4: having found the profit-maximising quantity of ticket sales you need to use the demand equation to find out what price to charge.

1   If all costs are fixed then MC = 0. From the demand curve equation we know that MR = 25 – q. Profits will be maximised when MR = MC; therefore profits will be maximised when:

$$0 = 25 - q$$

$$q = 25 \ (2{,}500 \text{ seats}).$$

From the demand curve, we know that the profit-maximising price will be p = 25 –0.5(25), that is P = £12.50.

2   The imposition of a levy effectively generates an MC of £1; therefore profits will now be maximised when:

$$1 = 25 - q$$

$$q = 24 \ (2{,}400 \text{ seats}).$$

From the demand curve we know that the profit-maximising price will be p = 25 –0.5(24), that is P = £13.

2.3 How much profit does the monopolist make?

Having determined the profit-maximising price and output strategy we must now determine how much profit is being made. To do this, an average cost curve must be introduced. Figure 17 is constructed by superimposing an average cost curve (AC) on Figure 16, in doing so care must be taken to maintain the geometric relationship between the average and marginal cost curves. The average cost curve will slope downwards until it is cut from below by the marginal cost curve at which point average costs of production will start to increase. (If you are in doubt see Figure 10 in Unit 3.)

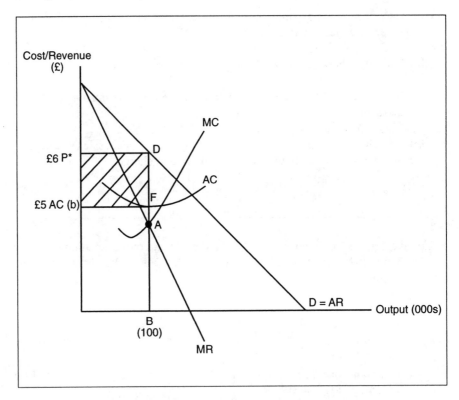

Figure 17: Monopoly and abnormal profits

Note that the term 'monopoly profit' and 'abnormal profit' can and are used interchangeably.

In Figure 17 the average cost curve is needed to inform us of the cost of producing (on average) each unit of output OB. This is determined at point F on the average cost curve, resulting in an average cost of production equal to AC(B). It may be useful at this point to introduce some illustrative values for output, price and average cost into the above example. In Figure 17 let us assume that the profit-maximising price is £6 and output 100. We will assume that average cost of production is £5 when output is 100. Hence:

Total revenue from sales   = £600 (100 × £6)

Total cost of production   = £500 (100 × £5)

Monopoly/abnormal profit   = £100

Note that the area of the hatched rectangle AC(B),P*,D,F illustrates the extent of monopoly profits.

Unlike the perfectly competitive firm discussed in the first section of this unit, a distinguishing characteristic of monopoly is the ability to sustain abnormal profits in the long run. In order to be able to do this the monopolist must be able to prevent new firms entering the industry and effectively competing the monopolist's abnormal profits away. You should now attempt Activity 7.

ACTIVITY 7

A monopolist who is currently maximising profits faces a special profits tax for its industry equal to 35% of profits. What will happen to price and output:

1   price will rise, output will remain the same

2   price will rise, output will fall

3   price will be unchanged, output will be unchanged

4   price will be unchanged, output will fall?

All that the tax will do is reduce after tax profits by 35%; therefore the price and output strategy that maximises profits before tax will maximise profits after tax. Hence the answer is 1.

2.4 Sources of monopoly power

LEGAL BARRIERS TO ENTRY
It may be the case that the monopolist is protected from competition by the existence of legal barriers to entry. These include **public franchises, patents** and **government licences**. A public franchise is a right granted by government which provides for a specific firm to produce a particular good or service and prevents all other firms from doing so. An example of this type of monopoly in the UK would be the Post Office, which, at the time of writing, still had a monopoly of first and second class mail. The extent of public franchise monopoly has been reduced in the

UK by the government privatisation policy, and where it still exists the public franchise monopoly is often subject to periodic competitive tendering. An example of this type of monopoly would be the monopoly position enjoyed by refuse collectors, who, in a large number of local authorities, are subject to regular competitive tendering.

Patents

A **patent** gives an individual or a firm the exclusive rights to the commercial exploitation of an idea. In economies with developed economic and legal systems, it is the most common way in which intellectual property rights are protected.

It is often argued that patents are necessary in order to provide an incentive for individuals and firms to engage in research and development which is both costly and risky in the sense that research may not result in commercially exploitable outcome(s). If a new idea can easily be copied, new firms may enter an industry so swiftly that whoever developed the new idea is insufficiently compensated for the risks and cost of innovation. The existence of a patent creates a period of time, typically 20 years in the UK, during which the original innovators can commercially exploit their idea. This may take the form of selling patent rights. In some cases the 20 year period can be extended, most notably in the pharmaceutical industry.

ECONOMIES OF SCALE

Before proceeding you may wish to review the concept of economies of scale by reading Unit 3 Section 5.2.

The cost conditions which exist in some industries may mean the minimum average costs are only obtained through large-scale production. It may be the case that the scale of production at which a firm must operate if it is to be competitive necessitates such vast levels of initial investment as to deter new entry. The extent to which this argument is convincing must be questioned due to the existence of transnational/multinational companies who have access to large sums of investment capital if the expected returns on capital are sufficiently enticing.

It may, however, be the case that an established monopoly may have lower costs than a potential entrant. This may be due to the fact that an established monopoly has developed production and marketing skills, they may also have established efficient component supply chains. So the incumbent monopolist may be able to repel any new entrant into the industry by engaging in a price war and practising **limit pricing**. In some instances the threat of a price war may be sufficient to deter new entry into the industry. The practice of limit pricing is illustrated in Figure 18.

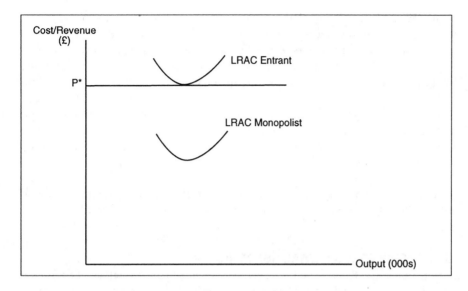

Figure 18: Limit pricing

In Figure 18, so long as the monopolist does not charge a price of P * or greater, the potential entrant cannot enter the market profitably. Note that the difference in average costs is due to lack of experience on the part of the potential entrant to the industry, rather than an inability of the entrant to produce at a comparable scale to the incumbent.

In extreme cases economies of scale may be so great that an industry may only be in equilibrium when there is one producer; such a situation is defined as **natural monopoly**.

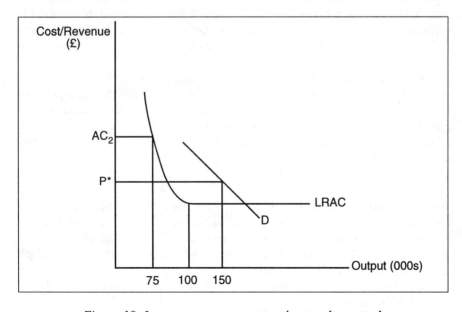

Figure 19: Long-run average cost and natural monopoly

Figure 19 can be used to explain the theory of natural monopoly the figure shows an L-shaped long-run average cost curve LRAC and a demand curve D. If we assume that the current monopoly supplier of the industry is supplying total market demand of 150,000 units at a price p*. If a firm were to enter this industry, attracted by the abnormal profits being earned by the incumbent, and both the new entrant and the incumbent took an equal share of market demand, that is they both produced 75,000 units, at a price of P* and under current cost conditions both firms would make losses. As Figure 19 shows if there were two producers in the industry they would incur average costs of AC_2 which exceed market price and hence they would make losses.

Note, therefore, that there is no price, given current demand conditions, which would allow both firms to cover their costs and therefore a natural monopoly exists.

OWNERSHIP OF A NATURAL RESOURCE

A monopolist may be protected from competition due to the ownership of a resource needed to enter the industry. The classic example is the Aluminium Company of America (Alcoa), which for a time controlled almost all sources of bauxite in the USA.

2.5 An evaluation of monopoly and perfect competition

In order to make a comparison of monopoly and perfect competition we will consider the price and output decision of a perfectly competitive industry which is operating with **constant costs**. (This is an assumption which I am going to make in order to simplify the following discussion.) I will then assume that this industry is taken over by a single producer operating under the same cost conditions and analyse the price and output decisions of the monopolist.

The assumption of constant cost production is an important one and means that we assume that a firm produces with constant marginal cost and therefore constant average cost of production. That is if marginal cost is constant at £5, then the 100th unit of output adds £5 to total costs and total costs increase from £495 to £500. You should now convince yourself that the average cost of producing 99 and 100 units of output is £5. (Average cost of producing 99 units = 495/99, average cost of producing 100 units = 500/100.)

We now consider firms operating in a perfectly competitive market under conditions of constant costs. All individual firms in the industry will have a marginal/average cost curve as shown in Figure 20(a). The horizontal aggregation of individual firms' marginal cost curves results in the industry supply curve which is illustrated in Figure 20(b). At this point you may wish to return to Figure 11, which illustrates the derivation of the industry supply curve in a perfectly competitive industry.

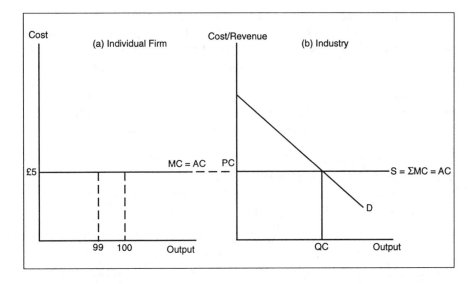

Figure 20: Perfect competition and long-run equilibrium

If the industry demand curve is now imposed on the industry supply curve we arrive at Figure 20(b), which suggests that the perfectly competitive industry will produce an output QC which will be sold at a price PC. If this industry is then (somewhat miraculously!) taken over by a monopolist the resulting outcome is illustrated in Figure 21(a).

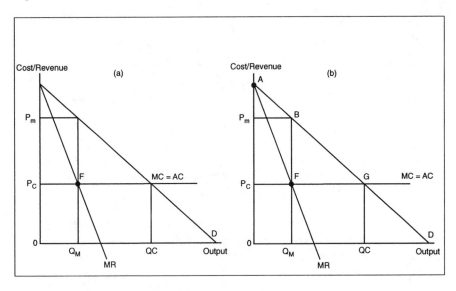

Figure 21: Monopoly and long-run equilibrium

The supply curve of the perfectly competitive firm is now the monopolist's average and marginal cost curves. The monopolist faces the same industry demand curve which has a corresponding marginal revenue curve MR. The profit-maximising level of output is therefore at point F, where MC = MR. This results in an output of Q_m which is sold at price P_m. It can therefore be seen that the monopolisation of an industry will result in less output being produced at a higher price than would be the case if the same industry were operating under perfectly competitive conditions.

In addition to the unfavourable price and output strategy of monopoly there are also welfare implications of monopoly, which are analysed in Figure 21(b). The welfare cost of monopoly can be evaluated by employing the concept of **consumer surplus**.

CONSUMER SURPLUS

If we reconsider our basic supply and demand analysis covered in Unit 2, Figure 22(a) shows that equilibrium is attained when demand equals supply at point A, resulting in an equilibrium price P* and an equilibrium quantity Q*.

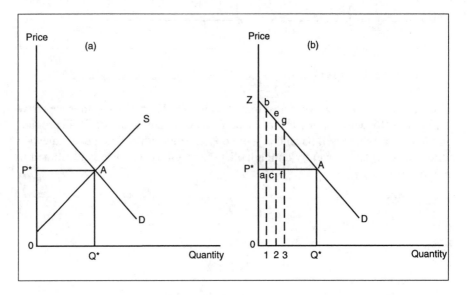

Figure 22: Consumer surplus

Figure 22(a) shows that consumers pay a price OP* for each unit of output OQ* which they consume. This results in total expenditure equal to (OP*) × (OQ*), which is represented by the area OP*AQ*.

Figure 22(b) examines the equilibrium combination of price and quantity in greater detail. Consider the first unit of output purchased. Consumers actually pay a price op* for that unit of output, but the demand curve suggests that they would be willing to pay OP* + ab.

For the second unit of output consumers would be willing to pay

OP* + ce.

For the third unit of output consumers would be willing to pay

OP* + fg.

The total amount which consumers would be willing to pay for output oq*, over and above that which they actually have to pay (op*Aq*), is represented by the triangle P*ZA. It is this area which represents consumer surplus. Consumer surplus can therefore be defined as:

'the difference between consumers' willingness to pay, for a given level of output, and what they actually have to pay'.

Operating under perfectly competitive conditions the industry depicted in Figure 21(b) will generate consumer surplus represented by the area A,G,P_c. The monopolisation of the industry reduces consumer surplus to A,B,P_m with a consequential loss of consumer surplus equal to P_m,B,G,P_c.

It is now important to identify where the 'lost consumer surplus' has gone. A portion of the 'lost consumer surplus' is transferred to the monopolist in the form of abnormal profits, in Figure 21 this is represented by the area P_m,B,F,P_c . This transfer of wealth from consumers, in the form of reduced consumer surplus, to the monopolist, in the form of abnormal monopoly profits, has implications for income distribution due to the fact that wealth is being diverted from a large group of consumers to a typically much smaller number of shareholders in the monopoly firm. In mitigation of the unfavourable distributional effects of monopoly it is often argued that shareholders in such companies are frequently large institutional investors such as pension funds and therefore the monopoly profits are benefiting a much more diverse body of individuals than may have been originally suggested.

The second portion of 'lost consumer surplus' to be considered is area B,F,G. This portion of 'lost consumer surplus' is known as the **deadweight loss of monopoly**. This is consumer surplus which is lost due to the fact that the monopolisation of the industry restricts output to q_m and increases price to p_m. Therefore consumers are not able to accumulate consumer surplus on units of output $(q_c - q_m)$because these units of output are not produced and sold.

Monopoly may impose further cost on society due to a lack of incentives for a monopolist to minimise costs of production. A perfectly competitive firm must continually strive to produce at minimum cost and innovate, where possible, in order to reduce costs, if it is to remain competitive. The monopolist, protected from competition by barriers to entry, can still earn large profits even if it is not using the most efficient techniques of production. Liebenstein (1966) used the term **x-inefficient** to describe a situation where monopolists fail to minimise average cost due to a lack of competitive pressure to do so. X-inefficiency may manifest itself in overstaffing, spending on prestigious head office buildings, as well as less effort being devoted to keeping technologically up-to-date and developing new markets. For example, x-inefficiency could be argued to have been present in the UK motor car industry given the increase in productivity which has been achieved at Ford, Rover and Vauxhall since Japanese car manufacturers located in the UK.

Now think what would happen if an inefficient monopolist were to take over a perfectly competitive industry. You might expect prices to go up, production to fall, loss of consumer surplus on 'lost' production and so on. Try Activity 8.

ACTIVITY 8

Amend Figure 21(b) to illustrate the consequence of the monopolisation of a perfectly competitive industry by an X-inefficient monopolist (assume production at constant cost under both competitive and monopoly conditions).

Clearly indicate on your diagram:

1 deadweight loss of monopoly

2 transfer of consumer surplus from consumers to the monopolist

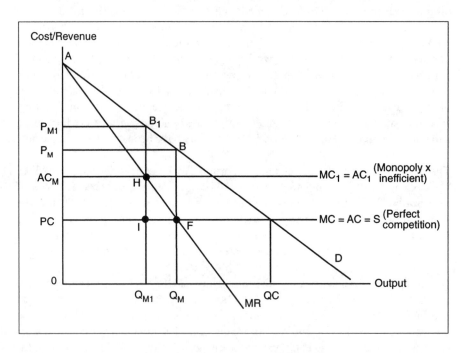

Figure 23: Monopoly and x-efficiency

If the monopolist were as efficient as the perfectly competitive firms monopolisation of the industry would result in output Q_M and price P_M as in Figure 21(b). The x-inefficient monopolist, however, will have higher marginal and average costs (MC_1 AC_1) than the perfectly competitive firm and this will result in output being further restricted to qm as shown in Figure 23 and price further inflated to P_{M1}. The consequences for consumer welfare of an x-inefficient monopolist is to reduce consumer surplus from A,B,P_M to A,B,P_{M1}. (You may wish to discuss with your tutors the significance of area AC_M,H,I,P_c.) Which measures the extra resource cost of producing output OQ_{M1} under monopoly conditions rather than conditions of perfect competition.

ARE THERE ANY POSITIVE ASPECTS OF MONOPOLY?

There are some advantages of monopoly which we must now consider. Firstly, a monopoly may be able to attain substantial economies of scale due to the operation of larger plant, an ability to centralise administration and an ability to avoid wasteful duplication of plant. The latter argument is/was often used to support the monopoly supply of utilities such as gas, water and electricity. If economies of scale are substantial monopoly provision of a good or service can lead to a more favourable price and output combination than would exist under competitive conditions. This situation is illustrated in Figure 24.

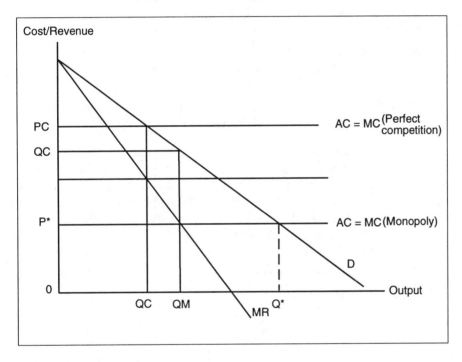

Figure 24: Monopoly and economies of scale

In the Figure 24 the constant cost assumption is maintained, and economies of scale result in the cost of monopoly production being substantially less than competitive production. Figure 24 illustrates that if economies of scale are sufficiently large, monopoly production can result in increased output at lower prices compared to competitive production. The situation would obviously be further improved if the monopolist could be forced to price as a competitive firm would. Such an equilibrium would result in output OQ* and price P*.

A second advantage of monopoly is that abnormal profits provide a source of funds which can be used to finance research and development expenditure. The monopolist also has an incentive to innovate and reduce costs since any increased profitability which is generated will not be dispersed amongst competing producers. We have already noted that innovators must be allowed to reap the benefits of their work in our discussion of patents above. Note that the impact of a patent is to effectively create monopoly rights to the commercial exploitation of an idea.

2.6 Monopoly and price discrimination

Price discrimination occurs when a seller charges different prices for its product which do not reflect any differences in costs of production. The motivation for such behaviour is to increase the marginal revenue obtained from the sale of extra units of output. In order for price discrimination to be practised by a monopolist, a number of conditions must hold.

● Firstly, **'arbitrage'** must not be possible, that is, consumers must not be able to purchase output in one market where prices are low and re-sell in markets where prices are higher.

● Secondly, demand elasticities must be different in each market. The monopolist will sell at a higher price in the market where demand is less elastic.

● Lastly, the seller must be able to exercise influence over market price and the seller must be able to distinguish between buyers.

If the monopolist can sell each unit of output separately, and he knows the maximum price each buyer would be willing to pay, then the monopolist is able to practice **'first degree price discrimination'**. Under these conditions the monopolists demand curve is now the monopolists marginal revenue curve, since in order to sell more output the monopolist only has to reduce the price of the next unit of output sold. First degree price discrimination means that the monopolist doesn't have to reduce the price of all units of output to increase sales.

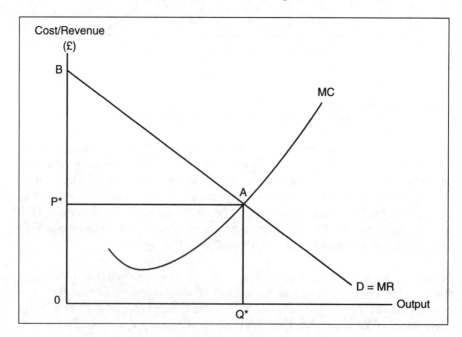

Figure 25: First degree price discrimination

As Figure 25 shows, profit-maximising output will now be oq*. However, rather than appropriating revenue equal to (0,p*,A,q*), the monopolist will be able to appropriate that which was previously consumer surplus, that is (p*,B,A). Hence, where a monopolist can practice first degree price discrimination total revenue will be equal to (0,B,A,q*). Note that in this extreme case, output is the same as it would be under perfect competition. There is a redistributive effect in that where first degree price discrimination is possible consumer surplus is appropriated by the monopolist. But there is no deadweight loss associated with the monopolisation of the industry.

Second degree price discrimination occurs when a firm charges customers different prices for the first tranche of output consumed and a different price for a subsequent tranche and so on. Such price discrimination is commonly practised in the tariffs charged by mobile phone network operators. The practice of accumulating air miles also effectively means that second degree price discrimination is being practised by most, if not all, major airlines.

Third degree price discrimination is where consumers are grouped into two or more independent markets and separate prices are charged in each market. An example of third degree price discrimination is the discriminatory pricing policy of the public utilities (gas, water and electricity) with respect to domestic and industrial users.

Figure 26 illustrates how a profit-maximising firm distributes total output between two separate markets.

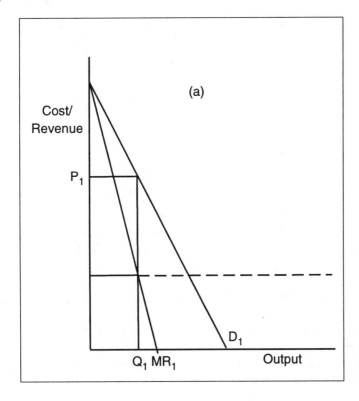

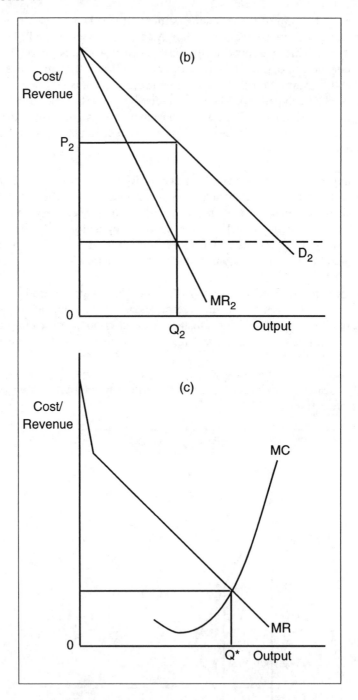

Figure 26: Price discrimination-the allocation of output between producers

Assume that Figure 26 (a) shows the demand schedule for domestic consumers for gas and (b) the demand schedule for industrial consumers of gas. Note that the elasticity of demand is different in each of the two separate markets. Figure 26 (c) shows the MR curve for the industry as a whole. This MR curve is constructed by horizontally aggregating the MR curves in each of the individual markets, that is $MR = MR_1 + MR_2$. In (c) the point at which the $MR = MC$ determines the profit-maximising output for the firm as a whole.

This output then has to be distributed between the two separate markets. This is done by equating the profit-maximising level of MC with MR_1 and MR_2 in each of the individual markets. This results in output q_1 and price p_1 in the market for domestic gas and a price p_2 and output q_2 in the market for industrial gas. Note that the total market output of gas $q^* = q_1 + q_2$.

REVIEW ACTIVITY 2

In the monopoly diagram below:

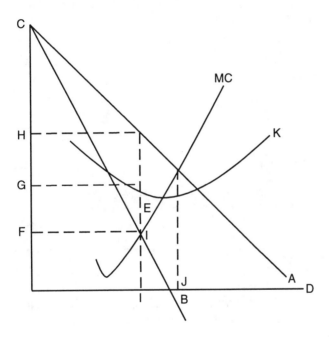

Label axis C and D.

Label curves A, B and K.

What is the profit-maximising level of output?

What is the allocatively efficient level of output?

At what price will output be sold if profits are to be maximised?

Draw a diagram to illustrate the concept of consumer surplus?

Summary

In this section we dealt with the concept of monopoly and its positive and negative aspects. We explained the difference between the firm's marginal revenue curve in the monopoly model compared to the model of perfect competition. We considered the basis of a profit-maximising monopolist's output and price decisions and exactly how much profit is made.

We went on to consider the sources of monopoly power and the protection from competition afforded by legal barriers to entry to the market, including franchises, patents and government licences. We compared monopoly and perfect competition and looked at the welfare implications of monopoly through the concept of consumer surplus. We also defined and explained the term 'x-inefficiency' as applied to a monopolist's failure to minimise average costs. Finally, we considered monopoly and price discrimination and distinguished between first, second and third degree price discrimination.

SECTION THREE

Imperfect Competition

Introduction

We have studied perfect competition and monopoly. In this section we turn to a form of market competition which lies between these two extremes. Such a market structure is referred to as **'oligopoly'** from the Greek, meaning 'few sellers'. We will define the charcteristics of an oligopolistic market structure. We will also discuss how oligopolists can increase profitability by colluding over prices, as well as the conditions under which collusion will break down.

An oligopoly exists when total output in an industry is dominated by a small number of firms, typically between three and seven firms. The extent to which an industry is an oligopoly or otherwise can be assessed by computing a **concentration ratio** for the industry. It is possible to calculate concentration ratios for any number of firms; however, if we were to compute the three-firm concentration ratio for a particular industry we would simply add together the market share of the three largest firms in the industry. The five-firm concentration ratio would be the summation of the market shares of the five largest firms in the industry.

In some oligopolistic industries firms may produce almost identical products (petrol, chemicals), whereas in other industries firms will produce differentiated products (cars, cigarettes). In the latter case, much of the competition between oligopolists will tend to be focused on promotion of brands of the same product.

The key characteristic of oligopolistic industries is the interdependence of firms, that is, any change in one firm's pricing policy or promotional activities will provoke a reaction from competitors. Therefore, an analysis of oligopoly cannot be based on the *ceteris paribus* assumption because if an oligopolist changes its pricing or promotional policies, other firms will react, 'other thing will not remain equal'.

3.1 Oligopoly and collusion

Since price competition will not benefit oligopolists, there is a strong incentive for oligopolists to collude over prices, since a reduction in price by one oligopolist would provoke similar reactions by other firms in the industry. This would result in what is commonly referred to as a **'price war'**, where the only beneficiaries would be the consumers.

The following discussion will explain how oligopolists can increase their profitability if they collude over prices. In its most extreme form all producers in the industry would come together and form a selling **'cartel'**, therefore the consumers in the industry would effectively be faced with a monopoly situation. Figure 27 illustrates the monopoly profits which the selling cartel could generate: we are suggesting here that the selling cartel can behave as a monopolist would.

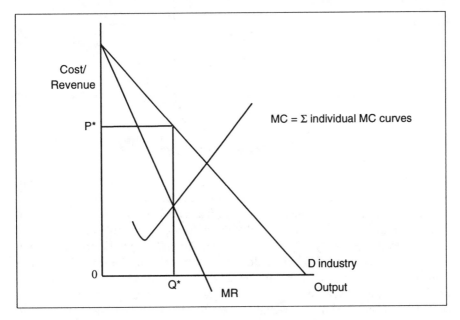

Figure 27: Selling cartels and monopoly pricing

The problems of operating an effective selling cartel begin when decisions have to be made about the manner in which output 0Q* is going to be distributed amongst the individual oligopolistic producers. One solution may be to allow the individual producers to compete using non-price competition for as much of output 0Q* as they can get. This, however, may result in producers spending, large amounts of the extra profits which the cartel has generated trying to capture as big a market share as possible. A second solution may be to distribute market share on the basis of historical market share, this is the most likely solution to be accepted in reality.

In the UK, cartels were prohibited by the 1956 Restrictive Trade Practices Act. This meant that firms could not formally enter into **'price fixing'** agreements. Therefore, firms would engage in 'tacit' collusion and agree to avoid price wars or competitive advertising campaigns. Where tacit collusion occurs pricing policies are often based on simple 'rules of thumb'. One such example is full cost pricing, whereby prices are set on the basis of adding a profit margin to long-run average costs of production, full-cost pricing is illustrated in Figure 28.

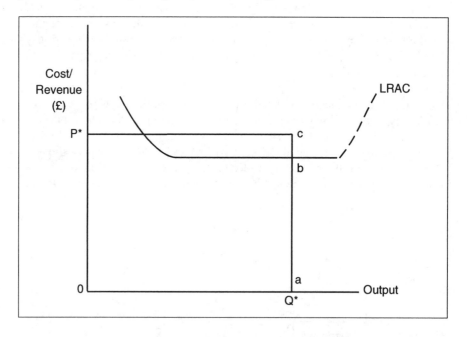

Figure 28: Full-cost pricing

In the above figure price p* is set by adding a profit margin (bc) to long-run average cost (ab) at a level of output which a firm would consider to be normal, q*. Normal in this context may be associated with a given level of capacity utilisation, that is, q* may be the output associated with producing at, say, 90% of capacity and it is this level of capacity utilisation which the firm regards to be normal. It may well be that the costs of all firms in the industry are not the same in such an instance. It may be the case that prices are set in accordance with a median cost producer, if this is the case efficient producers would enjoy a greater margin than (bc) and inefficient producers a smaller margin. Alternatively, price may be based on the costs of the dominant producer.

The ease with which firms can collude will increase the greater the number of the following conditions are met by the industry:

● The number of firms operating in the industry is small and all firms are well known to each other. This is often referred to as a **mature oligopoly**.

● Costs and methods of production are known and apparent to all firms in the industry. This is likely to be the case in mature oligopolies which employ standardised and non-changing production technologies.

● Firms produce similar products, that is, products which are not heavily differentiated.

● There is a dominant firm. If the dominant firm is the least-cost producer this can impose a discipline on price cartels, since if individual producers produce more than their allotted output the dominant firm can threaten to price at, or very near to, cost and therefore undercut all other producers.

● If industry demand is unstable this will place pressure on any collusive agreement. For example, if there are large reductions in demand, some individual producers may think that they can maintain their current levels of output by cutting prices and taking market share off competitors.

3.2 The breakdown of collusion, 'to cheat or not to cheat'

In some oligopolies very few of the above conditions will be present and in such cases the probability of price competition is greater. However, even where collusion exists, as the last of the conditions listed above suggests, market demand conditions may provide an incentive for an individual oligopolist to cheat. Whether or not an individual firm cheats will depend upon how it believes its rival will react.

Game theory has been developed in order to allow us to examine what is the optimal strategy for a firm given alternative predictions about competitors' reactions to different pricing strategies. Table 3 illustrates the simplest game of strategy where we assume that there are only two firms, each producing identical products with identical costs. The table shows what level of profits both firms will make, given the pricing strategy of the other firm. Therefore consider Firm 1: acting independently it knows that if it leaves its price unchanged it could get profits of £1 million if Firm 2 adopts a similar strategy. However, if Firm 2 cuts its price to £5 then Firm 1 will only make profits of £250,000. However, if Firm 1 cut its price to £5 and Firm 2 maintained its price at £10 then Firm 1, would make profits of £600,000. However, if Firm 2 also cut its prices both firms would make £500,000.

	Firm 1	
	£10	£5
Firm 2 £10	£1m each	£1.2m (1) £0.25m (2)
Firm 2 £5	£ 0.25m (1) £1.2m (2)	£0.5m each

Table 3: Profits for firm 1 and firm 2 under different pricing strategies

In the above example, if Firm 1 is risk-averse (that is, doesn't like taking risks) they will choose the strategy which will maximise their minimum return. Hence, if Firm 1 were to maintain its price at £10 its minimum return would be £250,000, the return if Firm 2 cuts its price. If Firm 1 cut its prices to £5 then its minimum return would be £500,000, the return if Firm 2 cuts its price. Hence, a risk-averse firm, such as Firm 1, would cut its prices to £5 since this is the strategy which maximises the minimum return.

Alternatively, you could adopt a different strategy which took a more optimistic approach, by making the assumption that your competitor behaves in a way which is most favourable to you. Hence if Firm 1 maintained its prices at £10 then it would assume that Firm 2 would maintain its prices at £10 giving each firm a profit of £1 million. However, if Firm 1 cut its prices on the (optimistic) assumption that Firm 2 would not, then Firm 1 would receive profits of £1.2 million. Therefore, an optimistic strategy would result in the same pricing policy as a pessimistic approach: to cut prices to £5. Where this is the case, namely that a risk-averse and risk-taking strategy prescribe the same pricing policy, the prescribed strategy is known as the dominant strategy.

However, given that the dominant strategy for individual firms acting independently results in each firm making £500,000, the benefits of collusion are obvious and would result in both firms doubling their profits to £1 million.

If both firms were to collude and charge £10, both firms would obviously benefit, however, both firms would have a large incentive to cut prices and cheat, since this would give the cheating firm a profit of £1.2 million. This incentive to cheat would ultimately lead to the dominant strategy being attained.

REVIEW ACTIVITY 3

The following table relates to the market share of the seven firms who supply concrete to the USA construction market.

FIRM	MARKET SHARE (%)
1	15
2	23
3	16
4	9
5	28
6	2
7	7

1 From the above data calculate:

   (a) the three-firm concentration ratio

   (b) the five-firm concentration ratio.

2 What factors will influence the ease with which firms in an oligopolistic industry can collude?

3 What can oligopolistic industries do to stop individual firms from cheating in a situation where prices have been fixed by price collusion?

Summary

In this section we studied the market structure known as oligopoly and defined its characteristics. We also explained how oligopolists can increase profitability by colluding over prices and outlined the factors leading to it. Finally, we indicated the conditions under which collusion will break down.

SECTION FOUR

Privatisation

Introduction

In this section we will discuss privatisation and identify three different forms of it. We will outline the different objectives of privatisation and how UK policy has sought to pursue these objectives.

Since the election of the first Thatcher administration in 1979 privatisation has been one of the most widely debated and written about subjects in economics. There are three different forms of privatisation.

4.1 The three forms of privatisation

1   **Denationalisation**, which is the form of privatisation with which most people are familiar. In the UK this type of privatisation has involved the high profile sale of state-owned assets such as British Telecom, British Gas, the Electricity Boards and Jaguar Cars. This form of privatisation involves state assets being sold to the private sector and hence large amounts of revenue flow into the Exchequer (government coffers).

2   **Deregulation**, which involves legislation being passed to allow for greater competition in the provision of goods and services. For example, the 1980 Transport Act deregulated the long-haul bus industry in the UK (the provision of coach journeys in excess of 30 miles). This industry provides an excellent case study of the long-run impact and evolution of deregulation policies because of the time which has elapsed since deregulation. Although policies of deregulation are not discussed in detail here, a number of articles are included under **Further Reading** at the end of this unit if you wish to pursue an interest in this aspect of privatisation.

3   The third form of privatisation is **contracting out**, which involves competitive tendering by private sector organisations for the right to provide state-financed goods and services. The most obvious forms of this type of privatisation would include the contracting-out of local authority refuse collection services, school meal services and hospital cleaning/laundering services. Again, this area will not be studied in detail, although references have been included at the end of the unit for those who wish to pursue the issue further.

4.2 The objectives of privatisation

The rest of this section will concentrate on the argument surrounding denationalisation. In the first instance we will examine the objectives of privatisation. The following analysis is based on a series of objectives which were put forward in Kay and Thompson (1986):

- economic efficiency
- generation of revenue for the Treasury
- promotion of popular capitalism
- reduction in the power of the trade unions
- reduction in government interference in industry.

We will discuss each of these in turn.

ECONOMIC EFFICIENCY

As economists economic efficiency is the objective of privatisation which we should be most keen to see attained. As our analysis of perfectly competitive and monopoly market structures indicated, we can identify, in the first instance, two types of efficiency. Firstly, **productive (technical) efficiency**, which occurs when output is produced at long-run average cost. Secondly, **allocative efficiency**, which occurs when price is equal to marginal cost.

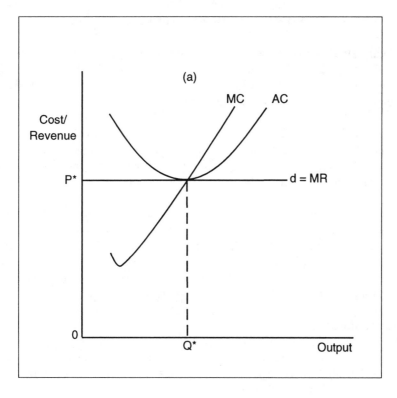

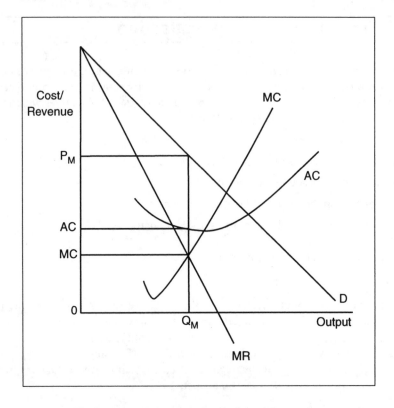

Figure 29: A comparison of perfect competition and monopoly

As Figure 29(a) shows, allocative and technical efficiency are simultaneously attained when there is long-run equilibrium in a perfectly competitive market. However, where a monopoly exists, as Figure 29(b) shows, price $P_M > MC$ and output is not produced at minimum average cost.

Policies of denationalisation are often justified on the grounds that they will allow for increased competition and, therefore, will deliver benefits in terms of productive and allocative efficiency which more closely represent those suggested by the model of perfect competition than the monopoly model.

So how does privatisation result in production at lower cost and prices which more closely reflect marginal cost? The answer given to this question is that privatisation will increase the competitive pressures felt by the managing directors of the newly privatised industries. But where does this competitive pressure come from? There are three main sources: product markets, capital markets and the market for corporate control. We shall deal with each in turn.

Product markets
If prior to privatisation the firm is a monopoly, and it is privatised into a competitive environment for product sales, then competition for sales will force the denationalised industry to cut prices in an effort to be competitive and hence will move prices closer to marginal cost.

However, in reality how many of the denationalised industries have been privatised into a competitive environment for product sales? In the case of the public utilities (gas, water, electricity and telecommunications) there was very little competition at the point of privatisation. If the government was really interested in promoting economic efficiency, policies of denationalisation would have been coupled with policies of deregulation at the point of privatisation. The fact that this did not occur may be due to what Kay and Thompson refer to as the 'paradox of privatisation', which notes that privatisation is a political, as well as an economic, process. Therefore, in order to get the managing directors of the privatised industries to countenance the process of privatisation it was necessary to forgo the economic benefits which would flow from increased liberalisation of industries at the point of privatisation. For example, why was Mercury not licensed to compete with BT for domestic telephone customers immediately after denationalisation in 1984? Why was British Airways allowed to keep monopoly rights over most of their most important European routes for a period of five years after privatisation?

The power of the managing directors in the political process of privatisation should not be underestimated since it is they who must ultimately sign the prospectus, without which the process of privatisation cannot proceed. This, therefore, gives the managing directors leverage over government ministers when deciding how, and on what basis, an industry will be privatised.

The benefits of increased liberalisation are apparent for everyone to see if you consider the marketing strategies which are currently being adopted in the telecommunications industry. Why are British Telecom so keen to provide us with cheap telephone calls to our loved ones? It is definitely *not* due to a philanthropic desire to improve our psychological well-being! BT has in fact cut the cost of telephone calls because of the increased competition it faces from Mercury, cable companies and the mobile phone network operators. Prices have also been forced down by the activity of regulators whose role is referred to below. (Further information on the work of the regulators can be obtained from the relevant Internet web site pages indicated under Further Reading at the end of the unit.)

Capital markets

The second source of competitive pressure for privatised firms will emanate from **capital markets**. That is, in order to attract investment funds, privatised industries will have to provide potential investors with a competitive rate of return on their investment. This will provide an incentive for privatised firms to be technically efficient since, by minimising average costs, profits will be increased and investors will be more willing to provide the firm with investment funds. However, if a firm is privatised as a monopoly there will be little incentive to minimise costs since competitive returns can be ensured by the generation of monopoly profits.

You should note that where the capital market discriminates efficiently between efficient and non-efficient producers, it will deprive the inefficient of investment capital which will ultimately, if no remedial action is taken, result in bankruptcy. This is due to the fact that firms who are successful in attracting investment funds will be able to invest in their products and processes of production, which will ultimately improve the firms' product market competitiveness and hence their profitability. Inefficient firms will not attract investment funds and ultimately their product and production techniques will become obsolete, resulting ultimately in bankruptcy.

THE MARKET FOR CORPORATE CONTROL

The third source of competitive pressure emanates from the **'market for corporate control'**. The value of a share on the stock market should reflect the expected future profitability of a firm. This is due to the fact that the ownership of a share creates a property right to a 'share' of the firm's profits. *(The 'efficient stock market hypothesis' suggests that a share price should reflect the present value of the future expected stream of a firm's profits. You may like to discuss this suggestion with your tutor, if possible, after you have studied the concept of present value in Unit 5.)* Therefore, if it is expected that the profits of a company will increase then the company's share price will increase, since investors will now be willing to pay more in order to get access to the higher profits.

A good example of this effect occurred in June 1995 when the regulator for the electricity industry announced the extent to which electricity prices were going to be regulated over the next 5 years. Price increases for the regional electricity companies were based on the RPI–x formula (discussed in detail in articles in the reader), which limits annual price increases to the retail price index *minus* the so-called **efficiency factor, x**. Obviously the bigger x is the smaller will be the annual increase in prices which the electricity companies are allowed to levy and hence the greater pressure there will be on their level of profitability. When the regulator, Professor Littlechild, announced a smaller efficiency factor X than the electricity companies and the stock exchange had forecast the price of electricity shares increased. This was due to the fact that expected future levels of profits had increased as a result of the regulator's announcement.

There are firms who monitor the performance of share prices with a view to acquiring other firms; such firms are sometimes referred to as **corporate raiders**. Corporate raiders operate relatively simple strategies to decide who they will acquire.

1   They monitor share prices in an attempt to identify shares which are underperforming, in other words currently trading at a price which is lower than their potential price, because of the inefficient manner in which the firm is currently being managed.

2   The corporate raider believes that if it takes the firm over, by purchasing the shares and then improving the management of the firm, it can improve profitability. The corporate raider can, therefore, make profit in two ways. Firstly, by taking the firm over at a low share price, enhancing efficiency, and then disposing of the company when share prices have increased, thereby making a capital gain on the difference in the price at which shares were purchased and disposed of.

Alternatively, the corporate raider can take profits in the form of dividends on shares. Note, however, that these dividends have been acquired cheaply since the corporate raider paid a price for the shares which reflected the old management's inefficiency rather than the profit potential of the share under new management.

Denationalisation allows a market for corporate control to exert its influence since the newly-privatised companies shares are openly traded on the stock exchange. Therefore, if managing directors do not perform efficiently with regard to the firm's profitability performance they may be subject to a takeover. This is not an inviting prospect for the current managing directors since in the event of a takeover they are almost certain to lose their job.

It is evident from the more recent privatisations that the government accepts the potential benefits of exposing privatised firms to the market for corporate control. The relatively recent water and electricity privatisations have generated regional companies and facilitated comparisons of managerial efficiency between them. This has directly exposed the managers concerned to the pressures of the market for corporate control. The issue of the market for corporate control is considered thoroughly in David Forrest's article (Resource Item 4.1) which appears in the Resource section at the end of this module. At the time of writing takeover activity has seen North West Water acquire MANWEB and a number of acquisitions have been referred to the Monopolies and Mergers Commission for consideration, for example, Wessex Water's proposed acquisition of South West Water. You should keep an eye on the business pages to keep up with the latest developments!

GENERATION OF REVENUE FOR THE TREASURY

Over the period 1979–94 the Treasury gained £55.2 billion from the sale of state assets. This has contributed significant sums of money to the Exchequer and has helped the Conservative party with its declared aim of reducing personal taxation. However, where the government has a declared aim of maximising the revenue from assets sales it has a conflict of interest with the first objective of privatisation which seeks to promote economic efficiency. This objective seeks to promote economic efficiency and dictates that you sell the nationalised industry into a competitive environment. However, if you wish to maximise the revenue from the sale of the privatised industry you would be better advised to sell it as a monopoly, which would generate more profits for shareholders and therefore command a higher share price at the point of privatisation.

PROMOTION OF POPULAR CAPITALISM

The first Thatcher administration (1979–83) could have been said to have almost stumbled across the policy of privatisation. You should note that while the Conservative Party manifesto of 1979 extolled the virtues of the private sector, the word privatisation did not appear. By 1983 this had changed and the Conservative Party, encouraged by the electoral popularity of the policy, were suggesting that we should become a nation of property owners (both in a real and financial sense). Individuals were encouraged to participate in a **'share-owning democracy'** and become **'active citizens'** in the new **'enterprise culture'**.

In 1982 Mr Nicholas Ridley, then Financial Secretary to the Treasury, stated:

'It must be right to press ahead with the transfer of ownership from state to private ownership of as many public sector businesses as possible.... The introduction of competition must be linked to a transfer of ownership to private citizens and away from the state. Real public ownership, that is ownership by the people, must be and is our ultimate goal.' (Treasury 1982)

The government will point to its objective of popular capitalism having been attained due to the fact that in 1994 share ownership in the UK had spread to 22% of the adult population compared to 7% in 1981(Griffiths and Wall, 1995). However, you should note the more detailed comments made in David Parker's article (Resource Item 4.2).

A further problem with the promotion of popular capitalism is the suggestion that the government may be able and willing to sell shares in privatised industries at a discount in order to promote popular capitalism. This suggestion is given a degree of support by some of the premiums which have been obtained by shareholders on the first day of trading. Again this issue is examined in greater detail in David Parker's article.

REDUCTION IN THE POWER OF THE TRADE UNIONS

The first Thatcher administration was elected with a mandate to redress the balance of industrial relations in the UK and, in the rhetoric of the time, to 'return to management the right to manage'. Privatisation was seen to contribute to this policy in so far as it exposed trade unions to the harsh realities of the private sector. No longer could trade unions make excessive wage claims without reference to the commercial implications of their actions. After privatisation the government would not be in a position to provide subsidies to underwrite excessive wage claims.

If unions made excessive wage claims they would result in a firm's costs of production and prices increasing. Ultimately this would result in reduced demand for output and therefore reduced demand for labour. Hence, if unions wanted to protect the employment prospects of their employees they had to accept wage claims which were in line with productivity growth.

REDUCTION IN GOVERNMENT INTERFERENCE IN INDUSTRY

It was argued that far too often the nationalised industries had been used to pursue governments macroeconomic policy objectives. Therefore, if inflation was deemed to be too high the prices of nationalised industries' output would be held down in order to dampen inflation. These nationalised industries would then be criticised for making losses! Alternatively, if the government wished to increase its receipts it could increase electricity or gas prices and effectively place an additional tax on the consumers of those utilities.

It was also argued that members of parliament could contest the commercial decisions of nationalised industry managers if they had political consequences of a detrimental nature. Hence a government MP would agree that the rationalisation of a particular industry was commercially sound as long as the rationalisation was not occurring in their constituency.

All of the above objectives of privatisation have influenced the process of privatisation to differing degrees at different times over the last 16 years. Hopefully an understanding of what privatisation is seeking to achieve will allow you to understand and evaluate the arguments which are put forward in the articles on the suggested reading list and in the reader.

REVIEW ACTIVITY 4

Because of the nature of the topic covered in Section 4 the review activities listed here are suggested essays, which you may like to construct plans for. In constructing these essay plans you will need to read the articles by David Forrest and David Parker (Resource Items 4.1 and 4.2 respectively, to be found at the end of the module.)

1 What are the objectives of current UK privatisation policy?

2 To what extent are regulators an effective substitute for 'real competition' in the product markets? Discuss your answer with reference to either the gas or electricity markets.

3 To what extent has privatisation widened share ownership in the UK? Why might wider share ownership be desirable?

Summary

In this section we discussed privatisation and identified three different forms of it. We outlined the different objectives of privatisation and how UK policy has been established in order to pursue those objectives. We also mentioned the role of the main regulatory bodies.

Unit Review Activity

There is no unit review activity for this unit because of the diverse nature of the subject matter.

Unit Summary

In the first three sections of this unit we examined three different theoretical models of competition: perfect competition, monopoly and oligopoly. We represented each in diagram form.

Specifically, we developed your understanding of how firms develop price and output strategies in response to different levels of market competition, and of the level and sustainability of profits in markets where there is a lot of competition or little competition

We explained why firms collude, the benefits of collusion and what factors may cause collusion to break down

In Section 4 we began to apply the theoretical knowledge developed earlier to the issue of privatisation. We looked at three different types of privatisation, at the objectives of privatisation and the market conditions which need to exist in order to achieve these objectives.

References

Griffiths, A and Wall, S, (1995), *Applied Economics: An Introductory Course*, Longman, 6th edn

Kay, J A and Thompson, D J, (1986), 'Privatisation: a policy in search of a rationale', *Economic Journal*

Liebenstein, H, (1966), 'Allocative efficiency or x efficiency', *American Economic Review*

Recommended Reading

The analysis of perfect competition and monopoly can be found in most standard introductory economic texts, for example:

Parkin and King, (1995) *Economics*, Addison-Wesley, 2nd edn

Sloman, (1995) *Economics*, Harvester Wheatsheaf, 2nd edn

The above texts will also provide an analysis of oligopoly.

The subject of privatisation and its constituent parts of denationalisation, deregulation and contracting out have been widely written about and there are numerous reference, you may wish to sample some of the following:

Jaffer and Thompson, (1986), 'Deregulating Express Coaches; a reassessment', *Fiscal Studies,* vol 7 no. 4

Provides an interesting case study of the deregulation of an industry and the impacts of that deregulation.

Beesley and Littlechild, (1983), 'Privatisation: Principles, Problems and Priorities', *Lloyds Bank Review*

A dated reference admittedly, but interesting since it suggests ways in which privatisation should be undertaken and can be used to evaluate subsequent policies. You should also note the discussion of regulation given that one of the authors subsequently became the regulator for the electricity industry.

The following four articles form an interesting case study of contracting out of refuse collection services:

1   Domberger, Meadowcroft and Thompson, (1986), 'Competitive tendering and efficiency: The case of refuse collection', *Fiscal Studies*, vol 7 no 4

2   Domberger, Meadowcroft and Thompson, (1988), 'Competition and efficiency in refuse collection: A reply', *Fiscal Studies*, vol 9 no 11

3   Ganley and Grahl, (1988), 'Competition and efficiency in refuse collection: A critical comment', *Fiscal Studies*, vol 9 no 1

4   Szymanski and Wilkins, (1993), 'Cheap Rubbish? Competitive tendering and contracting out in refuse collection 1981– 1988', *Fiscal Studies*, vol 14 no 3

For further information on the work of the regulatory bodies you may wish to consult the following Internet web sites:

1   British Telecom (regulated by OFTEL)

2   Electricity (regulated by OFFER): http://www.open.gov.uk./offer/offerhm.htm

3   You may also find http://www.open.gov.uk a good starting point to search for information on an extremely large number of government-related topics.

Answers to Review Activities

Review Activity 1

1   Perfectly competitive firms engage in business activity because they wish to maximise profits

2   Normal profit is the minimum level of profit a business person must receive in order to pursuade them to continue supplying output. That is, it is the minimum return the business person will accept in return for the risks they have taken in producing output. Profit are normal when p=AC. Abnormal profit exists when price exceeds average cost.

3   In the long run abnormal profit cannot exist because new firms will enter the industry enticed by the high levels of profitability. New firms will increase industry output (supply), which will force prices down. Prices will continue to fall until price is equal to average cost and hence the firm will earn a normal level of profit.

4   We need to make this assumption so that no buyer or seller is sufficiently large enough to influence market price (exert market power).

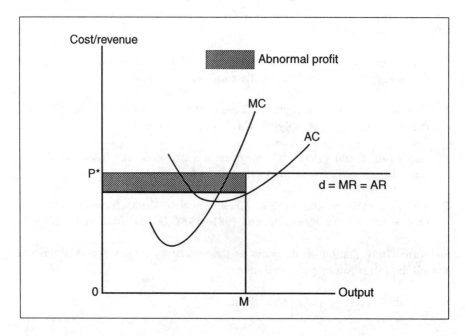

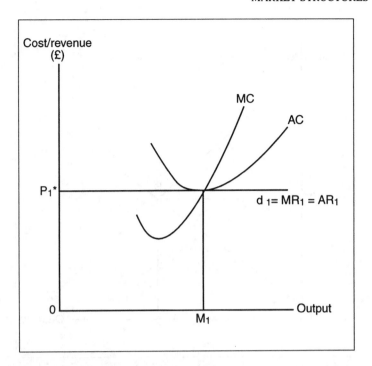

Review Activity 2

Axis C should be labelled Revenue (price/Cost £; axis D should be labelled Output).

Curve A is the demand or average revenue curve; curve B is the marginal revenue curve; curve K is the average cost curve.

I is the profit-maximising level of output.

J is the allocatively efficient level of output, since it corresponds with the point at which the marginal cost curve cuts the demand curve.

Output will be sold at a price equivalent to H if profits are to be maximised.

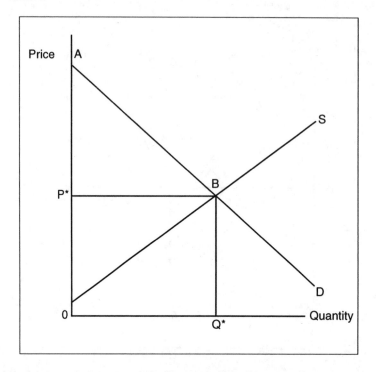

In the above diagram the equilibrium price is p* and equilibrium output q*. Area p*AB represents consumer surplus. That is the amount consumers were willing to pay for q* over and above what they actually have to pay.

Review Activity 3

1(a) The three-firm concentration ratio is 67%. That is, the sum of the market share of the three largest producers (28 + 23 + 16).

(b) The five-firm concentration ratio is 91%. That is, the sum of the market share of the three largest producers (28 + 23 + 16 + 15 + 9).

2   See Section 3.1:

The number of firms operating in the industry is small and all firms are well known to each other. This is often referred to as a **mature oligopoly**.

Costs and methods of production are known and apparent to all firms in the industry. This is likely to be the case in mature oligopolies which employ standardised and non-changing production technologies.

Firms produce similar products, that is, products which are not heavily differentiated.

There is a dominant firm. If the dominant firm is the least-cost producer this can impose a discipline on price cartels, since if individual producers produce more than their allotted output the dominant firm can threaten to price at, or very near to, cost and therefore undercut all other producers.

If industry demand is unstable this will place pressure on any collusive agreement. For example, if there are large reductions in demand, some individual producers may think that they can maintain their current levels of output by cutting prices and taking market share off competitors.

3   In order to stop firms cheating on any price agreement within an oligopolistic industry other members of the group have to develop deterrent strategies. This usually involves the dominant firm in the group threatening to slash prices unless all other members observe a degree of discipline with regard to their pricing policy. The dominant firm may be the producer who has the lowest average cost of the group and therefore could potentially set prices below the average cost of their fellow producers in the industry.

This is illustrated in the diagram below.

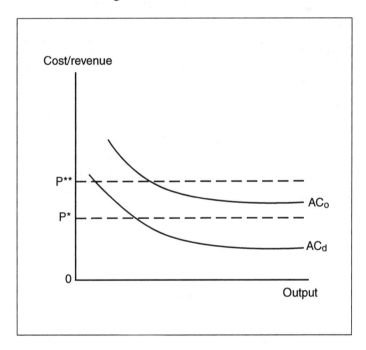

If AC_d represents the average costs of the dominant firm and AC_o represents the AC of all other producers, then a price of P* would make all producers other than the dominant firm incur losses. Faced with these losses firms who had cheated may be tempted to restore their prices to the agreed level P**. Note that, as with all deterrents, it can only be effective if the dominant firm is willing to impose the sanction. In the above example the dominant firm must be prepared to cut prices to P*.

Review Activity 4

The objectives of privatisation have been highlighted in this section. Many students fail to explain the ways in which the objectives may be attained. For example, where might we expect pressure for economic efficiency to come from (product, capital and corporate control markets)?

You may also wish to examine the extent to which the objectives of privatisation stated in this section may conflict. (Economic efficiency and maximising revenue for the Treasury, surely the latter objective provides an incentive to sell monopolies.)

In order to answer these questions you need to read: I can assure you that you will find no shortage of opinions! You may find it useful to visit some of the web sites I have listed under Further Reading, where you will find very up-to-date information.

UNIT 5
THE THEORY OF DISTRIBUTION

Introduction

In Unit 1 we saw that in order to produce output it was necessary to employ factors of production (land, labour, capital and entrepreneurial skills). This unit will examine how much each of these factors of production has to be paid in order to engage in the production of goods and services. We will begin in Section 1 by discussing the distribution of income in perfect and imperfect markets. In Sections 2–5 we will then examine:

- How wage rates are determined (Sections 2 and 3). That is what determines the income earned by labour.

- How interest rates are determined (Section 4). That is what determines the income of capital.

- How rents are determined (Section 5). That is what determines the income earned by land.

Clearly, these are all important issues for business people. Wages usually form the largest percentage of a firm's costs and hence their level is critical to a firm's competitiveness. The rate of interest and return on capital will determine whether or not investment is undertaken. Lastly, rents will exert an influence on a firm's location decision. In the following discussion we will examine the way in which incomes are distributed to labour, land and capital.

Objectives

At the end of the unit you should be able to;

- Explain how income is distributed in perfectly competitive markets for labour, capital and land.

- Appreciate that the assumptions which underpin the theory of perfect factor markets may be flawed. You should be able to evaluate the implication for income distribution if these assumptions are flawed.

- Describe the variables which influence the supply of labour to a particular occupation.

- Describe the variables which influence the demand for labour from profit maximising employers.

- Use the demand and supply theory developed in the previous two objectives to explain how wages are determined in imperfect labour markets.

- Describe the variables which determine the demand for capital.

- Explain the relationship between the supply of loanable funds and individuals' time value of money.

- Describe how demand and supply variables interact to determine land rents.

SECTION ONE

The Income Factors of Production

Introduction

In Section 1 our discussion will focus on three different elements of income distribution:

- We can examine how equally incomes are distributed among the population.

- We can examine the distribution of income between the factors of production: land, labour and capital.

- We can examine the distribution of income within a factor category. For example, why are doctors paid more than nurses, Premier League footballers more than university lecturers?

1.1 Distribution of income in perfect markets

In this section of our discussion we will assume that factors of production are bought and sold in a perfect factor market, that is, a market which is perfectly competitive. The assumptions which underpin the theory of perfect factor markets are similar to those which underpin the model of perfect competition.

ASSUMPTIONS

1   Both employers of the factors of production and owners of the factors of production are price takers: no one has the power to influence the factor price.

2   There is freedom of entry into and out of factor markets: we assume that capital and labour are not restrained from moving in and out of markets by unions, professional organisations or government. We also assume that land use can be changed without hindrance.

3   Workers have perfect knowledge of the wages and work conditions which exist in all parts of the labour market. Similarly, capital and labour are aware of the risks, returns and quality of factors in their respective factor markets.

4   All factor are homogeneous: it is assumed, for example, that all car workers are equally skilled and motivated.

We now consider how a perfect factor market operates, taking labour as an example. We assume that the price of labour will be determined by the supply and demand for labour. However we must note that the demand for labour is a 'derived demand', that is labour is not demanded for its own sake but for its ability to produce output. Hence the demand for car workers at Jaguar Cars will depend upon the demand for Jaguar Cars.

In Figure 1 the hourly wage rate is determined by the market as a whole. Both the employers of labour and employees must then accept this wage rate and in accordance with their own supply and demand schedules they then decide how much labour to demand and how much labour to supply. Hence the individual worker would supply $0Q_2$ hours of work and the individual employer would demand $0Q_1$ hours of work.

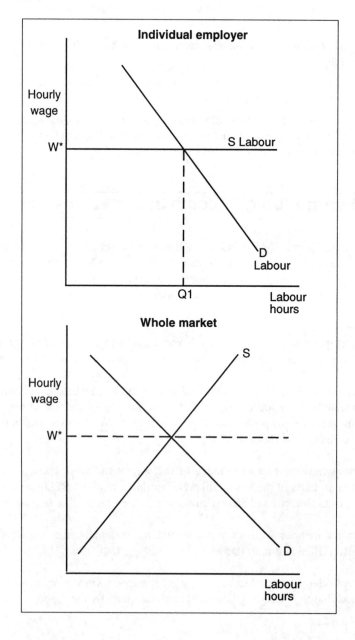

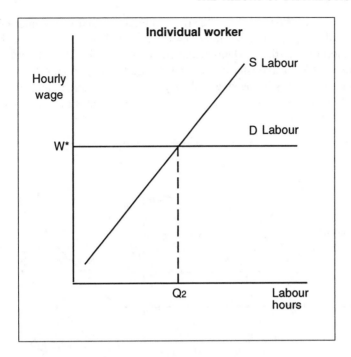

Figure 1:The determination of market wage rates

Now try Activity 1.

ACTIVITY 1

1 Let us assume that in a theoretical economy there are only two labour
   markets. The first labour market is for car workers, the second a labour
   market for steel workers. If both labour markets are perfectly competitive,
   what would you expect to happen if the hourly wage rate in the steel
   industry is £10 per hour and £15 per hour in the car industry?

Hint 1: revise the section on the assumptions which underpin the model of
perfectly competitive factor markets.

Hint 2: if the above assumptions (hint 1) hold then can wage rates in the two
different labour markets remain unequal?

Hint 3: how will wage rates in the different markets come together.

2 Do you think that the assumptions which underpin the perfectly competitive
   model of factor markets are realistic? What would be the consequence for
   income distribution if one or more of these assumptions did not hold?

Consider the two labour markets illustrated in Figure 2. In the car labour market the existence of a higher hourly rate should cause workers to exit the steel labour market and move to the car labour market. This will have the effect of reducing wage rates in the car industry due to an increased labour supply ($S_0 - S_1$). At the same time wage rates in the steel industry will increase due to a reduction in the supply of labour ($S_0 - S_2$). The net result is that wage rates in both markets come together at w*.

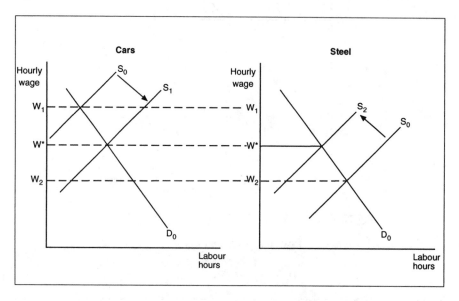

Figure 2: Wage equilibrium between labour markets

In reality, however, this is unlikely to happen as the cost of supplying factors may differ between different labour markets. For example, *ceteris paribus*, it is more pleasant to do a clean and safe job than a dirty and dangerous job. Hence the dirty and dangerous job would have to pay a higher wage rate in order to attract labour. In the above example we assume that individuals who are employed in the steel industry could easily transfer to employment in the car industry; we take no account of any training or education which might be necessary to allow such a transfer. We also fail to take account of factors such as geographical mobility: what if the steel industry is located in South Wales and the car industry in the West Midlands? Will workers be willing to move their homes and families?

1.2 Distribution of income in imperfect markets

In reality factor markets rarely, if ever, exhibit the characteristics which form the assumptions upon which the theory of perfect factor markets is based.

1   Various groups have economic power, for example large employers (Rupert Murdoch's News International), trade unions, and large owners of capital have significant economic power.

2   There may be restrictions on the movement of factors. Many governments restrict the quantity of capital which can be taken out of a country by imposing exchange controls. This may prevent capital from earning higher returns from investment opportunities overseas. Trade unions may attempt to restrict the employment of non-union labour.

3   Firms and households may have imperfect knowledge.

4   Economic agents may not always act to maximise their economic well being. For example firms may discriminate on the basis of race or gender irrespective of a worker's abilities, motivation and desire to work at the existing wage rate. Some owners of capital will only invest in ecologically or politically correct shares.

REVIEW ACTIVITY 1

Briefly discuss five ways in which you think markets for the factors of production could be made to more closely resemble 'perfect markets'.

SUMMARY

In this section we explained how income is distributed in perfect labour markets. We discussed the restrictive nature of the assumptions upon which the discussion of imperfect labour markets is based. Finally, we showed why labour markets have a tendency to be 'imperfect'.

SECTION TWO

Wage determination in perfectly competitive labour markets

Introduction

According to economic theory, wages which are determined in a perfectly competitive environment will be determined by the market demand and supply of labour. In this section we will examine the factors which determine the supply of, and demand for, labour.

2.1 The supply of labour

Firstly, consider the supply of hours by an individual worker to a given occupation. When making a decision about how many hours of labour to supply the individual worker has to take account of the fact that increased work hours reduces leisure hours. If we assume that leisure hours are subject to the **law of diminishing marginal utility** then, as increasing quantities of leisure hours are foregone, in order to supply more work hours, the marginal utility of the next leisure hour forgone will increase. (At this point you may wish to return to Unit 2 and revise the concept of marginal utility.) Essentially we are arguing that, as your leisure time is reduced, you will value any leisure hours which remain more highly.

Therefore, we argue that the individual worker will only supply increased work hours at a higher wage rate. The higher wage rate is necessary in order to compensate the worker for foregoing increasingly valuable leisure hours. The individual worker's supply of hours schedule is illustrated in Figure 3. For example, many workers receive increased hourly wage rates in order to persuade them to forgo their bank holidays or work 'unsociable' hours at weekends.

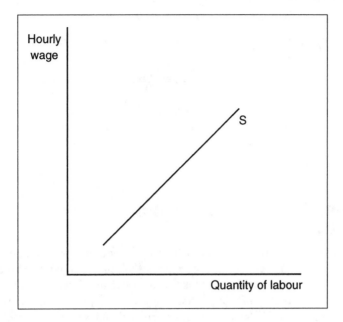

Figure 3: The individual supply of labour curve

The market supply curve for a given type of labour (for example, car workers) is obtained by aggregating over all individual worker supply schedules. It measures the number of workers who are willing to work at each wage rate. The result of such an aggregation is illustrated by the graph drawn in Figure 4 (c).

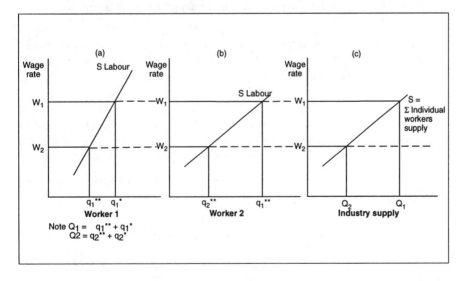

Figure 4: Industry supply of labour curve

The number of workers willing to supply their labour at each wage rate will depend on:

- the number of qualified workers
- the non-wage benefits of the job such as job security, fringe benefits and status
- the level of wages and non-wage benefits in alternative jobs.

A change in wages will cause a movement along the existing supply of labour schedule in Figure 4 (b), that is, as wages increase the number of workers available for work will increase. A change in any of the three factors listed above will shift the whole supply schedule.

2.2 Elasticity of labour supply

We will now consider the elasticity of supply of labour to a particular occupation. Here we need to consider the responsiveness of the supply of labour to a change in wage rates. The responsiveness of labour to a change in wage rates will depend critically on the mobility of labour, that is how easy is it for labour to respond to a change in wage rates. The greater the costs and difficulties of changing jobs and the longer the time period involved, the more immobile labour will be and the less elastic will the supply of labour be. For example, we would expect the supply of pathologists to be very inelastic since:

- It takes a long time to train pathologists and therefore a change in the wage rates paid to pathologists may only produce a significant increase in their supply in two or three years' time. This is the period of time it takes qualified doctors to specialise and train to become trained pathologists.

- The high level of training and education necessary for this particular job means that it is highly unlikely that car workers or steel workers are going to switch to becoming pathologists.

There are two main forms of **labour immobility: geographical** immobility, where workers are immobile between jobs in different regions of a country or between different countries; and **occupational** immobility, where workers are unwilling or unable to move between jobs which involve no geographical relocation.

ACTIVITY 2

1 Provide five reasons why workers may be geographically immobile.

2 Provide three reasons why workers may be occupationally immobile.

1   Workers may be geographically immobile for the following reasons.

   (i)   The cost and inconvenience of moving house. (How does negative equity affect the mobility of labour?)

   (ii)   Social and family ties.

   (iii)   Poor or overcrowded social infrastructure (schools, hospitals) in the region which labour is considering moving to.

   (iv)   Higher cost of living in the new region, which may in part be due to higher commuting costs.

   (v)   Workers may not be aware that jobs are available in other regions/countries.

2   Workers may be occupationally immobile for the following reasons.

   (i)   Lack of qualifications or training necessary to do an alternative job.

   (ii)   Less desirable fringe benefits in alternative jobs.

   (iii)   Lack of knowledge of available jobs.

(Please note that the above lists are in no way exhaustive and you may have provided responses which are equally valid. You may wish to discuss your responses with your tutors or class study groups, if this is possible.)

It was stated above that the time period being considered will also influence the elasticity of labour supply. For example, an occupation which has an inelastic supply of labour schedule in the short run may have a more elastic supply of labour schedule in the long run if more individuals can be persuaded to undertake training for that particular occupation. (The example relating to the supply of pathologists illustrates this point.) Now try Activity 3.

ACTIVITY 3

Compare the elasticity of the supply of:

1 nuclear power workers

2 shop assistants.

In both cases explain what factors are likely to influence the elasticity of supply (stating clearly any assumptions you have made about the nature of employment in each industry).

Your answer needs to consider the ease with which additional workers could be attracted to the industry. That is, is it necessary to increase wages substantially (an inelastic supply of labour) in order to attract additional workers.

If you are having difficulties with the terms elastic and inelastic supply of labour look at Figure 4(a), which shows an inelastic supply of labour schedule where the increase in the wage rate from w to w* provokes a relatively small response in the quantity of labour supplied. Figure 4(b) shows an elastic supply of labour schedule where the same increase in wages for w to w* provokes a much greater increase in the quantity of labour supplied. That is more workers offer themselves for work.

Your answer should also take account of the different training requirements for the two jobs and the potential source of labour supply for each occupation. The nature of the two jobs with respect to danger, fringe benefits, job satisfaction, etc. must also be considered.

2.3 Economic rent and transfer earnings

The earnings of any factor of production can be split into two constituent parts: **economic rent** and **transfer earnings**. The relative size of each of the two elements will be determined by the elasticity of supply of the factor.

- Economic rent is anything which a factor of production earns over and above transfer earnings.

- Transfer earnings are the minimum payments which a factor must receive in order to keep it in its present occupation.

For example, a university lecturer may earn £25,000 a year. The lecturer could earn £18,000 a year working in a research post and would transfer to that job if the current salary fell below £18,000. Therefore, the lecturer's transfer earnings are £18,000 and economic rent is £7,000.

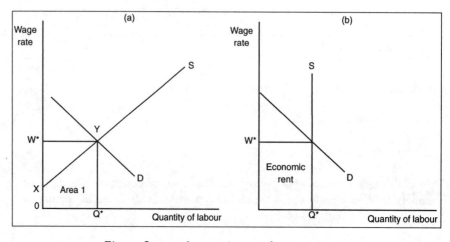

Figure 5: transfer earnings and economic rent

Now consider a market supply curve: area 1 in Figure 5 (a) represents transfer earnings. As we move along the supply curve from X to Y the wage rate has to increase in order to attract additional workers to the occupation. The supply curve indicates the amount which each individual worker has to be paid in order to induce that worker to enter the industry. Hence the area under the supply curve up to employment level Q* indicates the total transfer earnings of employees in this occupation.

However, all Q* workers receive the equilibrium wage rate w* and hence as a group the workers in this occupation earn economic rent equal to XW*Y. As Figure 5 illustrates, the more elastic the supply of labour to a particular occupation is, the greater will be the proportion of total wage income accounted for by transfer earnings.

Figure 5(b) examines the distribution of wage income between transfer earnings and economic rent when the supply of labour is perfectly inelastic. In such an instance the wage rate is determined solely by demand and all wage income is economic rent. The most quoted example of such a situation is the individual who possesses a unique talent, such as a rock star, a film star or a sports star. In such cases, as the individual becomes more popular, there is a higher demand for their services and hence the wage payments they can insist upon increase.

2.4 The demand for labour

Our previous analysis has concentrated on the supply side of the labour market, we will now consider the decisions which employers make when deciding how much labour to employ.

In the first instance we will consider the demand for labour from an individual firm. We will assume that the firm which is hiring labour has the objective of maximising profits. Thus the profit-maximising employer will, when employing more labour, take into account what the extra unit of labour adds to revenue and to cost. Intuitively, it would seem reasonable to suggest that an employer would be willing to employ an extra unit of labour if that unit of labour adds more to revenue than it does to costs.

Let us then consider what will determine the amount that increased employment of labour adds to a firm's total revenue.

1   We stated above that labour has a derived demand, therefore labour will only be demanded to produce extra output.

2   Recall from Unit 3 that the extra output which an extra unit of labour input produces is known as the **marginal product of labour**.

3   Therefore, the extra revenue that the employment of one more unit of labour will generate will be equal to the MPL multiplied by the price at which each unit of the extra output is sold.

4   This extra revenue which has been generated by the employment of an extra worker is known as the **marginal revenue product of labour (MRPL)**:

MRPL = MPL × p   (1)

Note that the variable p in equation (1) is the price of the extra output produced, it is not the price of labour (a very common mistake). In order to simplify the analysis it is assumed that the price at which extra output is sold is constant, that is the output which labour is producing is sold in a perfectly competitive market.

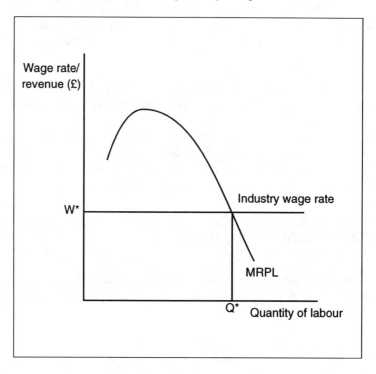

Figure 6: The equilibrium wage rate in a perfectly competitive labour market

Figure 6 shows the MRPL curve for an individual firm. The individual firm can hire labour at a constant wage rate since it is assumed that labour is hired in a perfectly competitive labour market. The profit-maximising employer will therefore employ 0q* units of labour up to the point where:

MRPL = W   (2)   W= wage rate

Note that the employer is effectively employing labour up to the point where MR (MRPL) = MC (W). That is up to the point where the marginal revenue generated by employing one more unit of labour (MRPL) is equal to the marginal cost of hiring one more unit of labour (W). Now try Activity 4.

ACTIVITY 4

Alpha Ltd. can hire workers in a perfectly competitive labour market at a wage rate of £10 per hour. The company sells its output in a perfectly competitive market at a price of 20p per unit. Given the following output and associated employment data for Alpha Ltd., calculate:

1 the MRPL at each level of employment

2 the number of workers Alpha Ltd. will employ (assume that Alpha Ltd. aims to maximise profits).

EMPLOYEES	OUTPUT	MPL	MRPL
0	0		
		?	?
1	60		
		?	?
2	130		
		?	?
3	220		
			?
4	280		
		?	?
5	330		
		?	?
6	370		
		?	?
7	395		

(Output data measures output per hour.)

1 The MRPL is calculated by multiplying the MPL by the constant product price of 20p. In order to calculate the MRPL it is therefore necessary to first calculate the MPL. Since the MPL is the increase in output when an extra worker is employed, we calculate MPL by looking at the difference in output levels when an additional worker is employed. Having calculated the MPL we

simply multiply this value by price (20p). The results of the calculation explained above are in the completed table below.

EMPLOYEES	OUTPUT	MPL	MRPL
0	0		
		60	£12
1	60		
		70	£14
2	130		
		90	£18
3	220		
		60	£12
4	280		
		50	£10
5	330		
		40	£8
6	370		
		25	£5
7	395		

2   A profit-maximising company will employ labour up to the point where W = MRPL. Since Alpha Ltd. has to pay workers £10 per hour it will employ workers up to the point where the MRPL = £10. Therefore Alpha Ltd. will employ 5 workers.

2.5 Will any workers be employed?

The above analysis needs to be qualified. Employing workers up to the point where MRPL=W leads to an optimal quantity of labour being employed. However under certain circumstances, which we will now examine, this optimal quantity of labour may be consistent with the firm making losses.

In order to develop our discussion it is necessary to introduce the **average revenue product of labour** (ARPL) curve. The concept of ARPL has exactly the same relationship with the average product of labour as the MRPL has with MPL, namely

$ARPL = APL \times p$ (3)

It therefore should not be surprising that the ARPL curve has the same relationship with the MRPL curve as the APL curve has with MPL curve. At this point you may wish to review Figure 1 in Unit 3. In both instances to arrive at the revenue product concepts you merely multiply the relevant product concept by a constant product price.

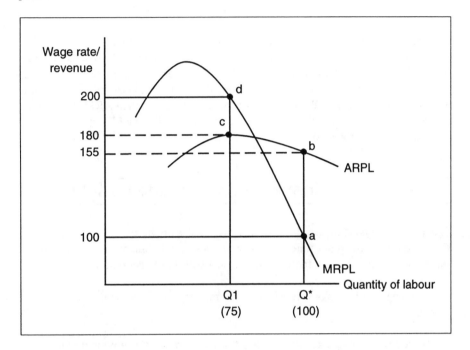

Figure 7: MRPL and the demand for labour

Figure 7 includes some illustrative values of employment and wage rates/revenues. At a wage rate of £100 the profit-maximising employer will demand 100 units of labour, determined by point (a) where the MRPL = W. Note that all 100 workers are paid a wage equal to the MRPL of the last worker employed, the 100th worker. Now consider the ARPL of the 100 workers who have been hired. The ARPL indicates on average what each of the 100 workers who have been employed are adding to the firm's revenues. Therefore, point (b) on the ARPL curve tells us that on average each of the 100 workers employed earns revenue equal to £155. Hence:

total wage bill when 100 workers are employed   =   £10,000

total revenue when 100 workers are employed   =   £15,500

Surplus   =   £ 5,500.

Now let us consider a situation where the wage rate doubles to £200. The profit-maximising employer, equating MRPL and the wage rate will demand 75 units of labour, determined by point (d) on the MRPL curve. However, when 75 units of labour are employed the ARPL will be determined by point (c) on the ARPL curve, and hence in this instance the ARPL is £180. Therefore:

total wage bill when 75 workers are employed   =   £15,000

total revenue when 75 workers are employed   =   £13,500

deficit   =   £1,500.

By employing 75 workers the employer would have to endure an excess of wage cost over revenues of £1,500. Obviously no rational employer would consider such a situation viable and hence no workers would be employed. So equation (2) above has a condition attached to it, namely that employers will hire labour up to the point where MRPL = W provided that the MRPL is less than ARPL. Therefore, only that section of the MRPL curve which lies below the ARPL curve will act as the demand curve for labour.

2.6 The determinants of the demand for labour

The above analysis has developed a downward-sloping demand curve for labour. What we must now determine is what will cause a movement along the demand curve for labour and what factors will cause a shift in the demand curve.

1   A change in the wage rate will cause a movement along the existing demand for labour curve.

2   If the MPL (some texts will refer to this as the **marginal physical product of labour**) changes the demand for labour curve will shift. An increase in MPL will cause the demand for labour curve to shift to the right.

3   If the price of output which labour is producing increases this will shift the MRPL curve (demand for labour curve) to the right.

DERIVING THE INDUSTRY DEMAND FOR LABOUR CURVE

In the preceding analysis we have assumed that the firm can sell extra output at a constant price because it is a small operator in a perfectly competitive market and hence any increase in the firm's output due to an expansion of employment has no impact on the market price of output. Hence, as the wage rate falls in Figure 8 (a) the increase in output associated with increased employment $0q_1$ to $0q_2$ to $0q_3$ has no impact on the MRPL curve.

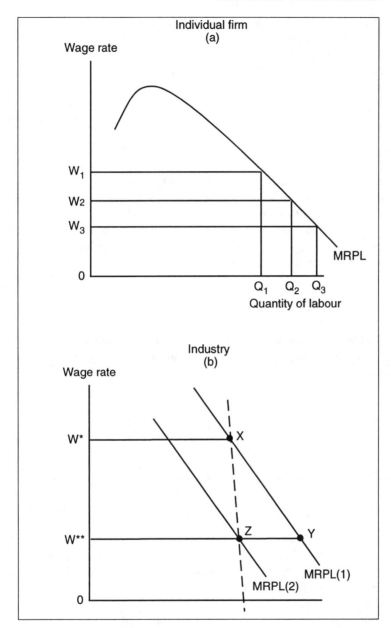

Figure 8: Deriving the industry demand for labour curve

However, as Figure 8 (b) shows, we cannot simply aggregate MRPL curves across all individual firms to arrive at the industry demand curve for labour. This is due to the fact that, as the wage rate drops from w* to w**, each individual firm will wish to expand along their MRPL curve from x to y. However, if every firm in the perfectly competitive industry does this, the industry supply curve will move to the right, causing the market price of the good being sold to fall. Hence the MRPL curve will shift inwards, to the left, in response to a fall in the price of the good being produced. Hence the industry demand curve is the broken line (xz).

WHY DO INEQUALITIES IN WAGE RATES EXIST?

In reality, wage equality or a tendency to wage equality will not exist as it does under the very restrictive assumptions of the model of perfectly competitive labour markets. This is due to the fact that the assumptions of the model are too restrictive and are highly unlikely to occur in reality: workers tend to have different abilities, there is less than perfect mobility of labour, all jobs are not equally attractive and workers and employers do not have perfect knowledge of labour market conditions.

However, even if the above conditions did hold, there would still be inequalities in perfectly competitive labour markets because of the time that it takes labour markets to adjust to changing conditions. Hence, in areas of high unemployment it will take time for workers to revise their wage demands downwards in response to an increased supply of labour and/or move to areas where work is available. In the same way, firms' decisions to relocate to areas where wage rates are lower also takes time. You should note that in reality a firm's relocation decision may not solely be determined by considerations of wage rates. Now try Activity 5.

ACTIVITY 5

On the basis of the above discussion, provide two characteristics which poorly paid workers will have and two characteristics which highly paid workers will have.

Poorly-paid workers will have one or more of the following characteristics:

1   Low demand for labour, due to a low demand for the product which labour produces, note that there is a derived demand for labour. Low labour productivity may also result in low demand for labour. (You may like to consider the extent to which low labour productivity is the 'fault' of labour.)

2   High supply of labour due to an excess supply of labour with the necessary skills or training to a particular occupation. A high supply of labour may also occur in areas where there is labour immobility and contracting industries.

Highly-paid workers will have one or more of the following characteristics:

1   A high demand for labour due to an expanding demand for output, and or workers who are highly productive.

2   Workers whose talents are in low supply, this factor will be enhanced if it takes a long period of time to train new workers and expand the supply of labour.

REVIEW ACTIVITY 2

1   In the following diagram, indicate the points at which, if workers were
    paid according to the principles of profit maximisation, they would
    generate revenues:

    (a) which were just sufficient to pay their total wage bill

    (b) which were less than their total wage bill

    (c) which were in excess of their total wage bill.

    In all cases assume that labour is recruited in a perfect labour market.

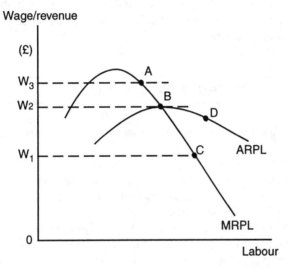

2   With the advent of mass production techniques what are the implications
    for the elasticity of supply in a large number of occupations?

3   Do you agree with the statement that 'nurses are paid too little'. Justify
    your response.

Summary

In Section 2 we explained how a worker's preference between leisure and income
influence their response to changes in wages. We described the factors which
influence the supply of labour and determine the elasticity of labour supply to a
particular occupation. We went on to define economic rent and transfer earnings.
Finally, we described those factors which will cause the demand for labour to
change and discussed a number of factors which will cause wage inequalities to
exist.

SECTION THREE

Wage determination in imperfect labour markets

Introduction

Our discussion above has suggested that the assumptions of a perfectly competitive labour market are too restrictive. The analysis in this section will relax some of the above assumptions. We will consider two different scenarios. The first will consider a situation where firms have monopoly power in the labour market, in the sense that they are the sole employers of labour. Secondly, we will consider a situation of monopoly in the supply of labour.

3.1 Monopoly demand for labour

When there is a sole employer of labour a situation of **monopsony** is said to exist.

As Table 1 illustrates, the industry supply of labour curve, which shows the supply of labour at different wage rates, is the same as the average cost of labour curve. That is, the wage rate represents the average cost to an employer of employing a given quantity of labour. However, the marginal cost of labour is made up of the extra wage which must be paid to the marginal employee (the last one employed) plus the extra which must be paid to all other employees: it is assumed that all employees have to be paid the same wage and so they gain when wages are raised to attract the marginal workers.

LABOUR SUPPLY	WAGE RATE	WAGE BILL	ACL	MCL
0	0	0		
				10
1	10	10	10	
				14
2	12	24	12	
				18
3	14	42	14	

LABOUR SUPPLY	WAGE RATE	WAGE BILL	ACL	MCL
				22
4	16	64	16	
				26
5	18	90	18	
				30
6	20	120	20	
				34
7	22	154	22	

Table 1

In the above table ACL = average cost of labour, where

$$ACL = \frac{\text{Total wage bill}}{\text{Labour supply}} \quad (4).$$

MCL = marginal cost of employing an extra worker and is equal to the change in the total wage bill when one extra unit of labour is employed. In the table above you should note that at all levels of labour input (supply) MCL is greater than ACL. Noting this last point, Figure 9 provides a representation of the typical MCL and ACL curves faced by a monopsonist. Superimposed on the two cost curves is the monopsonist's MRPL curve.

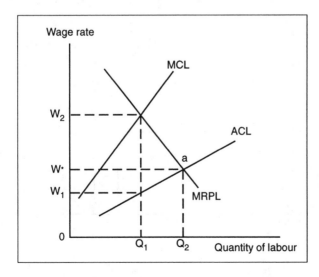

Figure 9: Monopsony and the supply of labour

In a perfectly competitive environment the industry would employ q_2 workers at a wage rate of W*: employment and wages would be determined by the point at which the industry demand is equal to supply for labour, point (a). The profit-maximising monopsonist will employ labour up to the point where the MCL is equal to MRPL: the monopsonist will employ q_1 workers. However, the monopsonist will not pay wages w_2 equal to the marginal cost of the last worker employed, it will pay wages equal to the ACL. That is, the employer will pay the wages which the industry supply curve dictates are necessary at employment level q_1. Therefore, the monopsonist employer will employ q_1 workers at a wage rate of w_1. The reason why the monopsonist employer can appropriate this extra surplus (equal to the difference between the ACL and MRPL, $w_2 - w_1$) out of labour is due to the fact that they are 'wage makers' not 'wage takers'. As individual employers they do not have to accept the wage rate set in a perfectly competitive environment. As Figure 9 illustrates, they do not face a constant MCL(wage rate).

3.2 Monopoly supply of labour

Now let us look at a situation where the supply of labour is under the control of unions. The analysis of monopoly labour supply is traditionally centred on the ability of unions as monopoly suppliers of labour to improve the terms and conditions of employment of their members. The extent to which unions can increase wages will depend on their ability to control the supply of labour and their memberships' willingness to undertake industrial action in support of higher wage claims.

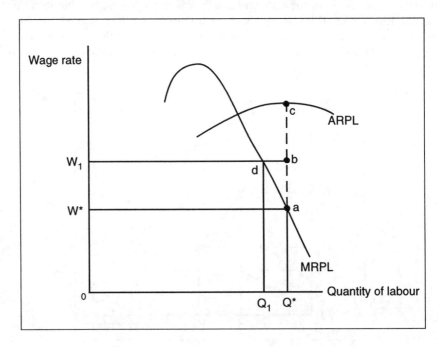

Figure 10: MRPL, ARPL and wage negotiations

Consider Figure 10: at a wage rate of w* the profit-maximising firm will employ $0q*$ workers, that is up to the point where the MRPL is equal to W*. If the firm in question operates in a perfectly competitive industry then the excess of ARPL over the MRPL, distance (ac), will generate revenue surpluses which are just sufficient to cover additional (non-labour) costs of production and provide a normal level of profit. Any attempt by unions to increase wages will only reduce employment as the demand for labour will contract backwards along the MRPL curve to point (d) and employment will fall to $0q_1$. Effectively, we are saying that firms who operate in the competitive environment listed above do not have the ability to pay higher wages and sustain employment levels, since to do so would mean accepting less than normal returns (profit).

However, if the firm in Figure 10 is a monopolist or operates in an oligopolistic industry, then the excess of ARPL over MRPL (ac) will generate surpluses which will cover all (non-labour) costs of production and provide abnormal profits. In this case, the union, as a monopoly supplier of labour, may be able to increase wages by appropriating some of the abnormal profits contained in (ac) for its members. For example, if the union is sufficiently militant and skilled in wage negotiation, it may force a solution such as that represented by point (b). At (b) the union would be negotiating for an increase in wages to w_1 and employment levels remaining at $q*$. Effectively, the union would be forcing the employer off his MRPL curve. The employer may be willing to do this so long as the distance (bc) covered all non-labour costs and provided a normal rate of return. If such a solution was to prevail the union would have in effect transferred all of the firm's abnormal profits to its members.

Unions who represent members who are employed in competitive industries can only increase wages without suffering reductions in the level of employment if workers increase their productivity. An increase in the MPL will shift the firm's and the industry's demand for labour curve to the right, which will lead to an increase in wages and employment.

REVIEW ACTIVITY 3

A firm uses only one variable factor of production, labour (L). The table below shows the different levels of daily output (Q) that will result from different numbers of workers being hired.

In the labour market the firm is a price taker and the going rate is £20 per day.

L	Q	PRICE
1	10	10
2	19	9
3	27	8

L	Q	PRICE
4	34	7
5	40	6
6	45	5
7	49	4

1 What is the profit-maximising level of output?

2 What would be the employment level if a national minimum wage of £25 per day were introduced?

Summary

In this section we explained how wage determination is influenced by monopsony and how wage determination is influenced by the monopoly supply of labour.

SECTION FOUR

The price of capital

Introduction

In this section we will explain the concept of present value and the relationship between it and compound interest. We will also develop an investment decision rule based on present value calculations. We will go on to define internal rates of return and calculate the IRR of a project. Finally, we will explain the relationship between the level of savings and interest rates.

As with the analysis above we will assume that the price for capital is determined in a perfectly competitive market and therefore the price of capital will be determined by the supply of and the demand for capital.

4.1 The demand for capital

The demand for capital is essentially an investment decision, that is to say we are examining the mechanisms which determine how many computers, machine tools or factories a particular firm is going to purchase. Therefore, as was the case with labour, the demand for capital is a derived demand, that is capital is not demanded for itself but rather for its ability to contribute to the production of output.

In order to analyse the demand for capital we must devise some mechanism by which firms can analyse how much investment they should undertake. Consider the following example: a firm can invest in a machine which costs £3,000. The machine will have a productive life of four years, after which it will be scrapped, the scrap value of the machine being £200. In each of the four years for which the machine is productive it adds the following amounts to the firm's total receipts, net of operating costs:

Year 1   £750

Year 2   £1,000

Year 3   £1,500

Year 4   £800

The firm will pay for the investment out of retained profits. The current deposit rate of interest is 10%.

How does the firm evaluate the above investment proposal? Well it could sum the returns to the investment (£4,050) and compare this with the cost of the investment. However, this would be an invalid way of assessing the investment proposal because of positive rates of interest (in this example equal to 10%). This effectively means that a pound's worth of income today is worth more than a pound's worth of income in twelve months time. Note that this is not due to the existence of positive rates of inflation; throughout this analysis we assume that the rate of inflation is zero.

£100 deposited in the bank at a 10% rate of interest is worth £110 after 1 year and £121 after 2 years. We assume that interest is compounded, the value of the savings after two years is equal to the value of savings after one year plus 10%. So a rational economic agent would be indifferent if offered the choice between £100 today or £110 in twelve months time. We therefore say that the **present value** of £110 due in twelve months' time is £100. The present value of £121 in two years' time is also £100.

The above savings calculations were based on the following compound interest equation:

$$A = P \times (1 + r/100)^n \quad (5)$$

where

A is the value of savings in n years time

P is the original sum deposited in the bank

r is the current deposit rate of interest

n is the number of years for which P is deposited in the bank.

If we now reconsider our investment proposal, the information which we have is telling us the returns that we are due in future years. Effectively we have a series of As in equation (5); what we now need to know is how much have we got to put in the bank today to get £750 in one year's time, £1,000 in two years' time, £1,500 in three years' time and £1,000 in four years' time. The return in the fourth year must include the scrap value (£200) of the machine. In order to do this we need to take equation (5) and make P the subject of the equation.

If we divide both sides of the equation by $(1 + r/100)$

then $P = \dfrac{A}{(1 + r/100)^n}$

where (P) is the present value of a return (A) due in (n) years time and r is now referred to as the rate of discount.

Hence the present value of the above investment returns would be calculated in the following way:

$$PV = \frac{750}{(1+10/100)} + \frac{1,000}{(1+10/100)^2} + \frac{1,500}{(1+10/100)^3} + \frac{1,000}{(1+10/100)^4}$$

$$PV = \frac{750}{(1.1)} + \frac{1,000}{(1.21)} + \frac{1,500}{(1.331)} + \frac{1,000}{(1.464)}$$

$$PV = 681.8 + 836.4 + 1,127 + 683.1$$

$$PV = £3,328.3.$$

The above result is stating that if we invest £3,000 today and we generate the expected returns listed above over the life of the machine that the expected returns will have a present value of £3,328.3. An alternative explanation would be that you would have to deposit £3,328.3 in the bank today in order to take the following sum of money out of the bank in future years:

Year 1   £750

Year 2 £1,000

Year 3 £1,500

Year 4 £1,000.

From the above discussion we can develop the following investment decision rule:

'if the present value of expected returns exceeds the cost of the machine (sometimes referred to as the **supply price**) then the investment proposal should be accepted'.

Often the above decision rule is couched in terms of net present value (NPV), where:

NPV = present value – supply price   (6).

The above decision rule then becomes:

NPV > 0 accept proposal   (7)

NPV < 0 reject proposal   (7a)

NPV = 0 indeterminate   (7b)

Now try Activity 6

ACTIVITY 6

Calculate the NPV of the following investment using a discount rate of (a) 8% and (b) 15% and advise as to the suitability of the project.

Project supply price = £10,000

Scrap value of investment at the end of project = £1,000.

Expected returns are quoted net of operating costs and taxation. Inflation is assumed to be zero:

Year 1 £2,000

Year 2 £4,000

Year 3 £4,000

Year 4 £2,000

Year 5 £1,000.

(a) The present value of returns at 8% is calculated thus (note you must add the scrap value to the return in year 5).

$$PV(8\%) = \frac{2{,}000}{(1.08)} + \frac{4{,}000}{(1.08)^2} + \frac{4{,}000}{(1.08)^3} + \frac{2{,}000}{(1.08)^4} + \frac{2{,}000}{(1.08)^5}$$

$$PV(8\%) = 1{,}851.85 + 3{,}429.36 + 3{,}175.36 + 1{,}470.04 + 1{,}361.19$$

$$PV(8\%) = 11{,}287.80$$

$$NPV = 11{,}287.80 - 10{,}000$$

$$NPV = £1{,}287.80.$$

As the NPV > 0 the project should be accepted.

(b) $$PV(15\%) = \frac{2{,}000}{(1.15)} + \frac{4{,}000}{(1.15)^2} + \frac{4{,}000}{(1.15)^3} + \frac{2{,}000}{(1.15)^4} + \frac{2{,}000}{(1.15)^5}$$

$$PV(15\%) = 1{,}739.13 + 3{,}024.57 + 2{,}630.06 + 1{,}143.51 + 994.35$$

$$PV(15\%) = 9{,}531.62$$

$$NPV = 9{,}531.62 - 10{,}000$$

$$NPV = £{-}468.38$$

As the NPV<0 the project should be rejected.

4.2 Internal rate of return (IRR)

An alternative approach to the present value calculations is to calculate the **internal rate of return (IRR)** of the project. The IRR will sometimes be referred to as the firm's **marginal efficiency of capital** and it is the rate of discount (interest rate) which makes the present value of returns to an investment project just equal to the project's supply price.

Therefore, in the above example we would attempt to calculate the rate of discount which made the returns to the project equal to £3,000, or in terms of NPV the rate of discount which makes the net present value of the project equal to zero.

If we consider the NPV calculation in Activity 7 when the rate of discount is reduced then the NPV of the project increases.

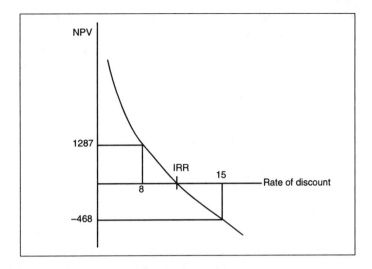

Figure 11: Net present value and internal rate of return

Figure 11 shows that as the rate of discount increases then the net present value of a project falls. Note that the relationship is not linear, this point will be important in the following analysis. The IRR of the project is the rate of discount which is consistent with NPV equal to zero (you should convince yourself that an NPV equal to zero is the same as the supply price of a project being equal to the present value of returns).

The relationship between NPV and the IRR outlined in Figure 11 can be used to make an estimate of the IRR for any given project, employing the technique of **'linear interpolation'**. In order to explain this technique, consider Figure 12.

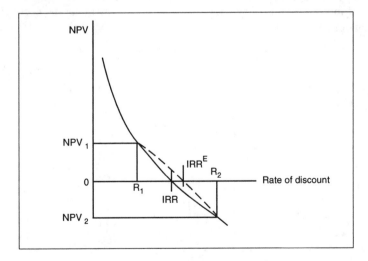

Figure 12: Estimating the IRR

Linear interpolation proceeds in the following way: a line is drawn on the NPV curve connecting the values of NPV at rates of discount of R_1 and R_2. The point at which the straight line cuts the discount rate axis is the estimated value of the IRR (IRR^E). As the diagram shows the IRR^E will be a slight overestimate because of the non-linear relationship between NPV and rates of discount. In order to calculate the exact point at which the straight line cuts the discount axis we use the expression:

$$IRR^E \text{ (estimate)} = R_1 + \frac{NPV_1}{(NPV_1 - NPV_2)} \times (R2 - R1) \text{ (8)}$$

Hence, in the above example, the IRR would be estimated at:

$$IRR^E = 10 + 10 \times \frac{(300)}{(300-116)} \times 10$$

$$IRR^E = 10 + 10 \times (0.72)$$

$$IRR^E = 17.2\%.$$

The IRR is effectively the return to the project. In order to make a decision about the suitability of the project the IRR has to be compared with the market rate of interest, as follows:

IRR > market rate of interest, accept the project

IRR < market rate of interest, reject the project

IRR = market rate of interest, indeterminate.

Note that if the IRR < market rate of interest we are effectively saying that you are better off investing in the project than in the bank.

As noted above, the IRR is **the marginal efficiency of capital** (MEC). A profit-maximising entrepreneur will invest capital up to the point where MEC is equal to the rate of interest, that is, where the marginal efficiency of capital is equal to the marginal cost of capital.

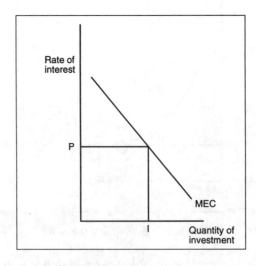

Figure 13: The marginal efficiency of capital curve

As Figure 13 shows, the MEC curve is effectively the **demand for capital curve,** since it shows the total demand for capital at different interest rates. In order for more investment to be undertaken the market rate of interest (the discount rate) must fall. Now try Activity 8.

ACTIVITY 8

Explain why the IRR may fall as more investment is undertaken

---

If we remember that the MEC is the IRR of an investment project, then why should the IRR of an investment fall as more investment is undertaken?

1   As the demand for capital goods increases with an increased level of investment then the price of capital goods will increase. With a higher supply price and a given level of expected returns, the IRR of a project must fall, therefore the investment will only be undertaken at a lower rate of interest.

2   If the demand for capital goods increases then the output of capital goods will increase and this may cause the price of output which capital goods produce to fall, thereby reducing the expected returns to an investment. With a given supply price, reduced expected returns will cause the IRR to fall and investment will only occur if the market rate of interest is low.

The above analysis shows that the demand for capital will increase as the market rate of interest falls. Let us now turn to the supply of capital.

4.3 Supply of capital

In this section we will consider the supply of funds which individuals make available for firms to borrow in order to finance investment.

The supply of loanable funds will depend on the rate of interest. The decision to save may be analysed in terms of a decision to forego consumption today (**save**) in order to enjoy higher levels of consumption at some point in the future. This in turn implies that individuals will only have an incentive to save if positive rates of interest exist. Essentially, in order to encourage an individual to save and forego current consumption, higher levels of consumption at some point in the future must be offered as compensation.

In order to get individuals to save, therefore, you have to overcome their **'time preference'** for current consumption. The stronger an individual's time preference for current consumption then the greater will be the rate of interest which it is necessary to offer that individual to induce them to save. Therefore, it would seem reasonable to suggest that savings will increase as interest rates increase, as more individuals will have their time preferences catered for at higher rates of interest.

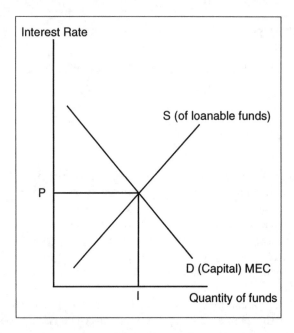

Figure 14: Interest rate determination-the supply and demand of loanable funds

Figure 14 shows the intersection of the supply of loanable fund schedule and the demand for capital schedule. At the point of intersection the market rate of interest is determined. This is the rate of interest which equates the demand for loanable funds (the demand for capital goods) with the supply of loanable funds. Effectively, it is the rate of interest which equates the IRR of the last investment project undertaken to the time preference (expressed as a rate of interest) of the individual who saves the last pound of loanable funds. Now try Activity 9.

ACTIVITY 9

What will happen to the market rate of interest if:

1 there is an increase in the price of raw materials used to make capital equipment

2 technical progress improves the efficiency of capital?

---

1   An increase in raw material prices will increase the price of capital equipment.

Ceteris paribus, this will force the IRR of all investment projects down and so the MEC curve, the demand for capital curve, will shift to the left, causing interest rates to fall.

2   If technical progress improves the efficiency of capital this will cause the expected returns to a project to increase and, with a constant supply price, this will cause the IRR of investment projects to increase. Therefore, the MEC curve, the demand for capital curve, will shift to the right.

REVIEW ACTIVITY 4

Calculate the NPV and the IRR of the following project which has the cash flows outlined below:

Year 0: (10,000)

Year 1: 2,000

Year 3: 3,000

Year 4: 5,000

Year 5: 4,000.

Base your NPV calculations on a rate of discount of 10%.

Summary

In this section we explained the concept of present value and understand the relationship between present value and compound interest and calculated the present value of a series of returns to an investment. We developed an investment decision rule based on present value calculations. We also defined IRR, internal rate of return and calculated the IRR of a project using the linear interpolation method. Finally, we explained the relationship between the level of savings and interest rates.

SECTION FIVE

The price of land

Introduction

This section seeks to apply the previous theoretical analysis to the pricing of land. That is land will be purchased up to the point where MC of land is equated with the MRP of land.

The income which is earned by landowners is referred to as **rent**. If we make the assumption that land has a perfectly inelastic supply then the price of land will be determined by the demand for land. The demand for land will reflect the marginal revenue product of land. The more productive land is or the more highly priced the good which is produced on the land then the greater will be the rent which land commands. Figure 15 illustrates how rents are determined

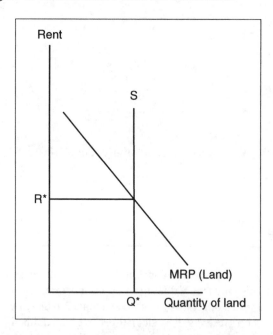

Figure 15: The determination of equilibrium land rents

ACTIVITY 10

Explain why the demand for land increases as rents fall.

Note that the demand curve for land is the MRP curve of land. Since we assume that land is subject to the law of diminishing returns then, as more land is employed, its marginal product will decline and hence the MRP of land falls as more land is employed in production.

As you are aware, not all land is rented, therefore how much should we pay for land which is purchased outright? How much should we pay for a piece of land which can earn rents of £2,000 per annum? The answer to this question is revealed by the following simple formula:

$$\text{Maximum value of land} = \frac{R}{r} \quad (9)$$

where R is the rent pa and $\bar{r}$ is the market rate of interest (deposit rate).

Hence, if current deposit rates are 6% then you should pay no more than £2,000/0.06 = £33,333 for the land.

Assume the individual had £33,333 to invest. If they deposited it in a bank it would earn £2,000 if the interest rate was 6%. Alternatively, the individual can buy the land, which will also provide returns of £2,000. Note that if the individual pays less than £33,333 for the land they are getting a better return on their investment than they would by placing their funds in a bank.

Recommended Reading

Griffiths, A, Wall, S, (1995), *Applied Economics: An introductory Course,* 6th edn. Longmans, Chapter 22

Paterson, I, Simpson, L, (1993), 'The Economics of Trade Union Power, in *Britain's Economic Miracle: Myth or Reality,*' Routledge

Parkin and King, (1995), *Economics,* Addison-Wesley, 2nd edn.134–141

Answers to Review Activities

Review Activity 1

Obviously my answers may not correspond to yours although that does not necessarily invalidate your answers.

Exchange controls could be removed. This would allow capital to flow more freely around the world. Presumably this would result in capital going to that part of the world where it could get the highest return. You may like to consider why governments impose exchange controls.

Steps could be taken to increase labours knowledge of job opportunities. This may mean that there would have to be greater investment in job centres and information technology to make workers aware of the job prospects which exist.

The government could take steps to enforce sex and racial discrimination legislation more forcefully. You should not underestimate the difficulties which may be encountered in trying to do so. However this should not be used as an excuse for not attempting to enforce compliance with existing legislation.

The 1980s saw a large body of opinion in support of the view that trade unions had too much power and a number of Employment Acts were passed to try and redress the balance.

Our analysis suggests that markets will not be perfect if there is markets power on the demand or supply side of the market. In relation to the labour market you might suggest that power on the supply side of the market has been addressed but the demand side has been left untouched.

Review Activity 2

1   (a) point B; (b) point A; (c) point C.

2   The advent of mass-production techniques is often accused of deskilling production. This effectively means that the level of skills required in any given production process have been drastically reduced. Accordingly, more people can offer themselves as workers in certain occupations because they are not excluded on the basis of lack of skill. Therefore, the answer to the question is that mass-production techniques have made labour supply more elastic in a lot of industries.

3   One side of the debate will provide arguments which state that nurses are paid a rate determined by the market. That is to say, the current wage rate is sufficient to recruit and sustain a level of supply into the nursing profession

which meets current demand. If there was a shortage of nurses then the market price would increase to reflect disequilibrium in the market.

The other side of the debate might say that the demand for labour in the nursing profession is underestimating the value of nurses because their services are not sold in an open market and therefore it is impossible to evaluate their MRP. It could be argued that if their output was correctly valued this would shift the 'demand for nurses' curve to the right and justify a higher rate of wages for nurses. It might be interesting to compare the pay rates of nurses in private hospitals with those in the NHS to see if the public sector market is currently undervaluing nurses.

Review Activity 3

L	Q	PRICE	TR	MRPL
1	10	10	100	
				71
2	19	9	171	
				45
3	27	8	216	
				22
4	34	7	238	
				2
5	40	6	240	
				−15
6	45	5	225	
				−29
7	49	4	196	

1   At a wage rate of £20 four workers will be hired since the MRPL(4) > 20 whereas MRPL(5) < 20.

2   At a minimum wage rate of £25 the fourth worker would not be employed since the MRP of the fourth worker, £22, is now less than the wage rate. Therefore, the effect of the minimum wage would be to reduce employment to 3.

Review Activity 4

NPV is calculated in the following manner:

$$NPV = -10,000 + \frac{2,000}{(1.1)} + \frac{3,000}{(1.1)^2} + \frac{5,000}{(1.1)^3} + \frac{4,000}{(1.1)^4} + \frac{4,000}{(1.1)^5}$$

NPV = £3,269.833

In order to calculate the IRR it is necessary to discount the above cash flows at two different rates of discount. In doing so we must discount at one rate which gives a negative NPV and one rate which gives a positive NPV. Having done this we can then use equation (8) to estimate the IRR of the project.

We already have one discount rate (10%) and an associated NPV of £3,269.834 from our calculations above. We know that as the rate of discount is increased the NPV of a project will fall. We need to discount the project's cash flow at a rate which will result in a negative NPV in order to calculate the IRR.

Through a process of trial and error we would find that a discount rate of 22% would result in an NPV of –£305.9. Note that all discount rates above 22% would also result in NPV which were negative.

We therefore have the necessary information to calculate the IRR of the above project:

$R_1 = 10$

$R_2 = 22$

$NPV_1 = £3,269.834$

$NPV_2 = -£305.8$.

By applying equation (8) we get:

$$IRR = 10 + \frac{3269.834}{3269.834 + 305.8} \times (22 - 10)$$

IRR = 20.97%.

UNIT 6

INTRODUCTION TO THE MACRO-ECONOMY

Introduction

You have been studying microeconomics. We have been concerned with the supply and demand for individual goods such as cars, beer or garden gnomes. We have also examined how wages are determined for doctors, teachers or builders in our study of the labour market. We now turn our attention to macroeconomics. We still examine demand and supply and the determination of prices but we will do so from the perspective of the whole economy. Now when we study demand we are concerned with **aggregate demand**, that is, the demand for all goods in the economy, and when we study supply, we are concerned with **aggregate supply**, the supply of all goods in the economy. We will examine how the aggregate output of all goods and services, measured by national income, is determined by the interaction of aggregate demand and aggregate supply.

In your microeconomics studies, we have discussed labour and capital and also the different types of market structure and how firms within these structures behave. We also looked at how government policy, for example, on taxation, affects outcomes. When studying macroeconomics, the role of government in our analysis is central. We will look at the main objectives of government economic policy and we will examine the debate between economists about which of these objectives are the most important and how best to achieve them.

We start with a very basic model of the economy, and examine how the total level of output in the economy, aggregate output or national income, is determined. We will then look at the debate between different types of economists about whether governments should try to influence the level of output in the economy and, if so, how best to do this.

This unit is divided into three sections.

Section 1 explains the structure of national income accounts. We will look at the ways in which national income is measured. We also consider ways of interpreting national income statistics as a measure of economic welfare.

Section 2 introduces a simple model of national income determination, the Circular Flow of Income. We will look closely at two different phenomena which influence national income. These are known as **injections** and **withdrawals**.

Section 3 introduces you to the major objectives of government economic policy. We will also look at the debate amongst economists about which of these objectives are the most important.

Unit Objectives

By the end of this unit you should be able to:

- define national income and explain the different ways that national income is measured

- differentiate Gross Domestic Product from Gross National Product

- explain the difference between real national income and nominal or money national income

- explain the Circular Flow of Income and show the importance of injections and withdrawals in the circular flow

- identify the major objectives of government economic policy

- differentiate between different types of economists such as Keynesians and monetarists.

SECTION ONE

National Income Accounts and Measurement of National Income

Introduction

What do we mean by **national income?** Have you ever considered how national income is measured or even why it is measured? In this section, we will attempt to answer these issues.

Imagine an economy with no government and no contact at all with other countries. Therefore we have only firms and households in this economy. This simple model of the economy is known as the **circular flow of income**. People in each household work for the firms to produce goods (output) and are paid wages for their labour. These wages make up each household's income. Each household then spends its income on the output produced by the firms. This process is illustrated in Figure 1.

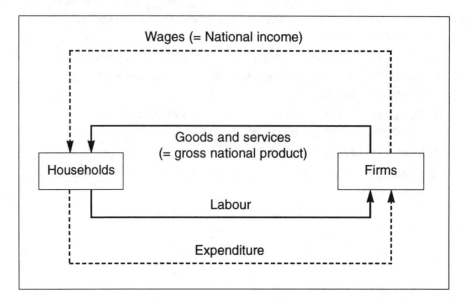

Figure 1: The circular flow of income.

Figure 1 shows our firms and households. The bold lines show the physical flows of labour and goods and services between firms and households. Each household provides labour services to the firms and the firms use this labour in the production of goods and services which are sold to the households. The dotted lines show the money flows between firms and households. The firms pay wages to households and households spend their wages (income) on the goods produced by the firm.

Let us assume that households spend all of their income on the goods produced by the firms. In other words, they do not save any of their income. We also assume that firms sell all of their goods so that no stocks are left unsold. Now, if households spend all their income on the goods produced then the total of all household incomes is equal to total expenditure in the economy. Furthermore if all goods are sold, then total expenditure must equal the value of goods produced.

Therefore in our simple economy we can see that:

Total income is equal to total expenditure and equal to total output.

We have made certain assumptions here which you may find unrealistic but in Section 2 we will relax these assumptions and you will see that this does not change our analysis.

We have established that, in a simple model of the economy, income equals expenditure equals output. If we accept this, we can measure either total income, total expenditure or total output in order to calculate **national income**. The national income accounts are a record of all of the calculations involved in such measurements.

Try the following activity.

ACTIVITY 1

Study Figure 1 and the text and decide which of the following statements is True and which is False.

1 The model assumes that all wages are spent on goods and services.

2 All the money earned by a firm goes to the employees.

3 Firms do not sell goods to overseas markets.

4 Firms are unable to sell all of the goods and services they produce.

---

1   True. In this model, all household income, that is, wages, is spent on goods and services. If you thought this statement was false, you may have thought that some money might be saved, or taken in taxes. Remember that in this model we begin by assuming that there are no savings or taxes. You might also have thought that some money went on entertainment, or holidays perhaps, well that counts as payment for a service.

2   True. All of the money earned by firms from selling goods and services is paid to the households as wages. Once again, you may have thought this statement was false, perhaps because you thought that the firm might use some of it's earnings on investment or research. In our simple model, we begin by assuming that no investment takes place.

3   True. We begin by assuming that our economy is isolated from other economies. No goods are sold to overseas markets.

4   False. We begin by assuming that firms do not have any stocks that they are unable to sell. All of the goods and services that they produce are sold.

1.1 National income accounts

National income accounts are prepared to assist in the assessment of a nation's economic performance. These accounts add together all financial transactions relating to goods and services within a specified period of time, usually one year. The accounts are published in both annual and quarterly format by the government central statistical office.

National income is the most common measure of the economic progress of a country. It gives an indication of what the country can afford in terms of things such as health spending which undoubtedly increase welfare. It also allows comparisons to be made between countries.

Naturally the flow of goods and services is extremely diverse. There are literally thousands of different goods in the economy. Examples are haircuts, fridges, books and maps. The only way to try to measure national income is by aggregating all of these goods by **monetary value**. This means multiplying the quantity of goods and services produced by the average price of those goods and services, which gives a measure called the **nominal national income**.

Increases in nominal national income may arise from an increase in the quantity of goods and services produced, an increase in the average price level of those goods and services, or some combination of both. Nominal national income, may therefore, be a poor indicator of the economic progress of an economy if an increase arises solely as a result of an increase in the average price level of goods and services.

Therefore, in order to determine how well the nation has progressed it is important to measure the **physical increase** in output of goods and services from one year to the next. The national income accounts therefore attempt to measure the actual or real volume of goods and services produced as well as the monetary value of goods and services produced.

The actual or real volume of goods and services produced is known as **real national income** and comparisons of real national income from one year to the next enable economists to measure accurately the economic progress of a nation in that period.

ACTIVITY 2

Which one of the following statements is correct?

The measure of nominal national income is:

1 the physical increase in output of goods and services.

2 the sum of all the wages and salaries paid to all workers.

3 the physical volume of all goods and services produced.

---

1   This is not correct. The nominal national income for a given year is NOT the increase in production over a given period, but the monetary value of production during that period. Choose another answer.

2   Yes, this is correct. The measure of nominal national income is the sum of all wages and salaries paid to workers. Remember that we defined national income as the value of all goods and services produced.

In our circular flow of income household, income is simply wages and salaries received as result of labour provided to firms. Now recall that households spend all of their income on the goods and services produced by firms. We also assumed that firms sold all goods and services produced. Therefore the total of all household incomes (wages and salaries) must equal the value of goods and services produced.

3   No, this is incorrect. The physical volume of goods and services produced is measured by real national income. Choose another answer.

1.2 Measurement of national income

We can define national income formally as the money value of finished goods and services produced within an economy during a given period of time, usually a quarter or a year. National income can be measured in three ways; each way should yield an identical value, although in practice, errors do occur. The three methods are the **output** method which adds together all of the 'value added' output of each sector of the economy within a given period; the expenditure method which adds together all the different categories of **expenditure** in an economy within a given period; or the **income** method which adds the total of all incomes from the production of goods and services in the economy.

Before examining each method in detail, we need to distinguish two types of valuation which are due to the fact that in the real world the price paid for goods by a consumer may be affected by taxes such as VAT or excise duties or subsidies paid to producers, and will therefore be different from the price received by the producer. The price received by the producer is a reflection of the cost of producing those goods. This is known as **factor cost**. Taxes such as these imposed on final expenditure will increase the price of products above the incomes paid to workers and suppliers of raw materials used in the production of those products. Subsidies will lower the price of products to below factor cost. The price paid by the consumer is the **market price**. Traditionally when we use the expenditure method, valuation is at market price; when we use the output or expenditure method, valuation is typically at factor cost.

We can write the relationship between the two types of valuation as:

Valuation at market prices = Valuation at factor cost + Taxes − Subsidies.

ACTIVITY 3

1   National income, valued at market prices, is £870,000. If total taxes are equal to £120,000 and total subsidies are equal to £95,000 then calculate national income at factor cost.

2   National income, valued at factor cost is £670,000 and national income valued at market prices is £790,000. Total taxes are equal to £165,000. Calculate total subsidies.

1   In order to answer this question you need to remember that:

Valuation at market prices = Valuation at factor cost + Taxes – Subsidies

The best way to proceed is to substitute the numbers you are given in the question. We need to calculate valuation at factor cost, say x, then substituting, we have.

$870,000 = x + 120,000 - 95,000$

$870,000 = x + 25,000$

$x = £845,000.$

Therefore national income valued at factor cost is £845,000

2   Once again remember that:

Valuation at market prices = Valuation at factor cost + Taxes – Subsidies

Therefore substituting in the same way,

$790,000 = 670,000 + 165,000 - y$

Where y represents total subsidies,

so, $790,000 = 835,000 - y$

and therefore, $y = £45,000.$

Total subsidies are equal to £45,000.

EXPENDITURE METHOD

National income can be measured by the sum total of all expenditure taking place in an economy within a given time period. By convention, total expenditure is classified into a number of categories:

- consumer expenditure
- general government final consumption
- investment expenditure
- net exports of goods and services abroad.

Consumer expenditure includes all consumer expenditure on goods and services produced in the domestic economy such as cars, fridges and haircuts. This does not include expenditure on house purchases which feature in a different category.

General government final consumption includes all expenditure by central and local government on goods and services. This also includes wages and salaries of government employees. It does not include income in the form of pensions, unemployment benefits or grants; these are known as **transfer payments**. This income is transferred from one section of the community to another and does not represent an increase in national income. For example, one person is paid wages each week. He or she will pay a proportion of this to the government in the form of income tax. The government will then use some of that tax to pay unemployment benefit, for example, to another person. Income is transferred from one person to the other but there is no overall increase in total income.

Investment expenditure may consist of investment in fixed capital such as buildings and machinery, and also includes house purchases by consumers. This whole category is known as **gross domestic fixed capital formation**. Fixed capital investment may be investment in new capital such as a new factory or a new piece of machinery which add to the capital stock, or it may be replacement investment, that is, investment in capital which replaces worn out capital. A different type of investment is the money tied up or invested in finished goods. These are called stock. Money is also tied up in 'unfinished goods' or 'work in progress', and raw materials used in the production process. When we talk about investment in stock in a given year, we mean the increase in stock during the year. If we included total stocks then we would be 'doublecounting' because some of the stock would have been purchased in the previous year and would have been included in that year's accounts. You should notice that stocks may actually fall during the course of a year and hence investment in stocks and work in progress may be negative. The addition of these categories gives the value of **total domestic expenditure**.

Try the next activity :

ACTIVITY 4

Match the items in List A to the items in List B

List A	**List B**
1 Investment expenditure	a. Cars, fridges and haircuts
2 Consumer expenditure	b. Suit manufacturer buys more material
3 General government final consumption	c. Mr Jones buys a house
4 Transfer payments	d. A new road
5 Investment in raw materials	e. A student receives his grant

1	goes with c	House purchases are classified as investment expenditure.
2	goes with a	Cars, fridges and haircuts are, of course, consumption goods.
3	goes with d	New roads are financed by local authorities. Therefore this falls into the category of general government final consumption.
4	goes with e	The payment of a student grant is a classic example of a transfer payment. Some of the tax revenue raised by the government from one section of the community, for example, the working population, is redistributed to another section, that is, students in the form of a grant.
5	goes with b	The suit manufacturer is buying raw materials for use in the production of suits. This constitutes investment in raw materials.

You should have found this activity fairly straightforward. We have not finished our discussion of total expenditure yet. We have considered the components of total domestic expenditure but in calculating national income we need to include one other category.

Net exports of goods and services abroad: some of the goods and services produced in the domestic economy are sold abroad. However, this still represents expenditure on domestically produced goods and is therefore included in the calculation of national income. Of course, domestic consumers will also spend some of their income on imports from abroad which are not produced in this country. This expenditure must be excluded from our national income calculation. Therefore net exports of goods and services abroad is calculated as the total expenditure on exports minus total domestic expenditure on imports.

Net exports of goods and services = Total expenditure on exports –
Total domestic expenditure on imports

We now have all the components that we can add together to give the national income. In the national accounts, the term we use for national income is **Gross Domestic Product** [GDP]. Once we have calculated GDP we can then use it to calculate **Gross National Product** [GNP]. GNP is a slightly different measure of national income. GDP gives an indication of the level of economic activity in the domestic economy and is therefore a useful indicator of domestic output and employment trends. Nevertheless national income can be affected by profits paid to, or received from, abroad and it is useful to define a measure that includes these types of receipts and payments. GNP is the measure that we use.

In order to get GNP, we have to calculate **net property income from abroad**. There will be firms in the domestic economy who have plants and factories abroad and this will generate a flow of income in the form of profit. Income will be coming into the country. On the other hand, there will be foreign firms who have plants and factories in the domestic economy that generate profit. This means income is leaving the country. The sum total of income coming into the economy less that going out from these sources is known as net property income from abroad. This total is then added to GDP in order to arrive at GNP.

Gross National Product = Gross Domestic Product + Net Property Income From Abroad

The 1988 figures for the UK are given in Table 1.

	£ Million
Consumer expenditure	293,569
General government final consumption	91,487
Gross domestic fixed capital formation	88,751
Value of physical increase in stocks and work in progress	4,371
Total domestic expenditure	478,538
Net exports of goods and services	83,339
Statistical discrepancy	2,056
Gross Domestic Product at Market Prices	**463,933**
Net property income from abroad	5,619
Gross National Product at Market Prices	**469,552**

Table 1

Source: CSO Blue Book, 1988

Note that a statistical discrepancy arises in Table 1. The data are collected from a very wide range of sources and discrepancies inevitably arise in the complex process of accounting for the whole economy.

ACTIVITY 5

You are given the following information concerning an economy.

Consumer expenditure	£200,000
General government final consumption	£85,000
Gross domestic fixed capital formation	£23,000
Value of physical increase in stocks and work in progress	£15,560
Total domestic expenditure on imports	£32,400
Total expenditure on exports	£52,900
Net property income from abroad	£7,500

All figures are expressed in market prices.

Calculate:

1 Total domestic expenditure.

2 Net exports of goods and services.

3 Gross domestic product.

4 Gross national product.

5 Gross national product at factor cost if total taxes in the economy are £132,000 and total subsidies are £53,000.

6 Proportion of GDP contributed by consumer expenditure.

7 Proportion of GDP contributed by general government final consumption.

---

1   Total domestic expenditure is the total expenditure by residents in the domestic economy on goods produced in the domestic economy. To answer this question, you must add consumer expenditure, general government final consumption, gross domestic fixed capital formation and the value of physical increases in stocks and work in progress. This is £200,000 + £85,000 + £23,000 + £15,560 = £323,560.

2   Net exports of goods and services is total expenditure on exports minus total domestic expenditure on imports. This is £52,900 – £32,400 = £20,500.

3   GDP is the total domestic expenditure plus the total for net exports of goods and services. In other words, simply add your answers from a and b. This is £323,560 + £20,500 = £344,060.

4   GNP is GDP plus net property income from abroad. This is £344,060 + £7,500 = £351,560.

5   The answer to d gives you a valuation at market prices. In order to value at factor cost, we must 'take out' taxes and 'add back' subsidies. GNP at factor cost is £351,560 – £132,000 + £53,000 = £272,560.

6   You have already calculated GDP as £344,060. Now we know that consumer expenditure is equal to £200,000. Therefore the proportion contributed by consumption to GDP is: 200,000/344,060 = 0.58.

7   GDP is £344,060 and general government final consumption totals £85,000 therefore the proportion contributed by general government final consumption to GDP is 85,000/344,060 = 0.25.

Well done if you got all these correct. If not, don't worry. Go back to the text and re-read anything you were unsure about. Also look again at Table 1 and see how the questions in the exercise tie in with these figures for the UK in 1988.

INCOME METHOD

A second method of calculating national income is to add together all incomes from the production of goods and services in the economy. This will also include various categories:

- personal income
- gross trading profits of companies
- gross trading profits of public corporations and general government enterprises
- rent
- adjustment for stock appreciation.

Personal income includes income received in the form of wages and salaries from employment or self-employment. This does not include income in the form of pensions, unemployment benefits or grants. As we have seen these are called transfer payments and this is simply income that is transferred from one section of the community to another and does not represent an increase in national income.

Gross trading profits of companies includes total profits of all non-government companies, that is, all privately owned firms. This profit may be distributed to shareholders and some may be paid out as interest to those who have lent money to the company.

Gross trading profits of public corporations and general government enterprises includes all profits of all companies owned by central government and local authorities. Examples of this type of business included British Rail and British Coal before their privatisation.

Rent includes firms that make most of their profit from the letting out of land or buildings. This figure also includes the profits of 'owner occupiers' that is, property or land used by firms who own that land or property. Obviously these firms do not pay rent to themselves and therefore an estimated or 'imputed' amount is calculated as what they would pay if their land or buildings were let to them. Similarly, this figure also includes property that is government owned and is occupied by government departments. This is known as an imputed charge for consumption of non-trading capital.

Finally, the figures also include an **adjustment for stock appreciation**. When stock prices rise then the value of all stock rises but this has no connection with changes in total output and must therefore be deducted from national income figures.

The 1988 figures for the UK are given in Table 2.

	£ Million
Income from employment	249,775
Income from self-employment	42,617
Gross trading profits of companies	70,242
Gross trading profits of public corporations	7,286
Gross trading profits of general government enterprises	−70
Rent	27,464
Imputed charge for consumption of non-trading capital	3,408
Less: Stock appreciation	− 6,116
Gross Domestic Product	394,606
Statistical discrepancy	181
Gross Domestic Product at Factor Cost	**394,787**
Net property income from abroad	5,619
Gross National Product at Factor Cost	**400,406**

Table 2
Source: CSO Blue Book, 1988

ACTIVITY 6

You are given the following data for an economy.

Income from employment	£100,000
Income from self-employment	£45,000
Gross trading profits of companies	£65,000
Gross trading profits of public corporations	£42,000
Gross trading profits of general government enterprises	£100
Rent	£13,950
Imputed charge for consumption of non-trading capital	£1,000
Stock appreciation	£2,500
Net property income from abroad	£1,000

All figures are expressed at factor cost

Calculate:

1   GDP.

2   GNP.

3   GNP at market prices if taxes in the economy are £34,670 and subsidies are £11,230.

1   To get GDP simply add together all of the figures except net property income from abroad, but remember that stock appreciation must be deducted from your total. This gives you a total of £264,550.

2   GNP is simply GDP, your answer to a, plus net property income from abroad. This is £264,550 + £1,000 = £265,550.

3   To get from factor cost to market price we need to deduct subsidies and add taxes. This gives us a total of £265,550 − £11,230 + £34,670 = £288,990.

Hopefully you had few problems with this activity!

OUTPUT METHOD

National income can also be measured by adding together the total output of all consumer goods and services and investment goods produced by all firms in the domestic economy during the course of the year. However, it is important that you notice that some firms produce goods which are then used in the production of other goods. Consider a firm that makes buttons. Some of these may be sold to suit manufacturers in the production of suits. If we measured the total value of all output produced by suit manufacturers and button manufacturers then we will be doublecounting as buttons will be valued twice, once as buttons and then again as part of a suit. Therefore to avoid this doublecounting, when we calculate the amount of output which contributes towards national income, we must only count the value of output added by each firm or industry in each stage of the production process. This 'value added' by an industry is the gross value of an industry's output less the cost of its inputs including purchases from other industries. We calculate the final output measure of national income by adding together the value added of all sectors of industry, commerce and the public sector.

The 1988 figures for the UK are given in Table 3.

	£ Million
Agriculture, Forestry and Fishing	5,625
Energy and Water Supply	21,485
Manufacturing	93,433
Construction	25,745
Distribution, Hotels and Catering	55,131
Transport and Communication	28,657
Banking, Finance, Insurance, Business Services	76,922
Ownership of Dwellings	21,407
Public Administration and Compulsory Social Security	27,023
Education and Health Services	35,237
Other services	25,785
Less: Adjustment for financial services	−22,204
Statistical discrepancy	181
Gross Domestic Product at Factor Cost	**394,787**
Net property income from abroad	5,619
Gross National Product at Factor Cost	**400,406**

Table 3

Source: CSO Blue Book, 1988

Note we have included an adjustment for financial services, that is banking, insurance or investment advice, for example. This represents transfers from one part of the industry to another, which is not an addition to national income.

ACTIVITY 7

You are given the following information about a simple economy. There are only three sectors in this economy and total output at factor cost for each is as follows.

Agriculture   £220,700

Transport   £136,250

Banking   £87,340

You are also told that GNP at factor cost is £523,650. Calculate:

1 GDP at factor cost.

2 net property income from abroad.

---

1   We know that GNP at factor cost is simply GDP plus net property income from abroad. If there are only three sectors then GDP is the sum of the totals for the three sectors. This is £220,700 + £136,250 + £87,340 = £444,290.

2   If GNP at factor cost is £523,650 then net property income from abroad is £523,650 − £444,290 which equals £79,360.

Nominal National Income and Real National Income

We have now examined the different ways of measuring national income. Before we leave this topic there is one final point to make about measuring it. National income has been defined as the money value of finished goods and services produced within an economy during a given period of time. The term used to describe this total is **nominal (or money) national income**.

There are therefore two ways that national income could increase in a given period:

● a rise in the physical quantity of goods produced by an economy.

● a rise in the average price level of all goods produced.

So if a nation produces exactly the same volume of goods from one year to the next but prices rise during that year, it may appear that national income has increased simply because the monetary value of national income has risen. This is one of the problems of calculating national income using **current prices**. So far, all the figures we have looked at are in current prices. Whenever we have calculated GDP or GNP whether at factor cost or market prices, we have calculated nominal or money figures. Another way of calculating national income is to revalue output at the price level for a specific year. The UK accounts use the year 1985. Therefore, we see how real production has changed. Not surprisingly, this measure of national income is known as **real national income**. Sometimes you may see this written in accounts as **national income at constant prices**.

To illustrate this, consider a simple example. A country produced 1,000 units of output in 1989 at £20 per unit. Therefore nominal or money national income is £20,000. If in the next year 1990, the country then produced the equivalent 1,000 units again but prices had risen to £40 per unit, then national income appears to have risen to £40,000. But this rise in national income is purely due to higher prices. The real national income for 1990 at constant 1989 prices would be unchanged at £20,000.

What happens if both output and prices double so that in 1990, 2,000 units are produced at £40 per unit? Nominal or money national income would be £80,000 but real national income at 1989 prices would be £40,000.

Generally then, we can usually learn more about the economic progress of a country by looking at real income measures rather than nominal or money measures. Both figures can be obtained from the national accounts in the UK.

ACTIVITY 8

In 1990, an economy produces 1,400 units of output at a price of £27 per unit.

1 Calculate money national income for 1990.

In 1991, the same economy produces 1,500 units at £32 per unit.

2 Calculate money national income for 1991.

3 Calculate real national income for 1991 at 1990 prices.

In 1992, the same economy produces 1,450 units at £34 per unit.

4 Calculate money national income for 1992.

5 Calculate real national income for 1992 at 1990 prices.

---

1 Money national income is total output multiplied by the price level. This is 1,400 multiplied by £27 which equals £37,800.

2 Money national income for 1991 is total output multiplied by the price level. This is 1,500 multiplied by £32 which equals £48,000.

3   Real national income at 1990 prices is the output produced in 1991 multiplied by the price level in 1990. This is 1,500 multiplied by £27 which equals £40,500.

4   Money national income for 1992 is total output multiplied by the price level. This is 1,450 multiplied by £34 which equals £49,300.

5   Real national income at 1990 prices is the output produced in 1992 multiplied by the price level in 1990. This is 1,450 multiplied by £27 which equals £39,150.

Hopefully you found this exercise fairly straightforward!

1.3 National income statistics and economic welfare

The concept of welfare concerns the well-being of society. It not only concerns other issues like levels of income and wealth but also health, working hours and law and order.

Most of us would agree that economic progress, measured by an increase in national income, is good for a country. Higher levels of national income suggest that an economy is producing more goods and becoming better off. However, economic welfare is not only determined by the output of goods and services, it is also affected by factors such as job satisfaction, quality of life, the state of the environment and also the distribution of income. None of these factors are measured in the national income statistics and so we cannot rely on them to tell us about the economic welfare of the citizens of a country.

Consider the quality of life. There is no doubt that if we all worked 100 hours per week then national income would rise, but would we be better off? Would the rise in national income be worth the hardship of working such long hours? The environment is also vital. If all our factories and industrial plants started to increase their production, national income would increase but pollution may also increase. This might affect the health of people living near to those plants. Would we be better off in this case? Some certainly would not be. The environment is important and we cannot assume that higher levels of national income compensate us for damage done by pollution.

The question of standards of living and the distribution of income is often considered most important of all. A rough approximation of the standard of living, called **per capita income**, is the average amount of national income received by each person, that is, the national income divided by the population figure. However, this is only an average figure and great inequalities can exist. For example, some company directors might receive an income of £1 million per year, while some pensioners receive less than £3,000. Again, because of inequalities, a rise in national income might benefit a small proportion of the population while the remainder were worse off. It is of little use to most of the citizens of a country if a rise in national income does not benefit them. So the per capita income only roughly approximates how well off people are.

A final problem may arise when national income statistics for different countries are used in order to make comparisons between those countries, on economic growth, for example. Different countries have different ways of measuring national income and use different methods of data collection. Because of this, the output of certain goods and services may go unmeasured in some countries. One example of this is non-marketed items. For example, if you employ a builder to extend your house then this will be recorded in the national income statistics. However, if you build the extension yourself then this will go unrecorded. The exclusion of this activity from the statistics means that the true level of production in the economy will be understated. Some countries may try to account for these non-market activities while others will not, so that figures are strictly comparable.

Furthermore, different countries may have different levels of 'underground' economic activity. The underground economy, sometimes referred to as the Black Economy, consists of illegal and undeclared transactions. For example, unemployed people who do small part-time jobs may not declare the income earned from these jobs because they will receive less unemployment benefit. If the income is undeclared then the activity is unrecorded. If there is a large underground economy in say, Italy, then the national income statistics of that country may seriously underestimate the true level of economic activity. As a result we cannot be sure that we are comparing like with like when we discuss the different growth rates in different countries.

In spite of these limitations, real national income remains the most common measure of the economic progress of a country. Recall that it does gives us an indication of what the country can afford in terms of items such as defence or health spending which contribute to the welfare of the economy and its citizens.

'GNP is far from being a perfect measure of economic welfare. Nor would it be possible to establish a measure of economic welfare that avoided the problems of making basic value judgments upon which everybody could agree. But it does provide a total measure up to a point, in a meaningful way, of very many of the items that do contribute to welfare and without which most people would consider themselves worse off.' Beckerman (1978) p. 60

REVIEW ACTIVITY 1

1 Define national income and briefly explain the three methods of calculating national income.

2 What are the two terms used in the national accounts to describe national income?

3 What is the difference between valuation at factor cost and valuation at market prices?

4 Why is real national income a better measure of a country's economic progress than nominal or money national income?

5 You are given the following information about an economy in the year 1990. There are four sectors in the economy and the output of each at factor cost is as follows:

Agriculture   £134,890

Forestry and Fishing £111,230

Construction   £45,875

Banking   £21,150

You are also told that net property income from abroad is £30,000 and that taxes in the economy are £18,000 and subsidies are £14,500. In 1991, net property income from abroad is zero and there is no change in the level of output produced but all market prices rise by 15%.

Calculate:

a   Nominal or money gross domestic product and gross national product at factor cost for this economy in 1990.

b   Nominal or money gross domestic product and gross national product at market prices for this economy in 1990.

c   Nominal or money gross domestic product and gross national product for 1991. Use valuation at market prices. You may need a calculator to answer this question.

d   Real gross domestic product and real gross national product in 1991 at 1990 prices. Again use valuation at market prices.

6 Explain using a simple example how the level of output in an economy can fall from one year to the next but nominal or money national income can actually rise.

7 Briefly outline why national income figures may not be an especially good indicator of the level of welfare in a country.

These questions broadly cover the whole section. You may have made one or two errors but don't worry. Just go back to the text to check where you went wrong. Well done if you made no mistakes.

Summary

We have learned how to define national income and we have looked at ways it is measured in the UK. Three methods are used: output, income and expenditure. You have also learnt to calculate and differentiate between GDP and GNP as measures of a country's economy. We also considered ways of interpreting national income statistics as a measure of economic welfare.

Section Two

National Income Determination and the Circular Flow of Income

Introduction

You briefly met the simple model of the circular flow of income as a view of national income determination in Section 1. Here we will look more closely at this model and two different phenomena which influence national income: **injections** and **withdrawals**.

2.1 Circular flow of income

Perhaps the best place to start in explaining exactly how national income is determined is the circular flow of income, a very simple model of an economy which you met earlier. In its simplest form, the circular flow of income assumes that, in the economy, there are just two sectors. You will recall that these are households and firms. There is no government and no overseas sector. People in the households work for the firms in the production of goods. For this service they receive wages. Households then buy those goods from the firms. In doing so they spend all the income they received in the form of wages. All the goods produced by the firms are purchased. In other words, there is no unsold stock. Finally the money received from the households is income to the firm which is then used in production of more goods and again paid out as labour to the workers. The whole process then continues. To illustrate the circular flow of income recall Figure 1.

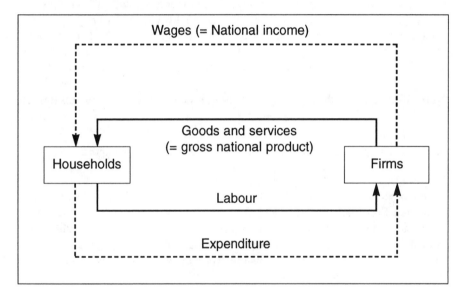

Figure 1: The circular flow of income.

The bold lines represent the flow of labour from households to firms and the flow of goods from firms to households. The broken lines represent the money flows, that is, wages paid by firms to households and expenditure by households on the output of the firms.

Because of our assumption that households spend all of their income and because firms sell all of the goods that they produce, then total income is equal to total expenditure and equal to total output.

We can write this formally as:

$Y = E = O$

where Y = income, E = expenditure and O = output.

In Section 1, we examined ways of measuring national income. We saw that there were three methods: the expenditure method, the output method and the income method. All of these methods gave us the same figure for national income (except for the statistical discrepancies!). National income will always equal national output which will always equal national expenditure. This is true for the simple circular flow of income and the whole economy. In fact, this is known as the **national income identity**. Remember, whenever we talk about the circular flow of income we are just discussing a very simple model of the economy.

WITHDRAWALS

Of course, the circular flow of income is only a model. We know that people do not spend all of their income, they save some. The simple model also ignores the fact that a government exists and some of the worker's income is paid to the government as taxation in order to help finance expenditure on defence and roadbuilding etc. Finally, there is also an overseas sector and households will not just buy from firms in the circular flow, they will also buy foreign goods or imports. So there are three factors which mean that money will be 'taken out' of the circular flow of income. These are saving, taxation and imports. Collectively they are known as withdrawals.

Total withdrawals in the economy are therefore savings plus taxation plus imports or

$W = S + T + M$

where W = total withdrawals, S = savings, T = taxation and M = imports.

INJECTIONS

While income will be taken out of the circular flow there will also be additions to the circular flow that arise outside it. We introduced a government into the model. Governments do not just tax people, they also spend. They finance roadbuilding and national defence, for example. In order to build roads, they employ workers and pay them incomes. So households gain income from the government which is outside our simple circular flow of income.

You will notice that we have introduced an overseas sector. An economy will not only buy goods from overseas, it will also sell goods to overseas markets. These are called exports and whenever a country exports goods then income comes into the circular flow from overseas.

Finally, firms do not only produce goods for households to consume. They also buy machinery and other types of capital which they will use in production. This is known as investment and investment will also bring money into the circular flow. Firms outside the circular flow will produce investment goods and will use workers from the households. Naturally they will pay them a wage for their labour and therefore households gain money from outside the circular flow.

Now we have three factors that 'inject' money into the circular flow. These are government expenditure, exports and investment. Collectively they are known as injections.

Total injections in the economy are therefore government expenditure plus investment plus exports or:

$$J = G + I + X$$

where J = total injections, G = government expenditure, I = investment and X = exports.

The interaction between injections and withdrawals will ultimately determine national income. We now introduce these injections and withdrawals into the circular flow in Figure 2.

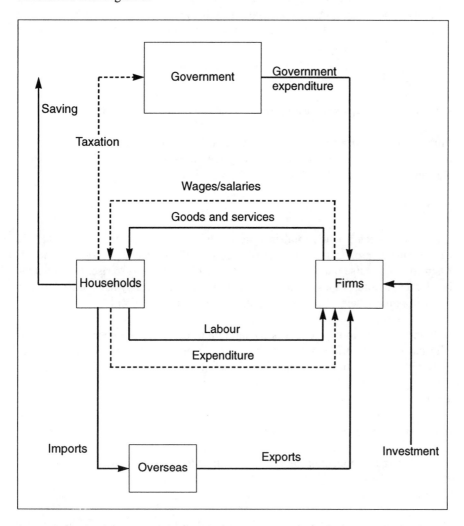

Figure 2: Circular flow of income with withdrawals and injections.

You should spend a few minutes looking through Figure 2 and the cash flows in order to make sure you fully understand injections and withdrawals into the circular flow of income.

2.2 Equilibrium national income

Equilibrium is a concept you have already looked at in your microeconomics studies. Equilibrium is a **state of rest**, where there is no reason for anything to change unless disturbed by an outside shock. When we have equilibrium in national income this means that national income will not change unless there is a sudden change in injections or withdrawals.

Obviously, in any economy, injections and withdrawals will occur simultaneously so that income will be entering and leaving the system. Equilibrium will occur when total injections equal total withdrawals. Any income received by households will be consumed or saved whilst a portion of that income will be paid to the government in taxation. Therefore we can write:

$$Y = C + S + T$$

where Y = income, C = consumption, S = savings and T = taxation.

Furthermore total expenditure in the economy is made up of consumption, investment, government expenditure and net exports (exports less imports) so that we can write:

$$E = C + I + G + X - M$$

Equilibrium occurs when total income (Y) is equal to total expenditure (E). If expenditure is greater than income then firms will be unable to satisfy demand. Therefore they raise output so that national income will start to rise. On the other hand, if expenditure is less than output then firms will find they have unsold stocks and will reduce their output so that national income starts to fall.

In both cases, national income is changing and therefore the economy is not in equilibrium. Equilibrium will occur when no tendency exists for income to change. This will occur when total expenditure is equal to total income. This is when:

$$Y = E$$

or, $C + S + T = C + I + G + X - M$

If we now deduct consumption (C) from both sides of this equation we can write:

$$S + T = I + G + X - M$$

Notice that we now have an expression in terms of injections and withdrawals. If we rearrange the equation slightly so that we write it with all injections on one side of the equation and all withdrawals on the other then we have:

$$S + T + M = I + G + X$$

Thus in equilibrium it must be the case that total injections are equal to total withdrawals.

National income will, of course, change over time and we can use the circular flow of income to explain how such changes come about. Firstly, consider a situation where we have equilibrium national income. In other words, national income is stable at a given level and will not change unless there is a 'disturbance'. For example, let total injections into the economy start to rise so that total injections are greater than total withdrawals. This increase in injections may arise for example because the government decides to spend more on roadbuilding. As injections are greater than withdrawals then more income will be coming into the circular flow than is leaking out so that total income in the circular flow will start to rise. As national income is rising then it is no longer stable and therefore the economy is no longer at a point of equilibrium. Eventually equilibrium will be restored at a higher level than previously.

Now consider the opposite case. People may decide to save more of their income, or alternatively, the government may decide to tax more so that total withdrawals are greater than total injections. In this case, more income will be leaking out of the circular flow than will be coming into it so that total income will start to fall. Again, this is not an equilibrium as national income is no longer stable. Eventually equilibrium will be restored at a lower level than previously.

It should be clear to you that equilibrium national income cannot occur when injections are not equal to withdrawals. Therefore once again we have our condition for equilibrium, that is, *national income is in equilibrium when total injections are equal to total withdrawals.*

National Income Equilibrium $W = J$

or alternatively $S + T + M = G + I + X.$

It is important that you understand this concept of **equilibrium national income**. It is also important that you are aware that it is only when injections equal withdrawals that we have equilibrium. We have mentioned the process where national income may be rising (when injections are greater than withdrawals) or where it may be falling (when withdrawals are greater than injections). This process is quite complex in practice and it is something we will return to in Unit 7.

ACTIVITY 9

Assume national income is in equilibrium. Which of the following would cause a change in the level of national income? State in each case exactly what is happening in terms of injections and withdrawals:

● an increase in the level of savings

● a decrease in the amount of goods sold to overseas markets.

An increase in the level of savings represents an increase in withdrawals from the economy. If there are no other changes then this would cause national income to fall.

A decrease in the quantity of goods sold to the overseas market would represent a fall in injections. If everything else remained constant, injections would now be less than withdrawals and so national income would fall.

This question should help you to understand how changes in injections and withdrawals lead to changes in national income. You should notice that we can only be absolutely sure of the effect of a rise in savings or a fall in exports if we assume that this does not cause a change in other injections or withdrawals. For example, we said that a fall in exports will cause a fall in the level of national income. However, if a firm realises it is exporting less it may immediately invest more to improve its product in an attempt to sell more abroad. Consequently the fall in injections (a drop in exports) prompts a rise in injections (a rise in investment) which may mean that national income will not fall. In each case when discussing a change in injections or withdrawals we assume that other things remain constant. This is known as the *ceteris paribus* assumption in economics and is something you will be familiar with from the microeconomics units.

ACTIVITY 10

National income is at a point of equilibrium when the following changes occur simultaneously:

More domestic goods are sold to the overseas market.

In money terms, the increase is £1250.

The government lowers taxation.

This raises total household income by £840.

Firms also decide to invest in more capital.

The increase in investment is £540.

Households decide to buy more foreign goods.

The increase in imports is £860.

Households also save more of their income.

Total savings rise by £350

After these changes, will national income rise or fall?

National income will be changing when injections and withdrawals are not equal. The best way to approach this question is to work out changes in total injections and withdrawals:

Injections:

>   Increased exports £1250
>
>   Lower taxes £840
>
>   Increased investment £540
>
>   *Change in total injections = £2630*

Withdrawals:

>   Increased imports £860
>
>   Increased savings £350
>
>   *Change in total withdrawals = £1210*

Clearly injections increase far more than withdrawals and so national income will be rising.

THE GOVERNMENT AND THE CIRCULAR FLOW

We have now looked at the circular flow of income which is the starting point for our studies of macroeconomic theory. The circular flow of income is a simplified model of the whole economy and provides a useful framework for our studies in the next units. Changes in injections or withdrawals can affect national income as we have seen. In the real economy, a change in investment can have far-reaching effects. An increase in taxation can also have a number of repercussions. You will know of some of these effects already.

Consider, for example what would happen if, *ceteris paribus*, the government increased taxation. Higher taxes means that households have less income available for spending or saving. In other words, an increase in taxation lowers household disposable income. We might therefore expect households to spend less because they have less income. They now buy less goods. In other words, demand will fall. Consequently firms have stocks of goods that they cannot sell. Now that demand has fallen, firms will not need to employ as many workers and so workers are sacked or made redundant. In other words, unemployment occurs. The process will not stop there. Households with unemployed workers have even less income and cut back on their spending which means firms may sell even less, and again start to sack workers. The whole process continues.

The point is that a change in injections or withdrawals can have far reaching effects. The taxation example is especially useful because it illustrates how government decisions can have a dramatic effect on the economy. Government decisions can, of course, benefit the economy. Continuing our example, if the government decides to embark on a motorway building programme it must hire workers to do this. The unemployed workers find jobs and receive wages. Household income rises and they buy more of the output produced by firms. Firms now start to hire more workers to meet this increased demand. Household income rises further and they buy more of the output of firms, once again, the whole process is repeated.

So the government, by taxing and spending in this way, can affect a number of outcomes. The level of national income can obviously be affected but so too can the levels of employment and unemployment, as can the profit levels of firms.

Finally, the government can use its tax and spending policy to **redistribute** income within the circular flow. The classic example of this is when those with higher incomes are taxed more than those with lower incomes. This tax revenue is then redistributed to people who do not work, in the form of unemployment benefits and pensions. In later units, we shall see that such transfers can have an important impact on the economy as well as being a vital aspect of government welfare policy.

We have taken this opportunity to examine ways in which the government can affect national income for two important reasons:

- the government may wish to use policies at its disposal, such as taxation and government spending, in order to achieve certain economic objectives such as full employment.

- a debate exists between economists about whether the government should intervene in the economy in order to achieve objectives like this. This debate also concerns what objectives, if any, the government should pursue and how best to achieve them.

It is to these two questions we will turn to in Section 3.

REVIEW ACTIVITY 2

1 Without looking at the figures in this section, draw the circular flow of income for an economy with no government or overseas sector. Carefully label the flows between households and firms. When you have done this, add the flows of injections and withdrawals from the government and overseas sector.

2 Explain the conditions under which national income will be in equilibrium. Give one example of how the government could raise national income to a higher equilibrium level.

3 Explain the difference between total income and disposable income for a household.

4 Explain why the national income of the overseas sector can affect the national income of the domestic economy.

5 National income is in equilibrium when you are given the following information about an economy:

Households decide to save less of their income and spend more. Total savings fall by £1100. Exports overseas rise by £300 but firms decide to cut investment spending by £440.

Will national income rise or fall?

6 Assume that all households save 20% of disposable income (after taxation). The tax rate is 25% and 15% of disposable income is spent on imports. If every worker in the economy is suddenly given a wage increase so that the total increase in income in the circular flow is £100,000, then, *ceteris paribus*, explain how injections and withdrawals change.

7 Is it possible that a reduction in taxation will not change national income?

These questions should have given you the chance to test your knowledge of this section. The material you have learnt will serve you well later in your studies, as it is an important foundation for much of the material that follows.

Summary

In this section, we introduced you to a simple model of national income determination. This is known as the circular flow of income. We looked closely at two different phenomena which influence national income: injections and withdrawals. These include various government and overseas factors and they affect whether national income rises or falls. You defined the concept of equilibrium national income.

SECTION THREE

Macroeconomic Issues and Controversies

Introduction

In the final section, we look at the major issues concerning the economy and we will consider the traditional objectives of government economic policy. You will also become familiar with the distinction between different types of economists, Keynesians and monetarists, and their areas of disagreement.

3.1 Macroeconomic issues

Though considerable debate exists amongst economists about the problems facing an economy, how best to deal with them and whether there is a role for the government, most economists would probably agree that the most important economic issues facing any economy today are:

- inflation
- unemployment
- economic growth
- balance of payments.

Table 3 shows the UK performance on each of these issues over the last fifteen years.

Year	Inflation(%)	Real GDP Growth (%)	Unemployment (%)	Current Account(£ m)
1980	18.0	−2.4	6.1	2,843
1981	11.9	−1.5	9.5	6,748
1982	8.6	2.0	11.0	4,649
1983	4.6	3.2	12.1	3,787
1984	4.9	2.4	12.6	1,832
1985	6.1	3.7	13.1	2,750

Year	Inflation(%)	Real GDP Growth (%)	Unemployment (%)	Current Account(£ m)
1986	3.0	3.3	11.9	−24
1987	3.7	4.1	10.8	−4,182
1988	4.9	3.8	8.3	−15,151
1989	7.7	1.8	5.7	−19,126
1990	9.5	0.4	5.8	−19,035
1991	5.9	−2.0	8.0	−8,176
1992	3.7	−0.5	9.7	−9,831
1993	1.6	2.3	10.3	−11,042
1994	2.5	3.9	9.3	−2,080
1995	3.4	2.3	8.2	−6,670

Table 3

Source: Economic Trends

INFLATION

Inflation can be defined as a process of persistently rising prices. When we hear that inflation is 10% for example, this does not mean that all prices are rising by 10% per annum. Inflation is a measure of average prices. In this case, on average, prices would be rising by 10% per annum.

In the UK, inflation is measured by changes in the **Retail Price Index** (RPI). This index measures the price of a representative 'basket of goods' that a typical individual would consume. Included in this 'basket' would be food, clothes, fuel, etc. As an example, the UK retail price index was 144.1 at the beginning of 1995 and 149.1 at the end of that year. Therefore the annual rate of inflation is calculated as: $100[(149.1 - 144.1)/144.1] = 3.4\%$ which you may notice from the table corresponds to the UK rate of inflation for 1995.

Notice that in our definition of inflation, we used the word 'persistently'. This is very important. If prices change 'once and for all', this is not inflation. The price change must be continual. Inflation means that there is a continual decline in the value of money which imposes a cost on society. Quite simply, if prices rise, then money will buy less. This cost of inflation will depend largely on whether the inflation is anticipated or unanticipated.

Anticipated and unanticipated inflation

Most people will be aware of any upward trend in prices. They will have some idea about the rate at which prices are rising. The average rate at which people believe that prices are rising is the **expected inflation rate**. If expectations of the inflation rate are correct then the actual inflation rate equals the expected inflation rate and inflation is said to be anticipated. **Anticipated inflation** is a rate of inflation which is correctly forecast by people. When inflation is anticipated then everyone knows what the rate of inflation is going to be in the future. In other words, the **actual rate of inflation equals the expected rate of inflation**. Therefore workers, for example, when bargaining for wage increases know exactly how much more pay is required to compensate them for increases in the cost of living. Hence, erosion of their living standards can often be avoided if inflation is anticipated.

However expectations are not always correct. If they are incorrect so that the actual rate of inflation exceeds the expected rate, then that part of inflation over and above the expected rate is said to be **unanticipated**. Most of the costs of inflation arise when inflation is unanticipated. In this case, price rises are a surprise to the public. Actual inflation does not equal expected inflation. In this case, workers may find that they have bargained for wage increases which do not compensate them for the higher costs of living. Living standards will fall.

Inflation can also be unfair. Weaker groups in society such as old people on fixed pensions cannot bargain for increases and often see their living standards fall. Inflation also causes further problems. Taxpayers often suffer. Most tax systems are progressive so that the rate of taxation increases as salaries increase. If workers bargain for higher wages to compensate them for higher prices, then they are not better off, they have just ensured that they are no worse off than previously. However the higher wages may take them into a higher tax 'bracket' so they are in fact worse off because they are paying proportionately more taxation!

Inflation can also lead to a misallocation of resources. As you have seen in your studies of microeconomics, economics is concerned with the efficient allocation of resources. If prices change rapidly in an unpredictable way it makes it more difficult to distinguish relative price changes which are the key to resource allocation in the market mechanism. Firms find it more difficult to make the correct economic decisions. For example, if the price of their output starts to rise do they take it as an indication that demand for the goods they produce is high and produce more, or do they just assume that inflation is the cause? Clearly inflation is a major problem in the economy.

Furthermore, as we saw earlier an economy exports goods and services which act as an important injection into that economy. If inflation occurs then the price of those exports will rise. It may be that those exports become uncompetitive. Foreign households will not buy domestic exports if they become too expensive. If exports decline as a result then workers producing those export goods become unemployed. Inflation can, therefore, cause unemployment.

Inflation may be **gradual** (or creeping) where prices rise slowly and persistently from year to year. Most European countries including the UK have experienced this type of inflation since World War II. In these cases, inflation rates will be low, perhaps 3 or 4%, although they can be higher. In the UK in 1975, inflation reached 24.2%; although rates even this high are rare in most parts of Europe.

A more sinister type of inflation is **hyperinflation**. In this case, price increases are extremely rapid. A European example of this phenomenon was the experience of Germany in the 1920s. Between 1922 and 1923, the inflation rate was approximately 10,200,000,000%! (Even this is modest compared with the experience of Hungary in the 1940s where inflation was one thousand billion times higher than Germany's experience.)

Later in this section, we will consider the debate between economists about the causes of inflation.

UNEMPLOYMENT

Unemployment is a measure of the number of people currently out of work who want to work. The number of unemployed in the UK in 1995 was approximately 2.4 million which represented 8.2% of the labour force. In the 1950s, unemployment in the UK averaged 1.2% of the workforce, in the 1960s it averaged 1.8%, in the 1970s it averaged 3.8%, and in the 1980s approximately 10%.

Economists identify different types of unemployment and we will look carefully at these later but here we define just two types:

- structural unemployment
- frictional unemployment.

Structural unemployment results from a long-term change in the structure of a country's industries. Over time, certain industries naturally decline as demand patterns change and technology progresses and this results in unemployment. Structural unemployment in recent years in the UK has occurred in the shipbuilding, textiles, coal and motorcycle industries. Certain regions such as the North east and North west have been particularly affected. Often workers unemployed as a result of structural changes do not have the skills to find work elsewhere. Alternatively, they may have the skills but there may be no suitable employment in the region where they live. The extent of structural unemployment will depend on how mobile workers are geographically and in terms of occupation. Those that can move to another area or can easily find another job because of their skills will tend to be unemployed for a shorter time than those who are unable to relocate or who have limited skills.

Frictional unemployment results from the fact that some people will always be 'between jobs'. Naturally people change their occupations at times during their working life. Often it takes time to move from one job to another so that there may be a short spell of temporary unemployment. This may be while they decide on the most suitable job or search out job opportunities.

The issue of unemployment is central to the debate between economists about the role of the government in the economy. We explore this issue in greater detail in this, and subsequent units.

ECONOMIC GROWTH

Economic growth is an increase in the real output of goods and services over a period of time, usually one year and in the UK it is measured by GDP and GNP. Economic growth is usually viewed as desirable for any country as it means that there are more goods and services for its residents to consume. High levels of growth tend to result in very low levels of unemployment which is obviously good for an economy and its inhabitants.

Growth tends to occur in cycles. High periods of growth are followed by low (or negative) periods of growth. Often economists use the terms 'boom' to describe a period of high growth and 'recession' to describe a period of low or negative growth. In the UK in 1995, the growth rate of GDP was 2.3%. The UK growth rate has always been cyclical with boom and recession following one another throughout the 1970s, 1980s and 1990s. In fact, the UK economic growth record since World War II has been rather poor compared with nations such as Japan and Germany.

Empirical research indicates that economic growth is influenced by a number of factors. Advances in technology or changes in the quantity or quality of factors of production used in producing goods will inevitably lead to increased growth. Naturally world trade conditions are also an important factor in determining growth. If all countries are experiencing high growth and levels of income then they will be consuming large quantities of goods including imports from other countries. There is a lot of potential for exporting in times of 'boom' which, as we have seen, is an important determinant of levels of income and hence economic growth. However to some extent, such studies have been unable to determine all factors contributing to economic growth and much of the variation in growth rates between different countries remains unexplained.

At this point we should note that increased noise, pollution and congestion as well as the depletion of natural resources are often undesirable side effects of economic growth.

There is considerable debate amongst economists about whether the government can act to improve a country's growth rate and how they should try to do so. We look at this debate in some detail later.

EXTERNAL BALANCE

In order to explain why external balance is important we need to begin with a brief explanation of the **balance of payments**.

Balance of payments

All economic transactions with the rest of the world are recorded in the balance of payments. External balance, often called **balance of payments equilibrium**, simply means that there is equality between imports and exports. You will study the balance of payments and the whole concept of international trade in more detail in Unit 10. However, here a brief description is sufficient.

The balance of payments is split into two accounts:

- the current account
- the capital account.

The current account records all international transactions and receipts in goods and services such as cars, bananas, televisions and insurance.

The capital account records all international flows of capital between the domestic economy and overseas whether they originate from the government or from firms or households in the economy.

An outward capital flow occurs when the residents of a country buy assets in a foreign country. Conversely, an inward capital flow occurs when residents of foreign countries buy domestic assets. **Net capital** flows are the difference between the two flows. If the net capital flow is positive, or in surplus, then the residents of the economy (including companies) are buying more foreign assets than are being bought by foreign residents.

The balance of payments is aptly named because it will always balance! When foreigners buy UK exports they will demand sterling in order to pay for those exports. Similarly, when UK residents demand foreign imports then the importers of these goods will require foreign currency to pay for them. To acquire this foreign currency they supply sterling. Therefore international transactions give rise to the demand for and the supply of sterling. The price of sterling in terms of foreign currency, that is, the **exchange rate** will move to ensure that the supply and demand for sterling are always equal so that the balance of payments balances. Note that this does not necessarily mean that the current account and the capital account will simultaneously balance but that any deficit on the current account (imports are greater than exports so that the supply of sterling is greater than the demand for sterling) will be offset by a surplus on the capital account (capital inflows exceed capital outflows so that the demand for sterling is greater than the supply of sterling).

We consider the external balance in more detail in Unit 10, here we briefly consider why it is important.

Importance of the external balance

In Section 2, we saw that imports are withdrawals from the domestic economy whilst exports are injections. *Ceteris paribus*, if exports exceed imports then national income will be growing. The domestic economy sells more goods and services than it buys. On the other hand, if imports exceed exports then, *ceteris paribus*, national income will be falling. Hence, it is often considered a problem if a country continually imports more than it exports. In technical jargon, this situation is termed a **current account deficit**. As we have seen, this deficit will be matched by a surplus on the capital account but this cannot go on forever. An economy cannot persistently buy more than it sells and live beyond its means. Eventually something must happen to correct persistent deficits.

In the UK, the external balance has always been a problem. For the year 1995 the current account was in deficit by £6,670 million. Many economists see these deficits as an explanation for the relatively poor economic performance of the UK over the last few decades. To understand this, consider how we might try to 'cure' an external deficit. To stop households buying imports we could raise taxes so that they have less disposable income. However less income means that they will consume less output in general including the output of domestic firms. Not only will households buy fewer imports but also fewer domestically produced goods. If domestic firms cannot sell all their output they may decide to use less labour. So unemployment will rise and national income will fall. So to cure the external deficit, we have had to reduce national income. This should illustrate to you how external deficits can act as a major constraint on economic growth.

Often higher levels of economic growth are associated with growing external deficits as higher levels of income means households buy more and more imports. We can suggest that external balance and high levels of economic growth are two things which rarely occur simultaneously.

ACTIVITY 11

1 Define inflation.

2 At the start of 1992 the RPI is 134, at the end of the year it is 141. Calculate the inflation rate for 1992.

3 Explain, in no more than 100 words, the difference between frictional and structural unemployment.

4 What does the balance of payments measure? What are the two accounts which make up the balance of payments?

5 Explain in a couple of sentences why rapid economic growth and balance of payments equilibrium might be incompatible.

---

1   Inflation is a process of persistently rising prices. If prices rise one year then never rise again this is not inflation but a once and for all rise in prices. Price rises must be persistent to be classed as inflation.

2   Inflation can be calculated as $[(141-134)/134] \times 100 = 5.22\%$.

3   Frictional unemployment refers to those workers who are between jobs. People change jobs over time and often it takes a while to find new work. Structural unemployment refers to those made unemployed as a result of changing patterns of demand or advances in technology. People made unemployed in this way are often unemployed for long periods because they lack the skills to find new jobs or they cannot move to areas where work is located.

4   The balance of payments records all economic transactions with the rest of the world. It is made up of two accounts: the current account, which records all

international transactions and receipts in goods and services; and the capital account which records all the flows of capital to and from abroad.

5   Often rapid economic growth will mean an increasing level of demand, some of which will come from abroad as imports. This increasing volume of imports will cause an external deficit. The government could try to cure the deficit by raising taxes but this would reduce income and lower economic growth.

3.2 Objectives of government economic policy

Now that we have identified the major economic issues facing an economy today, it is not too difficult to understand the objectives of government economic policy. Generally we assume that a government will try to achieve the following :

- a low and stable level of inflation
- a low rate of unemployment
- a satisfactory rate of economic growth
- an external balance (or balance of payments equilibrium).

To this list, often a fifth objective is added:

- an equitable distribution of income.

In order to achieve these objectives, a government has a number of measures it can take that fall into two groups:

- fiscal measures
- monetary measures.

Fiscal measures are the government's own financial operations, its income and expenditure, that is, taxation and spending. If it raises taxation, it withdraws money from the economy and the economy deflates, production falls, unemployment rises but inflation tends to stabilise. If it spends more by building roads or battleships then the economy inflates. Production rises, unemployment falls and inflation increases.

You will also have heard of 'fiscal policy'. Policy is a plan of action established to achieve certain objectives. Fiscal policy is the government's spending and taxation plans designed to achieve its objectives. It may be that the government believes that it should not use fiscal measures to attempt to control the economy in which case it would be said to follow a 'laissez-faire' (let them do what they want) fiscal policy.

Monetary measures for controlling the economy concern the control of the money supply. First, we will look closer at what is meant by money supply, then we can see what measures the government might take to control it and what kinds of policy it can follow.

Money is a medium of exchange which can take practically any form. Depending on the country you are in, money can be gold coins, cowry shells, blankets or decorated bits of paper (£10 notes). The physical medium of exchange — coins, cowries and notes — is called cash. If this cash is limited then the number of transactions that can occur is limited, the economy is deflated and prices are restrained. One way of controlling the economy would simply be to control the physical quantity of cash.

In a modern economy, cash is not the only or most important source of money: credit is. Governments can therefore control the money supply by controlling the creation of credit. It can do this in a number of ways. One way is to make it illegal for banks to lend money to customers for the purchase of cars. Another way is to raise the price of credit — **the interest rate**. These methods of controlling the cost and supply of money are called monetary measures.

Monetary policy is the plan the government has for controlling the economy by using monetary measures.

Later we look at how monetary and fiscal measures have traditionally been used by governments and we will also consider how economists view the use of these policies.

A LOW AND STABLE LEVEL OF INFLATION

We defined inflation as a process of persistently rising prices. Most governments now give a high priority to anti-inflation policies as a result of the marked increase in inflation experienced by the major industrial economies in the 1970s and 1980s compared to previous decades. Governments seek to minimise the rate of inflation because of the cost of persistently rising prices. As we have seen, inflation can lead to unemployment and resource misallocation and can be unfair.

A LOW RATE OF UNEMPLOYMENT

Unemployment imposes a burden on society. Not only is unemployment a waste of labour resources, it must be financed by the government. The government raises revenue for government expenditure from taxation. Some of this revenue will be spent on unemployment benefits. The higher the level of unemployment therefore the less revenue is available for expenditure on roadbuilding, education and health.

In order to reduce unemployment, a government might try to cut taxes or increase government expenditure to try to raise the level of national income. These measures achieve this objective by raising the level of demand in the economy. On the other hand, a government might try to improve job training schemes for unemployed workers or remove minimum wage legislation in order to improve the working of the labour markets.

A SATISFACTORY RATE OF ECONOMIC GROWTH

A government will want to achieve a satisfactory rate of economic growth in order to enhance the living standards of the country. It believes that higher growth tends to result in improved welfare. Furthermore higher rates of economic growth tend to result in lower levels of unemployment.

Economic growth is largely determined by the quality and quantity of the factors of production in an economy. Economic policy to raise growth rates can, again, operate at the macroeconomic or microeconomic level. At the macroeconomic level, economic growth may be stimulated by cutting taxes or raising government spending. This will raise the level of demand in the economy by raising incomes. Alternatively, at the microeconomic level governments might try to improve education, for example, in order to raise the quality of the nation's workforce.

EXTERNAL BALANCE (BALANCE OF PAYMENTS EQUILIBRIUM)

We noted earlier that an economy cannot persistently run a current account deficit because it will be living beyond its means. Any government will therefore want to try to ensure that the current account is not persistently in deficit. However, in practice, the government's ability to reduce deficits is limited. Generally, it may try one of three options, you will look at these in more detail in Unit 10. The first is to reduce the level of demand in the domestic economy to reduce the consumption of imports. This is known as **deflation**. However as we have seen deflation can cause other problems such as unemployment.

A second option is to try to limit the number of imports by imposing taxes on them to raise their price. An example of this is the use of **tariffs**. However, this may be unsatisfactory if it means consumers can no longer afford to consume foreign goods which may be of superior quality. Artificially raising import prices by such measures can lead to resource misallocation if consumers are forced to spend their income on lower quality goods simply because they are domestically produced.

A final option is to **devalue** the nation's currency. In other words, alter the exchange rate between the domestic currencies and the currencies of its trading partners. Consider the following simple example. The £1 is currently worth approximately $2. In other words, one pound sterling buys two US dollars on the foreign exchange markets. In order to buy an American television for $200, then a UK consumer must pay £100. In order to buy a UK video recorder for £150, an American consumer must pay $300.

Now what happens if the UK government decides to devalue the pound? This will mean that the pound will buy less dollars than previously. Assume the devaluation is such that £1 is now worth $1. In order to buy the American television, the UK consumer now needs £200. The price of American goods in the UK has gone up so that fewer will be purchased. In order to buy the UK video recorder, the American consumer needs £150. The price of UK goods in America has fallen.

So devaluation has made domestic goods relatively cheap compared to foreign goods. Devaluation therefore tends to encourage a switch in demand away from foreign goods towards domestic goods. This can often improve the current account balance.

You will look at the issues surrounding such policies in more detail in Unit 10.

AN EQUITABLE DISTRIBUTION OF INCOME

The government will always want to take into account the distributional effects of its policy. Income tax cuts may be used to increase demand and raise national income but they will increase the income gap between high and low income groups. The prime consideration here concerns what constitutes fairness or equity in terms of the distribution of income. High levels of economic growth may look impressive but it may be considered that all sections of the population should benefit from that growth.

POLICY PREFERENCES AND CONFLICTS OF OBJECTIVES

Governments and policymakers will naturally have their own opinions on which of these objectives are most important. It is extremely difficult, in practice, to achieve all of these objectives simultaneously. We have already seen that attempts to reduce a current account deficit can result in unemployment and reduced levels of economic growth. Perhaps the biggest conflict arises between inflation and unemployment. In times of low unemployment and high economic growth there is a higher level of income in the economy. There will be a lot of demand in the economy. Eventually there will come a point when firms can find no more labour to employ to help produce the goods to meet the high level of demand. To attract labour from other firms, or to encourage its current workers to work longer hours it will start to pay higher wages. These higher wages mean a firm's costs rise. In order to maintain profits, it will raise prices. Most firms in the economy will be faced with similar problems. Hence inflation results from low unemployment.

Governments could try to reduce the problem, perhaps by raising taxes, but this reduces demand and lowers income and can also lead to unemployment. Low inflation and low unemployment are very difficult to achieve at the same time. To confirm, you may like to look back at Table 3 to see that, broadly speaking, inflation falls when unemployment rises. When unemployment falls, inflation rises again!

If we accept that a government cannot achieve all the objectives at once then it is necessary for governments to prioritise. Decisions will depend on political beliefs, preferences and personal judgments. For most of the post war period, Conservative and Labour governments agreed on what the major objective should be.

'. . . the social democratic programme of all post war governments in Britain from the beginning of the fifties until 1979 was for. . . demand management to stabilize the economy and provide full employment.' Burton (1981)

However since the late 1970s, the main focus of economic policy has been on reducing the rate of inflation. Furthermore, there has also been a shift of thinking on the role of the government in the economy. Before 1979, the consensus was that the government should play an active role in attempting to influence the level of demand in the economy, using policies at its disposal. Generally, fiscal policy was seen as the most effective way of doing this, that is, the use of taxation and government spending to influence the level of demand in the economy. Since 1979, opinion has tended to favour a reduced role for the government in managing the economy. The popular belief is that it is not demand that needs manipulating, but the supply side of the economy which should be focused on. This means policies to improve the working of the labour market and to improve the quality of labour. Where macroeconomic policy is concerned, monetary policy, the use of interest rates, the money supply and the exchange rate, has generally become more in favour.

Next we turn to the economic debate between different types of economists about how the government should use economic policy to achieve its objectives.

ACTIVITY 12

1 List the five objectives of government economic policy.

2 Explain what is meant by:
   ● fiscal policy
   ● monetary policy.

---

1   The five objectives of government economic policy are: low and stable levels of inflation, low levels of unemployment, a satisfactory level of economic growth, external balance and an equitable distribution of income.

2   Fiscal policy is the government's spending and taxation plans designed to achieve its objectives. Monetary policy is the government's plan for controlling the economy by using monetary measures such as control of the money supply.

3.3 Macroeconomic debate

As you might suspect, there is a continuing debate amongst economists about how the economy functions and how active a role the government should play in attempting to influence it. In the broadest of terms, economists tend to fall into one of two categories: **Keynesians** and **monetarists**. Before we examine the differences between Keynesians and monetarists we will firstly look at the classical theory of economics.

CLASSICAL ECONOMICS
Classical economics developed in the eighteenth and nineteenth centuries. The most famous of all classical economists was David Ricardo (1772–1823). Classical economists believed that the government should take only a very small role in the economy. This was known as **laissez-faire**. They believed entirely in the power of the market. In other words, markets would move to equilibrium extremely quickly and there would never be an excess of supply or demand.

In your microeconomic studies, you saw that if demand was greater than supply at a given price then the price would rise. Alternatively, if demand was less than supply at a given price then price would fall. The classical economists believed that such processes occurred extremely quickly. In other words, they believed that markets would clear instantaneously and without need for government intervention.

Consider the labour market. You saw that if the price of labour is too high then there will be an excess supply of labour that is not employed at this wage. This is, of course, unemployment. The classical economists believed that this situation would not occur because the wage would fall immediately to ensure that the demand and supply for labour were equal. In other words, market forces act to remove any excess demand or supply in the market. This applies to the market for any good or service. There is no role for government intervention. Classical economists therefore predicted that the economy would always be at virtually full employment. There may be a small level of frictional unemployment as people changed jobs but nothing more.

As for inflation, the classical economists believed that the price level depended on the quantity of money in the economy. This was known as the **quantity theory of money**. In its purest form, the quantity theory of money says that increases in the supply of money lead to increases in the price level. For classical economists, the only role for the government was to ensure that the money supply was adequately controlled in order to prevent inflation occurring.

The classical economists also believed in the so-called 'classical dichotomy'. This stated that monetary and real forces were separate. What this meant was that the level of output and employment in the economy was determined solely by the forces of supply and demand whilst the level of inflation was determined by the money supply. Changes in the money supply would affect only prices, not output and employment levels. So a doubling of the money supply would lead to a doubling of all prices but this would not change the level of output and the level of employment.

Up until the end of the 1920s, the classical view of the economy seemed to be accurate. Unemployment tended to be extremely low. However, in the early 1930s the Great Depression affected the whole world. Levels of output slumped and unemployment reached record levels. In 1932 in the UK, approximately 22% of the labour force was out of work. The classical view of the economy, shared by the government at that time, was that unemployment could only be the result of wages being too high making an excess supply of labour. The government of the time believed that trade unions were preventing wages from falling. The dominance of classical thinking at the time was such that the government seemed powerless to do anything to reduce unemployment and raise national income.

The experience of the 1930s led one economist, John Maynard Keynes, to develop his own theory of the economy which attacked the very principles of classical economics.

KEYNESIAN ECONOMICS

Keynesian economics is the name given to the theories developed by John Maynard Keynes (1883–1946) in his classic book, *The General Theory of Employment,*

Interest and Money (1936). Keynes argued that the classical view that markets cleared rapidly was fundamentally wrong, particularly where the labour market was concerned. Keynes argued that while wages will rise rapidly when the demand for labour exceeded supply, they would be 'sticky' downwards. In other words, they would not fall when the supply of labour was greater than the demand for labour. He argued that workers would resist wage cuts so that unemployment would be a problem. Keynes argued that the government should take a major role in attempting to reduce this unemployment.

He argued that government should attempt to raise the level of demand in the economy by cutting taxation to stimulate spending, or by increasing government expenditure. Keynes favoured the use of fiscal policy to remove unemployment. He argued that without government intervention, unemployment would be persistent. Keynes felt that unemployment was a result of a 'demand deficiency' or insufficient demand. Keynes also felt that inflation was not likely to be a problem in times of high unemployment. Any inflation that would occur would only arise when full employment was reached. Inflation would occur if aggregate demand was higher than that level needed to generate full employment. In these cases, inflation would be caused by excess demand. Keynes called this **demand pull inflation**.

Keynes favoured the use of fiscal policy over monetary policy. He did not agree with the classical dichotomy which said that monetary policy could not affect output and employment. However he felt that monetary policy was a less powerful tool than fiscal policy for stimulating the economy.

The Great Depression had a lasting effect on the world economy and led to a decline in classical economic thinking. For the period from the end of World War II until the late 1970s, Keynesian economics reigned supreme. There was a broad consensus between all governments that the overriding objective of economic policy was to maintain full employment, or at least, as low a level of unemployment as was possible. In order to achieve this governments sought to influence the level of demand in the economy. This became known as 'demand management' or 'fine tuning' and fiscal policy, changes in taxation and government spending, was used to achieve this.

Throughout the 1950s and 1960s these policies were largely successful in keeping unemployment low. However, this demand management eventually ran into difficulty. In the UK, the chief problem was that periodically, because the economy was close to full employment, the external balance would fall heavily into deficit. The government would then have to reduce demand pressure by **deflating** the economy, that is, by reducing demand. So the economy entered a cycle of 'stop-go'. In other words, unemployment would be high so the government would increase spending and raise taxes. Unemployment would fall and the economy would be on a 'go' phase. Then gradually the current account would fall into deficit so that the government would have to raise taxes again and lower government spending. The economy entered a 'stop' phase. This pattern of 'stop-go' characterised the UK economy throughout the 1950s and 1960s.

However, far worse than this was the disturbing rise in inflation, coupled with a gradual rise in unemployment. This rise in both unemployment and inflation is known as **stagflation**. Demand management policies had, over time it seemed, become less effective in reducing unemployment and seemed powerless to do anything about the upward trend in prices.

Furthermore, the average growth rate of the UK economy throughout this period was appreciably below that of most other industrialised countries. Gradually, Keynesian economics came under attack from a group of economists who were deeply concerned about the economic performance of the UK and, most of all, the rising inflation level. These economists attacked the use of demand management to try to stimulate demand in the economy. They believed that inflation was the major problem facing the economy and that persistent demand management was responsible for rising prices. They also strongly favoured the use of monetary policy as a tool for stabilising inflation. These economists advocated so-called 'supply side' policies to remove unemployment by the abolition of minimum wages and the reduction of trade union power. Collectively, these economists are known as **monetarists**.

MONETARIST ECONOMICS

Monetarist economics, more commonly known as **monetarism**, is, in a sense, a return to the classical economic theory that was so predominant before the great depression. The most influential monetarist of all is the American Nobel prize winning economist Milton Friedman. Monetarists share with classical economists a belief in the quantity theory of money. You may recall that this states that changes in the money supply ultimately feed through into changes in prices. However such changes would not affect 'real' variables like the level of output or the level of employment.

Friedman undertook extensive research to prove that ultimately inflation followed increases in the money supply. The growth of inflation in the late 1960s and early 1970s in the UK was a result of neglecting to control the supply of money in the economy. This was because monetary policy had been largely ignored in the Keynesian era. In short, monetarists argue that inflation is simply 'too much money chasing too few goods'.

There was also an even more extreme version of monetarism developing in the 1970s in the USA. The proponents of this view also revived the theory of rapidly clearing markets and became associated with very distinctive policy views. This group were known as the **new classical monetarists** or simply **new classicals**, and we shall learn more about them later.

The election of the Conservative government under Margaret Thatcher in 1979 saw an end to the post war consensus that full employment was the overriding objective of economic policy. The new government followed the teachings of Friedman and abandoned demand management and the use of fiscal policy to fine tune the economy. Instead it relied on the quantity theory of money and supply side policies. This meant strict control of the money supply in order to reduce inflation and appropriate minimum wage and trade union legislation in order to improve the working of the labour market as a way of reducing unemployment.

Later we return to the debate and look closely at the results of the monetarist policies of the Conservative government of 1979. We now end this section with a brief description of the different types of economists that we focus on later in our studies.

Keynesian economists believe governments should take an active role in the economic management of the economy. They favour the use of fiscal policy to influence the level of demand and, hence output and employment in the economy. Monetary policy may also be used but is seen as a far less powerful tool. Inflation is not seen as a major problem. Demand pull inflation will only occur when full employment is reached. Generally these policies are associated with the political Left wing. In Unit 7 we will look closely at the basic Keynesian model of the economy.

Monetarist economists (including new classicals) believe the government should not attempt to manage the level of demand in the economy. Governments should focus on monetary policy and the money supply in particular in order to reduce inflation. Inflation is seen as the most important problem facing the economy. Unemployment should be tackled by attempting to improve the working of the labour market. This means reducing trade union power, abolishing minimum wage legislation and providing retraining schemes for unemployed workers. These policies are associated with the political Right wing.

REVIEW ACTIVITY 3

The following questions should prove to be fairly straightforward. However, you will probably have to review the text to answer them. Use the activity to make sure you clearly understand the terms we have studied in this section. Write no more than two or three sentences for each answer.

1 Explain what you understand by classical economics.

2 Outline the quantity theory of money.

3 Explain the difference between a Keynesian and a monetarist.

4 What is 'supply side' policy?

5 Explain what is meant by 'demand management'.

6 Define the term 'stagflation'.

Summary

In this section, you looked briefly at the two main theories of economics: Keynesian and monetarism. You examined how each approach advocates that a government acts in a particular way to control the economy.

Unit Review Activity

1 Define national income. How is national income measured in the UK?

2 You are given the following information concerning an economy.

Consumer expenditure	£350,000
General government final consumption	£70,000
Gross domestic fixed capital formation	£24,000
Value of physical increase in stocks and work in progress	£10,500
Total domestic expenditure on imports	£30,600
Total expenditure on exports	£54,750
Net property income from abroad	£2,500

All figures are expressed in market prices.

Calculate :

a   Total domestic expenditure.

b   Net exports of goods and services.

c   Gross domestic product.

d   Gross national product.

e   Gross national product at factor cost if total taxes in the economy are £150,000 and total subsidies are £76,000.

3 Explain the difference between a nominal and a real measure.

4 What are injections and withdrawals in the circular flow of income?

5 National equilibrium is at a point of equilibrium when the following changes occur simultaneously:

The overseas sector starts to buy less domestic goods.

In money terms the decrease is £750.

The government lowers taxation.

This raises total household income by £670.

Firms also decide to invest in more capital.

The increase in capital is £500.

Households decide to buy more foreign goods.

The increase in imports is £290.

Households also save more of their income.

Total savings rise by £300

After these changes, will national income rise or fall?

6 What do you understand by the 'classical dichotomy'?

7 If a government favours a Keynesian approach to economic policymaking, what would it consider to be the most important economic objective? How would it try to achieve this? What would a monetarist government do?

These questions, together with those earlier in the unit should enable to test yourself thoroughly and provide you with an important grounding in macroeconomics which should serve you well as you study the next four units.

Unit Summary

You have learned how to define national income and we have looked at ways it is measured in the UK. You have studied the circular flow of income, a basic model of the economy. We have discovered what sort of things can affect national income. These are known as injections and withdrawals. We have learned to identify when national income will rise or fall.

You have learned what the major economic issues are facing the government today and we have also seen what the main objectives of government economic policy are. We have also examined the controversy between Keynesian and monetarist economists

References

Keynes, JM, (1936), *General Theory of Employment, Interest and Money*, Macmillan, London

Beckerman, W, (1978), *An Introduction to National Income Analysis*, Weiderfield/Nicholson

Burton, J, (1981), The Thatcher Experiment: A Requiem?, *Journal of Labour Research*, George Mason University

Answers to Review Activities

Review Activity 1

1   Money or nominal national income can be formally defined as the money value of finished goods and services produced within an economy during a given period of time, usually a quarter or a year. National income can also be measured in constant prices. This is known as real national income.

The three methods of calculating national income are: the output method which adds together all of the 'value added' output of each sector of the economy within a given period, usually a year; the expenditure method which adds together all the different categories of expenditure in an economy within a given period; and the income method which adds the total of all incomes from the production of goods and services in the economy.

2   The two terms are Gross Domestic Product and Gross National Product. The difference between the two is net property income from abroad.

3   The price paid for goods by a consumer may be affected by taxes such as VAT or excise duties or subsidies paid to producers, and will therefore be different from the price received by the producer. The price received by the producer is a reflection of the cost of producing those goods. This is known as factor cost. Taxes such as those imposed on final expenditure will increase the price of products above the incomes paid to workers and suppliers of raw materials used in the production of those products. Subsidies will lower the price of products in terms of factor cost. The price paid by the consumer is the market price. The relationship between the two types of valuation can be written as: Valuation at market prices = Valuation at factor cost + Taxes − Subsidies.

4   Real national income is a better measure of a country's economic progress than money national income because a rise in real national income occurs only because of a rise in the level of output produced in the country. Money national income may rise even if the level of output is constant because the average price of all goods may rise. A country will therefore appear to be making progress when in fact it is not!

5   a Nominal gross domestic product at factor cost is simply the addition of the output of the four sectors of the economy. This is £134,890 + £111,230 + £45,875 + £21,150 = £313,145.

To get nominal gross national product add net property income from abroad, £313,145 + £30,000 = £343,145.

b We have values at factor cost so to value at market prices we simply add taxes and deduct subsidies for both gross domestic product and gross national product.

So nominal gross domestic product (at market prices) =
£313,145 + £18,000 – £14,500 = £316,645.

Nominal gross national product (at market prices) =
£343,145 + £18,000 – £14,500 = £346,645.

c Nominal gross domestic product for 1991 can be calculated again by adding
the output of our four sectors. Now though, prices are 15% higher so the
output of each sector will be raised by 15%. Agriculture for 1990 is £134,890,
if we raise this by 15% we get £155,124 (to the nearest whole number). If we
do the same for the other sectors we get the following totals:

Forestry and Fishing   £127,915
Construction   £52,756
Banking   £24,323

Therefore nominal gross domestic product equals £155,124 + £127,915 +
£52,756 + £24,323 = £360,118 and for the nominal gross national product we
have the same figure as net property income from abroad is zero.

d We are told that the real volume of output does not rise in 1991 therefore
real gross domestic product (market prices) for 1991 is the same as the
nominal figure for 1990. Real gross national product (market prices) for
1991 is slightly different from nominal gross national product (market
prices) in 1990 because in 1991 net property income from abroad is zero.

The answers are therefore, real gross domestic product (market prices) for
1991 is £316,645.

Real gross national product (market prices) for 1991 is also £316,645.

6   Consider this simple example.

In 1994 an economy produces 1,000 units of output. The market price of each
unit of output is £20. So that nominal national income is £20,000. In 1995 the
economy produces less than in 1994. It now produces 900 units. However
market prices rise to £25 per unit. So nominal national income actually rises to
£22,500. Price changes can be deceiving! (Notice real national income for 1995
at 1994 prices is £18,000 and this does show the fall in output.)

7   National income figures do not give a clear indication of living standards as
they do not measure factors which affect the quality of life such as pollution,
distribution of income, working hours and conditions of the population, etc.

Review Activity 2

1   Check back to Figures 1 and 2 to make sure you fully understand the flows of withdrawals and injections between households and firms and from the government and overseas.

2   National income will be in equilibrium when total injections (government expenditure, investment and exports) is equal to total withdrawals (taxation, savings and imports). The government could raise national income by cutting taxation. This would mean that households had a higher level of disposable income. Then they would spend more on the output of firms. In order to meet this higher demand, firms will hire more workers. These workers receive wages which raise household income. The whole process is then repeated and national income rises.

3   The distinction between total income and disposable income is made because of taxation. Total income is the income earned by the household before taxation. Disposable income is the income left after taxation. In other words, it is the total income available for spending and saving. Notice how a change in taxation changes only disposable income not total income.

4   The national income of the overseas sector can be an important influence on national income in the domestic economy. Consider a situation where the overseas sector suffers from a fall in the level of national income. This means that overseas households have less income to spend on all goods. This will mean they buy less of the exports of our domestic economy, which are, of course, imports for the overseas economy. Exports represent an injection and therefore injections into the domestic economy will start to fall. If injections fall then, *ceteris paribus*, national income falls.

Later in our studies of macroeconomics we will see how trade with the overseas sector is a very important determinant of the level of national income in an economy.

5   You have dealt with questions like this in earlier activities. The best approach is to work out total injections and withdrawals:
Injections:

Lower savings	£1100
Increased exports	£300
Total injections =	*£1400*

Withdrawals:

Lower investment	£440
Total withdrawals =	*£440*

Clearly injections increase by far more than withdrawals. As a result national income will rise.

6   The total rise in income is £100,000.

Taxation is 25% so that £25,000 is paid in taxation.

This means that of the increase in total income, only £75,000 is an increase in disposable income. Now of this, 20% or £15,000 is saved and 15% or £11,250 is spent on imports.

The final amount left, £48,750 is spent on the output of domestic firms.

Total injections into the economy = £100,000

Total withdrawals from the economy = £25,000 + £15,000 + £11,250 = £51,250.

National income will rise as a result of this increase in wages.

This question should not have given you too many problems. It illustrates how an increase in injections will also cause a consequent increase in withdrawals. This is something we will explore in more detail in the next unit.

7   It is possible, though probably unlikely, that a reduction in taxation, *ceteris paribus*, will have no effect on national income. However, the issue is worth exploring because the effect of changes in taxation on national income is important in the debate between different economists about how (or whether) the government should try to influence national income.

Assume the government cuts taxation. All households now have a higher level of disposable income. Assume that the total increase is £1,000. Households may spend all of this on the output of firms in the domestic economy. The change in injections total £1,000 while the change in withdrawals total exactly zero. National income would rise.

Alternatively, and more likely, households may save a small part of the increase, say £100 and they may spend a bit on imports, say £130. But as long as some of the increase is spent on domestic output then national income will rise. New injections total £1,000 and new withdrawals total £230. National income would rise.

However there is a final case where households spend all of the increase on imports or save it all, or some combination of the two so that none of the extra disposable income is spent on domestic goods. In this case the rise in injections of £1,000 is matched exactly by the increased withdrawals. Injections total £1,000 and withdrawals total £1,000. National income will not change.

This question is an interesting one. If the government seeks to reduce taxation in order to increase national income then how can it be sure that households will not save all the extra disposable income or spend it on imports?

Perhaps the best way to achieve the objective of higher income would be to cut the taxes of those on lower incomes. Consider a wealthy household with a high level of income. This household can afford most of the things it wants even without tax cuts. Now consider a low income household. This household has to cut back on its daily expenditure because of its low income. Any additional income would be most welcome for this household. Now, if the government cuts the taxes of all households by a small percentage what will happen? The high income household has little use for this extra small amount of income. It will probably save it. The low income household will, of course, spend the extra income. A proportion of the increase in income will not be passed on in the circular flow so that the increase in national income may be small.

If the government reduces taxes for low income households only, it can maximise the effect of those tax cuts on national income. The government can cut taxes by a larger amount than previously. The low income households will be very grateful for this extra cash which they go out and spend immediately. Thus most of the injection of tax cuts is passed back into the circular flow and not lost in withdrawals.

Review Activity 3

1   Classical economics is a body of theory that suggests that markets work efficiently without the need for government intervention. Classical economists believe in rapidly clearing markets. Inflation is determined according to the quantity theory of money, in other words inflation is caused by increases in the money supply. Classical economists also believe that 'real' variables such as output and employment levels are determined by supply and demand, while monetary variables can only affect inflation.

2   The quantity theory of money simply states that changes in the money supply lead to changes in the price level. A doubling of the money supply will lead to a doubling of all prices.

3   A Keynesian believes that governments should use fiscal policy to influence aggregate demand and hence employment and output. A monetarist believes governments should not try to influence aggregate demand but should control the money supply in order to keep inflation low. Supply side policy should be used to reduce unemployment.

4   Supply side policy refers to attempts to influence the working of the labour market. Examples include trade union legislation, training schemes for the unemployed, and minimum wage legislation.

5   Demand management refers to any policy that is used to try to influence the level of demand in the economy, usually fiscal policy is used. This means cutting taxation and raising government expenditure in times of high unemployment and raising taxation and reducing government spending if the external balance goes into deficit.

6   The term, stagflation, describes a simultaneous rise in inflation and

unemployment. The appearance of stagflation in the 1970s led to the downfall of Keynesian economic policymaking.

Unit Review Activity

1   National income can be formally defined as the money value of finished goods and services produced within an economy during a given period of time, usually a quarter or a year. National income can be measured by the income method, the expenditure method or the output method.

2   a Total domestic expenditure is the total expenditure by residents in the domestic economy on goods produced in the domestic economy. To answer this question you must add consumer expenditure, general government final consumption, gross domestic fixed capital formation and the value of physical increases in stocks and work in progress. This is £350,000 + £70,000 + £24,000 + £10,500 = £454,500.

b Net exports of goods and services is total expenditure on exports minus total domestic expenditure on imports. This is £54,750 – £30,600 = £24,150.

c Gross domestic product is the total domestic expenditure plus the total for net exports of goods and services. In other words simply add your answers from a and b. This is £454,500 + £24,150 = £478,650.

d Gross national product is gross domestic product plus net property income from abroad. This is £478,650 + £2,500 = £481,150.

e The answer to d gives you a valuation at market prices. In order to value at factor cost we must 'take out' taxes and 'add back' subsidies. Gross national product at factor cost is £481,150–£150,000 + £76,000 = £407,150.

3   A nominal measure is a measure in current prices; a real measure is a measure in constant prices. National income can be measured in nominal or real terms. Nominal national income for 1995 will be measured in 1995 prices. Real national income for 1995 will be measured in prices of a 'base' year, say 1985.

4   An injection into the circular flow of income is something that arises outside the circular flow and raises income inside the flow. Examples are investment, exports and government spending.

A withdrawal also arises outside the circular flow but will reduce income inside the flow. Examples include taxation, imports and savings.

5   National income will be changing when injections and withdrawals are not equal. The best way to approach this question is to work out changes in total injections and withdrawals:

Injections:

Lower taxes	£670
Increased Investment	£500
Total injections =	*£1,170*

Withdrawals:

Decreased exports	£750
Increased imports	£290
Increased savings	£300
Total withdrawals =	*£1,340*

Clearly withdrawals increase more than injections and so national income will be falling.

6   The classical dichotomy is the name given to the belief that real and monetary forces are separate. It basically embodies the beliefs of classical economists that 'real' variables like output and employment levels are determined by the forces of supply and demand while monetary variables such as inflation are determined by changes in monetary variables. This is closely related to the quantity theory of money which states that changes in the money supply (a monetary variable) lead to changes in inflation (a monetary variable) but they will not affect output or employment (real variables).

7   A government that favoured the Keynesian approach to economic policymaking would seek to maximise the level of employment in the economy. It would use taxation and government spending, fiscal policy, to achieve this. A monetarist government would see low inflation as the overriding objective of economic policy, it would achieve this by firm control of the money supply.

UNIT 7
NATIONAL INCOME DETERMINATION

Introduction

In Unit 6 we studied national prosperity, how it is measured, what factors affect it, and whether the government can influence it. You were introduced to a simple model of the economy, the circular flow of income, which shows how changes in national income come about. The circular flow of income is the foundation for what is known as the basic Keynesian model of national income determination. In this unit, we will look closely at this model to understand exactly how the economy reaches an equilibrium. We will also look at the concept and the components of aggregate demand and understand its importance in this model.

We will turn to the issue of government spending and fiscal policy, how spending is financed and consider the arguments for and against the use of demand management policy to influence the level of national income. Finally, we extend our model to include the external sector and see how changes in imports and exports influence aggregate demand and national income.

This unit is divided into four sections. Section 1 explains the basic Keynesian model of national income determination. We look at the concept of aggregate demand and its components. We define the marginal propensities to consume and save. You will become familiar with the Keynesian consumption function and we will see how changes in aggregate demand lead to changes in national income using the Keynesian cross diagram. We will also look at the multiplier process and understand its importance.

Section 2 looks more closely at the components of aggregate demand, principally consumption and investment. Having examined the Keynesian consumption function, we now look at alternative theories of consumption such as the permanent income hypothesis. We will also look at the determinants of investment expenditure.

Section 3 looks closely at the issue of using fiscal policy to influence the level of demand in the economy. We will look at ways the government finances changes in taxation and government spending and we will explore the debate between Keynesians and monetarists about the effectiveness of using fiscal policy to influence the level of demand and the consequences of this policy.

In Section 4, we extend our model to include an external sector and show how changes in imports and exports lead to changes in national income.

Unit Objectives

By the end of this unit you should be able to:

● define aggregate demand and identify the components of aggregate demand

- understand the Keynesian consumption function and use the Keynesian cross diagram to show how changes in aggregate demand lead to changes in national income

- explain the concept of the multiplier and be able to work out the value of the multiplier given the relevant data

- explain the permanent income hypothesis of consumption

- list the determinants of investment demand

- outline ways in which the government finances changes in taxation and government spending and demonstrate how fiscal policy can affect national income, output and employment levels in the Keynesian model

- outline the debate between monetarists and Keynesians concerning the effectiveness of using fiscal policy in order to influence the level of demand in the economy

- explain the importance of the external sector in determining national income.

SECTION ONE

Basic Keynesian Model of National Income Determination

Introduction

In this section we explain the basic Keynesian model of national income determination. We look at the concept of aggregate demand and its components. We define the marginal propensities to consume and save. You will become familiar with the Keynesian consumption function and we will see how changes in aggregate demand lead to changes in national income using the Keynesian cross diagram. We will also look at the multiplier process and understand its importance.

1.1 Components of aggregate demand

In the last unit, we looked at the circular flow of income in which we included only firms and households. We began with the assumption that households spend all of their income on the output of the firms but saw that if households chose to save some of their income then this would lead to a fall in output and income. Therefore in this simple model, output is said to be 'demand determined'. That is, ultimately the level of output produced and the level of national income are determined by the level of demand in the circular flow. In this model, supply is not a major consideration. It is assumed that supply can respond to changes in demand provided that there are unemployed or unused resources available. When we talk of demand we refer to the demand for consumption goods and services by households. However firms in the circular flow will also demand investment goods. In addition to this, the government can raise demand by spending, for example, on roads, housing and health. Finally, net exports (exports less imports) raise the level of demand in the economy. Collectively, consumption, investment, government expenditure and net exports are known as **aggregate demand**. However, we begin our discussion with the assumption that there exists no government or overseas sector so that demand arises only from consumption or investment.

CONSUMPTION AND INVESTMENT DEMAND

We will start by assuming that there is no government and no overseas sector, so that there are only two components to aggregate demand. These are the demand for consumption goods and services by households and the demand for investment goods such as machinery and buildings, by firms. We can therefore express aggregate demand as:

$$AD = C + I \quad (11)$$

where AD = aggregate demand, C = consumption and I = investment.

Later in Section 2 we look closely at theories of consumption and investment demand but here we will briefly look at determinants of these components of aggregate demand.

Consumption demand

Households receive income for providing labour to firms. Households can use this income to spend on any goods they choose such as food, cars, football matches and washing machines. Any income that is not spent will be saved. Households will plan how much of their income they wish to consume or save.

In this simple Keynesian model, it is assumed that if households receive more income then they will spend more. Research in a number of countries suggests that this is a reasonable assumption to make. People do consume more when they have a higher level of income.

Once we have made this assumption we can derive the **consumption function**. Households will plan how much of their income they will consume and how much they will save. The consumption function plots the amount of desired consumption by households at each level of income. In other words, *the consumption function shows the level of planned consumption at each level of income*. In such a simple model, with no government and no taxation, then disposable income is equal to national income. Figure 1 shows an example of a consumption function.

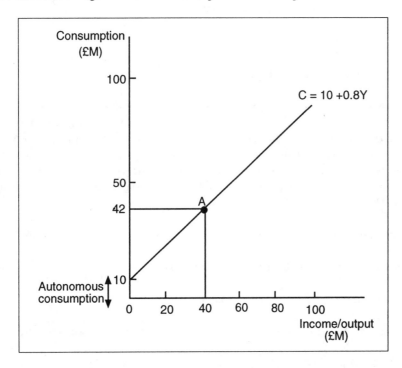

Figure 1: The consumption function shows the amount households would wish to spend at each level of income.

In Figure 1, consumption is measured on the vertical axis in millions of pounds and income is measured on the horizontal axis in millions of pounds. The consumption function is a straight line and the equation that describes this particular example is

$C = 10 + 0.8Y$ (2)

where C = consumption and Y = income.

This equation describes our straight line consumption function. We can use this to calculate the level of planned consumption, that is, the amount households want to spend, for different levels of income.

Notice that if income is equal to zero then consumption can be calculated:

$C = 10 + 0.8(0) = 10$

Remember, all figures are in millions of pounds. Planned consumption is equal to £10 million even when income is equal to zero. This amount of consumption equal to £10 million is unrelated to the level of income and is known as **autonomous consumption.**

However for any increase in the level of income above zero our equation tells us that 0.8 or 80% of this increase will be consumed. If the level of income is £40 million, then planned consumption will be:

$$C = 10 + 0.8(40) = 42$$

This is shown at point A in Figure 1.

In this equation for a straight line consumption function, the coefficient on income, in this case 0.8, is the slope of the function. It is also known as the **marginal propensity to consume.** The marginal propensity to consume is that proportion of an extra £1 of income that is consumed. In our example, an increase in income of £1 leads to an increase in consumption of 80 pence; hence the marginal propensity to consume is 0.8. However, if 0.8 of the extra £1 is consumed, then the remaining 0.2, or 20 pence, is saved.

In our example we can say that:

the marginal propensity to consume is equal to 0.8

the marginal propensity to save is equal to 0.2.

If we assume that all income is either consumed or saved then we can write:

$$Y = C + S \quad (3)$$

where Y = income, C = consumption and S = savings.

We can now use equations (2) and (3) to derive a **savings function.** If we rewrite equation (3), substituting for consumption from equation (2), we get:

$$Y = 10 + 0.8Y + S$$

We can rearrange this to solve for savings:

$$S = Y - 0.8Y - 10$$

We can write this as:

$$S = -10 + 0.2Y \quad (4)$$

Equation (4) is the savings function which is derived directly from our consumption function in equation (2). This tells us that at a zero level of income there is a negative amount of saving equal to £10 million. In other words, households are reducing assets to finance autonomous consumption. At an income level of £60 million, we can calculate savings as:

$S = -10 + 0.2(60) = 2$. This is shown as point A in Figure 2.

The slope of the savings function is the **marginal propensity to save**, in this case 0.2.

In a similar way to the consumption function, the savings function can be illustrated in Figure 2. On the vertical axis in Figure 2 we have planned savings measured in £ million and on the horizontal axis, income is measured in £ million.

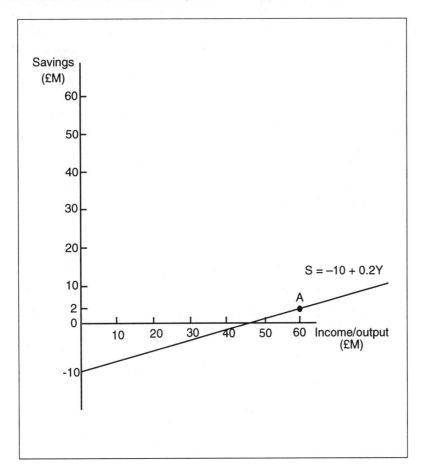

Figure 2: The savings function.

Investment demand

Although we will examine investment more closely in Section 2, for now we simply define investment as **firms' planned purchases of physical capital** such as buildings or machinery and increases in the stock of goods held for sale. In reality, investment demand will depend on how much output firms expect to sell in the future. In other words, it depends on expected future levels of income. But for now, as a first step, we will assume that investment is unrelated to the level of income, in other words, it is **constant** or **autonomous**. We now turn to the aggregate demand schedule and equilibrium national income.

1.2 Aggregate demand and equilibrium national income

AGGREGATE DEMAND SCHEDULE

We saw earlier that aggregate demand, in a simple two-sector model, was made up of planned consumption demand by households and planned investment demand by firms. We can now define aggregate demand more explicitly as **the amount that firms and households plan to spend on goods and services at each level of income**.

We can now use our consumption function and our assumption that, for now, investment is autonomous, to derive an **aggregate demand function**. This is depicted in Figure 3.

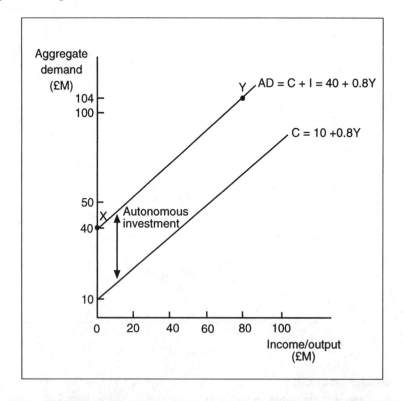

Figure 3: The consumption function and the aggregate demand function.

The vertical axis on Figure 3 measures aggregate demand and the horizontal axis measures income. The figure depicts our consumption function from Figure 1, labelled *C* and the aggregate demand function labelled *AD*. Notice that because we assume that investment is autonomous then the aggregate demand function is derived simply by adding vertically our constant level of investment to the consumption function. The aggregate demand function is therefore parallel to the consumption function. Let us assume that autonomous investment is £30 million.

Notice in Figure 3 that aggregate demand at a zero level of income is simply autonomous consumption, £10 million, plus autonomous investment, a total of £40 million.

Recall that from equation (1), we had:

$$AD = C + I$$

We can substitute in the consumption function from equation (2) and the autonomous level of investment to determine aggregate demand at any level of income.

$$AD = 10 + 0.8Y + 30 \quad (5)$$

At a zero level of income:

$$AD = 10 + 0.8(0) + 30 = 40, \text{ that is, £40 million.}$$

If income is equal to £80 million:

$$AD = 10 + 0.8(80) + 30 = 104, \text{ that is, £104 million.}$$

These two points are shown in the figure respectively, as points X and Y.

ACTIVITY 1

You are given the following consumption function: $C = 6 + 0.7Y$.

1 What is the amount of autonomous consumption?

2 What is the marginal propensity to consume?

3 What is the marginal propensity to save?

4 What is the level of consumption if the level of income is 50?

5 What is the level of consumption if the level of income is 90?

6 Derive the savings function and calculate the level of savings for the income levels 50 and 90.

All figures are in £ million.

1 Autonomous consumption is that level of consumption where income is zero, so autonomous consumption can be calculated as:

$$C = 6 + 0.7(0) = 6$$

2 Marginal propensity to consume is 0.7. For an extra £1 of income, then 70 pence is spent. For an extra £1 million of income to households, £700,000 extra will be spent.

3 Marginal propensity to save can be calculated easily as we know that the marginal propensity to consume and the marginal propensity to save must add up to one. Hence, the marginal propensity to save is 0.3. For an extra £1 of income 30 pence is saved. For an extra £1 million of income to households, £300,000 will be saved.

4 If income is 50, then consumption is:

$$C = 6 + 0.7(50) = 41.$$

5 If income is 90, then consumption is:

$$C = 6 + 0.7(90) = 69.$$

6 Income is either consumed or saved, so, $Y = C + S$

or, $Y = 6 + 0.7Y + S$

so, $Y - 0.7Y - 6 = S$

or, $S = -6 + 0.3Y$, this is the savings function.

If, $Y = 50$, $S = -6 + 0.3(50) = 9$.

If, $Y = 90$, $S = -6 + 0.3(90) = 21$.

SHIFTS IN THE AGGREGATE DEMAND SCHEDULE

Now that we have our aggregate demand function, we could ask if the function can shift over time? What would happen if autonomous investment suddenly increased from £30 million to £40 million? Now, at every level of income, aggregate demand would be higher.

Consider our previous examples. At a zero level of income, $AD = 10 + 0.8(0) + 40 = 50$, that is, £50 million. Alternatively, if income was equal to £80 million $AD = 10 + 0.8(80) + 40 = 114$, that is, £114 million.

At each level of income, aggregate demand rises by the increase in autonomous investment. This new higher aggregate demand schedule is shown in Figure 4 as AD_2 alongside the earlier schedule, AD_1.

Of course, reductions in autonomous investment or autonomous consumption will lead to a drop in the aggregate demand schedule. Keynes saw these kinds of changes in investment as the main source of shifts in the aggregate demand function.

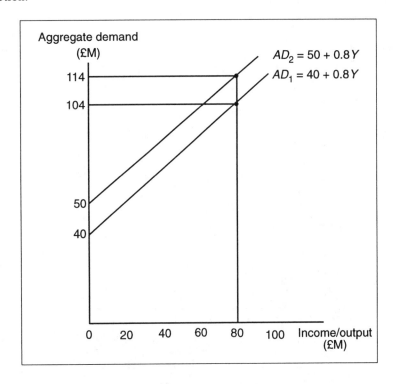

*Figure 4: Shifts in aggregate demand as a result
of changes in autonomous investment.*

In the two-sector model in Figure 4, with no government, only changes in autonomous investment or autonomous consumption can cause a shift in the aggregate demand schedule. Later in this unit we will see that government spending and export demand can also shift the aggregate demand schedule.

You should now be sure of what causes a shift in the aggregate demand schedule. Do not confuse this with movements *along* the schedule. Movements along the schedule are caused purely by changes in income.

EQUILIBRIUM NATIONAL INCOME
In our simple two-sector model of the economy, the output of firms is demanded by households. If households do not spend all their income, that is, they save some, then firms will not be able to sell all of their output and they will hire fewer workers. This will cause unemployment as we saw in Unit 6.

Equilibrium national income in our model can be defined as that point when planned aggregate demand of firms and households is equal to the level of output produced by firms.

In this situation, all demand by firms and households, consumption and investment, is satisfied. Figure 5 illustrates this equilibrium national income. This diagram is known as a **Keynesian cross diagram**.

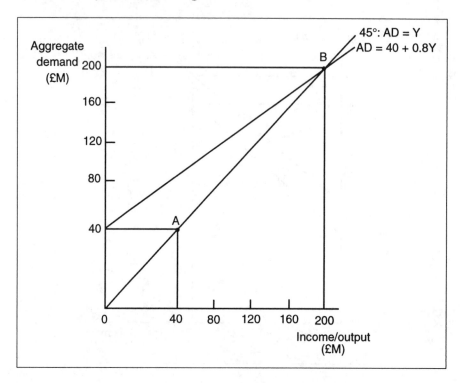

Figure 5: Keynesian cross diagram.

Aggregate demand is measured on the vertical axis and income on the horizontal axis. Remember as we saw in the last unit, income in this model will always equal output, hence the label on the horizontal axis. Figure 5 illustrates the aggregate demand function:

$$AD = C + I = 10 + 0.8Y + 30 = 40 + 0.8Y$$

To find the point of equilibrium when aggregate demand equals the level of output, we draw a line through the origin such that, at each point on the line, aggregate demand is equal to output. When we have equal scales on each axis then this occurs at 45 degrees.

The aggregate demand schedule is labelled AD. Point B is where the aggregate demand schedule intersects the 45-degree line. This is the only point on the aggregate demand schedule where income and planned aggregate demand are equal. This is **national income equilibrium**. In Figure 5, this is at a level of income of £200 million. Firms produce output of £200 million and aggregate demand is equal to £200 million.

In order to see this more clearly, consider the following. When income and output are equal to £200 million then:

$AD = C + I$, therefore

$AD = 10 + 0.8(200) + 30 = 200$, that is, £200 million.

In equilibrium, national income and output equals aggregate demand:

$Y = AD$ (6)

This equation is the national income equilibrium equation.

So, $Y = 10 + 0.8Y + 30 = 40 + 0.8Y$

$Y - 0.8Y = 40$

$0.2Y = 40$

$Y = 200$, that is, £200 million.

This is shown on Figure 5 as point B. Any other point on the aggregate demand schedule does not represent a point of equilibrium. All other points are points of disequilibrium because income and output are not equal to aggregate demand.

Notice from Figure 5 that at all levels of income and output of less than £200 million, aggregate demand is greater than income and output. You can see this because the aggregate demand function lies above the 45-degree line at all levels of income and output less than £200 million. In other words, there is excess demand. At this level of income and output households and firms cannot satisfy their demand. Too little output is produced. Firms would be expected then to increase output as it is easy to sell more.

At all levels of income and output above £200 million, aggregate demand is less than income and output. At all points where income and output are above £200 million the aggregate demand function lies below the 45-degree line. Here aggregate demand is not sufficient to enable firms to sell all of their output. There is too little demand. In this case, if firms cannot sell all their output then they are forced to cut back on production. Any such level of output (above £200 million) cannot therefore be an equilibrium level because output would tend to be falling as firms cut back output with insufficient customers to buy it all.

ACTIVITY 2

You are given the consumption function: $C = 6 + 0.7Y$. Autonomous investment is 45.

1 Calculate aggregate demand if income is 120.

2 What is the equilibrium level of income?

3 Draw the consumption function as accurately as possible.

4 On the same diagram, draw the aggregate demand schedule.

5 Indicate the equilibrium level of income on your diagram.

---

1   Autonomous investment is 45:

$AD = C + I$

so, $AD = 6 + 0.7Y + 45$.

If, $Y = 120$, $AD = 6 + 0.7(120) + 45 = 135$.

2   The equilibrium level of income is where aggregate demand is equal to income.

In equilibrium, $AD = Y$, so, $Y = C + I$

$Y = 6 + 0.7Y + 45$

$Y - 0.7Y = 51$

$0.3Y = 51$

$Y = 170$

3, 4, 5   See Figure 6.

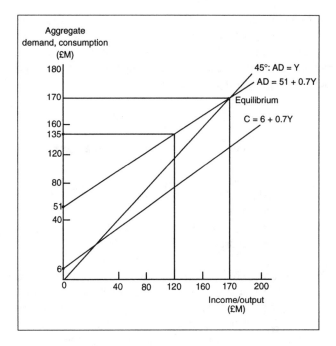

Figure 6: Consumption function and aggregate demand function.

ADJUSTMENT TO EQUILIBRIUM

Returning to our equilibrium position we need to ask how this equilibrium might come about. Figure 7 illustrates our Keynesian cross diagram and shows our equilibrium position at a level of income and output of £200 million.

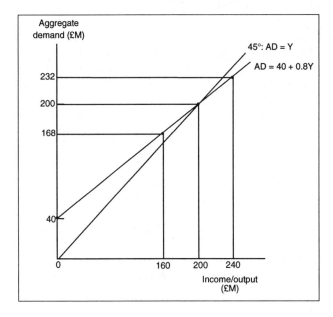

Figure 7: The equilibrium level of income is defined by the intersection of the aggregate demand function and the 45-degree line.

Now let us assume that output actually produced is £160 million. Figure 7 shows that, at this level of output, aggregate demand is greater than output. This is because the aggregate demand function lies above the 45-degree line at this point. However, we can use the aggregate demand equation, equation (5), to prove that aggregate demand is greater than output and income.

$AD = 10 + 0.8(160) + 30 = 168$, that is, £168 million.

Aggregate demand is £168 million; income and output are £160 million.

At this point, firms are producing all they can but they cannot satisfy demand. To do so they will need to run down their stock levels. However in the next period, they will raise output in order to meet higher levels of demand. Therefore, output starts to rise and will continue to do so until we reach national income equilibrium at point A where income and output are equal to £200 million.

Now consider a different situation, where income and output are equal to £240 million. Figure 7 shows that at this point aggregate demand is less than the level of income and output. The aggregate demand function is below the 45-degree line. However, once again, to satisfy yourself that aggregate demand is indeed less than income and output, use our aggregate demand equation:

$AD = 10 + 0.8(240) + 30 = 232$, that is, £232 million.

Aggregate demand is £232 million which is less than income and output at £240 million. Firms will be unable to sell all their output, they will gradually accumulate unsold stocks and will therefore start to reduce their output levels. They will continue to do so until equilibrium is reached once again.

Only at equilibrium are the plans of firms and households consistent with each other. Be careful that you understand that **national income equilibrium can occur at a level of income that does not guarantee full employment**. In our example, national income equilibrium occurs at a level of income of £200 million but this may not be a level of output that guarantees full employment. It is quite possible that an economy can be in equilibrium with unemployment present. There is no incentive to move from this position. Firms will not suddenly decide to produce more because if they did they would be unable to sell it. The problem, in this case, is the lack of aggregate demand. Keynesians describe this position as one of a **demand deficiency** and Keynesian economists see demand deficiency as the root of unemployment. We return to this issue in Section 3.

INJECTIONS, WITHDRAWALS AND EQUILIBRIUM

We can easily explain the analysis above in terms of the injections and withdrawals you met in Unit 6. Recall that injections were government expenditure, exports and investment. However, in this analysis we are assuming that there is no government or overseas sector so that the only injection we consider here is investment. Withdrawals consist of savings, taxation and imports. Again, with no government or overseas sector, for now, we consider only savings.

You may also recall that equilibrium national income occurred only when injections and withdrawals were equal. In our two-sector analysis, national income equilibrium occurs when:

$S = I$

where S = savings and I = investment.

To see this clearly, recall from equation (3) that:

$Y = C + S$

and from equation (1) that:

$AD = C + I.$

In equilibrium, aggregate demand is equal to income so that:

$Y = AD$

Therefore we can use equation (3) and rewrite equation (1) so that we have the following:

$Y = C + S$

$Y = C + I$

By definition, income will always be equal to planned consumption and savings. In equilibrium, income will equal planned consumption plus investment demand. Therefore, in equilibrium, savings and investment are equal.

You may recall that we saw the savings function in Figure 2 and we also assumed that investment was autonomous at a level of £30 million. We now depict the investment and savings functions in Figure 8. The savings function is labelled S and the investment function is labelled I.

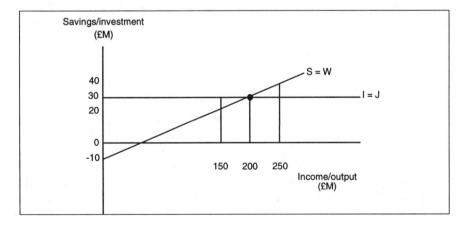

Figure 8: The intersection of the savings function with the injections function defines the equilibrium level of national income of £200 million.

On the vertical axis we have savings and investment, measured in £ million and on the horizontal axis we have income and output. National income equilibrium occurs where savings and investment are equal. This is at point A where income and output are equal to £200 million.

We could just as easily label our investment function as our injections function, J and our savings function as our withdrawals function, W. Recall that our savings function in equation (4) was:

$$S = -10 + 0.2Y$$

In equilibrium, therefore:

$$-10 + 0.2Y = 30$$

$$0.2Y = 30 + 10 = 40$$

$$Y = 200.$$

At levels of output and income below £200 million such as £150 million, investment is greater than savings, or in other words, injections are greater than withdrawals. At this point, the horizontal investment function is above the savings function. Recall that investment is autonomous and equal to £30 million while, at a level of income and output of £150 million, savings are equal to:

$$-10 + 0.2(150) = 20, \text{ that is, £20 million.}$$

Investment is greater than savings so that national income will be rising. This process will continue until savings are no longer less than investment; this occurs at an income of £200 million. We saw this in Unit 6.

On the other hand, at levels of output and income above £200 million such as £250 million, investment is lower than savings, or in other words, withdrawals are greater than injection. The horizontal investment function is below the savings function. Investment is equal to £30 million while, at a level of income and output of £250 million, savings are equal to:

$$-10 + 0.2(250) = 40, \text{ that is, £40 million.}$$

Investment is lower than savings so that national income will be falling. This process will take the economy back to equilibrium at an income of £200 million.

Note that we have been able to show that equilibrium national income is £200 million using either the 45-degree line diagram or an injections-withdrawals framework. They are different ways of using the same information to get at our required result.

ACTIVITY 3

In Activity 1, we saw that: $S = -6 + 0.3Y$.

1 Draw this function, together with the investment function for an autonomous level of investment of 45.

2 Calculate the level of savings at an income level 120.

3 In equilibrium, savings will be equal to investment. Use this to calculate the equilibrium level of income.

4 Indicate this point of equilibrium on your diagram.

1,4 Your diagram should look like Figure 9. Make sure that you label your axes clearly. The intersection of the savings function with the autonomous level of investment defines the equilibrium level of income of £170 million. The savings function $S = -6 + 0.3Y$ shows that for every increase in income of £1 then 30 pence is saved so that the slope of the savings function (the marginal propensity to save) is 0.3.

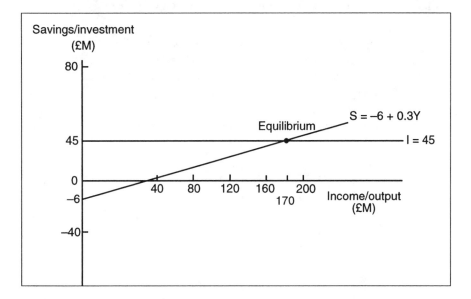

Figure 9: Equilibrium national income.

2   $S = -6 + 0.3Y$

=$-6 + 0.3(120) = 30$

3   In equilibrium, $S = I$. We know that $I = 45$ so we can write:

$$-6 + 0.3Y = 45$$

$$0.3Y = 51$$

$$Y = 170.$$

EQUILIBRIUM AND CHANGES IN AGGREGATE DEMAND

What will happen to our equilibrium position if the aggregate demand function falls due to a drop in autonomous investment? Recall that our AD function is:

$$AD = C + I$$

or, $AD = 10 + 0.8Y + 30$

In equilibrium we saw that:

$$AD = 10 + 0.8(200) + 30 = 200.$$

Now suppose firms are pessimistic about future prospects and decide to reduce investment from £30 million to £25 million, a drop of £5 million. What will happen? The aggregate demand function now becomes:

$$AD = 10 + 0.8Y + 25 = 35 + 0.8Y$$

Figure 10 shows our initial equilibrium at point X with income and output at £200 million. The aggregate demand function now drops down, a vertical shift of £5 million to AD_1. The new equilibrium is at point Y in the figure.

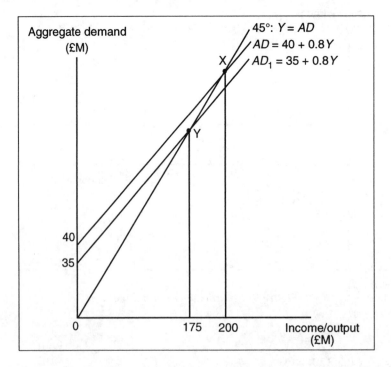

Figure 10: The decrease in autonomous investment from 35 to 40
causes a downward shift in the aggregate demand function.

The total change in income and output as a result of the drop in investment is £25 million, far greater than the initial drop in investment. Why is this the case?

At first, firms will not expect demand to change so they continue to produce output of £200 million. But aggregate demand has dropped by £5 million, that is:

$$AD = 10 + 0.8(200) + 25 = 195$$

So that firms have £5 million of unsold stock. They therefore decide to cut back on their production. Now they assume aggregate demand is £195 million so produce exactly this amount of output. Now, however aggregate demand is:

$$AD = 10 + 0.8(195) + 25 = 191, \text{ that is, } £191 \text{ million.}$$

So firms now have £4 million of unsold stock and decide to cut back further on production because of this rise in the level of stocks. They now assume aggregate demand is 191, so produce this amount of output. Now, though, aggregate demand has fallen again along the new aggregate demand schedule.

$$AD = 10 + 0.8(191) + 25 = 187.8, \text{ that is, } £187.8 \text{ million.}$$

Firms now have £3.2 million worth of unsold stock. They now decide to produce £187.8 million of output, but once again, aggregate demand has fallen.

$$AD = 10 + 0.8(187.8) + 25 = 185.24, \text{ that is, } £185.24 \text{ million.}$$

Once again leaving the firm with unsold stock. The unsold stock this time is £2.56 million.

Notice, that the amount of unsold stock gets progressively smaller each time. Eventually all output will be sold and there will be no unsold stock. At this point, there will be a new level of equilibrium.

Already, even though we have not yet reached equilibrium, the drop in income and output is: 200 − 185.24 = £14.76 million. Eventually the total drop in output and income will be far greater than the initial drop in autonomous investment. The fact that output and income fall considerably more than the initial fall in investment is because of the **multiplier process**.

The multiplier is the name given to the process whereby a fall in aggregate demand leads to a much greater fall in income and output before national income equilibrium is restored. In fact income and output will eventually fall by £25 million and a new equilibrium level of national income will be achieved at £175 million. We now see why.

1.3 The multiplier

If people decide, for whatever reason, to consume less and to save a higher proportion of their income, then the immediate result of this would be that there would be a drop in the sale of consumption goods. Firms producing these goods would find that they had stocks of unsold goods. Therefore they would reduce their output of these goods in response to the fall in demand. As this happened firms would start to lay off workers until they had just enough labour to produce the new, lower, level of output. There would be a lower level of overall income in the economy. But as incomes fell then there would be further falls in the level of consumption; and as consumption fell firms would cut back output and employment even further. This would generate another 'round' of falling incomes and consumption. The economy would enter a downward spiral in which the first round effect of a fall in consumption spending is multiplied by second and third round effects. The original drop in consumption is amplified.

In the Keynesian model any drop in demand therefore, has major 'knock on' effects. This effect is known as the **multiplier effect**. The multiplier tells us exactly how much output and income change as a result of a change in aggregate demand. Of course, the multiplier effect will not continue indefinitely. A reduction in income would not ultimately result in an income level of zero.

Equally, an increase in consumption for whatever reason has multiplier effects. The immediate result of an increase in consumption is that there would be an increase in the sale of consumption goods. Firms producing these goods would find that they have diminishing stocks of unsold goods. Therefore they would increase their output of these goods in response to the increase in demand. As this happened, firms would start to hire more workers so that they could produce the higher level of output. There would be a higher level of overall income in the economy. As incomes rose then there would be further increases in the level of consumption causing firms to increase output and employment further. The economy enters an upward spiral. Similarly, therefore, any increase in demand has multiplier effects. The economy would eventually settle at a new, higher, level of income. Essentially, the multiplier is a dynamic process taking place over a period of time. The final change in income and output is calculated by the following formula:

$$\Delta Y = \Delta AD \times [1/(1 - MPC)] \quad (6)$$

where ΔY = final change in output and income, ΔAD = initial change in aggregate demand, MPC = marginal propensity to consume. The value of the multiplier itself is: $[1/(1 - MPC)]$.

Of course, if income is either spent or saved then any income not saved is spent. Therefore, if 20% of income is saved (and therefore the MPS is 0.2) then 80% of income is consumed (and the MPC is 0.8). The sum of these marginal propensities, $0.8 + 0.2 = 1$. Whatever the marginal propensity to consume and the marginal propensity to save, they will always add up to one in a closed economy with no government or overseas sector. Therefore another way of writing the formula would be:

$$\Delta Y = \Delta AD \times [1/MPS] \qquad (7)$$

where MPS = marginal propensity to save.

From our example:

$$\Delta Y = -5 \times [1/(1 - 0.8)]$$

$$\Delta Y = -5 \times [1/0.2] = -5 \times 5 = -25$$

Equilibrium national income will be restored at a level of income £25 million less than the previous level of £200 million. This is £175 million. Remember, in equilibrium, aggregate demand will be equal to income and output. To prove this is a new equilibrium:

$$AD = 10 + 0.8(175) + 25 = 175$$

Alternatively savings will be equal to investment:

$$S = -10 + 0.2(175) = 25.$$

ACTIVITY 4

1 In the earlier activities of this section we saw that the equilibrium level of income was 170. Autonomous investment was 45. Using the same consumption function, let there be an increase of autonomous investment from 45 to 49. Calculate the new equilibrium level of output. Draw the shift from the old equilibrium to the new equilibrium in a diagram.

2 Now assume we are back at our initial equilibrium with autonomous investment of 45. If autonomous investment falls to 39, what is the new equilibrium level of income? Draw this equilibrium position on your diagram.

---

1   $C = 6 + 0.7Y$

The multiplier is therefore $1/(1 - MPC) = 1/(1 - 0.7) = 1/0.3 = 3.33$.

Investment increases by 4 so income will change by:

$$4 \times 3.33 = 13.33$$

The new equilibrium level of income will be $170 + 13.33 = 183.33$.

Alternatively, aggregate demand now becomes:

$$AD = 6 + 0.7Y + 49 = 55 + 0.7Y.$$

If $Y = AD$ in equilibrium then:

$Y = 55 + 0.7Y$

$Y - 0.7Y = 0.3Y = 55$

$Y = 55/0.3 = 183.33$

b   If investment falls by 6 then income changes by:

$-6 \times 3.33 = -20$

So, the new equilibrium level of income is $170 - 20 = 150$.

Alternatively, aggregate demand now becomes $AD = 6 + 0.7Y + 39 = 45 + 0.7Y$.

In equilibrium, $Y = AD$ then:

$Y = 45 + 0.7Y$

$Y - 0.7Y = 0.3Y = 45$

$Y = 45/0.3 = 150$.

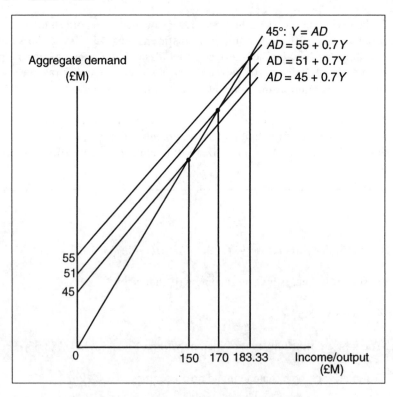

*Figure 11: Consumption function with increases
and decreases of autonomous investment.*

THE MULTIPLIER AND WITHDRAWALS

We now know that the multiplier tells us by how much national income will change as a result of a change in aggregate demand. But what determines the extent of the increase in national income? Consider an increase in aggregate demand. This will lead to a rise in income. Some of this increase in income will be passed back into the circular flow in the form of consumption, however some of the increase will be withdrawn as savings. Obviously the more that is withdrawn then the less that is passed back into the circular flow. Therefore the higher the marginal propensity to save then the more of any increase in income is saved and the eventual increase in national income is lower.

Here we see that the impact of the multiplier is determined by withdrawals. The higher the withdrawals, the lower the value of the multiplier.

In our earlier example, we saw that the value of the multiplier was 5, that is, $1/[1 - MPC] = 1/[1 - 0.8] = 5$. The reason that it is so much greater than one is because any shift in aggregate demand, in this case autonomous investment, causes further changes in consumption demand. The higher the marginal propensity to consume is, then as any initial increase in investment leads to an increase in income, more of this increase is consumed within the circular flow of income. Hence, the multiplier is higher.

We can also think about this in terms of the marginal propensity to save where saving is the only withdrawal in this simple model. Earlier we defined the value of the multiplier as $1/MPS$, so the higher the marginal propensity to save, that is, the more an increase in income leaks out of the circular flow as a withdrawal, then the lower is the multiplier. Consider a situation where households save 50% of their income rather than 20% as we have considered so far. The multiplier value is $1/0.5 = 2$. Previously, we had a value of 5 for the multiplier when the marginal propensity to save was 0.2.

In Figure 12 we show the effect of an increase in autonomous investment in two different situations. Firstly, we use our initial consumption function $C = 10 + 0.8Y$ so that:

$$AD = 10 + 0.8Y + 30 = 40 + 0.8Y.$$

In this case the marginal propensity to save is 0.2 (marginal propensity to consume is 0.8).

Secondly, we use a very similar function but where the marginal propensity to save is 0.5 (marginal propensity to consume is 0.5), that is, $C = 10 + 0.5Y$ so that:

$$AD = 10 + 0.5Y + 30 = 40 + 0.5Y.$$

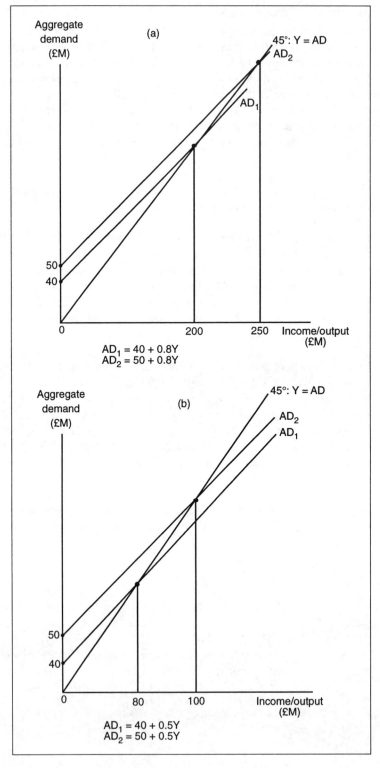

Figure 12: Increases in autonomous investment.

Notice that in diagram (a), equilibrium national income is at £200 million. An increase in autonomous investment of £10 million, so that investment increases to £40 million, leads to an increase in income and output of:

$10 \times (1/0.2) = 50$, that is, **an increase in income of £50 million.**

Equilibrium is reached at a level of income and output of £250 million.

Now in diagram (b), initial equilibrium is at a level of income and output of £80 million, that is, $AD = C + I$

$AD = 10 + 0.5(80) + 30 = 80.$

Now an equivalent increase in autonomous investment of £10 million, in this case, leads to an increase in income and output of:

$10 \times (1/0.5) = 20$, that is, **an increase in income of £20 million** so that the new level of equilibrium national income is £100 million.

Clearly, the higher the marginal propensity to save, the greater are the withdrawals from an increase in aggregate demand, and the lower is the value of the multiplier.

The value of the multiplier therefore depends on withdrawals. The more withdrawals there are then the lower the value of the multiplier. In Sections 3 and 4, we see how the multiplier value is affected by the extension of our model to the government and external sector, this means that imports and taxation will be further withdrawals in our model.

REVIEW ACTIVITY 1

You are given the following consumption function: $C = 5 + 0.8Y$. Autonomous investment is 70.

1   Calculate the level of consumption and aggregate demand at an income level of 160.

2   Calculate the level of consumption and aggregate demand at an income level of 230.

3   What is the marginal propensity to consume? What is the marginal propensity to save?

4   Derive the savings function and calculate the level of savings at income levels of 80 and 170.

5   Calculate the equilibrium level of national income.

6   Calculate the value of the multiplier

7   Given your answer to 5 calculate the new level of equilibrium income if autonomous investment rises from 70 to 76.

8   Now use your answer to 7 to calculate the new equilibrium level of national income if investment falls from 76 to 73.

9   Draw the consumption function and show the equilibrium positions from 5 and 7.

10 Which of the following statements best describes the multiplier?

    a   The multiplier is the process whereby an increase in investment leads to an increase in employment.

    b   The multiplier tells us by how much savings change as a result of an increase in aggregate demand.

    c   The multiplier effect shows the increase in firm's profits as a result of an increase in consumption.

    d   The multiplier tells us exactly how much output and income change as a result of a change in aggregate demand.

Summary

You have investigated the basic Keynesian model of national income determination. We looked at the concept of aggregate demand and its components. We defined the marginal propensities to consume and to save. You now understand the Keynesian consumption function and see that changes in aggregate demand lead to changes in national income using the Keynesian cross diagram. You looked at the important multiplier process.

SECTION TWO

Consumption and Investment Demand

Introduction

In this section, we look more closely at the components of aggregate demand, mainly consumption and investment. Having examined the Keynesian consumption function, we now look at alternative theories of consumption that include the permanent income hypothesis. We will also look at the determinants of investment expenditure.

2.1 Consumption demand

In our simple two-sector model of the economy, consumption and investment are the two components of aggregate demand. Here, we consider consumption. Theories of consumption demand lie at the heart of the debate between Keynesian and monetarist economists over the effect of government policy. In our consideration of the Keynesian model, we assumed that people would consume more at higher levels of disposable income. However, we need a more detailed understanding of consumption behaviour to fully understand the policy debate. We look more closely at the Keynesian theory of consumption, and an alternative theory of consumption associated with monetarists called the **permanent income hypothesis**.

KEYNESIAN CONSUMPTION FUNCTION

For Keynesian economists, consumption by each individual is determined by the level of disposable income of that individual. This is more commonly known as **personal disposable income**. Remember that disposable income is the income left over after payment of taxes. In Section 1, we assumed no government and therefore no taxation, so that disposable income was simply equal to income. Of course, in a world with taxation, disposable income will be less than income.

The Keynesian theory says that as disposable income rises consumption will increase but it will account for a decreasing proportion of income. At the same time, savings will account for an increasing proportion of income. In simple terms, this means that people with higher incomes will save a greater proportion of their income than people on lower incomes.

Earlier we defined the marginal propensity to consume as the proportion of a £1 increase in disposable income that is consumed. Now we define a closely related concept known as the **average propensity to consume**. This is simply consumption expenditure expressed as a proportion of disposable income, that is:

$APC = C/Y$

where APC = average propensity to consume.

If we return to our consumption function of Section 1, at income Y, consumption is given by:

$C = 10 + 0.8Y$

The marginal propensity to consume in this function is 0.8. However the average propensity to consume depends upon the level of income. Consider a level of income of £100 million, consumption is:

$10 + 0.8(100) = 90$, that is, £90 million,

thus, $APC = 90/100 = 0.9$.

Now consider a higher level of income of £200 million, consumption is:

$10 + 0.8(200) = 170$, that is, £170 million,

thus, $APC = 170/200 = 0.85$.

Now consider a higher level of income of £400 million, consumption is:

$10 + 0.8(400) = 330$, that is, £330 million,

thus, $APC = 330/400 = 0.825$.

The average propensity to consume falls as income rises. Thus Keynes stated that at higher levels of income an increasing fraction of total income is saved and a decreasing fraction consumed. At high levels of income, much of that income will be saved and it may be that demand is therefore insufficient to generate a level of output consistent with full employment. This is a potential source of unemployment for wealthier nations.

The Keynesian theory of consumption places a lot of emphasis on current levels of income as a key determinant of consumption. Because of this, the theory is often known as the **absolute income hypothesis**.

The theory has important policy implications. If current disposable income can be changed then consumption can be changed. So a government can use fiscal policy to alter the level of consumption and therefore aggregate demand. Consider a situation where unemployment exists. In order to reduce this, governments could lower taxation and therefore raise disposable income. In the Keynesian model, consumption and hence aggregate demand rises. The level of national income also increases and unemployment is likely to fall. This is a classic case of demand management. We return to this issue in Section 3.

Like any theory, the absolute income hypothesis is subject to criticism. Researchers studied years of historical data to see if the theory explained the facts well. In fact, over the period of time examined, current disposable income did not explain consumption very well. For example, even though incomes grew, *APC* did not fall. This problem led to the development of alternative theories of consumption.

ACTIVITY 5

Given our consumption function from earlier activities, $C = 6 + 0.7Y$, calculate the average propensity to consume (APC) at the following levels of income:

1   50

2   90

3   170.

---

1    $APC = C/Y$

    $C = 6 + 0.7(50) = 41$

    $APC = 41/50 = 0.82$

2    $C = 6 + 0.7(90) = 69$

    $APC = 69/90 = 0.77$

3    $C = 6 + 0.7(170) = 125$

    $APC = 125/170 = 0.74$

PERMANENT INCOME HYPOTHESIS

The problems of the Keynesian consumption function led to the development of new theories of consumption. The 1950s saw the development of two very similar theories. In *A Theory of the Consumption Function* (1957), Milton Friedman developed his **permanent income hypothesis** and during the same period Franco Modigliani, together with Richard Brumberg, developed the so-called **life cycle theory of consumption** in *Utility Analysis of the Consumption Function: An Interpretation of Cross-section Data* (1954).

These theories are so similar that we consider them under the same heading. The basic point about these theories is that **consumption depends, not on current personal disposable income but on the total income expected over the consumer's life.** Individuals have an expectation of how much income they will receive during their lifetime and on the basis of this expectation they plan a lifetime consumption pattern. Because of the existence of banks that allow people to borrow and lend, then people's consumption at any point in time will not be restricted by their level of income at that time. Therefore individuals will even out their lifetime consumption pattern by borrowing in times of low income, and saving in times of high income. Figure 13 illustrates the pattern of consumption, savings and income over the lifetime of a typical individual.

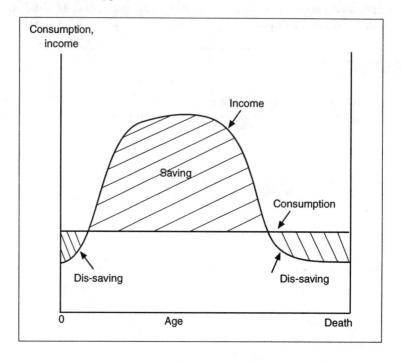

Figure 13: A lifetime pattern of consumption and saving.

Figure 13 shows age on the horizontal axis and consumption and income on the vertical axis. We can see that income increases typically during the early working years, reaches a peak then starts to decline in retirement. During the early stages of their working life, individuals will borrow in anticipation of higher income later. In the periods of higher income, individuals earn enough income to pay off the debts from the early years and to save. Once the individual reaches retirement age they use their savings to finance their consumption, a process known as **dis-saving**.

The key point about the theory is that consumption patterns relate, not to current levels of disposable income but to the total income expected over the entire lifespan, in other words, wealth. As a result of this, individuals will not change their consumption if current income changes, unless they see that change in income as being permanent and affecting their lifetime wealth. Friedman hypothesised that increases in current disposable income because of taxation cuts would be seen as temporary or transitory and not affecting wealth. As a result, consumption would not respond to these tax cuts unless they were seen as permanent. In short, these theories developed by Friedman and Modigliani suggest that Keynesian demand management policies are unlikely to be successful because of the dependence of consumption, not on current disposable income, but on wealth. The theories of Friedman and Modigliani form part of the monetarist arguments against Keynesian policy. We consider this point in more detail in Section 3.

2.2 Investment demand

In everyday language people often confuse investment with savings. Be careful that you do not fall into this trap! When we talk about 'investing money in a bank account' what we really mean is **saving**. Economists use the term **investment** to describe additions to the capital stock of the economy – factories, machines, offices and stocks of materials used to produce other goods and services. It also includes additions to the stock of housing.

An important distinction should be made between **gross** investment and **net** investment. The value of the capital stock will fall over time due to general wear and tear and obsolescence. Economists use the term **depreciation** to describe this. Gross investment refers to the total purchases of all capital goods in a given period. Net investment is gross investment less depreciation. Net investment does not include investment to replace worn out capital stock and therefore measures the change in the capital stock from one period to another.

DETERMINANTS OF INVESTMENT EXPENDITURE

Investment expenditure accounts for approximately one fifth, or 20% of total expenditure in the UK. Here we try to answer the question:

- What factors influence the level of investment in the economy?

We begin by looking at two of the most influential theories of investment:

- Classical Loanable Funds Theory
- Keynesian Marginal Efficiency of Capital Theory.

Classical Loanable Funds Theory

Before Keynes developed his theories, investment was explained according to the loanable funds theory. Firms often have to borrow to finance investment projects. Naturally, they have to pay a rate of interest on their borrowing. In a sense, we can think of the rate of interest as the price of borrowing for investment. If firms have to pay a high rate of interest on their borrowing, then they may be discouraged from undertaking investment. Hence at high rates of interest, investment will be low. On the other hand, at lower rates of interest, firms can borrow cheaply and will be encouraged to invest more. At low rates of interest, investment will be higher.

Some firms, however, will not borrow to invest. Instead they use any surplus cash they may have to buy capital goods. For those firms, the interest rate is the **opportunity cost** of investment. At high interest rates, firms can earn a high rate of interest by lending their surplus cash and not investing. Generally therefore, investment will be lower at high interest rates. At low interest rates, firms are less likely to be able to earn a high return from their surplus cash so choose to invest instead. Therefore at low rates of interest, according to this theory, investment is higher. The relationship between investment and interest rates is shown as the curve labelled Inv in Figure 14. The curve can be thought of as the **demand curve for investment,** or **loanable funds.**

The figure also shows an upward sloping curve labelled *Sav*. This shows how savings by households will rise as the rate of interest rises. If households can earn a high rate of interest then obviously they are more likely to save. At lower rates of interest, they save less. This curve is the supply of savings, or as it is better known, the **supply curve of loanable funds**.

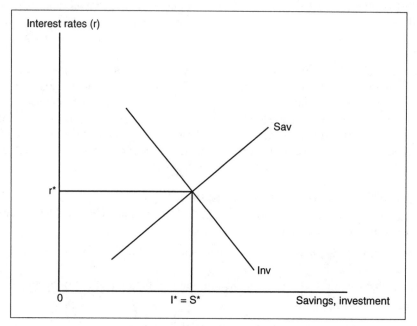

Figure 14: The supply of loanable funds (savings) and the demand for loanable funds (investment) determine the rate of interest.

In Figure 14, on the horizontal axis we have savings and investment and on the vertical axis, we have the rate of interest. As in any market, the equilibrium price, or in this case, the equilibrium rate of interest, is determined by the supply and demand for loanable funds. This is shown as r* and therefore the total amount of investment in the economy is I*, and the total level of saving is S*. It is worth mentioning that this is also the classical theory of how interest rates are determined.

Keynesian Marginal Efficiency of Capital Theory
The Keynesian theory of investment is like the classic loanable funds theory in one important respect. It also states that investment would be higher at low rates of interest and lower at high rates of interest. However Keynes explained this in terms of the **marginal efficiency of capital** (MEC) .

The marginal efficiency of capital is the rate of return expected on an extra unit of investment. Imagine a firm that is considering an investment project with a MEC of 15%. If the rate of interest in the economy is 20%, then the firm will make a loss if it undertakes the project. It will pay an interest rate of 20% on its borrowing, yet it will earn only 15% on the project. Of course, at any one time, there will be a large number of firms, each considering different projects with different MECs. The lower the rate of interest then more of these projects will be profitable and more investment will take place. Similarly, the higher the rate of interest then fewer projects will be profitable and less investment will take place. Figure 15 illustrates a marginal efficiency of capital schedule, MEC and shows the relationship of the marginal efficiency of capital to the rate of interest.

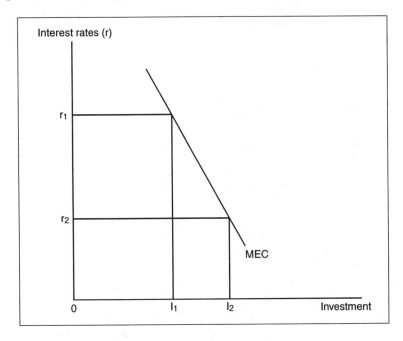

Figure 15: The marginal efficiency of capital schedule.

Figure 15 shows that the amount of investment depends upon the relationship between the marginal efficiency of capital and the current interest rate in the market. The equilibrium level of investment occurs when the rate of interest is equal to the marginal efficiency of capital. As the figure shows, at an interest rate r_1 then the level of investment is I_1. If the interest rate falls to r_2 then investment increases to I_2.

We assume that the rate of interest is that rate at which firms borrow money. However, many firms in the UK will finance investment from retained profits. This fact does not alter the relationship between the MEC and the interest rate. Firms that have retained profits have a choice about what to do with the money. They can use it to finance investment or they can save it. The higher the rate of interest then the more attractive saving is. Alternatively, we can say that the higher the rate of interest then the higher will be the opportunity cost of investment and therefore the lower will be the amount of planned investment in the economy.

Importance of expectations in the Keynesian model
Keynes felt that the most important influence on investment was **expectations**. He argued that changes in expectations about future prospects would lead to shifts in the MEC curve. Figure 16 illustrates this.

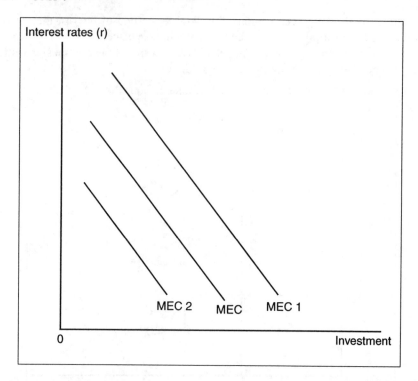

Figure 16: Changes in firm's expectations of future business prospects can cause shifts in the MEC schedule.

Figure 16 shows our marginal efficiency of capital curve, MEC, from Figure 15. Assume that the government announces plans to reduce taxation and increase government spending. Firms may expect that as a result of these changes, demand will increase and therefore that prospects for business in the future are good. They will now wish to increase their investment to enable them to meet the higher level of demand. The MEC curve will shift to MEC_1.

Alternatively, if firms are pessimistic about the future, perhaps because the government has announced plans to cut spending and raise taxation, then they will reduce their investment and the MEC curve would shift to MEC_2.

The MEC curve can shift at any time due to changes in firms' expectations of future prospects, so that the level of investment demand may be very unstable.

Keynes felt that expectations were the most important factor determining investment demand. He argued that, even at high interest rates, if expectations were optimistic then investment demand could be high. At the same time, at low interest rates, if expectations were pessimistic then investment demand could be low. Thus, **for Keynesians, investment demand will tend to be unstable and not necessarily closely related to interest rates**. We return to this point later in our studies as it has important implications for economic policy.

ACTIVITY 6

Redraw Figure 15 and show the effect of the following on the MEC schedule:

1 a decrease in general business confidence

2 a decrease in the productivity of labour.

1   A decrease in general business confidence will mean that less investment will take place at each interest rate. The MEC schedule will shift to the left.

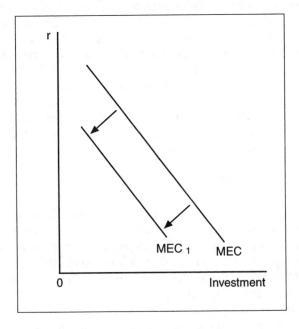

Figure 17: MEC schedule with a decrease in business confidence.

2   A decrease in the productivity of labour will cause firms to substitute capital for labour so that more investment will take place at each level of the interest rate. The MEC schedule will shift to the right.

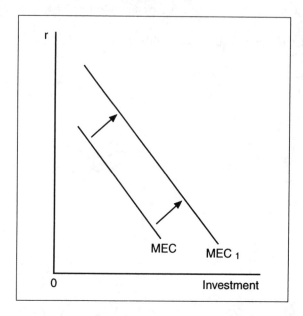

Figure 18: MEC schedule with a decrease in the productivity of labour.

Accelerator principle

We now know that classical (and monetarist) economists see interest rates as the key determinant in explaining investment demand. Keynesians agree that interest rates have some influence but see the state of expectations and business confidence as the key to investment. Keynesians therefore believe that it is not so much current output and income but **future** output and income that is important. Nevertheless, it is extremely likely that **changes** in the level of output do affect investment demand, and this is explained by the **accelerator principle**.

The accelerator principle suggests that the level of investment varies with the rate of change of income or output rather than with the rate of interest. To illustrate the principle consider this simple example.

A firm makes ironing boards. Assume that the firm needs one machine to produce £1 million of output per year and that each machine lasts 20 years. We will also assume that no machine needs replacing over the time period in consideration (therefore we consider only net investment). In year 1, the firm has £20 million worth of orders. It already has 20 machines so that no investment takes place. In year 2, orders are unchanged so that there is no need to invest. In year 3, orders increase to £24 million so that the firm needs to invest in another four machines if it is to fulfil orders. In year 4, orders increase still further to £30 million. The firm invests in another six machines so that it can fulfil these orders. In year 5, orders remain at £30 million so that there is no need to invest in that year. Finally in year

6, orders fall to £28 million. The firm has too much capital stock and does not, therefore, need to invest. This is all summarised in Table 1.

Year	Annual output	No of machines	Investment
1	20	20	0
2	20	20	0
3	24	24	4
4	30	30	6
5	30	30	0
6	28	28	0

Table 1

In our example, a change in demand leads to a change in investment. If there is no change in demand then there is no investment. Furthermore in percentage terms the changes in demand lead to much bigger changes in investment. For example, the 25% increase in demand in year 4 (from £24 million to £30 million) leads to a 50% increase in investment in that year (from four machines to six machines).

The accelerator theory therefore predicts that investment spending in the economy is likely to be far more volatile than demand. The accelerator theory can be expressed formally as:

$$I_t = b(C_t - C_{t-1})$$

where I_t = Investment in year t, $C_t - C_{t-1}$ = change in consumption during year t, b = accelerator coefficient or capital-output ratio. The capital-output ratio is the amount of capital needed in the economy to produce a given quantity of goods. If £2 of capital is needed to produce £1 of goods, then the capital-output ratio is 2.

The accelerator theory predicts therefore, that changes in the level of investment are related to past changes in consumption. The theory is, however, quite simplistic. For example, there will almost certainly be a time lag involved between changes in demand and changes in investment. This lag will vary between different firms and industries and the theory cannot be adapted to incorporate these lags. Furthermore, there will always be firms with excess stocks of capital. If there is an increase in demand then these firms will utilise this excess capital and will not invest. Finally, different firms will have different expectations about whether increases in demand are likely to be sustained or short lived. Therefore, firms who anticipate that the increased demand will be short lived will not invest. Nevertheless, despite these problems, evidence suggests that a link does exist between changes in demand and investment.

ACTIVITY 7

The accelerator theory can be expressed:

$$I_t = b(C_t - C_{t-1})$$

If $b = 3$ and you are told that in year 0, consumption was equal to £10 million and thereafter grew at a rate of 10% per annum then calculate the level of investment in years 1 to 4.

In year 0, consumption is £10 million. It grows 10% in the next year so that in year 1 it is equal to £11 million (£10 m + £1 m). Investment in year 1 is therefore calculated as $I = 3(11 - 10) = 3$, that is, £3 million.

In year 1, consumption is £11 million. It grows 10% in the next year so that in year 2 it is equal to £12.1 million (£11 m + £1.1 m). Investment in year 2 is therefore calculated as $I = 3(12.1 - 11) = 3.3$, that is, £3.3 million.

In year 2, consumption is £12.1 million. It grows 10% in the next year so that in year 3 it is equal to £13.31 million (£12.1 m + £1.21 m). Investment in year 3 is therefore calculated as $I = 3(13.31 - 12.1) = 3.63$, that is, £3.63 million.

In year 3, consumption is £13.31 million. It grows 10% in the next year so that in year 4 it is equal to £14.641 million (£13.31 m + £1.331 m). Investment in year 4 is therefore calculated as $I = 3(14.641 - 13.31) = 3.993$, that is, £3.993 million.

Hopefully you were able to manage this question without too much difficulty!

REVIEW ACTIVITY 2

1 What are the determinants of consumption demand?

2 If the permanent income hypothesis is correct, why will Keynesian attempts to influence demand by cutting taxation not work?

3 What are the determinants of investment demand?

4 Which of the following would not cause the investment demand curve to shift to the right?

   a an increase in GDP

   b an increase in the general level of wages

   c an increase in the interest rate

   d improved business confidence.

Summary

We have now completed our study of investment demand. The key determinants of investment according to the theories we have considered are:

- the rate of interest
- business expectations and confidence
- changes in consumption.

SECTION THREE

Keynesian Model and Fiscal Policy

Introduction

In this section, we look closely at the issue of using fiscal policy to influence the level of demand in the economy. We look at ways the government finances changes in taxation and government spending and we explore the debate between Keynesians and monetarists about the effectiveness of using fiscal policy to influence the level of demand and the consequences of such policy.

3.1 Keynesian model and unemployment

In Section 2, we became familiar with the basic Keynesian model of aggregate demand. We defined the concept of aggregate demand and, assuming that supply responds to changes in demand, saw how changes in aggregate demand led to increases in national income and output. We defined the multiplier and saw how changes in autonomous components of aggregate demand such as autonomous investment led to much greater changes in national income and output.

Ultimately, in this model, aggregate demand is the key determinant of the level of national income. Here we continue our analysis of the Keynesian model by considering how fiscal policy can be used to influence national income, output and employment levels.

UNEMPLOYMENT IN THE KEYNESIAN MODEL

Earlier we defined national income equilibrium as that level of income where the level of aggregate demand is exactly equal to the level of output produced by firms in the economy. However we also said that there is no guarantee that at this equilibrium level of income, all labour in the economy will be employed, that is, there will be no unemployment.

In Unit 6, we looked at the simple circular flow of income. Households supplied labour to the firms who used this labour to produce goods. The firms paid wages to the households who then spent all of their wages on the output of the firms.

Now let us relax the assumption that households spend all of their income on the output of firms. Instead we assume that they save a proportion of that income. Now firms will be unable to sell all of their output and will accumulate unsold stocks. In this case, the economy will not be in equilibrium. Income (output) is not equal to aggregate demand. Firms will start to cut back on production and reduce labour. National income will start to fall. Eventually equilibrium will be restored at a lower level of national income. Once the economy has settled at this new lower level of national income there will be some workers who no longer have jobs.

For Keynes this was the chief economic problem. The economy could be at a state of rest in equilibrium, with no tendency to move from that point, and workers could be unemployed. Keynes said that such unemployment arose because of an insufficient level of demand in the economy. More commonly, this is known as a **demand deficiency**. Keynes argued that in such a case governments should use fiscal policy to increase aggregate demand in the economy to raise income and output and lower unemployment.

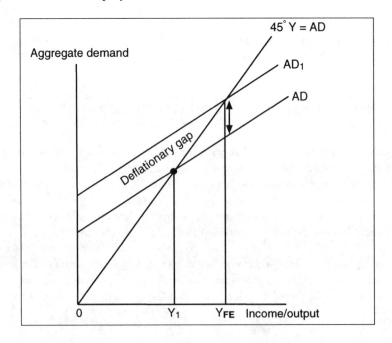

Figure 19: Keynesian cross diagram.

Figure 19 reproduces our familiar Keynesian cross diagram. As before, income and output are measured along the horizontal axis. Aggregate demand is measured on the vertical axis. Equilibrium national income is at the income level Y_1 where the aggregate demand schedule, AD cuts the 45-degree line. Notice that we have also labelled a higher level of income Y_{FE}. This is the level of income that generates full employment or a zero level of unemployment. In the Keynesian model, at this level of output, there may be a small level of frictional unemployment that is not affected by changes in aggregate demand.

Figure 19 shows that, at the equilibrium level of income Y_1, there is unemployment. Aggregate demand needs to be higher so that the level of output Y_{FE} can be achieved. If aggregate demand could be raised to AD_1 this level of income could be achieved. The gap between AD and AD_1 is known as the **deflationary gap**. The deflationary gap measures the increase in aggregate demand necessary to restore full employment.

UNEMPLOYMENT AND FISCAL POLICY

As we have seen, Keynes felt that there was a serious possibility that unemployment would become persistent. He argued that in equilibrium there was no automatic tendency for this unemployment to fall, therefore the government should intervene in order to raise aggregate demand to eliminate the deflationary gap. In our consideration of the Keynesian model so far, we have assumed that no government or overseas sector exists. We now relax our assumptions and introduce the government. We discuss the implications of introducing the overseas sector in Section 4.

As you are probably aware, the introduction of a government means that we now have to include taxation and government spending into our analysis. Government spending is an injection into the economy and a component of aggregate demand. Taxation is a withdrawal.

In Section 1, we defined aggregate demand in equation (1) as:

$$AD = C + I$$

Now, by introducing the government we rewrite this equation as:

$$AD = C + I + G \quad (9)$$

where G = government spending.

How could the government achieve an increase in aggregate demand? There are a number of possibilities, it could:

- reduce taxation in order to raise disposable income
- increase government spending
- try to increase the level of investment by allowing generous tax benefits

to firms that invest in capital plant and machinery.

Ultimately, government spending has to be paid for by taxation or borrowing. We will discuss the implications of this for investment and aggregate demand later. Initially we look at the ways in which the government can raise aggregate demand including changes in government spending and changes in taxation that do not affect investment.

Reductions in taxation

We now examine the effects of changes in taxation on consumption and aggregate demand. In order to finance expenditure the government raises taxes. Some of the tax revenue will be redistributed among the population as pensions, child benefit and unemployment. Collectively, these are known as **transfers**. Any tax revenue raised but not redistributed in the form of transfers, is known as **net taxation**. In reality, household disposable income is reduced by net taxation.

$$Y_d = Y - T \quad (10)$$

Where Y_d = disposable income, Y = income and T = net taxation revenue.

There are a number of different forms of taxation in the economy, and we consider these shortly. For now we assume that taxation is imposed on income and is a fixed proportion of income. In other words, government net taxation revenue is given by:

$$T = tY \quad (11)$$

where T = net taxation revenue, Y = income and t = tax rate.

Let us assume that $t = 25\%$ so that if income rises by £1 then government net tax revenue rises by 25 pence.

We can now substitute equation (10) into equation (9) which gives us:

$$Y_d = Y - tY = Y(1 - t) \quad (12)$$

Any increase in income of £1 results, in our example, in an increase in disposable income of 75 pence. The remaining 25 pence goes to the government as revenue.

Previously we saw that the consumption function was made up of two components. Autonomous consumption and consumption which depends on the level of income. Specifically in equation (2) we saw that:

$$C = 10 + 0.8Y \quad (2)$$

With an autonomous level of investment of £30 million, this gave us an equilibrium level of income of £200 million.

We continue to assume that consumption is a function of income. However now consumption depends on disposable income, so we rewrite our consumption function as:

$$C = 10 + 0.8Y_d \quad (13)$$

Or we can write this as:

$$C = 10 + 0.8(1 - t)Y = 10 + 0.8(0.75)Y$$

$$C = 10 + 0.6Y \quad (14)$$

Compare equation (14) with (2). You will notice that consumption has been reduced by 0.2Y. Earlier we talked about the marginal propensity to consume as an indicator of what people would spend of their available income. Now we will see how the *MPC* concept is modified to account for the change in consumption under taxation.

Remember that *MPC* is the increase in consumption from an increase in disposable income of £1. In the absence of taxation, *MPC* is 0.8. Now that taxation is introduced the *MPC* falls to 0.6. We now define this new marginal propensity to consume as *TMPC*. We use this *T* to remind us that in the presence of taxation the value of *MPC* will change. Then:

$$TMPC = MPC(1 - t) \quad (15)$$

You may recall that *MPC* defines the slope of the consumption function. By introducing taxation, our consumption function has a flatter slope. The effect of introducing taxation into the analysis is to increase the withdrawals in the economy. Previously, if households received an extra £1 of income then 80 pence would be spent and the remaining 20 pence would be saved, that is, withdrawn. Now if households receive the extra £1 then 25 pence is immediately withdrawn in taxation. Of the remaining 75 pence 80%, or 60p is consumed and 20%, or 15p is saved. Taxation reduces both consumption and saving from the extra £1 of income. Figure 20 shows our original consumption function defined by equation (2) and our new function defined by equation (14).

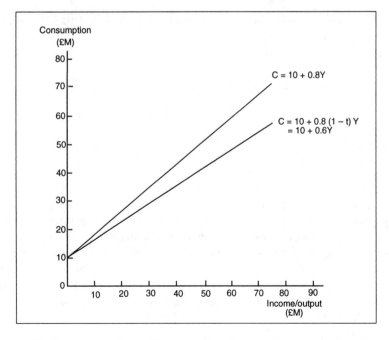

Figure 20: Income taxation will change the slope of the consumption function.

Now that we know how changes in taxation can affect aggregate demand, we can consider how the government can remove a deflationary gap by reducing taxes. Recall our consumption function defined by equation (14). Now if we continue to assume an autonomous level of investment of £30 million and a zero level of government expenditure then our aggregate demand function can be written as:

$$AD = 10 + 0.6Y + 30 = 40 + 0.6Y \quad (16)$$

This is shown in Figure 21.

The equilibrium level of income is where aggregate demand is equal to output and income, that is, where:

$$AD = Y$$

so we can rewrite equation (16) as, $Y = 10 + 0.6Y + 30 = 40 + 0.6Y$

Therefore, $Y - 0.6Y = 40$

so that, $Y = 100$, that is, £100 million.

The equilibrium level of income is shown in Figure 21 at point A.

Before we introduced taxation, we saw that the equilibrium level of income was £200 million. Clearly if the introduction of taxation can reduce national income in this way, then by reducing taxation, national income can be increased.

To consider by how much income will rise as a result of a cut in taxation we must return to the multiplier. You may recall that in Section 1, equation (7), we defined the multiplier as:

$$\Delta Y = \Delta AD \times [1/(1 - MPC)]$$

Now that we have introduced taxation into our analysis, this formula will alter. Now we rewrite the expression as:

$$\Delta Y = \Delta AD \times 1/(1 - TMPC) \quad (17)$$

You will recall that $TMPC = MPC(1 - t)$.

We begin from a tax rate of 25% and we continue to use our consumption function:

$C = 10 + 0.8Y_d$. Autonomous investment is equal to £30 million. National income as we have seen is £100 million.

Now let the government reduce taxation from 25% to 15%, a reduction of 10%. Consider this carefully. If national income is £100 million and the tax rate is 25% then government tax revenue is 0.25(100 million) = £25 million. A reduction in the tax rate of 10% reduces tax revenue and raises disposable income by £10 million. However aggregate demand will not rise by £10 million. As investment is autonomous the only component of aggregate demand that will change is consumption. Now if individual disposable income rises by £10 million and we have MPC of 0.8 then consumption, and therefore aggregate demand, will rise by just £8 million. The other £2 million is saved by households.

So using our multiplier from equation 3.9:

$\Delta Y = \Delta AD \times 1/(1 - TMPC)$

so, $\Delta Y = 8 \times 1/(1 - TMPC)$

Now $TMPC = MPC(1 - t)$

$\qquad\qquad = 0.8 \, (1 - 0.15)$

$\qquad\qquad = 0.68$

so, $\Delta Y = 8 \times 1/(1 - 0.68)$

$= 25$, that is, an increase in national income of £25 million.

Therefore the new equilibrium level of national income will be £125 million. To see this, remember that in equilibrium $Y = AD$, and in our example:

$AD = 10 + 0.8(1 - 0.15)Y + 30$

so, $AD = 40 + 0.68Y$

In equilibrium, $Y = 40 + 0.68Y$, so $0.32Y = 40$.

$Y = 125$. This is shown as point B. Figure 21 illustrates this.

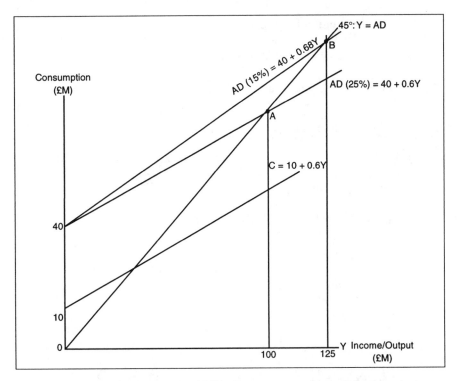

Figure 21: At a tax rate of 25% the aggregate demand function is
AD(25%). This generates an equilibrium level of income of £100 million.
If the tax rate changes to 15%, then the aggregate demand function
shifts to AD(15%). This intersects the 45–degree line at point B
generating a higher equilibrium level of income of £125 million.

The aggregate demand function with a tax rate of 25% is labelled $AD(25\%)$. The equilibrium level of income is £100 million. The change in the tax rate alters the slope of the consumption function and hence the aggregate demand function. The new aggregate demand function is labelled $AD(15\%)$ and the new equilibrium level of income of £125 million is shown.

Clearly by reducing taxation, national income is increased. The reduction in taxation raises the disposable income of households. Some of this increase will be spent and the rest will be saved. As households raise their level of spending then firms experience an increase in demand and notice a fall in stock levels. Therefore they will raise output and will hire more labour in order to do so. As they hire more labour then the newly employed workers receive incomes in the form of wages. Naturally, they will spend most of this income and add further to the increase in demand. As a result of the multiplier effect the final increase in national income will be far greater than the initial increase in aggregate demand.

ACTIVITY 8

You are given the following consumption function: $C = 5 + 0.5Y_d$. The tax rate is 10% and the level of autonomous investment is zero.

1 Calculate the equilibrium level of income with and without the tax.

2 Calculate the value of the multiplier with tax.

3 Calculate the new equilibrium level of national income if the tax rate falls to 5%.

4 Illustrate your answers to 1 and 2 in a Keynesian cross diagram.

---

1   In equilibrium, $Y = AD$

Without taxation, $Y = 5 + 0.5Y$ as $Y = Y_d$ if there is no tax,

so, $0.5Y = 5$

$Y = 10$ (point A in Figure 22)

With taxation, $Y = 5 + 0.5Y_d$

so, $Y = 5 + 0.5(1 - t)Y = 5 + 0.5(0.9)Y$

$Y = 5 + 0.45Y$

$0.55Y = 5$

$Y = 9.1$ (point B in Figure 22)

2   Multiplier value is $1/(1 - TMPC) = 1/(1 - 0.45) = 1.82$.

3   Tax rate $= 5\%$

In equilibrium, $Y = 5 + 0.5(0.95)Y = 5 + 0.475Y$

so, $Y - 0.475Y = 5$

$0.525Y = 5$

$Y = 9.52$.

To see this another way, tax rate falls from 10% to 5% so that tax revenue falls and disposable income rises by, $0.05(9.1) = 0.455$.

However, aggregate demand does not rise by this amount as the MPC tells us that 50% of the increase in income will be saved so demand rises by only $0.5(0.455) = 0.2275$.

Aggregate demand rises by 0.2275 and from the multiplier formula we can see that national income will rise by $0.2275 \times 1/(1 - 0.475) = 0.42$. So national income rises $9.1 + 0.42 = 9.52$.

4

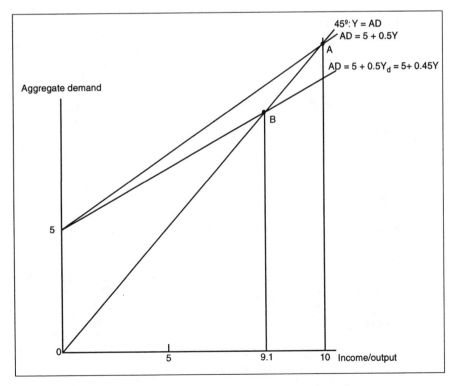

Figure 22: New equilibrium level of income with reduction in tax.

We can look at the effects of taxation on national income in another way. In Section 1, we examined national income equilibrium in terms of injections and withdrawals. Although we have introduced a government sector we are assuming for now that government spending is zero, so that the only injection is investment. As for withdrawals, we now have taxation as well as savings.

Recall that equilibrium national income occurred only when injections and withdrawals were equal. In our previous analysis, national income equilibrium occurred when:

$S = I$

where S = savings and I = investment.

Now we rewrite this as:

$S + T = I$ (18)

We also saw that:

$Y = C + S$

We rewrote this equation as:

$Y = C + S + T$

In equation (9), we saw that $AD = C + I + G$, we assume that $G = 0$, so that:

$AD = C + I$

In equilibrium, $Y = AD$ so that:

$C + I = C + S + T$

By definition:

$I = S + T$ (19)

Equation 3.11 reminds us that in equilibrium, injections are equal to withdrawals.

If we return to our tax rate of 25% we calculated an equilibrium level of income of £100 million. To see that equation (19) holds we need to define a savings function. In equation (13), we saw that:

$C = 10 + 0.8Y_d$

In equation (4), we saw that:

$S = -10 + 0.2Y$

Having introduced taxation this becomes:

$$S = -10 + 0.2Y_d = -10 + 0.2(1 - t)Y = -10 + 0.2(0.75)Y = -10 + 0.15Y \quad (20)$$

As for taxation, the tax rate is 25% and the equilibrium level of income is £100 million so that taxation revenue is 0.25(100). If we substitute these figures into equation (19):

$I = -10 + 0.15(100) + 0.25(100) = 30$, that is, £30 million. We know that autonomous investment is £30 million so that equation (19) holds.

Now if the rate of taxation drops by 10% to 15%, equilibrium income will be at a higher level but equation (19) must still hold, that is, $I = S + T$.

We know $I = 30$, and the savings function from equation (20), $S = -10 + 0.2Y_d$

so, $S = -10 + 0.2(1 - t)Y = -10 + 0.2(0.85)Y = -10 + 0.17Y$.

As for taxation, this is proportional to income. In equation (11), $T = tY$.

Using a 15% tax rate, equation (19) can be written:

$$30 = -10 + 0.17Y + 0.15Y$$

$$30 = -10 + 0.32Y$$

$$40 = 0.32Y$$

$$Y = 125.$$

As we proved earlier the new national income equilibrium is £125 million.

Figure 23 illustrates our initial injections and withdrawals in the absence of taxation. Equilibrium national income is £200 million. This is, of course, the position depicted in Figure 8.

Figure 23 then shows the effect of imposing a tax rate of 25%. The withdrawals function shifts upwards to W_1 and national income equilibrium falls to £100 million. This withdrawals function, W_1, is $S + T$, and we have seen that in this case, $S = -10 + 0.15Y$, and $T = 0.25Y$,

so that, $S + T = W_1 = -10 + 0.15Y + 0.25Y = -10 + 0.4Y$.

The third situation is also shown where taxation falls to 15%. The slope of the withdrawals function changes so that W_2 is the new withdrawals function and national income rises to £125 million. This withdrawals function is $S + T$ where, in this case:

$S = -10 + 0.17Y$ and $T = 0.15Y$, so that, $S + T = W_2 = -10 + 0.32Y$.

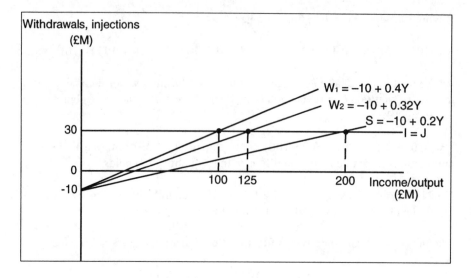

Figure 23: The effect of changes in taxation on the withdrawals function.

The whole point of this discussion is to show the effect of taxes on national income. Clearly tax cuts raise national income. The exact rise in the level of national income depends on the value of the multiplier.

ACTIVITY 9

The consumption function $C = 5 + 0.5Y_d$. The autonomous level of investment of zero, and the tax rate is 10%.

1 Calculate the savings function.

2 Use the injections and withdrawals approach to calculate the equilibrium level of income.

1   $Y = C + S + T$

and we know, $T = 0.1Y$

so, $S = Y - C - T = Y - 5 - 0.5(1 - t) \, Y - 0.1Y$

$= Y - 5 - 0.45Y - 0.1Y = -5 + 0.45Y$

2   In equilibrium, injections will be equal to withdrawals:

$S + T = I$

But investment is zero,

so, $S + T = 0$

$-5 + 0.45Y + 0.1Y = 0$

$-5 + 0.55Y = 0$

$0.55Y = 5$

so, $Y = 9.1$.

Changes in taxation to achieve full employment

We have looked at the effect of taxation on national income. Now we consider how changes in taxation can affect the level of employment. Let us assume that, for a particular year:

- full employment occurs when national income is £160 million.
- autonomous investment is fixed at £30 million.
- taxation is currently at 15%.

By how much must the government reduce taxes in order to restore full employment? The easiest way to answer this question is to use our equation for aggregate demand:

$AD = C + I$

In equilibrium, $Y = AD$ so, $Y = C + I$.

We can rewrite this in full:

$Y = 10 + 0.8(1 - t)Y + 30$.

Y needs to be 160, so we can write: $160 = 10 + 0.8(1 - t)160 + 30$

so, $160 = 40 + 0.8(1 - t)160$, or, $160 = 40 + 128(1 - t)$

so, $120 = 128(1 - t)$

$(1 - t) = 120/128 = 0.9375$

$t = 1 - 0.9375 = 0.0625$.

The tax rate must fall to 6.25% to restore full employment at a level of income of £160 million.

ACTIVITY 10

You are given the following consumption function: $C = 8 + 0.6Y_d$. The tax rate is 30%. Autonomous investment is 20.

1 Calculate the equilibrium level of income.

2 Full employment is reached when national income is equal to 60. Calculate by how much taxes should fall to achieve this.

1 In equilibrium, $Y = AD$

so, $Y = 8 + 0.6(1 - 0.3)Y + 20$

$Y = 28 + 0.42Y$

$0.58Y = 28$

$Y = 48.27$

2 In equilibrium, $Y = AD$ so, $Y = C + I$, we can rewrite this in full:

$Y = 8 + 0.6(1 - t)Y + 20$

Y needs to be 60 to ensure full employment so we can write:

$60 = 28 + 0.6(1 - t)60$

$60 = 28 + 36(1 - t)$

$32 = 36(1 - t)$

$(1 - t) = 32/36 = 0.89$

so, $t = 1 - 0.89 = 0.11$. The tax rate must fall to 11% to restore full employment at a level of income of 60.

Increases in government spending

We have now seen how the government can raise national income by reducing taxes. However, governments can also raise national income by spending on projects such as roadbuilding or defence. This type of government expenditure will add directly to aggregate demand and influence the level of national income.

So far we have assumed that government spending is equal to zero. Let us now assume that government spending is £20 million. We will also assume that the level of government spending is independent of the level of national income. In other words, government spending is autonomous. Our final assumption is that the tax rate is zero. Therefore our aggregate demand function can now be defined as:

$AD = C + I + G$ (21)

or, $AD = 10 + 0.8Y + 30 + 20$

$AD = 60 + 0.8Y$

Again, all figures are expressed in £ million.

In the absence of government spending (and taxation) we saw that the equilibrium level of income was £200 million. Changes in government expenditure which are autonomous are dealt with in exactly the same way that we dealt with changes in autonomous investment earlier in Section 1. Recall that our equation (7) defined the multiplier as:

$\Delta Y = \Delta AD \times 1/(1 - MPC)$

So an increase in autonomous government spending of £20 million constitutes an increase in aggregate demand of £20 million. In equilibrium, income will rise by:

$+ 20 \times 1/(1 - 0.8) = 100$

So that national income rises from £200 million to £300 million. To prove this:

In equilibrium, $Y = AD$:

$Y = 10 + 0.8Y + 30 + 20$

$Y = 60 + 0.8Y$

$Y - 0.8Y = 60$

$0.2Y = 60$

$Y = 300$, that is, £300 million. Figure 24 shows the increase in income as a result of the increase in government spending.

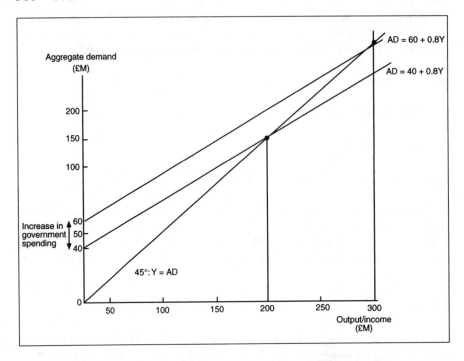

Figure 24: An increase in government expenditure will cause an upward shift in the aggregate demand function.

Another way of seeing this is in terms of withdrawals and injections. In general, withdrawals are savings and taxation but since we now assume zero taxation our only withdrawal is savings. Our injections will be investment and government spending. In equilibrium, withdrawals and injections will be equal so that:

$$S = I + G$$

We saw in equation (4) that our savings function was:

$$S = -10 + 0.2Y$$

Before the government raised spending, the only injection was investment of £30 million. We can now write:

$$S = -10 + 0.2Y = I + G$$

or, $-10 + 0.2Y = 30 + 20$

$-10 + 0.2Y = 50$

$0.2Y = 60$

$Y = 300.$

Figure 25 shows this shift in the equilibrium position using our injections and withdrawals diagram.

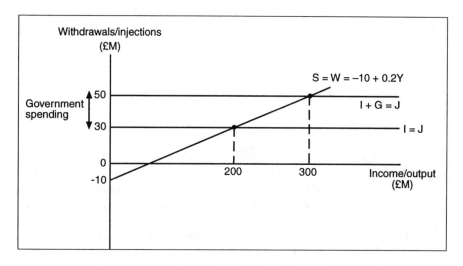

Figure 25: Increase in government spending using withdrawals and injections.

Before we close this discussion, let us consider the effects of simultaneously raising taxes and raising government expenditure. Let us begin with our assumptions from Section 1. Government spending and taxation are zero and autonomous investment is £30 million.

$$AD = C + I = 10 + 0.8Y + 30 = 40 + 0.8Y.$$

And as we have seen equilibrium national income is £200 million.

Now let the government raise taxation from zero to 20%. This will raise tax revenue and reduce disposable income by 0.2(£200 million) = £40 million. At the same time, the government raises government spending from zero to £40 million. In a situation where the increase in taxation is exactly equal to the increase in government expenditure we have what is known as a **balanced budget**. At first glance, you may think that national income will not change in this case. Let us find out:

$$AD = C + I + G$$

so, $AD = 10 + 0.8Y_d + 30 + 40$

$$AD = 80 + 0.8(1 - t)Y$$

$$AD = 80 + 0.8(1 - 0.2)Y$$

$$AD = 80 + 0.64Y$$

In equilibrium, $Y = AD$, so, $Y = 80 + 0.64Y$

$Y - 0.64Y = 80$

$0.36Y = 80$

$Y = 222.22$, that is, £222.22 million.

So, the balanced budget has led to an increase in national income of £22.22 million. Now we will consider why and by how much additional spending with a balanced budget will raise national income.

An increase in government spending of £40 million directly adds £40 million to aggregate demand. Now you might think that taking £40 million in tax would reduce aggregate demand by the same amount, leaving the situation effectively as it was before the increase in spending and tax. It doesn't! Can you see why?

Before the increase in tax, people had £40 million more disposable income. But as the *MPC* is 0.8, then only 80% or £32 million of this income was consumed. Therefore reducing disposable income by £40 million reduces consumption (and hence aggregate demand) by £32 million. Some of the reduction in disposable income as a result of the increase in taxation will be offset by reductions in savings by households. The effect of the spending therefore is to raise aggregate demand by £40 million, and the taxation has reduced it by £32 million, a net effect of an £8 million increase in aggregate demand.

We can now utilise the multiplier to confirm the new equilibrium level of income.

$\Delta Y = + 8 \times 1/(1 - TMPC)$

$= + 8 \times 1/(1 - 0.64) = 22.22$, that is, an increase in national income of £22.22 million. This generates a higher level of income of £222.22 million.

Figure 26 illustrates our initial aggregate demand function in the absence of taxation and government expenditure. This is labelled AD, where $AD = 40 + 0.8Y$. The equilibrium level of income is shown as £200 million. This is labelled A. We then show the new aggregate demand function with the balanced budget. This is AD_1, where $AD_1 = 80 + 0.64Y$. The new equilibrium level of income is £222.22 million, this is labelled B.

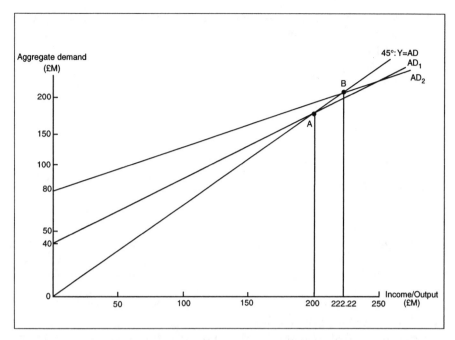

Figure 26: The balanced budget causes the aggregate demand function to shift from AD1 to AD2 and equilibrium moves from A to B, equilibrium national income increases from £200 million to £222.22 million.

ACTIVITY 11

You are given the following consumption function: $C = 15 + 0.8Y$. Autonomous investment is 12. Government spending and the tax rate are zero.

1 Calculate the equilibrium level of income.

2 The government now raises government spending from zero to £13.5M By how much must it raise taxes so that the budget is balanced? Calculate the change in income as a result of the balanced budget.

1   In equilibrium, $Y = AD$

   $Y = 15 + 0.8Y + 12 = 27 + 0.8Y$

   $0.2Y = 27$

   $Y = 135$

2   Government spending increases to £13.5M. So a balanced budget raises tax so that tax revenue increases by 13.5. National income is 135 so the tax rate must be 13.5/135 = 10%.

Now $C = 15 + 0.8Y_d = 15 + 0.8(1 - 0.1)Y = 15 + 0.8(0.9)Y$

So that $AD = 15 + 0.72Y + 12 + 13.5$

$AD = 40.5 + 0.72Y$

In equilibrium, $Y = AD$

$Y = 40.5 + 0.72Y$

$0.28Y = 40.5$

$Y = 144.6$

So a balanced budget raises national income from £135M to £144.6M.

FISCAL POLICY, AGGREGATE DEMAND AND THE AGGREGATE SUPPLY CURVE IN A KEYNESIAN MODEL

Earlier you saw that by using fiscal policy, that is, changes in taxation and government spending, the government can raise national income. So far we have assumed that output is solely determined by aggregate demand and that aggregate supply, the total output supplied in the economy, simply responds to changes in aggregate demand. We now look at aggregate supply in this Keynesian model and see how changes in aggregate demand affect aggregate supply and the price level.

In the Keynesian model, prices are assumed to be fixed if the level of national income is such that there is unemployment. Only when there is full employment will prices rise in response to any increase in aggregate demand. Let us return to our initial consumption function:

$C = 10 + 0.8Y$

We assume no taxation and an autonomous level of investment of £30 million. In this case, the equilibrium level of income is £200 million. We will assume that this is also the level of national income that ensures full employment. Initially government spending is zero, but now suppose the government tries to raise spending to £20 million. If aggregate supply could rise then we can calculate the new level of equilibrium income:

$AD = 10 + 0.8Y + 30 + 20$

so, $AD = 60 + 0.8Y$

In equilibrium, $Y = AD$, so, $Y = 60 + 0.8Y$

$0.2Y = 60$

$Y = 300$, that is, £300 million.

However, because the economy is at full employment we know that this rise cannot occur. Therefore aggregate demand has risen but aggregate supply is unable to respond. As a result, the price level increases. The difference between our initial level of aggregate demand and the new higher level of aggregate demand as a result of the increased government spending, is known as the **inflationary gap**. Figure 27 illustrates this.

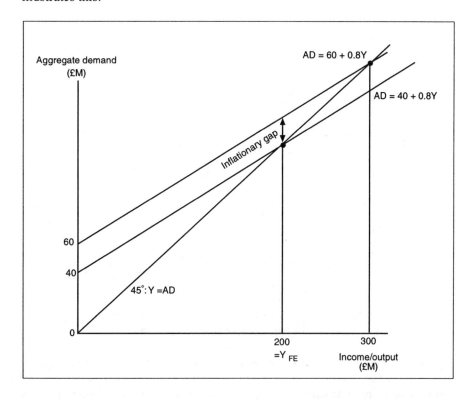

Figure 27: The inflationary gap.

The initial equilibrium level of income is shown at £200 million. Now with increased government spending of £20 million, the new level would be £300 million if supply could respond. The inflationary gap measures the 'gap' or difference between the full employment level of national income (£200 million) and the higher national income level which would be achieved if supply could respond (£300 million). This is shown in Figure 27 and it arises because aggregate demand is higher than necessary to bring about full employment.

You can see that in the Keynesian model, unemployment and inflation cannot occur at the same time. Unemployment is caused by too little demand (demand deficiency) and inflation is caused by too much demand (excess demand). In this model, prices can only rise when there is no more unemployment and aggregate supply can rise no further. If there is some unemployment then aggregate demand can be increased and prices will not rise. Unemployment will fall and national income will rise. Once full employment is reached, further increases in aggregate demand cannot raise national income and will simply cause inflation. This should give you some idea about the shape of the Keynesian aggregate supply curve. Figure 28 shows aggregate demand and supply in the Keynesian model.

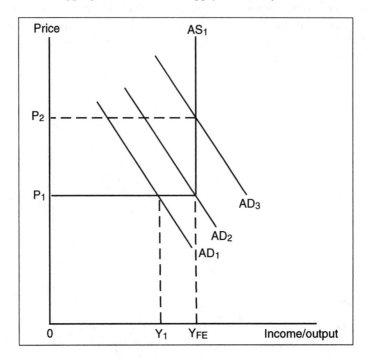

*Figure 28: Changes in aggregate demand and the
Keynesian aggregate supply schedule.*

Before we examine the aggregate supply curve, we need firstly to explain the downward sloping nature of the aggregate demand schedule. The aggregate demand schedule is the total demand for all goods and services in the economy: that is by consumers, by firms, by the government and by foreigners. Consider the schedule AD_1 in Figure 28 and let us look at why the schedule slopes downwards.

The total level of spending will depend on people's money incomes and the prices that they have to pay. For any given level of money incomes, the higher the level of prices then the less people will be able to buy. So if prices rise then less will be purchased and aggregate demand will be lower. Therefore one explanation of the downward sloping aggregate demand curve is an **income effect**. There will also be **substitution effects** which reinforce the downward sloping nature of the aggregate demand curve. For example, if the price level rises then people will buy more foreign produced goods, that is, imports, and foreigners will buy fewer UK exports so that the demand for domestic goods falls. In addition to this, higher prices will erode the value of peoples' savings in banks and building societies. Many people will cut back on spending because their real wealth is lower. Once again, higher prices leads to a reduction in aggregate demand.

The combination of these substitution and income effects is that the aggregate demand curve slopes downward. This is shown as AD_1.

We now turn to the aggregate supply curve and consider how increases in aggregate demand affect the price level. Figure 28 shows the Keynesian aggregate supply curve which is horizontal for all levels of income and output until full employment is reached at Y_{FE}. At this point, supply can no longer increase and becomes vertical. This is labelled AS_1.

Suppose we have an initial level of income of Y_1 where income is below the full employment level, aggregate demand can be raised by cutting taxes or raising expenditure. AD_1 shifts to AD_2. This raises income to the full employment level Y_{FE} but does not affect prices which are fixed at P_1. However further increases in aggregate demand to AD_3 cause an increase in prices to P_2 with no change in income. The point is that, in this Keynesian model, provided that unemployment exists then governments can raise aggregate demand without causing prices to rise. However once full employment is reached then further attempts to increase aggregate demand will simply raise the price level.

In Unit 9, we look more closely at the concept of aggregate supply. Later in this unit we look at problems of using fiscal policy to change aggregate demand and income. In particular, we focus on the monetarist criticisms of using fiscal policy in this way.

Now we look at the different types of taxation used by the government and the way in which the government finances its expenditure.

3.2 Government budget

As you saw in Unit 6, fiscal policy was the major tool of economic policy used since World War II to manage the level of demand in the economy. Keynesian economic thinking was dominant. Keynesians emphasised the power of fiscal policy. Monetary policy, at that time, was seen as a less effective tool with which to manage demand.

The chief reason for using fiscal policy was demand management. Fiscal policy was used to 'fine tune' the economy. Over time economies often go through natural cycles of recession followed by boom followed by recession etc. This is known as the **trade cycle**. Keynesians naturally see the trade cycle as a result of fluctuations in investment over time. Fiscal policy was seen as a vital element in smoothing out the trade cycle. If the economy was in a boom period and near full employment then there was the danger of inflation. Additionally at high levels of demand there was a serious risk of external deficit. In these cases, the government could raise taxes and reduce government spending to prevent what is known as 'overheating'. On the other hand in a recessionary period, taxes would be cut and government spending raised in order to boost aggregate demand. When fiscal policy is used like this it is known as **discretionary fiscal policy**. This is shown in Figure 29. The continuous line shows the effects of the trade cycle in the absence of Keynesian fine tuning policy while the broken line shows how fiscal policy can be used to 'dampen' down the effects of the cycle.

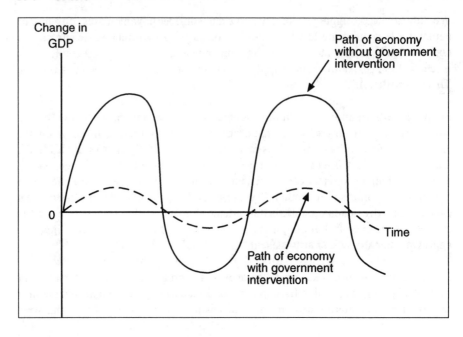

Figure 29: Discretionary fiscal policy.

We have already mentioned that government expenditure, G is financed from tax revenue, T. The government budget is concerned with the amount that the government spends and raises in tax revenue. The government budget position is measured by: $G - T$.

If tax revenue exceeds the amount the government spends in a given period,

that is, $T > G$ then we say there is a **budget surplus**;

if, $T = G$ then there is a **balanced budget**;

if, $T < G$ then we say there is a **budget deficit.**

Before we consider ways of measuring the government budget we briefly look at the different types of taxation the government uses to raise revenue.

TAXATION

Broadly speaking, we can split taxation into three categories:

- direct taxation
- indirect taxation
- taxes on wealth.

Direct taxation – direct taxes are taxes on earnings and income such as income tax. The rate of income tax paid by individuals depends upon their level of income. Higher income individuals pay a higher rate than lower income individuals. This is known as a **progressive tax**. If individuals own property they will have to pay tax on any rent they may receive. They also pay tax on earnings from financial investments such as share dividends. Another example is tax on company profits which is known as corporation tax. National insurance is another example of direct taxation.

Indirect taxation — Indirect taxes are those taxes on expenditure on goods and services. The most familiar example of this is value added tax or VAT. VAT is levied on most types of goods, although certain goods such as books and children's clothes are not subject to VAT. Other forms of indirect tax, known as duties, are levied on alcohol, petrol and tobacco, for example.

Taxes on wealth — In addition to direct and indirect taxation, local and central governments also raise revenue by taxing property (council tax) and transfers of wealth (capital gains tax and inheritance tax).

Taxation as an automatic stabiliser

Whilst tax revenue is raised in order to finance government expenditure, governments also use taxation as an **automatic stabiliser** in the economy. An automatic stabiliser is something that reduces the effect on national income of a large sudden change in the economy, called a 'shock'. Shocks, such as a sudden drop in autonomous investment, can have harmful effects on national income, the price level and the level of employment. Let us examine how an automatic stabiliser can reduce the effect of a shock.

In our discussion of the Keynesian model of national income determination, we saw that changes in autonomous expenditure such as investment can affect national income. Consider our example of the consumption function again:

$$C = 10 + 0.8Y$$

Let taxation be zero and autonomous investment be £30 million. Now let autonomous investment fall by £10 million to £20 million.

According to our multiplier national income falls by:

$$\Delta Y = \Delta AD \times [1/(1 - MPC)]$$

$$= -10 \times 1/(1 - 0.8) = -50, \text{ that is, income falls by £50 million.}$$

Now let's see what would have been the case if tax at 20% had been in place during the fall in autonomous investment. Our consumption function becomes:

$$C = 10 + 0.8Y_d = 10 + 0.8(1 - t)Y = 10 + 0.64Y$$

In this case an equivalent fall in autonomous investment of £10 million causes a fall in national income of: $-10 \times 1/(1 - 0.64) = -27.77$, that is, a fall in income of just £27.77 million.

The tax effectively reduces the amount of change in national income that arises from a change in autonomous investment. This is how tax can be seen as an automatic stabiliser. Shocks will affect aggregate demand. In our example, the drop in autonomous investment will cause a fall in aggregate demand, which is represented by an inward shift in the aggregate demand schedule. As aggregate demand falls then government tax revenue falls and this mitigates against the fall in national income.

Taxation is not the only form of automatic stabiliser. Another is unemployment benefit. As national income falls and unemployment rises then the amount of unemployment benefit paid by the government rises. This also mitigates against the fall in national income.

FINANCING THE GOVERNMENT BUDGET

If the government follows a Keynesian policy of cutting taxes and raising government expenditure in times of recession then it may well have a budget deficit, a situation where tax revenue is insufficient to finance government spending. In fact, the Keynesian policy of cutting taxes and raising government expenditure in order to influence demand is often referred to as **deficit financing**. Since World War II in the UK, a budget deficit was usual although it did go into surplus in the late 1960s and mid 1980s.

How can the government spend more than it has in revenue? Like any of us, it borrows. The government borrows by issuing securities. It sells these securities to the public and financial institutions and raises money to finance spending. These securities are effectively a promise to repay or more commonly, an IOU. If the government wishes to borrow for a long period, for example 5, 10 or even 50 years, it issues government bonds or 'gilts'. These gilts entitle the holder, that is the lender, to receive an annual interest payment during the period of the loan. At the end of the loan period, the government pays back the sum borrowed. Alternatively, the government can borrow in the short term, perhaps for a period of months. To do this it issues 'treasury bills' which usually do not pay interest. For example, the government might issue a treasury bill of £500 for repayment in six months time. No-one will lend £500 free to the government for six months so instead the government sells the bill at a discount. Assume that the current rate of interest on other similar assets is 12% per year. Then at the start of the six month period the bill will be worth £470. The £30 difference between £500 and £470 represents the interest on the bill. £30 interest for 6 months is the equivalent of £60 interest for the year where £60 is 12% of £500.

Clearly, if the government wishes to finance a large budget deficit then it must persuade people to buy more and more of these securities. It has to make the securities increasingly attractive. To achieve this, it often raises the rate of interest paid on the securities. We examine the effects of government borrowing later.

MEASURING THE BUDGET DEFICIT IN THE UK

If the government has a budget deficit each year then the amount of debt owed grows. This total amount is recorded as the **national debt**. The national debt is made up of the total stock of gilts and treasury bills held by the public and financial institutions. Whenever a budget deficit occurs the national debt grows. When a budget surplus is achieved then a small part of the national debt is paid off.

When we talk of the government budget we are referring to the budget of the central government. However, in addition to this the national accounts also record the deficit of the whole public sector, known as the **public sector borrowing requirement**, the PSBR.

The PSBR is made up of the borrowing requirement of the central government, (the budget deficit), the borrowing requirement of local authorities and the borrowing requirement of public corporations. The PSBR tells us exactly how much the government needs to borrow to finance its spending plans.

The PSBR is closely related to the budget deficit, and the UK has had a PSBR for most years since World War II. However, in the late 1960s and late 1980s, the PSBR became negative. In other words, the public sector had sufficient tax revenue to finance its spending plans and pay back some of its previous borrowing. In such periods, there is no PSBR but instead, a PSDR, **public sector debt repayment**.

We might be alarmed if the budget deficit or PSBR grew year after year because eventually the debt has to be paid back. Persistently high deficits might indicate that at some stage in the future the government will need to raise taxes or cut public spending in order to pay off the accumulated debt. There is some truth in this and persistently high deficits are worrying. However the measure that we should observe is the deficit as a percentage of GDP. This figure gives a better measure of the ability of the economy to pay off the debt. Only if the deficit as a percentage of GDP grows continually does it become a serious problem.

Table 2 (over page) shows the PSBR as a percentage of GDP for the period 1968–1994.

The disturbing rise in the PSBR as a percentage of GDP in the early 1990s has worried many economists. This was a result of the severe recession in the UK in this period. As output fell and unemployment rose the government spent more on benefits yet received less in tax revenue as firms' profits and the number of people in employment fell. As a result, the early 1990s saw the Conservative government introduce some tax raising measures for the first time since approximately 1980.

BUDGET DEFICIT AND FISCAL POLICY

What information does the budget deficit, or PSBR, reveal about the government fiscal policy position? Does a high deficit indicate that the government is pursuing an **expansionary** fiscal policy in order to raise the level of aggregate demand? Does a small deficit, or surplus, indicate that the government is pursuing a **contractionary** fiscal policy in order to reduce aggregate demand to prevent the economy from overheating?

By itself the deficit alone is not a good measure of fiscal position. The deficit can change for reasons that have nothing to do with fiscal policy. If the overseas sector goes into recession and buys less of the domestic economy's exports then the domestic level of income will fall as injections fall. Unemployment may rise in the export industries and aggregate demand will fall as household income falls. The government will spend more on unemployment benefit and tax revenue will fall.

Year	PSBR/GDP(%)
1968	3.3
1969*	−1.3
1970*	−0.1
1971	2.6
1972	3.4
1973	6.2
1974	8.5
1975	10.6
1976	8.0
1977	4.2
1978	5.5
1979	7.2
1980	5.9
1981	4.8
1982	2.0
1983	4.5
1984	3.7
1985	2.4
1986	0.7
1987*	−0.3
1988*	−2.8
1989*	−2.1
1990*	-0.4
1991	1.5
1992	5.5
1993	7.8
1994	6.4

* A negative figure indicates PSDR

Table 2

Source: CSO Annual Abstract of Statistics

The deficit will increase with no change in government policy.

When the economy is doing well, or is in a boom period, then spending on unemployment benefits will be falling and tax revenues will be high. In this case, the deficit will be low or negative, that is, there will be a budget surplus. Therefore the budget deficit alone tells us little about government policy. It is extremely difficult to tell whether the government is pursuing a discretionary fiscal policy in order to fine tune the economy or to manage the level of demand.

3.3 Fiscal policy debate

We have now studied the Keynesian model in some detail and we have seen how the government can change tax rates and levels of spending in order to influence the level of aggregate demand. In the period since World War II until the late 1970s, successive governments used fiscal policy in a discretionary way in order to maintain a low level of unemployment and in order to prevent the economy from overheating to the extent that inflation and external deficits became a problem. For much of this period, both unemployment and inflation in the UK remained relatively low but unfortunately the UK economic performance was poor compared with that of other industrial nations.

The major cause for concern was the tendency of the economy to run into external deficit whenever full employment was approached. The government would have to raise taxes and reduce spending in order to reduce the level of demand so that import demand fell. This would tend to raise unemployment again. Once the external deficit had been reduced then taxes would be cut and spending raised to boost demand again. This cycle of raising then reducing aggregate demand became known as 'stop-go' and characterised the UK economy throughout the 1950s and 1960s.

In the 1970s, inflation rates began to increase. Keynesian theory said that inflation would only occur when the economy was near to full employment. But in the 1970s, inflation and unemployment began increasing at the same time. This process was known as **stagflation**. Keynesian theory was unable to explain this and so confidence in the use of discretionary fiscal policy began to decline. The election of the Conservative government in 1979 saw a total abandonment of discretionary fiscal policy and demand management and an increasing emphasis on the importance of monetary policy. Why did discretionary fiscal policy become a problem? We now turn to the problems of using fiscal policy to manage the level of demand.

EFFECTIVENESS OF DISCRETIONARY FISCAL POLICY
There are a number of problems associated with using fiscal policy in a discretionary manner to influence aggregate demand. We can consider these under the following headings:

- time lags

● measurement uncertainty

● side effects.

Time lags

In Figure 29 we saw how fiscal policy can be used to fine tune the economy and reduce the output effects of the trade cycle. The problem with this is that aggregate demand can change for any number of different reasons, and changes often take time to recognise because economic statistics take a long time to collect. Furthermore once the government cuts taxation and raises government spending, there is a time lag before aggregate demand increases. So for example, if there has been a period of unemployment and low aggregate demand the government may wish to act. The most up to date economic data it has is six months old and will therefore not show if the trade cycle is starting to improve. The economy may be going into a boom period. If the government now boosts aggregate demand the boom will be made worse. Inflation and external deficit problems will be exacerbated.

On the other hand, the trade cycle may start to go into a recession after a long boom period. The government however may not have the data to see this and it does not realise that the boom has turned into a recession. In order to stabilise the effects of the perceived boom it raises taxes and cuts expenditure. These policies start to influence aggregate demand just as the trade cycle pushes the economy into recession. Hence the recession is made worse. Unemployment is higher and output lower than it would have been had the government not intervened. Clearly, discretionary fiscal policy can be destabilising. Figure 30 illustrates this point. Notice how this figure contrasts with Figure 29.

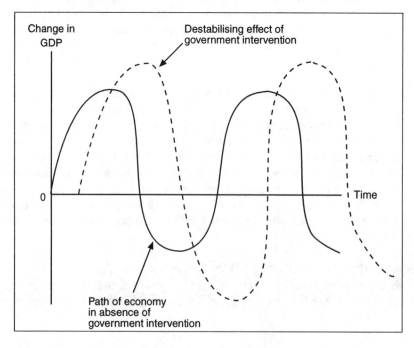

Figure 30: The effects of policy lags on the economic cycle.

Measurement uncertainty

In order to use fiscal policy to remove deflationary gaps the government needs accurate data on the size of these gaps. It also needs an accurate estimate of the multiplier in order to estimate the effects of its policy. Such data will be hard to find and at best will only be approximate. If the data is at all inaccurate the government may cut or raise taxes and government spending too much. If the government wishes to reduce unemployment, it may cut taxes by too much. This will mean there is a higher level of aggregate demand than is necessary to bring about full employment. In this case, inflation will start to rise and the external balance may start to go into deficit. On the other hand, if the government tries to reduce inflation in times of full employment it might reduce spending and raise taxes too much causing a serious recession. Once again, discretionary fiscal policy can be destabilising.

Side effects

Discretionary fiscal policy does not work in isolation. Using deficit financing to influence aggregate demand may have unwanted side effects. We have mentioned that the government finances borrowing by selling gilts and treasury bills to the public and financial institutions. The interest rate it pays on these securities is a key determinant of the level of market interest rates in the economy. We return to this point in more detail in Unit 8. If the government wishes to increase the size of the deficit in order to boost aggregate demand, then it will need to pay higher interest rates in order to persuade lenders to buy the securities. This will tend to raise the general rate of interest in the whole economy. A problem here is that higher interest rates tend to reduce investment demand as we saw in Section 2. Investment demand is a key component of aggregate demand. So the government may boost aggregate demand but the effects of the increase will be mitigated by the reduction in investment demand. Monetarists argue that this is one of the major problems of demand management. They argue that higher interest rates as a result of using deficit financing, 'crowd out' investment demand.

Monetarists also argue that deficit financing can be inflationary. We explore this point in more detail later. Instead of borrowing to raise money for government spending and tax cuts, the government, wishing to avoid high interest rates may simply print money to pay for its spending plans. As we have seen, monetarists believe firmly in the quantity theory of money which states that increases in the money supply cause inflation. Monetarists argue that inflation is an inevitable result of deficit financing and point to the UK stagflation in the 1970s to illustrate this.

As a final point, you should recall also that monetarists believe that the key determinant of consumption is not disposable income but permanent income or wealth. They argue therefore that tax cuts are futile as a way of raising aggregate demand as they do not affect wealth.

REVIEW ACTIVITY 3

1 You are given the following information: $C = 40 + 0.75Y_d$. $I = 30$, $G = 30$. Taxation is zero.

   a Calculate the equilibrium level of income and the value of the multiplier.

   b Autonomous investment rises from 30 to 35. Calculate the new equilibrium level of income.

   c The government now decides to introduce taxation. It introduces a tax rate of 20%. Calculate the equilibrium level of income and the value of the multiplier. Autonomous investment is still 35.

   d How much would the government have had to increase expenditure in order that the new tax rate was part of a balanced budget? What is the equilibrium level of income in this case?

   e Using your answer to c, if full employment is at a level of income of 360, how much must taxes fall from 20% to generate full employment?

   f Illustrate your answers to a, b and c using a Keynesian cross diagram.

2 You are given the following information: $C = 25 + 0.8Y_d$. $I = 15$, $G = 10$. Taxation is zero.

   a Derive the savings function and use this to calculate the equilibrium level of income.

   b Taxation is now increased to 10%. Investment rises to 20. Use this information to calculate the equilibrium level of income.

   c What is the value of the multiplier?

   d Illustrate your answers in a diagram.

3 Using a Keynesian aggregate supply curve explain briefly how changes in aggregate demand can reduce unemployment and cause inflation.

4 Explain, in one paragraph, the term 'deficit financing'.

5 In no more than 250 words, explain the problems of using fiscal policy to 'fine tune' the economy.

6 Which of the following statements is false?

   a An increase in government expenditure will probably reduce unemployment.

   b Fiscal policy encompasses both taxation and public expenditure.

   c A balanced budget is when increases (or reductions) in government expenditure are matched by increases (or reductions) in taxation.

   d 'Deficit financing' is the name given to government policy to reduce the external deficit.

Summary

In this section, we have studied in some detail the way fiscal policy can be used to influence aggregate demand. We have also examined problems which may limit the effectiveness of this policy. In the next unit, we look in more detail at monetarist criticisms of Keynesian demand management. However, we now examine the effect of imports and exports in the Keynesian model.

SECTION FOUR

Imports and Exports in the Keynesian Model

Introduction

In this final section, we extend our model to include an external sector and show how changes in imports and exports lead to changes in national income.

4.1 Imports, exports and aggregate demand

So far in our study of the Keynesian model we have not considered the overseas sector. In other words, we have considered a closed economy. We now include the overseas sector in our model and consider the determination of national income in an open economy. We have already seen in Unit 6 that imports represent a withdrawal from the economy while exports represent an injection. We consider how changes in imports and exports affect aggregate demand and hence, national income. In Unit 10, we will consider the external sector in far more detail, here we simply see how imports and exports help determine national income.

We have so far considered aggregate demand as being made up of consumption, investment and government expenditure. To this we now add net exports. This is in effect the external balance of the domestic economy. **Net exports** is the demand for exports less the demand for imports. Or in economist's jargon, the demand by the overseas sector for domestically produced goods less the demand by the domestic economy for goods produced overseas. We can now write aggregate demand in the open economy as:

$$AD = C + I + G + X - M \qquad (22)$$

where X = exports, M = imports and $(X - M)$ = net exports.

Furthermore in equilibrium we know that injections and withdrawals are equal so that in equilibrium we have:

$$S + T + M = I + G + X \qquad (23)$$

In Unit 10, we look more closely at the determinants of imports and exports. Here we assume that the key determinant of imports is the level of national income. The higher the level of national income then the higher the level of consumption and the higher the level of imports. As for exports, these are determined by the income of the overseas sector and are not affected by the income of the domestic economy. In this model, exports are autonomous.

Figure 31 illustrates that imports rise as national income rises while exports are autonomous. At higher levels of national income, the external balance often goes into deficit. At lower levels of national income, the external balance is more likely to be in surplus.

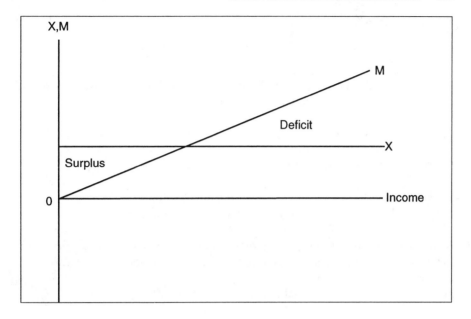

*Figure 31: As national income rises then import demand
increases and the external balance goes into deficit.*

How does the inclusion of exports and imports affect the level of national income?
Consider the following situation in which we calculate national income when
exports and imports are both nil.

$C = 20 + 0.8Y_d$

$I = G = 20$ and the tax rate is 20%.

In equilibrium, $Y = AD = C + I + G + X - M$

so, $Y = AD = 20 + 0.8(1 - 0.2)Y + 20 + 20 + 0 - 0$

$Y = 60 + 0.64Y$

$Y - 0.64Y = 0.36Y = 60$

$Y = 166.67.$

Now let us introduce exports. Assume that exports rise from zero to 30. We ignore
imports for the moment. Now we can write aggregate demand as:

$AD = C + I + G + X$

In equilibrium, $Y = AD = C + I + G + X$

$Y = 20 + 0.8(1 - 0.2)Y + 20 + 20 + 30$

$Y = 90 + 0.64Y$

$Y - 0.64Y = 0.36Y = 90$

$Y = 250$

Income rises to 250 because the inclusion of exports adds to aggregate demand. We can see this by using our multiplier formula:

$\Delta Y = \Delta AD \times 1/(1 - TMPC)$

So, $\Delta Y = + 30 \times 1/[1 - 0.8(1 - 0.2)] = 30 \times 1/0.36 = 83.33$

We saw that when exports and imports were nil, $Y = 166.67$. Adding the increase in income due to exports $(83.33) = Y + Y = 166.67 + 83.33 = 250$.

Now what happens if we include imports? Imports depend on the level of income. Let us assume that 10% of income is spent on imports, so that we can write:

$M = 0.1Y$, where $0.1 =$ marginal propensity to import (MPM).

We can write aggregate demand as:

$AD = C + I + G + X - M$

$= 20 + 0.8(1 - 0.2)Y + 20 + 20 + 30 - 0.1Y$

$= 90 + 0.64Y - 0.1Y$

$= 90 + 0.54Y$

In equilibrium, $Y = AD$ so, $Y = 90 + 0.54Y$

$Y - 0.54Y = 0.46Y = 90$

$Y = 195.65$.

The inclusion of imports reduces national income because it acts as a withdrawal. Recall that the value of the multiplier depends on withdrawals. The more withdrawals there are then a greater proportion of any increase in income is withdrawn from the economy and the lower is the overall multiplier effect on national income. Now that we include imports, the value of the multiplier becomes:

$1/[1 - (TMPC - MPM)]$ (24)

Before we introduced imports, we saw that the level of national income was 250. The introduction of imports, where imports are 10% of income, means that aggregate demand is directly reduced by $0.1(250) = 25$. So the change in income is:

$-25 \times 1/[1 - (0.64 - 0.1)] = - 25 \times 1/0.46 = - 54.35$, and $250 - 54.35 = 195.65$.

Figure 32 illustrates our initial equilibrium at point A. The introduction of exports causes a parallel upward shift in the aggregate demand curve to AD_J. Equilibrium is at point B. Finally, introducing imports alters the slope of the aggregate demand function and equilibrium now occurs at point C.

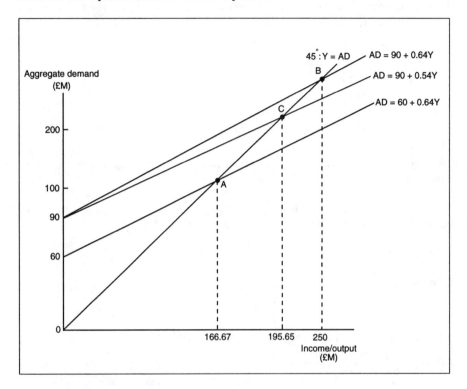

Figure 32: Aggregate demand function with introduction of imports and exports.

As before we can consider this in terms of injections and withdrawals. In our initial situation, withdrawals are savings and taxation while injections are government expenditure and investment. In equilibrium, $S + T = I + G$, $T = 0.2Y$, $I = 20$, $G = 20$.

As for savings, remember: $Y = C + S + T$, so, $S = Y - C - T$:

$S = Y - 20 - 0.8(1 - 0.2)Y - 0.2Y = Y - 0.2Y - 0.64Y - 20$

$S = -20 + 0.16Y$

So withdrawals, W are equal to $S + T = -20 + 0.16Y + 0.2Y = -20 + 0.36Y$. This schedule is shown in Figure 33 as is the injections schedule J, where $J = I + G = 40$. Equilibrium is where the two schedules intersect at point A, at a national income of 166.67. To see this:

$S + T = I + G$

$-20 + 0.36Y = 40$

$0.36Y = 60$

$Y = 166.67.$

Now the introduction of exports of 30, raises our injections function to 70 and we can determine the new equilibrium:

$S + T = I + G + X$

$-20 + 0.36Y = 40 + 30 = 70$

$0.36Y = 90$

$Y = 250$

This equilibrium is shown at point B where the withdrawals schedule intersects the new injections schedule $J_1 = I + G + X$.

Finally introducing imports affects the withdrawals schedule which now becomes: $S + T + M = -20 + 0.36Y + 0.1Y = -20 + 0.46Y$. In equilibrium,

$-20 + 0.46Y = 70$

$0.46Y = 90$

$Y = 195.65$

This is shown at point C at the intersection of J_1 with $W_1 = S + T + M$.

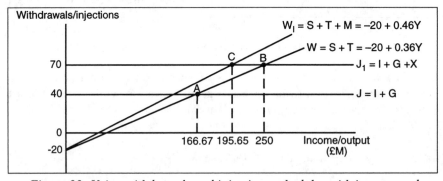

Figure 33: Using withdrawals and injections schedules with imports and exports.

REVIEW ACTIVITY 4

You are given the following information: $C = 30 + 0.75Y_d$. $I = G = 25$. $T = 0.2Y$.

1 Calculate equilibrium national income.

2 If exports are 20 and 10% of income is spent on imports, calculate the new equilibrium level of income and illustrate your answers in an injections and withdrawals diagram.

Summary

We have extended our model to include an external sector and shown how changes in imports and exports lead to changes in national income. In the next unit, we turn to a vital issue that, so far, we have largely ignored, the issue of money. We will look more closely at some of the points of controversy between Keynesian and monetarist economists.

Unit Review Activity

Read the article 'Stabilisation policy' by R Thomas, *The Economic Review*, March 1988, Item 7.1 in your Resource File. Then answer the following questions in about 250 words each.

1   In discretionary fiscal policy, what is an inside lag? What is an outside lag?

2   Explain why fiscal policy, when the article was written, was likely to be destabilising

Unit Summary

In Section 1, we studied the basic Keynesian model of national income determination. We defined aggregate demand and saw how changes in aggregate demand led to much larger changes in national income as a result of the multiplier process. We also saw that full employment was not guaranteed in national income equilibrium.

In Section 2, we looked closely at Keynesian and monetarist theories of consumption and investment demand.

In Section 3, we saw how discretionary fiscal policy can be used in order to manage the level of demand and fine tune the economy. We also saw that this policy could lead to instability because of the presence of lags. We also considered monetarist criticisms of using Keynesian discretionary fiscal policy.

In Section 4, we examined the Keynesian model in an open economy framework by introducing imports and exports into the model.

Recommended Reading

Lipsey, RG and Chrystal, KA, (1995), *An Introduction to Positive Economics.*

Sloman, J, (1995), *Economics,* Prentice Hall/Harvester Wheatsheaf.

Answers to Review Activities

Review Activity 1

1   $C = 5 + 0.8Y$, so, at an income level of 160, $C = 5 + 0.8(160) = 133$

   $AD = C + I = 5 + 0.8Y + 70 = 75 + 0.8Y$

   so, $AD = 75 + 0.8(160) = 203$

2   $C = 5 + 0.8Y$ so, at an income level of 230, $C = 5 + 0.8(230) = 189$

   $AD = C + I = 75 + 0.8(230) = 259$

3   $MPC = 0.8$ and $MPS = 0.2$

4   $Y = C + S$, so, $Y = 5 + 0.8Y + S$

   so, $Y - 0.8Y - 5 = S$

   $S = -5 + 0.2Y$

At an income level of 80, $S = -5 + 0.2(80) = 11$

At an income level of 170, $S = -5 + 0.2(170) = 29$

5   There are two ways to do this. We can use our aggregate demand equation $AD = C + I$. In equilibrium, aggregate demand is equal to income and output, $AD = Y$.

So we can write $Y = C + I$, or, $Y = 5 + 0.8Y + 70$

$Y - 0.8Y = 75$

$0.2Y = 75$

$Y = 375.$

Another way is to equate savings and investment, $S = I = -5 + 0.2Y = 70$

$0.2Y = 75$

$Y = 375.$

6   The multiplier formula is $1/MPS$, so $1/0.2 = 5$.

7   The change in income from a change in autonomous investment is:

$\Delta Y = \Delta I \times (1/MPS)$

This can be calculated as $+6 \times 5 = 30$.

So the new equilibrium level of income is $375 + 30 = 405$, the aggregate demand function is now $AD = 81 + 0.8Y$.

8   Now if investment falls from 76 to 73 then the change in the equilibrium level of income is $-3 \times 5 = -15$, therefore the new equilibrium level of income is 405 $-15 = 390$. The aggregate demand function becomes $AD = 78 + 0.8Y$.

9

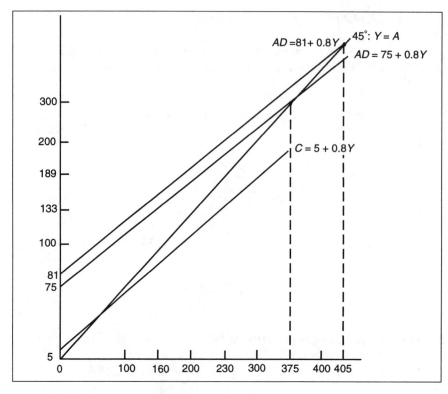

Figure 34: The consumption function.

10   You were asked which of the following statements best describes the multiplier.

a   *The multiplier is the process whereby an increase in investment leads to an increase in employment.* This is incorrect. You may have thought that this statement was correct because an increase in investment almost certainly will lead to an increase in employment and this in turn will cause national income to increase. However, this is only one part of the multiplier process which is concerned with increases in national income. The multiplier includes this but is more generally concerned with how an increase in any component of aggregate demand, not just investment, will lead to an increase in national income and employment. Choose another answer.

b   *The multiplier tells us by how much savings change as a result of an increase in aggregate demand.* This is incorrect. It is true that savings will be affected by an increase in demand because as national income rises then so will savings. However, it does not describe the multiplier process. Choose another answer.

c   *The multiplier effect shows the increase in firm's profits as a result of an increase in consumption.* This is incorrect. Increases in consumption may raise firms' profits but the multiplier process says nothing about the profitability of firms. Choose another answer.

d *The multiplier tells us exactly how much output and income change as a result of a change in aggregate demand.* This is the correct answer. Any change in aggregate demand will lead to a change in national income. The multiplier process tells us exactly how much income changes as a result of this change in aggregate demand. Well done if you got this correct the first time. If you didn't, make sure that you fully understand why the other responses are incorrect.

Review Activity 2

1 According to Keynesians, the key determinant of consumption is current disposable income. Monetarists, such as Milton Friedman, believe that permanent income, or wealth, is more important.

2 If the permanent income hypothesis is correct then tax cuts will have much less influence on consumption and aggregate demand than Keynes suggested. Tax cuts raise current disposable income but unless these cuts are seen as permanent, and therefore affecting wealth, then they will not affect consumption. Most people know that governments change every few years and therefore tax policies also change. Tax cuts are rarely permanent.

3 Although classical and Keynesian theory differ, the two theories agree that the rate of interest is an important determinant of investment demand. Keynesians also stress the importance of expectations. The accelerator theory suggests that changes in consumption will have an effect on investment demand.

4 a This will probably lead to a shift in the investment schedule to the right. A higher level of GDP will probably indicate a higher level of demand. Firms may expect to be able to sell more and as a result choose to invest more in order to produce a higher quantity of goods.

b A rise in wages will encourage firms, where possible, to use more capital at the expense of labour. So the investment demand schedule will shift to the right.

c An increase in interest rates will cause a drop in investment. There will be a movement down the investment demand schedule and investment will fall. The investment demand curve will not shift.

d Improved business confidence will have an effect similar to that of a. Firms, anticipating a higher level of demand will probably invest more so that they can produce more to satisfy the higher level of demand. The investment demand curve would shift to the right. Therefore, c is the correct answer.

Review Activity 3

1   a $AD = C + I + G$

$= 40 + 0.75Y_d + 30 + 30$

Now we can simplify this, bearing in mind that in the absence of taxation, $Y = Y_d$

$AD = 100 + 0.75Y$

In equilibrium, $Y = AD$

$Y = 100 + 0.75Y$

$Y - 0.75Y = 0.25Y = 100$

$Y = 400$

Multiplier $= 1/(1 - MPC) = 1/(1 - 0.75) = 4$

b   Investment rises from 30 to 35. We can determine the new equilibrium level of income in two different ways. Firstly, in the same way we solved a:

Now, $AD = 40 + 0.75Y_d + 35 + 30$

$= 105 + 0.75Y_d$

$Y = AD$ and without taxation, $Y = Y_d$

so, $Y = 105 + 0.75Y$

$Y - 0.75Y = 0.25Y = 105$

$Y = 420$

Alternatively, we can simply use our multiplier value and equation (7)

$\Delta Y = \Delta AD \times (1/1 - MPC)$ (7)

so, $\Delta Y = 5 \times 4 = 20$

Therefore equilibrium national income rises $400 + 20 = 420$.

c   Our aggregate demand function before tax is:

$AD = 105 + 0.75Y_d$

Now with taxation of 20%, we can rewrite this as:

$AD = 105 + 0.75(1 - 0.2)Y$

so, $AD = 105 + 0.6Y$

In equilibrium, $Y = AD$, so, $Y = 105 + 0.6Y$

$Y - 0.6Y = 0.4Y = 105$

$Y = 262.5$

Multiplier value is now $1/(1 - TMPC)$ where $TMPC = MPC(1 - t)$

so, multiplier value is $1/[1 - 0.75(1 - 0.2)] = 1/0.4 = 2.5$.

d   The government introduced tax of 20%. Before the tax, national income
     was 420 so at a tax rate of 20% then the tax revenue to the government and
     the reduction in disposable income was equal to:

$0.2(420) = 84$.

In order to balance the budget, the government would have needed to
raise government expenditure by 84. In this case, we could rewrite
aggregate demand as:

$AD = C + I + G$

$= 40 + 0.75Y_d + 35 + (30 + 84)$

$= 189 + 0.75Y_d = 189 + 0.75(1 - 0.2)Y = 189 + 0.6Y$

In equilibrium, $Y = AD$, so, $Y = 189 + 0.6Y$

$Y - 0.6Y = 0.4Y = 189$

$Y = 472.5$

Given a national income level of 420, an increase in taxation from zero to
20% and a simultaneous increase in government expenditure of 84, an
increase in national income to 472.5 results.

e   Returning to our answer to c, an introduction of taxation at a rate of 20%
     results in an equilibrium level of national income of 262.5. Now full
     employment is at an income level of 360.

In equilibrium, $Y = AD$, so, it will be the case that:

$$360 = 40 + 0.75(1 - t)360 + 35 + 30 = 105 + 270(1 - t)$$

$$360 - 105 = 255 = 270 (1 - t)$$

$$1 - t = 255/270 = 0.944$$

$$t = 0.056 \text{ or } 5.6\%.$$

f

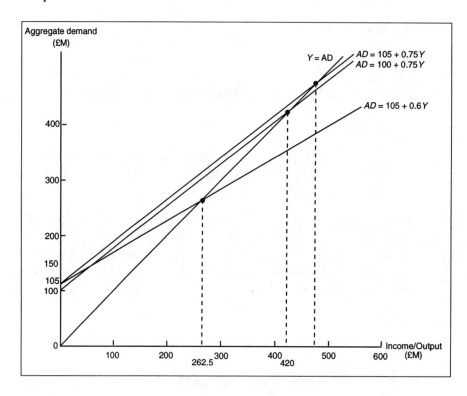

Figure 35: Keynesian cross diagram.

2   a $Y = C + S + T$, now, $T = 0$ so, $Y = C + S$ and $Y = Y_d$

$$Y = 25 + 0.8Y_d + S$$

$$Y = 25 + 0.8Y + S$$

so that in terms of saving, $S = Y - 25 - 0.8Y = -25 + 0.2Y$

Our savings function is: $S = -25 + 0.2Y$

In equilibrium, injections are equal to withdrawals. In this case, injections are investment and government spending, and withdrawals are savings. Therefore, $S = I + G$, so, $-25 + 0.2Y = 15 + 10 = 25$.

$0.2Y = 50$

$Y = 250.$

b   Taxation is introduced at 10% and investment increases to 20.

In equilibrium, $S + T = I + G$, so, $- 25 + 0.2Y + 0.1Y = 20 + 10 = 30$

$-25 + 0.3Y = 30,$

$0.3Y = 55$

$Y = 183.33.$

c   In a tax situation, the multiplier is $1/(1 - TMPC)$, now $TMPC = MPC(1- t)$, which in this case is: $0.8(1 - 0.1) = 0.72$

so, the multiplier is $1/(1 - 0.72) = 3.57.$

d

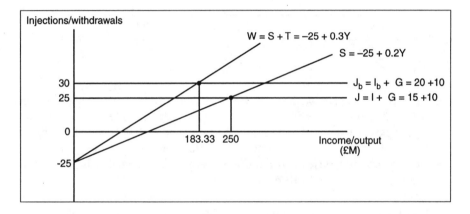

Figure 36

Your answers to the next three questions may differ from the following but they should cover these points.

3

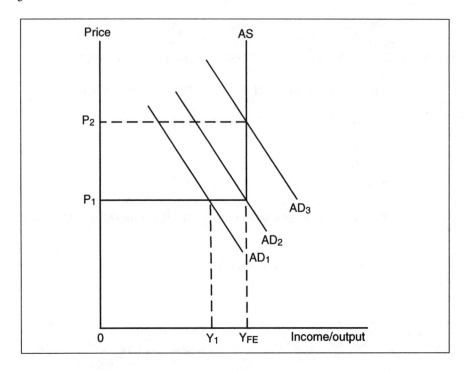

Figure 37: Keynesian aggregate supply curve.

Figure 37 shows price on the vertical axis and national income on the horizontal axis. The current level of national income, Y_1, is determined at the intersection of the aggregate demand and aggregate supply curves. This level of income is below that necessary to generate full employment, Y_{FE}. If the government cuts taxes and/or raises expenditure the aggregate demand curve will shift from AD_1 to AD_2 and full employment can be achieved. However, if the government miscalculates how much it needs to raise aggregate demand then it may cause inflation. It might increase aggregate demand to AD_3. This generates full employment but raises the price level from P_1 to P_2.

4   Deficit financing uses fiscal policy in order to raise the level of demand. Often this type of policy causes a budget deficit. Aggregate demand will be low and unemployment high in a recession. In this case, there may be a budget deficit as expenditure on unemployment benefit will be high and tax revenue will be low as many people are unemployed and do not pay tax and company profits will be lower in recession. Although a deficit exists, the government will cut taxes and increase spending in order to reduce unemployment thereby increasing the budget deficit. Hence the term 'deficit financing'. Deficit financing is an inevitable result of demand management and the use of discretionary fiscal policy.

5   While the use of fiscal policy in order to fine tune the economy can be successful in maintaining a low level of inflation and unemployment, often

there are problems associated with this policy.

Firstly, the data used by the government in order to decide by how much it needs to change tax rates or government spending are often out of date, or inaccurate. Therefore the government may implement changes too late, or alternatively miscalculate the extent of changes necessary to achieve its objectives. This can be destabilising.

Monetarists also criticise the use of discretionary fiscal policy on a number of grounds. Firstly, they argue that deficit financing leads to higher interest rates if the government has to sell more bonds to finance borrowing. This will reduce investment, a vital component of aggregate demand. Any change in aggregate demand as a result of fiscal fine tuning will be mitigated by this 'crowding out' effect. Further, monetarists argue that if tax cuts or increases in spending are financed by printing money then this will lead to inflation.

Finally, monetarists argue that consumption depends on permanent income or wealth and not on disposable income. Changes in tax rates do not affect permanent income unless they are seen as permanent and will therefore not affect consumption.

6   a   True. Higher public expenditure will raise aggregate demand and national income so that unemployment will fall.

    b   True. Fiscal policy refers to government taxation and public expenditure policies.

    c   True. A balanced budget is when a change in government spending is exactly matched by an offsetting change in taxation. If the government, for example, reduces government expenditure by £1 million then a balanced budget would imply a reduction in taxation so that disposable income is raised by £1 million.

    d   False. Deficit financing concerns the government attempts to reduce unemployment by cutting taxation and raising government expenditure. This type of policy often results in a budget deficit where tax revenue is insufficient to pay for government expenditure. $Y = 200$.

Review Activity 4

1   $AD = C + I + G = 30 + 0.75(1 - 0.2)Y + 25 + 25$

In equilibrium, $Y = AD$, so, $Y = 80 + 0.6Y$

$Y - 0.6Y = 0.4Y = 80$

$Y = 200$

2   Now $AD = C + I + G + X - M = 80 + 0.6Y + 20 - 0.1Y = 100 + 0.5Y$

In equilibrium, $Y = AD$, so, $Y = 100 + 0.5Y$

$Y - 0.5Y = 0.5Y = 100$

You should be aware that the fact that income has not changed is a 'chance' result. In other words, it arises purely from the information and numbers you are given. You should not conclude that the introduction of an external sector would always result in an unchanged level of national income.

In order to illustrate this, you need to calculate the injections and withdrawals functions. For part 1, withdrawals $= S + T$.

$S = Y - C - T = Y - 30 - 0.75(1 - 0.2)Y - 0.1Y = Y - 0.6Y - 0.1Y - 30$

$= -30 + 0.3Y$

so, $W = S + T = -30 + 0.3Y + 0.1Y = -30 + 0.4Y.$

Injections are $I + G = 25 + 25 = 50$, so, in equilibrium:

$-30 + 0.4Y = 50$

$0.4Y = 80$

$Y = 200$. This equilibrium is shown as point A.

In part 2, the withdrawals schedule changes to W_1 where:

$W_1 = S + T + M = -30 + 0.4Y + 0.1Y = -30 + 0.5Y$

And injections change to J_1 where $J_1 = I + G + X = 50 + 20 = 70$.

In equilibrium, $-30 + 0.5Y = 70$

$0.5Y = 100$

$Y = 200$. This is shown as point B in Figure 38.

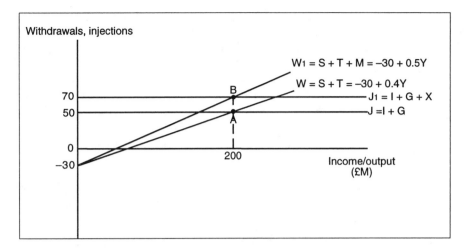

Figure 38

Unit Review Activity

1   When the government wishes to influence the level of aggregate demand in order to fine tune the economy, it needs economic data to tell it how much to raise spending, or how much to cut taxes etc. This data takes a long time to collect and when it reaches the government it may already be out of date so that the government may be acting on data that is no longer relevant. This delay in collection is an inside lag.

Once policy is enacted it does not affect aggregate demand immediately. Policy changes take time to take effect. The government may cut taxes if the trade cycle has pushed the economy into recession. By the time the tax cuts start to work, the economy may be on an upswing so that the effect of tax cuts exacerbates the boom and is destabilising, perhaps causing an external deficit or inflation. The lag that occurs between policy being implemented and actually starting to work is known as an outside lag.

2   At the time the article was written, government policy was to maintain a fixed public sector deficit. This meant that if the economy was in a boom period then tax receipts would start to rise and government expenditure would fall as benefit payments dropped. This would reduce the deficit. The government would therefore raise spending in order to keep the deficit constant. This meant raising aggregate demand in a boom which was likely to worsen it. On the other hand, if the economy was in a recession then tax receipts would start to fall and government expenditure would rise as benefit payments increased. This would increase the deficit. The government would therefore cut spending in order to keep the deficit constant. This meant reducing aggregate demand in a recession which was likely to worsen it. Such a policy was therefore destabilising.

UNIT 8
THE ROLE OF MONEY AND THE FINANCIAL SYSTEM

Introduction

Having studied the Keynesian theory of national income determination and explored some of the areas of debate between Keynesians and monetarists we now turn to the issue of money. It is very difficult to imagine an economy without money. We do not often stop to think why money is used and what the consequences would be if money did not exist. If you want to buy a good you exchange money for that good. How would you acquire that good if money did not exist ? How would you know the price of the good ? After all, prices are expressed in terms of money. Having considered this and having considered why money exists we need to ask why does the seller accept money from you in exchange for the good ?

In this unit we will examine the role of money and we will see how the money supply is determined. As with other commodities there is a demand for, and supply of, money. We will explore these in detail and we will see how monetarists and Keynesians disagree as to the importance and the effects of monetary policy.

This unit is divided into three sections:

Section 1 defines money and examines the functions of money. A simple financial system is outlined and we develop a simple model of credit creation. We then look at the financial system in the UK and examine how the supply of money is determined.

Section 2 considers Keynesian and monetarist theories of the demand for money and considers the connection between money, aggregate demand and inflation.

Section 3 focuses on monetary policy and traces the development of post-war monetary policy in the UK. We also examine the UK experience of monetarism in the 1980s.

Objectives

By the end of this unit you should be able to:

- list and explain the functions of money
- outline the main components and functions of the UK financial system
- explain how banks create credit.
- compare and contrast Keynesian and monetarist theories of money demand
- demonstrate how changes in the money supply affect aggregate demand
- explain the importance of the liquidity trap

- explain why monetarists and Keynesians disagree over the importance of monetary policy
- describe the problems that arise in controlling the money supply
- outline the UK experience of monetarist policy.

SECTION ONE

Money and the Financial System

Introduction

So far in our studies of economics we have touched only briefly on the topic of money. In this unit, we will spend some time looking at the functions of money and we will explore in some detail how money influences national income. As you might expect this role of money is the subject of considerable controversy. Keynesians argue that money has very little effect on the level of national income and, for that matter, on the price level. Monetarists disagree entirely: they argue that changes in the money supply will ultimately affect only prices and not national income. They agree that in the short term changes in the money supply may affect national income but, for reasons we will explore later, these changes in national income will be short lived and that in the longer term, only the price level will be affected. In other words Monetarists argue that 'money is neutral in the long run'.

In this section we will look at the definition and the functions of money and then outline a simple financial system and a simple model of credit creation. We will then look at the financial system in the UK and examine how the supply of money is determined.

1.1 Money and the functions of money

WHAT IS MONEY ?

Money can be defined as **any asset which is generally acceptable as a means of payment**. This definition describes the most important function of money: money as a **medium of exchange**. Consider an economy without money. How would individuals buy and sell goods? The only way to trade would be by bartering, literally swapping one good for another.

If you wished to sell a car you would need to find someone who wished to buy a car and who also had a good that you wanted in exchange for your car. This is known as 'double coincidence of wants'. It would be extremely time consuming to have to go through such a process each time you wished to make a trade. The whole process suffers from having no accepted medium of exchange.

The existence of money therefore saves time and makes the whole trading process more efficient. You spend money in order to buy the goods you want. The seller of those goods does not need to worry whether you have anything that he wants in exchange for those goods. He accepts money safe in the knowledge that he can use that money to buy any goods that he wants.

In the nineteenth century gold and silver coins were used as money. In prisoner of war camps cigarettes were used as money. These are classic examples of **commodity money** where an ordinary good (gold or cigarettes) serves as a medium of exchange. In order that these goods can be used as money, society must obviously reduce the other uses of that good or devote resources to producing more of the good. As an example, one of the uses of a cigarette is to smoke it. If people did not cut back on their smoking then eventually all the cigarettes would disappear and they would not function as money. At any one time more cigarettes than are needed for smokers are in existence so that they can serve as money and this extra supply takes up resources to produce it. As a way of overcoming this problem **token money** is used. Token money is a means of payment which has a value far in excess of its cost of production or in excess of its value in uses other than money. For example, a £50 note costs very little to produce (far less than £50) and if it is not used as money it is effectively a piece of paper which is of little use. Of course as token money is so cheap to produce then anyone can produce it. To make token money work, its production must be restricted so that private supply (i.e. forgery) is illegal, and it must also be defined as **legal tender** so that everyone will accept it as payment for goods and services.

OTHER FUNCTIONS OF MONEY

As well as acting as a medium of exchange, money also fulfills a number of other functions.

These are:

- a store of value
- a unit of account
- a means of deferred payment.

We now consider these individually,

- **Money as a store of value:** money can be held to make future purchases. If money did not act as a store of value then nobody would accept money in exchange for goods because that money would be worthless when they tried to buy goods with it the following week. Therefore, if money was not a store of value then it could not act as a medium of exchange. As well as money there are other stores of value such as houses, works of art and bank accounts. Money is just one asset in which wealth can be held. In fact, if money is held as a store of value it pays no interest and falls in value because of inflation and so it is actually inferior in this function than some of the other assets we have named. On the other hand, it has the advantage that it can be turned quickly into goods that one wants, whereas houses take time to sell and therefore there is a delay before one can spend the wealth accumulated earlier. The ease with which an asset can be turned quickly into goods is known as liquidity. Money is the most liquid of the various assets in which wealth may be held.

- **Money as a unit of account:** money serves as a 'yardstick' in which transactions can be valued in accounts, whether those accounts are the national income accounts or the accounts of a small firm. If an apple costs 30 pence and an orange 15 pence, we know that the value of one apple equals the value of two oranges.

  In times of extremely high inflation, money ceases to act as a unit of account. Prices change so rapidly that an apple costing 30 pence in the morning might only buy one orange in the evening.

- **Money as a means of deferred payment:** this function is similar to that of a store of value but in this case refers to the payment of loans over a period of time, such as a long-term loan, or mortgage for the purchase of a house, when the amount to be repaid is stated in money terms.

DEFINITIONS OF MONEY

We have now considered what money is and have examined the functions of money. When we think of money we often think only of the notes and coins that we carry around, however this is an extremely narrow definition because there are other assets to consider. Consider a bank account. Account holders are provided with a cheque book and they can use cheques to purchase goods and services. Cheque book money is therefore a medium of exchange . However, it is not perfect because people and firms can refuse to accept cheques in a transaction. A bank account also functions as a store of value, a unit of account and a means of deferred payment.

There are a number of assets which can be considered to be money and in practice a number of definitions are used to define money more clearly. The most common definitions are:

- narrow money
- broad money.
- **Narrow money:** this refers to money used for transactions purposes. In the UK there are two measures of narrow money, M1 (M – one) and M0 (M – zero). M1 includes notes and coins in circulation and in banks' tills, banks balances at the Bank of England (of which we will hear more later), and sterling **sight deposits** of domestic households held at banks. A sight deposit is an account on which cheques can be drawn and from which money can be withdrawn on demand without prior notice. M0 just includes notes and coins in circulation and in banks' tills and bank balances at the Bank of England.

● **Broad money:** consists of narrow money plus balances held as savings and not necessarily for transactions purposes. Such balances are known as **time deposits** because they cannot always be withdrawn on demand. A period of notice is required. Sometimes even broader definitions are included which include deposits with other financial intermediaries. One of the broadest measures used in the UK was sterling M3 or £M3, though this is not the broadest measure. £M3 consists of M1 plus UK private sector (households' and firms') time deposits plus UK public sector sterling deposits and all savings accounts. A yet broader measure is M4, which consists of £M3 plus building society deposits.

Over the years the various definitions of money have been constantly updated and redefined, which illustrates how difficult it is to define money properly in a modern, ever-changing financial environment. Such definitions are often difficult for authors as well as students to remember!

' The inescapable conclusion is that there can be no unique definition of broad money. Any choice of dividing line between those financial assets included in, and those excluded from, broad money is to a degree arbitrary and is likely over time to be invalidated by developments in the financial system.'
(Bank of England *Quarterly Bulletin*, May 1987, p. 219)

The functions of money and the distinction between broad and narrow money are extremely important. To make sure that you have understood the first part of this section, try the following activity. Neither question should take more than about five minutes.

ACTIVITY 1

1 Outline the difference between narrow money and broad money.

2 Money functions as a medium of exchange. Explain what this means.

My answer is given below. You may have something different; this is fine, as long as you make sure that you have included all the important points.

1 Narrow money is money used for transactions purposes. When we talk of narrow money we are thinking of notes and coins in circulation and sight deposits at banks, i.e. deposits on which cheques can be drawn and from which money can be withdrawn on demand. The UK has two measures of narrow money . The most narrow is M0, which is simply notes and coins in circulation. A slightly broader definition is M1, which is M0 plus sight deposits.

Broad money consists of narrow money plus balances held as savings. Savings are not necessarily held for transactions purposes. In other words, they are held as a store of value. Such balances are known as time deposits because they cannot always be withdrawn on demand. A period of notice is required. In the

UK there are a number of measures of broad money. Sterling M3 or £M3 was one of the broadest measures used up until the mid-1980s. This measure included M1 plus public sector deposits, seven-day deposits and all savings accounts, including wholesale deposits, i.e. large deposits by companies and financial institutions. A more commonly used broad measure is M4, which includes £M3 plus all building society deposits.

2   A medium of exchange is something which is generally acceptable as a means of payment. If you wish to purchase a good then you can do so by exchanging the correct amount of money. Consider a situation where there is no medium of exchange. The only way to acquire the goods you want is to swap any good you have for the good you want. This is time consuming and inefficient. You need to find someone who has the good that you want *and* who wants the goods that you have in exchange. This is known as a 'double coincidence of wants' and arises because there is no acceptable medium of exchange.

1.2 Outline of a financial system

FUNCTIONS OF A FINANCIAL SYSTEM

A financial system typically consists of a set of markets and institutions which provide the following services:

- **Financial intermediation between borrowers and lenders :** it provides a means whereby money from those who wish to lend is transferred to those who wish to borrow.

- **A payments mechanism :** i.e. a system of transmitting payments. By the use of cheques, debit cards, credit cards, standing orders etc., money is transferred from one person or institution to another without the need to rely on cash.

- **Financial markets:** these enable holders of wealth to change the various assets, such as government bonds for example, that make up their wealth. The set of assets that make up an individuals or a firms wealth are known as a **portfolio** of assets. Financial markets enable individuals and firms to buy and sell assets in order to change their wealth portfolio.

- **Financial services:** such services enable firms and individuals to obtain financial advice on insurance or pensions for example, or buy foreign currency.

STRUCTURE OF A FINANCIAL SYSTEM

We will now look at each financial institution and their relationship to one another. There are a number of different types of institution in a financial system. These can be broadly defined under the following headings:

- **The central bank:** the central bank of the UK is the Bank of England. This institution stands at the centre of the financial system and is responsible for the supervision of the financial system and also the operation of monetary policy. That is not to say that it determines monetary policy, but that it carries out the monetary policies of the elected government of the day, such as issuing currency and setting the level of interest rates. The central bank also acts as a banker to the government and to other banks. The government bank account is held at the Bank of England and all other banks retain accounts there.

Today there is considerable debate as to the degree to which the central bank should be subjected to political control. In the UK the Bank of England is under the control of Her Majesty's Treasury which is in turn under the control of the Chancellor of the Exchequer. Thus, ultimately, in the UK, monetary policy is determined by the government. This is not the case in all other countries. In Germany and New Zealand, for example, the central bank has responsibility for monetary policy and is independent of the government. There is a significant body of opinion which favours an independent Bank of England.

- **Banks:** the major functions of banks are the operation of current (cheque) accounts and deposit accounts, the provision of personal loan facilities and financial advice to customers, and the provision of a payments mechanism. We will consider the operation of banks in more detail later in this unit.

- **Other financial institutions:** there are other institutions, as well as banks, which accept deposits and make loans. Building societies are probably the best example: they accept deposits and make loans for house purchases. Another example is a finance house, which are often referred to as **secondary banks**. Finance houses traditionally specialise in hire purchase and leasing contracts. They are able to attract money by offering higher rates of interest than the banks. They also borrow funds from the money markets (which we turn to shortly). Often these institutions do not operate within the payments mechanism like banks so that deposits held with finance houses are not generally accepted as a means of payment. However, these deposits can be withdrawn on demand and therefore converted very quickly into money.

In practice it is difficult to draw a clear dividing line between these institutions and banks. For example, an increasing number of building societies provide facilities for making payments.

- **Liquidity:** this refers to the speed and the certainty with which an asset can be converted into cash whenever the asset holder desires. Cash itself is the most liquid asset of all. Other assets such as sight deposits are very liquid. An asset such as a house, for example, is less liquid. Houses cannot always be converted quickly into cash.

Banks provide different assets with varying degrees of liquidity. As we have said, a sight deposit is a highly liquid asset because it can be converted into cash on demand, but a time deposit is a less liquid asset because account holders must give a period of notice before withdrawing cash.

We now turn to the issue of financial intermediation.

FINANCIAL MARKETS AND FINANCIAL INTERMEDIATION

A number of financial markets exist in which assets can be bought or sold, thus enabling holders of wealth to adjust their holdings of different types of assets (in other words, their portfolios). Typically, markets include those for money (short-term bank deposits), foreign currency and capital (long-term finance). Foreign exchange markets enable individuals to exchange one currency for another. The capital market consists of a **primary** market where firms issue securities (shares and bonds) in order to raise finance, and a **secondary** market, which is where existing securities are bought and sold.

In modern economies lending is not carried out directly between the borrower and the lender but instead passes through financial intermediaries, an example of which is a bank. Those who have surplus cash deposit the cash in a bank as savings. These are the lenders. The bank then lends those funds to borrowers in the form of loans. This act is known as **financial intermediation.** Figure 1 shows the simple structure of financial intermediation.

Figure 1: The basic structure of financial intermediation

BENEFITS OF FINANCIAL INTERMEDIATION

Financial intermediation occurs when a bank or other institution 'comes between' or mediates between, a number of lenders and a number of borrowers. Mediation has a number of advantages over transactions between individual borrowers and lenders. These advantages are :

- maturity transformation
- risk transformation
- co-ordination of lenders
- reduced costs.

We will look at these in turn.

- **Maturity Transformation:** the process whereby short-term loans are converted into long-term loans.

Maturity refers to the period of a loan. At the end of the period the loan is said to **mature** and the loan must be repaid.

Usually a borrower, such as a home buyer or a business, wants a loan for a substantial period, 20-25 years in the case of a house mortgage. So they are long-term borrowers. However the main source of funds are members of the public who have a little money to spare. These lenders don't want to tie all their money up for a long time but want immediate or short-term access to it. They are only willing to be short-term lenders. The problem is, how can the contradictory wants of long-term borrowers and short term lenders be met ?

The solution is this. An intermediary, a bank or building society, say, instead of trying to match a single short-term lender with a single long-term borrower, accepts deposits for short periods from a large population. The identity of the depositor and the amount they deposit may be constantly changing, but so long as a stable proportion of the population is lending even small amounts for a short time, the bank will have constant access to funds. Long-term loans can be made from this constant supply of funds. You will see that, by using an intermediary who accepts deposits from many lenders, short-term deposits can be transferred into long-term loans. This is known as **maturity transformation**.

● **Risk transformation:** whenever a financial institution, say a bank or building society, makes a loan it is taking a risk. How can it be sure that the lender will repay the loan when it matures ? Therefore, when making a loan the bank or building society takes the risk that the lender will **default** on the loan.

In order to minimise this risk, the financial intermediary will perform a number of checks to assess the credit-worthiness of the lender. It has the expertise and facilities to properly assess risk and decide to which firms and individuals it would be prudent to make loans. It would be impossible for a sole lender to assess risk in this way. A sole lender would have neither the time or the facilities to check credit references etc. At the same time, the intermediary can provide the depositor with a risk-free deposit. This means that the lender can deposit his or her cash with the financial institution safe in the knowledge that he or she can withdraw that cash whenever they so wish. There is no possibility that the bank will be unable to repay the lender. This is known as **risk transformation**.

Risk and maturity transformation occur because the **intermediary** has a large number of depositors against which loans have been created. Because of this large number the intermediary is not likely to be faced with a large number of withdrawals at the same time. At the same time, because of the large number of loans, the failure of one loan is unlikely to have a serious effect on the operation of the intermediary.

● **Coordination of lenders:** generally borrowers, such as firms or house buyers, will want to borrow large sums of money. However, individual lenders will usually only save small amounts of money at one time. The financial intermediary is able to satisfy the needs of borrowers by 'parcelling up' a series of small deposits to make a larger loan. The classic example here are loans for house purchase. Each individual deposit is likely to be much smaller than the loan, which is an amalgam of a series of smaller deposits.

● **Reduced costs:** if there was no such thing as financial intermediation then somebody wishing to borrow, say £500, would need to search out somebody who wanted to lend £500. The borrower would have to spend time, and possibly money, travelling around and making enquiries in order to find a suitable lender. The lender would also have to spend time and money searching out a borrower. In other words, the process of lending and borrowing would be both expensive and time consuming.

The presence of financial intermediation saves both lenders and borrowers having to seek each other out. Lenders simply deposit their cash with the bank or building society and allow that institution to lend out the funds to borrowers. You can think of financial institutions as a sort of 'exchange' for borrowing and lending. Financial intermediation therefore reduces the cost of transferring funds from lenders to borrowers.

Hopefully you are now able to understand the benefits provided to both lenders and borrowers by financial intermediaries. The following activity should ensure that you have fully digested the information presented in this section. Once again, your answer is unlikely to be exactly the same as mine; however, provided that you include the most important points then you can allow yourselves a pat on the back.

ACTIVITY 2

Explain, in no more than 200 words, the terms 'maturity transformation' and 'risk transformation'.

Maturity transformation refers to the process whereby financial intermediaries 'borrow short and lend long'. Borrowing, of course, refers to deposits from the public which are repayable on demand. Lending is usually made over a much longer period. The intermediary knows he can do this because of the very large number of depositors. Any day-to-day withdrawals will be matched by day-to-day deposits.

Risk transformation refers to the process whereby the intermediary borrows and provides the lender with an asset that is virtually risk free, i.e. a deposit account on which the intermediary is extremely unlikely to default. At the same time the intermediary has the expertise to properly assess risk and make loans to risky firms and individuals. This would be impossible for a sole lender.

1.3 A model of credit creation

In Section 1.1 we looked at the issue of token money. Token money developed out of the activities of goldsmiths who accepted deposits of gold and other precious metals for safe keeping. Naturally they would issue a receipt for this gold which was known as a **promissory note**, or more simply, a **note**. Over time, these notes became used like money is today. If an individual had 50 bars of gold deposited with a goldsmith, he would have perhaps 50 notes, each being a receipt for one bar of gold. If that individual wished to buy some land for a price of, say, one bar of gold, he would then give the seller a note in exchange for the land. The seller would then go to the goldsmith and would get one bar of gold in return for the note, alternatively he could use the note to buy goods from someone else. The notes were therefore used as money.

Goldsmiths realised that, at any one time only a very small proportion of people, say 10%, would want to reclaim their gold. The remaining 90% could be lent out. Therefore, goldsmiths would retain 10% of deposits and lend out the rest. Each deposit of gold was the responsibility of the goldsmith who would eventually have to pay it back. The deposits were therefore the **liabilities** of the goldsmith. At the same time, of course, those deposits of gold could be used to make loans, so were also an **asset.**

If goldsmiths lent out gold that gold was used in transactions by the borrower. The borrower would exchange the gold for goods and the recipient of the gold would then redeposit it with the goldsmith. The goldsmith would issue a note as a receipt and would then lend out 90% of the new deposit. The whole process would be repeated again and again. The goldsmith would always retain 10% of deposits so each deposit of say £10 of gold would lead to £9 of notes being issued. The goldsmith therefore created credit. The money supply expanded because of the loans made by the goldsmith.

Today, this **credit creation process** is the key determinant of the supply of money in the economy though of course, today it is banks and not goldsmiths who take the deposits. Furthermore, it is no longer the case that all notes are backed up by deposits of gold. Any notes *not* backed up by gold are known as **fiduciary issues**. Banks create credit, not on gold deposits, but on Bank of England notes so that all currency is fiduciary issue. Ultimately, the amount of credit created depends on the amount of deposits retained and not lent out. The Bank of England controls the money supply by imposing a limit to the proportion of deposits that can be lent out.

Now consider one large bank which is the only bank in the economy. Every individual and firm in the economy uses this bank. Assume the bank has initial deposits of £1,000 cash so that assets are equal to £1,000 and liabilities are equal to £1,000. Assume that from past experience the bank knows that, at any one time, 10% of deposits will be withdrawn. So that, of the initial cash, £900 can be lent out. This amount is then used by borrowers to spend on goods. Those who receive the money then deposit it with the bank so that the whole £900 is re-deposited. Now 90% of this amount, £810, can be lent out and the remaining £90 is retained to meet withdrawals. Eventually this £810 comes back to the bank and 90%, £729, is lent out again and the remainder is retained. At the end of the process, with total cash of £1,000 in the system then the bank is able to make £9000 of loans. This ratio of cash retained to total deposits, in this case 10%, is known as the **cash ratio.**

You can see that the higher the cash ratio the smaller the amount of loans that can be made and hence less credit can be created. If the bank had a cash ratio of 20% then with total cash of £1,000 in the system then the bank will be able to make £4,000 of loans. If the cash ratio was 5% then with total cash of £1,000 in the system then the bank can make £19,000 of loans.

Credit creation is a process that takes time. A deposit of £1000 does not lead to the creation of £9000 credit immediately ; this amount builds up over a period. If you study the model you will see that the length of this period depends on the level of economic activity - the frequency of transactions that are made between people. So for a given change in bank deposits, the amount of credit will change more or less rapidly depending on the current level of economic activity.

The cash ratio limits the amount of credit that is created. When the cash ratio is high the amount of the deposit retained is high, and the amount of credit created is comparatively low. (We will see later that other factors also affect the amount of the deposit that is retained, and so these other factors also affect the amount of credit created).

By imposing a certain cash ratio on the banks the Bank of England can limit this process of credit creation, and therefore control, to some extent, the money supply in the economy.

Using our 10% cash ratio the bank balance sheet started as:

Assets   **Liabilities**

Cash £1,000   Deposits £1,000

By the end of the process the balance sheet looks like this:

Assets   **Liabilities**

Cash   £1,000   Initial deposits   £1,000

Loans   £9,000   Created deposits £9,000
          £10,000   £10,000

The cash ratio puts a limit on the amount of credit that can be created. The cash ratio can be expressed in the equation:

$D = C \times 1/R$ (**1**).

D = Total deposits, C = cash held by the bank, R = the cash ratio; $1/R$ is the credit creation multiplier. Now assume that more cash is deposited in the system. The effect upon the level of deposits can be calculated using the equation:

$\Delta D = \Delta C \times 1/R$ (**2**).

Equation 2 can also be use to calculate the effects of a fall in the amount of cash in the system.

In the example above we have assumed just one bank exists, however the analysis is easily adapted to a system where there are many more banks.

The simple cash ratio shows how the central bank can limit the amount of credit created in the economy. In the 1990s the Bank of England does not impose a cash ratio as such but requires that all banks hold 0.35% of deposits in a 'special' accounts at the central bank. These accounts earn no interest and are often referred to as **non-operational accounts**. Naturally, all banks will retain some cash in order to meet day-to-day cash withdrawals, and guidelines as to exactly how much cash to hold are given by the central bank.

It should now be clear that the cash ratio determines the amount of credit that banks can create and hence how much the money supply can be expanded by bank activity. The next activity will ensure that you have understood the credit creation process.

ACTIVITY 3

1 A bank has initial deposits of £2,000 and a cash ratio of 5%. Calculate :

   (i) the amount of loans it can make

   (ii) the increase in the amount of loans it can make if there is a sudden increase in deposits of £1,000.

2 Another bank has deposits of £5,000 and a cash ratio of 2%. Calculate the amount of loans it can make.

3 Explain how it is that when Mr. Smith deposits £100 in a bank or building society time deposit, he locks up his capital but increases the national money supply.

Remember first of all that: D = Total (initial plus created) deposits, C = Cash held by the bank and R = cash ratio; so that, in this example, C = £2000 and R = 0.05.

1 (i) We utilise the equation 1: $D = C \times 1/R$; so that $D = 2,000 \times 1/0.05 = 2,000 \times 20 = £40,000$.

£40,000 is the figure for total deposits. £2,000 existed at the start so that £38,000 of deposits have been created by loans.

(ii) In order to answer this question we can use equation 2: $\Delta D = \Delta C \times 1/R$; so that $\Delta D = 1,000 \times 1/R = 1,000 \times 1/0.05 = £20,000$.

The bank can now make another £19,000 of loans (remember that £1,000 is not lent out).

2   Total deposits $= 5,000 \times 1/0.02 = £250,000$ so that the total amount of loans is £245,000.

3   When Mr. Smith deposits his £100 with the bank or building society he can be sure that his capital is safe. The bank or building society provides him with a risk free asset so that his account can be converted to cash as and when he wishes. However, that £100 represents an addition to deposits for the bank or building society and enables it to create more credit. If, for example, it has a cash ratio of 10% then it can make a further £900 of loans, which leads to an increase in the national money supply as we have seen.

PROFITABILITY AND LIQUIDITY

When banks make loans to individuals they charge an interest rate that yields them a profit. Clearly, the more loans that banks can make then the more profit they will make. However, because they have to retain some cash to meet the central bank's requirement, and because some cash is naturally kept in order to meet day-to-day withdrawals, then a limit is placed on the amount of profit that can be made. There is said to be a trade-off between **profitability** and **liquidity**. The bank wants to make profit but at the same time it must have sufficient cash to meet central bank guidelines and day-to-day requirements. Banks therefore have to conduct their activities so that they are both profitable and liquid at the same time. We will consider this in more detail when we examine the assets and liabilities of banks. However, highly liquid assets such as cash, are less profitable because they earn less interest (cash of course, earns no interest). Less liquid assets such as loans over 25 years for a mortgage are more profitable.

The ratio of liquid assets held to illiquid assets is known as the **liquidity ratio**. The higher the liquidity ratio, the lower the profitability and vice versa. Of course, if the liquidity ratio is too low then there exists the possibility that banks will not be able to meet demands for day-to-day withdrawals by the public. Such a situation could lead to a severe loss of confidence in the banking sector and could seriously destabilise the economy. Hence the Bank of England offers guidelines to the banks as to the liquidity ratio that they should maintain. Naturally, banks will have a certain liquidity ratio that they will maintain in order to be prudent.

1.4 The financial system

So far we have looked at the different types of financial institution and outlined a simple model of a financial system. We will now look at the financial system of the UK in more detail and we pay close attention to the following matters:

- the role of banks within the financial system
- the discount market
- the role of the Bank of England within the financial system
- the determination of the money supply
- the connection between the money supply and fiscal policy (You may recall that monetarists criticised the use of deficit financing on the grounds that it was inflationary and that it led to the 'crowding out' of investment).

BANKS WITHIN THE FINANCIAL SYSTEM

We have seen how the process of credit creation causes changes in the supply of money in the economy. Not surprisingly, bank deposits (which includes initial deposits and those created by banks), form the largest component of the money supply so that it is not too difficult to understand that the banks have a key role to play in the determination of the supply of money.

Banks, along with other financial institutions, form what is known as the **monetary sector** (sometimes also known as the **banking sector**). The activities of the monetary sector are supervised by the Bank of England. In order to be known as a 'bank', a licence must be granted by the Bank of England, and certain criteria regarding asset structure, the amount of capital, and the range of services available must be met. We will concentrate mainly on what are known as **clearing banks**. These are the banks that you will be familiar with from the high street, such as Midland, NatWest, Lloyds, Barclays, TSB, Royal Bank of Scotland and others.

Just as you or I may have an account with a high street bank, such as Midland or TSB, so these banks hold accounts at the Bank of England. If Midland repays money it owes TSB, then the accounts of both banks at the Bank of England are adjusted.

THE CLEARING BANKS

Clearing banks are so called because, collectively they operate a central *clearing house* in London. The clearing house is where the debts between different clearing banks are settled daily. As an example of how it works, consider two banks, Midland and TSB. The account holders, i.e. the customers of these banks, will send cheques to each other as payment for goods and services. Of course cheques will also be passed between customers of the same bank but we will ignore these for now. All the Midland cheques received by TSB customers are paid into branches of the TSB then sent to the TSB head office so that they can be added up. Exactly, the same thing happens to TSB cheques received by Midland customers. At the end of each day all cheques are sent to the London clearing house. The total sum of the cheques for each bank are compared. Suppose TSB customers have received £2 million in total from Midland account holders while Midland bank holders have received £1.5 million from TSB account holders. We can think of this simply as Midland owing £2 million to TSB and TSB owing £1.5 million to Midland. Midland will settle this debt by making a single payment of £0.5 million to the TSB. The accounts of each bank at the Bank of England are adjusted accordingly. Once the process is complete the banks make the necessary adjustments to the accounts of their individual customers.

Although we have suggested here that the process is manual (which would explain why a cheque takes three days to clear), the process is increasingly done electronically. Debit cards, such as Switch or Delta, and direct debits and standing orders are dealt with purely electronically.

As a final note, we did mention that customers of the same bank will also write cheques to each other. Because these do not involve debts between different banks then the clearing system is not involved. The cheques are cleared within the bank and may be much quicker.

THE ASSETS AND LIABILITIES OF BANKS

We have discussed how financial intermediation is one of the major functions of financial institutions and banks in particular. Banks act as a 'middleman' between lenders and borrowers and engage in maturity and risk transformation as we have seen.

We have mentioned some of the functions of banks and seen how the activity of banks can influence the national money supply. We shortly examine how the monetary authorities (the government and the Bank of England) seek to influence the ability of the banks to create credit. So that you are able to fully understand this process we will now examine the different **assets** and **liabilities** of banks that form the balance sheet of UK banks.

ASSETS

In order to be both profitable and liquid, banks will hold a number of different assets at any one time. Ideally, banks will wish to hold only profitable assets but these will tend to be less liquid so that the liquidity ratio may be too low. Therefore, some highly liquid assets will be held even though they make no profit for the banks. The assets we will look at are:

- cash
- operational balances at the Bank of England
- market loans
- bills of exchange
- investments
- advances.
- **Cash:** notes and coins kept in the banks' tills in order to meet day-to-day withdrawals by members of the public. Cash is the most highly liquid of all assets, and, because it has to be retained by the bank, will earn no profit.
- **Operational balances at the Bank of England:** these are effectively the banks' bank accounts at the Bank of England. In fact, the Bank of England is often referred to as the 'bankers' bank'. Banks hold these accounts for prudential reasons, for example, in case they find that the cash held in their tills becomes depleted, perhaps because many people

withdraw large amounts of cash on the same day. In such a case the banks would withdraw some of these operational balances in order to 'top up' their tills. Such accounts earn no interest and can be withdrawn on demand so are a highly liquid asset. The amount held depends upon the bank in question and how much cash they believe they will need daily. Generally, banks will want to minimise the amount of assets held in such a way as they earn no interest.

In addition to the operational account, banks hold 0.35% of all assets in *non*-operational accounts at the Bank of England. This is imposed by the Bank of England as a way of safeguarding against the banking system becoming illiquid. Once again, these accounts earn no interest and furthermore, cannot be withdrawn by banks.

● **Market loans:** these are made up of loans by the banks to other financial institutions. Some of these loans are short term and are repayable on demand or at short notice. The most liquid loans are those made to discount houses, which form a large part of the London money market. We will examine the importance of the money market shortly.

Liquid loans are known as **money at call and short notice**. This is generally lent overnight and for no more than 14 days. If the bank has money at call or short notice and finds itself short of cash then it demands repayment of the loans. Discount houses are, therefore, an important component of the whole banking system and banks have to keep 2.5% of their deposits with the discount houses.

Market loans also consist of loans between banks. If one bank has excess cash it can make a loan to a bank that is short of cash. Market loans are possibly the main source of liquidity for banks.

● **Bills of exchange:** are effectively promises to pay a certain sum of money on some future fixed date. They can be issued by the government (treasury bills), local authorities (local authority bills) or by firms (commercial bills). A borrower, such as a company seeking finance for investment, issues a certificate in exchange for cash from the lender. When the specified future date arrives the bill reaches **maturity** and the borrower pays the money back with a specified interest payment.

Government-issued treasury bills, which we mentioned briefly in the previous unit, are a short-term source of finance, as are local authority bills. Both of these are issued for three months. Commercial bills issued by firms for any period between one month and a year, are becoming increasingly used as a way of financing trade.

● **Investments:** generally include banks' holdings of government bonds which, as we saw in the previous unit, are sold by the government in order to finance spending and changes in taxation. Government bonds are issued as a longer-term source of finance for the government and tend to be illiquid but the closer a bond is to maturity then the more liquid it is.

● **Advances:** loans of all types, such as mortgages, personal loans and overdrafts, to both households and firms. They are the major source of profit for banks because they earn interest. They make up the largest proportion of all assets held by banks.

ACTIVITY 4

List two differences between market loans and bills of exchange

---

1   Market loans are loans between banks and financial institutions or other banks. Bills of exchange are held by banks in exchange for loans to the government, local authorities or firms.

2   Bills of exchange have varying degrees of liquidity. Government and local authority bills are issued for three months. However, firms can issue bills for just one month (a liquid asset) or up to 12 months (an illiquid asset). Market loans are generally repayable within 14 days and are therefore highly liquid.

RESERVE ASSETS

The banks must be liquid to the extent that they must always hold enough cash (or assets that can be easily turned into cash) in order to meet day to day customer demands. Such assets that are highly liquid, for example cash, money at call and short notice, bills of exchange and government bonds with less than a year to maturity, are known as **reserve assets** and until 1981 all banks were required to keep a **reserve assets ratio** of 12.5%. In other words, reserve assets held had to be at least 12.5% of deposits. Today, the requirements are that:

● banks hold 0.35% of all assets in non-operational accounts at the Bank of England

● banks keep 2.5% of their deposits with the discount houses.

Other than these requirements, the banks themselves decide on how much of their assets to retain in a highly liquid form, though the Bank of England will keep a close watch on all banks to ensure that the whole system is sufficiently liquid.

Having considered the asset side of the banks balance sheet we now turn to an examination of the liabilities.

LIABILITIES

The two most important liabilities of the banking sector are:

● deposits

● certificates of deposit.

● **Deposits:** by far the largest component of bank liabilities are the deposits of the public and of firms, which account for almost 80% of all liabilities of banks. Broadly speaking, deposits can be classed as **time**

deposits or **sight deposits**. Time deposits are not repayable on demand. Members of the public wishing to withdraw cash must give a period of notice. Such deposits earn a rate of interest. Sight deposits usually earn no interest and are repayable on demand. Since the late 1980s, however, the distinction between time and sight deposits has become less obvious. Increasingly, for example, sight deposits pay a rate of interest.

Some deposits are from other banks and financial institutions. In the last few years there has been a significant increase in borrowing and lending between banks.

● **Certificates of deposit (CDs):** these are issued by banks to customers for large fixed-term deposits. Customers will generally be firms. The certificates can be traded, so they are a liquid asset for the depositor, though they are not at all liquid for banks.

ELIGIBLE LIABILITIES

The banks are overseen and supervised by the Bank of England which may seek to influence the level of deposits in order to control the money supply. Those deposits which are closely monitored by the central bank are known as **eligible liabilities**.

The main way in which banks make profits is by charging interest for loans, overdrafts and mortgages. They also make charges for services such as safe deposits and currency exchange, and they impose penalties for dishonoured cheques and unauthorised overdrafts. In order to obtain the money that they lend, banks themselves will often have to borrow money and they will either do this by borrowing from other banks or borrowing in the discount market, which we discuss shortly. Naturally they will be charged interest on this borrowing and they will also have to pay interest on their customer's deposits. Clearly, in order to be profitable the rates charged by the bank must be greater than the rates they pay on their own borrowing.

Now try Activity 5 to ensure that you understand the difference between bills, bonds and certificates of deposit.

ACTIVITY 5

Complete the following sentence.

Gaiety Underwear wish to purchase a large shipment of Far Eastern garments from their wholesaler. They could raise finance for this by issuing a.

(a)   treasury bill

(b)   bond

(c)   commercial bill

(d)   certificate of deposit

The correct answer is (c). Firms issue commercial bills in order to raise short-term finance for projects such as this. (a) is incorrect: treasury bills are issued by the government; (b) is incorrect: bonds are issued to finance long-term investment, such as the purchase of capital machinery; (d) is incorrect: a certificate of deposit is issued by a bank to customers who make large fixed-term deposits.

We now turn to a closer examination of the London money market which is a vital component of the banking system.

1.5 The London money market

The London money market is a market for short-term loans. The Bank of England operates in the money markets in order to conduct monetary policy. The market consists of two sub-markets: the **discount market** and the **parallel money markets**.

THE DISCOUNT MARKET
Figure 2 illustrates how the discount market works.

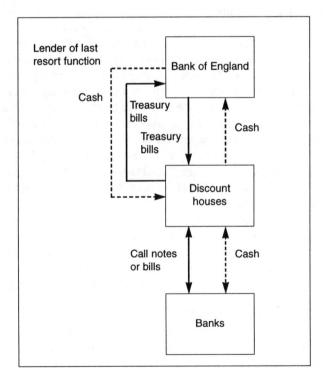

Figure 2: The discount market

The figure illustrates how the discount houses act as a 'buffer' between the Bank of England and the banks in the discount market. Discount houses borrow money at very short notice. Banks, for example, lend money overnight (money at call). These funds represent very short term surplus cash held by the banks. The discount houses use this cash to buy treasury bills; in other words, they make short term loans to the Bank of England who are acting for the government. Discount houses can only lend short term because they only borrow short term.

On certain days banks lend surplus cash to the discount houses and on other days they will want to withdraw their funds so that they have enough cash in their tills to pay customers withdrawing cash from their accounts. Occasionally, the discount houses themselves may be short of cash at the same time as the banks. They cannot obtain money at call so instead they must borrow from the Bank of England.

This is one of the most vital functions of the central bank - that of **'lender of the last resort'**. If the discount houses are short of cash there is a danger that the whole market could become illiquid. In such a case the central bank will step in and guarantee liquidity. The Bank of England will buy back treasury bills from the discount houses and therefore supply cash to the discount houses. However, the Bank reserves the right to charge a penal rate of interest. This was known as **bank rate** in the period before 1971 and **Minimum Lending Rate (MLR)** between 1971 and 1981. This means that the discount houses lose money if they have to rely on loans from the central bank.

In this way the Bank of England can influence the rate of interest in the market. Influencing interest rates is one component of monetary policy, which we will examine in more detail later. However, if the government wishes to raise the rate of interest, it will create a shortage of cash in the discount market by selling more treasury bills to the public. As people buy these bills they draw cheques on their accounts with the banks which reduces banks' balances at the Bank of England. In order to restore these balances banks will borrow from the discount houses by selling bills. The discount houses, faced with this demand for cash from the banks will become short of cash and will be forced to borrow from the Bank of England who will charge a high rate of interest. Now in order to make a profit the discount houses will have to recoup this loss. They do this by offering lower prices for the bills sold to them by banks. Banks will now find themselves losing profit, so they raise the rate of interest they charge to their customers for their loans, overdrafts and mortgages. In this way the government acting through the Bank of England can influence interest rates in the economy. We will look at this process and the implications of this in more detail when we consider monetary policy.

THE PARALLEL MONEY MARKETS

We will not look at these markets in great detail, except to say that they include markets in foreign currencies, local authority bills, certificates of deposit, and various types of loans such as large loans between banks or between companies. It also provides a market in short-term borrowing in order to finance hire purchase.

These markets have expanded and become more important since the 1980s, largely because government policy has allowed the opening of the market to include international dealings. The Bank of England oversees the money markets but does not act as a lender in the last resort.

Having now considered the banks and the money markets we turn to the role of the Bank of England.

THE BANK OF ENGLAND

The Bank of England is the central bank of the UK. It was founded in 1694 and nationalised in 1946. The Bank of England (or, more simply, the Bank) fulfills two major roles. The first is to oversee and supervise the whole financial system, the second is to act as the bank of the government and to carry out the government monetary policy.

We have already briefly mentioned that central banks in some other countries are independent of the government, and although there are those who believe that the Bank of England should be independent, currently the Bank is controlled by the government and works closely with the Treasury, the government department responsible for economic policy.

The Bank has a number of functions within these two roles:

- **The bankers' bank:** all banks and financial institutions keep deposits at the Bank. As we have seen, all banks keep *operational* and *non-operational* balances at the Bank; these balances are the bank's bank accounts at the Bank of England. Operational accounts earn no interest and can be withdrawn on demand. In addition, to preserve the liquidity of the system, banks are required by the government to hold 0.35% of all their assets in non-operational accounts at the Bank. These accounts earn no interest and cannot be withdrawn.

- **The government's bank:** the Bank holds the government accounts, receiving income, for example, from tax revenue and also paying for government expenditure. The Bank also manages the national debt on behalf of the government. The **national debt** is the accumulated debt of the whole of the public sector. This role involves the Bank issuing bonds and treasury bills, paying interest on these and redeeming them, i.e. paying off their values as they mature. The Bank also manages the government borrowing programme if the government runs a budget deficit it must finance the deficit by borrowing. To do this the Bank organises the sale of government bonds (gilts) or treasury bills on the government's behalf.

- **Operation of monetary policy:** the Bank is responsible for the implementation of government monetary policy. We will look at this in some detail shortly.

- **Note issue:** the Bank has the sole right to issue bank notes in England and Wales (in Scotland notes are issued by the clearing banks). It prints notes and coins and oversees their release in accordance with the wishes of the government.

- **Supervision of the system :** the Bank lays down guidelines or 'prudential standards of liquidity' for the banks in terms of how much of their assets should be kept in a liquid form. This is known as **prudential control**.

- **Lender of the last resort:** the Bank provides liquidity to the discount houses when they have to pay back money at call and short-term loans to the banks. This function is vital as a way of maintaining confidence in the money markets and banking system in general.

- **Foreign dealings:** the Bank holds gold and foreign currency reserves in what is known as the **exchange equalisation account.** It uses these to buy or sell sterling on the foreign exchange markets in order to influence the value of the exchange rate. You will study this in Unit 10.

We have now completed our study of the London money markets, though we will return to this topic when we examine monetary policy. To ensure that you have fully digested this material, try the following activity

---

ACTIVITY 6

Assume that the monetary authorities (the government and Bank of England) want to raise interest rates. List the steps in the process through which they can achieve this.

Step 1: government, via the Bank of England, sells more treasury bills to the public.

Step 2: members of the public pay for these bills by issuing cheques on their bank accounts.

Step 3: banks' balances at the Bank of England are reduced.

Step 4: banks will borrow from the discount houses in order to restore these balances. They sell bills to the discount houses.

Step 5: discount houses become short of cash and are forced to borrow from the Bank of England who will charge a penal rate of interest .

Step 6: The discount houses will have to recoup this loss. They do this by offering lower prices for the bills sold to them by banks.

Step 7: banks lose profits. They raise the rate of interest charged to customers for their loans, overdrafts and mortgages.

Interest rates are therefore raised by the initial sale of treasury bills to the public.

Do not worry if you had used more or less than seven steps to summarise the process. The idea of the activity was to make sure that you are fully able to understand each stage of the process whereby increased sales of Treasury bills to the public results in higher interest rates in the economy.

1.6 The money supply

The importance of the supply of money to the economy is the subject of considerable debate. Keynesians argue that the money supply has a small role to play in the determination of the level of output and prices, but is not especially important. In the post-war years when successive governments followed Keynesian economic policies, little attention was paid to the quantity of money in the economy. However, with the emergence of increasing levels of inflation in the 1970s and the election in 1979 of the Conservative government committed to monetarism, the money supply became the focus of economic policy. Monetarists see inflation as the major economic problem and believe that it can only be controlled by controlling the money supply.

In order to control the money supply you have got to know what it is that you are trying to control. We have seen that there are a confusing number of definitions of the money supply (i.e. M0, M1, £M3). If the government wishes to control the supply of money then it must choose which one of a number of measures it will use. The Conservative government of 1979 focused on sterling M3, a very broad measure. However, deciding which measure to control and then attempting to control it is by no means straightforward and we will look closely at the difficulties experienced by the 1979 administration later in this unit.

In Section 1 we saw how the banks affected the supply of money in the economy. Now we will look at some other factors which affect the money supply.

DETERMINATION OF THE MONEY SUPPLY

The money supply in the economy is affected by a number of factors, such as bank deposits, government policy and also factors external to the U.K economy. We will not consider external factors in this section as the external sector is considered in unit 10. We begin by considering the effect of bank deposits.

In Section 1.3 we looked at a simple model of credit creation to see how bank lending affects the money supply. The money supply is also affected by other factors including bank deposits and government policy – both of which we will look at in this section – and external factors which we will look at in unit 10.

In our model of credit creation we saw that the amount of credit banks can create depends on the cash ratio they choose to maintain. But the chosen cash ratio is not the only factor that influences the amount banks can lend. The amount they can lend is constrained by

- the amount of their assets that they choose to hold in a liquid form
- the amount they are required to hold in deposits at the Bank
- the amount that the public wishes to borrow that a bank undertakes is affected by government

Liquidity of Assets – The banks may hold their assets in the form of cash, which is the most liquid asset of all. They would then be able to lend a large proportion of those assets. Alternatively they may hold less liquid assets such as government bonds and would be unable to lend quite so much. Thus the money supply is determined partly by the banks preference to hold liquid assets as opposed to long term assets.

Of course, the banks will vary the proportion of liquid to illiquid assets according to business circumstances. So in preparation for Christmas, for example, when many customers will want to withdraw cash, banks will convert some of their liquid assets into cash. (This is not a case of the banks affecting the money supply – it is their provision to meet the requirements of customers to withdraw their own cash).

Deposits at the Bank – The banks are required to maintain non-operational accounts with the Bank. These accounts cannot be withdrawn for the banks' use nor can they be included in the basis of calculating lending based on the cash ratio. So the bigger the deposits, the less the banks can lend.

The public's desire to borrow – the banks can only lend what people want to borrow. When people feel financially insecure they may fear getting into debt ; or when interest rates are high they may wish to defer borrowing till better times. To combat customer reluctance to borrow, banks may reduce interest rates but this may lower profits so they will not do this readily. Banks may try to make the public borrow more by lowering the rates of interest on loans but there is a limit to this because they will not want to lose profits. So the simple model of credit creation is less simple in practice ! However, we can say that if banks decide to change the amount of their assets that they retain in liquid form then this will affect the money supply.

The influence of government – The government can influence the supply of money in several ways.

- Selling securities to the Bank
- Selling bills to the open market
- Selling gilts

each of these has different effects which we will turn to next.

EFFECTS OF DIFFERENT METHODS OF FINANCING THE PSBR
Selling securities to the Bank of England

Firstly, the government could sell securities such as gilts and treasury bills to the Bank of England. The Bank will buy the securities and credit the government account at the Bank with the relevant amount, say £1 million. The government then spends this money on roadbuilding or defence, etc. and the money finds its way to firms and households as profits and wages. This money is then paid into those firms and households bank accounts and the banks then deposit this money into their own accounts with the central bank so that the banks balances rise by £1 million. Clearly, bank liabilities have risen by £1 million as their deposits have risen by this amount and also their assets have increased by £1 million as they now have an extra £1 million in their central bank accounts. The money supply will increase by at least

£1 million, and probably more, as these new deposits represent an increase in liquid assets for the banks. As we saw from our cash ratio, any cash increase will lead to an expansion of the money supply by far more than that increase in cash.

Selling bills to the money market

Another way of financing the PSBR would be to sell bills to the money market. The Bank of England would act on behalf of the government and sell Treasury bills to the discount houses. The discount houses borrow money at call from the banks to pay for these or sell bills to the banks to acquire the cash. The banks pay by drawing on their accounts with the Bank of England. Therefore, the banks now have £1 million worth of bills or call notes but have £1 million less cash in their balances with the central bank. However, once the government spends the money on its roadbuilding, for example, the money finds it way back to the banks. The banks then deposit this £1 million from their customers in their accounts at the central bank so that these balances have not altered. They still have, however, the call notes and bills which can then be called in so that liquid assets have risen by £1 million. This expansion of liquid assets causes an increase in the money supply of at least £1 million.

Selling gilts to the banks

The government could finance the PSBR in a different way, by selling £1 million worth of gilts, that is long-term securities, to the banks. As before, the banks reduce their balances at the central bank by £1 million but this will be restored when the money finds its way back into customer accounts as a result of government expenditure. Liabilities rise by £1 million as a result of the increased deposits and assets rise by £1 million as a result of the acquisition of gilts. However, now banks will have a greater proportion of illiquid assets in their balance sheets as these gilts are relatively illiquid so that they may have to reduce their lending to maintain a prudent liquidity ratio. This method of financing the PSBRis not likely, therefore, to have any significant effect on the money supply.

Selling bills to the public

As well as these methods, the government could sell bills to the public, but this is not likely to affect the money supply because the public will reduce their accounts by the £1 million to pay for the bills and the £1 million will find its way back to the banks as a result of the government expenditure. So there is no change in the banks' liquid assets.

Selling bills and gilts overseas

One final way of financing the PSBR is to sell bills and gilts to the overseas sector. The effects of foreign dealings on the supply of money are considered in Unit 10. However, briefly, the sale of securities leads to an inflow of foreign currency which is then converted into domestic currency. There is, therefore, an increase in the supply of money though the process is somewhat more complex than we suggest here. Furthermore, if the economy is part of an agreement to maintain a fixed value of the currency (for example, if the government is part of an exchange rate mechanism similar to that operating currently in Europe), then the authorities will need to buy and sell the domestic currency on the foreign exchange market in order to maintain the fixed value. If the currency starts to decline below the fixed value then the authorities buy that currency using foreign exchange reserves. This buying raises the value of the currency and as the buying of domestic currency reduces the amount of that currency on the foreign exchange market then the money supply falls. If the currency starts to rise above the fixed value then the authorities sell that currency for foreign exchange reserves. This selling lowers the value of the currency and, as the selling of domestic currency raises the amount of that currency on the foreign exchange market, the money supply rises.

Clearly, the way that the government finances its borrowing will determine the effect on the money supply. In practice, the government cannot easily choose who it sells securities to, so that at least some effect on the money supply is likely. Monetarists argue that the way in which deficits have been financed in the UK has led to increases in the supply of money, and therefore inflation, via the mechanism described by the quantity theory of quantity theory of money. Government monetary policy, which is directly concerned to some extent with influencing the money supply, will be explored later in this unit.

We also mentioned that external factors can affect the money supply in the economy. We explore this in some detail in Unit 10. In Section 2 of this unit we will examine the theories of the demand for money and then consider equilibrium in the money markets. We will then turn to a consideration of how changes in the money supply can affect aggregate demand and prices.

Now try Activity 7 to ensure that you have understood the discussion about money supply.

ACTIVITY 7

Outline, in no more than about 300 words, three factors that might influence the money supply.

A number of factors will influence the money supply.

Firstly, the banks will wish to retain a certain proportion of their assets in a highly liquid form. It may be that the government *imposes* a certain ratio that the banks must conform to as part of its monetary policy. Either way, the ratio of liquid assets to total assets will limit the amount of credit that can be created. The higher the proportion of assets that is retained in a liquid form, then the lower the amount of credit that can be created. Obviously, the amount of credit that can be created is to some extent determined by the number of people seeking loans. People will be more keen to borrow at lower interest rates. So the rate of interest can influence the money supply via its effect on the demand for loans. We will study this in more detail later in the unit.

Secondly, government fiscal policy can also influence the money supply. If the government has to borrow then the way that it will do so can affect the money supply. It is likely that government borrowing will have at the very least some small effect on the money supply. Higher borrowing will tend to raise the money supply.

Thirdly, external factors will also influence the supply of money, for example if the government finances part of its borrowing by selling securities to the overseas sector, or if the government is forced to intervene in the foreign exchange markets in order to preserve a fixed value for the domestic currency.

REVIEW ACTIVITY 1

1 Outline the functions of money.

2 Describe the benefits of financial intermediation.

3 A bank has initial deposits of £50,000 and a cash ratio of 8%.

Calculate :

   (i) the amount of loans that can be made

   (ii) the increase in the amount of loans it can make if there is a sudden increase in deposits of £10,000.

4 List the functions of the Bank of England.

5 Outline the process whereby a sale of government securities to the banking sector can lead to an increase in the money supply.

Summary

In this section we discussed the definition and the functions of money. We outlined a simple financial system and a simple model of credit creation. Finally, we looked at the financial system in the UK and examine how the supply of money is determined.

SECTION TWO

Money Demand, Aggregate Demand and Money Market Equilibrium

Introduction

We will now turn to the issue of the demand for money. When we defined money in Section 1 we saw that there were a number of definitions, such as M0 or M1, each including different assets such as sight or time deposits. In this section, the demand for money refers to the demand to hold *cash* rather than other financial assets such as shares or bonds.

As for any good, there is a market for money and equilibrium in the market is determined by the interaction of supply and demand. The demand for money is a subject that is hotly debated amongst economists and in examining the different theories of the demand for money we will begin to see why monetarists and Keynesians disagree, not only on the importance of the money supply, but also on the relative importance of monetary and fiscal policy.

In Section 2 we will study three theories of the demand for money, which we will call:

- the classical quantity theory
- the Keynesian theory
- the monetarist theory (often known as the restatement of the quantity theory).

We will also look at the relationship between the demand for money and aggregate demand, and finally we will study monetarist and Keynesian theories of inflation.

2.1 Theories of the demand for money

The demand for money is not like the demand for any other good. Most goods are demanded in order to consume. The **demand for money** is the demand to hold wealth in the form of money rather than other financial assets. Furthermore, the demand for money is said to be a demand for *real* balances. This means that individuals are not interested in the amount of cash they hold but more in the amount of goods that that money can buy. Obviously, the amount of goods that a sum of money can buy will depend on the price level. At a higher price level individuals will need to hold more money to buy the same goods than they would at a lower price level. Real money balances are calculated by dividing nominal money balances by an appropriate price index such as the retail price index.

THE CLASSICAL QUANTITY THEORY

The **classical quantity theory** sees the main role of money as a medium of exchange. In other words money is used purely in order to buy goods and services. Individuals will only hold money in order to finance expenditure, so that an individual's money holdings are directly related to the value of the transactions that the individual carries out. Put simply, if the individual has more money than he needs to finance his transactions then he will get rid of this excess cash by spending it. On the other hand, if the individual is short of cash he will reduce his expenditure. Money is just a substitute for goods.

Aggregate demand for money is simply the sum of all individuals' demand for money. In equilibrium the demand for money is equal to the supply of money. Classical theorists argued that if the demand for money were greater than the supply of money, then individuals would dispose of the excess money by spending more. However, society as a whole cannot dispose of its excess money as one person's expenditure is another person's receipts ! Therefore, if people are buying more goods, then demand is rising and so the aggregate price level will rise. The quantity theory of money is therefore a theory of inflation and until the 1930s it was *the* theory of inflation. In this example we also see how changes in the money supply can lead to increases in aggregate demand. We explore this point later.

Classical economists expressed their ideas formally using the equation:

$$M \times V = P \times T \ (3).$$

M = money supply, P = price level, V = velocity of circulation. This is the number of times that money goes around the economy in a period of time or the number of times that a £1 changes hands in that period. T = The number of transactions carried out in a given time period.

This equation is known as **the equation of exchange** and is the basis of the quantity theory of money. The equation of exchange is in fact an identity! It will always hold. Both sides of the equation measure the same thing.

In order to illustrate exactly what this means, consider a very simple economy where there are four individuals A, B, C and D. Let D produce goods that C wants and C produce goods that B wants. B produces goods that A wants and A produces goods that D wants. In each case the value of the goods concerned is £100. So the total value of goods exchanged is £400. However, it would only be necessary to have a stock of money of £100 to finance this expenditure as D would pay A £100 and then A would pay B £100 etc. Total income generated is £400. Notice here that this is because the money supply in the economy is a *stock* but income and expenditure are *flows* over time.

In terms of our equation, we have M equal to £100 and V equal to 4. Furthermore, the price level, P, is equal to £100 and the number of transactions, T, is equal to 4, so that $M \times V = P \times T$. $P \times T$ is simply the total value of all transactions.

A very slightly more complex example may also help explain this equation. The following data shows all transactions in an economy in a given period.

Four maps sold at £11 each = £44

Two books sold at £8 each = £16

Three ties sold at £4 each = £12

One mirror sold at £8 = £8

Total transactions sum to £80

You are also told that the money stock is £40

This information enables us to work out the other values in our equation

$M \times V = P \times T$.

The purchase of each single item constitutes a transaction so that from our data the number of transactions is 10 $(4 + 2 + 3 + 1)$. We now know that

$40 \times V = P \times 10$.

Since $P \times T$ is the total value of all transactions, which is equal to £80, then the general price level (or, if you prefer, the 'average' price level, P) must be £8.

Therefore, $40 \times V = 80$; V, the velocity of circulation is equal to 20.

Providing we can measure the stock of money, if we know the value of $P \times T$, we can measure the velocity of circulation. Of course, $P \times T$ is the total value of all transactions in the economy, which is of course, GDP(something we examined in Unit 6). Therefore the velocity of circulation can be, calculated.

However, classical economists took this identity one stage further and developed it into a theory. The theory was the **quantity theory of money**, which stated that changes in the money supply caused changes in the price level, i.e. inflation. In order to develop this theory they made three assumptions:

1   The quantity of money was said to be exogenous. This means that the quantity of money, M, is not related to other variables in the equation, P, V or T. The money supply is determined 'outside' the equation, for example by the government.

2   The velocity of circulation, V, is constant. The velocity of circulation is determined by institutional factors such as how often people get paid and the timing of income receipts and expenditure. The less often people get paid then the longer they will hold onto money and hence the lower will be V. The

more often people are paid then the shorter the period they hold money and hence the higher the value of V. Classical economists argued that such factors were not likely to alter over a short period of time s⌃ that V would be fixed in the short term.

3   The number of transactions, T , would be fixed. Classical economists theorised that the economy would always be at a level of output such that there would be full employment. In such a case the number of transactions could not possibly rise as the economy was at full capacity. Classical economists did not think that the number of transactions would fall because this would lead to unemployment, a factor they ignored.

Equation 3, the equation of exchange, can now be rewritten as:

$$P = (V/T) \times M \quad (4).$$

If both V and T are fixed the value of (V/T) is fixed. Therefore, the price level, P, is directly related and proportional to the supply of money. Any increase in the supply of money would cause prices to rise. The quantity theory is a theory of excess monetary demand or 'too much money chasing too few goods'. We will see later how this differs from the Keynesian theory, which sees inflation, not as a result of monetary forces, but of real forces, that is, as a result of demand and supply conditions in markets.

Of course, any theory is really only as good as the assumptions on which it is based. The first major problem with the theory is that unemployment does occur so that the number of transactions, T, is generally not fixed. Secondly, the velocity of circulation, V, may not be fixed either. Research suggests that V tends to fluctuate in the short run. If V and/or T were not constant then changes in the money supply may not lead to changes in prices. If the government expanded the money supply then the velocity of circulation or the number of transactions could fall so that the value of MV and PT do not change.

So far in this discussion we have considered the quantity theory of money but have not really considered how this relates to the *demand* for money. A later version of the quantity theory known as the 'Cambridge version' was developed in the 1920s by adapting the quantity theory. A group of economists at Cambridge University reformulated the theory, replacing the number of transactions with national income. The number of transactions refers to *all* transactions in the economy and therefore includes purchases of intermediate goods, such as raw materials. We are more interested, however, in the level of output of the economy. The definition of transactions was restricted to include only those involving the sale of final goods and services.

The equation of exchange then became:

$$MV = PY \quad (5).$$

Y = real national income, so PY is equal to nominal (or money) national income.

This was then rewritten as:

$M = (1/V)PY = kPY$, where $k = (1/V)$.

In equilibrium, the supply of money, M, will be equal to the demand for money, MD, so we now have,

$MD = kPY$ (**6**).

The underlying assumptions of the Cambridge version are the same as the quantity theory, so that $(1/V)$ or k will be a constant. What the equation says is that the demand for money is a constant proportion of nominal national income. In other words, the demand for money is stable and predictable and can be calculated from the national income accounts.

If the demand for money is a constant proportion of national income then increases in the money supply will lead directly to increases in aggregate demand. As the money supply increases then individuals will find themselves with more money than they wish to hold. They will spend their excess holdings of money so that aggregate demand rises and prices rise.

In this theory, then, monetarists see money only as a medium of exchange whereby money is only demanded in order to finance expenditure. The quantity held to finance transactions is directly related to national income.

Now try Activity 8 to check your understanding of what we have discussed.

ACTIVITY 8

1 Explain in about 150 words why it is so important to monetarist economists that, in the quantity theory of money, the velocity of circulation and the number of transactions are constant.

2 The following data show all transactions in an economy in a given period.

Eight books sold at £10 each = £80

Two pairs of shoes sold at £8 each = £16

Three televisions sold at £60 each = £180

One mirror sold at £4 = £4.

You are also told that the money stock is £140. Calculate the values of P and V and, hence, MV = PT.

3 In the previous question, if we agree with classical and monetarist economists, what is the effect of an increase in the money supply from £140 to £200 ?

1   If we have a variable velocity of circulation or volume of transactions then the link between the money supply and prices may break down. Consider the following data:

M = 100, V = 4, P = 16 , T = 25. Clearly we have $100 \times 4 = 16 \times 25$.

Monetarists and classical economists argue that an increase in the money supply will directly effect prices as V and T are constant, so that if, say, the money supply was to double to 200, the effect would be:

$200 \times 4 = P \times 25$ so $800 = P \times 25$. Therefore, P has risen to $800/25 = 32$.

According to monetarist theory, an increase in the money supply leads to a 'one for one' increase in prices. In this case, a doubling of the money supply leads to a doubling of prices.

Now what if we relax the monetarist assumptions ?

What if the doubling of the money supply causes a 50% drop in the velocity of circulation ?

M rises to 200 and V falls to 2, so that $200 \times 2 = 8 \times 25$.

There is no change in the price level. Similarly, a doubling of the money supply could lead to a doubling of the number of transactions and therefore not affect the price level. This, argue Keynesians, is a likely scenario in times of unemployment. Unemployment is, of course, ignored by monetarists and classicals so that T is constant.

2   From our data the number of transactions is $14 \ (8 + 2 + 3 + 1)$, so that we now know

$140 \times V = P \times 14$.

The total value of transactions, PT, from our data is £280 $(80 + 16 + 180 + 4)$

so the general price level P must be $280/14 = 20$. Therefore:

$140 \times V = 280$.

V, the velocity of circulation is equal to 2.

3   From the previous question, we have:

MV = PT or $140 \times 2 = 20 \times 14$.

Monetarists and classical economists believe that V and T are constant, so our values for V and T do not change as a result of an increase in the money supply. Therefore, if the money supply increases to 200 the only change will occur in the price level.

We have:

$200 \times 2 = P \times 14$

$$400 = P \times 14$$

so P = 28.57, a rise from the previous level of 20.

Notice that the percentage rise in the price level of 42.85% exactly matches the percentage rise in the money supply.

THE KEYNESIAN THEORY OF MONEY DEMAND

The classical quantity theory of money said that money was held only to finance transactions. Keynesians called this the **transactions motive** for holding money. Keynes agreed that people would hold money to finance transactions but argued that there would be two other motives for holding money: the **precautionary motive** and the **speculative motive**.

The transactions motive, or demand for money, was directly related to the level of national income. The higher the level of national income, the greater the quantity of money held for transactions purposes.

The precautionary demand for money arises because people will want to retain money to meet unexpected expenditure. The future is uncertain and expenditures that cannot be planned in advance may arise. Therefore, people hold some money as a precaution. Once again, Keynes felt more money would be held for this reason at higher levels of income.

Whilst income would be the key determinant of the transactions and precautionary demand for money, interest rates might also be a factor. At higher interest rates individuals will want to hold less cash because the more cash they hold the more interest they will be losing. Economists say that, at higher interest rates, the **opportunity cost** of holding cash is higher.

The most important departure of Keynesian theory from the classical theory arises out of the speculative motive for holding money. The theory of the speculative demand for money which we now discuss is often referred to as **liquidity preference**. In this theory money can be held as a substitute for other assets, of which **bonds** were considered the most important. Indeed, the Keynesian theory of liquidity preference is developed in a world where just two financial assets are considered: money and bonds.

We have already mentioned government bonds or gilts in our consideration of fiscal policy. Here money is held, not to finance transactions, but for speculative reasons. The demand for money to be used entirely for speculative reasons is also often referred to as demand for **idle** balances. (Not surprisingly, money demand in order to finance transactions or for precautionary reasons, is known as demand for **active** balances.)

Bonds are financial assets which provide a fixed return based on the value of that bond. This fixed return is also known as a 'coupon'. Borrowers issue bonds in exchange for cash. The bond is held for a period of time during which the lender receives a fixed return based on the value of the loan. At the end of the period of time the bond matures and the loan is repaid.

For example, a £100 bond with a coupon value of £10 would provide the bondholder (the lender) with income of £10 per year during the life of that bond. Bonds are usually issued for a fixed period and at the end of the period the issuer of the bond (the borrower) would redeem the bond i.e. repay the loan of £100 on which the bond was issued.

One very important point to note is that the *price of a bond is inversely related to the rate of interest*. Consider the bond example above with a £10 coupon. This is based on a bond value of £100 so that the return on the bond or interest is 10%. Now consider a situation where the interest rate on all other financial assets rises to 20%. The original bonds are now unattractive to investors. Investors start to sell their bonds, which pushes the price downwards. The price will continue to fall until the bonds become as attractive as other assets. This is when the bonds also pay a 20% rate of interest. How does this come about ? The £10 coupon is fixed. Therefore, the value of the bonds falls until the £10 coupon represents a 20% interest rate. This means that the price of the bond falls to £50. So if interest rates rise then bond prices fall. On the other hand, consider a situation where the interest rate on all other financial assets falls to 5%. The original bonds are now very attractive to investors. Investors start to buy bonds which pushes the price upwards. The price will continue to rise until the bonds become just as attractive as other assets. This is when the bonds also pay a 5% rate of interest. Therefore, the value of the bonds rises until the £10 coupon represents a 5% interest rate. This means that the price of the bond rises to £200. So if interest rates fall then bond prices rise.

Now that we have established this relationship we can consider the speculative demand for money. Figure 3 illustrates the speculative demand function. The horizontal axis measures the speculative money demand while the vertical axis measures interest rates.

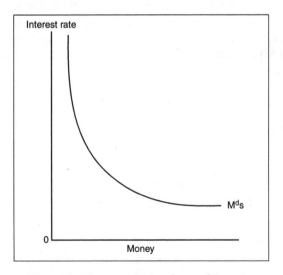

Figure 3: The speculative demand function

At high rates of interest the speculative demand, M^ds, is low, whilst at lower interest rates the speculative demand is high. How does this situation arise ? The speculative demand centres around individuals' ***expectations*** of future changes in interest rates. If the rate of interest is high then individuals might expect that it is likely to fall. In such a case bond prices will rise. Individuals will therefore prefer to hold bonds rather than money. Individuals will exchange their money now for bonds so that when bond prices do rise they can sell their bonds at the higher price and make **capital gains** (profits). Therefore individuals hold little cash at high interest rates. On the other hand if the rate of interest is low then individuals might expect that it is likely to rise. In such a case bond prices will fall. Individuals will therefore prefer to hold money rather than bonds. Individuals will sell their bonds now for cash. They will sell them before prices actually fall to avoid making a **capital loss** on their bonds. Therefore, at lower rates of interest individuals hold more money.

Of course, each individual will have different expectations of what will happen to interest rates. However, in the Keynesian theory, at low interest rates most individuals will expect rates to rise and will prefer to hold money, whilst at higher rates most individuals will expect rates to fall and will prefer to hold bonds. If you examine Figure 3 carefully you will notice that at lower interest rates the speculative demand for money curve becomes horizontal. This means that at very low interest rates everyone expects interest rates to rise and bond prices to fall, so that individuals will only want to hold money. This is known as the **liquidity trap**. Effectively, therefore, there is a lower limit to the interest rate. At this point the speculative money demand curve is horizontal so that the interest elasticity of money demand is infinite. No one believes interest rates can fall further. Everyone believes that bond prices are about to fall, so they simply hold cash.

Now that we have examined the three Keynesian motives for holding money we can define the overall money demand schedule. We have seen that the transactions and precautionary demand for money depend on the level of income not on interest rates. The money demand schedule for these two motives is illustrated in Figure 4. The demand for money for transactions and precautionary motive for money demand schedule is labelled $M^d y$. This function is vertical as it does not depend on the rate of interest.

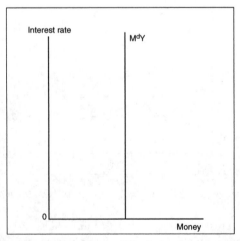

Figure 4: M^d y encompasses the transactions and precautionary demand for money

In deriving a total money demand schedule, the amount of money demanded for the three motives is summed horizontally at each rate of interest. Figure 5 shows the dotted curves M^dy (transactions and precautionary demand) and M^ds (speculative demand) and the total money demand function M^D.

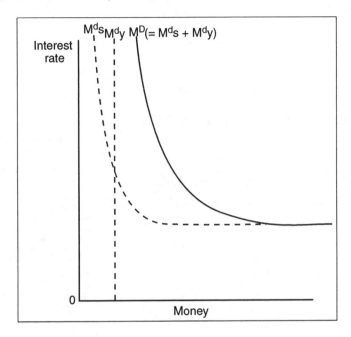

Figure 5: The money demand function, M^D is the horizontal summation of the transactions and precautionary demand for money, M^dy and the speculative demand for money, M^ds

Try this quick activity to see if you have understood the Keynesian demand for money theory. The activity should take you no more than five minutes.

ACTIVITY 9

1 At an interest rate of 5%, the demand for money for transactions and precautionary purposes is £100 million and the demand for money for speculative purposes is £50 million. Calculate the total demand for money at interest rates of 5%.

2 If interest rates rise, underline the likely effect on each of the following; will they rise/fall/stay the same?

(a) M^ds; (b) M^dy; (c) M^D.

1   The total demand for money is simply the sum of the transactions and precautionary demand (£100m) and the speculative demand (£50m). The answer is, therefore, £100m + £50m = £150m.

2   (a) M^ds (speculative demand) will fall.

   (b) M^dy (transactions and precautionary demand) will stay the same.

   (c) M^D (total demand for money) will fall. Remember that $M^D = M^ds + M^dy$, so that if M^ds falls and M^dy is unchanged, then M^D will fall.

SHIFTS IN THE DEMAND FOR MONEY SCHEDULE

The demand for money schedule (M^D) will shift if there is a change in either income or prices. If there is an increase in income the demand for money function will shift out to the right. Figure 6 illustrates the effects of an increase in income. The money demand function (M^D_1) is drawn for a given income level. If income rises then the money demand function shifts to the right to M^D_2.

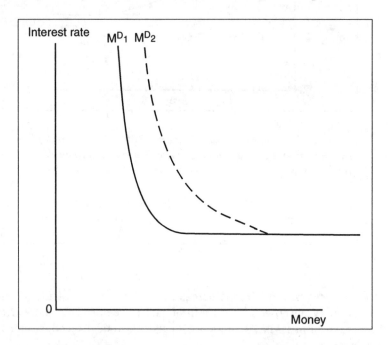

Figure 6: An increase in income causes the money demand schedule to shift to the right

Similarly, a fall in income would cause the speculative money demand curve to shift to the left.

The price level will also cause the demand for money schedule to shift. So far we have ignored prices (this is because the Keynesian analysis assumes fixed prices). However, what will happen if prices do rise ? We defined money demand to be a demand for *real* balances. At a higher price level individuals will need to hold more nominal money to buy the same goods than they would at a lower price level. If the price level were to increase, individuals would hold more cash and the money demand function will shift to the right. Similarly, if the price level were to fall, the money demand function would shift to the left .

IMPLICATIONS OF THE CLASSICAL AND KEYNESIAN THEORIES

Now let us see what the implications of the two theories are, starting with the classical theory. In this theory, if the government increased the money supply, individuals would spend it. This is because in the classical theory money is only held to finance transactions. If the economy is at full employment, as classical theory assumed, then output cannot rise. Therefore, aggregate demand would rise as individuals spent their excess money and this would cause prices to rise. There is, therefore, a crucial link in classical theory between money, aggregate demand and inflation.

Figure 7 shows a vertical aggregate supply curve labelled AS. This is vertical to reflect the classical assumption of full employment. In such a case output is fixed and cannot respond to price increases. The aggregate demand curve is shown as AD_0 and the intersection of the two curves gives a price level P_0 and an income level Y_0 . Now, in the classical model, if the money supply increases then individuals will spend their excess holdings and this causes aggregate demand to rise to AD_1 and prices to rise to P_1. The increase in the supply of money causes a shift in aggregate demand and leads to inflation.

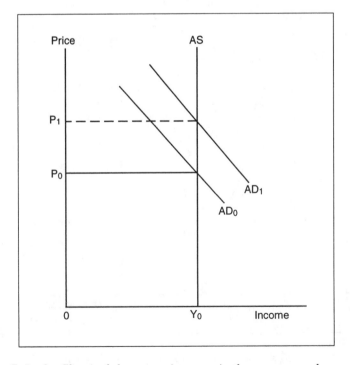

Figure 7: In the Classical theory, an increase in the money supply causes the aggregate deamnd schedule to shift from AD_0 to AD_1. Income is unchanged but prices rise from P_0 to P_1.

How does this compare with the Keynesian theory ? In the Keynesian theory money is held not only for transactions purposes, but also for speculative reasons. So if the government increased the supply of money then individuals might not spend their excess money holdings but use them to speculate. If the interest rate was low then, as the government increased the supply of money, individuals would simply hold it in preference to bonds. This is the liquidity trap. Of course, some cash would be used to finance transactions and also held for precautionary reasons but any *increase* in the money supply would simply be held as idle balances by investors expecting interest rates to rise and bond prices to fall. Therefore, at low interest rates the link between money and aggregate demand breaks down. Money will not affect aggregate demand at low interest rates.

Figure 8 illustrates this: the money demand schedule (M^D) is shown and we assume that the money supply is determined by the government and that the government can fix the supply as it wishes. In other words, the money supply is exogenous. This is shown as M^S. Now we have drawn this intersection of the two curves along the horizontal portion of the money demand curve so that the economy is in a liquidity trap at interest rate r_0. If the government increased the money supply so that M^S shifts to M^S_1 then individuals would simply hold this extra cash as idle balances and not spend it. Aggregate demand and prices would not be affected. In the Keynesian analysis the quantity theory of money may not hold. Keynes therefore dealt a blow to classical theory.

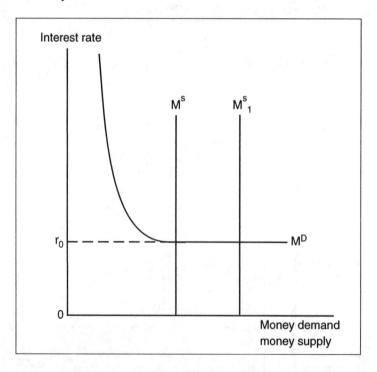

Figure 8: In the presence of a liquidity trap, an increase in
the money supply has no effect on the interest rate.

ACTIVITY 10

1 Government bonds with a nominal value of £50 pay a fixed coupon of £4. Interest rates on other assets rise to 10%. By how much will the price of bonds change?

2 Explain why, according to Keynesian theory, money demand is low at high interest rates and high at low interest rates.

3 Show the effects of a fall in the price level on the Keynesian money demand schedule.

4 Why is the liquidity trap central to the debate between economists over the effectiveness of monetary policy?

---

1 Bond prices will fall until the rate of interest on bonds is equal to that on other assets. Individuals sell bonds and the price falls. It stops falling when the £4 coupon represents an interest rate of 10%. Bond prices fall to £40.

2 In the Keynesian theory, at high interest rates and hence low bond prices, individuals will be expecting interest rates to fall so that bond prices rise. Therefore, they will want to hold bonds because they will make a capital gain if they hold bonds and the price rises. Hence, individuals will hold little money so that money demand is low at high interest rates. At low interest rates and high bond prices, individuals will be expecting interest rates to rise so that bond prices fall. Therefore, they will want to hold money because they will make a capital loss if they hold bonds and the price falls. Hence, individuals will hold mainly money so that money demand is high.

3 The demand for money is a demand for real balances. This means individuals are not especially bothered by the amount of cash they hold but more with the amount of goods that cash will purchase. If prices fall then individuals can make the same amount of purchases with less cash so that the money demand curve will shift to the left as shown in the diagram below. MD_0 shifts to MD_1.

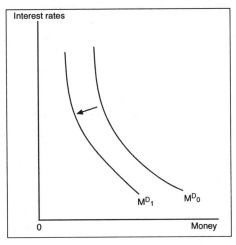

4   The liquidity trap describes the situation where all individuals believe that interest rates are so low that they can only rise. In a recession, a government may try to lower interest rates by increasing the money supply. They may do this in order perhaps to raise aggregate demand via consumption and investment demand. In Keynesian theory, however, the increase in the money supply does not lower interest rates because everyone holds the extra cash as idle balances. Individuals believe interest rates will rise and bond prices will fall so that they will prefer to hold only cash. The increased money is not spent so that consumption does not rise. Interest rates do not fall. Hence, investment is unaffected. In addition to this because there is no shift in demand then prices are not affected as monetarists predict. The link between money and prices and aggregate demand breaks down. This means that, in certain circumstances, monetary policy might not have any effect on aggregate demand.

Having examined the Keynesian theory of money demand we turn finally to the monetarist theory of money demand, more commonly known as the restatement of the quantity theory, which is attributable to Milton Friedman. Having done this we then return to the link between money and aggregate demand.

THE RESTATEMENT OF THE QUANTITY THEORY

Keynes had argued that money demand will vary with the interest rate and was therefore not stable. Interest rates in practice tend to be volatile so that the demand for money would be constantly changing. This conflicted directly with the classical quantity theory which relied on a stable velocity of circulation and hence demand for money. Friedman's task in developing the restatement was to show that the demand for money was stable after all. Friedman's new theory was developed in an article called 'The quantity theory of money: a restatement', *Essays in the Quantity Theory of Money*, M. Friedman (ed.), University of Chicago Press (1956).

In order to achieve this, rather than attempt to destroy Keynesian theory, he built upon it. He agreed that money was a substitute for interest-bearing assets such as bonds but he argued that it was also a substitute for many other types of asset such as company shares, houses, washing machines etc. In arguing this Friedman was saying that the rate of interest, vital to Keynesian analysis, was relatively insignificant as it would only influence one of a large number of asset decisions.

In the Keynesian theory, a rise in interest rates would cause a fall in the demand for money. In Keynesian theory, since there are only two assets under consideration then a change in interest rates is likely to have a significant effect on money demand. Higher interest rates means that bond prices fall. Investors will expect that the next likely move in bond prices will be upward. So they buy bonds and reduce their holdings of money. In the Friedman theory, a much larger number of assets is under consideration and a rise in interest rates might affect each asset in a number of ways. If interest rates rise then people may decide that their mortgages are too expensive. They might sell their houses and decide to buy better motor cars. Alternatively, other people might decide to sell their houses and buy an interest bearing bond. For Keynes the choice was bonds or money, but for Friedman the choice was far more extensive. Because there are so many different assets the effect of interest rates on money demand would be negligible.

Friedman argued that the key determinant of money demand was wealth or permanent income, something you studied in the last unit. This permanent income would be relatively stable over an individual's life so that the demand for money would also be stable. The demand for money function would then be constant with the interest rate perhaps having some minor significance. If the interest rate changes there will be very little change in the demand for money. Money demand is, therefore, interest inelastic and is depicted in Figure 9. The monetarist demand for money function is far steeper than its Keynesian counterpart and there is no liquidity trap.

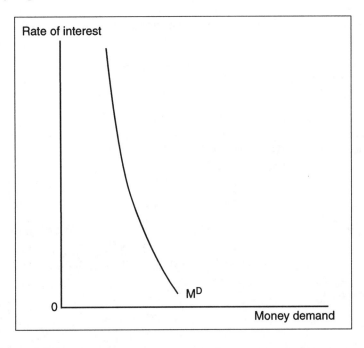

Figure 9: The monetarist demand for money function, M^D is steeper than the Keynesian version. There is no liquidity trap.

In this model, if the government increased the supply of money then individuals would retain some of the extra cash but would also spend some of it on other assets: cars, shares, fridges, etc. and this increase in demand would be reflected in higher prices. Friedman accepted that there may also be an increase in output and national income but that, by and large, the increase in the money supply would lead to higher prices. Friedman argued that increases in the supply of money would affect the price level and output level after *long* and *unpredictable lags*. In other words, an increase in the money supply would not have immediate effects (the lags could be between one and two years) and it would be very difficult to assess by how much the price level and/or the output level would be affected. Friedman therefore argued that policy should not be discretionary but that governments should follow policy rules. For example, the government should allow the money supply to grow at a constant rate per year. This would prevent the economy being destabilised by continual changes in the growth rate of the money supply, which would have lagged and unpredictable effects.

In summary, therefore, we can say that the classical and monetarist theory of money demand is that money demand is a stable function of income and that increases in the money supply raise aggregate demand and prices. Keynesian theory suggests that the key determinant of money demand is interest rates and that the demand for money is therefore volatile and unstable. Increases in the money supply may or may not affect aggregate demand while the effect on prices (which we have not yet considered in the Keynesian model) will depend on whether or not aggregate demand increases and, if so, whether or not the economy is at full employment.

Now try Activity 11 to check your understanding of the three theories we have just discussed.

ACTIVITY 11

The table below lists the three theories we have discussed in the left-hand column, and various issues about which each of these theories makes a prediction. Summarise the text you have been studying by filling in the table. Allow about 20 minutes for this.

Predictions

Theory	Effect of an increase in the money supply on interest rates	Effect of an increase in the money supply on aggregate demand	Effect of an increase in the money supply on the price level
Classical	1 (a)	2 (a)	3 (a)
Keynesian	1 (b)	2 (b)	3 (b)
Monetarist	1 (c)	2 (c)	3 (c)

For example, the first empty cell (1a) is in the classical row and is in the column labelled 'Increase in money supply on aggregate demand'. In this box write in the effect on aggregate demand of an increase in the money supply as predicted by the classical theory. In the cell below (1b) write in the prediction of Keynesian theory, and so on.

I hope you enjoyed that activity. Your answers had to be squeezed into a small space and will have summarised a lot of text. I have provided fuller answers and would not expect you to have written as much as me.

1 (a) The effect of an increase in the money supply on interest rates is to lower the rate of interest in the classical model

1 (b) In the Keynesian model, the answer is not obvious. If interest rates are high

so that the economy is not in a 'liquidity trap' increases in the money supply will lower interest rates. If the economy is in a liquidity trap then increases in the money supply will have no effect on interest rates.

1 (c) In the monetarist model an increase in the money supply has the same effect as in the classical model. Interest rates fall.

2 (a) In the classical model, money is held for transactions purposes only so that as the money supply increases individuals find that they are holding excess money. They spend this excess money and aggregate demand rises.

2 (b) In the Keynesian model, the answer is less obvious. If the economy is not in a liquidity trap then at least some of the increase in the money supply will be used for transactions purposes so that aggregate demand rises. However, if the economy is stuck in a liquidity trap then increases in the money supply will be held for speculative reasons. All investors expect interest rates to rise and bond prices to fall. They will not want to hold bonds and will simply hold any increase in the money supply rather than spending it. Aggregate demand would not rise.

2 (c) The monetarist theory predicts the same as the classical theory. Increases in the money supply lead to increases in aggregate demand.

3 (a) In the classical theory, the quantity theory of money holds. Any increase in the money supply will lead to an increase in the price level. As the money supply increases individuals find that they are holding excess money. They spend these extra holdings and aggregate demand rises. Now in the classical model, full employment is assumed so that this increased demand does not lead to an increase in supply. The price level therefore rises.

3 (b) In the Keynesian theory the effect on the price level is, once again, less obvious. In 2 (b) we saw that an increase in the money supply may not affect aggregate demand if the economy is in a liquidity trap. In such a case the price level would not change. If the economy was not in a liquidity trap then aggregate demand would rise but even then the effect on the price level is not clear. If the economy is at full employment then the price level will rise. If, on the other hand, unemployment exists, then supply will rise in response to the increase in aggregate demand and the price level will not be affected.

3 (c) Once again, the monetarist theory predicts the same as the classical theory. An increase in the money supply will cause prices to rise.

In completing the boxes you will have referred back to a lot of material and hopefully this will have enhanced your understanding of the different theories of the demand for money.

We will now go on to examine equilibrium in the money market and then the connection between the money market and aggregate demand.

2.2 Money market equilibrium and aggregate demand

MONEY MARKET EQUILIBRIUM

As with any market, equilibrium is determined by the interaction of supply and demand. Equilibrium in the money market is achieved through changes in the rate of interest. Consider Figure 10, which shows a money demand (M^D) and money supply schedule (M^s). Equilibrium is at the interest rate r_0.

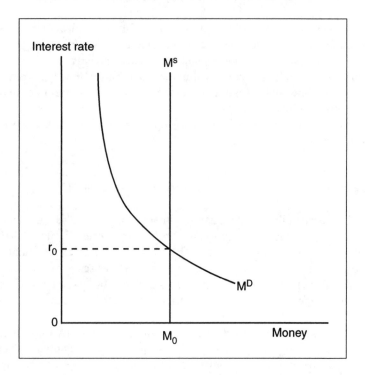

Figure 10: Money market equilibrium

If the rate of interest was above r_0 individuals would be holding more money than they wished. These "excess" holdings would be used to buy other assets such as shares, bonds etc., which would raise the price of these assets and therefore lower the rate of interest until equilibrium was restored. Alternatively, if the rate of interest were below r_0 then individuals would have insufficient money holdings. They would sell any other assets that they were holding such as shares, bonds etc. which would lower the prices of these assets and therefore increase the rate of interest until equilibrium was restored. The equilibrium quantity of money is M_0.

So far in our studies we have talked of *the* rate of interest. Of course, in reality, there are a number of interest rates. Different assets have different interest rates. The interest rate on building society deposits will differ from that on gilts, which will differ from that on Treasury bills, etc. In discussing the theory we are therefore referring to an average rate of interest on all assets, and money market equilibrium will be achieved when the total demand for, and supply of money are equal.

THE MONEY MARKET AND AGGREGATE DEMAND

Changes in the money supply will affect aggregate demand directly and indirectly. The direct effect from an increase in the money supply arises because individuals will have more to spend if the government increases the money supply. They will increase their spending on goods and services so that aggregate demand increases directly. The effect of this was illustrated in Figure 7.

There is also an indirect effect on aggregate demand which arises from the effect of an increase in the money supply on the rate of interest. You will recall from the previous unit that investment demand depended on the rate of interest. Investment demand is a vital component of aggregate demand, so that changes in the money supply which affect interest rates will also affect investment and aggregate demand. Figure 11 shows how an increase in the money supply will lead to a fall in the rate of interest which causes an increase in investment.

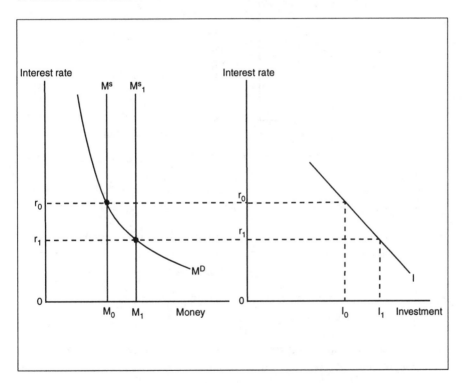

Figure 11: Increases in the money supply lower the rate of interest which will lead to an increase in investment.

The left-hand graph shows the effect of an increase in the money supply from M^S to M^S_1 in the money market. The interest rate falls from r_0 to r_1 and the equilibrium money supply rises from M_0 to M_1. The right-hand graph shows how this reduction in the interest rate causes an increase in the amount of investment from I_0 to I_1.

Similarly, a reduction in the money supply will raise interest rates which will reduce investment. Figure 12 shows how the increase in investment leads to an increase in national income using the Keynesian cross diagram which you became familiar with in Unit 7.

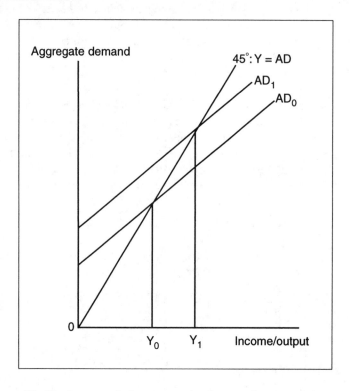

Figure 12: The increase in investment leads to an increase in aggregate demand from AD_0 to AD_1 which raises national income from Y_0 to Y_1.

The increase in investment causes an upward shift in the aggregate demand schedule from AD_0 to AD_1 which leads to an increase in national income from Y_0 to Y_1.

ACTIVITY 12

Explain, using appropriate diagrams, how a reduction in the money supply will affect aggregate demand.

If the government reduces the money supply then this can affect aggregate demand in two ways. Firstly, higher interest rates will reduce investment so that aggregate demand falls. Furthermore, if the money supply falls then individuals will find that they are holding less money than they would like. To restore their holdings they cut back on their consumption. Hence there is a dual effect on aggregate demand as investment and consumption fall.

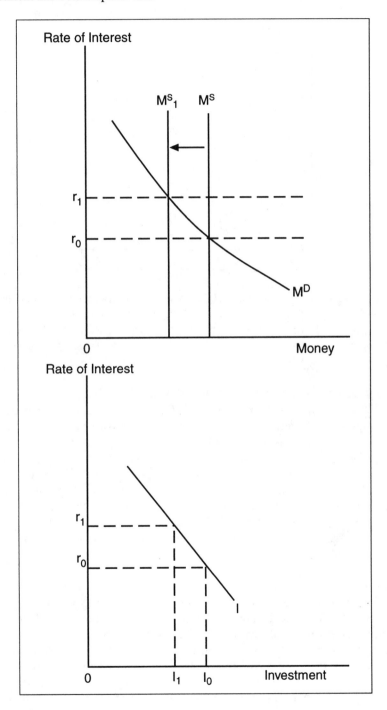

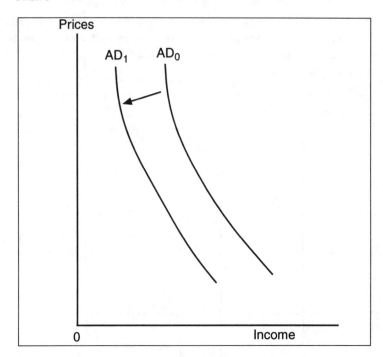

The diagram shows the effect of the reduced money supply. In the left-hand graph, the money supply curve M^S shifts left to M^S_1 so that interest rates rise from r_0 to r_1. In the centre graph we see the effect this has on investment which falls from I_0 to I_1. The right-hand graph shows the effect on the aggregate demand curve, AD_0 shifts to AD_1.

MONEY SUPPLY GROWTH AND THE ECONOMY

Of course, in reality the money supply is not fixed but is continually growing. The money supply has to grow in order to keep pace with a growing economy. Consider a situation where the economy grows by 10% over a year. The demand for money which increases in proportion to income will also increase by 10% so that if the government does not increase the money supply by at least 10% then the interest rate will begin to rise and this will tend to depress investment. Furthermore, as the money supply falls relative to output then individuals find they have to reduce expenditure to restore their cash balances. Consumption will fall. Therefore, aggregate demand falls and the level of output and income will fall. Unemployment may rise.

On the other hand, if the government increases the money supply by more than 10%, then the money supply will grow relative to output. The demand for money will grow by 10% in line with the higher income (because people need more cash for their greater volume of transactions), but the supply of money increases even more, so the interest rate will begin to fall. This will tend to boost investment. Furthermore, as the money supply rises relative to output then individuals find they have excess money balances. They increase their expenditure to get rid of the excess cash and so consumption increases and aggregate demand and output rise. There may also be an effect on the price level. However, the exact increases in output and the price level may be difficult to predict. This is what Friedman meant when he spoke of the unpredictability of the effects of changes in the money supply.

The authorities may seek to control aggregate demand by manipulating the rate of interest. By reducing the supply of money the government can force interest rates upwards which will tend to depress investment demand and thus reduce aggregate demand. In response, the public might want to finance consumption by debt or loans; however, higher interest rates will discourage borrowing so aggregate demand remains subdued. Interest rates therefore affect the aggregate demand curve by influencing both investment and consumption behaviour.

In the last unit we saw that Keynesians seek to influence the level of aggregate demand in order to 'fine - tune' the economy. We also saw that Keynesians tended to use fiscal policy in order to achieve this. Monetary policy, of which changes in the money supply are a prime example, was rarely used at all. Why was this the case ?

Keynesians argue that monetary policy is a less effective tool for increasing aggregate demand for a number of reasons. Firstly, the presence of the liquidity trap means that changes in the money supply may well be ineffective as a way of influencing aggregate demand.

As we saw in the previous unit, Keynesians argue that the key determinant of investment demand is expectations or business confidence. There may be a situation where interest rates are low but investment is also low because firms are pessimistic about the future prospects of the economy. In such a case the government may try to encourage investment by expanding the money supply. However, if the interest rate is so low that the economy is 'stuck' in the liquidity trap, such a policy will not influence aggregate demand. Figure 13 illustrates this.

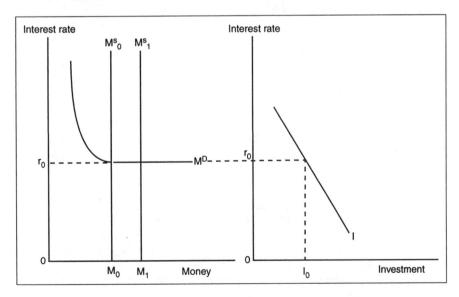

Figure 13: In the presence of a liquidity trap, an increase in the money supply has no effect on investment and aggregate demand.

The increase in the money supply, from MS_0 to MS_1, does not affect the interest rate. The interest rate is so low that all individuals believe that it will rise and therefore expect bond prices to fall. Therefore the increase in the money supply is held in idle balances. Aggregate demand does not change. Keynes felt that such a situation would be likely to occur in a recession. Interest rates are so low that all individuals expect them to rise and therefore retain money for speculative purposes. Increasing the money supply has no effect on interest rates or aggregate demand. In such a case, fiscal policy is the only way of increasing aggregate demand. It will raise business confidence and shift the investment demand curve to the right.

Keynesians also argue that changes in the money supply are a poor tool to influence aggregate demand because of the *instability* of the money demand schedule. They argue that expectations about changes in interest rates, inflation and exchange rates (something we do not consider here) will influence individuals decisions regarding how much income to hold in speculative or idle balances. Such balances may well be large. Because of the volatility of these variables, and because of the large size of these balances, the money demand function is likely to be unstable and to shift around a lot so that the effects of increases in the money supply cannot be predicted.

Consider Figure 14, which shows the effects of an increase in the money supply from MS_0 to MS_1. The government wishes to lower interest rates in order to influence aggregate demand. The money demand schedule is given by MD_0 so that an increase in the money supply from MS_0 to MS_1 will lower interest rates from r_0 to r_1. However, if the money demand schedule shifts to MD_1, then the attempt by the government to lower interest rates will be unsuccessful as interest rates shift to r_2, which is higher than r_0.

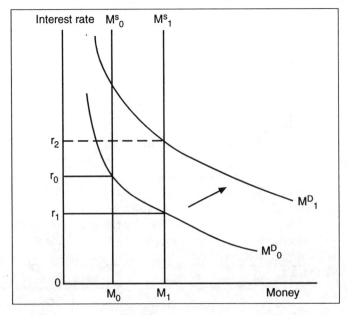

Figure 14: If the money demand function is unstable then attempts by the government to lower the interest rate from r_0 to r_1 are unsuccessful.

Because of the instability of money demand, the effects of monetary policy cannot be predicted. Hence, Keynesians argue that monetary policy is a less useful tool than fiscal policy to steer aggregate demand.

On the other hand, monetarists, as we have seen, argue that the demand for money function is stable. They argue that the key role of money is as a medium of exchange so that the effects of monetary policy are predictable. They argue that increases in the money supply may have some effect on output, but will ultimately lead to higher prices via the quantity theory of money.

We have now studied the different theories of the demand for money and also considered the effects of the money markets on aggregate demand. We now turn to a consideration of the different theories of inflation. Inflation is a phenomenon we defined in Unit 6 as a process of persistently rising prices. We now examine what causes inflation.

2.3 Theories of inflation

Whenever we study the topic of money and aggregate demand it is vital that we give consideration to inflation. According to Keynesians and monetarists inflation is caused by excess demand. However, the theories are fundamentally different because monetarists argue that inflation is caused by excess *monetary* demand, while Keynesians argue that inflation is caused by excess *real* demand.

MONETARIST THEORIES OF INFLATION
'Inflation is always and everywhere a monetary phenomenon' (Milton Friedman).

As we have seen, for monetarists the key to inflation is the money supply. The original quantity theory of money suggested that increases in the money supply caused increases in the price level. Output was not affected because the economy was already at full employment. If the government increased the money supply then individuals would be holding excess money balances. In monetarist theory, money is held only to finance transactions so that these excess holdings are spent on goods and services, so that aggregate demand rises. Output cannot rise, so that the effect is higher prices. We saw this process illustrated in Figure 7.

In Friedman's later version of the quantity theory, the increase in the money supply may have a small effect on output but will mainly cause higher prices. Therefore, the monetarist theory is often drawn with an upward-sloping supply curve to show that there may be a small output effect from the increase in the money supply. Figure 15 illustrates an upward sloping supply curve, AS. The intersection of AS with the aggregate demand curve, AD_0 determines the equilibrium price level, P_0 and output level, Y_0.

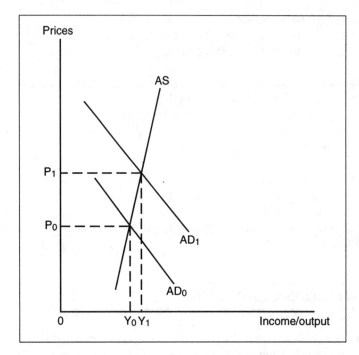

Figure 15: In Monetarist theory, increases in the money supply
will have a much larger effect on prices than on output.

Look at Figure 15. The effect of an increase in the money supply is to raise aggregate demand from AD_0 to AD_1. People find that they are holding more money than they wish so they dispose of it by spending on goods and services. The increase in aggregate demand causes prices to rise from P_0 to P_1. There is a small increase in output from Y_0 to Y_1 but the major impact of the increase in the money supply is to raise prices.·

Inflation is caused by an expansion of the money supply and for monetarists the money supply is the key to inflation, which is simply 'too much money chasing too few goods'. For monetarists, the way to control inflation is by controlling the money supply.

Keynesians disagree with this theory for a number of reasons. Firstly, as we have seen, they argue that money is not held only to finance transactions but also for speculative reasons. Therefore increases in the money supply may not cause increases in prices if the increased money is held in idle balances and not spent. In fact, Keynesians argue that, because the demand for money function is unstable, then the effects of increases in the money supply are unpredictable. They argue that, in certain cases, increases in the money supply can affect aggregate demand via interest rates, which will affect investment demand (obviously, when interest rates are high enough so that the liquidity trap is not a problem). They believe that aggregate demand will rise without an accompaning rise in prices provided that unemployment and hence, spare capacity, exists in the economy. The traditional quantity theory stated that there would be no output effect from an increase in the money supply, though Friedman, in his restatement, did acknowledge that there may be a small output effect of a money supply increase.

KEYNESIAN THEORIES OF INFLATION

We saw in the last unit that, for Keynes, inflation and unemployment are effectively opposite sides of the same coin. Unemployment is caused by deficient demand, while inflation is caused by too much demand. Ultimately, however, this excess demand originates in the real, not the monetary, side of the economy.

Figure 16 illustrates the Keynesian cross diagram which you became familiar with in Unit 7. On the vertical axis we have aggregate demand. You will recall that the components of aggregate demand (AD) are consumption demand (C), investment demand (I), government expenditure (G) and Net exports (X– M).The full employment level of output is shown as Y_{FE}. Assume that the current level of aggregate demand is AD_0. This aggregate demand schedule intersects the 45 degree line at point X and this results in a level of income corresponding to full employment (Y_{FE}). However, if aggregate demand now increases to AD_1, perhaps because of an increase in investment demand (for example), then there is an excess of demand. Equilibrium is now achieved at point Z. The output level Y_1 results. However because the economy has no unemployed resources it cannot respond to the increased aggregate demand by increasing the physical volume of goods and services. The excess demand leads to an increase in prices so that nominal (money) national income rises. However, there is no real increase in the output of the economy.

Remember that nominal national income is simply the price level multiplied by the physical quantity of goods and services produced in the economy (real output or income). Therefore, a rise in the price level, in this case, raises nominal national income to Y_1.

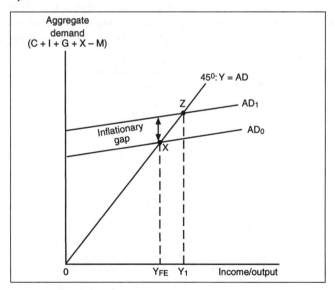

Figure 16: Keynesian "demand pull" inflation.

In this Keynesian theory inflation is caused by an excess of physical demand over supply and does not arise from monetary forces. This Keynesian theory is known commonly as 'demand pull' inflation.

Keynesians also argue that while demand forces may often lie behind inflation, cost factors may be important. Inflation can also arise as a result of supply side factors. Many Keynesians, in fact, argue that this 'cost push' inflation is a better explanation of rising prices than demand pull inflation. This is because at various points in time inflation and unemployment have occurred simultaneously.

In this theory, inflation is a result of monopoly power in both goods and labour markets. Strong trade unions are able to bargain for large wage increases which add to firms' costs. Monopoly firms are able to pass this increase in costs onto consumers as higher prices. The theory suggests that unions compete with each other in wage bargaining, so that if one union wins say, a pay increase of 5%, then another will use 5% as a minimum from which pay negotiations will start.

Of course, wages will naturally rise over time because of inflation. Workers receive a nominal or money wage. If inflation is running at 10% and those money wages do not rise or rise by less than 10% then *real* wages will be falling. Unions will need to ensure that their members get a 10% rise in money wages to maintain the same real wage and living standards. It is when unions start to compete for money wage increases over and above 10% that inflationary pressure arises.

Cost push inflation is a supply-side phenomenon, which is illustrated in Figure 17. The diagram shows an aggregate demand curve AD and a Keynesian 'L-'shaped aggregate supply curve, AS_0. (The shape of the Keynesian aggregate supply curve was explained in Unit 7. Make sure that you can remember why it is shaped like this.)

If unions push for wage increases then firms' costs rise. As you will be aware from your microeconomic studies, such cost increases cause a fall in the quantity supplied at each price level so that the aggregate supply curve shifts upwards to the left to AS_1. This causes an increase in the price level from P_0 to P_1 and a fall in output from Y_0 to Y_1.

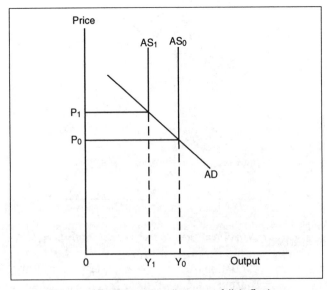

Figure 17: Keynesian "cost push" inflation

We have now completed our studies of different theories of inflation. However, inflation is a topic to which we will return in the next section when we examine monetary policy. We will look closely at monetary policy in the UK in recent years and we will also look at the attempts by the incoming Conservative government of 1979 to control inflation as part of the so called ' Medium Term Financial Strategy'.

REVIEW ACTIVITY 2

Read Resource Item 8.1: 'The Demand for Money : Problems and Issues' by Ray Barrell from the *Economic Review* and answer the following questions. Each answer should be no more than 200 words.

1 The author states that a concern for Keynes was that 'A speculative wave could raise the demand for money and ....unless prices were always perfectly flexible, it would have to be accompanied by a fall in real output and employment.' Explain how this process would occur.

2 Does empirical work tend to agree with Keynesian or monetarist theory ?

Summary

In this section we discussed the issue of the demand for money. When we defined money in Section 1 we saw that there were a number of definitions, such as M0 or M1, each including different assets such as sight or time deposits. In this section, the demand for money referred to the demand to hold *cash* rather than other financial assets such as shares or bonds.

We found that the demand for money is a subject that is hotly debated amongst economists and in examining the different theories of the demand for money we began to see why monetarists and Keynesians disagree, not only on the importance of the money supply, but also on the relative importance of monetary and fiscal policy.

We studied three theories of the demand for money: the classical quantity theory, the Keynesian theory and the monetarist theory (often known as the restatement of the quantity theory).

We also looked at the relationship between the demand for money and aggregate demand, and finally we discussed monetarist and Keynesian theories of inflation

SECTION THREE

Monetary Policy

Introduction

Section 3 focuses on the different types of monetary policy and traces the development of post-war monetary policy in the UK. We also examine the UK experience of monetarism in the 1980s, and the success or otherwise of the so-called Medium Term Financial Strategy (MTFS).

Monetary policy is the use, by the authorities, of monetary variables, such as the money supply and interest rates to achieve economic objectives. In many respects monetary policy is considered to be far more important in the 1990s than it was in the 20 to 30 years after World War Two. At that time governments sought to influence aggregate demand using fiscal policy (i.e. taxation and government expenditure), and monetary policy was, at best, a supplementary tool. Monetary and fiscal policy were considered to be totally independent. The role of monetary policy was largely to ensure that fiscal policy ran smoothly. That is, to preserve orderly financial markets so that the government could sell gilts and treasury bills at favourable prices and interest rates in order to finance the PSBR. At this time, the actual quantity of money in the economy, the money supply, was not considered important. Governments, influenced strongly by Keynesian economic theories, thought that the money supply was impossible to control properly and simply allowed the money supply to adapt to the level of economic activity.

After 1979, the new Conservative government, committed to monetarist policies, placed far more importance on monetary policy. Their most important objective was to control inflation and they tried to achieve this by controlling the money supply as measured by sterling M3 or £M3. (In Section 1 we explained that sterling M3 or £M3, consists of four elements : notes and coins in circulation plus banks balances at the Bank of England plus sterling sight and time deposits and savings accounts).

The government philosophy was not to manage the level of demand in the short term but instead to provide a sound and stable economic environment in which business could flourish in the medium term. This policy was the centrepiece of the so-called Medium Term Financial Strategy (MTFS). The government would announce, in advance, targets for the money measure £M3 for the next few quarters (three month periods) ahead. The target would be progressively reduced in accordance with the desire to lower inflation. The idea was that firms, unions, households, etc. would expect lower inflation in future in line with the falling rate of growth in the money supply and would therefore moderate their wage demands and price increases accordingly. In other words, the government sought to create expectations of lower inflation. The issue of expectations is central to the monetarist-Keynesian debate and is something we will focus on in detail in the next unit.

Monetarists believe that monetary and fiscal policy are linked in such a way that governments cannot conduct fiscal policy without affecting to some extent, the money supply. They argue that the use of Keynesian demand management techniques in the 1950s, 1960s and early 1970s led to excessive government borrowing, which inflated the money supply and led to inflation. As we saw in the first section of this unit, deficit financing may be inflationary depending on how it is financed. At times in the 1970s increases in the PSBR did seem to be associated with increases in the money supply though at other times there seemed to be little relationship between the two variables.

We will now go on to explore the different types of monetary policy used in the UK in recent years and we will also assess the success or otherwise of the MTFS in the early 1980s.

3.1 Monetary control techniques

In the first section of this unit we saw how banks are able to create credit and therefore increase the supply of money. However, banks cannot create unlimited credit. The government imposes a limit as to how much of their assets should be retained in liquid form. Furthermore, they will want to maintain a 'prudent' liquidity ratio. The greater the proportion of assets retained in a liquid form the lower will be the ability of banks to create credit. Not surprisingly, therefore, monetary policy has often been used to influence the ability of banks to create credit so that the money supply can be controlled. The problem with attempting to reduce the ability of banks to create credit in this way is that banks are often able to find a way around the policy. If people want to borrow money and banks want to lend then it will be difficult for the Bank of England to control every part of the financial system to prevent them from doing so.

We also saw that the way in which the PSBR is financed can also affect the supply of money so that monetary control can be achieved by adjusting the method of financing. We saw that if the government sells gilts or treasury bills outside the banking system then the money supply will not increase. But in order to encourage the buying of these assets the government has to offer higher interest rates on them which has a depressing effect on investment and aggregate demand known as "crowding out". Clearly, a reduction in the PSBR is desirable to reduce monetary growth and avoid such crowding out. The 1979 Conservative government saw the reduction of the PSBR as crucial to money supply control and the 1980 MTFS specified target growth rates for both £M3 and the PSBR.

Monetary policy is also often directed at the control of interest rates rather than the money supply and we explore this separately. Broadly speaking, monetary policy in the UK has altered at the beginning of each decade and we will now examine the post-war history of monetary policy directed at the control of the money supply from the 1950s to the 1980s.

MONETARY CONTROL IN THE 1950S

In the 1950s, the authorities (the government and the Bank of England) operated a 28% liquid assets ratio. This meant that the banks had to retain 28% of their assets in a liquid form. Whenever liquid assets fell below the required quantity banks would have to reduce their lending. At the same time in order to further limit the banks ability to create credit, the authorities used **open market operations** to influence the supply of cash in the banking system. Open market operations are the buying and selling of government securities on the open market, i.e. to the general public. However, in this context, such selling and buying was not in order to finance a PSBR but purely a way of controlling the money supply. The public buy the securities using cheques drawn on their bank accounts. These cheques are paid into the government's account at the Bank of England so that both sides of the banks balance sheets are reduced. Assets fall as the banks' balances at the Bank of England fall and liabilities fall as customer deposits fall. In principle, the banks would be forced to reduce lending in order to maintain their asset structure within the imposed ratio. However, the banks were usually able to get round this problem by recalling money at call from the discount houses so that the discount houses would be short of cash. The Bank of England would then act as lender in the last resort to supply cash to the market. This, of course, would undermine the whole objective of the open market operations, which was to reduce the quantity of cash in the system.Open market operations may also be used in cases where the government wishes to increase the money supply. In such a case it will buy back securities thus raising the levels of cash in the market.

The problem with monetary control techniques during this period was that economic thinking at the time did not recognise a link between the PSBR and monetary policy. Open market operations were often undermined by the sale of government securities to the banking sector as a way of financing government borrowing. Ultimately, the government wanted to be able to sell bonds and bills in order to finance borrowing. It therefore sought to keep interest rates fixed at a given level so that its borrowing would not be expensive. Generally therefore, monetary policy during this time was rarely effective as a way of restricting the ability of banks to create credit therefore in 1960 a new policy of 'special deposits' was introduced.

MONETARY CONTROL IN THE 1960S

Special deposits were introduced in 1960 as a more effective way of influencing the ability of banks to create credit. Special deposits were introduced as a supplementary scheme to operate alongside the 28% liquid assets ratio. Banks were required to deposit a given percentage of their deposits in special accounts at the Bank of England. These accounts were then frozen so that they represented highly illiquid assets for the banks. They were also a very simple way of reducing a bank's liquidity and ability to create credit. In fact, calls for special deposits probably had little effect on the banks' total lending because banks usually had a stock of liquid assets such as treasury bills, acquired previously from government attempts to finance borrowing. These assets were sold in exchange for cash thus undermining the special deposit scheme.

MONETARY CONTROL IN THE 1970S

As a result of the ineffectiveness of previous monetary policy the authorities introduced 'Competition and Credit Control' (CCC) in 1971. The basis of this policy was to abolish the existing liquid assets ratio, and replace it with a 12.5%

reserve assets ratio which stipulated that all banks were to retain specified reserve assets of 12.5% of their deposits. The assets included in this ratio were: bank balances at the Bank of England, treasury bills and other short-dated government stock, in other words those assets that could easily be influenced through government open market operations and so-called **funding**.

Funding refers to a situation when the authorities issue more gilts and long-dated stock and less treasury bills and short-dated stock. The effect of funding is that banks will hold a larger proportion of relatively illiquid assets and will be forced to reduce lending in order to maintain a prudent liquidity ratio.

In practice, CCC did not work well. It was undermined by the removal of controls on bank lending during this period. Lending expanded dramatically and at the same time the PSBR grew quite considerably so that the whole policy was undermined and later abandoned in 1981 by the new Conservative government.

MONETARY CONTROL IN THE 1980S

The Conservative government elected in 1979 was firmly committed to the control of the money supply and outlined the planned changes in monetary policy in their Green Paper on Monetary Control published in 1980. The government outlined targets for the broad money measure £M3. The authorities believed that the best way to achieve control of £M3 was to limit growth of the narrow money supply or monetary base (in section one we defined narrow money as money used for transactions purposes, of which there are two measures M1 and M0). In principle, as cash is ultimately a liability of the government, then it should be fairly easy to control; however, in order to control it correctly, the Bank of England would need to abandon the lender of last resort function whereby cash would always be made available to the banking system in the event of a shortage.

Although the government claimed to be firmly committed to the control of the broad money measure £M3, in fact, by 1983 all targets were abolished. By and large, the government found £M3 very difficult to control and though inflation did fall in the 1980s, this was more to do with the severely deflationary policies followed in this period. Demand was reduced by reductions in public spending and increases in the rate of interest. Unemployment rose so that inflation inevitably fell.

The government did adopt a policy of monetary base control because this would have meant accepting volatile interest rates. Furthermore, the authorities were not prepared to abandon the traditional role of the Bank as a lender in the last resort.

ACTIVITY 13

Explain, in no more than four or five sentences, what you understand by the term 'open market operations' and how they might affect the money supply.

As always with written questions such as this, I am sure that your answer will be different to mine. Make sure, however, that you clearly understand the way that open market operations can affect the money supply.

Open market operations are the buying and selling of government securities such as gilts and treasury bills on the open market, i.e. to the general public. If the government sells securities this will tend to reduce the money supply because it will reduce bank lending. The public pay for the securities using cheques drawn on their bank accounts. These cheques are paid into the government's account at the Bank of England so that both sides of the banks' balance sheets are reduced. Assets fall as the banks balances at the Bank of England fall and liabilities fall as customer deposits fall. Banks are forced to reduce lending in order to maintain their asset structure within the prudent or government imposed ratios. The authorities can similarly raise the money supply by buying securities on the open market.

3.2 Interest rate control

The equilibrium quantity of money and rate of interest are determined by the interaction of the supply of, and demand for, money. However, the authorities may sometimes try to control interest rates through their activity in the money markets. Let us see how this might work.

If the banks are short of cash they may call in their loans of money at call from the discount houses. If the discount houses are short of cash they will borrow from the Bank of England who will provide cash as lender of last resort to the market. In providing this cash the Bank can choose the rate of interest it charges to the discount houses. This rate will then have a 'knock-on' effect on other rates throughout the economy.

Before 1971 the rate at which the Bank provided liquidity as a lender in the last resort was known as **bank rate**. If the Bank changed bank rate all the banks would automatically change their interest rates on customer borrowing and deposits by the same amount. In order to stay competitive, other institutions, such as building societies, would have to change their rates. Therefore, the Bank could control interest rates throughout the economy by changing bank rate.

Between 1971 and 1981, bank rate was replaced by Minimum Lending Rate (MLR) as part of Competition and Credit Control. Under this scheme, the banks did not need to alter their own rates automatically following a change in MLR. The philosophy behind this change was to allow a more competitive environment ; however, in practice, the banks did follow the change in MLR.

The Bank usually backed up changes in MLR with open market operations. For example, a tighter monetary policy would involve an increase in MLR. This would be backed up by sales of treasury bills and gilts on the open market, which would lower their price and therefore raise the interest rate on them. As the public pay for these bills and bonds they issue cheques drawn on their bank accounts which reduces the banks' liquidity so that the banks are forced to recall money at call from the discount houses. If the discount houses are now short of liquidity they will be forced to borrow from the Bank, of England at the new higher MLR. To avoid having to do this they will be prepared to pay a higher interest rate on their borrowing at call from banks. Banks thus divert money towards the discount market, leaving less cash available for loans to customers. This reduced supply of funds for loans tends to drive up the rate of interest. Therefore, ultimately, the rise in MLR was accompanied by a rise in general rates throughout the economy. Furthermore, when MLR rose, the banks took this as a sign that monetary policy was going to be tighter. Therefore, in anticipation of a rise in interest rates in the money market, they would raise their interest rates. MLR was abandoned after 1981. However, the authorities still intervene in the money markets by buying and selling treasury bills : in order to influence interest rates and the degree of liquidity in the market.

In order to see how the authorities might try to influence interest rates and the degree of liquidity in the market consider a situation where the Bank wishes to tighten monetary policy by raising interest rates. The way it will do this will depend on whether the discount houses have excess cash or a shortage of cash. If the discount houses are short of cash then they will be forced to borrow from the Bank. In practice the Bank will purchase bills from the discount houses. The Bank will only buy bills at a certain price. The lower the price they buy at the greater the interest rate. Hence, the Bank can raise interest rates in this way. On the other hand, if the discount houses have surplus cash then the Bank can alter the price of bills, and hence the rate of interest, by altering the quantity of bills for sale. The greater the quantity of bills supplied the greater the increase in the interest rate. The overall effect of the actions of the Bank are illustrated in Figure 18.

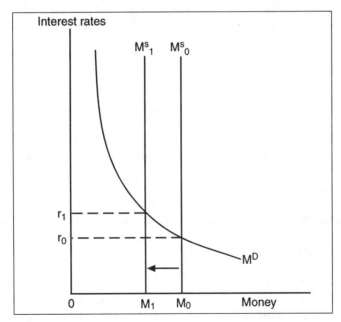

Figure 18: A reduction in the money supply from M^S_0 to M^S_1, due to a sale of bills by the central bank, causes interest rates to rise from r_0 to r_1.

The Bank's sale of bills reduces the money supply from MS_0 to MS_1, which drives interest rates up from r_0 to r_1.

Often the authorities will seek to influence the interest rate in order to affect the value of the currency on the foreign exchange market. This is an aspect of monetary policy that is explored in Unit 10.

We can now illustrate the changing nature of monetary policy in the UK in the post-war period. Before 1981, with the dominance of Keynesian economic thinking, monetary policy was directed, not to control of the money supply, but towards the maintenance of a suitable interest rate for government borrowing. The government did not want high interest rates so it would, therefore, ensure that there was no shortage of liquidity in the market. This is illustrated in Figure 19.

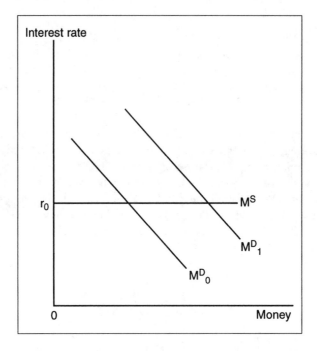

Figure 19: If the authorities are always prepared to supply money to the system then interest rates can be maintained at r_0.

In seeking to maintain the interest rate r_0, the government will, therefore, always supply cash to the system to prevent a rise in interest rates, which would raise the cost of government borrowing and hence the national debt. Even if there was an increase in the demand for money, as shown by the shift in money demand from MD_0 to MD_1, interest rates would not increase because of the perfectly elastic money supply.

After 1981 the government planned to move to a **monetary base control system** whereby the authorities seek to limit the narrow money supply. This would have meant fixing the money supply, abandoning the lender of last resort function and and allowing the rate of interest to change as a result of changes in the demand for money. In Figure 20 the increase in money demand from MD_0 to MD_1 leads to a sharp rise in interest rates from r_0 to r_1, because the authorities do not supply cash to the system as a lender in the last resort. The money supply is effectively fixed at m_0.

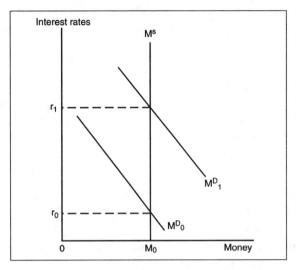

Figure 20: In a monetary base control system, the authorities abandon the lender of last resort function. Increases in the demand for money lead to sharp increases in the rate of interest.

In practice, after 1981, the government did not operate a system of monetary base control but allowed interest rates to operate within some 'target band'. Therefore, the supply of cash was completely elastic within this range. If the interest rate appeared to move outside the range then cash would readily be supplied. Figure 21 illustrates this.

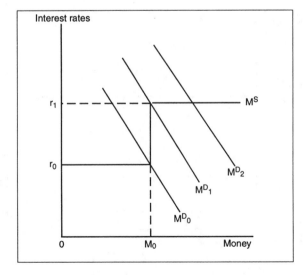

Figure 21: Interest rates are allowed to move within a "target band" between r_0 and r_1.

Suppose the government wishes to maintain interest rates within the range r_0 to r_1. Providing money demand does not vary outside the range of MD_0 to MD_1, the supply of cash will be inelastic so that rates can vary but stay within the target band. However, if money demand was to increase to MD_2 then the authorities would supply cash in order to prevent rates rising beyond r_1.

At the same time, the authorities would not wish to see rates fall below r_0. If rates were to fall to less than r_0 this might encourage consumers to borrow more money in order to finance consumption. As banks lend to these consumers then credit is created and the money supply expands so that inflation occurs. Therefore, at low levels of money demand the authorities would always be willing to supply cash.

To test that you have understood how interest rate control operates, try the following activity which should take no more than ten minutes.

ACTIVITY 14

Assuming that the government maintains an interest rate target, as in the UK before 1981, explain how changes in the demand for money might affect output. Use a diagram to illustrate your answer.

(**Hint:** Output will only change, via investment, if interest rates change.)

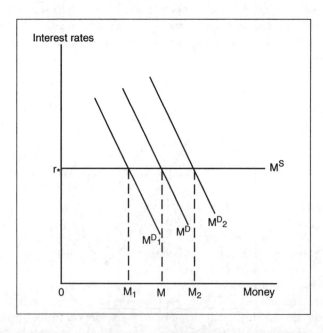

If the government maintains a fixed interest rate target then it will always supply cash to the system so that there is never a cash shortage or surplus. In short, the money supply is perfectly elastic, as the diagram shows. The government seeks to target the interest rate at r∗. If money demand falls from M^D to M^D_1 there is no change in interest rates so there will be no effect on investment and hence no effect on output.

Another way of looking at this is to think of the quantity theory of money. If money demand falls then individuals are spending more. The velocity of circulation rises. However, the quantity of money falls from M to M_1, so that the rise in M offsets the fall in V. In the equation $MV = PT$, MV does not change so PT does not change. There is no effect on output.

Similarly, if money demand rises to M^D_2 there is no change in interest rates and therefore no effect on output. People are holding more money and spending less. Velocity of circulation falls. However, the money supply has risen to M_2, which offsets the fall in velocity. Output is unaffected.

If your answer is nothing like mine do not panic ! Simply refer back to the text and then read through my answer again. I am sure that you will grasp it second time around !!

3.3 Problems of monetary control

The control of the money supply in order to reduce the rate of inflation is extremely difficult for any government, both practically and politically.

Political problems arise from the need to keep a tight rein on the PSBR. As we have seen, a high PSBR will often lead to an expansion of the money supply. Therefore any government committed to the control of inflation will want to reduce the PSBR. This can prove difficult for a number of reasons.

Firstly, some components of government spending are very difficult to control. In the last unit we considered automatic stabilisers such as unemployment benefit and a progressive tax system. In times of recession, rising unemployment and falling income, government expenditure on unemployment benefit rises automatically to offset the decline in income. Therefore, as the economy goes into recession, the government will spend more on unemployment benefit and receive less in the form of tax revenues, so that the PSBR rises automatically. It would prove politically damaging to reduce spending on unemployment benefit or raise tax rates in times of recession.

Another problem for the government is *where* to make cuts in public expenditure. Many areas of government expenditure, such as education or health, are politically very sensitive. Any government that cuts spending in these areas is likely to become extremely unpopular. The need to retain the support of the electorate is vital for any government. This need for popularity explains a further problem with attempting to control the PSBR. Often governments wish to cut taxation in order to win popularity. Cuts in tax rates regularly occur in the year or so prior to a general election. Naturally, lower tax rates reduce government revenues so that the cost of being elected to power is an increased PSBR.

Equally problematic are the practical difficulties of monetary control. In the early 1980's the authorities wished to control the narrow money supply (M0) as part of their wider policy of monetary control. How might this be achieved ?

The authorities could impose a statutory cash ratio on the banks. In other words they could insist that the banks retain a certain proportion of their liquid assets with the Bank of England. Then, the authorities would use open market operations to control the supply of cash to the system.

However, if the banks can attract more cash from the public, or, alternatively, persuade the public to withdraw less cash, for example by making sight deposits more attractive, then the controls will not be successful. Furthermore, if the cash ratio is not imposed on all financial institutions it will not be successful. The idea of the control is to reduce lending and credit creation, but if certain institutions (for example, building societies) are not subject to the ratio, they will attract more demand for loans at the expense of banks, so that total loans are not reduced. This is a classic case of something known as 'Goodhart's Law' named after Charles Goodhart, a former Bank of England economist. Goodhart's Law states that attempts to regulate one part of the banking system merely diverts business to other parts of the system.

Banks can offset the effect of the controls by holding cash in excess of the minimum stipulated. Therefore, they are able to resist open market operations and expand lending by reducing their cash ratios toward the minimum rather than be forced to reduce lending.

Perhaps the greatest problem for any government wishing to control the monetary base is the role of the Bank of England as a lender in the last resort. This traditional role means that cash will always be provided to the system in the event of a shortage, so that strict monetary base control is always likely to be undermined.

Ultimately, the authorities want to reduce the amount of lending by banks. Because of the practical difficulty of trying to control the money supply, the authorities often attempt to reduce the demand for money. The demand for money can be reduced by raising interest rates, which can be achieved without too much difficulty by the Bank raising the rate at which it lends to the money markets.

As you might expect, this policy is also problematic. If the authorities drive up interest rates to discourage borrowing investment demand will be reduced and aggregate demand will fall. The economy may well go into recession. Firms that have taken large loans to finance capital investment find that the cost of that investment has risen. They may raise prices to maintain profits. Hence, inflation may follow higher interest rates. Furthermore, high interest rates are politically unpopular. People with mortgages find that their repayments have risen. People who have loans or overdrafts face higher penalties. As a result, incomes fall, which will affect consumption and aggregate demand.

In addition, high interest rates attract capital from abroad, which leads to a rise in the rate of exchange. We will explore this in detail in Unit 10. However, at higher exchange rates, domestic exports become more expensive and foreign imports become cheaper. Unemployment may occur if export industries start to lose business to foreign competition.

Finally, as we noted in our discussion of monetary policy and aggregate demand, the money demand curve may be unstable so that the authorities cannot accurately predict the effects of policy on interest rates.

Clearly, there are a number of difficulties associated with attempts to control the money supply. It is against this background that we close this unit with an assessment of the attempts by the Conservative government of 1979 to control the money supply. The policies of this government in the first few years after their election are often referred to as 'the monetarist experiment'.

3.4 The monetarist experiment

'To master inflation, proper monetary discipline is essential, with publicly stated targets for the rate of growth of the money supply. At the same time, a gradual reduction in the size of the government's borrowing requirement is also vital.' (Conservative Party Manifesto 1979.)

The Conservative government of 1979 made control of inflation the central objective of economic policy. Tight control of the money supply and PSBR was to be accompanied by labour market policies designed to make the labour market more efficient and responsive to market forces. We will consider labour market policy in the next unit. For now we concentrate on the objective of low inflation. The way this was to be achieved was via control of the broad money supply, sterling £M3. The policy was known as the Medium Term Financial Strategy (MTFS).

The government set advance target ranges for the £M3 and PSBR growth rates. The target ranges were reduced progressively in line with the policy of reducing inflation. The idea behind this was to create expectations of low inflation in the future. This was intended to persuade trade unions and firms to reduce their wage demands and prices in line with the lower inflation.

The relevant data for the period is shown in Table 1.

	1980/1	1981/2	1982/3	1983/4	1984/5	1985/6
£M3 target range (% growth)	7–11	6–10	8–12	7–11	6–10	5–9
£M3 actual (% growth)	19.4	12.8	11.2	9.5	9.7	13.6
PSBR target range (% of GDP)	3.25	4.25	3.5	2.75	2.25	2.0
PSBR actual (% of GDP)	5.4	3.4	3.1	3.2	3.2	–

Table 1

The table shows that for the period 1980-2 the government 'overshot' the target ranges for the money supply. This failure to achieve preset targets is important. The government had to prove its commitment to the reduction of inflation in order to encourage expectations of lower inflation. If the government is unable to fulfill its targets then public confidence in the ability of the government to reduce inflation is eroded. This may explain why wage demands were not moderated in line with the falling money targets, with the result that the economy entered a severe recession.

In the period 1982–5 the government apparently met targets. However, the target ranges for these years were revised upwards after the failure to meet earlier targets. Such 'shifting of the goalposts' further undermined the credibility of the government policy.

The PSBR target was achieved in only two of the five years shown. Although the government cut expenditure and raised taxes, the severe recession in the early 1980s , meant that the government was faced with higher benefit payments and lower tax revenues, thereby raising the PSBR.

The early 1980s witnessed the most severe recession in the UK since the 1930s. Furthermore, despite the low inflation objective, inflation rose dramatically in the first two years of the Conservative administration.

The government cut public spending and raised the VAT rate so that fiscal policy depressed aggregate demand. Furthermore, interest rates rose considerably in an attempt to reduce the level of borrowing. The effect of this was to cause a collapse in investment demand, which added to the massive decline in aggregate demand and rising unemployment. The rise in interest rates did not have the desired effect. Firms finding themselves in financial difficulty because of high interest rates and low demand resorted to 'panic' borrowing in order to gain funds to see them through the difficult period. As a result, the money targets were missed.

To make matters worse, oil prices rose in this period. Britain is an oil exporter and this meant that the external balance moved into surplus. This, combined with the high interest rates, led to an inflow of foreign capital which led to a rise in the exchange rate. British exports became uncompetitive so that unemployment rose further. Meanwhile, the rise in VAT and oil prices started to put upward pressure on prices. Between 1979 and early 1981 unemployment rose from 4.7% of the labour market to 10%. Eventually, after 1982, inflation fell. This was hardly surprising given the depth of the recession in this period.

Table 2 shows the annual percentage growth rates of inflation and the government monetary target £M3. It also shows the growth rate of the narrow money measure M0

Year	£M3	M0	Inflation
1973	27.0	*	9.1
1974	12.3	*	16.0
1975	10.4	*	24.2
1976	8.5	*	16.5
1977	7.7	*	15.9
1978	12.7	12.0	8.3
1979	11.1	12.1	13.4
1980	16.2	5.6	18.0
1981	12.3	1.7	11.9
1982	8.8	1.7	8.6
1983	10.2	5.9	4.6
1984	9.7	14.4	5.0
1985	13.4	3.7	6.1
1986	19.0	5.1	3.4
1987	22.8	4.3	4.2
1988	20.5	7.7	4.9

Table 2

*M0 data is unavailable before 1978.

This data is reproduced in Figure 22.

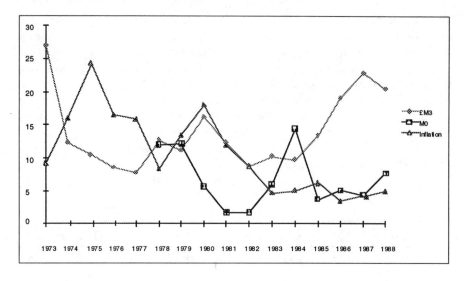

Figure 22: £M3,M0 and Inflation. 1973 – 1988.

The graph shows two interesting aspects of government policy in the early 1980s. Firstly, although the government believed that inflation could be controlled by £M3, there is no obvious direct relationship between the two variables. Take the years 1973-77, inflation is rising sharply while £M3 is falling. Friedman had, of course, spoken of long and variable lags between changes in the growth rate of the money supply and changes in the rate of inflation. However, a glance at the data shows no clear evidence of a relationship. In the period after 1983 £M3 starts to rise while inflation is falling. We therefore need to consider whether the government chose the correct money supply measure to target.

Secondly, the failure of the government to meet the targets in the early 1980s might appear to suggest that monetary policy was fairly loose in this period. However, a glance at the M0 data in this period shows that the narrow money supply was in fact falling considerably. The government, failing to meet its £M3 target, tightened policy further by raising interest rates and reducing public expenditure. The narrow money data, however, shows that policy was very tight indeed. This dramatic decline in the money supply explains the collapse of aggregate demand in this period.

By 1985 the monetarist experiment was over. Though the government continued to see low inflation as the most important objective of economic policy, monetary targets were abandoned. Unemployment remained high until 1987, and started to fall when government policy reverted to the more discretionary stance of the 1950s and 1960s.

How do we assess the monetarist experiment ? Clearly, the government did not expect the economy to enter such a deep recession and underestimated the effects that this would have on the PSBR. Furthermore, it seems clear that the government may well have been focusing on the wrong money supply target as an indicator of policy tightness. This is highlighted by the infamous 'hairshirt' budget of 1981 when, in the middle of the deepest recession for 50 years, the government cut government expenditure and raised taxes further. Such demand deflation at a time of rising unemployment, showed that the Keynesian era was well and truly over. The government was clearly attempting to restrain £M3 when a glance at the figures for M0 would have shown them how tight policy was.

Milton Friedman, the most influential monetarist of all, criticised the government for using fiscal policy as a tool with which to control the money supply. He argued that monetary base control, control of the narrow money measure M0, was the best method.

The effects of the policy were made worse by the rise in oil prices which partly contributed to the rise in the value of sterling and caused a collapse in exports. However, the government had also raised interest rates to unprecedented levels (16% in October 1980), which had seriously depressed aggregate demand and contributed to the recession.

By 1981 inflation was 12%, higher than when the Conservatives came to power. Unemployment was approaching three million and the economy was in the depths of a severe recession. The government had overshot its targets and the policy had been criticised by the most eminent monetarist of all.

It is therefore difficult to conclude that the monetarist experiment was anything other than a failure. As we have seen, by the mid 1980s the policy was abandoned and, though there was no explicit policy announcement, government policy reverted to traditional demand management.

In completing our study of the importance of money and monetary policy we have effectively completed our examination of the demand side of the economy. In the next unit we explore the "supply side" of the economy and we examine Keynesian and monetarist debates regarding the labour market.

REVIEW ACTIVITY 3

Read Resource Item 8.2, 'Monetary Targets – A Short History' by David Savage, from the *Economic Review* and answer the following questions.

I hope that the article did not prove to be too heavy. The article is a useful reference because it neatly summarises the monetarist approach to the problem of inflation and then evaluates monetarist policy. Not surprisingly the questions that I have set direct you to these points. Your task is to answer these three questions. You should spend no more than five minutes on the first two questions and 10-15 minutes on the final question.

1   Outline the three monetarist assumptions upon which the monetarist solution to the problem of inflation is based.

2   How does the author explain the 'relegation' of monetary targets ?

3   Summarise, in no more than 200 words, the author's evaluation of monetary
    targets.

Summary

In Section 3 we focused on the different types of monetary policy: the use, by the
authorities, of monetary variables, such as the money supply and interest rates to
achieve economic objectives. We traced the development of post-war monetary
policy in the UK. We looked at monetary control policies, techniques and problems
in the 1950s, 1960s, 1970s and 1980s. We also discussed the UK experience of
monetarism (the 'monetarist experiment') in the 1980s, and the success or otherwise
of the so-called Medium Term Financial Strategy (MTFS).

Unit Review Activity

Once again I have selected an article for you to read ! Hopefully you have enough
energy after studying such a long unit. Having read the article try the two short
questions then compare your answers with mine. As usual, if your answers are very
different go back to the article then reread my answers to see why we differ.

Read Resource Item 8.3, ' Macroeconomic Policy since 1979' by Michael Wickens
from the *Economic Review* and answer the following questions.

1   Describe the links between the money supply and the rate of inflation revealed
    by the data.

2   Outline what the author believes was the major cause of the recession in
    1980–1?

Unit Summary

In Section 1 of this unit we defined money and studied the functions of money. We
also outlined a simple financial system and discovered how banks can create credit.
We also studied the financial system of the UK and looked in more detail at the
credit creation process.

In Section 2 we studied the different theories of the demand for money and examined the link between money, aggregate demand and prices.

In Section 3 we looked at monetary policy in the UK in the post war period and we paid particular attention to the attempts to implement monetarism in the UK in the early 1980s.

References

Friedman, M, (1956), 'The quantity theory of money: a restatement', *Essays in the Quantity Theory of Money*, M. Friedman (ed.), University of Chicago Press.

Recommended Reading

There are a number of good economics textbooks which cover the material in this unit. The most useful that I have found are

King, D and Parkin, M, (1992), *Economics*, Addison Wesley, Chapters 27, 28 and 32.

Sloman, J, (1994), *Economics*, Second Edition, Chapters 18 and 19, Prentice Hall.

Answers to Review Activities

Review Activity 1

1   The functions of money are :

   Medium of exchange: money is acceptable as a means of payment in transactions.

   Store of value: money can be held to make future purchases. If money is held in an individuals wallet it does not become valueless. If money did not act as a store of value then nobody would accept money in exchange for goods because that money would be worthless when they tried to buy goods with it the following week. Therefore if money was not a store of value then it could not act as a medium of exchange. Money is not the best store of value as it pays no interest and falls in value because of inflation and so it is actually inferior in this function to some of the other assets we have named.

Unit of account: this means that money serves as a "yardstick" in which transactions can be valued in accounts whether those accounts be the national income accounts or the accounts of a small firm. Without valuation in terms of money it would be very difficult to compare production of physical quantities of different goods or commodities.

Means of deferred payment: this function is similar to that of a store of value but in this case refers to the payment of loans over a period of time such as a long-term loan, or mortgage for the purchase of a house, when the amount to be repaid is stated in money terms.

2 Remember that your answer may differ from mine, but , so long as you have most of the main points, do not worry. Make sure that you consider the following :

maturity transformation

risk transformation

reduced costs

co-ordination of lenders (or 'parcelling').

Financial intermediation performs a number of useful functions.

(i)   Maturity transformation refers to the process whereby financial intermediaries ' borrow short and lend long'. Borrowing , of course, refers to deposits from the public which are repayable on demand. Lending is usually made over a much longer period.

(ii) Risk transformation refers to the process whereby the intermediary borrows and provides the lender with an asset that is virtually risk free, i.e. a deposit account on which the intermediary is extremely unlikely to default. At the same time, the intermediary has the expertise to properly assess risk and make loans to risky firms and individuals. This would be impossible for a sole lender.

(iii) Parcelling up: a third benefit of financial intermediation is that the financial intermediary can 'parcel up' a series of small deposits and make a larger loan.

(iv) Finally, the existence of financial intermediaries saves lenders having to spend time and resources seeking out borrowers, and also saves them having to assess the credit-worthiness of the borrower.

3   (i)   D = C × 1/R; so that D = 50,000 × 1/0.08 = 50,000 × 12.5 = £625,000.

£625,000 is the figure for total deposits. £50,000 existed at the start so £575,000 of deposits have been created by loans.

(ii) $\Delta D = \Delta C \times 1/R$; so that $\Delta D = 10,000 \times 1/R = 10,000 \times 1/0.08 = £125,000$. The bank can now make another £115,000 of loans. The first £10,000 is not lent out.

4   My answer is presented here. As always, check that you include the same points.

The Bank of England has a number of roles:

(i)   It is the bank of the government. It holds the government accounts, receiving income, for example from tax revenue and also paying for government expenditure.

(ii)   The Bank also operates the government monetary policy by acting in the money markets to influence interest rates or the supply of money.

(iii)   The Bank is responsible for seeing that the government can achieve its borrowing. It will therefore buy and sell gilts and bonds to the money markets, the banking sector or the public. It will also try to ensure that interest rates in the market are conducive to the amount of borrowing.

(iv)   The Bank also manages the national debt on behalf of the government. The national debt is the accumulated debt of the whole of the public sector. This role involves the Bank issuing bonds and treasury bills, paying interest on these and redeeming them i.e. paying off their values, as they mature.

(v)   The Bank has the sole right to issue bank notes in England and Wales. It prints notes and coins and oversees their release in accordance with the wishes of the government.

(vi)   The Bank also supervises the whole financial system. It lays down guidelines or 'prudential standards of liquidity' for the banks in terms of how much of their assets should be kept in a liquid form. This is known as prudential control.

(vii)   The Bank acts as lender of the last resort to the banking system. The Bank does not lend directly to the banks but does so through the discount houses. This function is vital as a way of maintaining confidence in the money markets and banking system in general.

(viii) The Bank also holds gold and foreign currency reserves in what is known as the exchange equalisation account. It uses these to buy or sell sterling on the foreign exchange markets in order to influence the value of the exchange rate.

5   This question tested how well you have understood the effects of financing the PSBR on the money supply. Do not worry if you found this a little difficult. Refer back to the text for guidance if necessary. Your answer should be something like the following.

Suppose the government finances borrowing by selling securities of, say, £1 million to the banks. Banks reduce their balances at the central bank by £1 million. However, the government then spends on various projects and money is paid to households in the form of wages and this is then paid into customer accounts with the banks. Bank liabilities rise by £1 million as a result of the increased deposits and assets rise by £1 million as a result of the acquisition of government securities. If the government sells only long-term bonds, i.e. gilts to banks then banks will have a greater proportion of illiquid assets in their balance sheets as these gilts are relatively illiquid. They may have to reduce their lending to maintain a prudent liquidity ratio. If the government sells short-term treasury bills then, obviously, banks will hold a greater proportion of liquid assets in their balance sheets. Clearly, the effect on bank lending and the money supply will depend on the type of assets the government issues in order to finance borrowing.

Review Activity 2

1   If money demand rises, perhaps due to a speculative wave where individuals decide to hold more money at a given interest rate, then the money demand curve will shift to the right. If the money supply is constant or increases proportionately less than money demand, then the money supply will be too small to satisfy the level of demand. Individuals start to reduce their spending in order to bring money balances to the new higher desired level. As they do so the velocity of circulation falls. In terms of the quantity theory of money, $MV = PT$, if V falls and if P is not flexible, then the only way the identity can hold is if T falls. Since T is effectively real output and income, then falls in T imply that employment is also likely to fall.

2   Empirical work on the demand for money is not conclusive. In the periods where the economy was fairly stable the money demand seemed to be stable, which would tend to favour the monetarist argument. However, evidence from the early 1970s, at a time when the economy was subject to major external shocks, such as the oil price increase, and when the money supply was rapidly expanding, is that money demand was less stable. In some respects, these inconclusive results favour the Keynesian view, which tends to argue that money demand may be stable for a time but may be subject to sudden, unpredictable instability. This would mean that the effects of policy would be unpredictable.

Review Activity 3

1   Firstly, the money supply is a key determinant of the level of prices and nominal income. This is of course implicit in the quantity theory of money. Secondly, the economy is inherently stable and will tend towards full employment. Finally, policies designed to stabilise the economy have the opposite effect. They will destabilise, because of lags and inflation.

As a result of these ideas, monetarists say that policy should be based on fixed rules. Say, a fixed annual growth rate for the money supply and a fixed ratio of the PSBR to GDP will be maintained. In other words, discretionary policy should be avoided.

2   Monetary targets were 'relegated' because of the unhappy experience during the first two years of the MTFS. Doubts arose over the ability to control the money supply and over the reliability of changes in the money supply as an indicator of the tightness of monetary policy. For example, in this period prices were rising at a much faster rate than the growth rate of narrow money.

3   The author argues that measurement of the money supply is extremely difficult and such measures may not be a guide to monetary conditions in the economy. He argues that the problems of controlling the money supply were greatly underestimated and this explains the lack of success in meeting the targets. The link between money and prices, so vital to the monetarist argument, has not always held up well. The government-preferred measure of the time, £M3, explains inflation well, albeit with a two year lag, in the 1960s and early 1970s but less so in the early 1980s. Finally, historical evidence does not prove that the monetarist assertion of an inherently stable economy holds. In the 1930s, for example, there was a long period of high unemployment and low output.

Thus, many of the key assumptions on which monetary targeting was based are invalid.

Unit Review Activity

1   Changes in the money supply, according to monetarists, will cause changes in the price level after a lag of one to two years. The data shows a strong correlation between £M3 and inflation before 1982, but the relationship is poor thereafter. However, the data suggests a strong link between narrow money (M0) and inflation. The sharp drop in M0 after 1979 leads to a sharp drop in inflation after 1981.

2   The author believes that the chief cause of the recession in 1980-1 was the sharp rise in the price of oil. This caused domestic production costs to rise so that industry was forced to cut back on production. Furthermore, by this time, the UK was an oil exporter so that the price rise boosted export revenues and led to an increase in the value of sterling on the foreign exchange market. This

made exports relatively expensive compared to imports so that UK manufacturing output started to fall.

UNIT 9
NATIONAL INCOME DETERMINATION AND AGGREGATE SUPPLY

Introduction

We have completed our study of the demand side of the economy and now turn our attention to the **supply side**. According to Keynesian economic theory, national income is determined by demand side factors, such as the demand of the public for goods and services. The supply side is due to a response from firms and entrepreneurs to this demand. Keynesian theory largely ignores the role of the supply side in determining national income. However, the supply side does have an important role to play and in this unit we will look closely at this.

Consider inflation. In the Keynesian model, this results from excess demand. But another way of looking at this is to think of inflation as a result of insufficient supply, caused by the inability of the supply side to respond to an increase in demand. Therefore, we can see inflation as a result of excess demand or insufficient supply.

The supply side is also important when we consider the issue of external balance. If demand is buoyant in the economy and the economy is at full employment so that domestic demand cannot be fully satisfied, then domestic consumers will purchase more imports which may cause an external imbalance.

Whether we accept this or not, there is no doubt that in the late 1960s and 1970s the importance of the supply side became increasingly apparent. During these years the economy was stuck in a **stop-go** cycle and unemployment and inflation were high at the same time, this situation is known as **stagflation**. The emergence of stagflation meant that Keynesians had to rethink. Inflation was increasingly explained as a result of cost factors on the supply side, perhaps associated with excessive union power or monopoly power. As we have seen, this was known as **cost push** inflation and in some senses it represents the first attempt by Keynesians to consider the supply side of the economy.

The Conservative government of 1979, committed to monetarism, embarked on a series of supply side policies in order to improve the labour market. In doing so it was following the classical economic theory that the labour market should be allowed to operate freely without 'imperfections'. We will look at these imperfections and the government policy in this unit.

We begin with an examination of the labour market and see how Keynesian and monetarist economists explain the determination of aggregate supply. We then introduce the **Phillips curve** and discuss how this has influenced economic policymaking since the 1950s. We also consider supply side policy, and examine the Conservative government's supply side policies in the early 1980s.

This unit is divided into three sections. Section 1 explains the classical and Keynesian theories of the labour market and of aggregate supply.

Section 2 considers the importance of the distinction between short-run aggregate supply and long-run aggregate supply and discusses what factors shift the aggregate supply curve.

Section 3 introduces the Phillips curve which suggests that there is an inverse relationship between the rate of change of money wages and the level of unemployment. We will look at the effect of discretionary demand management policy within this framework and use the Phillips curve to show the effect of monetarist policies in the UK in the early 1980s. Finally, in this section, we examine supply side policy such as trade union and minimum wage legislation.

Unit Objectives

By the end of this unit, you should be able to:

- explain the difference between real and money wages
- draw the Keynesian and classical aggregate supply curves
- explain how unemployment arises in the classical model
- distinguish between short-run and long-run aggregate supply
- define the Phillips curve and understand the importance of expectations
- distinguish between rational and adaptive expectations
- explain the rationale for supply side policy.

SECTION ONE

Theories of Aggregate Supply

Introduction

In this section, we explain the classical and Keynesian theories of the labour market and of aggregate supply.

1.1 Classical theory of aggregate supply

Aggregate supply is the total production of goods and services in the economy. The greater the quantity of goods and services available to individuals, the greater are living standards. In this section, we look at factors which promote improved living standards in a country. We will also examine why fluctuations in aggregate supply occur. We begin our study of aggregate supply by looking at classical theory. Monetarists also adopt this theory so you can think of it as the **monetarist theory of aggregate supply**.

SHORT-RUN PRODUCTION FUNCTION

In your microeconomic studies you looked at the labour market in terms of the labour market for individual occupations. In this unit, we consider an aggregated labour market of all the suppliers (workers) and demanders of labour (firms) in the economy. We will start however with a concept you will be familiar with, the **production function**. You will recall from your earlier economics studies that we defined a short run and a long run. In the long run, all factors of production are variable. However, in the short run at least one factor of production is fixed. We will assume just three factors, labour, land and capital, and we will also assume that capital and land are fixed in the short run. The **short-run production function** (SRPF), therefore, shows the amount of output that can be produced in the economy with all land and capital fixed and **labour as the only variable factor**.

Figure 1 illustrates a short-run production function. Output is measured on the vertical axis and labour is measured on the horizontal axis. Output increases as labour input increases. Notice the shape of the function. Because of the principle of diminishing marginal returns, the slope of the curve becomes flatter as more and more labour is added to the fixed factors. This means that each successive worker adds less to output than the previous worker.

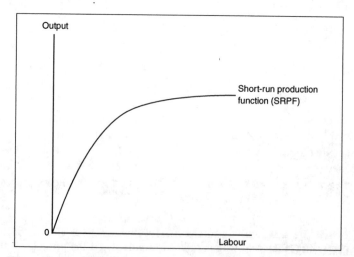

Figure 1: The SRPF shows the amount of output produced in the economy with capital fixed. Labour is the only factor of production that can be varied in the short run.

Remember that this analysis considers the whole economy. It is an **aggregate** short-run production function. In this analysis, we make no distinction between different types of labour. All workers are assumed to be identical in terms of ability and skills.

ACTIVITY 1

The short-run production function describes:

1 the quantity of goods produced in the economy in the short term.

2 the quantity of goods produced in the economy.

3 the quantity of goods produced in the economy for each possible amount of labour used, assuming that only the quantity of labour varies.

---

1 This is incorrect. The response is incomplete. Although the short-run production can be thought of as describing the quantity of goods and services produced in the economy in the short run, it shows how much can be produced with one factor of production (capital) fixed.

2 This is incorrect. The response does not describe short-run aggregate supply. The quantity of goods produced in the economy is simply 'aggregate supply', although the statement does not tell us about whether it is long-run or short-run aggregate supply.

3 This is the correct answer. Short-run aggregate supply is the quantity of goods produced in the economy assuming that one factor of production (capital) is fixed so that only the quantity of labour varies.

DEMAND FOR LABOUR

In the model the demand for labour, like any other commodity, depends on the price of labour. The price of labour is, as always, expressed in terms of wages. However, in this model the important variable is the **real wage**. The nominal or **money wage** is simply the amount of money paid to workers in return for their labour. The real wage is that nominal wage measured in terms of the amount of goods that can be purchased. In other words, the real wage is the nominal wage deflated by the price level. Formally, if we call nominal or money wages, W and the price level by P then real wages are (W/P).

If the price level rises and money wages are constant or rise by a smaller proportion than the price level then real wages fall. Alternatively, if the price level falls and money wages are constant or fall by a smaller proportion than the price level then real wages will rise. Obviously, if the price level is constant then a rise or fall in money wages leads to a rise or fall in real wages.

ACTIVITY 2

In 1979 the price level was 100. In 1989 it was 150. Over the same period, money wages rose from 1500 to 4500. Which statement(s) are correct?

1 Real wages rose by 50%

2 Money wages rose by 200%

3 Real wages rose by 100%

4 Price level rose by 50%

5 Money wages fell by 200%

1   Real wages are equal to money wages W divided by the price level P. In 1979 real wages were equal to $(1500/100) = 15$. In 1989, real wages are equal to $(4500/150) = 30$. Therefore, the rise in real wages from 15 to 30 represents an increase of 100%, that is, $[(30 - 15)/15] \times 100 = 100$. Response a is incorrect.

2   Money wages were equal to 1500 in 1979 and 4500 in 1989. Therefore, money wages have risen by 200%, that is, $[(4500 - 1500)/1500] \times 100 = 200$. Response b is correct.

3   This answer is correct. Real wages rise from 15 in 1979 to 30 in 1989. This is a rise of 100%, that is, $[(30 - 15)/15] \times 100 = 100$.

4   The price level is equal to 100 in 1979 and 150 in 1989. This is a rise of 50%, that is, $[(150 - 100)/100] \times 100 = 50$. Response d is correct.

5   From the answer to b, this is clearly incorrect.

When real wages are high, fewer people will be able to get work and when real wages are low, more people will be employed. Figure 2 shows the demand curve for labour D_L, with the quantity of labour on the horizontal axis and the real wage on the vertical axis.

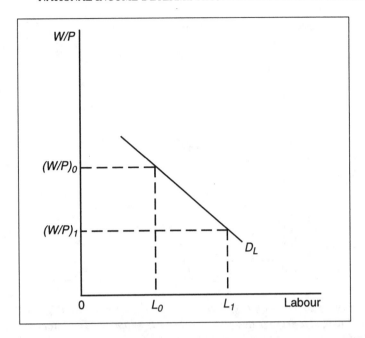

Figure 2: The demand for labour. As real wages fall the quantity of labour demand increases.

At the real wage $(W/P)_0$, the quantity of labour demanded is L_0. Now if the real wage falls to $(W/P)_1$, for example, because the price level rises or nominal wages fall, then the quantity of labour demanded will rise to L_1.

At all times in this analysis, remember that we are talking about the whole economy and the whole labour market so that when we refer to real or money wage, we are referring to the **average** rate throughout the economy.

SUPPLY OF LABOUR AND LABOUR MARKET EQUILIBRIUM

Now that we have examined the demand for labour we must consider the supply of labour. Once again, the analysis is similar to that for any other good. People of working age will have to allocate their time between work and leisure. The theory asserts that, as wages rise people will want to spend more time in work because leisure becomes more expensive. Similarly, at lower wages, people prefer to spend less time working and more time in leisure pursuits because the rewards for working, wages, are lower. As economists say, the suppliers of labour, workers, will want to supply more labour when real wages are higher, whilst at lower real wages, they will reduce the supply of labour. Therefore the labour supply curve will be upward sloping. Figure 3 shows the supply of labour curve S_L and our demand for labour curve D_L. The intersection of these curves determines the equilibrium real wage $(W/P)^*$ and the equilibrium quantity of labour employed L^*.

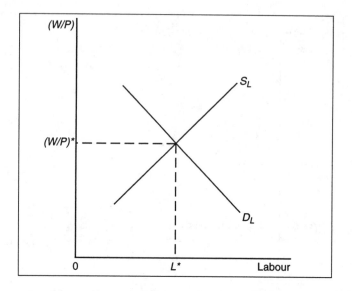

Figure 3: The supply of labour curve (S_L) shows that at higher real wages a greater quantity of labour is supplied. The intersection of the supply of labour and the demand for labour determines the equilibrium real wage (W/P)* and quantity of labour employed.

Of course, suppliers of labour (workers) cannot force employers to give them jobs so that it is the demand for labour that governs the quantity of labour employed in equilibrium. Furthermore, in classical theory the labour market is assumed to be highly efficient so that the real wage instantaneously achieves this equilibrium. Generally, the analysis assumes that the adjustment takes place via changes in money wages. The price level does not change. In other words, money wages in this model are **perfectly flexible**. Therefore according to classical theory, a situation will never exist where real wages are too high so that there is an excess supply of labour and unemployment, or where real wages are too low so that excess labour demand exists. In these cases, the money wage will very quickly adjust so that any excess of supply or demand is eliminated.

In order to see if you have understood this section on the classical theory of aggregate supply try this short activity.

ACTIVITY 3

Indicate whether the following statements are true or false:

It follows from the assumptions of classical theory that:

1 If the price of goods and services goes up then money wages go up instantly

2 There is no unemployment

3 If many English workers emigrated to Australia real wages would be unaffected.

1   This is true. A rise in the price of goods and services means that real wages will
    fall. In this case, the demand for labour would exceed the supply of labour.
    Money wages would rise to 'choke off' this excess demand. Equilibrium would
    be restored when real wages returned to their previous level.

2   This is true. In the classical theory, unemployment will not exist.
    Unemployment is an excess supply of labour. In the classical model, any
    excess supply of labour would be instantly eliminated by a fall in money
    wages.

3   This is false. Figure 4 illustrates; the supply of labour curve for England is S_L
    and the demand for labour curve is D_L. The equilibrium real wage (W/P) and
    quantity of labour employed L are shown. If many English workers emigrated
    then the labour supply would be reduced. This is represented by a leftward shift
    in the supply of labour curve from S_L to S_{L1}. The real wage is raised from (W/P)
    to $(W/P)_1$. The equilibrium quantity of labour employed is L_1.

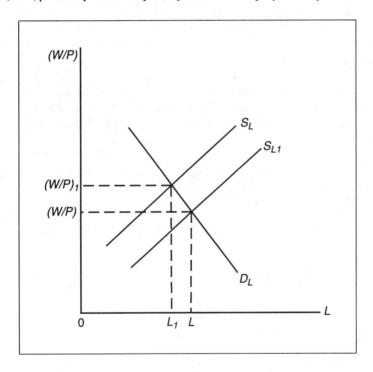

Figure 4: If many workers emigrate labour supply is reduced, S_L shifts to S_{L1}.
The real wage increases and the equilibrium quantity of labour falls to L_1.

Hopefully you were able to determine which statements were correct. Now that we
have considered the labour market we will use this to develop the aggregate supply
curve in the classical model.

CLASSICAL AGGREGATE SUPPLY CURVE

The aggregate supply curve shows the quantity of output supplied at each different
price level. Earlier when we looked at the short-run production function we studied

the relationship between production and the quantity of labour employed, now we
will look at the relationship between production and prices. This is shown by the
aggregate supply curve which shows the quantity of output supplied, that is, the
amount of goods and services produced by firms at each different price level.

What does the graph of production and prices look like? Will the level of production
be affected by changes in the price level? Will prices affect wages, and the level of
wages affect employment and the level of production? Let us look at this step by
step.

The aggregate supply curve is derived from the labour market and the production
function. Figure 5 has four quadrants. The bottom left quadrant is the starting
point for our analysis. This shows our labour market in equilibrium at a real wage
$(W/P)^*$ where the equilibrium quantity of labour employed is L^*. Let us assume that
the money wage is 400 and the price level is 100 so that this equilibrium real wage
is 4. The quantity of labour employed at this real wage L^*, is transferred to the
quadrant above in the top left which shows our short-run production function.
The short-run production function shows us the equilibrium quantity of output
produced by the quantity of labour L^*. This quantity of output, read from the
vertical axis, is Y^*.

We now transfer this level of output across to the top right quadrant. Here we have
output on both axes and a 45-degree line through the origin. If we use the same scale
on each axis then we can use the 45-degree line to transfer Y^* to the horizontal axis.

We can now draw the aggregate supply curve in our remaining bottom right
quadrant, with output on the horizontal axis and the price level on the vertical axis.
The output level Y^* is shown in the final quadrant.

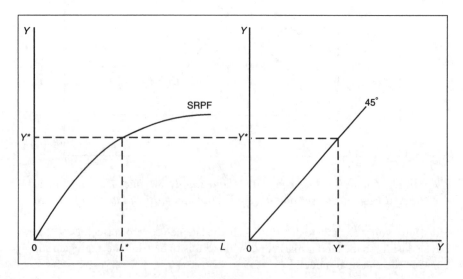

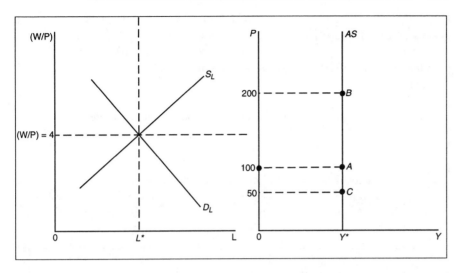

Figure 5: Derivation of the classical aggregate supply curve (AS).

On the vertical axis we have our price level of 100. Point *A* is clearly one point on our aggregate supply curve. Now what happens to output in this model as the price level changes? Suppose prices double from their initial level of 100 to a new level of 200. In the classical model, money wages will instantaneously rise by exactly the same proportion so that real wages are unchanged. Money wages therefore rise to 800 so that the real wage is still 4. This means that if the real wage does not change then there is no change in the equilibrium quantities of labour and output. We now locate point *B* in the bottom right quadrant as another point on the aggregate supply curve. Output at this point is Y^* and the price level is 200.

Now consider a drop in the price level from 200 to 50. Money wages will now fall instantaneously by exactly the same proportion so that real wages are unchanged. Money wages therefore fall to 200 so that the real wage is still 4. This means again that, as there is no change in the real wage then there is no change in the equilibrium quantities of labour and output. We now locate point *C* in the bottom right quadrant as yet another point on the aggregate supply curve. Output at this point is Y^* and the price level is 50. If we join our points *A*, *B* and *C* we derive our aggregate supply curve *AS*. Quite clearly, in this classical model, the aggregate supply curve is vertical or perfectly inelastic with respect to the price level. Whatever the level of price, the amount of output is Y^*. The nature of the supply curve arises from the assumption that money wages are perfectly flexible and adapt to changes in price to ensure that the labour market is never in disequilibrium.

This level of output Y^* is that level of output that generates full employment. In the classical model, disequilibrium situations, such as excess supply or demand will never exist. Unemployment, an excess labour supply, represents a labour market disequilibrium and will therefore never exist in the classical model.

ACTIVITY 4

In the classical model, money wages are equal to 500 and the price level is equal to 200.

1 If the price level rises to 300 what will happen to money wages?

2 If the price level falls to 50 what will happen to money wages?

1   The real wage is $(500/200) = 2.5$. In the classical model, money wages will adjust immediately following a change in the price level, to ensure that real wages do not change. Therefore, if the price level rises to 300, then money wages will rise to $300 \times 2.5 = 750$.

2   If the price level falls to 50 then money wages will fall to $50 \times 2.5 = 250$.

AGGREGATE SUPPLY AND CHANGES IN CAPITAL STOCK

In deriving our aggregate supply function, we assumed that labour was the only variable factor of production. If we assume that all factors are variable then the aggregate supply function will be affected. In the longer term, firms will be able to replace and update worn out capital stock. They may also expand their stock of capital by buying more machinery for example. In other words, in the long term, the supply of capital in the economy grows. How will this affect aggregate supply? Figure 6 reproduces Figure 5 but shows a second production function $SRPF_1$ which corresponds to a higher level of capital stock. This lies above our first short-run production function at all times. This means that, for the same quantity of labour, more output can be produced because of the higher capital input. As a result, the labour market equilibrium generates a higher level of output Y_1, reading off $SRPF_1$, this results in a shift of the aggregate supply curve to Y_1 as shown.

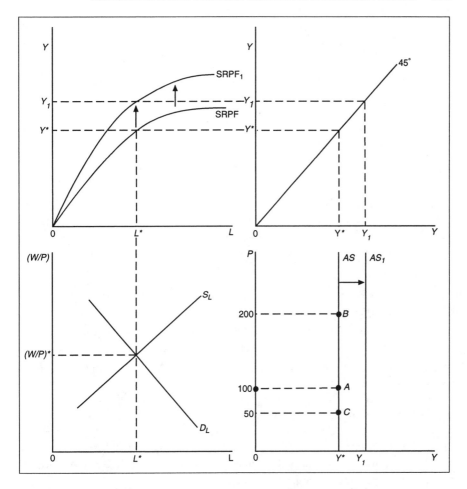

*Figure 6: An increase in the capital stock causes a
shift in the long-run aggregate supply curve.*

A number of factors may lead to shifts in the aggregate supply curve. As well as
increases in the capital stock, technological progress and increases in the ability of
the labour force will have similar effects.

ACTIVITY 5

1 Draw the classical aggregate supply function and an aggregate demand
  curve. In the last unit we saw that, in classical theory, an increase in the
  money supply led to an increase in aggregate demand. Therefore, show the
  effect of an increase in the money supply in your diagram.

2 Use your diagram to show the effect of an improvement in technology.
  Remember that an improvement in technology would shift the short-run
  production function upwards.

1

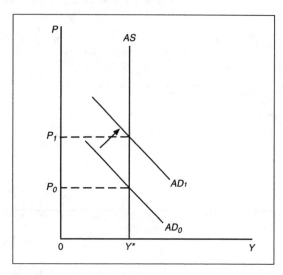

*Figure 7: The classical aggregate supply curve is AS which shows an
equilibrium level of Y*. An increase in the money supply which
raises aggregate demand from AD to AD₁ will raise the price
level P₀ to P₁, but output is unaffected.*

The increase in the money supply causes an increase in aggregate demand.
Remember that, in classical theory, if the money supply increases then aggregate
demand will increase as people find they are holding more money than they want.
They get rid of this excess cash by spending on goods and services. This is shown
by a rightward shift from AD_0 to AD_1. This has no effect on output but raises the
price level from P_0 to P_1. Increases in the money supply have no effect on output
and the level of employment in this model. Economists call this the **neutrality of
money**. Money is neutral in the classical model.

2

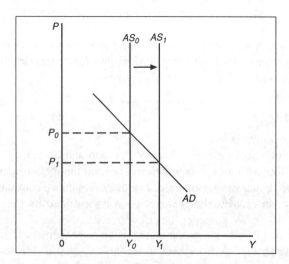

*Figure 8: The improvement in technology causes a rightward shift in the
aggregate supply function. If aggregate demand is unchanged then the
effect is to raise output from Y₀ to Y₁ and to reduce the price
level from P₀ to P₁.*

If your answers were correct, it shows that you have a good grasp of this difficult concept. If you had problems, look again at the figures and explanations.

UNEMPLOYMENT IN THE CLASSICAL MODEL

Unemployment is a serious social problem as well as a waste of human economic resources. Unemployment imposes a cost on everyone because ultimately welfare benefits paid to the unemployed are financed by taxation. The issue of unemployment is closely related to that of aggregate supply. The greater the quantity of labour employed then the higher is aggregate supply; high levels of unemployment will therefore tend to reduce aggregate supply.

Unemployment is defined as the number of people out of work at a point in time. Unemployment will increase if the number of workers losing jobs is greater than the number of people gaining jobs. It is important to remember that the number of unemployed workers in the economy does not correspond precisely to theoretical concepts of unemployment used by economists.

Economists define different types of unemployment and we examined some of these in Unit 6. **Structural unemployment** occurs as certain industries decline over time as demand patterns change and technology progresses; **frictional unemployment** results from the fact that, as people change their occupations during their working life, they may have short periods of unemployment while 'between jobs'.

Classical and Keynesian economists also have their own definitions of unemployment. We will examine Keynesian unemployment in the next section but here we examine the cause of unemployment from a classical perspective.

It may seem odd that we consider unemployment in the classical model when we have already stated that classical economists assume that flexible money wages will ensure that unemployment never exists. However, classical economists assumed that the labour market would be perfectly efficient and would not have any **imperfections**. The existence of imperfections may cause unemployment in the classical model. Imperfections are anything that interferes with the market mechanism. What sort of things might this include? We consider three examples here:

- minimum wages
- trade unions
- unemployment benefit.

Although we discuss these under a classical heading, monetarists also argue that these factors will cause unemployment. The three factors we consider here were at the centre of a series of labour market reforms initiated by the Conservative government of 1979. We consider the effect of each of these in turn.

Minimum wages

Figure 9 illustrates our familiar labour demand and supply curves D_L and S_L. Equilibrium real wages and labour demand are $(W/P)^*$ and L^* respectively.

Minimum wages are set by the government at a higher level than the market determined level. Consider a minimum real wage established at (W/P)min above the equilibrium level.

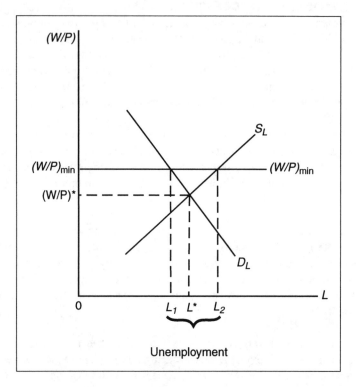

Figure 9: Demand for labour and supply of labour curves intersect at an equilibrium real wage $(W/P)^*$ and an equilibrium quantity of labour employed, L^*. A minimum wage set above the equilibrium real wage $(W/P)_{min}$ causes unemployment.

At this minimum wage, the quantity of labour supplied L_2 is greater than the quantity of labour demanded, L_1. The amount of labour measure by the 'gap', $L_2 - L_1$ represents the amount of unemployment created by this minimum wage. Thus the imposing of a minimum wage prevents the market mechanism from working and represents an imperfection that causes unemployment.

Trade unions

Trade unions which are common in the labour market act as agents for workers in the negotiation of work and employment contracts. Naturally, they will try to secure the best wages and conditions for their members. Often they impose minimum qualifications for certain jobs. Once employed the workers become part of the union. The British Medical Association defines minimum educational requirements in allowing somebody to become a doctor. The effect of such measures is to reduce the labour force available to perform that job. In effect, the labour supply is restricted. Figure 10 shows our familiar labour demand and supply curves as well as our equilibrium real wages and labour demand.

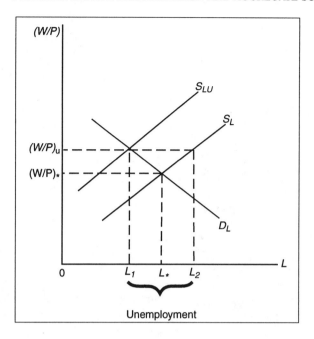

Figure 10: Trade unions act to restrict the supply of labour

The effect of the union is to restrict the labour supply. This means that the labour supply curve is forced up from S_L to S_{LU}. This raises the real wage to $(W/P)_U$ and reduces the level of labour demanded to L_1. At this higher real wage, with no union, the supply of labour would be L_2. The effect of the union is to create a level of unemployment, $L_2 - L_1$. Of course, trade unions do not exist in every sector of the economy. However if some of the unions that exist act in this way then the average real wage in the economy will be raised and this will lower the level of employment.

Unemployment benefit

Unemployment benefit, paid to individuals unable to find work, provides them with a minimum income while they look for a job. Classical theorists argue that if unemployment benefits are too high compared with real wages, then unemployed people will have less incentive to find jobs. In principle, individuals will want to find work quickly so that they can earn a real wage and improve their living standards. However, if the level of benefit is high relative to real wages, then individuals will be encouraged to spend more time unemployed. The incentive to work will be reduced. Let us see how this happens and the effects of paying unemployment benefit on real wages and on the total number of people employed.

Figure 11 depicts a labour demand curve D_L. This shows the amount of workers that employers want at each level of the real wage. The figure also shows a labour supply curve S_L which shows the number of people wanting to work at each level of the real wage. The intersection of D_L and S_L tells us what the equilibrium real wage will be and what quantity of labour will be employed at this real wage. The equilibrium real wage is $(W/P)^*$ and the quantity of labour employed is L^*.

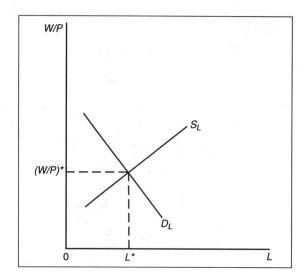

Figure 11: The intersection of the labour demand curve and the labour supply curve determines the equilibrium real wage and the quantity of labour employed.

Now what happens when we introduce benefits? This will not affect the number of workers needed by employers but the theory is that it will affect their willingness to work. Monetarists assume that people do not want to work but in order to get money they will give up some of their leisure time in return for a wage. However, if the individual is 'paid' without doing anything, then according to this view, he or she will not want to surrender any free time until the reward for doing so becomes worthwhile. This can only happen when real wages are greater than benefits. The supply of labour is affected as shown by curve S_{LB} in Figure 12.

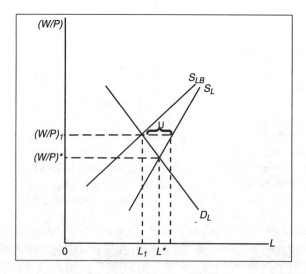

Figure 12: The introduction of benefits causes S_L to shift to S_{LB}. This raises the equilibrium real wage and lowers the quantity employed. The unemployment created is shown by the horizontal distance, U.

S_{LB} shows the amount of labour workers are willing to supply at each real wage in the presence of unemployment benefits. The gap between S_{LB} and S_L at each real wage shows the amount of labour that chooses not to work and instead registers as unemployed and claims benefits.

Let us look more closely at S_{LB} to explain why it is assumed to take the shape shown. Notice that S_{LB} is not parallel to S_L. The larger the gap between the two curves, S_L and S_{LB} , then the lower the real wage. Unemployment benefits not only encourage workers to spend longer searching for jobs but more specifically, at low real wages there will be a disincentive to take jobs. Faced with a choice between taking benefits or a low paid job which may pay only slightly more than the benefit level, then many will choose benefits. Therefore the lower the real wage the smaller the number of individuals willing to take jobs. Obviously, at higher real wages this disincentive effect is reduced so that the effect on the labour supply is smaller.

The effect of the benefit is to reduce the amount of labour demanded to L_1 and to raise the real wage to $(W/P)_1$. The amount of unemployment created is shown as the horizontal distance, U, between the curves S_L and S_{LB}.

If the demand for labour fell at each real wage the level of unemployment would rise as more workers choose to register as unemployed and accept benefits rather than work for a low real wage. If the demand for labour rose at each real wage the level of unemployment would fall as more and more workers would choose to take jobs in order to receive higher real wages.

To sum up, in the classical theory, flexible money wages ensure that the aggregate supply curve is perfectly **inelastic**. Furthermore, there will be no unemployment in this model providing that the market mechanism is allowed to work. In the presence of market imperfections, such as trade unions, minimum wages or benefits, unemployment may exist.

In classical theory, if the government wishes to reduce unemployment then it should reduce these imperfections. Measures might include the abolition of minimum wage legislation, trade union reform and reform of the unemployment benefit system.

ACTIVITY 6

Assume that an economy has a high level of unemployment benefit which is then reduced by the government. Using the same axes:

1   Sketch graphs showing the equilibrium position for labour demanded and supplied at various levels of real wages and benefits.

2   Now plot the labour supply curve with high benefit payments

3   Plot a third labour supply curve with lower benefits

For 1, 2 and 3, show the equilibrium real wage and quantity employed.

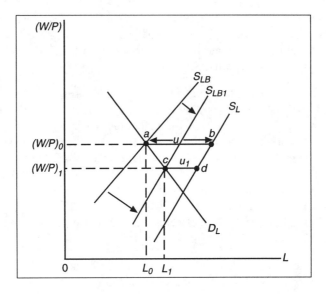

Figure 13: Labour demand and supply with high and low benefits

The economy is at point *a*. The supply of labour curve is S_L and the supply of labour curve in the presence of unemployment benefit is labelled S_{LB}. The demand for labour curve D_L is shown. Before the benefit reduction the quantity of labour employed is L_0 and the real wage is $(W/P)_0$. Unemployment is shown by the horizontal distance *ab*. A reduction in benefit shifts S_{LB} to the right to S_{LB1}. The incentive to work is raised. The curve pivots towards the S_L curve as the incentive to take low paid jobs is especially raised. Unemployment falls. The real wage falls to $(W/P)_1$ and the quantity of labour employed rises to L_1. Unemployment is now measured by the horizontal distance *cd*.

1.2 Keynesian theory of aggregate supply

Now that we have seen how aggregate supply is determined in the classical model we turn to the Keynesian theory of aggregate supply. In doing so, we use exactly the same tools to derive the aggregate supply curve. The production function is exactly as we have already described. The crucial difference lies in the labour market. Keynes agreed that when employers want more labour than is available (or in an economist's terminology, when there is an excess demand for labour) then money wages will rise so that the real wage rises to eliminate the excess demand. In other words, money wages are **flexible upwards**. However, Keynes argued that when there was an excess of labour supply money wages would **not** fall so that real wages would not adjust. Keynes believed that workers would resist cuts in money wages. Therefore in this model, money wages are **sticky downwards**.

How does this affect the labour market? Figure 14 illustrates. The labour demand and supply curves are labelled D_L and S_L respectively. To begin our analysis, assume the equilibrium real wage is $(W/P)^*$ and the equilibrium labour quantity is L^*. Now assume that for some reason, the price level falls so that the real wage rises to $(W/P)_1$.

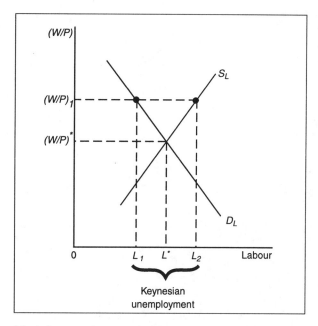

Figure 14: A drop in the price level causes real wages to rise if money wages are 'sticky' downwards. This creates unemployment.

At this new higher real wage, the demand for labour is greater than the supply of labour. Specifically, at this real wage the demand for labour is L_1 and the supply of labour is L_2. The quantity of labour, $L_1 - L_2$, represents this excess supply of labour and is known as **Keynesian unemployment**. This term is used to distinguish it from the classical unemployment we have just considered. In the classical model, this excess would be instantaneously eliminated by a downward adjustment in the money wage so that the real wage falls to $(W/P)^*$. In the Keynesian model, because money wages are sticky downwards, the unemployment persists.

We now derive the Keynesian aggregate supply curve in exactly the same way we derived the classical supply curve, using the production function and the labour market. Figure 15 shows the same four quadrants that we saw in our consideration of classical aggregate supply. Our analysis begins in the bottom left quadrant in our labour market. Let us assume once again that the initial price level is 100 and that the money wage level is 400 so that the equilibrium real wage is 4. This equilibrium real wage generates an equilibrium quantity of labour employed of L^* and an equilibrium level of output of Y^* from the short-run production function. Recall that Y^* is the full employment level of output. Using our 45-degree line in the top right quadrant, we transfer this level of output onto the horizontal axis and then into the bottom right quadrant. If we now show the price level of 100 in this quadrant we derive point A on the Keynesian aggregate supply curve.

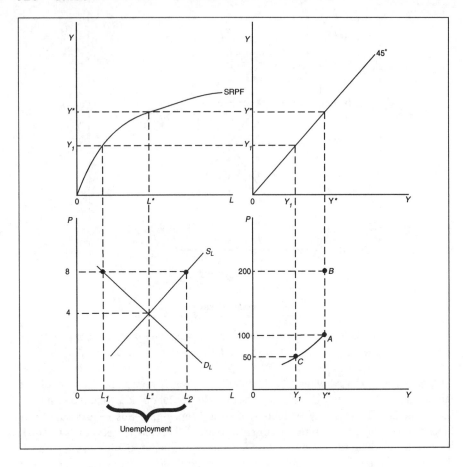

Figure 15: Derivation of the Keynesian aggregate supply curve

Now let the price level rise from 100 to 200. Just as in the classical model, the money wage will be perfectly flexible in an upward direction and will rise by the same proportion to maintain an equilibrium real wage of 4. Therefore money wages rise to 800. We now show 200 as the price level in the bottom right quadrant and locate point *B* on the Keynesian aggregate supply curve. At any price level above 100, then the Keynesian aggregate supply curve is vertical like its classical counterpart. This is because for **prices above** the equilibrium level, money wages are **flexible**.

Now consider our initial position again. Let prices fall from 100 to 50. Now money wages are sticky downwards so that money wages do not fall from the level 400. Therefore the real wage rises to $(W/P)_1 = (400/50) = 8$. At this new higher real wage, the supply of labour L_2 exceeds the demand for labour L_1. The amount of labour $L_2 - L_1$ represents the level of unemployment in this model. As for output, this level of labour employed L_1 can be transferred to the top left quadrant and the production functions shows that this generates an output level of Y_1. If we now use our 45-degree line we can transfer this level of output to the bottom right quadrant. If we show the price level of 50 here then we can locate point *C* on the Keynesian aggregate supply curve.

The Keynesian aggregate supply curve can now be shown clearly if we join these points. It differs from the classical aggregate supply curve in that, below that price level which generates full employment and output of Y^*, the supply curve slopes upwards.

In general this Keynesian aggregate supply curve is shown as a backward L-shaped curve. We met this in Unit 7. This curve is shown in Figure 16 and is labelled KAS.

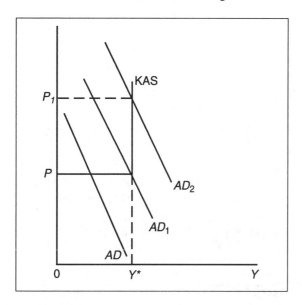

Figure 16: Keynesian aggregate supply curve is KAS. It is vertical at the level of output Y^*, full employment. Once this level of output is reached, increase in aggregate demand raises the price level.

The shape of the aggregate supply curve means that changes in aggregate demand such as that shown from AD to AD_1 will not raise the price level as long as output is below the full employment level of output, Y^*. Once the full employment level of output is reached then further increases in aggregate demand such AD_1 to AD_2 will raise prices from P to P_1.

Contrast this with the classical theory of aggregate supply. In this theory, increases in the level of aggregate demand will automatically lead to higher prices as shown in Figure 17.

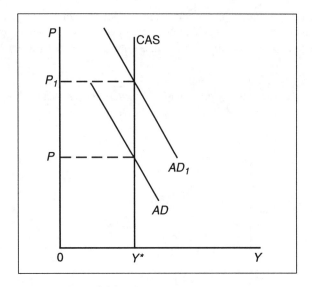

Figure 17: Classical aggregate supply curve is CAS. Increase in aggregate demand will affect only the price level.

The classical aggregate supply is labelled CAS. The increase in aggregate demand from AD to AD_1, causes an increase in the price level from P to P_1.

REVIEW ACTIVITY 1

In classical theory, a change in the money supply does not affect the level of output or the level of employment. It will only affect the price level. Economists say that money is neutral in classical theory. Use a diagram to show whether or not money is neutral in the Keynesian model.

Summary

What we have considered so far are the 'pure' Keynesian and classical views of aggregate supply. In doing so we have made no distinction between short-run aggregate supply and long-run aggregate supply. In the next section, we examine these closely as they are fundamental to the monetarist-Keynesian dispute over the effectiveness of economic policy.

SECTION TWO

Short-run and Long-run Aggregate Supply

Introduction

In this section, we look at the distinction between short-run aggregate supply and long-run aggregate supply and consider its importance. We discuss what factors shift the aggregate supply curve.

In Unit 8, we distinguished between Keynesian and classical views of aggregate supply. In this unit, we develop a general theory of aggregate supply known as the **neo-Keynesian synthesis** . This rather grand name is given to a theory of aggregate supply which incorporates parts of both the Keynesian and classical theory. The theory is one of short- and long-run aggregate supply.

When we refer to the short run in economics we generally define it as a situation where a firm has at least one factor of production that is fixed. In macroeconomics, the short run is a period over which the prices of goods and services change in response to changes in demand and supply but money wages do not change. Often, unions and workers sign money wage contracts for a period of time that cannot be renegotiated until the contract expires so if prices rise during the life of the contract then real wages will fall.

Obviously, in order to protect real wages and living standards, unions will have to negotiate wage contracts on the basis of their **expectations** of what will happen to prices in future. The long run in macroeconomics is a time period in which wages adjust to changes in supply and demand.

2.1 Short-run aggregate supply

What does the short-run aggregate supply curve look like? Consider a single firm. If the price of its output starts to rise then as far as the firm is concerned, the real wages of its workers will fall. The firm continues to pay workers the same money wages but the output produced by those workers can now be sold at the higher price. Firms will therefore hire more labour and increase output. On the other hand, if the price of output falls then real wages will rise so that less labour will be demanded and output will fall. Clearly then, at higher prices output rises and at lower prices output falls. This will be the same for all firms in the economy so that the short-run aggregate supply curve looks like a 'standard' upward sloping supply curve. A short-run aggregate supply curve, SAS, is shown in Figure 18.

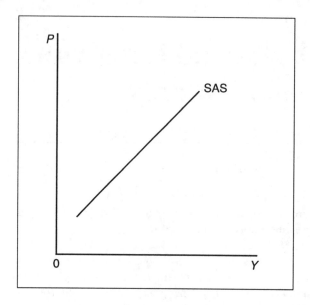

Figure 18: The short-run aggregate supply curve, SAS

At higher prices then, output is raised and the level of employment rises. As prices fall then output is reduced and unemployment rises. In deriving the short-run aggregate supply curve we assume rigid or fixed money wages. The analysis of short-run aggregate supply is similar to the Keynesian theory of aggregate supply.

2.2 Long-run aggregate supply

In the long run, money wages adjust to fully reflect any changes in prices. Money wages are therefore fully flexible. In other words, the real wage will be constant and the long-run aggregate supply curve is vertical just like the classical aggregate supply curve. The long-run aggregate supply curve defines the potential limit to output of the economy and is that level of output where money wages have fully adjusted to any changes in prices. It is often called the long-run **equilibrium level of output.**

Because money wages are fully flexible in the long run then if any unemployment exists at this equilibrium level of output then this will be due to labour market imperfections such as trade union activity, minimum wage legislation or the existence of unemployment benefits. Figure 19 shows both a long-run aggregate supply function, LAS, and our short-run aggregate supply function, SAS.

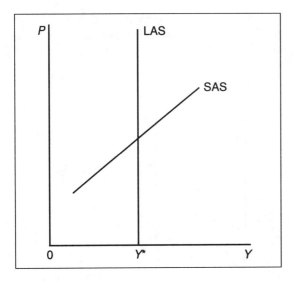

Figure 19: Short-run aggregate supply curve
and long-run aggregate supply curve

At Y^*, any unemployment that exists will be due to the existence of labour market imperfections. The name given to this unemployment is the **natural rate of unemployment**. We study this more later, for now it is sufficient to say that, providing the economy is free from government intervention then the economy will settle at equilibrium with this level of unemployment. In other words, if the government does not attempt to influence aggregate demand by the use of discretionary fiscal policy then unemployment will settle at the natural rate.

2.3 Shifts in aggregate supply

The following factors will cause changes in the aggregate supply curve:

● changes in money wages

● changes in the quantity or quality of factors of production

● technological changes

● labour market reforms

● expectations.

We now consider each of these in turn.

CHANGES IN MONEY WAGES

If money wages change, the short-run aggregate supply curve (SAS) will shift. Changes in the price level will cause movements along SAS but changes in money wages will cause shifts in SAS. Consider a rise in wage rates. If prices do not change then real wages rise and this puts upward pressure on a firm's costs. Firms therefore want to supply less at each price level. Figure 20 shows an initial price level of P_0. If money wages rise then the short-run aggregate supply curve will shift upwards and to the left to SAS_1 and the price level rises to P_1. Conversely, a fall in wage rates would cause the SAS to shift downwards and to the right and prices would fall.

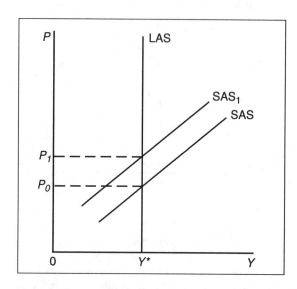

Figure 20: Increases in money wages will cause the short-run aggregate supply curve to shift upwards to the right. Output is unaffected but the price level rises.

Changes in money wages will shift the short-run aggregate supply but not the long-run aggregate supply curve. Make sure you understand why this is the case. Long-run aggregate supply is the quantity of output produced when wages have fully adjusted to achieve the natural rate of unemployment. When the economy is producing its long-run aggregate supply curve, any change in money wages is matched by changes in prices. Real wages and output remain constant.

CHANGES IN THE QUANTITY AND QUALITY OF FACTORS OF PRODUCTION AND TECHNOLOGICAL CHANGES

The effects of these two factors are so similar that we consider them together. If the quality of the labour force is improved, for example, by education, then the economy can produce a greater quantity of output at any price level. Similarly, if the quality of the capital stock is improved by advances in technology then a greater quantity of output can be produced at any price level. Improvements such as these will cause both the long- and short-run aggregate supply curves to shift as illustrated in Figure 21.

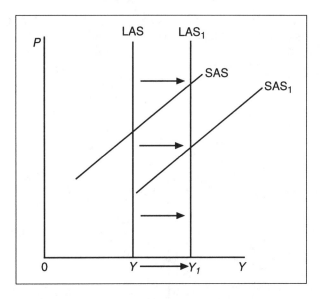

*Figure 21: Changes in the quantity and quality of factors of production
raise the quantity of output that can be produced at each price level.
Both the SAS and the LAS shift to the right.*

As Figure 21 shows both the LAS and SAS shift so that the long-run output of the economy increases from Y to Y_1. Obviously, at a higher level of income then the natural rate of unemployment is reduced.

LABOUR MARKET REFORMS
Under this broad heading, we can consider factors such as removal of minimum wages, trade union reform in order to reduce union power and also changes in the benefit system in order to improve incentives. These reforms are designed to make the labour market more efficient so that any unemployment is largely frictional. The effect of these reforms can be illustrated using Figure 21. By removing any unemployment that occurs as a result of imperfections then output rises and the natural rate of unemployment falls.

EXPECTATIONS
Whenever aggregate demand changes both trade unions and firms will have expectations about what will happen as a result of this change. For example, firms might believe that an increase in aggregate demand will result in increased demand for their own product. They will therefore invest in capital in order to satisfy the increased demand for their products. The short-run aggregate supply curve will shift to the right as firms supply more output at each price level. On the other hand, if firms believe that the increase in aggregate demand will not result in higher sales of their products and will simply result in higher prices, then they will choose not to invest because, unless they can sell extra output, there is no need for new productive capacity.

What about unions and workers? If they believe that prices will rise then they will start to demand higher money wages to maintain the level of real wages. This will raise firms' costs so that firms will want to produce less at each price level. The short-run aggregate supply curve will shift to the left. Figure 22 illustrates this situation. Assume an economy at point A. The government then raises aggregate demand. If unions and workers expect the increase in aggregate demand from AD to AD_1 to raise the price level then the short-run aggregate supply curve will shift from SAS to SAS_1. The economy goes to point B. Notice how the expectations of higher prices are fulfilled!

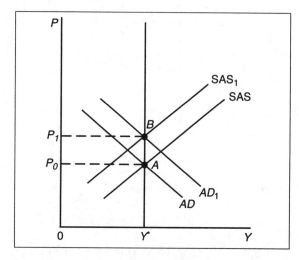

Figure 22: An increase in demand will cause the AD curve to AD_1. If firms' workers expect prices to rise then the SAS will shift up to SAS_1.

There will be a short-run aggregate supply curve for each expected price level. The intersection of a particular short-run aggregate supply curve with the long-run aggregate supply curve shows the expected price level of that short-run curve. This is illustrated in Figure 23.

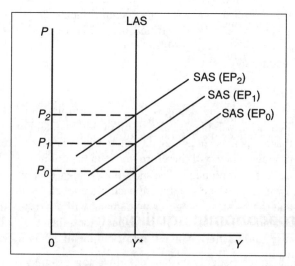

Figure 23: A short-run aggregate supply curve corresponds to each expected price level. The price level expected is determined by the intersection of each SAS with the LAS.

Figure 23 shows the long-run aggregate supply curve and three short-run aggregate supply curves. Each curve corresponds to different price level expectations. For example, the short-run aggregate supply curve corresponding to an expected price level of P_0, SAS(EP_0), intersects the LAS at a price level of P_0. If higher prices are expected then the short-run curve shifts up to SAS(EP_1) which intersects the LAS at P_1.

The issue of expectations is extremely important in macroeconomics and we explore this topic in more detail later in this unit.

Having examined the different theories of aggregate supply, we now turn to the issue of macroeconomic equilibrium in an aggregate demand and supply framework.

ACTIVITY 7

Explain the term **natural rate of unemployment** in approximately 150 words.

The natural rate of unemployment is the rate of unemployment that the economy settles at in the absence of government attempts to influence aggregate demand. The natural rate of unemployment corresponds to that output level where money wages have fully adjusted to changes in prices. We can also say that at this output level, expected prices equal actual prices.

The natural rate of unemployment may be made up of frictional unemployment, that is individuals who are 'between jobs', and any unemployment that arises from minimum wage legislation, trade union behaviour or the nature of the benefit system. Attempts to reduce the natural rate of unemployment, and therefore raise the long-run aggregate supply, tend to involve supply side reforms such as the abolition of minimum wages, trade union reform or a reduction of benefit levels.

2.4 Macroeconomic equilibrium

Having studied aggregate supply in some detail we now examine **macroeconomic equilibrium**. Figure 24 shows our long- and short-run aggregate supply curves and the aggregate demand curve *AD*.

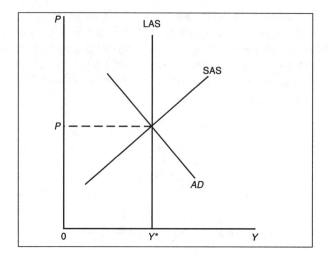

Figure 24: Macroeconomic equilibrium is achieved at Y*
where unemployment is at the natural rate

The intersection of *AD* and the short-run aggregate supply curve, SAS occurs on the long-run aggregate supply curve, LAS. The amount of output, *Y** is achieved and the price level is *P*. This is known as **full employment equilibrium**. Although this suggests that there is no unemployment at this level of income there may be some frictional unemployment or unemployment arising from labour market imperfections such as minimum wages. You may find it less confusing therefore to think of *Y** as the **natural rate of unemployment equilibrium**.

A different scenario is depicted in Figure 25. Here the intersection of *AD* and SAS generates a level of output of Y_1 which is below *Y**. The horizontal distance, $Y_1 - Y^*$, reflects the presence of a **deflationary gap**. Remember we looked at deflationary gaps in Unit 7. Unemployment is above the natural rate and the price level P_1, is now lower than it was in Figure 24.

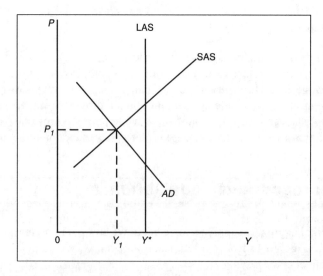

Figure 25: Macroeconomic equilibrium is achieved at Y_1. Y_1 is
below Y* so that unemployment is above the natural rate.

Finally, we show the opposite case in Figure 26 where the level of output is above that which generates the natural rate of unemployment. The intersection of AD and SAS results in an output level Y_2. The horizontal distance $Y^* - Y_2$ reflects the presence of an **inflationary gap**. Unemployment is below the natural rate. This puts upward pressure on prices which rise to P_2.

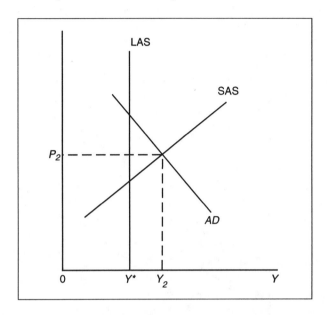

Figure 26: Macroeconomic equilibrium is achieved at Y_2. Y_2 is above Y^* so that unemployment is below the natural rate.

CHANGES IN AGGREGATE DEMAND AND AGGREGATE SUPPLY

We have seen in the last three figures, some examples of different equilibria. We now look at how the economy moves from one equilibrium position to another following changes in aggregate demand or aggregate supply. We start with aggregate demand and consider the effect of a decrease in aggregate demand and an increase in aggregate demand in turn.

Decrease in aggregate demand

Figure 27 shows the long-run aggregate supply curve LAS and the short-run aggregate supply curve SAS. The aggregate demand curve AD is shown. Let us start from an initial position where equilibrium is achieved at a level of output that generates the natural rate of unemployment. This is point A. If the government raises taxation then this will reduce aggregate demand. The aggregate demand curve AD curve will shift to AD_1. Equilibrium is now achieved at point B: Output falls from Y^* to Y_1. Prices fall from P_0 to P_1.

What happens next? Firstly, as prices have fallen then real wages have risen. Hence, firms will hire less labour so that the reduction in output is associated with an increase in unemployment above the natural rate. If money wages do not fall to restore real wages at the previous level then this unemployment will persist and the economy will be stuck in recession. However, if money wages do fall to restore the previous real wage then firms costs will fall and this will cause the short-run aggregate supply curve to shift from SAS to SAS_1. Because money wages fully adjust then the new equilibrium will be restored at $Y*$ on the long-run aggregate supply curve. Prices fall to P_2 and final equilibrium occurs at point C.

Clearly therefore, the response of money wages to changes in the price level is crucial. If they adjust fully then the level of output is not adversely affected by the reduction in aggregate demand ; however if they are 'sticky' then the economy will suffer from unemployment and a low level of output. In other words the economy will enter a recession

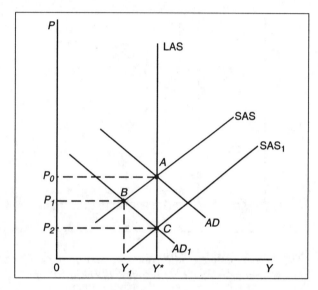

Figure 27: Decrease in aggregate demand: output falls, price level falls.

Now we have looked at the effect of a decrease in aggregate demand we consider the effect of an increase in aggregate demand.

Increase in aggregate demand

Figure 28 depicts our initial position A once again. What happens if aggregate demand increases to AD_1? The economy now experiences rising prices and output rises to Y_2. The economy experiences 'demand pull' inflation. Equilibrium occurs at point B. Higher prices means that real wages have fallen so that firms demand more labour and unemployment falls. If money wages do not rise to restore real wages to the previous level then the economy will be in a boom period. However, if money wages do rise to offset the price increase then the short run aggregate supply curve will shift up to SAS_1 as firms' costs rise. Equilibrium will be restored at point C with output $Y*$ but prices at a higher level P_2.

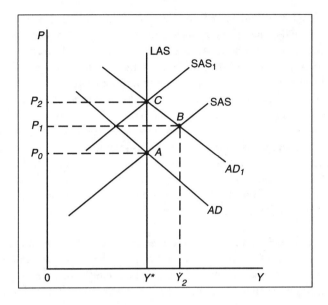

Figure 28: Increase in aggregate demand.

Let us now consider how expectations might affect our analysis. In particular we will see how stagflation can occur. You remember that stagflation is simultaneous unemployment and inflation

EXPECTATIONS AND STAGFLATION

Figure 29 shows our familiar situation. The economy is at point A. Output is Y_1 below Y^* so that unemployment is above the natural rate.

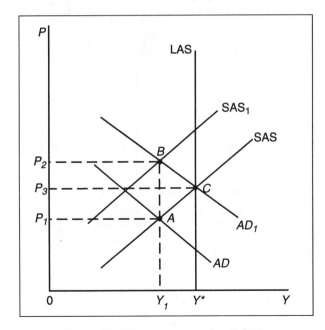

Figure 29: Expectations and stagflation

The government may now seek to reduce unemployment and increase output by raising aggregate demand. If the government cuts taxes and increases spending then aggregate demand may rise to AD_1. However, unions and workers may expect higher prices as a result and start to demand higher money wages. The aggregate supply curve shifts to SAS_1. The increase in money wages offsets the increase in prices so that real wages are unchanged. Firms do not hire more labour and the level of output is unchanged. The economy goes to point B. The effect of the increase in aggregate demand is simply higher prices. This analysis demonstrates how **stagflation**, simultaneous rising prices and unemployment, can occur. Clearly, expectations are vital. If unions and workers had not expected higher prices then they would have not demanded higher money wages and the SAS curve would not have shifted. The economy would have gone to point C. Output would have risen to Y^* and prices would have risen to P_3.

The government can never effectively measure the state of expectations in the economy so it cannot be sure of the effect of its policy on output and prices. This is one of the reasons that monetarists criticise demand management policy. They argue that it has unpredictable effects and is therefore potentially destabilising.

ACTIVITY 8

An economy is in equilibrium with unemployment at the natural rate, so that $Y = Y^*$. Draw a diagram to illustrate this situation. Now assume that the government wants to lower the price level and decides to reduce aggregate demand. Show the effects of this on your diagram if unions and workers expect lower prices; and if unions and workers do *not* expect lower prices

---

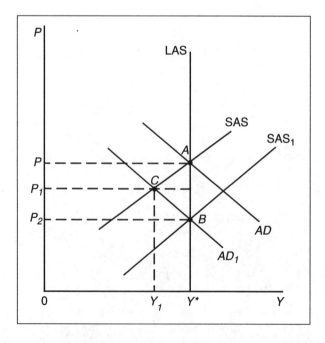

Figure 30: Macroeconomic equilibrium with unemployment at the natural state, with effects of reducing aggregate demand.

Figure 30 shows the economy at position A on the long-run aggregate supply curve. If the government tries to reduce the price level by cutting aggregate demand then AD goes to AD_1.

If unions and workers expect lower prices then the short-run aggregate supply curve SAS will shift to the right, SAS_1. Equilibrium is achieved at point B. Output remains at Y^* and the price level falls to P_2.

If unions and workers do not expect lower prices then the short-run aggregate supply curve SAS will not shift. The reduction in aggregate demand will mean that equilibrium will be achieved at point C. Output falls below Y^* so that unemployment rises above the natural rate. The price level is P_1.

Your figure should look something like Figure 30. Questions like this are useful for you because they are a good test of whether you have understood the text. If your answer is not correct then do not panic, the topic is tricky if it is new to you. Come back to the exercise and try it again later.

WAGE-PRICE SPIRAL

We have examined some of the consequences of changes in aggregate demand. However, aggregate supply may also change, for example, if the price of raw materials changes. This can lead to a **wage price spiral**. Consider Figure 31. The economy is at point A. Output is Y^* and prices are P_0

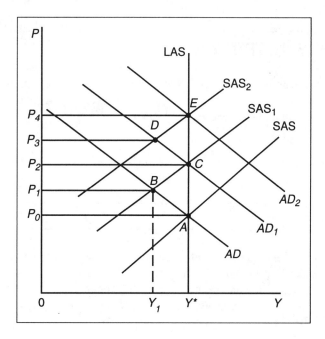

Figure 31: Wage-price spiral

Now consider the effect of a change in short-run aggregate supply. Suppose the price of raw materials rises sharply which raises firms' costs. This situation arose in the UK in 1973. At that time, the UK was an oil importer so that higher oil prices meant higher costs. Firms will now want to produce less at each price level. How will this affect the short-run aggregate supply?

The short-run aggregate supply curve will shift up from SAS to SAS_1. The economy will move to point B and enter a period of stagflation. Prices rise to P_1 and output falls to Y_1 so that unemployment starts to rise. This is an example of 'cost push' inflation that we became familiar with in Unit 8.

What will happen if the government responds by trying to raise aggregate demand in order to reduce unemployment? The aggregate demand curve shifts to AD_1 and the economy goes to point C. Output rises to Y^* and prices rise to P_2. However, workers realise that this is going to raise prices even more so that real wages will fall. Therefore they start to demand higher money wages to compensate. The short-run aggregate supply curve shifts up further to SAS_2. The economy goes to D. Output starts to fall again towards Y_1 and prices rise further to P . Once again the government may try to expand demand to AD_3 which will take the economy to point E with output at Y^* and prices even higher at P_4. Once again, higher prices will encourage workers to demand higher money wages and the short-run aggregate supply curve will drift up further.

What we have described here is a **wage-price spiral**. Our analysis shows approximately what happened to the UK economy in the period after the 1973 oil shock.

REVIEW ACTIVITY 2

Assume an economy is in equilibrium with output at the natural rate of unemployment equilibrium. Show the effect of a decrease in the money supply that is expected; and unexpected.

Summary

Having examined aggregate demand and supply and looked at the effects of changes in aggregate demand and supply, in the next section, we look at the effect of changes in aggregate demand from a slightly different perspective. Essentially we are looking at the same problem using slightly different tools. The main tool we will use is the **Phillips curve**.

SECTION THREE

The Phillips Curve

Introduction

In Unit 7, we saw that in Keynesian theory, unemployment and inflation are effectively opposites, that is, unemployment arises from a deficiency of demand and inflation from too much demand. This implies that, to some extent, unemployment and inflation can be traded off against one another. In other words, a government can expand demand to eliminate unemployment as long as it is prepared to accept a rise in inflation. Conversely, a government can reduce demand to lower inflation but this will be achieved at the expense of higher unemployment.

In 1958, Professor A W Phillips (1914–1975) published the results of his research which suggested that money wage rates rise faster when unemployment is at low levels. Phillips used data from the UK for the period 1861–1957. By plotting the data, Phillips concluded that there was an inverse relationship between changes in money wages and the level of unemployment.

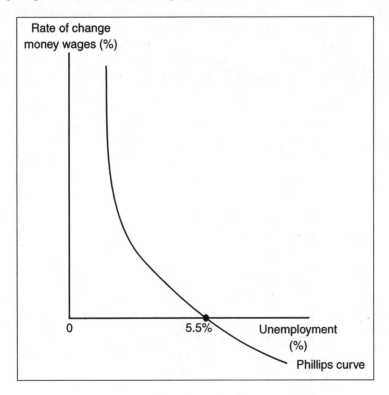

Figure 32: A typical Phillips curve depicts an inverse relationship between unemployment and the rate of change in money wages

Figure 32 shows the typical Phillips curve. Simply put, the Phillips curve shows that when unemployment is high, money wages will not be rising very quickly while if unemployment is low, money wages will begin to rise more rapidly. The relationship between the rate of change of money wages and unemployment is such that Phillips estimated that, for the UK, money wages would not change if unemployment was 5.5%. In other words, according to Phillips, money wages would be constant when unemployment was equal to 5.5% of the labour force.

Over the period studied, changes in money wages were generally about 3% higher than the rate of inflation. It was quite clear that there was a direct relationship between the rate of change of money wages and the rate of inflation. Usually, in fact, the Phillips curve is discussed in terms of inflation and unemployment rather than changes in money wages and unemployment.

We now examine the implications of the Phillips curve in terms of the monetarist-Keynesian debate.

3.1 Keynesians and the Phillips curve

The Phillips curve was seen to favour Keynesian analysis. Economists believed that the Phillips curve could be used to advise a government how much inflation would increase if unemployment was to be reduced by a certain percentage. The curve is non-linear. This is important. At low levels of unemployment, attempting to reduce unemployment even further would cause inflation to rise by a much larger amount than a similar reduction at a higher level of unemployment. This point is illustrated in Figure 33.

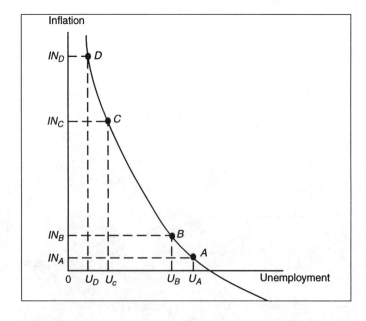

Figure 33: Reductions in unemployment and the Phillips curve

Consider an economy at point A. Unemployment is at a level U_A and inflation is at a level IN_A. Now, if aggregate demand is expanded to reduce unemployment to U_B, then inflation will rise to IN_B. The economy goes to point B. Now consider point C. If the government attempts to reduce unemployment by exactly the same amount as previously from U_C to U_D this will only be achieved with a much higher increase in inflation from IN_C to IN_D.

The Phillips curve was used by Keynesians to justify their theories of inflation. In fact the curve can accommodate both the Keynesian 'demand pull' and 'cost push' theories of inflation.

At low levels of unemployment, national income, output and aggregate demand will be high and this explains rapid increases in prices if the government seeks to reduce unemployment further. Thus the Phillips curve provides support for the **demand pull theory of inflation**.

How can we explain cost push inflation in terms of the Phillips curve? Well at low levels of unemployment trade union power will be high. Why is this? If unemployment is high then unions cannot afford to demand high wage increases as employers will simply recruit from the large pool of available labour who will accept lower wages in order to get jobs. On the other hand, unions will be able to push for higher wage increases at low levels of unemployment as employers will find it difficult to find workers who will accept lower wages. These higher wages raise firms' costs and force them to raise prices to maintain profits. Thus the Phillips curve can be seen in terms of **cost push inflation**.

The Phillips curve suggests that unemployment will only be rising if inflation is falling and inflation will only be rising if unemployment is falling. The two will not rise simultaneously. However, in the 1970s unemployment and inflation began to occur simultaneously in **stagflation**. This could not be explained in terms of the standard Phillips curve unless there was more than one Phillips curve for an economy. Consider Figure 34.

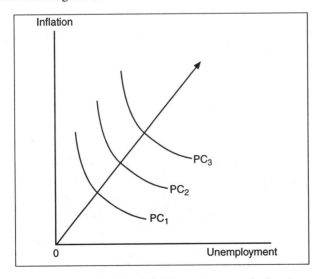

*Figure 34: A family of Phillips curves, each showing
a higher 'unemployment-inflation trade-off'*

Figure 34 shows a 'family' of Phillips curves each showing unemployment and inflation trade-offs at progressively higher levels of each. It could be that the economy was gradually drifting onto higher and higher Phillips curves along a path shown by the arrow. But how would this process occur? Furthermore, why would it occur? The monetarist theory offered an explanation.

ACTIVITY 9

The Phillips curve is a relationship between unemployment and the price level. Is this statement true or false?

The statement is false. The Phillips curve is a relationship between unemployment and the inflation rate. The inflation rate is the percentage **change** in the price level. You should be careful not to mistake inflation for the price level.

3.2 Monetarists and the Phillips curve

Milton Friedman attempted to explain the existence of stagflation in a 1968 paper 'The Role of Monetary Policy'. He argued that any trade-off between unemployment and inflation would exist only in the short run and that in the long run no such trade-off would exist. He thus defined a short-run Phillips curve and a long-run Phillips curve. Each is depicted in Figure 35.

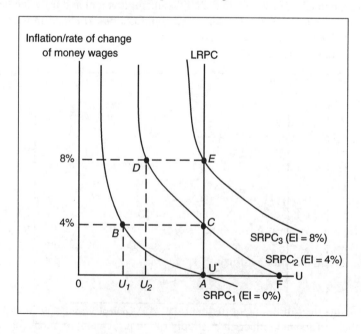

Figure 35: Short-run and long-run Phillips curves and effects of expectations

Figure 35 shows three short-run Phillips curves ($SRPC_1$, $SRPC_2$ and $SRPC_3$) and a long-run Phillips curve (LRPC). Notice that on the vertical axis we have both the rate of inflation and the rate of change of money wages. Each short-run Phillips curve corresponds to a different level of **expected inflation**.

$SRPC_1$ intersects the LRPC along the horizontal axis and therefore corresponds to a zero level of expected inflation. $SRPC_2$ intersects the LRPC at an inflation level of 4% and therefore corresponds to a 4% level of expected inflation. $SRPC_3$ intersects the LRPC at an inflation level of 8% and therefore corresponds to an 8% level of expected inflation.

The long-run Phillips curve shows that, in the long run, no inflation-unemployment trade-off exists. The intersection of LRPC with the horizontal axis defines the natural rate of unemployment, U^*. At this level of unemployment, inflation will not be increasing or decreasing in the absence of government attempts to stimulate aggregate demand. Often therefore the natural rate of unemployment is called the **non-accelerating inflation rate of unemployment** or NAIRU. There is no 'trade-off' along this long-run Phillips curve. The short-run Phillips curves however, show that the trade-off will exist in the short run. You should notice a strong similarity between this analysis and our study of long- and short-run aggregate supply. In many respects, we are conducting the same analysis using Phillips curves.

The key to Friedman's analysis is the way in which **expectations** are formed. Consider the economy at point A. Here unemployment is at the natural rate and the inflation rate is zero. The economy is on the LRPC and $SRPC_1$ which is the short-run Phillips curve corresponding to an expected inflation rate of zero. Firms and employers expect the zero level of inflation to continue. Because the economy is on the LRPC, this position is stable and the economy could stay at this point permanently in the absence of government intervention.

Now let the government try to reduce the level of unemployment by increasing aggregate demand. To do this the government may reduce taxes or raise spending. As we have seen this will almost certainly lead to an increase in the money supply. Initially, the level of unemployment may fall to U_1 and inflation and the rate of change of money wages will rise to, say, 4%. The economy goes to point B. However, according to Friedman, this situation cannot persist indefinitely. The economy is no longer on the LRPC, so this position is unstable.

Workers will only supply more labour if real wages have risen. Initially, they may not realise that both money wages and the price level have risen by 4% so that real wages have not risen at all. In other words, they mistake the 4% rise in money wages as a 4% rise in real wages. This is because they are expecting zero inflation. Economists call this **money illusion**. Therefore workers will be prepared to supply more labour.

This explains the fall in unemployment. However, after a period of time workers realise their errors and reduce their supply of labour. Unemployment starts to rise and continues until the natural rate of unemployment is restored. The economy goes to point C. Unemployment is back at the natural rate but inflation is now 4% higher. The economy is now on a higher short-run Phillips curve SRPC$_2$ which corresponds to an expected inflation rate of 4%. This position is stable and the economy could remain here permanently if the government did not intervene again.

Workers will now expect 4% inflation to continue into the future. Once again, the government may try to expand demand to reduce unemployment. The economy moves from point C to point D. Inflation and the rate of change of money wages rise to 8% while unemployment falls to U_2. This fall in unemployment again results from money illusion. Workers believe that the increase in money wages to 8% is a real wage rise because they continue to expect a 4% level of inflation. However, once again, as the economy is not on the LRPC then the position is unstable. Over time workers realise their money illusion and the economy drifts to point E. Unemployment returns to the natural rate but inflation now runs at 8%. The economy is now on SRPC$_3$ which corresponds to an expected inflation rate of 8%.

ACTIVITY 10

Which of these statements is correct?

When the economy is on the long-run Phillips curve (LRPC):

1 Inflation is accelerating.

2 Unemployment is zero.

3 Unemployment is at the natural rate.

4 Inflation is zero.

---

1   is incorrect. When the economy is on the LRPC the rate of inflation is stable, neither accelerating or decelerating. In fact, when the economy is on the LRPC then the level of unemployment at this output is known as the **non-accelerating inflation rate of unemployment**.

2   is incorrect. Unemployment is at the natural rate. This unemployment is a result of labour market imperfections such as minimum wage legislation or trade union activity.

3   is correct.

4   is incorrect. When the economy is on the LRPC the rate of inflation is neither increasing or decreasing but it is not necessarily equal to zero.

The monetarist theory suggests that the unemployment-inflation trade-off is a short-run phenomenon only. The government can only keep unemployment permanently below the natural rate if they continually expand the money supply to keep inflation at a higher rate than expectations. Notice that inflation expectations in this theory always lag the actual inflation rate by one period before catching up. For example, when the economy is at point *B* the actual rate is 4% but firms and workers expect only zero inflation. Eventually, when expectations catch up then the economy goes to point *C*. Similarly, when the government expands the economy to point *D* then actual inflation of 8% exceeds the expected rate of 4% for a time. Expectations then catch up and the economy goes to point *E*.

Unemployment is only below the natural rate when the actual rate of inflation is above the expected rate. Therefore only by continually increasing the rate of increase of the money supply to keep actual inflation above expected inflation can the government permanently reduce inflation below the natural rate. This would, of course, result eventually in **hyperinflation**, if the government permanently increases the growth rate of the money supply.

Only points that are on the LRPC are stable. Once the economy has reached a certain inflation rate such as point *C* then the only way that the economy can get back to zero inflation is by deflation. In this case, the economy suffers a period of unemployment above the natural rate.

From point *C*, if the government reduced aggregate demand and raised taxes then unemployment would start to rise and prices and money wages would fall. The economy would drift to point *F* where unemployment is well above the natural rate. Although prices are falling, because of money illusion, money wages take time to adjust downwards so that the economy enters a **recession**. During this period of recession the inflation rate falls. Eventually the economy will go back to point *A*.

This analysis of the Phillips curve became known as the **expectations augmented Phillips curve**. In this model, inflation expectations are constantly catching up with the actual inflation rate. Expectations are said to be **adaptive** because they are based on the past behaviour of inflation. The presence of adaptive expectations enables a government to exploit a short-run trade-off between inflation and unemployment. The monetarist theory therefore suggests that increasing the money supply in order to raise aggregate demand will succeed in the short run but in the long run will be ineffective. When changes in the money supply do not influence output and employment, economists say that money is **neutral**. Therefore in this monetarist theory **money is neutral in the long run but not in the short run**.

However, while many monetarists accept Friedman's view, there is little agreement on the amount of time that the expected inflation rate will take to catch up with the actual rate of inflation. Therefore, a money expansion will be characterised by a rise in both output and the rate of inflation, then, after a period of time, output will start to fall again. In Friedman's words, the lags will be 'long and variable'.

ACTIVITY 11

Draw a long-run Phillips curve and a series of short-run Phillips curves for progressively higher levels of expected inflation. Show how a government can only reduce unemployment permanently below the natural rate by progressively accelerating the inflation rate. Carefully indicate the path of the economy on your diagram.

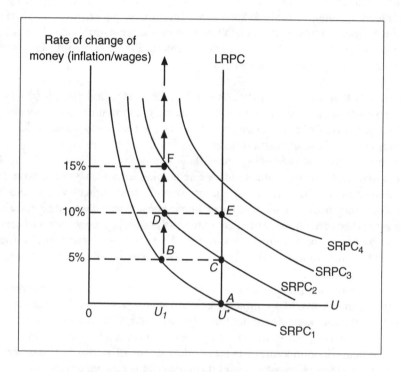

Figure 36: Long-run and short-run Phillips curve for
progressively higher levels of expected inflation

The economy is at point A with unemployment at the natural rate. The expected level of inflation is zero which corresponds to $SRPC_1$. The government expands demand to reduce unemployment to U_1. However, in doing so inflation accelerates to say, 5%. The economy goes to point B on $SRPC_1$. Actual inflation (5%) exceeds expected inflation (zero). Workers and firms suffer money illusion and output rises and unemployment falls. However when expectations catch up, then the economy will start to drift towards point C. To prevent this the money supply is expanded further to take the economy to point D with an actual rate of inflation of 10%. The level of unemployment remains at U_1. Actual inflation of 10% exceeds the expected level of 5% and generates money illusion. Once again if expectations catch up then the economy will go to point E so the government expands the money supply to take the economy to point F where inflation is 15%. The process continues. The path of the economy from A is shown by the line of arrows. The only way unemployment can be permanently reduced below the natural rate is to create higher and higher inflation.

NEW CLASSICAL THEORY

The monetarist theory rose to prominence and had a great influence on UK government economic policy from 1979. Keynesian theory went into decline. However, there were a group of monetarist economists in the USA who took an even more extreme view than Friedman. These economists were termed **new classicals**.

New classical economists argued that expectations were not adaptive but **rational.** Friedman's version of events suggested that workers and firms could be continually 'fooled' in the short run. By increasing the money supply so that actual inflation would be higher than expected inflation, then unemployment could temporarily be reduced below the natural rate. Money illusion would occur each time the government tried to reduce unemployment. The new classical economists argued that firms and workers would not suffer persistent money illusion. The government may be able to fool them once but they would not be able to do so continually. Firms and workers would learn from their past mistakes. Therefore over time if the government persistently tried to reduce unemployment below the natural rate then firms and workers would immediately expect higher inflation. Workers would not be prepared to supply more labour because they know that real wages will not be increasing and firms will not hire more labour because they know that real wages have not fallen. Hence the effect of attempts to stimulate aggregate demand by raising the money supply are simply to raise inflation immediately. **There would be no effect on unemployment and no effect on output even in the short run. Money is neutral in the short run and the long run**. In terms of Figure 35 if the economy was at point A and the government cut tax rates and increased spending then the economy would go immediately to C. If the government tried the policy again then the economy would go directly to E.

New classical economists argue that the Phillips 'curve' is a vertical line running through the natural rate of unemployment. The new classical theory has implications for governments seeking to reduce inflation. Consider Figure 37. The long-run Phillips curve, LRPC and two short-run Phillips curves are shown. $SRPC_1$ corresponds to a zero level of expected inflation and $SRPC_2$ to a 6% level of expected inflation.

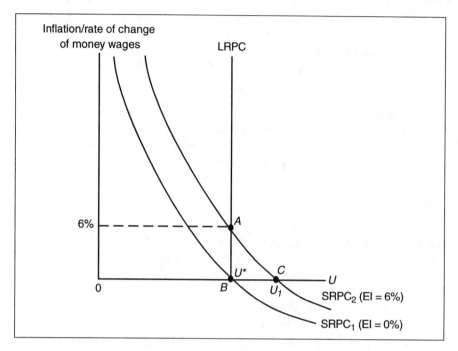

Figure 37: Neo-classical view of the Phillips curve as a vertical line running through the natural rate of unemployment

Assume the economy is at point *A*. Unemployment is at the natural rate and inflation is 6%. Expected inflation is 6%. The economy is on $SRPC_2$ which corresponds to this expected inflation rate of 6%. Now if the government announces plans to reduce aggregate demand so that inflation returns to zero then one of two scenarios could occur.

In the first scenario, if expectations are rational and firms and workers believe the government then they expect zero inflation immediately so they are prepared to accept lower money wages than they would otherwise. Expected inflation is now zero in view of the government announcement. The short-run Phillips curve corresponding to expected inflation of zero is $SRPC_1$. The economy immediately moves from *A* to *B*. Inflation is reduced and no change in unemployment occurs.

However, a second scenario might arise. What if firms and workers do not believe the government announcement? In the past, the government may have lacked monetary discipline and have a poor inflationary record. Firms and workers may not believe that the government announcement is **credible**. They continue to expect 6% inflation and do not lower wage demands.

If the government then reduces aggregate demand and cuts the money supply, the economy does not go onto the lower short-run Phillips curve $SRPC_1$. Instead it drifts to point *C* on $SRPC_2$. Inflation falls towards zero but unemployment rises to U_1 above the natural rate. Workers continue to demand higher money wages because they expect inflation to continue rising at a rate of 6%. However, because the money supply has been reduced, inflation starts to fall below 6%. As a result, real wages rise and firms are forced to make workers redundant.

This analysis is useful in considering the recession in the UK in the period after 1979. The UK economy was suffering from relatively high inflation, though unemployment was approximately at the natural rate. The new government tried to reduce inflation by cutting the money supply. It announced these plans in advance in the **medium term financial strategy** (MTFS). Theoretically firms and workers would expect lower inflation in line with the reduction in the money supply. Aggregate demand would be reduced and the economy would settle at a lower inflation rate with no change in output and unemployment.

In fact this did not happen. When aggregate demand was reduced, expectations did not adjust. Workers and firms continued to expect higher prices. Inflation did start to fall but only after output had been massively reduced and unemployment had risen dramatically. Expectations proved to be adaptive. People continued to expect higher inflation. This was because the government announcements lacked **credibility**.

Workers and firms were used to high inflation. They did not take the government announcement seriously. In the early 1970s, the Conservative government led by Edward Heath had also announced that it would try to reduce inflation but when unemployment started to rise as a result of the reduction in aggregate demand it had reversed its policy. This experience led people to regard announcements such as that of the MTFS with little confidence even though Mrs Thatcher had promised 'no U-turns'.

The reduction in aggregate demand occurred over a period of time so that unemployment climbed gradually. By 1981, the economy was in the depths of a serious recession yet aggregate demand was cut further in the budget of that year. Why was this? Almost certainly because despite the massive cuts in aggregate demand up to that point, money supply targets had been missed, so to prove credibility, aggregate demand had to be cut further to bring the money supply under control.

Effectively, the government led the economy into a serious recession in order to show how serious it was about reducing inflation. This approach was encouraged by the government economic advisers of the time, the most influential of whom was Patrick Minford, a confirmed new classical economist.

Under the assumption of adaptive expectations a deep recession was inevitable because expectations always lag actual events by one period. To avoid the recession the government made policy announcements to encourage expectations to adjust quickly but this failed because of lack of credibility.

However, it is certain that, although the government expected output to fall and unemployment to rise, they vastly underestimated by how much.

". . . the experience has been chastening. Though some of us did expect the implementation of a monetary strategy designed finally to bring the great inflation of the 1970s to an end to have significant adverse effects, none of us expected the deep and prolonged depression that ensued."

David Laidler, UK monetarist economist, *Oxford Review of Economic Policy* (1985).

ACTIVITY 12

Explain clearly, using a diagram, exactly why, under rational expectations, governments cannot permanently reduce unemployment below the natural rate. You may need about fifteen minutes or so to do this activity.

Under **adaptive expectations**, firm's and worker's expectations of inflation constantly lag behind the actual inflation rate which results in money illusion. Eventually expectations catch up. But firms and workers do not 'learn' from their mistakes. They can be continually fooled by governments.

Under **rational expectations**, firms and workers do learn. The government may be able to fool them once but will not be able to do so continually. Under rational expectations workers and firms learn from errors they made. They realise they have been 'surprised' by the government policy and will not be fooled again.

Therefore if expectations are formed rationally, the government can only expand output and unemployment by increasing the money supply if it is a 'surprise'. If the increase in the money supply is fully expected then the short-run Phillips curve will shift upwards and to the right and only the price level will change.

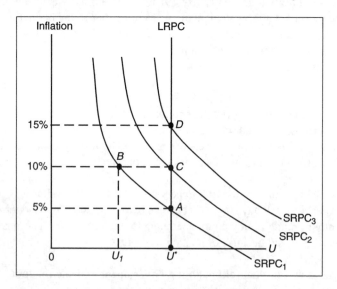

Figure 38: Reducing unemployment

Consider our Figure 38. The economy is at point A on $SRPC_1$. Unemployment is at the natural rate and the inflation rate is 5%. If the government unexpectedly raises aggregate demand then output and inflation may rise and unemployment will fall to U_1. The economy will go to point B. The rate of inflation is now 10%. However, firms and workers will soon realise they have suffered money illusion and the economy will return to the LRPC at point C on the higher short-run Phillips curve $SRPC_2$. The government will be unable to achieve such an increase in output again in this way. If it tries to expand demand again, workers will simply expect higher inflation and the curve $SRPC_2$ will shift up to $SRPC_3$. Money wages will rise immediately to offset the higher price level. Real wages will be unchanged and there will be no change in output or unemployment. The economy will go straight to point D. Inflation would increase to 15%

The lesson of rational expectations is that only **unexpected** increases in aggregate demand via increases in the money supply can affect output and unemployment. If the increase in demand is expected then output is unaffected. This directly contradicts Keynesian theory. If output is low and unemployment high then Keynesians argue for an increase in aggregate demand. On the other hand, if the economy is experiencing a boom then Keynesians argue for a decline in aggregate demand. The problem is that rational individuals will anticipate the government policy in advance. Economic data is widely available and reported in the financial pages of the quality papers. If output is falling and unemployment rising then people expect an increase in demand, if output is rising and unemployment falling then people expect a reduction in demand.

We have made a clear distinction between the monetarists led by Friedman and the new classical economists. However, both believe in **classical dichotomy** which states that money affects only monetary variables such as the price level and does not affect real variables such as output or employment. The key difference is that new classicals believe that expectations are not adaptive but rational. This means that the money supply will have no effect on real variables even in the short run while monetarists believe that a short run effect may be present.

Both types of economist argue that the only **permanent** way to reduce unemployment is by attempting to reduce the natural rate which can be achieved by a series of labour market reforms such as benefit reforms, the abolition of minimum wage legislation and improvements in institutions that match workers to jobs such as job centres. Collectively, these measures are known as **supply side reforms**. Macroeconomic policy should simply seek to control the money supply in order to maintain low inflation. Governments should seek to balance budgets and not use deficit financing to influence aggregate demand. Both argue that discretionary demand management should be avoided because of the inflationary consequences.

3.3 Supply side policy

Supply side policy as you might expect is designed to improve the supply side of the economy. There are a number of policies that may come under this heading. We will mainly consider the supply side policies that were followed by the Conservative government of 1979. The reason for this is that before 1979, supply side policy was given a role secondary to that of demand management. Governments in the post-war period relied on two main types of supply side policy: **investment incentives** and **incomes policies**.

INVESTMENT INCENTIVES

As a key component of aggregate demand, the government was keen to stimulate investment where possible. This meant offering tax incentives to encourage firms to invest. We do not need to worry about these in any detail. The main point is that firms investing in new plant and machinery paid less taxation for a period of time.

INCOMES POLICIES

We have seen from our study of the Phillips curve that the government in the 1950s and 1960s believed that unemployment and inflation could be 'traded-off', in other words, the government could expand demand to lower unemployment at the expense of higher inflation.

Often the government tried to use incomes policies to keep inflation down. This meant imposing a limit on pay increases, after agreement with the unions. The intention was to prevent inflation rising whenever the government tried to reduce unemployment by expanding aggregate demand. Unfortunately, in this period these policies tended to work only for a short period of time. The government could only impose effective restraints on public sector workers. Eventually public sector trade unions would see private sector workers getting higher wage increases because they were not subject to the government imposed limit. Public sector unions would go on strike to get higher money wages. Eventually, unions would compete with each other in their wage bargaining and the policy would disintegrate. This is exactly what happened at the end of 1978 in what became known as the 'winter of discontent'. Unions had gone along with the Labour government incomes policy for a period of time but as inflation increased they went on strike to protect real wages. The UK was paralysed by a series of strikes and many believe that the whole affair played an important part in the defeat of the Labour Party in the 1979 general election.

The new Conservative government abandoned incomes policies. Monetarists are committed to allowing the market mechanism to work. Incomes policies are, of course, a direct attempt to override the market mechanism. An expansion of aggregate demand would raise the price level so that real wages would fall. This was because the government restricted increases in money wages. Lower real wages would result in excess demand for labour and in the absence of intervention, money wages would rise until the real wage was back at the equilibrium level. The incomes policy prevented this happening.

This interference with the market was in direct contradiction with the philosophy of the new government which was to allow the labour market to move freely. The new government argued that monetary discipline was the way to control inflation and in line with monetarist philosophy did not believe that unemployment could be permanently reduced by demand management policy. The only way to reduce unemployment permanently was to reduce the natural rate of unemployment and therefore raise the long-run aggregate supply of the economy. Therefore, the new government embarked on a series of labour market reforms designed to remove 'imperfections'.

The philosophy of the Conservative government is contained in the following statement by Patrick Minford one of the key government advisers of the time.

"The labour market is just like any other market except that it is the most interfered with market we've got in the economy. First, there are minimum wages. Secondly, there are unions that restrict the supply of labour in very many areas of the economy. Thirdly, the government sets a minimum social wage in the form of social security benefits ... These things constitute massive interference in the market.

Unemployment is a response to the interaction of supply forces and basic demand forces . . . the way to get unemployment down ... is to tackle the underlying causes of the market distortion ... to get at the reasons why wages will not fall to levels at which labour will be more competitive ... If you try and stimulate demand by engineering a rise in public expenditure, you will not have changed the underlying situation ... Unemployment will go back up."

(Source: *Open University Series on Unemployment*)

LABOUR MARKET REFORMS
Broadly speaking labour market reforms can be classified under three headings: **trade union reform, removal of minimum wages** and **benefit and tax reform**.

Trade union reform
We saw in Section 1 how trade unions can restrict the quantity of labour and therefore raise real wages. The effect of this restriction means that non members of unions are unable to find certain jobs and are therefore unemployed. By reducing unions' power so that they cannot restrict the quantity of labour then any unemployment that results from union behaviour will be reduced

Removal of minimum wages
We saw earlier that minimum wage legislation can create unemployment because invariably minimum wages are set at a level above that which equates the demand with the supply of labour. Unemployment results. By removing this legislation then this unemployment can be eliminated.

Benefit and tax reform
Reforms under this headings are designed to improve the incentives of unemployed workers to take jobs. Monetarists argue that if the difference between the level of unemployment benefit available and the average level of wages is too low then some may decide that they are 'better off' remaining unemployed. One way to solve this **poverty trap** is to cut unemployment benefit. The effect of this is shown in Figure 39.

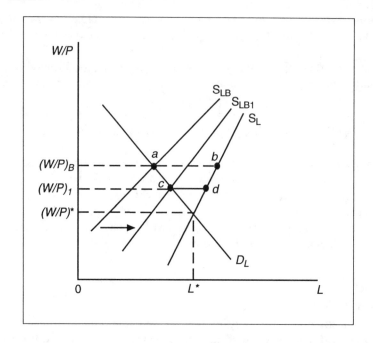

Figure 39: Reducing unemployment benefit reduces the number unemployed as a result of 'disincentives' from ab to cd

Recall from Figure 11, that we have the labour demand curve D_L and two labour supply curves. The curve S_L is the labour supply curve in the absence of unemployment benefit. These two curves determine the equilibrium quantity of labour demanded, L^* and the equilibrium real wage, $(W/P)^*$. The curve S_{LB} shows the effective labour supply curve in the presence of unemployment benefit. Benefit reduces the amount of labour supplied at each real wage and this is more pronounced at lower wages so that S_{LB} is not parallel to S_L. The lower the real wage the greater the reduction in the number of individuals willing to take jobs. Obviously, at higher real wages this disincentive effect is reduced so that the effect on the labour supply is smaller.

The effect of unemployment benefit is to reduce the amount of labour supplied and to raise the real wage to $(W/P)_B$. The amount of unemployment created is shown as the horizontal distance ab. A reduction in unemployment benefit would cause S_{LB} to shift because it would increase the incentive to work. S_{LB} shifts to the right to S_{LB1}. The equilibrium real wage falls to $(W/P)_1$ and the quantity of unemployment falls. The new lower level of unemployment is measured by the horizontal distance cd.

This is, however, a drastic solution to the problem of unemployment. There is no reliable evidence to indicate that welfare benefits have a large disincentive effect. Furthermore, as technology progresses over time many workers may find that their skills become obsolete and they may find it very difficult to find new employment. These policies would be very hard on these workers. After 1979, the gap between average real wages and benefit levels did grow but unemployment did not fall as predicted.

At the same time as reforming the benefit system, another suggested measure was to cut income taxes to encourage unemployed workers to take jobs. Obviously, an unemployed worker is more likely to take a job if his 'take home' pay is higher. This policy would reinforce the benefit reforms and would be most effective if tax rates were reduced for the low paid to help eliminate the poverty trap. The Conservative administration did reduce income taxes dramatically but did not concentrate on the tax rate paid by low paid workers so it is debatable whether the poverty trap was reduced. Of course, reductions in income taxes are also designed to improve the incentives of those already in jobs and make them more productive and encourage them to work longer hours. Therefore this policy should be seen from the wider perspective of improving the efficiency of the supply side rather than just seeking to reduce unemployment.

REVIEW ACTIVITY 3

Assume an economy with output at Y^* and unemployment at the natural rate. The price level is quite high. Show how a reduction in aggregate demand, coupled with supply side reform which improves work incentives and abolishes minimum wages can reduce inflation without causing a recession.

Before you attempt this question you may find it useful to look back at our examination of long-run and short-run aggregate supply in Section 2.

If you find this activity difficult then use the following hints. Read hint 1 and then try to answer the question. If you still have a problem then read hint 2 .

Hint 1   Remember that supply side policy will shift the short- and long-run aggregate supply schedules to the right.

Hint 2   If you are still having difficulty then show the reduction in aggregate demand on your diagram. Then look at the actual price level (where the aggregate demand curve cuts the short-run aggregate supply curve) and compare this with the expected price level (where the short-run aggregate supply curve cuts the long-run aggregate supply curve). If the expected price level is not equal to the actual price level then this will cause the short-run aggregate supply curve to shift.

Summary

The benefit of supply side policy should be clear to you. Prices can be reduced without the need for recession. Furthermore output can be raised in the long term, and unemployment reduced, without the need for demand management policy.

However, you should be notice that despite the commitment to supply side reform, unemployment rose steadily from 1979 to a peak in 1986. Much of this was due to the collapse in aggregate demand during this period. The recession had serious effects on the supply side of the economy. Many workers became long-term unemployed and their skills became obsolete. Much of the industrial capacity of the economy was eroded. Therefore when demand was expanded near the end of the 1980s, the economy could not fully satisfy this with the result that the external balance went sharply into deficit. This naturally placed great limitations on the potential growth of the economy.

On a positive note, labour productivity was considerably higher in the 1980s than in the previous two decades though this may be as a result of technological advancements rather than any supply side policy.

The Conservative government was elected in 1979. Economic policy stood on two pillars. Macroeconomic policy would be directed to the control of the money supply in order to reduce inflation. Fiscal policy would be adjusted in line with this objective. In other words, discretionary fiscal policy was to be abandoned in favour of balancing the budget. Microeconomic policy would focus on the supply side and a series of reforms was put in place to improve the efficiency of the supply side.

Though Margaret Thatcher was replaced by John Major in 1990, low inflation remains the central objective of Conservative macroeconomic policy although strict control of the money supply was abandoned in the mid-1980s. The government remains committed to improving the supply side of the economy particularly by improving incentives via the tax system.

We have now completed our studies of macroeconomics within a 'closed' economy and we now consider the external sector. To a large extent we have avoided considering issues such as exchange rates, devaluations and depreciations. However, these issues are extremely important and any government must seek not only to influence internal objectives such as inflation or unemployment, but must also operate within an international context. This is our subject in Unit 10.

Unit Review Activity

Read Resource Item 9.1 'A cruise around the Phillips curve', *The Economist*, February 19, 1994. Answer the following questions.

1   Why does the author suggest that the Phillips curve worked well in earlier years?

2   What sort of issues, according to the article, will affect the natural rate of unemployment?

3   What is the 'sacrifice ratio'?

4   How important is government credibility in affecting the sacrifice ratio?

Unit Summary

In Section 1, we studied the Keynesian and classical theories of aggregate supply and we saw that the key distinction between the two theories lies in the treatment of money wages. In the classical model, money wages are perfectly flexible so that any change in price is offset by a change in money wages. Real wages and therefore labour demand, output and employment are unaffected by price changes. In the Keynesian model, money wages are only flexible upwards. If price falls then money wages will not fall so that real wages rise. This leads to a reduction in the quantity of labour employed and the level of output and employment.

In Section 2, we examined the distinction between short-run and long-run aggregate supply and we looked at the factors that cause shifts in the short- run aggregate supply curve in particular. We also looked at the effect of changes in aggregate demand and short-run aggregate supply.

In Section 3, we introduced the Phillips curve as an apparent relationship between the level of unemployment and the rate of change of money wages (or inflation). We then introduced the monetarist expectations-augmented Phillips curve and saw that changes in the money supply affect the price level but only temporarily affect the level of output and employment. Finally, we looked at new classical theory where changes in the money supply directly affected prices but had no effect on output or employment even in the short term.

References

Laidler, D, (1985), *Monetary Policy in Britain – Success and Shortcomings,* Oxford Review of Economic Policy

Friedman, M, (1968), *The Role of Monetary Policy*, American Economic Review

Minford, APL, (1990), Open University Series on Unemployment

Phillips, AW, (1958), *The Relationship between unemployment and the rate of change of money wage rates in the United Kingdom 1861–1957,* Economica

Answers to Review Activities

Review Activity 1

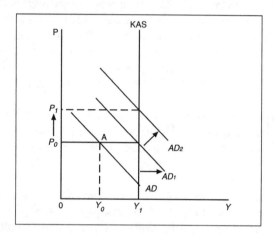

Figure 40: Keynesian model

If money is neutral then changes in the money supply affect only prices and not output or employment levels. In the Keynesian model, money is not neutral if there is unemployment. In this case, the economy will be on the horizontal section of the aggregate supply curve, such as point A in the figure. Increases in the money supply shift the aggregate demand curve and output rises from Y_0 to Y_1 as shown. Prices do not rise. However, when full employment is reached, further increases in the money supply affect only prices so that now money is neutral. Prices rise to P_1 from P_0 but output is unaffected.

Review Activity 2

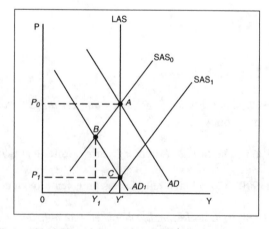

Figure 41: Macroeconomic equilibrium with expected and unexpected money supply

Figure 41 illustrates both cases of expected and unexpected money supply. The economy is at point A. The reduction in the money supply reduces aggregate demand from AD to AD_1. If this decrease in the money supply is fully expected then everyone will expect lower prices to result so that money wages fall to maintain the real wage. In this case, the economy goes straight to point C. The lower money wages lower firms' costs so that the short-run aggregate supply curve shifts down to SAS_1. Output and employment are not affected but the price level falls to P_1.

On the other hand, if the reduction is not expected then money wages do not fall immediately to offset the drop in prices. Real wages have risen. Firms demand less labour so that output falls to Y_1 and unemployment will rise above the natural rate. The economy goes to point B. Now if trade unions and workers resist money wage cuts then this situation may persist. But if money wages are flexible then as they fall the demand for labour rises and output rises again as the economy goes to point C.

Review Activity 3

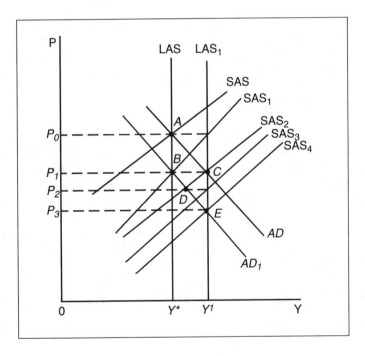

Figure 42: Reducing inflation without causing a recession

Figure 42 shows the economy at point A. The price level is P_0. The supply side reform raises the long-run potential of the economy and causes the long-run supply curve to shift from Y^* to Y^*_1. Recall that the short-run aggregate supply curve also shifts from SAS to SAS_1. The reduction in aggregate demand takes the economy to point B. Output is now below the long-run potential but has not fallen from its initial level, Y^*. Prices have fallen to P_1.

Notice that the economy is at point B on SAS_1. SAS_1 cuts the new long-run aggregate supply curve at a price level of P_0. The expected price level is therefore P_0 but the actual price level is P_1. As expectations catch up with the actual level then SAS_1 shifts down to SAS_2 and cuts the long-run aggregate supply curve at point C. We can see that at this point the expected price level is P_1. The economy, however goes to point D where AD_1 cuts SAS_2. The expected price level is P_1 but the actual price level is clearly lower at P_2. Once again expectations adjust downwards. Eventually the economy settles at point E on SAS_4 with output at $Y*_1$.

Unit Review Activity

1   The author believes that the Phillips curve worked well for a while because inflation was low and relatively stable so that expectations of inflation tended to be close to actual inflation. When inflation became more volatile then expectations were affected so that the 'stable' relationship between unemployment and inflation broke down.

2   The natural rate of unemployment will be affected by generous unemployment benefits, minimum wage legislation, poor education and training, and other obstacles to labour mobility such as lack of information for job seekers, or lack of rentable accommodation. We don't mention this last factor in our unit. The more geographically mobile the labour force is then the lower the natural rate of unemployment.

3   The 'sacrifice ratio' is the relationship between reductions in inflation and the increase in unemployment needed to achieve that reduction. For example, country A may be able to reduce inflation by 5% but at the expense of a 3% rise in unemployment. Country B may have to raise unemployment by 6% to achieve an equal reduction in inflation. Country B has the higher sacrifice ratio.

4   The more credible is the government then the lower the sacrifice ratio. If a government announces an intention to reduce inflation from say 10% to 5% and the announcement is believed then immediately money wages will fall in the expectation of lower prices. Real wages do not change. Output and unemployment do not change and prices fall. If the government lacks credibility then money wages will not adjust so that when prices fall the real wage rises. Firms demand less labour and output falls and unemployment rise as prices fall.

UNIT 10
INTERNATIONAL TRADE

Introduction

So far in your studies of economics, with a few exceptions, you have assumed that an economy exists in isolation. In this unit we will discover the advantages of trading with other nations and examine the trading patterns of the UK.

We will also analyse how such international transactions are priced and recorded. In particular, we will examine the exchange rate, the various ways in which it is quoted and how it can be used to compare the international competitiveness of nations.

The problems caused by balance of payments deficits and surpluses will then be considered and we examine the policies available to governments to correct such problems. We will conclude our discussion of the Balance of Payments by discussing the conflict between policies used to cure external deficits and surpluses and policies used to attain domestic economic goals, such as stable prices and low unemployment.

Finally, we will consider how the value of the UK pound sterling and the US dollar have changed since 1944. We will also look briefly at the future of exchange rate management in Europe.

Section 1 uses a simple economic model to demonstrate that countries can benefit through increased consumption by trading with other countries. We will then examine the pattern of UK trade with the rest of the world. We will also look at measures countries can take to restrict, or prevent, trade with another country in certain goods.

Section 2 introduces the exchange rate and discusses the various ways in which it can be expressed and determined. We will also examine how the price of a country's currency determines the amount of goods a country exports to and imports from other nations. Finally, we will add imports and exports to the Keynesian model of national income determination which we looked at in Unit 6.

Section 3 examines the way international trade between countries is recorded in the balance of payments. We will also discover why it can be problematic for a country to import more goods than it exports, or, to a lesser extent, why it might be a problem for a country to export more goods than it imports. We will also discuss policies available to governments to correct balance of payments problems and the conflicts which arise with the attainment of the domestic economic goals introduced in Unit 6.

Section 4 charts the history of the exchange rate between 1944 and the mid-1990s. The experiences of the UK, USA and Germany are drawn upon to highlight the links between interest rates, domestic economic policy and the exchange rate. Finally, we look at the future prospects of the European currencies.

Objectives

By the end of this unit you should be able to:

- appreciate why countries trade
- list the UK's major trading partners
- define comparative and absolute advantage
- list the measures available to governments to restrict trade
- interpret exchange rate quotations
- differentiate between real and nominal exchange rate quotes
- define exchange rate appreciation and depreciation
- distinguish between fixed and floating exchange rate regimes
- list the factors which have a positive and negative influence on imports and exports
- determine aggregate demand in an open economy
- define the balance of payments and its constituent parts
- explain the problems of balance of payments deficits and surpluses
- suggest remedies to cure balance of payments problems and cite examples from recent economic history in support of your suggestions
- highlight the links between interest rates, domestic economic policy and the exchange rate using examples from recent exchange rate history
- argue for and against fixed and floating exchange rates.

SECTION ONE
Why Do Countries Trade?

Introduction

In this section we will use a simple economic model to demonstrate that countries can benefit through increased consumption by trading with other countries. We will then examine the pattern of UK trade with the rest of the world. We will also look at measures countries can take to restrict, or prevent, trade with another country in certain goods.

1.1 Gains from trade

We will begin this section by considering a simple world consisting of two countries, Pilsner and Oregano, each of which has a limited amount of labour and capital resources which it can use to produce two goods: beer and pizza. Each of the countries has an advantage in the production of one of the goods. In this section we will introduce a measure of such production advantage and demonstrate that by concentrating production on the good in which they hold the advantage and by trading with other nations the country can be better off.

The country of Pilsner can produce beer and pizza at any point inside or on the production possibility frontier shown in Figure 1.

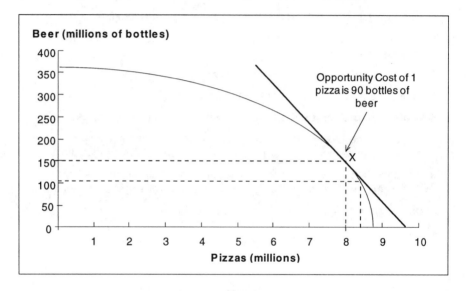

Figure 1: Opportunity cost in Pilsner

The people of Pilsner are consuming all the beer and pizza that they produce and are operating at point X in the figure. Therefore, Pilsner is producing 150 million bottles of beer and 8 million pizzas each year.

From the figure it can be seen that, in order for Pilsner to produce an extra half a million pizzas, it must reduce its production of beer by 45 million bottles. Similarly, in order to increase production of pizzas by 1, Pilsner must reduce beer production by 90 bottles.

Therefore the opportunity cost of 1 pizza is 90 bottles of beer. The opportunity cost can be calculated by calculating the slope of the production possibility frontier at point X.

The country of Oregano also produces beer and pizza. Its production possibility frontier is shown in Figure 2. Like the people of Pilsner, the people of Oregano consume all the beer and pizza they produce and are operating at point y. Therefore, Oregano is producing 180 million bottles of beer and 4 million pizzas.

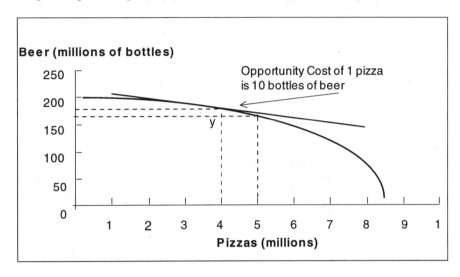

Figure 2: Opportunity cost in Oregano

From Oregano's production possibility frontier we can calculate that the opportunity cost of one pizza is 10 bottles of beer.

The opportunity cost of beer and pizza in Pilsner and Oregano is summarised below in Table .

	Pizza	Beer
Oregano	1 pizza costs 10 bottles of beer	10 bottles of beer costs 1 pizza
Pilsner	1 pizza costs 90 bottles of beer	90 bottles of beer costs 1 pizza

Table 1

From the table we can see that pizzas are cheaper in Oregano than in Pilsner: 1 pizza costs 10 bottles of beer in Oregano and 90 bottles of beer in Pilsner. But beer is cheaper in Pilsner than in Oregano: 1 pizza buys 90 bottles of beer in Pilsner but only 10 in Oregano.

COMPARATIVE ADVANTAGE
A country has a **comparative advantage** in producing a product if it can produce that product at a lower opportunity cost than any other country.

Therefore:

- Oregano has a comparative advantage in pizza production
- Pilsner has a comparative advantage in beer production.

Oregano could buy 90 bottles of beer from Pilsner at a cost of 1 pizza. The equivalent amount of beer would cost 9 pizzas in Oregano. Pilsner could buy 1 pizza from Oregano at a cost of 10 bottles of beer. The same pizza would cost 90 bottles of beer in Pilsner. In this situation it makes sense for Oregano to buy beer from Pilsner and for Pilsner to buy pizza from Oregano.

The demand for beer and pizza in Pilsner and Oregano will be determined by preferences in the two countries. However we may assume hypothetical demands for beer and pizza in Pilsner and Oregano which will lead to pizzas being exported from Oregano and beer being exported from Pilsner. Figure 3 illustrates how the market for pizza would possibly operate.

The quantity of pizzas traded is measured on the horizontal axis and the price of pizza (expressed as the number of bottles of beer each pizza costs) is measured on the vertical axis.

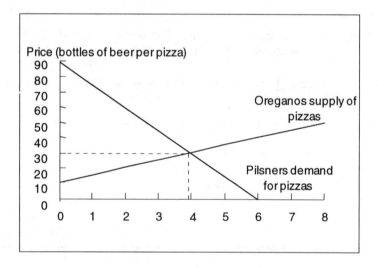

Figure 3: International trade in pizzas

If no trade between Pilsner and Oregano takes place then the price of a pizza in Pilsner is 90 bottles of beer. The lower the price of a pizza (in terms of bottles of beer) the greater is the quantity of pizza that Pilsner will import from Oregano.

This type of relationship is illustrated by the downward-sloping curve that shows Pilsner's import demand for pizzas. As the price of pizza decreases, the quantity of imports demanded by Pilsner increases.

Oregano responds in the opposite direction. The higher the price of pizzas the greater is the quantity of pizzas that Oregano will export to Pilsner. This relationship is illustrated by the upward-sloping curve that shows Oregano's export supply of pizzas.

Equilibrium in the market for pizzas occurs when the import demand curve intersects the export supply curve In this case, the equilibrium price of a pizza is 30 bottles of beer. At this price 4 million pizzas are exported by Oregano and imported by Pilsner. Notice that the price at which pizzas are traded is lower than the initial price in Pilsner but higher than the initial price in Oregano.

How does Pilsner pay for its pizzas ? By exporting the commodity in which it has a comparative advantage - beer. For each pizza Pilsner has to pay 30 bottles of beer. Thus for 4 million pizzas they have to pay 120 million bottles of beer. Therefore, Pilsner exports 120 million bottles of beer to Oregano.

Oregano is exchanging 4 million pizzas for 120 million bottles of beer and Pilsner is exchanging 120 million bottles of beer for 4 million pizzas. Trade is balanced between Oregano and Pilsner. The value received for imports equals the value paid for imports.

In an economy that does not trade with other economies the production and consumption possibilities are identical. That is, the economy can only consume what it produces. But with international trade an economy can consume different quantities of commodities from those that it produces. The production possibility frontier describes the limit of what a country can produce but it does not describe the limits to which it can consume.

With international trade both countries can exchange beer for pizza at a price of 30 bottles of beer per pizza. These trading prices are illustrated by the dashed lines in Figure 4.

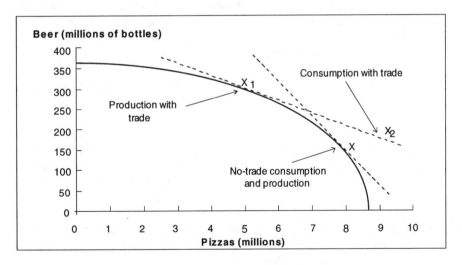

Figure 4: Production and consumption in Pilsner with trade

With international trade, the producers of pizzas in Oregano can now get a higher price for their output. Therefore, they increase pizza production. At the same time, beer producers in Oregano are now getting a lower price for their beer and so they reduce production.

Producers in Oregano adjust their output until the opportunity cost in Oregano equals the opportunity cost in the world market. Opportunity cost in the world market is identical for both countries and is represented by the slope of the dashed lines in Figure 5.

For Oregano the opportunity cost of producing a pizza equals the world opportunity cost at point y_1.

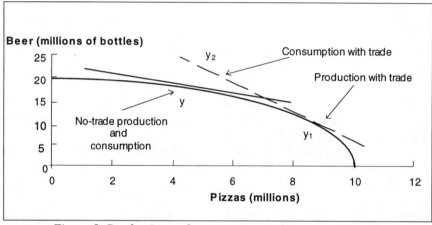

Figure 5: Production and consumption in Oregano with trade

In Pilsner, pizzas are now less expensive, and beer more expensive, than before. As a consequence, producers in Pilsner decrease pizza production and increase beer production. They change their production levels until the opportunity cost of producing beer equals the opportunity cost on the world market.

For Pilsner the opportunity cost of producing a pizza equals the world opportunity cost at point x_1 (Figure 4).

We saw earlier that Oregano exports 4 million pizzas a year to Pilsner and Pilsner exports 120 million bottles of beer a year to Oregano. Thus, Pilsner's consumption of beer is 120 million bottles *less* a year than it produces and its consumption of pizzas is 4 million a year *more* than it produces. Therefore, Pilsner consumes at point x_2 (Figure 4).

Furthermore, Oregano's consumption of beer is 120 million bottles *more* a year than it produces and its consumption of pizzas is 4 million a year *less* than it produces. Oregano consumes at point y_2 (Figure 5).

We can, therefore, compare Oregano and Pilsner's consumption patterns with and without trade (see Table 2).

	Consumption/ production without trade	Production with trade	Consumption with trade
Oregano	180 million bottles of beer 4 million pizzas	90m bottles of beer 9m pizzas	210m (90m + 120m) bottles of beer 5m (9m – 4m) pizzas
Pilsner	150 million bottles of beer 8 million pizzas	300m bottles of beer 5m pizzas	180m(300m – 120m) bottles of beer 9m (5m + 4m) pizzas

Table 2

We can clearly see that Pilsner gains from trading with Oregano.

ACTIVITY 1

1   Describe the effects of trading with Pilsner on Oregano's producers of beer and pizza.

2   How much more beer and pizza is the country of Pilsner able to consume in a world with trade than a world without trade ?

Without trade, Oregano consumes and produces 180m bottles of beer and 4m pizzas. With trade, Oregano biases production towards the good in which it has a comparative advantage and produces 90m bottles of beer and 9m pizzas. Therefore there will be a movement in resources from the beer industry to the pizza industry.

By trading with Pilsner it is able to consume 210m bottles of beer and 5m pizzas. Depending on the demands for beer and Pizza in Pilsner. Consequently, Oregano consumes an extra 30m bottles of beer and an extra 1m pizzas *more* than it consumed in a world without trade.

ABSOLUTE ADVANTAGE

A related concept to comparative advantage is **absolute advantage**. A country has an absolute advantage over another in the production of a particular good if its output per unit of input is higher for that good.

Let us make the simplistic assumption that the only input required to produce beer and pizza is labour. Furthermore, let us suppose that in Oregano fewer workers are required to produce any given amount of beer and pizza than in Pilsner. In this situation Oregano has an absolute advantage over Pilsner in the production of both goods.

However, the absolute cost of production is irrelevant in determining gains from trade. It does not matter how much labour, or any other factors of production, are required to produce beer and pizza. What is important is how many pizzas must be given up to produce an additional bottle of beer.

Oregano may have an absolute advantage in the production of both goods; however, they cannot have a comparative advantage in the production of both goods. Therefore, despite Oregano's absolute advantage in both goods they will still export pizzas to Pilsner and import beer from Pilsner.

ACTIVITY 2

Suppose that the production conditions prevailing in two countries, A and B, are as follows.

Country	One day's labour produces:
A	600 tons of rice or 200 metres of silk
B	200 tons of rice or 100 metres of silk

Determine whether either country has an absolute advantage in the production of rice and silk.

Clearly, labour is more productive absolutely in country A than in country B, in both the production of rice and in the production of silk. One day's labour in country A produces more rice and more silk than it does in country B. Country A, therefore, has an absolute advantage in the production of both goods.

1.2 The UK pattern of trade

Having argued the case for trade we can now show who the UK actually trades with. From Figure 6 we can see that the UK has trade links with countries all round the world. Its chief trading partners are in the EC and its next largest market is North America.

What is evident from this figure is that, overall, the UK runs a deficit with most of its trading partners, the exception being the wealthy oil-producing states. That is, it imports more goods and services from the world economies than its exports to them.

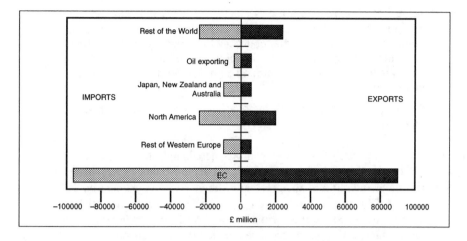

Figure 6: The pattern of UK trade in 1995

1.3 Trade restrictions

Governments may restrict international trade in order to protect domestic industries from foreign competition. The restriction of international trade is called **protectionism.**

The method of protection chosen may affect demand or supply. Demand may be influenced by tariffs and subsidies. Supply can be influenced by the introduction of, quotas, voluntary export restraints, administrative restrictions and embargoes.

- **Tariff:** a tax imposed by the importing country when a good crosses an international boundary. The effectiveness of the tariff in reducing imports is dependent upon its size and upon the elasticity of demand for the imported good. If demand for the imported good is price inelastic (insensitive to changes in price) then import demand will not fall by a large amount. In fact, due to the increased price the value of imports (price × quantity) may well rise. However, if the demand for the imported good is price elastic (sensitive to changes in price) then import demand will fall and domestic consumers will switch to domestically produced goods.

- **Subsidy:** financial assistance provided by government to boost exports (for example, VAT remission) or facilities to enable a company to price its goods competitively in the world market. Similarly, subsidies to domestic firms may enable them to compete more easily with imported goods.

- **Quota:** a quantitative restriction on the import of a particular good. It specifies the maximum quantity of a particular good that may be imported in a given period of time.

- **Voluntary export restraint (VER):** an agreement between two countries in which the exporting country agrees to restrain the volume of its own exports. For example, in 1981 the Japanese agreed to restrict the number of car exports to the UK.

● **Administrative restrictions:** regulations that discriminate against foreign goods in favour of home goods. For example, a Japanese trading practice (considered by other countries to be unfair) has been the use of licensing and the withholding from foreigners of details of impending changes to licenses, whilst warning domestic producers of changes well in advance.

● **Embargo:** a situation where some goods are completely banned from entry into an economy.

Nowadays trade restrictions are becoming increasingly rare in the industrialised world. Because of the benefits of free trade (as demonstrated above), many Western countries have entered into an agreement (the General Agreement on Tariffs and Trade – GATT), the aim of which is to limit government intervention in international trade. Since the formation of GATT, in 1947, several rounds of negotiations have taken place and have resulted in tariff reductions.

REVIEW ACTIVITY 1

Economy A has 1,200 hours of labour available. It can produce two goods, apples and bananas. The production of one apple requires three hours of labour, whilst the production of one banana require two hours of labour.

1   Fill in the gaps in the table below, ensuring that Economy A utilises its full labour capacity of 1,200 hours.

Apples produced	Bananas produced
0 apples = 0 hours	600 bananas = 1200 hours
50 apples = 150 hours	
100 apples = 300 hours	
150 apples = 450 hours	
200 apples = 600 hours	
250 apples = 750 hours	
300 apples = 900 hours	
350 apples = 1050 hours	
400 apples = 1200 hours	0 bananas = 0 hours

2   Draw a graph to show Economy A's production possibility frontier. Note that we have assumed for ease of exposition that Economy A's production possibility frontier is linear.

3 What is the opportunity cost of apples in terms of bananas in Economy A? What is the opportunity cost of bananas in terms of apples ?

4 A second economy, Economy B, has a labour force of 800 hours. In Economy B the production of an apple requires 5 hours of labour and a banana 1 hour. Economy B's production possibilities are detailed in the table below.

Apples produced	Bananas produced
0 apples = 0 hours	800 bananas = 800 hours
50 apples = 250 hours	550 bananas = 550 hours
100 apples = 500 hours	300 bananas = 300 hours
150 apples = 750 hours	50 bananas = 50 hours
160 apples = 800 hours	0 bananas = 0 hours

What is the opportunity cost of apples in terms of bananas in Economy B? What is the opportunity cost of bananas in terms of apples?

5 Which economy has a comparative advantage in the production of apples?

6 Which economy has a comparative advantage in the production of bananas?

7 What trade patterns might result from this situation?

Summary

In this section we used a simple economic model (the trading activities of the countries Oregano and Pilsner) to demonstrate that countries can benefit through increased consumption by trading with other countries.

We then examined the pattern of UK trade with the rest of the world. Finally, we looked at the measures countries can take to restrict, or prevent, trade with another country in certain goods: tariffs, subsidies, quotas, voluntary export restraint , administrative restrictions and embargoes.

SECTION TWO

The Exchange Rate

Introduction

In this section we will introduce the exchange rate and discuss the various ways in which it can be expressed and determined. We will also examine how the price of a country's currency determines the amount of goods a country exports to and imports from other nations. Finally, we will add imports and exports to the Keynesian model of national income determination which we looked at in Unit 6.

2.1 What is the exchange rate?

Typically, prices of internationally-traded goods are not quoted in terms of bottles of beer per pizza. Instead each country has a currency in which its products are priced. In order to purchase a country's products you therefore have to obtain its currency by exchanging your own currency for its currency. The number of units of foreign currency you obtain in return for a unit of your own currency is known as the **exchange rate**.

An American company importing goods from Germany with their price quoted in Deutschmarks buys marks in order to pay for the goods. An American company exporting goods to Germany, again with the price denominated in marks, receives Deutschmarks, which it then sells in exchange for dollars. These transactions are made in the **foreign exchange markets**.

The foreign exchange market is the framework of individuals, firms, banks and brokers buying and selling currencies. The foreign exchange market for any one currency, for example, the French franc, consists of all the locations in which the French franc is dealt.

The foreign exchange market is made up of commercial banks, foreign exchange brokers and other authorised agents. These groups are kept in close contact with one another and with developments in the market via telephone, computer terminals, telex and fax.

Important foreign exchange markets are to be found in London, New York, Tokyo, Zurich and Frankfurt. Further markets exist in Amsterdam, Paris, Toronto, Brussels, Milan, Bahrain, Hong Kong and Singapore. The overlapping of time zones in these centres means that, apart from weekends, there is always one centre which is open

2.2 Exchange rate quotes

The exchange rate is simply the price of one currency in terms of another. Since the exchange rate between two currencies is the price of one currency in terms of another there are two ways of expressing it:

- **indirect quote:** foreign currency units per unit of the domestic currency. Taking the pound as the domestic currency, on 16 May 1996 approximately US$1.5 were required to obtain one pound, i.e. ($/£) = 1.5.

- **direct quote:** domestic currency units per unit of foreign currency. Again taking the pound as the domestic currency, on 16 May 1996 approximately £0.67 was required to purchase one dollar, (£/$) = 1/1.5 = $0.67.

Note that the direct and indirect quotes are reciprocals of each other and that an indirect quote from the viewpoint of the one country is the direct quote from the viewpoint of another country.

In the UK the indirect method of quotation is adopted whilst in continental Europe the direct method of quotation is used. While it is not important which method of expressing the exchange rate is employed, it is necessary to be careful when talking about a rise or fall in the exchange rate because the meaning will be very different depending upon which definition is used.

A rise in the pounds per dollar [(£/$)] exchange rate from, say, £0.67/$1 to £0.70/$1 means that more pounds have to be given to obtain a dollar. This means that the pound has depreciated in value or, equivalently, the dollar has appreciated in value.

However, a rise in the dollars per pound ($/£) exchange rate from $1.5/£1 to $1.53/£1 would mean that more dollars are obtained per pound, so that the pound has appreciated or, equivalently, the dollar has depreciated.

In general, all else being equal, a depreciation of a country's currency makes its goods cheaper for foreigners, whilst an appreciation of a country's currency makes its goods more expensive for foreigners.

Two numbers are usually given in any exchange rate quotation (for example, DM 2.3122 – 2.3142/£) The left-hand figure in an exchange rate quote is known as the **bid rate** and the right-hand figure as the **ask rate**.

- The **bid** rate is the rate at which a bank will *sell* the currency (i.e. the bank will sell DM's in exchange for pounds at 2.3122DM/£)

- the **ask** rate is the rate at which the bank will *purchase* the currency in exchange for pounds (i.e. the bank will buy DM's and sell £'s at 2.3142DM/£)

The difference is known as the **bid ask spread** and represents the gross profit margin of the bank. Whether using the indirect or direct quotation method the smaller number is always termed the bid rate and the higher the ask (or **offer**) rate.

You would expect the 'profit margin' on heavily traded currencies such as the DM and the Yen will be less than the 'profit margin' on thinly-traded currencies such as the Danish Kroner.

ACTIVITY 3

1   You are given the following exchange rate quotes:

DM 2.2634 – 2.2655 /£ and ¥ 135.321 – 135.516/ £.

Identify the bid rates and the ask rates and explain what each of these mean.

2   (a) How many DM would you receive in return for £1m ?

   (b) How many yen would you receive in return for £1m ?

3   (a) If you immediately sold the DM obtained above at the quoted rate how many pounds would you receive ?

   (b) If you immediately sold the yen obtained above at the quoted rate how many pounds would you receive ?

---

1   DM bid: 2.2634 DM/£; ask: 2.2655 DM/£

¥ bid: 135.321 DM/£; ask: 135.516 DM/£

The dealer will purchase pounds from you/sell you DM at the rate 2.2634DM/£.

The dealer will purchase DM from you/sell you pounds at the rate 2.2655DM/£.

The dealer will purchase pounds from you/sell you yen at the rate 135.321 ¥/£.

The dealer will purchase yen from you/sell you pounds at the rate 135.516 ¥/£.

2   (a)   2.2634 DM/£ × £1m. = DM 2,263,400

   (b)   135.321 Y/£ × £1m. = ¥135,321,000

3   (a)   DM 2,263,400 ÷ 2.2655 DM/£ = £ 999,073

   (b)   ¥ 135,321,000 ÷ 135.516 ¥/£ = £ 998,561

2.3 Alternative exchange rate regimes

An exchange rate regime is a description of the conditions under which national governments allow exchange rates to be determined. One important feature of an exchange rate regime is **convertibility:** the degree to which a currency of one country may be changed into the currency of another.

FIXED EXCHANGE RATE REGIME
In a **fixed exchange rate regime** national governments agree to maintain the convertibility of their currency at a fixed exchange rate (a currency is convertible if the government agrees to buy or sell as much of the currency as people wish to trade).

For example, between 1949 and 1967 the dollar/pound exchange rate was fixed at $2.80/£. In order to keep the exchange rate fixed at a given level the monetary authorities must intervene in the foreign exchange market. Using the analogy that the exchange rate is just the price of a good, then when there is increased demand for a good at the current price there is pressure for the price to rise. Conversely, when there is reduced demand for a good at the current price there is pressure for the price to fall. Therefore, when there is increased demand for pounds at the current exchange rate (i.e. there is excess demand) the monetary authorities must sell pounds if they want to keep the exchange rate fixed. Similarly, when there is reduced demand for pounds at the current exchange rate the monetary authorities must buy pounds if they want to keep the exchange rate fixed.

The buying and selling of currency by the monetary authorities is termed foreign **exchange market intervention**.

Under a fixed exchange rate system the value of the currency can be changed by the monetary authorities announcing their willingness to trade domestic currency against foreign currency in unlimited amounts at a new exchange rate. The monetary authorities would then intervene at a different level in order to keep the exchange rate fixed.

Under a fixed exchange rate regime, a **devaluation** (revaluation) is a reduction (increase) in the exchange rate that governments commit themselves to maintain.

FLOATING EXCHANGE RATE REGIME
In a **pure-floating exchange rate regime** the exchange rate is allowed to attain its free market equilibrium level without any government intervention. **Dirty floating** describes an exchange rate regime in which intervention is used to offset large speculative movements in the exchange rate in the short run, but where the exchange rate is gradually allowed to find its equilibrium level in the longer run. Under a floating exchange rate regime, a **depreciation** (appreciation) is a reduction (increase) in the exchange rate brought about by market forces.

2.4 The real exchange rate

In 1975 the dollar/sterling exchange rate was $2.22/£ (i.e. £1 bought $2.22 and $1 bought £0.45). In 1982 it was down to $1.75 (i.e. £1 now bought only $1.75 and $1 now bought £0.57). Such a fall in the international value of sterling makes British goods cheaper for US citizens and US goods more expensive for British citizens.

However, this is not the complete picture. During these years Britain had a higher inflation rate than the US and so the price of UK goods was rising more quickly than the price of US goods. Thus, other things being equal, the demand for UK goods would have decreased, while US goods would have appeared cheaper to the British, who would therefore be expected to buy more US goods.

Whether British goods became more or less competitive against US goods depended on whether the increase in Britain's competitiveness arising from a fall in the actual exchange rate (commonly referred to as the **nominal exchange rate**) was larger than the reduction in Britain's international competitiveness arising from higher inflation than the US.

International competitiveness is measured by the **real exchange rate**. The real exchange rate measures the relative price of goods from different countries when measured in a common currency.

For example, the real exchange rate between the US and Britain can be expressed as:

$$\text{Real exchange rate} = \frac{(\text{£ price of UK goods})}{(\text{\$ price of US goods})} \times (\text{\$/£}) \text{ exchange rate.}$$

An increase in the real exchange rate increases the price of UK goods relative to US goods when measured in the same currency and so makes the UK less competitive, relative to the US.

Conversely, a fall in the UK's real exchange rate against the dollar makes the UK more competitive, relative to the US. Table 3 shows the change in the real exchange rate between 1976 and 1981. Over this period the real exchange rate increased from 1.56 to 1.82. UK goods became significantly less competitive because, in a common currency, their price increased relative to the price of US goods.

	1976	1981
$/£	1.81	1.75
UK price level (1980=100)	59.6	121.5
US price level (1980=100)	69.1	117.1
Real exchange rate between the $ and £	1.56	1.82

Table 3

The fall in the nominal exchange rate was not sufficient to offset the much higher inflation rate in the UK compared to the US.

2.5 The effective exchange rate

The **effective exchange rate** of the UK measures the value of the pound against a 'basket' of foreign currencies. The basket consists of each of the UK's leading trading partners. The more important a nation is as a trading partner the more 'weight' it has in the 'basket'.

For example if the UK traded equally with only three nations, the USA, Germany and France, the effective exchange rate would be:

$$(1/3) \times S(\$/£) + (1/3) \times S(DM/£) + (1/3) \times S(FFr/£) =$$

$$(1/3) \times 1.5157 + (1/3) \times 2.3132 + (1/3) \times 7.8356 = 3.89.$$

The effective exchange rate is usually expressed as an index, with the base year equal to 100. An increase in the index indicates that the pound has increased in value against its trading partners whilst a decrease in the index indicates that the pound has fallen in value against its trading partners.

The value of the sterling index on 16 May 1996 was 84.4 (based on 1990=100). This indicates that since 1990 sterling has fallen in value by 15.6% (100-84.4) against its major trading partners.

ACTIVITY 4

The table shows the UK and US price levels and exchange rates in 1976 and 1981. Use this information to answer the following questions.

	1976	1981
$/£	1.81	1.75
UK price level (1980 = 100)	59.6	121.5
US price level (1980 = 100)	69.1	117.1
Real exchange rate between the $ and £	1.56	1.82

1   Calculate the percentage change in (i) UK prices and (ii) US prices.

2   Assume that price levels have changed as shown in the table, but

> exchange rates have remained the same. State whether the cost of US goods to UK residents would now be more or less expensive than the equivalent UK good. Illustrate your answer by considering a watch that cost £50 in the UK in 1976 and $90.5 in the US in 1976.
>
> 3   In order for the sterling cost of the watch to be the same in the UK and US in 1981 would the nominal dollar-sterling exchange rate have to rise or fall ? What level would it have to change to ? Does this represent an appreciation or a depreciation of sterling against the dollar ?
>
> 4   The real exchange rate has changed as shown. State the effect this has had on UK competitiveness.

1   (i) Prices in the UK have increased by 104% [(121.5 – 59.6) ÷ (59.6)]

   (ii) Prices in the US have increased by 69% [(117.1 – 69.1) ÷ 69.1]

2   Less expensive. Consider a watch that cost £50 in the UK and $90.5 in the US in 1976. The prices of the same watch in 1981 are £102 (£50 + 104%) in the UK and $153 in the US. At an exchange rate of $1.81/£ the US watch costs £84.55. Therefore, if the exchange rate remains unchanged, because US inflation is lower than UK inflation, it will now be cheaper to buy the watch in the US.

3   Fall! It would have to fall to $1.5/£ for the sterling cost of the watch to be £102 in both the UK and the US. This represents a 17 % [(1.5 - 1.81) ÷ 1.81] depreciation in the value of sterling against the $. The underlying rationale for this depreciation is that, on average, inflation has been higher in the UK than in the US. Therefore, in order to compensate for this and to maintain purchasing power parity the value of sterling against the dollar must fall.

4   Less: an increase in the real exchange rate, by increasing the price of UK goods relative to US goods when measured in the same currency, makes the UK less competitive relative to the US.

2.6 The demand for exports and imports

We have explained why countries trade with one another and how such trade is implemented via the foreign exchange market. We will now identify what impact the level of the exchange rate prevailing in the foreign exchange market has on import and export demand.

The demand for UK products will be determined mainly by the level of income in the rest of the world and the UK's real exchange rate. In particular, the demand for UK exports will be high when:

- the level of income in the rest of the world is high
- the level of the UK's real exchange rate is low.

For imports, the reverse is true. The demand for foreign products by UK residents will be determined mainly by the level of UK income and the UK's real exchange rate. In particular, the demand for imports into the UK will be high when:

- the level of domestic income is high
- the level of the UK's real exchange rate is high.

2.7 Foreign trade and income determination

For simplicity in introductory macroeconomics it is common to assume that we are considering a closed economy - one without overseas trade. In this section we will remove this assumption and consider how foreign trade influences national income.

We saw earlier that national income is determined by the following identity:

$$Y = C + I + G + (X - M).$$

That is, an economy's income is equal to the sum of consumption expenditure in the economy, investment in the economy, government expenditure in the economy and net exports (exports minus imports).

For the moment we are only going to consider the relationship between national income (GDP) and net exports, this relationship is referred to as the **net-export function**. If we assume that foreign incomes and the real exchange rate are constant. We can imagine a linear relationship existing between domestic GDP and real imports (i.e. as domestic GDP rises, imports also rise). Moreover, since we are assuming that foreign income and the real exchange rate are constant as GDP rises, the level of exports remains constant.

Using hypothetical data, based loosely on UK 1995 statistics, the relationship between GDP and net exports is depicted in Table 4.

Real GDP	Real exports	Real imports	Net exports
350	167	112	55
400	167	128	39
450	167	144	23
500	167	160	7
550	167	176	9
600	167	192	-25
650	167	208	-41

Table 4

Figure 7 depicts this information in the form of a graph.

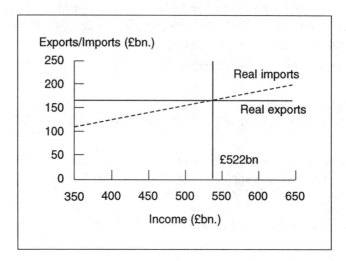

Figure 7: Exports and imports

Study Figure 7. Notice the following points:

● The export demand function is horizontal since export demand is independent of the level of domestic income.

● The level of imports rises steadily as income rises. The slope of the import demand schedule is called the **marginal propensity to import**. The marginal propensity to import is the fraction of each additional pound of national income that residents wish to spend on extra imports. In the above example a £50bn increase in domestic income increases imports by £17bn. The marginal propensity to import is therefore 0.34.

The level of exports is equal to the level of imports when national income is £522bn.

If we now assume an investment level of 50, government expenditure of 50, an autonomous consumption level of 50 and a marginal propensity to consume of 0.30, we can add foreign trade to the closed-economy Keynesian model developed in unit 7 and use the framework to determine the equilibrium level of national income in an open economy.

The relationship between GDP (Y), consumption (C), investment (I) exports (X) and imports (M) is depicted in Table 5.

Y	C	I	G	X	M	C+I+G + X–M
0	50	50	50	167	0	317
50	85	50	50	167	–16	336
100	120	50	50	167	–32	355
150	155	50	50	167	–48	374
200	190	50	50	167	–64	393
250	225	50	50	167	–80	412
300	260	50	50	167	–96	431
350	295	50	50	167	–112	450
400	330	50	50	167	–128	469
450	365	50	50	167	–144	488
500	400	50	50	167	–160	507
550	435	50	50	167	–176	526
600	470	50	50	167	–192	545
650	505	50	50	167	–208	564

Table 5

Figure 8 shows this information in the form of a graph.

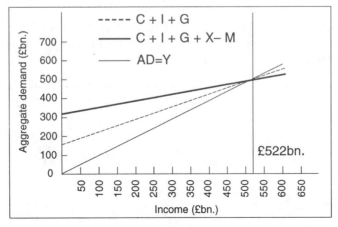

Figure 8: Equilibrium in an open economy

Starting from the $Y = C + I + G$ schedule introduced earlier, we now add on the net exports schedule (X-M). If net exports were independent of domestic income the effect of this would be a parallel shift up or down in the $Y = C + I + G$ schedule.

However, Figure 8 shows that at low levels of income, net exports are positive. Aggregate $Y = C + I + G + X - M$ will then exceed $Y = C + I + G$. As income rises import demand rises and the level of net exports falls. At the income level of £522bn. net exports are zero and the $Y = C + I + G$ and $Y = C + I + G + X - M$ schedules intersect each other. Beyond this income level, net export demand is negative and the $Y + C + I + G + X - M$ schedule falls below the $Y = C + I + G$ schedule.

Therefore, the introduction of net exports to the closed-economy Keynsian model introduced in Unit 7 brings about a 'pivot-shift' in the aggregate demand schedule.

Now try the following activities to ensure that you have understood the main points discussed in this section.

REVIEW ACTIVITY 2

1   Given the following information determine the equilibrium level of National Income.

Investment = £200bn.

Autonomous Consumption = £50bn.

Marginal Propensity to Consume = 0.45.

Marginal Propensity to Import = 0.40.

Government Expenditure = £400bn.

Export Revenue = £250bn.

2   What would be the impact on National Income of a change in UK consumers tastes which increases the Marginal Propensity to Import from 0.40 to 0.65

REVIEW ACTIVITY 3

In the following table insert a '+' sign if you believe their exists a positive relationship between the economic variables listed in the first column and the economic variables listed at the top of the next two columns. Insert a '−' sign if you believe a negative relationship exists.

	Demand for UK Exports	Demand for UK Imports
World GDP		
UK GDP		
UK Real Exchange Rate		

Summary

In this section we discussed the exchange rate and the various ways in which it can be expressed and determined. We also looked at how the price of a country's currency determines the amount of goods a country exports to and imports from other nations. Finally, we added imports and exports to the Keynesian model of national income determination which we looked at in Unit 6.

SECTION THREE

The Balance of Payments

Introduction

In this section we will examine the way international trade between countries is recorded in the balance of payments. We will also discover why it can be problematic for a country to import more goods than it exports, or, to a lesser extent, why it might be a problem for a country to export more goods than it imports. We will discuss policies available to governments to correct balance of payments problems and the conflicts which arise with the attainment of the domestic economic goals introduced in Unit 6.

3.1 What is the balance of payments?

The accounting record of all a country's commercial transactions with respect to the rest of the world is called the balance on international transactions or more commonly the **balance of payments.**

Taking the UK as the domestic country and the US as the 'rest of the world', all international transactions that give rise to an inflow of pounds to the UK are entered as credits (+) in the UK balance of payments accounts. Outflows of pounds are shown as debits, and are entered with a minus sign (–).

Similarly, inflows of dollars to the US are credits in the US balance of payments accounts but outflows are debits.

The balance of payments is divided into two principal divisions: the **current account**, which is the record of all purchases and sales of goods and services with respect to the rest of the world, and the **capital account**, which represents the flow of financial assets - either bought or sold outright.

3.2 The current account

Visible trade balance	−10,594
Invisible trade balance	+3,790
Investment income	+10,519
Transfers	−5,399
Current account balance	**−1,684**
Net transactions in UK external assets	−39,363
Net transactions in UK external liabilities	+35,802
Net Financial Transactions	**−3,561**
Balancing item	**5,245**

Table 6: The UK balance of payments accounts in 1994 (£m)
(Source: Office of National Statistics)

The current account of the balance of payments records international flows of goods and services, and other net income from abroad, divided into visible and invisible trade:

- **visible trade:** exports and imports of goods (cars, food steel, etc.)
- **invisible trade:** exports and imports of services (banking, shipping, tourism, etc.).

In 1994 net exports of UK goods amounted to – £10,594m, displayed as a debit (outflow of pounds) in the balance of payments accounts. In comparison the invisible trade balance amounted to a surplus of £3,790m, displayed as a credit (inflow of pounds).

The current account also takes into account **transfer payments** between countries (foreign aid, the budget contribution to the EC) and **net property income** (which arises when residents of one country own income-earning assets in another country).

Combining all of the above, the UK's current account on the balance of payments was £1,684m. in deficit in 1994.

3.3 The capital account

The **capital account** of the balance of payments records international transactions in financial assets.

It includes the following:

- **Transactions in external assets:** this records the total value of assets (for example, factories, land, shares) in other countries bought by UK citizens minus the value of assets in other countries that UK citizens have sold. This may also include changes in the governments holdings of foreign currencies, i.e. reserves.

- **Transactions in external liabilities:** this records the total value of UK assets acquired by foreign citizens minus the value of any assets that foreign citizens have sold.

Adding together the items from net investment, trade credit, and other net transactions in financial assets, we obtain a net outflow of £3,561m on the capital account of the UK balance of payments in 1994 (i.e. the UK capital account was in deficit in 1994).

BALANCING ITEM

The **balancing item** is a statistical adjustment which would be zero if all previous items had been correctly measured. It reflects a failure to record all transactions in the official statistics. This may be due to the fact that statistics are obtained from a number of sources, and that there are often delays before items are recorded. There are often omissions too. In 1994 the balancing item was £5,245m.

3.4 Change in reserves

In 1994 the UK level of official foreign currency reserves fell by £1,045m, that is, on average the monetary authorities were buying pounds and selling foreign currency. These transactions are included under the heading 'net transactions in external assets' in the balance of payments.

The amount the reserves change by will vary, depending upon whether the currency is determined under a fixed or floating exchange rate regime.

FLOATING EXCHANGE RATES

Suppose first that the exchange rate is freely floating and there is no government intervention in the foreign exchange market. The government is neither adding to or running down the foreign exchange reserves. The exchange rate adjusts to equate the supply of pounds and the demand for pounds in the foreign exchange market.

The supply of pounds arises from imports to the UK (paid for in sterling) or purchases of foreign assets by UK residents. It measures the outflows from the UK, the negative items on the balance of payments accounts for the UK.

The demand for pounds arises from UK exports (paid for in sterling) and purchases of UK assets by foreigners, and measures the inflows to the UK, the positive items on the UK balance of payments accounts.

With a freely floating exchange rate, the quantities of pounds supplied and demanded are equal. Hence inflows equal outflows and the balance of payments is exactly zero. There is no government intervention in the foreign exchange market and therefore no change in reserves.

Since the balance of payments is the sum of the current account and the capital account, under floating exchange rates a current account surplus must be exactly matched by a capital account deficit, i.e. an increase in the country's holdings of foreign assets.

FIXED EXCHANGE RATES

When there is a fixed exchange rate, the balance of payments need not be zero.

When there is a balance of payments deficit, total outflows exceed total inflows on the combined current and capital accounts. How is this deficit financed ?

When there is a balance of payments deficit the supply of pounds to the foreign exchange market exceeds the demand for pounds. Hence, the balance of payments deficit is equal to the excess supply of pounds in the foreign exchange market. To maintain the fixed exchange rate, the central bank has to offset this excess supply of pounds by buying an equivalent quantity of pounds. This is achieved by the central bank running down its foreign exchange reserves, buying pounds and selling foreign currencies.

Conversely, when there is a balance of payments surplus the government is intervening in the foreign exchange market to add to foreign exchange reserves.

The interaction of the supply and demand for pounds and the need for intervention can be illustrated easily with the aid of a simple diagram. Consider Figure 9. In this diagram, S refers to the supply schedule for pounds, D refers to the demand schedule for pounds and S* refers to fixed exchange rate level (foreign currency per unit of domestic currency, for example, $/£).

The supply of pounds on the foreign exchange results from UK residents selling pounds and buying foreign currency in order to purchase foreign goods and assets. The supply schedule is upward sloping, indicating that as the exchange rate increases (i.e. sterling is appreciating and the foreign currency is depreciating) the desire to purchase foreign goods and assets increases.

The demand for pounds on the foreign exchange market arises from foreign residents selling foreign currency and buying pounds in order to purchase UK goods and services. The demand schedule is downward sloping, indicating that as the exchange rate decreases (i.e. sterling is depreciating and the foreign currency is appreciating) the desire to purchase UK goods and assets increases.

The left-hand side of Figure 9 shows the case of a balance of payments surplus (at the exchange rate S* the demand for pounds exceeds the supply for pounds). In order to keep the exchange rate fixed the Bank of England thus has to purchase an amount of pounds (ab) by drawing on its foreign exchange reserves.

The right-hand side shows the case of a balance of payments deficit (at an exchange rate S* the supply of pounds exceeds the demand for pounds). In order to keep the exchange rate fixed, the Bank of England has to supply additional pounds (cd) on the market, and will acquire foreign currencies in exchange. It can use these to build up reserves or to pay back foreign loans.

If the exchange rate was being determined under a pure-float exchange rate regime the exchange rate prevailing in the foreign exchange market would be the level determined by the supply and demand schedules in Figure 9.

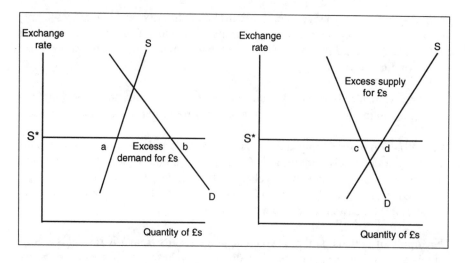

Figure 9: The demand and supply schedules for pounds

Maintaining a fixed rate will cause changes in the money supply. If the rate is maintained above the equilibrium (right hand figure), there is a balance of payments deficit. The Bank of England buys pounds. It therefore withdraws them from circulation and reduces the money supply.

The decrease in the money supply causes the rate of interest to increase. Consequently UK assets will be more attractive than their international counterparts, thereby causing an increase in the demand for £s which will help soak up their excess supply. Furthermore, deflationary monetary policies restrain GDP and lead to a decrease in imports and consequently a decrease in demand for foreign currency.

If the rate is maintained below equilibrium so that the value of sterling is artificially low (left-hand figure), there is a balance of payments surplus. The Bank of England supplies additional pounds (which are spent by foreigners on UK exports etc. and are thus injected into the UK economy). It therefore increases the money supply.

Here the rate of interest falls, causing a reduction in the demand for pounds. Higher GDP also leads to an increase in imports and consequently an increase in demand for foreign currency.

If the Bank of England did not want the money supply to alter, it would have to counter these effects with other monetary measures: for example, open market operations. Thus, when there is a deficit and money supply falls, the Bank of England could buy back government bonds from the general public, thereby restoring the money supply to its original level.

The process of countering the effects on the money supply of a balance of payments deficit or surplus is known as **sterilisation**.

Although the UK was officially pursuing a floating exchange rate regime in 1994, the Bank of England did in fact intervene in the foreign exchange market. On average it was selling foreign currency and buying pounds and thus maintaining the exchange rate at a slightly higher level than it would have been under a free float.

3.5 General principles of correcting balance of payments problems

As outlined above, a balance of payments deficit or surplus is usually considered more of a problem under a fixed exchange rate regime rather than under a floating exchange regime. In a pure-float exchange rate regime the exchange rate adjusts so that the supply and demand for the currency equate in the foreign exchange market.

In general the demand for the domestic currency is brought about by foreign buyers purchasing domestic goods. In order to purchase the goods they must sell the foreign currency and buy the domestic currency. Likewise, if a foreign investor wishes to invest in a domestic asset he must sell his foreign currency and purchase the domestic currency.

Therefore, an increase (decrease) in overseas demand for domestic goods or an increase (decrease) in investment from overseas will increase (decrease) the demand for domestic currency on the foreign exchange market and consequently bring about a rise (fall) in the value of the domestic currency.

By contrast, the supply of the domestic currency results from domestic buyers wishing to purchase foreign goods, the price of which is denominated in foreign currency. In order to purchase the goods they must sell the domestic currency in exchange for the foreign currency. Likewise, if a domestic investor wishes to purchase a foreign asset he must first of all buy the foreign currency in exchange for the domestic currency.

Therefore, an increase (decrease) in demand for foreign goods or an increase (decrease) in investment overseas will increase (decrease) the supply of the domestic currency on the foreign exchange market and consequently bring about a fall (rise) in the value of the domestic currency.

In principle, as an exporter's currency increases in value, its exports will be more expensive to overseas buyers, therefore reducing demand. Moreover foreign goods will be cheaper to domestic buyers, therefore imports will increase. The effect of the appreciation of the domestic currency will also impact on the capital account, as falling domestic interest rates may bring about an outflow of funds seeking a higher return elsewhere. This leads to a fall in demand for the domestic currency and an increase in demand for foreign currencies.

Similarly, as the value of the currency falls foreign goods will be cheaper to foreign buyers and exports will increase. Foreign goods will be more expensive to domestic buyers and imports will fall. The depreciating currency may lead to an inflow of 'hot money' attracted to higher domestic interest rates. This leads to a rise in demand for the domestic currency and a fall in demand for foreign currencies.

When the exchange rate is fixed the government must intervene in the foreign exchange market, either by buying the domestic currency in the case of a deficit, or selling the domestic currency in the case of a surplus.

A short-run deficit or surplus does not pose a problem as this can easily be accommodated through the running down of reserves in the case of a deficit, or reserve augmentation in the case of a surplus.

However a reserve loss cannot be maintained indefinitely. Eventually the government must adopt a more proactive policy such as devaluation, deflation or import controls. The type of policy adopted must be chosen so as not to conflict with the internal economic goals of full employment and price stability.

ACTIVITY 5

The citizens of Eden, whose currency is the run, conducted the following transaction in 1995:

Imports of goods and services	1,250 run
Exports of goods and services	1,985 run
Borrowing from the rest of the world	400 run
Lending to the rest of the world	100 run
Increase in official holdings of foreign currency	150 run

1   Using the outline given below set out the balance of payments accounts for Eden.

Eden balance of payments, 1995 run

Exports

Imports

Current account

Overseas borrowing

Overseas lending

Capital account

Balance of payments

Change in official reserves

2   Carefully consider the balance of payments accounts and select which one of the following exchange rate regimes is being followed by the government of Eden:

    (a)   fixed exchange rates

    (b)   dirty-floating exchange rates

    (c)   pure-floating exchange rates.

3   In about 50 words, explain your selection in (b) above.

1   **Eden Balance of Payments, 1995**

Exports	+1985
Imports	−1250
Current Account	**+735**
Overseas Borrowing	−400
Overseas Lending	+100
Capital Account	**−300**
Balance of payments	**+435**
Change in official reserves	**+150**

2   (b) dirty-floating exchange rates.

3   Since the balance of payments is in surplus the demand for the domestic currency is greater than the supply of the domestic currency (through demand for foreign currency). This will lead to the appreciation of the run. If the government of Eden wished to keep the exchange rate fixed, they would have to sell 435 run on the foreign exchange markets. In which case reserves would increase by the foreign currency equivalent of 435 run. Since reserves have only increased by 100 run we must assume that the run is determined by a 'dirty-floating' exchange rate regime

3.6 Deficit problems

In the case of an external deficit the supply and demand for the domestic currency do not equate at the current exchange rate. In fact, the supply of the domestic currency in the foreign exchange market is greater than the demand for the domestic currency – at the current exchange rate. We can therefore say that there is 'excess supply' of the domestic currency on the foreign exchange markets.

An excess supply of the domestic currency will put pressure on the exchange rate to depreciate. If the monetary authorities wish to keep the exchange rate fixed they must absorb this excess supply by purchasing the domestic currency and selling the foreign currency on the foreign exchange markets.

If this so-called 'intervention' is not sterilised it will reduce the monetary authorities' stock of foreign currency reserves and reduces the money supply in the economy. This monetary effect further assists in the correction of the deficit problem by increasing interest rates.

The increase in interest rates may reduce capital outflows and attract foreign investment, thereby increasing the demand for the domestic currency and absorbing the excess supply.

Furthermore, in a Keynsian sense, higher interest rates stifle investment and reduce national income and then (via the marginal propensity to import) lower import demand. Lower imports will then reduce the supply of the domestic currency on the foreign exchange markets.

According to the monetarist theory, a reduction in the money supply below that of money demand may deflate the economy. This deflation may lead to unemployment in the economy. The likelihood of unemployment resulting from the use of non-sterilised intervention to cure a balance of payments deficit will very much depend on domestic conditions within the economy. For example, such a policy will not be problematic if the economy is at or near full employment.

If the deficit problem persists (and reserves continue to dwindle or foreign debts mount) then the domestic government will be forced to adopt more proactive policies designed to restrict the supply of the domestic currency on the foreign exchange markets. Such policies may be designed to restrict demand for the foreign imported goods, such as quotas and tariffs, or they may be designed to deter domestic investors from investing overseas, such as exchange controls.

Such policies have two main effects on the current account: an income effect (**expenditure reducing**) and a substitution effect between domestic and foreign goods (**expenditure switching**).

- **Expenditure reducing:** deflationary policies will reduce national income. This will reduce expenditure, including expenditure on imports. This will shift the sterling supply curve (see Figure 9) to the left. The bigger the marginal propensity to import, the bigger the reduction in import expenditure and the larger the shift.

However, although deflationary policies may improve the balance of payments, unemployment is likely to rise and the rate of growth to fall.

- **Expenditure switching:** if deflationary policies reduce the rate of inflation, domestic goods will become cheaper relative to foreign goods and foreign goods will become more expensive relative to domestic goods.

Foreign consumers will switch to UK exports. The more elastic their demand, the bigger the switch. UK consumers will switch to domestically-produced goods. Again the more elastic their demand the bigger the switch. Such events will reduce the conflict between balance of payments and employment objectives.

Expenditure switching could also be achieved by the use of restrictions on imports, such as tariffs and quotas. However, this would conflict with the objectives of free trade.

A devaluation of the domestic currency may be resorted to. A successful devaluation will alleviate the 'excess supply' by increasing exports and decreasing imports. A devaluation will only be successful if something known as the **'Marshall-Lerner condition'** is satisfied and if there is sufficient capacity in the economy to meet the increased import demand from overseas and/or produce goods that were previously imported. (The Marshall-Lerner condition is discussed under devaluation, below.)

However, devaluations are inconsistent with the ethos of fixed exchange rate regimes. If overseas holders of the domestic currency, particularly central banks, lose confidence in the currency (if a currency can be devalued it can be devalued again) then this may cause a 'run' on the currency as they try to sell the currency on the foreign exchange market. This will further exacerbate the problem and, consequently, devaluations are only used as a last resort.

DEVALUATION

If a nation operating a fixed exchange rate system drops the external value of its currency then exports will appear cheaper to foreigners while imports will appear more expensive to domestic customers.

This measure is therefore an expenditure switching policy. Its efficacy is dependent upon the elasticities of demand for imports and exports. The Marshall-Lerner criterion states that devaluation will only improve the balance of payments if the sum of the elasticities of demand for exports and imports is greater than unity. A payment surplus could be cured by a revaluation if the same criteria were met.

The importance of this condition can be demonstrated easily with a simple example.

Example

You are given the following information on a hypothetical world economy consisting of two countries, the US and the UK, each of which trade in two goods, fish and computers.

Sterling/dollar exchange rate is $3/£.

The price of UK fish exports to the US is £10/kg.

The price of US computer exports to the UK is $600/unit.

Current US demand for fish = 20 kgs.

Current UK demand for computers = 5 units.

Using this information we can calculate the UK Trade Balance. From Table 3.2 below we can see clearly that the UK is running a trade deficit with the US.

UK Import Expenditure	5 units × $600 ÷ $3/£	(£1000)
UK Export Receipts	20 kgs × £10/kg	£200
Exports – Imports		(£800)

Table 7

In order to improve this trade deficit the monetary authorities may decide to devalue the value of sterling against the dollar. The effectiveness of such a policy will depend on the magnitudes of the elasticity's of exports and imports. This relationship is demonstrated in cases 1 and 2 below.

Case 1: (the sum of the elasticities of exports and imports exceed unity)

Current US demand for fish = 20 kgs.

Current UK demand for computers = 5 units.

The UK import elasticity for computers (US exports) = –1.2.

The US import elasticity for fish (UK exports) = –5.

Sterling is devalued from $3/£ to $2/£.

The devaluation raises the sterling price of computers from £200 to £300 (e.g. by 50%) and lowers the dollars price of fish from $30 to $20 (e.g. by 50%).

This devaluation reduces the UK demand for computers by 60% (–1.2 × 50%) to 2 units and increases the US demand for fish by 250% (–5 × –50%) to 70 kg

The impact on the UK current account is as follows.

UK Import Expenditure	2 units × $600 ÷ $2/£	(£600)
UK Export Receipts	70 kgs × £10/kg	£700
Exports – Imports		£100

Table 8

The UK Balance of Payments thus moves from a deficit of £800 to a surplus of £100.

Case 2: (the sum of the elasticity's of exports and imports are less than unity)

The UK import elasticity for computers (US exports) = 0.

The US import elasticity for fish (UK exports) = –0.5.

The devaluation again raises the sterling price of computers from £200 to £300 (e.g. by 50%) and lowers the dollars price of fish from $30 to $20 (e.g. by 50%).

This devaluation leaves the UK demand for computers unchanged at 5 units and increases the US demand for fish by 25% (–0.5 × –50%) to 25 kgs.

The impact on the UK current account is as follows.

UK Import Expenditure	5 units × $600 ÷ $2/£	(£1500)
UK Export Receipts	25 kgs × £10/kg	£250
Exports – Imports		(£1250)

Table 9

Thus the UK Balance of Payments therefore deteriorates from a deficit of £800 to a deficit of £1250.

Therefore the normal devaluation response (case 1) and the perverse devaluation response (case 2) may be generalised into the Marshall-Lerner condition.

Devaluation will only improve a country's Balance of Payments if the sum of the domestic and foreign elasticity's of demand for imports exceeds unity.

ACTIVITY 6

In which of the following cases will devaluation of sterling be successful in curing a Current Account deficit:

1   UK Elasticity of Demand for Imports = –0.4
    World Elasticity of Demand for UK exports = –0.5

2   UK Elasticity of Demand for Imports = –1.0
    World Elasticity of Demand for UK exports = –2.0

3   UK Elasticity of Demand for Imports = –0.1
    World Elasticity of Demand for UK exports = 0.

4   UK Elasticity of Demand for Imports = –0.3
    World Elasticity of Demand for UK exports = –0.6

5   UK Elasticity of Demand for Imports = –2.0
    World Elasticity of Demand for UK exports = –1.5

Recall that the Marshall-Lerner criterion states that devaluation will only improve the balance of payments if the sum of the elasticities of demand for exports and imports is greater than unity.

Therefore a devaluation will be successful in curing a Current Account deficit in cases (b) and (e). In both cases the absolute value of the sum of the UK Elasticity of Demand for Imports and the World Elasticity of Demand is greater than 1.

THE J-CURVE

It has frequently been observed that measures taken to rectify a balance of payments deficit have often led to an immediate deterioration of the current account followed by a subsequent recovery. If this is charted we obtain the J-curve effect illustrated in Figure 10.

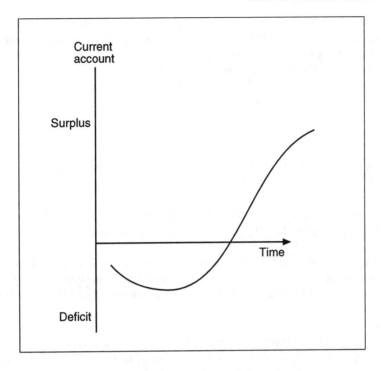

Figure 10: The J-curve effect

Why this occurs can best be understood by splitting the subsequent events up into three periods – the short term, the medium term and the longer term.

THE SHORT TERM
The initial response to a devaluation may be quite slow. For instance there may have been a lot of contracts agreed at the old exchange rate or it may take some time to build up the productive capacity to meet the increased demand for exports.

If the domestic prices of export goods are unchanged, and the quantity of exports has yet to respond to the new prices, export revenues will only be slightly higher. However, if import quantities have also not changed by much but the import prices have risen by the amount of the devaluation then the value of imports may have risen substantially. Therefore the current account may move into deficit in the short term.

However, in the longer term, as purchasers and suppliers adjust the quantities of imports and exports, higher export quantities and lower import quantities are likely to move the current account into surplus.

THE MEDIUM TERM
Recall the national income identity introduced in Unit 7:

$$Y = C + I + G + (X - M).$$

X represents the level of exports, M represents the level of imports, Y represents national income (typically measured by GDP - see Unit 6), I represents the level of investment in the economy, G represents the level of government expenditure and C represents the level of consumer expenditure.

The national income identity can be reformulated as follows:

$$X - M = Y - (C + I + G)$$

i.e. balance of payments deficit/surplus = national income (GDP) – total domestic expenditure (TDE).

From this formulation we can say that the balance of payments will be in deficit if total domestic expenditure is greater than national income.

Thus we can argue that devaluation will only be successful if TDE does not absorb the whole of GDP. For this condition to be fulfilled there must be spare capacity in the economy, otherwise output will not be able to rise to meet the increased demand for exports.

This approach underlines the necessity to have spare capacity in the economy before devaluing the currency. It may be necessary to accompany the devaluation with expenditure reducing policies to reduce domestic absorption.

Beginning at full employment, a devaluation accompanied by higher taxes will increase the demand for net exports without increasing total aggregate demand. Since there is no upward pressure on domestic prices, the increased international competitiveness can be sustained in the medium term.

THE LONGER TERM

Eventually domestic firms that import raw materials will want to pass on these costs in higher prices. Workers who buy imported consumer goods will demand higher wages to offset the increased cost of living. In turn, these price and wage increases will lead to other firms and other workers responding in a similar manner.

Thus the eventual impact of a devaluation will be an increase in all other nominal wages and prices in line with the higher import prices, returning the real exchange rate to its near initial value.

EXAMPLE

A classic example of the short, medium and long-term effects in action can be seen by analysing the 1967 devaluation of sterling.

Balance of Payments problems had existed in the UK throughout the 1950s and 1960s. Yet from 1949 until 1967 the pound dollar exchange rate was fixed at $2.80.

Because of sterling's role as a reserve currency amongst commonwealth countries, devaluation was avoided as it would immediately reduce the value of these countries' reserves. They might then lose confidence in sterling and decide to convert their reserves into gold or dollars. Such selling would cause a crisis, forcing further devaluation. Consequently, deflationary policies were preferred as a solution to balance of payments problems.

But finally, in November 1967, the long-resisted devaluation came. The pound was devalued from $2.80 to $2.40. Table 10 shows the effect of the devaluation on the current account.

	1967	1968	1969	1970
Current account (£m)	–£294m	–£286m	£463m	£731m
Balance of payments (£m)	–£671m	–£1410m	£687m	£1287m
Public sector borrowing requirement (PSBR) as a % of GDP	5.3%	3.4%	–1.2%	0%
Real exchange rate (1975 = 100)	109	102	102	103

Table 10

The first row shows that it took two years before the current account moved from deficit into surplus. The annual data given in the table do not fully capture the J-curve effect.

However, a J-curve effect is evident from examination of the evolution of the current account during 1967 and 1968. In particular, the current account deficit was £59m in the third quarter of 1967 (i.e. 1967Q3) and £219m in 1967Q4 - the short term effect outlined above. This was followed by a transformation of the 1967 current account deficit of £294m into a current account surplus of £731m in 1970 – the J-curve effect outlined above.

In 1967 UK unemployment was low and the economy was close to full employment. The economy had few spare resources to meet the increased demand for exports or import substitution. In 1968 and 1969 fiscal policy (as indicated by the figures in table 3.5 showing the PSBR as a percentage of GDP falling from 3.4% to –1.2%) was tightened, reducing domestic consumption and allowing for an improvement in net exports (the medium term effect).

The final row indicates the long-term effect. It shows that instead of using the 15% devaluation to reduce export prices, UK exporters responded by raising prices and profit margins. Consequently, only about half of the competitive advantage was passed on to foreign purchasers as lower foreign prices for UK goods. Furthermore, by 1970 the real exchange rate had begun to rise again as workers asked for cost of living increases to meet higher import prices.

3.7 The problem of a balance of payments surplus

While it is generally accepted that a persistent balance of payments deficit, through the erosion of reserves, is a problem, it is much less obvious that a surplus can also pose problems.

The reasons why running a persistent balance of payments surplus is a problem are as follows:

1 **One country's surplus is another country's deficit:** it is impossible for all countries to simultaneously run a balance of payments surplus. If countries refuse to reduce their persistently large surpluses, then deficit countries will find it difficult to reduce their deficit. This may force them to impose restrictions on imports and all countries may suffer from the resultant collapse in world trade.

2 **The 'Dutch disease':** the growth of Britain oil trade surplus in the 1970s and 1980s together with an influx of 'hot-money', caused the exchange rate to rise to a level which decreased the competitiveness of non-oil visible exports in world markets, and increased the competitiveness of imports in the UK economy.

Thus, much of the benefit of North Sea oil revenues were lost in financing industrial imports, leading to a rundown of the economy and an increase in the number of unemployed.

This syndrome is known as the 'Dutch disease', after the experience of the Netherlands following the discovery of natural gas in the North Sea in the 1950s.

3 **Inflationary consequences:** in Keynsian analysis a balance of payments surplus represents an injection of demand into the economy, causing demand pull inflation, if output cannot be raised to meet demand.

4 **When the balance of payments is in surplus there is excess demand for the country's currency at the current exchange rate.** If the exchange rate is determined under a fixed or dirty-floating exchange rate regime the monetary authorities will be forced to intervene in the foreign exchange market and sell the domestic currency in return for foreign currency. This builds up the country's foreign currency reserves but at the expense of an increase in the

country's money supply, which may lead to inflation. This inflation will in the end 'solve' the surplus problem by making home country goods more expensive, relative to foreign goods.

3.8 Surplus problems

In the case of an external surplus the supply and demand for the domestic currency do not equate at the current exchange rate. In fact the demand for the domestic currency in the foreign exchange market is greater than the supply of the domestic currency – at the current exchange rate. We can therefore say that there is 'excess demand' of the domestic currency on the foreign exchange markets.

This will put pressure on the exchange rate to appreciate. If the monetary authorities wish to keep the exchange rate fixed they must meet this excess demand by selling the domestic currency and buying the foreign currency on the foreign exchange markets.

If this so-called 'intervention' is not sterilised then this increases the monetary authorities' stock of foreign currency reserves and increases the money supply in the economy. This monetary effect further assists in the correction of the surplus problem via its impact in decreasing interest rates.

The decrease in interest rates may lead to an outflow of capital from the domestic economy, thereby increasing the supply of the domestic currency and absorbing the excess demand.

Furthermore, as we saw in Unit 7, lower interest rates tend to increase investment and hence increase national income and then, via the marginal propensity to import, increase import demand. This will then increase the supply of the domestic currency on the foreign exchange markets.

In a monetarist sense, an increase in the money supply above that of money demand may led to price inflation in the domestic economy.

Therefore, inflation may be an artefact of the use of non-sterilised intervention to cure a balance of payments surplus. The extent of the inflationary problem will very much depend on domestic conditions within the economy. For example, this policy will not be problematic if the economy is in a slump.

If the increase in the money supply experienced above is 'sterilised' then the economy will remain in external surplus. This policy may be preferred if domestic economic conditions are strong.

If a surplus problem persists the domestic government will be forced to adopt more proactive policies designed to increase the supply of the domestic currency on the foreign exchange markets (by stimulating the demand for foreign currency). Such policies may be designed to increase the demand for foreign goods or, by lowering the interest rate, making investments from overseas less attractive.

For example, if the surplus is export-driven then assuming there is spare capacity in the economy, the monetary authorities could introduce an expansionary fiscal policy with lower taxes and high government expenditure. This will then boost the internal economy and stimulate import demand.

Alternatively, if the surplus is driven by 'hot money' entering the economy to take advantage of high interest rates, the monetary authorities could reduce interest rates (a policy referred to as easing monetary policy) making sterling less attractive to investors and reducing the inflow of the so-called 'hot money'.

The external value of the currency may be changed in order to overcome surplus problems. In this case, to alleviate the excess demand for the currency at the existing exchange rate, the currency must be revalued. A successful revaluation will alleviate the 'excess demand' by decreasing exports and increasing imports. As noted earlier, the revaluation will only be successful if the Marshall-Lerner condition is satisfied. In particular, if the Marshall-Lerner condition is not satisfied, import and export demand will not respond in a manner that will improve the current account.

Now try the following activities to ensure that you have understood the main points arising from the discussion in this section.

ACTIVITY 7

Distinguish between expenditure switching and expenditure reducing policies.

Expenditure switching policies attempt to persuade domestic consumers to switch from foreign goods to domestic goods in the case of a trade deficit, or from domestic to foreign in the case of a surplus. Expenditure reducing policies decrease the total amount of economy which via the marginal propensity to import reduces expenditure on exported goods.

ACTIVITY 8

If a country devalues its currency, explain why the following statements are probable consequences:

1   its goods will become cheaper for foreign consumers and firms

2   foreign goods will become cheaper for domestic consumers and firms

3   exports will increase

4   imports will decrease

5   net exports (exports – imports) will increase.

1 By definition, a devaluation of one currency against another means that a unit of the domestic currency now buys less foreign currency than it did previously. Equivalently a unit of foreign currency now buys more domestic currency than it did previously. Consequently, due to the increased spending power of the foreign currency, domestic goods will now appear cheaper to foreign firms and consumers.

2 Following the above argument, as a result of the reduced spending power of the domestic currency, foreign goods will now appear more expensive to domestic consumers and firms.

3 The export elasticity of demand is negative. Therefore a reduction in the price of exports will lead to an increase in exports. This is assuming, of course, that there is sufficient spare capacity in the domestic economy to meet the increased export demand.

4 The import elasticity of demand is negative. Therefore an increase in the price of imports will lead to a decrease in imports. This is assuming, of course, that there are domestic suppliers of goods that consumers and firms may switch to.

5 If the Marshall Lerner condition - the sum of the elasticities of demand for exports and imports is greater than unity - is satisfied, the increase in export receipts will outweigh the reduction in import expenditure and net exports will increase.

REVIEW ACTIVITY 4

List three requirements that must be satisfied in order for a devaluation to improve a country's trade balance.

Summary

In this section we examined the way international trade between countries is recorded in the balance of payments. We found out why it can be problematic for a country to import more goods than it exports, or, to a lesser extent, why it might be a problem for a country to export more goods than it imports. We discussed the policies available to governments to correct balance of payments problems and the conflicts which arise with the attainment of the domestic economic goals.

SECTION FOUR

Recent Exchange Rate History

Introduction

In this section we will chart the history of the exchange rate between 1944 and the mid-1990s. We will draw on the experiences of the UK, USA and Germany drawn to highlight the links between interest rates, domestic economic policy and the exchange rate. We will look at the European Monetary System and its key features, as well as the future prospects for the main European currencies. Finally, we will discuss the advantages and disadvantages of floating and fixed exchange rates.

4.1 The Bretton Woods system

The system adopted in 1944 is called the **gold standard exchange**. It is also commonly referred to as the **Bretton Woods system**, after the town in New Hampshire, USA where its details were worked out.

Under the Bretton Woods system there was a fixed dollar/gold exchange rate ($35 per ounce). Furthermore, the USA guaranteed that it would freely convert dollars into gold. In turn, all other countries pegged their exchange rates to the US dollar and were required to keep the exchange rate within 1% of a fixed parity. The exchange rate between other currencies could then be calculated by their common relationship with the dollar.

For example if the DM/$ exchange rate is 4DMs per $ and the $/£ exchange rate is $2.80s per £, then it follows that the DM/£ exchange rate is 11.2 DMs per £. That is £1 is equal to $2.80 and $1 in turn is equal to 4 DMs. It follows then that £1 is equal to $4 \times 2.80 = 11.2$ DMs.

$$S(DM/£) = S(DM/\$) \times S(\$/£)$$

$$= 4 \text{ DM}/\$ \times \$2.80/£ = 11.2 \text{ DM}/£$$

In order to maintain parity with the dollar each country had to intervene in the foreign exchange market. The intervention was conducted in dollars and so each central bank had to keep dollar reserves.

Therefore, if there was excess demand for dollars at the current exchange rate which was putting downward pressure on the value of the domestic currency relative to the dollar, then the central bank would have to sell dollars (and run down its reserves in the process) to maintain the fixed exchange rate. Similarly, if there was excess supply of dollars at the current exchange rate, which was putting upward pressure on the domestic currency relative to the dollar. The central bank would have to buy dollars (and augment reserves in the process) in order to maintain parity with the dollar.

For example, from 1949 to 1967 the dollar/£ exchange rate was fixed at $2.80/£. The Bank of England, therefore, had to intervene in the foreign exchange market to ensure that the exchange rate stayed within ± 1% of this level ($2.772/£ − $2.828/£). Thus, if there was an increase in the demand for pounds, the Bank of England had to intervene in the foreign exchange market at the upper support level of $2.828/£ and supply (in exchange for dollars) the pounds necessary to prevent the exchange rate going above this level.

A consequence of this is that should the US run a balance of payments deficit, overseas central banks would be forced to buy dollars (sell domestic currency) in order to prevent their currencies from appreciating relative to the dollar. This process had the effect of increasing the domestic money supply, possibly leading to inflation.

If there was a persistent tendency for an exchange rate to reach its upper or lower levels, indicating a fundamental disequilibrium, then the Bretton Woods system allowed currencies to revalue or devalue, depending on the circumstances. For example, the dollar value of the pound was reduced in November 1967 from $2.80 to $2.40. However, as pointed out above, a devaluation is only successful in curing a balance of payments deficit if the Marshall Lerner conditions are satisfied.

However devaluation was intended as a last resort. Prior to that, governments were supposed to pursue expenditure reducing, deflationary and reflationary policies.

Since dollars had become the world's medium of exchange, the US could never run out of foreign exchange reserves. This willingness to hold dollars as reserves meant that the US government could simply finance a balance of payments deficit by printing more dollars. So long as the US ran small balance of payments deficits this wouldn't be a problem as they held enough gold reserves to meet conversion demands.

However, in the mid 1960s the US began to run much larger payments deficits with the rest of the world (partly to finance the Vietnam War). This increased the dollar holdings of overseas central banks and meant that US gold reserves were becoming inadequate to guarantee convertibility.

This situation led to a 'run on gold' as central banks became worried that the convertibility of dollars to gold was to be suspended, leaving them with dollars, which, clearly, from the persistent US balance of payments deficits, were overvalued.

Some relief came in 1970 with the creation of Special Drawing Rights (SDRs), the currency of the International Monetary Fund (IMF). The value of the SDR was set at the equivalent of 1/35 oz of gold (note that 1 oz = $35) and it was used to create 'paper gold'.

However, the writing was on the wall for the Bretton Woods system. On 15 August 1971 the US, in response to huge trade deficit figures, announced the inconvertibility of dollars to gold – the key aspect of the system. The 10 largest nations met in Washington DC in December 1971 to resolve the situation. As a result of the subsequent **Smithsonian Agreement**, the US raised the price of gold to $38 per ounce (i.e. $35 dollars no longer bought an ounce of gold and so the dollar was devalued). Each of the other countries revalued its currency by up to 10% and increased the upper and lower limits to ±.

By 1973 the dollar was again under heavy selling pressure and the price of gold was raised further in February 1973, to $42.22 per ounce. Eventually, in March 1973, after the currency markets were closed for two weeks, the Bretton Woods system was ended as countries decided to float their exchange rates. In fact, sterling was floated earlier, in June 1972.

4.2 The oil price shock

The OPEC oil price increase in 1973/74 caused huge balance of payments deficits for oil importers and corresponding balance of payments surpluses for the OPEC countries. A natural response would have been for the oil-importing countries to depreciate their currencies, making their domestic goods more competitively priced in the world market, and increasing the price of exports.

However, the demand for oil is highly inelastic; a depreciation would have made things worse as it could have caused a further rise in inflation, little increase in exports and could well have initiated a series of competitive devaluations.

The OPEC countries could not spend all of these surpluses on additional imports. Firstly, they did not have the capacity to consume such a huge increase in imports, and secondly, the oil importing countries did not have the capacity to supply such a huge increase in exports.

A large part of the oil surpluses were therefore invested in short-term dollar and, to a lesser extent, sterling deposits. This created a large pool of funds which Western banks could use for speculation on the world's financial markets. This money could be switched quickly from one financial centre to another to take advantage of favourable interest rates and exchange rates.

This created a massive capacity for banks to adopt speculative attacks on currencies, thus making it difficult for countries to control exchange rates by normal intervention. Reserves and access to foreign loans were often inadequate to prevent the speculative selling. Governments therefore had to rely much more on using interest rates to counteract the speculative flows.

The problem with using interest rates to control the exchange rate in this situation is that the interest rate required to stem capital flows may be wholly inappropriate for existing internal economic conditions.

Moreover, the use of higher interest rates to prevent the outflow of speculative money may cause other countries to raise their interest rates in competition. Such beggar-thy-neighbour policies would lead to world recession.

Until 1975 the UK was able to defend the exchange rate through the inflow of the oil surpluses and through foreign borrowing for intervention in the foreign exchange market. However, in 1975 the value of sterling began to fall (see Figure 11). This continued into 1976 leading eventually to crisis in November 1976 when the UK negotiated a loan from the International Monetary Fund (IMF). The resulting rescue package included an insistence on the adoption of monetary targets through higher interest rates. The exchange rate 'bottomed out' at the end of 1976.

4.3 The rise of sterling: 1976–81

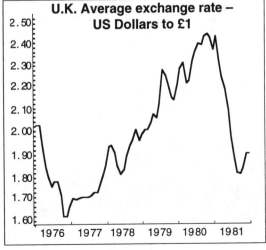

Figure 11: The rise of sterling 1976–81

The intervention of the IMF, together with the growing importance of North Sea oil, brought about renewed confidence in sterling which began to appreciate in value. In fact, in 1977 the Bank of England intervened in the foreign exchange market by selling sterling to prevent the exchange rate rising too much. Note from Figure 12 the increase in UK reserves throughout 1977.

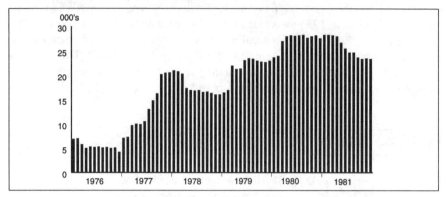

Figure 12: UK official reserves (in US$m) by month from 01/01/76-31/12/81

The resultant receipt of foreign currencies was used to build up reserves and pay off some of the foreign loans the UK acquired in the early 1970's to defend sterling.

We can see from figure 11 above that throughout this period, the pound was largely allowed to float freely (an example of a 'pure-floating' exchange rate regime) on the foreign exchange markets (note the long periods where the level of reserves stayed constant). From October 1976 to November 1980 the dollar/sterling exchange rate increased from $1.6367/£ to $2.4168/£.

The reason for this dramatic appreciation in the value of sterling was largely two-fold.

Firstly, North Sea oil revenue was making an increasingly significant contribution to the current account of the balance of payments (see Figure 13). Moreover, the fact that the UK was now an oil exporter allowed sterling to survive the second oil price shock in 1979 (the price of oil rose from $13 per barrel in mid-1978 to $19 per barrel in 1979 and to $31 during 1980).

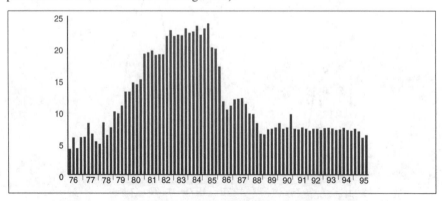

Figure 13: Oil exports as a percentage of total UK exports per
quarter from 01/01/76–31/12/95

Secondly, the Thatcher government which came to power in 1979, moved the policy of Monetary Targeting to the centre of UK economic policy, through the Medium Term Financial Strategy (MTFS). In order to meet its monetary targets the government increased interest rates, with short term interest rates reaching over 17% in late 1979. This obviously led to large capital inflows and an appreciation of the exchange rate. Had the government wished to prevent this increase in the exchange rate it would have had to intervene in the foreign exchange markets by selling sterling. This would have had led to unwanted increases in the money supply. The government, therefore, could not target both the exchange rate and the money supply. It chose the money supply and let interest rates, and hence the exchange rate, rise.

ACTIVITY 9

Look at Figures 11 and 12. Describe briefly the actions the Bank of England could have undertaken in the foreign exchange market to avoid the value of sterling rising between 1978 and 1981.

For the majority of this period the Bank of England did not intervene on the foreign exchange markets. If it wished to keep the value of the pound down it would have had to sell domestic currency, in exchange for foreign currency (which would increase reserves) on the foreign exchange market.

4.4 'Reagonomics': 1981–5

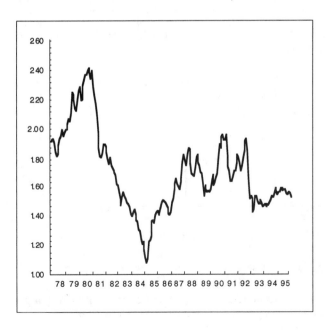

*Figure 14: (a) United States Dollar effective exchange rate,
monthly index (b) UK Average exchange rate – US dollars to £1*

We can see from Figure 14 that the US dollar appreciated substantially between January 1980 and May 1985. The main reasons this occurred was the divergent macroeconomic policies pursued by the US and the rest of the world (see Table 11).

	1980	1981	1982	1983	1984	1985	1986
US budget deficit ($bn)	−76.2	−78.7	−125.7	−202.5	−178.3	−212.1	−212.6
Average annual US interest rates (%)	11.75	13.42	10.88	8.50	8.75	7.67	6.25
Average annual Japanese interest rates (%)	8.15	6.35	5.50	5.38	5.00	5.00	3.58
Average annual German interest rates (%)	7.29	7.50	6.96	4.17	4.29	4.29	3.58

Table 11

With the election of President Reagan in November 1980, the USA adopted policies which became known as 'Reaganomics': tight monetary policy and a loose fiscal policy. Tax cuts and increased government expenditure led to a growing budget deficit, increasing from $76bn in 1979 to $213bn in 1986.

Because of the commitment to monetarism the budget deficit couldn't be monetized and had to be financed largely by borrowing. This led to high interest rates and attracted foreign capital to the US, producing a capital account surplus.

However, high aggregate demand led to a rise in imports and a current account deficit.

The effect of the capital inflows increased demand for the domestic currency on the foreign exchange markets and everything else unchanged would usually drive up the value of the currency (an appreciation).

The effect of the increased demand for imports would be to increase the supply of the domestic currency on the foreign exchange market and, with everything else unchanged, this would usually drive down the value of the currency (a depreciation).

However, these capital inflows were so large that they caused the dollar to appreciate, despite the current account deficit. This case demonstrates that short-term exchange rate movements are often brought about by capital account changes rather than current account changes.

It must be remembered that, if the value of the dollar is increasing in the foreign exchange market against its trading partners, then the value of its trading partners' currencies must be depreciating in value.

In particular, the value of sterling fell from $2.40 at the beginning of 1981 to a low of $1.05 in February 1985. Further depreciation (and dollar appreciation) was averted in February 1985 through the action of a number of European central banks and the Bank of Japan, who sold a total of $11bn over a period of a few days. This action was a result of the **Plaza Accord**, an agreement by the finance ministers of the five largest industrial nations to drive down the value of the dollar. Continued selling by the world's major central banks drove down the value of the dollar. By 1987 it had returned to its 1980 level.

4.5 The shadowing of the DM

In the late 1980s the value of sterling was again beginning to rise. With entry into the Exchange Rate Mechanism pending, the Chancellor, Nigel Lawson, wanted to keep the value of sterling pegged to the DM. Learning from the experience of the early 1980s, whereby it was demonstrated that movements in the exchange rate were largely due to capital account changes, the Chancellor attempted to prevent the rise in the value of sterling through a loose monetary policy. In particular, interest rates were reduced from 11% in October 1986 to 7.5% in May 1988.

These interest rates were still high in comparison to other nations, and so there was strong upward pressure on the value of sterling. Therefore, in order to keep the value of sterling 'pegged' at around DM2.90/£ - DM3.00/£, the Bank of England sold vast amounts of sterling. Thus, in contrast to the period in the early 1980s when a pure-float exchange rate policy was adopted, an extremely 'dirty-float' exchange rate policy was followed, and , as we can see from Table 12 (opposite), reserves more than doubled between January 1987 and June 1988. You may recall from section 3.4 that unless the foreign exchange intervention is **sterilised**, foreign currency purchases lead to an increase in the domestic money supply.

The loose monetary policy, combined with foreign currency purchases, led to a dramatic increase in the growth of the money supply and domestic credit (the so called 'Lawson boom'). The domestic economic problems which ensued – rising inflation and a deteriorating current account balance – meant that the policy of shadowing the DM had to be abandoned in favour of the attainment of domestic economic policy goals.

ACTIVITY 10

Construct a supply and demand diagram for sterling against the DM which represents the period of "shadowing the DM". Clearly label a feasible equilibrium exchange rate if the pound had been left to float during this period.

We can see from Table 12 that reserves more than doubled between January 1987 and June 1988. This indicates that the monetary authorities were selling sterling during this period in exchange for foreign currency. We may conclude therefore that at the prevailing exchange rate, DM2.90 – DM 3.00/£, there was excess demand for sterling.

Sterling was therefore being kept artificially low and a plausible equilibrium exchange rate would have been a rate in excess of DM3.00 that would have equated supply and demand.

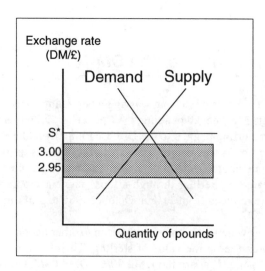

	DM/£	UK reserves ($m)
15/01/87	2.798	21952
15/02/87	2.788	22257
15/03/87	2.920	27039
15/04/87	2.953	29807
15/05/87	2.983	34679
15/06/87	2.963	34364
15/07/87	2.973	34915
15/08/87	2.966	34365
15/09/87	2.981	34808
15/10/87	2.993	41399
15/11/87	2.985	41281
15/12/87	2.987	44326
15/01/88	2.977	43093
15/02/88	2.982	42927
15/03/88	3.071	47519
15/04/88	3.138	47857
15/05/88	3.166	48533
15/06/88	3.125	48519

Table 12

4.6 The European Monetary System

The aim of the European Monetary System (EMS) is the promotion of monetary stability in Europe. Its key element is the Exchange Rate Mechanism (ERM) an agreement under which member countries keep their currencies within agreed limits against each other. Other important aspects of the system are the European Currency Unit (the ECU) and the European Monetary Co-operation Fund (EMCF).

The Exchange Rate Mechanism (ERM) is a system of fixed exchange rates between ERM currencies, but where fluctuations are permitted within specified limits. For example, when the UK joined the ERM in October 1990 its 'central parity' against the DM was DM2.95/£, with the band of fluctuations initially set at 6%.

The central parities can be adjusted from time to time by agreement with other member states.

If any currency reaches its lower or upper limit against any other ERM currency, then the central banks of the relevant country's must intervene on the foreign exchange market, by buying the weaker currency and selling the stronger currency, to keep the currency within the band of fluctuation.

The EMCF provides a "very short-term financing facility (VSTF)" , which provides unlimited credit to finance such obligatory intervention.

The European Currency Unit (ECU) is a basket currency. It consists of a specified amount of each of the EMS currencies, with the amounts chosen so as to reflect each country's economic weight.

Sometimes rather than quote the complete set of bilateral central rates in the parity grid, it is easier to just quote the exchange rate between the ECU and each of the EMS currencies.

The EMS comprising of the nine EC member states (Belgium, Denmark, France, Germany, Ireland, Italy, Luxembourg, Netherlands and the UK) came into existence in March 1979. All the countries except the UK also joined the ERM and adopted fluctuation bands of $177 \pm 2.25\%$ (Italy initially adopted a fluctuation band of $\pm 6\%$).

Spain joined the ERM in June 1989 with a fluctuation band of $\pm 6\%$ the UK joined in October 1990 with a fluctuation band of $\pm 6\%$ and finally Portugal joined in April 1992, also with a fluctuation band of $\pm 6\%$.

The UK had initially thought it unwise to peg the value of sterling, a "petrocurrency", to other non-oil currencies. The rationale was that non-oil currencies were unlikely to be affected in the same manner as sterling was by the price of oil.

A further obstacle to entry to the ERM was the historically high rates of inflation in the UK relative to the ERM countries. In particular if the UK were to peg its exchange rate to a country whose annual rate of inflation is 5% lower than the UK level then in order to maintain international competitiveness sterling should depreciate by 5% per annum.

However in October 1990 it was widely believed that inflation had been beaten and so the UK joined the ERM at a central parity of DM2.95 with a $\pm 6\%$ band of fluctuation. In fact we can see from the table 13 below that it has had a great deal of success in reducing inflation as ERM member countries imported monetary prudence from Germany.

	UK	Germany	France	Italy	Belgium	N'lands	Denmark	Spain
1980	13.92	4.09	9.98	15.56	4.76	4.84	–	11.62
1981	8.80	4.55	9.62	14.43	5.59	4.90	8.66	10.78
1982	7.04	4.04	9.57	11.94	6.42	4.72	7.57	10.82
1983	3.33	2.61	6.92	11.54	5.86	2.06	5.49	8.94
1984	3.73	1.89	5.92	8.32	5.00	2.55	4.81	8.71
1985	4.67	1.67	4.60	6.41	3.82	1.81	3.78	6.69
1986	2.57	0.08	1.99	4.93	1.14	0.24	2.56	6.57
1987	3.10	0.03	2.53	3.26	1.17	−0.59	3.03	4.07
1988	3.25	0.86	1.92	3.67	0.76	0.50	3.41	3.44
1989	5.85	1.99	2.60	4.89	2.19	0.78	3.53	4.97
1990	6.89	1.97	2.54	4.48	2.46	1.74	2.08	5.00
1991	4.83	2.33	2.48	4.90	2.55	2.22	1.83	4.51
1992	2.96	4.24	1.89	4.06	1.86	2.55	1.74	4.60
1993	1.18	3.35	1.56	3.18	2.09	1.90	0.88	3.36
1994	1.81	2.12	1.28	2.96	1.88	2.13	1.46	3.61
1995	2.61	1.37	1.30	3.88	1.12	1.54	1.61	3.56

Table 13: Annual inflation rates of EMS member countries, 1980–1995

The earlier UK experience of shadowing the DM demonstrated to many people that ERM membership would involve a loss of monetary policy independence, as interest rates are adjusted to maintain the exchange rate within its band of fluctuation. In fact as the UK economy moved into recession the government was unable to make the substantial cuts in interest rates required to boost investment and aggregate demand, as if the UK lowered its rates too far the resultant capital outflows would push the pound down to the bottom of its 6% band.

The government therefore could not target both the exchange rate and the money supply. This time it chose the exchange rate.

The ERM ran into trouble during 1992. Britain was in severe recession with unemployment rates higher than at any time since the depression of the 1930s. Italy was also experiencing recession. These conditions were coincident with reunification in Germany. The financing of the reunification process led to a growing budget deficit and high German interest rates. The high German interest rates put upward pressure on the DM, forcing Britain and Italy to raise interest rates if they wanted to keep their exchange rates within the ERM.

With the domestic conditions of Britain and Italy not being able to withstand such an increase in interest rates, the view of the foreign exchange market was that sterling and the lire would eventually devalue. Consequently speculators sold British Pounds and Italian lire hoping to gain from eventual devaluation (e.g. selling a large quantity of pounds and lire at the current exchange rate in exchange for a safe currency such as the DM then profiting when the devaluation has been forced by buying pounds and lire back at a lower level). The scale of intervention required by the UK and Italian monetary authorities to remain within the bands of fluctuation was so large that the UK and Italy were forced to withdraw from the ERM in September 1992 and float against other ERM currencies.

Turmoil returned in the summer of 1993. In similar circumstances to those the previous year in the UK, domestic economic conditions in France required a cut in interest rates. As in the previous year this would only be possible if Germany also cut interest rates, which it would not do. Again speculators began to sell the weak currency (the Franc) in expectation of a devaluation. In an attempt to rescue the ERM, the EC finance ministers agreed to widen the fluctuation bands to ± 15%.

In December 1991 the leaders of the EC countries met at Maastricht in Holland to negotiate a treaty (the Maastricht Treaty) on European Monetary Union (EMU) , and the consequent creation of a single currency, single central bank (the European Monetary Institute) and a single monetary policy.

A key step towards European Monetary Union is the convergence of members' economies (remember the conflicts of September 1992 when a number of economies had vastly dissimilar economic circumstances). In order to progress to EMU a country must meet five convergence criteria.

1. Inflation – inflation should be no more than 1.25% above the average rate of the three lowest inflation rates of the European Union.

2. Interest Rates – The rate of interest on long term government bonds should be no more than 2% above the average of the three countries with the lowest interest rates.

3. Budget Deficits – budget deficits should be no more than 3% of GDP.

4. National Debt – national debt should be no more than 60% of GDP.

5. Exchange Rate – the currency should have been a full ERM member for two years.

EMU is scheduled to begin on January 1st, 1999 with the creation of a new currency called the Euro. Whilst exchange rates will be irrevocably fixed at this point notes and coins will not be changed until 2002.

The decision on who should be included is to be made in 1998 on 1997 economic data. Economic Forecasts for 1997 from the Organisation of Economic Development (OECD) are included in the table below.

	Budget Deficit (% GDP)	Debt (% GDP)	Inflation[a]	Long Term Interest Rates[b]
Germany	–2.3	58.6	2.1	6.3
France	–3.0	53.5	2.0	6.8
Italy	–5.4	125	3.7	10.4
UK	–2.8	54.7	2.3	7.9
Austria	–4.7	74.6	2.3	6.6
Belgium	–3.2	131	2.2	6.8
Denmark	–0.5	72.4	3.1	7.5
Finland	–0.1	69.0	2.6	7.3
Greece	–7.7	108	6.5	-
Ireland	–2.8	81.9	1.4	7.7
Luxembourg	0	7.6	1.9	6.8
Netherlands	–2.4	77.0	1.7	6.3
Norway	+2.1	45.0	2.7	6.8
Portugal	–3.7	69.0	3.6	-
Spain	–4.1	68.6	3.1	9.7
Sweden	–3.3	80.7	3.2	8.8

Table 14

Notes:[a] average of three lowest countries 1.67%. Inflation rates must therefore be less than approximately 3%.

[b] average of three lowest countries 6.4%. Long term interest rates must therefore be less than approximately 8.4%.

The shaded blocks indicate where the Maastricht criteria is expected to be met. Thus we can see that only two countries Germany and France meet the Maastricht criteria and are also currently members of the ERM. In fact, it is debatable whether France will meet the Budget Deficit target of 3%, as this is based on an optimistic forecast of GDP growth in France in 1997.

On this basis EMU will consist of Germany (and Luxembourg whose currency is not a member of the ERM but is pegged to the DM). However the criteria may be watered down to allow more countries to join.

ACTIVITY 11

Explain, in no more than 100 words, why you think the Maastricht Treaty includes criteria on:

1   low interest rates and

2   low inflation rates?

---

1   If a country has significantly higher interest rates than the other Maastricht Treaty signatories then it may attract 'hot-money' from overseas, which will put pressure on the domestic interest rate to appreciate. Moreover, the outflow of funds from other currencies may put downward pressure on its value.

2   If a country has significantly higher inflation than its trading partners then there will be pressure on the country's currency to depreciate by an amount equal to the inflation differential.

4.7 The exchange rate debate

THE CASE FOR AND AGAINST FLOATING EXCHANGE RATES

Floating exchange rates ensure balance of payments equilibrium
Under a pure-floating exchange rate regime a balance of payments imbalance will be rectified automatically through the forces of supply and demand on the exchange rate. For example, if a currency has a balance of payments deficit, then, all else equal, the currency should depreciate until the demand for the domestic currency (from overseas investors and from overseas buyers of domestic goods) equates with the supply of the domestic currency (from domestic buyers of foreign goods and domestic residents investing overseas). Conversely, a balance of payments surplus should be eliminated by an appreciation of the currency.

No conflict with internal policy
When a country has a floating exchange rate a balance of payments deficit is corrected through the market mechanism described above. When a country has a fixed exchange rate, however, the policies adopted to cure the deficit may be in conflict with the domestic economic objectives.

For example, if the central bank intervenes in the foreign exchange market by selling the domestic currency to meet an excess demand for it, the domestic money supply will increase, which may lead to inflation.

This was exactly the conflict facing the Conservative government in the early 1980s, when it was using a policy of monetary targeting to reduce inflation. There was pressure on sterling to appreciate. If the government wished to defend sterling then it would have to intervene on the foreign exchange markets and, consequently, increase the domestic money supply. The government, therefore, could not target both the exchange rate and the money supply. It chose the money supply and let interest rates, and hence the exchange rate, rise.

Therefore, under a floating exchange rate regime interest rate policy is not determined by the need to protect the exchange rate.

If, instead, the government elects to use expenditure-reducing policies to cure the deficit, such as deflating the economy to reduce import demand, this may result in unpleasant domestic conditions, such as unemployment.

Floating exchange rates insulate economies

A floating exchange rate helps to insulate the domestic economy from foreign price shocks. If there is an increase in foreign prices under *fixed* exchange rates then the prices of imported goods will increase accordingly. However, domestic goods will now be less expensive to foreign consumers and hence more competitive.

Consequently under fixed exchange rates an increase in foreign prices may lead to a balance of payments deficit and require the monetary authorities to intervene in the foreign exchange market by selling the domestic currency. This will increase the domestic money supply and lead to a rise in the domestic price level. Hence, fixed exchange rates lead to the importing of foreign price inflation/deflation.

In this situation, if the exchange rate is floating, market forces will force the exchange rates to appreciate until parity is restored.

Lower reserves

Floating exchange rates (should) mean that there is a smaller need to maintain large reserves to defend the currency. Their reserves, can, therefore, be used more productively elsewhere. However, the recent UK experience of a dirty-floating exchange rate regime has been one of increased intervention in the foreign exchange market. This can be attributed largely to the dramatic growth in foreign exchange market turnover and the increased need to intervene in the market to offset speculative movements in the exchange rate.

Uncertainty

It is often argued that floating exchange rates increase business uncertainty and lead to less trade and investment than under fixed exchange rates. Certainly, this is one of the motivations for the wish to have a single currency in Europe.

If the exchange rate is fixed, you know exactly how much domestic currency you will get from selling goods overseas or from returns on overseas investments. With floating exchange rates there is a risk that the currency that you are receiving will fall in value and so reduce the domestic currency proceeds.

However the market mechanism has taken care of this uncertainty by allowing overseas traders and investors to 'hedge' their risk using a wide variety of financial instruments, such as forward contracts, options and futures. Hedging involves buying a financial instrument that will yield a profit in certain circumstances which are unfavourable to you. For example, in the case above, if the domestic value of the currency you are receiving has fallen, and you have hedged this risk, then the 'hedge' will yield a profit. Therefore, overall, you receive the same amount of domestic currency as if the currency had been fixed.

Speculation

It is argued that a floating exchange rate promotes an increase in currency speculation. This often leads to strong or weak currencies, even when this is not justified by the prevailing levels of interest rates, unemployment, the current account and economic growth.

This is undoubtedly true, as the experience of the UK in 1980/81 demonstrated. Attracted to the high UK interest rates at the time, 'hot-money' flowed into the UK, driving the exchange rate up to $2.40/£.

However, in a pure floating regime speculators profit at the expense of another foreign exchange market 'player', not at the expense of the government. This is in contrast to the experience under the Bretton Woods and ERM systems where in 1967 and 1992, speculators were selling sterling to the Bank of England in the expectation of a devaluation of the pound. Having forced a devaluation they were then able to realise a capital gain by buying back sterling at a lower price. In this situation it is the central bank that loses, not another speculator.

Lack of discipline

There is a counter argument to that of floating exchange rates insulating an economy from foreign inflation. Some economists believe that floating exchange rates are to blame for inflation and that fixed exchange rate regimes possess a deflationary bias.

In a floating exchange rate regime it is possible that such an inflation problem will be ignored until it reaches extremely high levels. Although we did argue earlier that this is an advantage of floating exchange rates, as it allows the government autonomy in domestic economic policy.

If a country has high inflation relative to its trading partners the currency will depreciate in value, leading to higher import prices. This will further fuel domestic inflation, which may lead to a spiral of increasing inflation and exchange rate depreciation.

THE CASE FOR AND AGAINST FIXED EXCHANGE RATES

The advantages and disadvantages of fixed exchange rates are directly, but inversely, related to the advantages and disadvantages of floating exchange rates, some of which have already been discussed.

Fixed exchange rates promote international trade and investment

There is little argument that fixed exchange rates provide the best environment for the conduct of international trade and investment. In fact, from this point of view, a single currency is the optimal exchange rate regime.

The debate is more to do with the costs (discussed below) associated with joining a fixed exchange rate or single currency regime.

Discipline

The commitment to a fixed exchange rate regime imposes a degree of discipline on domestic macroeconomic policy that is absent under a floating exchange rate regime.

In particular, if a country adopts a policy of excessive monetary growth and allows its inflation rate to exceed that of its trading partners, its exports will fall and its balance of payments will be in deficit. In order to cure the deficit the government could adopt expenditure-reducing (for example, deflation) or expenditure-switching (devaluation) policies. Both strategies are highly visible and would indicate economic mismanagement, a risk governments may not be willing to take if they want to get re-elected !

This feature of fixed exchange rates is evident from the ERM, whereby high inflation countries were able to import monetary stability from Germany and lower the rate of inflation.

Conflict with domestic economic policy

Under a fixed exchange rate regime in order to maintain the external value of a currency in the face of downward market pressure the central bank must intervene on the foreign exchange markets and buy the domestic currency. A consequence of this is that the domestic money supply will fall and increase interest rates.

This was exactly the situation facing the UK in 1992. High German interest rates were attracting 'hot-money' to Germany, leading to upward pressure on the DM (with equivalent downward pressure on the other ERM currencies). In order to keep sterling within the band of fluctuation, interest rates would have to increase.

However, domestic circumstances called for a reduction in interest rates in order to stimulate aggregate demand. This policy conflict eventually led to sterling leaving the ERM in September 1992.

Thus, it is not possible to use the interest rate as a domestic policy tool whilst also keeping the exchange rate fixed. As in previous episodes of history, the exchange rate was allowed to find its own level, while the interest rate was used to solve the domestic economic problems.

Now try the following activities to ensure that you have understood the main points discussed in this section.

ACTIVITY 12

Explain why, when a country's currency is allowed to float, there is no conflict with:

1   the growth of the domestic money supply and

2   the level of domestic interest rates.

---

1   When a country allows its currency to float it is not required to intervene on the foreign exchange markets by buying or selling the domestic currency. There will therefore be no impact on the domestic money supply.

2   When a country allows its currency to float the monetary authorities will be able to set the level of domestic interest rates to meet domestic economic targets without worrying about the effect their actions may have on international capital flows.

ACTIVITY 13

Explain why a UK exporter/importer may feel more comfortable trading internationally when Sterling is determined in a fixed exchange rate regime than in a floating exchange rate regime.

Quite simply, under a fixed exchange rate a UK exporter knows exactly the domestic currency value of its exports and, similarly, an importer knows exactly the domestic currency cost of its imports.

REVIEW ACTIVITY 5

Using an example from recent exchange rate history and in no more than 50 words comment on the validity of the following statement: "A tight monetary policy coupled with loose fiscal policy will lead to a depreciation of the domestic exchange rate".

Summary

In this section we traced the history of the exchange rate between 1944 and the mid-1990s. We highlighted the experiences of the UK, USA and Germany in order to show the links between interest rates, domestic economic policy and the exchange rate. We then described the European Monetary System, including the Exchange Rate Mechanism and the plans for European Monetary Union. Finally, we considered the pros and cons of fixed and floating exchange rates

Unit Review Activity

1   Define (a) comparative advantage: (b) absolute advantage.

2   Describe the differences between the foreign exchange market activities of a government whose currency is determined under a fixed exchange rate regime and one whose currency is determined under a pure-floating exchange rate regime.

3   (a) What is the balance of payments accounts ?

   (b) Give some examples of credit and debit items in the UK balance of payments accounts.

   (c) What are visibles and invisibles ?

   (d) What is the difference between the balance of trade and the current account balance ?

4   Put yourself in the position of the Governor of the Bank of England.

   You are facing upward pressure on the value of the pound and are required to intervene on the foreign exchange markets to prevent the value of the pound from rising. Will your activities impact on the domestic money supply?

Unit Summary

In Section 1 we learnt why countries trade with one another. We also noted which areas of the world the UK has trading links with.

In Section 2 we were introduced to the exchange rate and how it is quoted . We also introduced a measure of international competitiveness - the real exchange rate.

In Section 3 we looked at how a country's external transactions are recorded. We have considered the impact the choice of exchange rate regime has on a government's role in the foreign exchange market. We also analyzed the problems of balance of payments imbalances and discussed possible policies to cure deficits and surpluses.

In Section 4 we examined recent exchange rate history. We also discussed the European Monetary System. Finally, we highlighted the advantages and disadvantages of fixed and floating exchange rate regimes.

Recommended Reading

Special Issue on European Monetary Union, *Economic Affairs*, Summer 1996, Vol. 16, No. 3, p. 4–38.

Reddaway, B, 'The Balance of Payments and the Exchange Rate', *The Economic Review*, Vol. 12, No. 3, p. 35–37.

Hutton, J,'Three decades of the Balance of Payments, Exchange Rates and Unemployment', *The Economic Review*, Vol. 10, No. 4, p. 2–6.

'The role of the exchange rate in monetary policy', Speech by the Governor of the Bank of England to the ACI Annual Conference, *Bank of England Quarterly Bulletin*, (August 1994), p. 255–258.

'Changeover to a single currency' *Bank of England Quarterly Bulletin*, (February 1996), p. 88–90.

'The foreign exchange market in London', *Bank of England Quarterly Bulletin*, (November 1992), p. 408–412.

'The Maastricht Agreement on European Monetary Union' *Bank of England Quarterly Bulletin*, (February 1992), p. 64–68.

Roarty, M.J, 'The New Protectionism and Developing Countries', *The Economic Review*, p. 21–24.

Answers to Review Activities

Review Activity 1

1

Apples produced	Bananas produced
0 apples = 0 hours	600 bananas = 1200 hours
50 apples = 150 hours	525 bananas = 1050 hours
100 apples = 300 hours	450 bananas = 900 hours
150 apples = 450 hours	375 bananas = 750 hours
200 apples = 600 hours	300 bananas = 600 hours
250 apples = 750 hours	225 bananas = 450 hours
300 apples = 900 hours	150 bananas = 300 hours
350 apples = 1050 hours	75 bananas = 150 hours
400 apples = 1200 hours	0 bananas = 0 hours

2

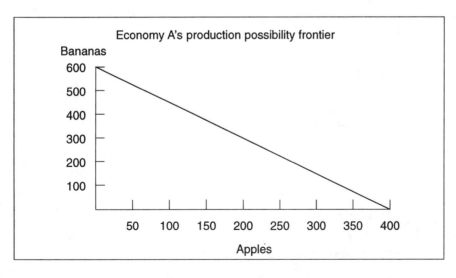

Economy A's production possibility frontier

3   The opportunity cost of an apple in Economy A is 1.5 bananas, i.e. to produce
    50 additional apples they must reduce banana production by 75. Therefore, to

produce an additional apple they must reduce banana production by 1.5.

By the same token the opportunity cost of a banana is 2/3 apples. i.e. they must reduce apple production by 2/3 in order to produce an additional banana.

4 The opportunity cost of an apple in Economy B is 5 bananas. By the same token the opportunity cost of a banana is 1/5 apples, i.e. they must reduce banana production by 5 in order to produce 1 more apple. Similarly, they must reduce apple production by 1/5 in order to produce 1 more banana.

5 Since the opportunity cost of an apple is lower in Economy A (1.5 bananas) than in Economy B (5 bananas) Economy A has a comparative advantage in the production of apples.

6 Since the opportunity cost of a banana is lower in Economy B (1/5 apples) than in Economy A (2/3 apples) then Economy B has a comparative advantage in the production of bananas.

7 Each economy will concentrate on the production of the good in which it has a comparative advantage in production. Economy A will increase production of apples and import bananas from Economy B . Economy B will increase production of bananas and import apples from Economy A. The quantity of apples and bananas each country imports will be dependent upon the demand for apples and bananas in the two economies.

Review Activity 2

1   Using the Identity:-

$$Y = C + I + G + X - M$$

Then,

$$Y = 50 + (0.45 \times Y) + 200 + 400 + 250 - (0.40 \times Y)$$

$$Y = 900 + 0.05 \times Y$$

Thus,

$$Y = 900 \div 0.95 = £947bn.$$

2   Now,

$$Y = 900 + 0.45 \times Y - 0.65 \times Y$$

$$Y = 900 \div 1.2 = £750 \ bn.$$

The increased desire to purchase foreign goods with each additional pound of income leads to a reduction in national income from £947bn. to £750bn.

Review Activity 3

	Demand for UK Exports	Demand for UK Imports
World GDP	+	
UK GDP		+
UK Real Exchange Rate	−	+

Review Activity 4

1   The Marshall-Lerner condition must be satisfied.

2   There must be spare capacity in the economy to meet increased export demand.

3   Domestic firms must not use the devaluation as an opportunity to raise prices and so erode the competitive gain.

Review Activity 5

This statement is incorrect. The experience of the US in the early 1980's demonstrated that when there is downward pressure from import expenditure and simultaneous upward pressure from capital flows the pressure from the capital flows will be the dominant force.

Unit Review Activity

1   (a) A country has a comparative advantage over another in the production of a good if it can produce it at a lower opportunity cost, i.e. if it has to give up less of other goods in order to produce it.

(b) A country has an absolute advantage over another in the production of a good if it can produce it with less resources than the other country.

2   In a fixed exchange rate regime governments agree to maintain the

convertibility of their currency at a fixed exchange rate, by buying and selling domestic currency on the foreign exchange market. When there is reduced demand for the domestic currency at the current exchange rate the monetary authorities will absorb the excess domestic currency by buying it on the foreign exchange market. When there is an increased demand for the domestic currency at the current exchange rate the monetary authorities will meet the extra demand by selling the domestic currency on the foreign exchange market. In a pure-floating exchange rate regime the exchange rate is allowed to attain its free market equilibrium level without any government intervention.

3 (a) The balance of payments are a systematic record of all transactions between domestic residents and residents of foreign nations, over a given time period.

(b) All transactions are recorded in domestic currency. Credit items have a positive sign and debit items a negative sign. Credit items include exports of goods and services and earnings of interest from overseas and investment from overseas. Debit items include imports of goods and services, dividend payments made to overseas residents and domestic investment made overseas.

(c) Visibles: these include the export and import of tangible items. For example, basic raw materials, manufactured goods, fuels etc.

Invisibles: these include (i) earnings from and payments for private sector services, such as financial services and travel services; (ii) government sector services, such as running overseas embassies, (iii) interest, profits and dividends arising from international financial activities, (iv) private sector current transfers, such as gifts overseas and aid donations, (v) government sector current transfer payments, such as official overseas aid and payments relating to the EC budget.

(d) The balance of imports and exports in visible trade is called the balance of trade. The aggregation of the visible and invisible balances yields the current account balance.

4 In order to keep the value of the currency down the central bank would have to sell domestic currency on the foreign exchange market. This necessarily implies an increase in the domestic money supply.

RESOURCES

▷ RESOURCE 1.1

By Nigel Lawson
Source: Market
Capitalism and Moral
Values, Samuel
Britton and Alan
Hamlin. Edward
Edger 1995.

Some reflections on morality and capitalism

Introduction

Some 15 years ago, towards the end of the unhappy life of the last Labour Government, I contributed to a book of essays published under the somewhat apocalyptic title, *The Coming Confrontation* and sub-titled, *Will the Open Society Survive to 1989 ?*

I chose as the theme for my own essay what I termed 'The Moral Dimension'. I began by asserting what seemed to me to be a paradox:

There can by now be no doubt that collectivism has failed. Throughout the nations of the industrialised world, the people are freer and their living standards higher the less far-reaching is the degree of state ownership, direction and control of the economy. Yet, throughout the industrialised world, the frontiers of the state, so far from being rolled back, are almost everywhere being further extended (Lawson, 1978)

After examining various possible reasons for this paradox, I concluded that the principal explanation lay in the fact that:

It is the moral dimension that lies at the heart of the matter. For man is a moral animal, and no political or economic order can long survive except on a moral base ... (Yet) the apologists of capitalism have hoped to win the day on the merits of its fruits, and have unwisely allowed the moral dimension to go by default. The apologists of the barren tree of socialism, by contrast, have played the moral card for all it is worth - and a good deal more besides (Lawson, 1978).

In this chapter I shall be revisiting this topic and - in the light of ten years' experience as a Minister - be reflecting further on the relationship between capitalism and morality.

For the avoidance of doubt, incidentally, I use the term 'capitalism' to describe an economic order based on free markets and private property - not, let me add, in some theoretical or ideal sense, but in the only way in which any system should be judged, namely as we know it in the real world. And by 'the world' I do indeed mean the world - the capitalism of Japan, for example, as much as that of the United States.

Much has changed since 1978. The seemingly inexorable extension of the frontiers of the state has been emphatically reversed. Throughout the Western world, and notably since the coming into office of the Thatcher Government in the UK in 1979 and the Reagan Administration in the USA in 1981, capitalism has appeared to be in the ascendant and socialism in retreat. Nor has this trend been confined to the Western world. During the course of the 1980s much of the developing world, too, came belatedly to recognize the benefits, and adopt the policies, of the market economy. As an intermittent attender at meetings of Commonwealth Finance Ministers, I can vouch for a quite remarkable change over that period.

But the most dramatic development has been the great changes in Central and Eastern Europe, where the collapse of communism and the command economy has revealed a landscape of economic failure, poverty and environmental degradation on a scale that few had believed possible. It is perhaps not surprising to find that the most passionate supporters of the capitalist market economy today are to be found among the ablest of the new leaders of these countries. Nor, incidentally, are recent events in China without interest.

There is nothing particularly surprising about the unrivalled practical success of market capitalism. It is not surprising that people give of their best in a climate of freedom, within a legal and institutional framework of order and justice. Nor is it in any way surprising that the rational decisions needed to make a modern economy even half-way efficient can be taken only by a multiplicity of decision–makers armed with the knowledge provided by a myriad of market prices.

What is surprising is that, despite all this, and the important events of the past decade, which have led even the British Labour Party to reconsider its commitment to socialist egalitarianism and hostility to the market economy, the 'atmosphere of hostility to capitalism' which Schumpeter remarked upon some 50 years ago is still so pervasive.

And the reason for this is clear. While its material success, and its demonstrable superiority over all known alternative economic systems, is no longer open to question, capitalism is still widely seen as morally suspect.

(In parenthesis, I must confess that I find myself distinctly uneasy about the tendency towards the collectivization of morality; in which moral censure is reserved for governments and politico-economic systems, with individuals seen as innocent victims. We would do better to stick to the traditional idea of morality as a matter of individual personal responsibility).

Be that as it may, why should capitalism be seen as morally suspect, given its unrivalled and proven ability to improve living standards and eliminate large–scale poverty, and its unique harmony with the political virtues of freedom and democracy?

In part, the explanation clearly lies in sloppy thinking. There is a frequent tendency to contrast, consciously or subconsciously, the market capitalism we know, with all the faults and flaws we see around us, with some ideal economic order which would, almost by definition, be free of these imperfections. In fact, of course, in an imperfect world, the only valid comparison is with other systems as they actually operate (or have operated) in practice.

Similarly, there is a parochial predilection to blame the moral failings of man, which – not surprisingly – are evident throughout the world, on the nature of the politico-economic system in place where the critic happens to reside.

But in the case of the alleged moral failings of capitalism, it has to be conceded that there is rather more to it than that.

Morality, as most people see it, is a matter partly of motivation and partly of outcomes. And market capitalism is widely seen as defective in both respects.

Self-interest

So far as motivation is concerned, it is seen as a system based on self-interest, the very antithesis of morality – for what is the essence of a moral code if it is not the curbing of selfishness and self-gratification?

As for the outcome, while the population as a whole might benefit from capitalism, that benefit is shared to an unequal extent that many feel *ipso facto* immoral.

It is these two characteristics, self-interest and inequality, that largely explains the alleged moral deficiencies of capitalism. Let me take them each in turn.

A regard for one's self-interest is a prominent feature in the make-up of almost all mankind. It is not the only feature, but it is a uniquely powerful one. Moreover, it is hard to see how, without it, a large-scale free society could possibly be governable. A socialist or statist government, besides its apparatus of restrictions and controls, creates, through the tax system and grants of one kind and another, inducements designed to encourage those forms of economic behaviour it believes to be desirable. But unless people sought to advance their self-interest, these inducements would clearly be ineffective.

The characteristics of market capitalism is not that it alone is based on the idea of channelling self-interest for the greater good – not that there is anything wrong with that. It is rather that it is a unique mechanism for doing so directly, with the least interposition of government.

Why, then, is market capitalism alone thought to be based on the allegedly morally disreputable concept of the pursuit of self-interest?

Partly, perhaps, because Adam Smith, more than 200 years ago, was so disarmingly honest about it. Those who seek to commend a politico-economic system are expected to be decently hypocritical, and to flatter their audience by speaking in loftier tones.

But is it also partly because, whereas capitalism is customarily discussed in terms of the motives of the governed, socialism is usually considered in terms of the motives of this in government.

Even that, however, is very much a distinction without a difference. There is little practical evidence that politicians and bureaucrats are wholly altruistic beings, on a higher moral plane than vulgar businessmen – as that admirable television documentary, *Yes, Prime Minister*, has well illustrated.

It is true that in a country such as ours, where pecuniary corruption is rare, there is the distinction that, whereas businessmen seek financial reward, politicians seek votes. But that is no basis for according moral superiority to a system in which more decisions are taken by politicians and bureaucrats, and fewer by businessmen and ordinary people.

Moreover, there are important positive moral arguments in favour of market capitalism, quite apart from the freedom and liberty on which it is based, and the beneficent results to which it has led, to which I have already alluded

In the first place, there is the extent to which it gives greater freedom than other systems – albeit still within strict limits, set by the rule of law – for the peaceful pursuit of self-interest, in practice that means the natural desire of men and women to benefit not merely themselves but also their family, in particular, their children.

To my mind this is a vitally important extension, not to be dismissed as genetic selfishness. When parents neglect their children (or worse), as in recent well-publicized 'home alone' cases and the like, we do not regard this as a lack of genetic selfishness, but with horror as morally unacceptable behaviour. Sub-ordinating one's own personal interest to that of one's family is not the beginning and end of altruism, to be sure; but it *is* the beginning, as it is the foundation and cradle of social behaviour.

The family, which looms large in the scheme of market capitalism, is not only the foundation of a stable society, but an important bulwark against tyranny – as, of course, is the institution of private property, the more widely spread the better. Hence the infallible rule that tyrannies always seek to weaken, if not destroy, the family. Jung Chang, in her remarkable book *Wild Swans,* shows particular poignantly how Maoist communism felt obliged to wage war on the family loyalties so deeply rooted in Chinese culture, and quotes a line in a song much heard on the eve of the devastating Cultural Revolution: 'Father is close, and Mother is close, but neither is as close as Chairman Mao'.

Another key feature of market capitalism is the private sector, non-monopolistic, firm. Capitalism is sometimes portrayed either as monopolistic exploitation or an unattractive competitive jungle, where the values of co-operation are lost in a free-for-all. What this overlooks is that the private sector firm itself provides a model of effective co-operation, which the preoccupation of economists (inasmuch as they are interested in the firm at all) with the company as a single corporate personality, seeking to maximize its profits as it lurches along its U-shaped cost curve, should not be allowed to obscure.

These two institutions, the family and the firm, come together, of course, in that much-derided corporate entity, the family business. While more important at earlier stages of development than later stages, and in some cultures more than in others, I suspect that the value of the family business and the culture it represents has been insufficiently recognized.

Egalitarianism

But while the misguided moral critique of market capitalism as irredeemably selfish has been allowed to acquire considerable resonance, an even more powerful ground for moral disfavour has been the inequality to which it leads.

Yet in these terms, the closer the charge is examined the less impressive it appears. There is clearly no principle of equality that has any conceivable merit. Equality in misery is of no value to anyone. And equality of opportunity – an admirable aspiration, provided it is sought by levelling up rather than levelling down – is clearly a different matter altogether. Indeed, given the widely different capacities of different individuals, not to mention the inescapable caprice of chance, the one thing that genuine equality of opportunity can be guaranteed to produce is inequality of outcome.

Nor, incidentally, is it clear whether equality should be considered within the context of the nation and society in which we live, or in the wider context of the world as a whole. Even in the narrower context, it is doubtful if there can be more than a tiny minority of eccentrics who wish to see a society in which absolute equality is the rule. Yet once it is accepted that there must be inequality, the principle of equality (if there ever was one) has been abandoned, and we are left not with morality but with something that looks rather like an amalgam of aesthetics and envy.

Not that absolute equality, or anything approaching it, is possible anyway (which is one good reason why it has never existed anywhere, at any time). For one thing, there is more than one dimension of equality: it is not simply a matter of income and wealth. In particular, the closer to pecuniary equality a government seeks to move, the greater the coercive power needed to achieve this, and the greater the inequality of power between government and governed.

Moreover, absolute equality, even in the sense in which it is theoretically attainable, must of necessity lead to misery. If there is to be no greater reward for work or saving or effort of any kind than is received by those who decline to work or save or make any effort, then remarkably little work, saving or effort will be undertaken. This is not simply an elementary economic proposition. It is also intimately connected with a more robust moral sentiment: that associated with equity and desert. If two people are working at the same job, with equal skill, and one chooses to work overtime while the other does not, failure to pay the former more would be seen as not merely self-defeating but grossly inequitable.

It is true that large disparities in rates of pay can give rise, particularly when hyped up by the populist press, to storms of apparent moral outrage. But this has nothing to do with attachment to any principle of equality. People do not expect some third division nonentity to be paid the same as Eric Cantona, or a chorus girl the same a Pavarotti. While we are all equal under the law and in the sight of God, we are not all equally good footballers or singers; and people well understand that pay relates to performance, as measured in the market-place, rather than to moral worth. Simple envy aside, the outrage is based either on ignorance of the reason for the high pay, or on disapproval of the individual receiving it – or the way he makes his money, or both.

Not that any specific inequality is necessarily justified even in economic terms: it may well not be. The argument for market capitalism is not that it is infallible – no human construction could possible be infallible – but that it is superior to any other politico-economic order.

For these reasons, the egalitarian argument is usually couched in terms not of equality *tout court* but rather those of *more* equality. One problem with this, however, is the *insatiability* of egalitarianism. Once the legitimacy of egalitarianism is accepted, however much equality there is, the cry will always be for more of it. If and when taxes come down, it will be held that the worse off should be the beneficiaries: when they go up, it will be held that it is the better off that should bear the burden. That is how the UK ended up, at the close of the 1970s with the absurd top rates of income tax of 75 per cent on earning and 98 per cent on savings. income.

The Government of which I was a member felt that this was far too high, and I myself played a part in reversing the process. I recall vividly how this was characterized by my egalitarian critics as 'handouts for the rich' and, as such, self-evidently immoral. The concept that egalitarianism might have gone too far was not one that they could accept.

It is the combination of the insatiability of egalitarianism with the impossibility of achieving equality that causes the elevation of equality into the touchstone of political morality to be a recipe for maximizing discontent. In a sense, indeed, it is positively immoral. A moment ago I referred to envy. Anthony Crosland, in the original (1956) edition of his important book *The Future of Socialism*, openly discussed the necessity for the Labour Party to base its appeal on envy – although in later editions he prudently abridged this section. Even so, in his 1975 Fabian Tract, *Social Democracy in Europe*, he was obliged to admit that egalitarianism was not primarily concerned with improving the lot of the less well off: '... the argument for more equality is based not on any direct material gain for the poor, but on the claims of social and natural justice.'

Natural justice it cannot be; and 'social justice' is simply a term dreamed up to mean the same as, but to sound more impressive than, greater equality – rendering that part of his assertion an empty tautology.

Nevertheless, Crosland's claim is useful in making the distinction, which as an honest man he was obliged to do, between equality and the relief of poverty. Market capitalism is the best system ever devised for the avoidance of large-scale poverty and for enabling the poor to improve their lot. But what it manifestly does not ensure is the elimination of poverty altogether.

That is why the voters rightly expect of any government that it should operate a social security system for the relief of poverty, and why all governments, however wedded to market capitalism, in practice do so. There are obviously a number of practical questions involved in this. It is not merely a case of how poverty is to be defined (certainly not in terms of the average wage), but also whether relief should be targeted or part of some universal benefit (overwhelmingly the former, I believe), whether other dimensions should be taken into account (age certainly should, and the 1985 social security reforms erred in this respect); whether relief for the unemployed poor should be linked to some form of workfare (I believe it should), and so on.

But the key point is this. So far from making a case against market capitalism, the existence of an underclass is a challenge to find a means of minimizing its size and saving those in it from degradation without in any way undermining market capitalism or detracting from the benefits that system has proved itself to be uniquely capable of providing. Just as the sensible successful businessman who seeks to help those less fortunate will do so not by changing the way he runs his business but by applying part of his personal wealth to philanthropy, so the wise government will best help the poor not by interfering with the market but by creating a well-designed social security safety net alongside it.

I have referred more than once to the success of market capitalism – a success that is now recognized even by the more thoughtful members of the Labour Party. For example Professor Raymond Plant, *inter alia* Chairman of the Labour Party's working party on electoral systems, wrote recently that:

Both the intellectual and political case against common economics and central economic planning has been won. The intellectual debate since Reagan, Thatcher and the changes in Eastern Europe is no longer about central economic planning or the case for the market but much more about the range of social and political institutions within which markets are embedded, the scope and purposes of these institutions, and their relationship to the market economy (Plant, 1992).

Market capitalism, to give it its proper name (or, more fully, democratic market capitalism), has, compared with all other known systems, scored on every front: freedom, opportunity, protection of the environment, the living standards of the average family. In this last context, it has proved itself to be a more favourable environment for economic growth than any other the world has known.

Growth

But is it the case, as some argue, that it is only the fact of economic growth that makes market capitalism politically acceptable? The argument here is, essentially, that the unequal distribution of wealth is acceptable, and the system seen as having legitimacy, only because it is in principle open to anyone to improve their position without disadvantaging others – since the possibility of growth, which market capitalism is best able to realize, ensures that economic change is not a zero-sum game.

Thus when (the argument continues) the Malthusian nightmare becomes reality, as in a finite world it must, and growth comes to a full stop (not to say goes into reverse), market capitalism will ceased to be morally acceptable: the whole basis of its legitimacy will have disappeared.

Strictly speaking, it is no part of government's job to seek to bring about the maximum practicable growth in recorded GNP. The government's job, in the economic field is to create the legal and institutional framework required for market capitalism to thrive, together with the other essential element of the required framework – needed, incidentally, for social as well as economic reasons – namely, price stability.

Whatever the case for government intervention in the working of the capitalist market economy for social purposes, to intervene in order to boost economic growth is doubly perverse – first because, as I have just maintained, growth as such should not be an objective of government policy; and secondly because experience has shown that the capitalist market economy is (for good reasons) better able than government action to produce growth.

The point here is that the government's responsibility is to create the conditions in which individuals can generate growth, if that is what they desire, in the way in which they desire it. And they surely do and will continue to do so, even though the form may change. Despite Christianity's uneasiness with market capitalism, it was Pope John Paul II who declared that creativity was the essence of man, which implies the need for the freedom to create; and it is man's creativity which produces growth.

Certainly, if and when the combination of rising population and finite resources leads to an end to growth and to a world of falling material living standards, discontent with market capitalism may well increase - as indeed would discontent with any other economic system that happened to prevail at the time. The extent of the discontent might depend, of course, on the pace of the decline and the extent to which (as a result of technological progress) it is accompanied by increasing leisure time which can be spent in ways that make minimal demands on resources.

But it is difficult to see why this should fatally undermine the legitimacy of the capitalist market system. For the essence of the market economy, and its great moral attribute, is voluntarism: the fact that economic transactions are freely undertaken because each side benefits. This would continue to be true even if and when overall growth has ceased.

All this, moreover, is in any case a very long way off. We may live in a world of finite resources, but the price mechanism ensures that we respond to scarcity by becoming progressively less wasteful - see, for example, the steadily diminishing energy content of output. And, in general, in what is sometimes termed somewhat optimistically 'the information age', the material content of growth appears to be diminishing. Only a very small portion of the market value of a pop video, for example, is attributable to its visible plastic form.

For all of these reasons, it would be the height of folly to doubt legitimacy of market capitalism in the world in which we live because of the problems that would arise – problems, incidentally, that would bedevil far more than market capitalism – were the Malthusian nightmare to become, one day, reality.

Conclusion

Throughout modern history, market capitalism has sought to rest its case on its material success – a relative success which, over the past five years, events in Central and Eastern Europe have shown in a particularly telling light. Socialism, by contrast, has been forced by practical failure onto the high ground of morality.

Perhaps we could leave it there. Perhaps we should adapt the description of the Roundheads and Cavaliers in *1066 And All That*, and accept that capitalism is right but repulsive, whereas socialism is wrong but romantic. But I would not feel comfortable in doing so. Success, which is inevitably incomplete anyway, will sooner or later always be taken for granted, and then the moral assault, if unanswered, will gain ground. At the very least, if we are to live within a market capitalist system, it is unsatisfactory that we should have doubts about its moral foundations. One or two recent speeches, even by some members of the present Government, betray a worrying insecurity in this context.

In this essay I have not sought to enumerate the moral values that tend, in practice, to be associated rather more with democratic market capitalism than with any other known politico-economic order: such attributes as probity, integrity, honesty, fair-dealing, trust, respect for others (including their property) and the like – still less have I sought to discuss whether these values are adopted for their own sake or because experience teaches us that honesty is the best policy (both elements are clearly, it seems to me, present).

In particular, I have dealt only cursorily with the profound connection between market capitalism and the moral value of freedom and voluntarism. I have done so partly because I have become increasingly aware over the years that there is no single moral value which can serve as the sole foundation for a political, economic or social system, or for the conduct of personal life, and that the search for one is a wild goose chase. And I have done it partly because I felt it more important to examine the alleged moral defects of market capitalism.

It is obvious that I write from a particular perspective, which may not be universally shared. Morality, in any case, is a field in which it is particularly easy for intelligent people to reach divergent conclusions. But at least, in seeking to repudiate the moral critique of capitalism, and to suggest that it should not be held responsible for the moral imperfection of man, I do not need to win my case. For even a stand-off in the moral dimension is enough to allow market capitalism's undoubted superiority in the world of practical achievement to win the day.

Bibliography
Crosland, C.A.R. (1975), *Social Democracy in Europe*, London: Fabian Society.
Lawson, N. (1978), 'The Moral Dimension' in *The Coming Confrontation: Twelve Essays by Different Authors*, London: Institute of Economic Affairs.
Plant, R. (1992), *Autonomy, Social Rights and Distributive Justice*, London: IEA Health and Welfare Unit.
Schumpeter, J.A. (1943), *Capitalism, Socialism and Democracy*, London: George Allen & Unwin.

▷ RESOURCE 8.1

Source: Barrell, R (1985) The Economic Review, vol 2, no 3, January, p. 10 –13, Phillip Allan Publishers.

The Demand for Money: Problems and Issues

The development of the theory of the demand for money is summarised in order to highlight the empirical problems raised in the search for a demand for money schedule, and the interaction between a theory of the demand for money and a policy of control of the money supply.

Discussion of the nature of the demand for money came to prominence during the Keynesian Revolution in macroeconomics in the 1930s. Although Keynes was not the first economist to discuss the demand for money, his contribution was to put it at the centre of the stage as a (potentially) important source of disturbance to the equilibrium of the economy. The subsequent debate in this area has centred around the stabilising or destabilising nature of money.

The Roots of the Study of Money Demand
Early approaches to the study of macroeconomics were based around the Quantity Theory of Money. This theory has a long history, and its clearest statement can

be found in the works of the Scottish philosopher David Hume in the 1750s. He put forward the view that the level of prices in a country would be determined partly by the level of stock of money in the economy. If output were reasonably stable around full employment, then the price of goods would be determined by the demand for money of individuals relative to the stock of money available to them. If individuals' demand for money were constant, then fluctuations in the quantity of money would determine the price level. In the classical Quantity Theory, money and gold were virtually synonymous because the financial system had hardly started to develop. This tendency to identify money with gold continued into the early twentieth century, and it is only in the last forty years that economists have begun to take account of the complexities of financial systems, a step that has been vital in improving our knowledge of the influence of money on prices.

The theory of the demand for money in the Quantity Theory was implicit in its construction. Hume did not try to explain why people held money, and nor did many of his successors. The Quantity Theory is often associated with the name of Irving Fisher, a US economist writing mainly in the early twentieth century. He described the theory by using familiar symbols. He suggested that the level of nominal transactions in the economy, expressed as the number of transactions (T) multiplied by the price level per transaction (P), was determined by two factors. The first was the quantity of money in circulation (M) and the second was the number of times each unit of money was used in a year (V). This latter magnitude, known as *velocity*, was assumed by Fisher to be basically fixed by the transactions technology in the economy, and as this depends on the legal system, the banking structure, and so on, Fisher assumed it would change only slowly over time. Because V was thought to be stable, the major determinant of the level of nominal income ($P \times T$) was seen as the quantity of money. Fisher's objective in his work was to demonstrate that the quantity of money causes prices to be at a particular level, and he used his famous quantity

equation:

$$MV = PT$$

to explain the level of and fluctuation of prices. To do this he assumed that transactions were basically fixed at full employment.

A knowledge of the Quantity Theory is vital to an understanding of the debates over the demand for money. Firstly, it is important because $MV = PT$ can easily be transformed into the simplest theory of the demand for money. Dividing both sides by V, we can write:

$$M = \frac{1}{V} PT$$

which can be seen as a money demand equation, according to which the demand for money in the economy will depend on the level of prices, the level of transactions and on the velocity of circulation in the economy. Much subsequent discussion of the importance of money demand developed in response to this equation, because many workers in the field have asked whether or not it is possible to treat velocity as constant. Keynes' attack on his predecessors was largely based on the premise that it was unwarranted to treat velocity as stable, and that it was possible to demonstrate that it was likely to be unstable. To do this, Keynes produced one of the first discussions of the reasons why people hold money. It is his fascinating discussion of money demand that is the keystone to Keynes' attack on the Quantity Theory of Money.

The Keynesian Tradition in Money Demand

Keynes' approach to money demand did not arise in isolation but was a development of a long Cambridge tradition. Alfred Marshall and A.C. Pigou had both written on the 'cash balance' approach to the Quantity Theory. They stressed that it was important to understand why people held money if one wanted to understand the determination of the price level, and their equation explained individuals' holdings of money (M) by assuming that it would be a constant proportion (k) of their nominal income (PY). They used the equation

$M = k\,PY$

to explain the determination of the price level in the economy, but it was the ex-banker Henry Lavington who first saw that this could be seen as a money demand equation, and he was also the first Cambridge economist to discuss the dependence of the cash balance proportion, *k,* on the interest rate. As a practical banker, he was aware that individuals were willing to economise on their cash holdings in response to high interest rates. (This is a rare example of economists learning from the banking world.)

Keynes extended this approach considerably and more importantly completely reorientated the study of money demand. His first objective was to show that money could be a major destabilising force in the economy, and that this resulted largely from the instability and unpredictability of the demand for money in a modern economy. He discussed an economy in which many financial assets other than gold existed, so in explaining the demand for money it is necessary to explain why people hold money and not some other financial asset. the important distinction for Keynes was between assets whose capital value was certain and assets whose capital value was not. The former assets, which were basically currency and deposits with banks, were identified as money, and the latter were the speculative assets (known as bonds) that some individuals might wish to buy.

Three reasons for holding money were postulated: for transactions, as a precaution, and for speculation. Keynes never appeared to doubt that the transactions demand for money was very stable and very predictable; for most people the transactions demand dominated their money holdings. It may have been influenced by factors such as the interest rate, but it was for most purposes a constant proportion of money income. Keynes pointed out that individuals hold money for more than transactions purposes, however. Firstly, most individuals would hold or carry money balances as reserve against unforeseen eventualities: the world is an uncertain place, and one never knows when a bill may arrive or an offspring need

bailing out of gaol! Clearly the need for precautionary reserves could rise if the world came to be perceived as a more uncertain place. This could be especially important at the beginning of a depression when individuals might choose to move into money. These sorts of fluctuations in money demand could easily have an effect on the economy, with a rise in money demand of this sort having a depressing effect as individuals cut consumption to raise their money balances.

The second new reason for holding money put forward by Keynes was for speculation. The essential question is, why do people hold an asset such as money which earns no return, rather than bonds which do earn a return? Obviously speculators prefer to earn interest, but sometimes interest-earning assets such as government bonds may seem very unsafe because their price is liable to fall. At times like this, speculators will do their best to hold money so as to reduce risk to their capital, despite the loss of interest. Speculative money demand can be seen as very unstable. By its very nature, a speculative market lives on rumours and suppositions, and even if speculators are on average right about future events, their reactions can still lead to very large fluctuations in money demand.

Sometimes, Keynes supposed, speculators might all get caught in 'liquidity traps', where everybody believes interest rates have reached their lowest possible level, so that bond prices (which are inversely related to the interest rate) are at their highest and no further speculative gains can be made. Keynes neither thought this a very likely event nor did he consider the liquidity trap important. For him the potential large-scale instability of money was far more important. A speculative wave could raise the demand for money, making the existing stock of money inadequate for current transactions. This fall in velocity would have to be accompanied by a fall in nominal income and unless prices were always perfectly flexible, it would have to be accompanied by a fall in real output and employment. By introducing speculative money demand, Keynes had turned the

Quantity Theory on its head and demonstrated that unstable money demand could explain fluctuations in the economy. Keynes' description does not *fully* represent the complexity of the modern financial world (and this has caused many problems in recent analysis), but it does mark a major move forward from the simplistic descriptions of the quantity theorists.

The Search for a Stable Money Demand
Early empirical studies of a demand for money seemed to be searching for a relationship between the quantity of money held and the interest rate and the level of income. Indeed, it was shown that over the long run in both the US and the UK the quantity of money held did depend positively on the level of income and vary inversely with the interest rate. In the first edition of David Laidler's excellent book, *The Demand for Money* (Wadsworth, 1970), it was possible for him to point to a multiplicity of studies that demonstrated

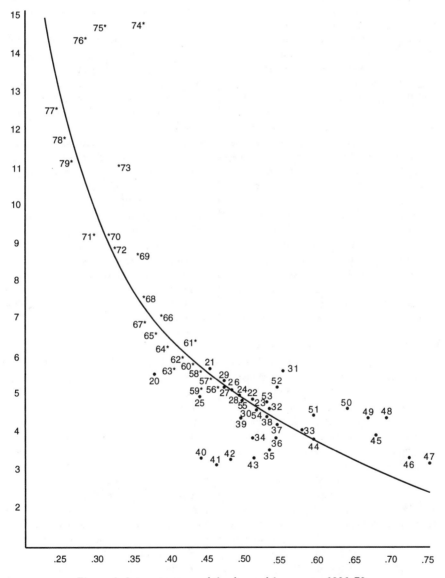

Figure 1: Interest rates and the demand for money, 1920–79
Source: Artis and Lewis 1981

that money demand had been stable.

These results seemed to be contrary to the basic Keynesian position and they supported the position adopted by Milton Friedman in his 1956 essay, *The Quantity Theory of Money: A Restatement*. Friedman claimed that Keynes and the Keynesians had overstated their case, and although he admitted that Fisher's simple quantity theory was inadequate, he claimed that it was easy to restate the theory in a more satisfactory form. His restatement is really just a return to pre-Keynesian theory, but the factors influencing money demand are more fully spelled out. Money demand is seen to be related to the rates of return on alternative assets such as equities, bonds, etc., as well as depending on the price level, the rate of inflation, the level of income, and the state of tastes and technology. Friedman claimed that if all these factors were taken into account, then it would be seen that the demand for money was reliable and predictable.

Empirical work in the area seemed to demonstrate that the quantity theory approach was, after all, adequate as a description of money demand and of fluctuations in money income. But economists in Britain were rather late in accepting these ideas, partly because of the influence of the Radcliffe Report on the workings of the Monetary System (1959). The economists behind the Report believed that velocity could vary without limit and as such took a rather extreme Keynesian position. By 1970 the Bank of England had come round to a belief in the importance of money and in the stability of money demand. This change in belief was associated with a change in policy and in operating procedures. In the early 1970s the Bank believed that the income elasticity of demand for money was rather high (around 2) and so in 1972–73 they allowed the money supply to grow rapidly because income growth was expected to be rapid. This 'Barber boom' episode was important for two reasons. Firstly, it persuaded most economists in the UK that excess money does cause inflation. Secondly, we learnt that our belief in the stability of money demand was not well founded, and was

probably wrong. During the relatively calm periods of the 1950s and '60s money demand had seemed stable because little was happening, but after 1973 it became difficult to predict how much money individuals would choose to hold.

In the long run the ratio of money held to income does seem to have been related in a stable way to the rate of interest, as can be seen from Figure 1, adapted from M. Artis and M. Lewis' book, *Monetary Control in the United Kingdom* (Philip Allan, 1981). Only in 1973–75 do the points lie far away from a simple relationship shown by the curve. But this demonstrates the point that Keynes was trying to make. We cannot rely on an immutable demand for money because it will be subject to sudden and unexpected speculative and precautionary surges. (It is rather nice that the first 'surge' happened just after most economists became convinced of its impossibility. Economists were confident they were able to predict the course of money demand, but they totally failed to do so during 1973–75.)

There were, of course, a number of attempts to explain why the empirical studies were unable properly to predict the amount of money demanded. It could have been because the definition of money being used in the studies was inadequate and thus led to a misrepresentation. Because financial institutions have steadily become more complex, it is increasingly difficult to identify just one asset as 'money'. The definition most commonly used (currency plus current accounts plus deposit accounts) may exclude relevant assets, and it could be that if they were included, then the demand for 'money' would again be seen as stable. This may be so, but if one wishes to use 'money' for macroeconomic policy, then it would be useful to know what it is before something goes wrong. Alternatively the explanation of money demand may have been inadequate because some important determining factors had not been looked at. It may be possible that expected inflation, for instance, was an important variable in the early 1970s and its omission caused problems, but this seems unlikely as individuals were holding too much money. The empirical conclusion to the debate, albeit a provisional one, is that money demand is very complex and could be subject to sudden shifts.

Policy Issues

The difficulties in predicting the demand for money have important policy implications. It may make a policy of fixed money supply rules, such as that adopted by the current Government, much more difficult to operate. A 5% growth in £M3 means very different things for the level of aggregate demand and the rate of inflation if money demand *falls* by 10% rather than *rises* by 10%. The possibility of unstable money demand suggests that the government should always stand by to take action to keep the economy on course, even if it does not normally expect to intervene on a day-to-day basis.

Monetary control is liable to stay an important issue for the foreseeable future. There is little evidence that electric money (electronic transfers of credit cards etc.) or credit cards have had much influence on individuals' desires to hold these particular assets. Holdings of currency alone are around 5% of GNP and they show little sign of declining. Even if individuals decide to hold fewer current accounts at banks, they will still wish to hold assets that, with

changes in technology, are becoming more and more money-like. The monetary authorities are now, for example, taking serious notice of the demand for Building Society deposits when determining monetary policy. Changes in banking technology seem to be reinforcing Keynes' position that the demand for money may be unstable. Sudden changes of mood in markets can now be much more easily transformed into massive flows of funds. New developments make it even more important to understand money demand but also make it increasingly difficult to rely on the stability of the object(s) under study.

References

Artis, M. & Lewis, M. (1981) *Monetary Control in the United Kingdom*, Philip Allan

Friedman, M. (1956) 'The quantity theory of money: a restatement', *Essays in the Quantity Theory of Money*, M. Friedman (ed.), University of Chicago Press

Laidler, D. (1970) *The Demand for Money,* Wadsworth

Ray Barrell is currently Economic Adviser at H.M. Treasury; he has previously taught at the Universities of Southampton, Brunel and Stirling. His major interests are in monetary economics and policy.

Monetary targets – a short history

RESOURCE 8.2 ◁

Savage, D (1984) The Economic Review, vol 2, no 1, September , pp. 3-7, Phillip Allan Publishers.

Setting a target rate of growth for the money supply has become a familiar part of macroeconomic policy making and the major expression of monetary policy. This familiarity should not hide the fact that there are two reasons which make policy making with monetary targets particularly difficult. First, the money supply is not a policy instrument which can be set directly by policy makers. In contrast to a tax rate which is directly under the governments control, the money supply can only be influenced indirectly by means of, say, changes in interest rates. Secondly, 'hitting' a monetary target is not the ultimate aim of

any policy. A monetary target is only an *intermediate* target which is important because of its influence on something else.

Policy making with monetary targets is, in effect, a two-stage procedure. The policy maker has first to decide what growth rate for the money supply is most likely to achieve ultimate objectives, such as price stability, high employment and external balance. S/he has then to manipulate instruments over which s/he does have close control (a short-term rate of interest, for example) in order to achieve that growth rate.

Approaches to Monetary Policy

During the 1960s and 1970s monetary policy tended to focus directly upon particular, immediate problems. These included, during the period of fixed exchange rates, protection of the level of foreign exchange reserves. The Bank of England would raise the bank rate to counter an outflow of gold or dollars arising from, for example, a deficit in trade or an increase in interest rates abroad. Monetary policy was also used at times to affect internal demand, though it was generally considered less effective than fiscal policy for this purpose. Bank rate was regarded as one of the instruments available for checking a tendency either towards inflation or recessions. But, because the impact of changes in interest rates was considered too weak and uncertain to rely on alone, bank rate changes were usually supported by direct controls on credit. Statutory hire purchase controls (on the minimum deposit rate and length of repayment period) were frequently used to influence consumer spending. Bank lending, particularly to persons, was also regulated at times by ceilings on advances and by 'persuasion'.

Monetary policy was not used smoothly but was often intended to have something of a shock effect as policy makers looked for quick, tangible results. In recent years, however, monetary policy has been planned on a much more extended time scale. Since 1976, growth rates for the money supply have been specified at least one year, and sometimes several years, into the future. These have not always been rigorously adhered to, but in principle they limit the use of monetary policy for regulating short-term changes in the economic situation.

Viewed purely as a change in the technical operation of monetary policy, there is no reason why the adoption of monetary targets should have been accompanied by a change in ultimate objectives. Monetary targets could, in principle, be linked to objectives for real output growth and employment rather than price stability. But in practice their adoption was a step towards giving greater priority to stopping inflation.

These changes in the priorities and mechanisms of monetary policy had their origin in the experience of the late 1960s and early 1970s. Although, in common with other industrial countries, Britain had suffered almost continuous inflation since the war, it became a much more urgent problem during this period. There was mounting criticism of economic policy as it had been practised up to that time. It was claimed that attempts to stabilise short-term fluctuations in demand through adjustments in fiscal and monetary policy had been perversely destabilising in practice. It was also argued that policy of sustaining a high level of demand through thick and thin in the interests of full employment had caused, or at least 'validated', upward pressure on wages and prices. Incomes policies had not been as successful as had been hoped, except for limited periods.

Monetarist ideas, which purported to offer a simple solution to the problem of inflation, gained increasing influence. From a practical point of view, three of these ideas are of particular consequence. The first is the great importance attached to the money supply as a determinant of the aggregate level of nominal income and of the price level – in contrast to the conventional wisdom of the earlier postwar period that monetary influences are not very powerful and are concentrated on a relatively small proportion of total demand. Second, there is a belief that the economy is inherently highly stable and, if left to itself without interference from government policy, would tend towards a high level of employment. It follows from this that policies to stabilise the economy are unnecessary and, in the long run, inflationary. Furthermore, monetarists argue that such policies are likely to be poorly timed and actually destabilising. This argument is based on the fact that while the effects of changes in the money supply are predictable in the long run, they work their way through the economy with time lags which are long and unpredictable. These ideas were marshalled in support of a policy of keeping the money supply growing at a steady and predictable rate, year in and year out.

Many people were attracted to

monetarism by an apparently strong empirical relationship between money and prices. As inflation became higher and more volatile, people also became aware of the inherent difficulty of basing monetary policy on interest rates. This difficulty arises from the fact that most logic which suggests a relationship between interest rates and economic activity does not refer to the nominal rates observed in the market but to 'real' rates - nominal rates adjusted for changing expectations of inflation (which cannot be observed nor very reliably measured). Focusing policy on the money supply, instead, seemed to be a way of escaping this problem.

Monetary Targets

Monetary policy seems to have moved informally towards greater emphasis on the monetary aggregates from the early 1970s. Explicit targets were first announced in December 1976 in a letter of intent to the International Monetary Fund associated with the application for a £3.9 billion loan. A list of all subsequent monetary target announcements is shown in Table 1. The first targets were expressed in terms of domestic credit expansion (DCE). (This and

other terms are defined more fully in Table 2.) This is because policy at that time was aimed at rectifying a large deficit on the balance of payments. As the balance of payments swung into surplus on current account, the focus of attention soon switched from DCE to targets for the broadly defined money stock (£M3).

The next major landmark was the announcement of the medium-term financial strategy in the March 1980 Budget. That strategy represented an altogether more sweeping departure from traditional policy making. The importance of the money supply as the ultimate determinant of inflation was accepted. The choice lay between an immediate stop on any increase in money, as advocated by Professor Hayek, and a gentler deceleration, an approach associated with professor Friedman. The latter choice having been made, gradually diminishing rates of increase in the money supply (£M3) were announced at once for four years ahead.

The role of fiscal policy in the strategy was a purely subordinate one. Targets for the PSBR (declining annually as a proportion of GDP) were set so that the burden of achieving the monetary targets

Date announced	Period	Aggregate	Target[a]	Outturn[a]
December 1976	April 1976 – April 1977	DCE	9	4.9
		£M3	9–13	7.7
March 1977	April 1977 – April 1978	£M3	9–13	16.0
April 1978	April 1978 – April 1979	£M3	8–12	10.9
November 1978	October 1978 – October 1979	£M3	8–12	13.3
June 1979	June 1979 – April 1980	£M3	7–11	10.3
November 1979	June 1979 – October 1980	£M3	7–11	17.8
March 1980	February 1980 – April 1981	£M3	7–11	22.2
March 1981	February 1981 – April 1982	£M3	6–10	13.5
March 1982	February 1982 – April 1983	M1	8–12	12.1
		£M3	8–12	10.9
		PSL2	8–12	10.8
March 1983	February 1983 – April 1984	M1	7–11	13.5
		£M3	7–11	9.5
		PSL2	7–11	13.2
March 1984	February 1984 – April 1985	M0	4–8	–
		£M3	6–10	–

Note: (a) Percentage growth at an annual rate, seasonally adjusted (save for DCE, £billion at an annual rate).

Table 1: Monetary Targets and Actual Outturns

should not rest on high interest rates. Although fluctuations around the PSBR path were to be tolerated in the light of variations in economic activity, 'there would be no question of departing from the money supply policy'.

The strategy got off to an inauspicious start, the financial targets being exceeded by very large margins in the first year. The actual rate of growth of £M3 was more than twice the target rate (see Table 1). The 1981 Budget reaffirmed the principles behind the original strategy, but raised the projected path for the PSBR; the permitted range of increase for £M3 for the next period remained as it was and was not reduced to claw back the excess of the previous period.

Further adjustments to the strategy were made in the 1982 Budget. The single target for £M3 was replaced by multiple targets for M1, PSL2 and £M3. After another substantial overshoot in 1981/2, the permitted rate of increase in the money supply (on all definitions) was set at 8–12% by contrast with the 7–11% of the 1980 strategy. There were no substantial changes in 1983, but the 1984 Budget dropped PSL2 from the list of designated aggregates and M1 was replaced by the monetary base, M0, as a measure of narrow money.

On a practical level, it has been clear for quite some time that the focus of Bank of England attention has moved away from monetary targets back towards the level of interest rates and the exchange rate. 'Defensive' interest rate changes in responses to changes in world rates have been a prominent feature of monetary policy since late 1981. This reassignment of policy, away from domestic monetary objectives to stabilising the exchange rate, may probably be ascribed in part to an asymmetry in the willingness of the authorities to permit large changes in sterling: while they were prepared, by and large, to tolerate appreciation in 1979 and 1980, there has been concern at times over the past three years that sharp depreciations would worsen inflation.

But, perhaps most fundamentally, the relegation of the role of monetary targets reflects doubts, compounded by the unhappy experiences of the first two years

of the medium-term financial strategy, about the reliability of monetary aggregates as indicators, and their controllability. £M3 grew very rapidly in 1980 and 1981, but other indicators gave contradictory readings. Interest rates were very high for a period of recession (not only in nominal terms but also in relation to inflation) and the narrower aggregates, M0 and M1, were growing much more slowly than prices. Another manifestation that monetary policy was very tight was a chronic over-valuation of the pound. There is little doubt that this was a cause of recession and, more especially, of a calamitous decline in British manufacturing industry. Doubts about the reality of £M3 as an indicator were increased further by a series of 'distortions' to it during this period, including those arising from the ending of exchange controls in October 1979 and the lifting of the 'corset' in June 1981. If circumstances were particularly unkind to the choice of £M3, as the centrepiece of the Government's new strategy, the episode is a warning of a fundamental problem with monetary targets. In a highly sophisticated and evolutionary financial system, to base policy on a particular monetary aggregate is to build upon shifting sand, since the meaning of the aggregate, and its relation to the economic situation, are liable to change. Change occurs because banks and other financial institutions strive to exploit profitable new opportunities and overcome constraints. This problem is by no means confined to broader aggregates. (The reliability of M1 as a measure of transactions balances has been undermined in recent years as interest-bearing sight deposits grow in importance and building societies compete with banks to provide transactions services.) Nor is it confined to this country; similar difficulties have been encountered in the United States.

Evaluation

The arguments that led to the adoption of targets seem much less believable today. First, while the problem of measuring real interest may not have diminished, it has become abundantly clear that measuring the money supply is not straightforward either.

Monetary base (M0)	The total of assets that are, or could potentially be, employed as cash reserves by the banking system. It includes the cash in banks' tills, deposits with the Bank of England (which can be readily converted into till money), and currency in circulation with the public. The last component is by far the largest, accounting for 90% of the total.
Money stock (M1)	The narrow definition of money. It is the sum of notes and coin in circulation (which are circulated in M0) and sterling sight deposits held by domestic residents.
Money stock (£M3)	The broad definition of money. It consists of notes and coin in circulation plus all sterling bank deposits held by the private and public sectors. £M3 equals M1 plus public sector deposits, which are relatively unimportant, 7–day deposits and savings accounts, which are for the most part small savings from the personal sector, and wholesale deposits, which are large deposits by companies and financial institutions.
Private sector liquidity (PSL2)	A broader aggregate still, which includes liquid assets which are relatively close substitutes for bank deposits. PSL2 equals £M3 plus Treasury bills, building society deposits, National savings and certificates of tax deposit.
Domestic credit expansion (DCE)	Ignoring some necessary statistical qualifications, DCE may be regarded as the increase in the money supply plus the balance of payments deficit (or minus the surplus). Thus, a DCE target limits monetary target according to the balance of payments situation. If there is a deficit, the growth in the money supply must be less than the target for DCE, whereas the permissible growth in the money supply is greater than the DCE target if there is a surplus. The introduction of a DCE target means, in effect, that instead of having as its primary objectives high employment or price stability (the consequences for the external balance being secondary), monetary policy is assigned the role of restoring external balance (with effects on domestic objectives being correspondingly relegated).
Public sector borrowing requirement (PSBR)	One definition of the government's budget deficit. (There are several others.) The PSBR is total government expenditure (on goods and services, pensions, interest, etc.) minus total receipts (from taxes, rents, etc.) plus net lending to the private sector. By accounting convention, sales of state-owned assets reduce the PSBR.

Table 2: Explanation of terms

While it is always possible to choose a particular aggregate and measure it, there can be little confidence that the aggregate chosen will remain a consistently good guide to the impact of monetary policy on the economy.

Second, the problems of controlling monetary aggregates were greatly underestimated. As Table 1 shows, the authorities' track record at hitting targets has been poor. To some extent this has been attributable to a lack of total commitment to targets. But it also reflects practical operational problems, arising from the fact that the relationships between fiscal policy and interest rates, the instruments actually under the authorities' control and the monetary aggregates, act in a slow and imprecise way.

Third, the alleged relationship between money and prices has not held up at all well in recent years. If £M3 is the preferred definition, then the most convincing correlation for the 1960s and 1970s is achieved by assuming a substantial time lag, of the order of two years, between money and prices. On this interpretation, the rapid expansion in £M3 during 1972-3, for example, is held responsible for high inflation in 1974–75. However, this leaves the problem of explaining the sharp deceleration in inflation in 1982 and 1983, which also followed rapid growth in £M3. If the relationship between £M3 and the retail price index (RPI) has broken down recently, the opposite seems to be true of the relationship between M1 and the RPI. The slowdown in M1 growth of 1978-81 anticipates the falling rate of inflation from 1980 onwards, just as some would predict; but this relationship is much less clear in the 1960s and early 1970s.

Last, but by no means least, the case for fixed monetary rules rests on the belief that the economic system will, if left to itself, produce tolerably high levels of activity and employment. Experience, first of recession and then of unemployment materially greater than at any time since the 1930s, shows the economy to be much less stable than the monetarists have pictured it.

The present status of money aggregates is really that of indicators, not binding constraints or firm targets of policy. That is to say, they may be thought at times to convey information about the ease or tightness of financial conditions in the economy and, depending on other considerations such as the strength of sterling or the level of interest rates, they may exercise some influence on policy. But there is no presumption that the authorities would, as a matter of course, take action to prevent a breach of one or more of the target ranges.

If monetary targets are not a very active influence on the day-to-day conduct of monetary policy, they are of undoubted importance as a symbol of the Government's resolve to contain inflation. In discussion of inflation during the 1950s and 1960s it was often argued that workers pressed for higher money wages, and businesses felt free to pass on the increased costs in the form of price increases because the government was committed to maintain the money demand necessary to avoid unemployment. It has been suggested by some that by showing that the government is not prepared to underwrite inflation in this way, publicly announced monetary targets have an important educational function and the threat they pose to unemployment will, of itself, modify the inflationary bias in wage bargaining. Viewed in this way, monetary targets are the latest in a series of attempts (through persuasion, exhortation, forms of incomes policy) to resolve the conflict between the objectives of high unemployment and low inflation by disciplining the attitudes and expectations that carry the rise in wages and prices on even in the presence of unemployment.

David Savage works at the National Institute of Economic and Social Research and is currently Editor of the National Institute Economic Review. His principal areas of expertise are monetary theory and macroeconomic policy.

Macroeconomic Policy since 1979

RESOURCE 8.3 ◁

Wickens, M (1988)
The Economic
Review, vol. 5, no 5,
May , pp. 2–5,
Phillip Allan
Publisher.

The present government claims to have been responsible for a dramatic improvement in the UK economy since 1979, whilst its political opponents claim that the government's policy has caused an equally dramatic deterioration. This article reviews macroeconomic developments in the economy since 1979 and discusses both the policies adopted and the theories underlying them.

The Conservative government of Mrs Thatcher was first elected in May 1979, and was re-elected in June 1983 and June 1987. Before taking office, the Conservatives' diagnosis of the economy was that Britain was the 'sick man of Europe' with low economic growth, high inflation, a strike-prone labour force and a population who looked increasingly to the state for the provision of services. Government policy since 1979 has aimed at changing all of this. In 1988, and for the last few years, economic growth has been comparable with the high rates of the 1950s, inflation has been low, the number of strikes has decreased, the basic rate of taxation is lower and the proportion of National Income borrowed by the government has fallen. As

a result the Prime Minister and the Chancellor of the Exchequer have been offering advice to other countries on how they can achieve the 'British miracle'. Even the other political parties have taken note, and at the last election it was clear that the differences between their macroeconomic policies and those of the Conservatives had narrowed.

Despite its apparent success, the government has been heavily criticised for poor management of the economy from the moment they first announced their policies. In the early 1980s when inflation reached 24% for a time, GDP was falling and unemployment was rising rapidly, criticism was strident and widespread. Today critics point to a high level of unemployment, especially in the regions, and to concerns about the level of expenditures on public services such as education and the health service.

Who is right? Is the government justified in claiming that it is government policies which have brought about the economic successes? Are their critics correct in blaming government policy for the present high level of unemployment and

	GDP at factor cost	Consumer expenditure	General government consumption expenditure	Private sector fixed capital formation	Public sector fixed capital formation	Changes in stocks	Exports of goods and services	Imports of goods and services	Balance of trade
1977	193.9	124.9	46.2	–	–	2.6	59.6	52.2	7.4
1978	199.5 (5.6)	131.7 (6.8)	47.2 (1.0)	29.2	13.5	2.2 (-0.4)	60.7 (1.1)	54.2 (2.0)	6.5 (-0.9)
1979	203.8 (4.3)	137.6 (5.9)	48.2 (1.0)	30.4 (1.2)	13.2 (-0.3)	2.5 (0.3)	63.2 (1.5)	59.9 (5.7)	3.3 (-3.2)
1980	199.6 (-4.2)	137.2 (-0.4)	49.0 (0.8)	29.6 (-0.8)	12.2 (-1.0)	-2.8 (-5.3)	63.1 (-0.1)	57.9 (-2.0)	5.2 (1.9)
1981	197.5 (-2.1)	136.9 (-0.3)	49.0 (0)	27.7 (-1.9)	10.1 (-2.1)	-2.5 (0.3)	62.7 (-0.4)	56.4 (-1.5)	6.3 (1.1)
1982	199.4 (1.9)	138.2 (1.3)	49.6 (0.6)	29.5 (1.8)	9.9 (-0.2)	-1.1 (1.4)	63.2 (0.5)	59.5 (3.1)	3.7 (-2.6)
1983	207.1 (7.7)	143.8 (5.6)	50.5 (0.9)	29.9 (0.4)	11.8 (1.9)	0.7 (1.8)	64.7 (1.5)	62.8 (3.3)	1.9 (-1.8)
1984	210.9 (3.8)	146.9 (3.1)	50.9 (0.4)	33.7 (3.8)	11.8 (0)	-0.1 (-0.8)	69.0 (4.3)	68.5 (5.7)	0.5 (-1.4)
1985	219.0 (8.1)	152.0 (5.1)	51.1 (0.2)	36.1 (2.4)	10.2 (-1.6)	0.6 (0.7)	73.3 (4.3)	70.6 (2.1)	2.7 (2.2)
1986	223.4 (4.4)	159.2 (7.2)	51.6 (0.5)	36.2 (0.1)	10.4 (0.2)	0.6 (0)	75.3 (2.0)	74.8 (4.2)	0.5 (-2.2)

Note: Figures in parentheses are changes from previous year.
Table 1: Expenditure on Gross domestic product (£bn, 1980 prices)
Source:Data Supplement

for the recession of 1980/1? Or are factors outside government control responsible both for the apparent successes and the apparent failures? In this article I shall review the main macroeconomic developments of the UK economy and government macroeconomic policy since 1979. I shall outline the macroeconomic theories that underlie the government's policies, and comment on how well these theories conform to our experience since 1979. I shall attempt to determine to what extent government policy has had any influence on events and how events have shaped policy. I shall *not* discuss the merits of the government's choice of policy priorities, but take them as given. The main macroeconomic objective has clearly been the control of inflation. In a clear break with the postwar Keynesian tradition, the government has argued that the unemployment rate is determined by market forces and cannot be controlled by government.

Some Basic Statistics

The key macroeconomic statistics for the period 1977-86 are set out in tables 1 and 2. In 1978, before the Conservatives took office, the growth rate of real GDP was 2.8%, inflation as measured by the GDP deflator was 12%, unemployment was 5.1%, government expenditure on goods, services and investment was 30% of GDP, government borrowing was 5.7% of GDP and there was a very small current account surplus. Apart from the inflation rate, 1978 was clearly a good year for the economy. By 1981, after over two years in office, the growth rate was −1.0% (real GDP was lower than in 1978), the inflation rate was 10% (having been 19% in 1980), unemployment was 9% and rising, the current account was in surplus and the real exchange rate was 19% higher than in 1978, implying a loss in competitiveness. In 1986, the most recent year for which complete National Income accounts are available, the growth rate of real GDP was 2.0%, inflation was 3%, unemployment was 11.6%, government expenditure was 28% of GDP, government borrowing was 0.7% of GDP, the current account was marginally in deficit and the real exchange rate was 13% lower than in 1981 and 3.5% higher than in 1978. In 1987 both the growth rate and inflation rate increased slightly, and by December 1987 the unemployment rate fell to 9.4%.

A preliminary conclusion for the period as a whole is that, with growth, government expenditure, the current account and competitiveness similar in 1986/7 to their 1978 values, the principal successes of the

	Growth of M0 (%)	Growth of M3 (%)	Inflation rate* (%)	Short-term interest rate** (%)	Long-term interest rate*** (%)	PSBR as % of GDP (%)	Effective exchange rate (1980 = 100)	Real exchange rate (1980 =100)	Unemployment rate (%)
1977	10.9	9	12	6.4	12.7	4.2	84	80	5.2
1978	15.4	15	12	11.9	12.5	5.7	85	85	5.1
1979	13.6	13	13	16.5	13.0	7.4	91	90	4.6
1980	4.1	20	19	13.6	13.8	5.9	100	100	5.6
1981	2.6	14	10	15.4	14.7	4.9	99	101	9.0
1982	3.5	9	7	10.0	12.9	2.1	95	98	10.4
1983	6.0	11	6	9.0	10.8	4.5	86	91	11.2
1984	5.8	10	5	9.3	10.4	3.7	82	88	11.2
1985	4.2	13	6	11.5	10.6	2.5	83	90	11.5
1986	5.4	19	3	10.9	9.9	0.7	76	88	11.6

Note: *GDP deflator
     **Treasury Bill rate
     ***Gilts rate

Table 2: Selected Economic Indicators
Source: Data Supplement

government have been a threefold cut in the inflation rate and the achievement of a balanced budget. The main cost of these successes has been a doubling of the rate of unemployment. Due to increases in labour productivity the rise in unemployment has not been fully reflected in a loss of output (real GDP), which has risen by 18% since 1978, though arguably output might have been even higher if unemployment had been less.

The Basis of the Government's Policy

The theoretical underpinnings of the government's early position were provided by monetarism. According to monetarism, inflation is caused by excessive money growth. To reduce inflation it is necessary (and sufficient) to decrease the rate of growth of the money supply. This is expected to raise the rate of unemployment and to reduce output temporarily. The quicker the public revises its expectations about inflation, the less will be the cost in terms of higher unemployment and lost output. Monetarism also claims that neither monetary nor fiscal policy has any effect on unemployment or output except in the very short term. Thus, monetary policy should be aimed at the control of inflation and fiscal policy should be constrained by the need to balance the budget. By setting clearly defined targets for the rate of growth of the money supply and attaining them, the public will believe in the anti-inflation policy and will rapidly adjust their expectations of inflation. In this way the unemployment and output costs of reducing inflation will be kept to a minimum.

All of Sir Geoffrey Howe's Budget speeches reflect these monetarist tenets. Nor was he alone in being under the influence of monetarism. A large number of the industrialised countries were pursuing similar policies. Even the previous Labour government was not completely immune, for when it asked for assistance from the IMF in 1976 this was given on condition that stricter monetary policies were followed.

Did Monetarism Work?

Can monetarism explain the behaviour of inflation since 1978 and does it provide a viable basis for policy? In Table 2 the inflation rate and the rate of growth of M3 (the measure of money supply initially favoured by the government) are reported. According to the theory, there will be a one- to two-year lag in the response of inflation to a change in the supply of money. If expectations are revised quickly this will be reduced. The data reveal no obvious lag. Up to 1982 there is a strong correlation between inflation and the rate of growth of M3, but after 1982 the two move in opposite directions. If monetarism is to be believed, the very high rate of growth of M3 in 1986 should have caused substantial inflation in 1986 or 1987, but it didn't.

Even if there were a well-defined connection between inflation and monetary growth there remains the problem of controlling the money supply. This proved to be virtually impossible and undermined the credibility of the government's monetary policy. Different measures of money have been targeted, such as narrow money M0 and broad money such as M3, but all without success. (For discussion of the measurement of monetary aggregates, see the article by Michael McCrostie in this issue of *The Economic Review*.) One reason is that the public alters its holding of one type of money compared with another depending on their relative rates of return. M3 includes interest-bearing deposits. As the interest rate on deposits increases relative to other assets, more of these deposits will be held and non-interest-bearing deposits will be less attractive. Table 2 shows that nominal interest rates have remained high over the period 1984-6 even though inflation has fallen, while real interest rates have been high since 1983. This may have helped reduce M0 and increase M3. Provided the public continues to maintain its balances and not spend them, inflation will not occur. If there are signs that the public wishes to reduce M3, possibly because interest rates have fallen, the growth of the money supply may need to be slowed to avoid inflation.

It has been argued that evidence in support of the claim that inflation is caused by monetary growth simply reflects the fact that the higher the price level the greater is the transactions demand for money, thereby reversing the direction of causation. Assuming that M0 is largely transactions balances, this counter-argument suggests that increases in the price level should either precede or be contemporaneous with increases in M0. The evidence of Table 2 offers support for this view since the growth in M0 and the inflation rate are highly correlated.

To sum up so far, since taking office the government's main priority has been to reduce the rate of inflation by controlling the rate of growth of the money supply in accordance with monetarist principles. But while inflation has decreased, the growth rate of M3 has not. Thus, whatever the cause of the fall in inflation, it seems that it is not entirely due to the government's original policy. Partly as a result of the failure of the link between M3 and inflation, and partly to avoid the embarrassment of consistently missing its monetary targets, around 1985 the government altered its views on the conduct of monetary policy.

The Recession of 1980-1

The basic facts of this recession were set out above. Let us examine 1980 in more detail. In Table 1 the changes in real GDP and its main components are reported. GDP fell by £4.2 billion, or by 2.1%, compared with 1979. The main component of GDP to fall was changes in stocks (or inventories) which was £5.3 billion less in 1980 than in 1979. There was also a fall in both private and public sector investment. Government expenditure on other goods and services actually rose, and the trade account was in surplus due to a fall in imports which was brought about by the recession. It would appear therefore that the recession was not caused by fiscal policy, though clearly the cut in government investment did not help. Nor was monetary policy tight in 1980 despite the high inflation rate, for the real stock of money stayed approximately constant, as shown in Table 2.

If the recession was not caused by either fiscal or monetary policy, what was the cause? The principal exogenous influence on the UK economy in the period 1979-81

was the doubling of the price of oil in 1979. This had several repercussions. First, and most obvious, domestic production costs rose sharply, and these increased costs were passed on as higher prices, thereby adding to the inflationary pressure already being exerted by rising wage rates. This increase in costs partly accounts for industry wishing to run down its inventories.

Second, by 1979 the UK had become a major exporter of oil, so that the price rise acted to increase oil export revenues even though the quantity of oil exports fell. The increase in oil revenues was an important factor in the 19% appreciation of sterling referred to earlier. This loss of competitiveness further reduced the demand for UK goods and helped bring about the fall in both inventories and manufacturing output. In fact, manufacturing output fell by 17% from the date of the oil price rise in 1979 to the end of 1981.

Initially, faced with cost increases and reduced competitiveness, firms tried to ride out the storm by borrowing, thus adding to the demand for money. As we have seen, monetary policy was accommodating, with M3 growing at the same rate as prices, so this increased demand was satisfied. But towards the end of 1981, the government reassumed its anti-inflationary stance and tightened monetary policy. This, together with the pressure on demand arising from the extra borrowing, caused real interest rates to rise sharply. Firms were therefore forced to cut output and lay off workers, with the result that unemployment jumped by 3.4% from 1980 to 1981.

We can therefore sum up the cause of the 1980/1 recession and the role of the government's policies as follows. The recession was due primarily to the oil price increase rather than to government policy. Private sector inventories fell sharply, partly in response to the oil price rise and partly as a result of gloomy anticipations of future demand – without this, arguably, the recession might have been avoided. The increase in the oil price raised the general price level. In 1980 monetary policy was accommodating. This helped firms' short-term finances and kept unemployment from rising. No doubt remembering 1974, when after the first oil price shock inflation briefly reached around 40%, in 1981 the government reverted to its previously announced anti-inflationary stance and tightened monetary policy considerably. This caused an increase in borrowing costs and in unemployment. Thereafter the government continued to pursue its policies of reducing inflation and cutting the budget deficit, whilst reiterating its belief that it couldn't affect the unemployment rate.

Schools Brief: A cruise around the Phillips curve

RESOURCE 9.1 ◁

The Economist,
London, 1994.

One of the most important questions in applied economics is whether governments can reduce unemployment by tolerating a higher rate of inflation. This week's brief on labour-market economics looks at a controversy that is nearly 40 years old.

In 1958 Bill Phillips, a New Zealand economist, published "The Relation Between Unemployment and the Rate of Change of Money Wages in the United Kingdom, 1861–1957."

This paper secured its author's immortality. Phillips had spotted a striking regularity: there appeared to be a stable trade-off between inflation and unemployment – the more you had of the one, the less you had of the other.

For Britain, during the long period Phillips studied, an unemployment rate of about 2.5% was associated with a rise in wages of about 2% each year. Allowing for productivity growth, that was roughly consistent with stable prices. By and large, higher rates of unemployment were observed when prices were falling; lower rates were observed when prices were rising. The lower the rate of joblessness, the higher the rate of inflation.

Figure 1 plots inflation (looking directly at prices, not wages) and unemployment in America during the 1960s. The points fall on a fairly neat, downward-sloping line. Here too the "Phillips curve" seems to work. And its implication is clear: governments can cut unemployment by tolerating a higher rate of inflation. It follows that the challenge for macroeconomic policy is to strike the right balance between those two evils.

Governments may disagree about how to do so, according to moral and political judgments about which parts of society should carry how much of a burden. But as far as the economics is concerned, the choice that lies before policymakers is fairly straightforward.

Think again

Until the end of the 1960s, few would have disagreed with this view. That changed because the simple Phillips curve faced two separate, but equally withering, attacks: one from economic theory, the other from the real world. The theoretical attack was all the more impressive because it came first – at a time when the statistics appeared to say that the Phillips curve still worked. In 1968, in separate articles, Milton Friedman and Edmund Phelps pointed out that the theory underlying the Phillips curve made no sense. The crucial point is that it is real wages, not money wages, that matter both to workers and to employers.

Suppose that inflation – in both prices and wages – rises by five percentage points. Instead of going up to 5% this year, prices rise by 10%; instead of going up by 7% this year, wages rise by 12%. In real terms, however, nothing whatever is different. The real wage is the same as it would have been otherwise. The demand for labour and the supply of labour both depend on real wages, not money wages, so they too will be the same. That being so, there is no reason to expect the level of employment to change. The Phillips curve cannot be right.

But there is a complication. This fixity of real wages and employment is the position "in equilibrium" a term which, in

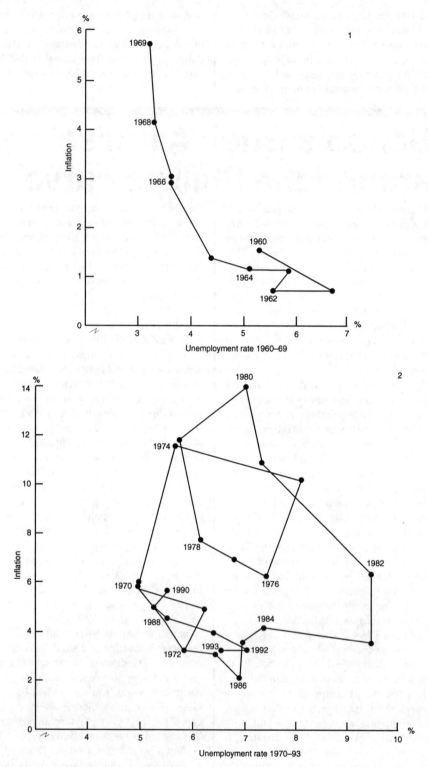

Figures 1 and 2: The vanishing Phillips curve American unemployment against inflation, annual averages

this branch of economics, means "when workers' expectations about inflation turn out to be correct". For instance, if prices are stable year after year, and workers expect them to carry on being stable, those expectations will keep on being right. That is an equilibrium. If prices rise reliably by 10% year after year, and are expected to continue doing so, that too is an equilibrium. In both cases, prices and other money-denominated things (eg, money wages) are changing, but real things (eg, real wages and employment) aren't. So unemployment will be no lower than in the zero-inflation case. In equilibrium, unemployment is the same, regardless of inflation.

However, as Messrs Friedman and Phelps accepted, in moving from one equilibrium to another the Phillips-curve relationship can be briefly true. Suppose prices rise unexpectedly – and, in the first instance, wages do not. In other words, wages fall in real terms. The demand for labour will rise. Further suppose that workers, whose expectations are in a twist, are slow to realise that their wages have fallen in real terms – that is, they suffer from "money illusion". They will not reduce their supply of labour. As a result, the increase in the demand for labour will cause employment to expand. More workers will have jobs than before, but they will be paid less in real terms.

In this way, an unexpected rise in inflation can cut unemployment. But consider what happens if inflation now holds steady at its new, higher rate. Workers realise that their wages have fallen in real terms. They bid for higher pay, to catch up. And as they succeed, and real wages return to their initial level, the demand for labour falls back, likewise to its initial level. Once the money illusion has dissipated – once the economy is back in "equilibrium" – everything "real" (notably real wages and employment) is as before. Only the rate of inflation is different: it is permanently higher.

The Friedman-Phelps critique looked watertight. Almost before other economists had finished thinking it through, conclusive evidence in support of it began to arrive.

Figure 2 extends the inflation and unemployment figures of Figure 1 into the 1970s and 1980s. Unemployment is anything but constant: it moves around a lot. So does inflation. But Figure 2 looks nothing like Figure 1. Inflation and unemployment, the two great evils, are no longer linked in such a way as to suggest an exploitable trade-off.

Why did the Phillips curve work so well in earlier years? The most likely answer is that the relationship was an accident that depended on special circumstances prevailing before the 1970s. Inflation was low and relatively stable; expectations of future inflation were similar. After 1970 inflation in America and other industrial countries became more volatile – and much higher on average than before. Expectations were subject to frequent shocks. In this new world, the appearance of a stable relationship between inflation and unemployment vanished.

Go forth and multiply

The simple Phillips curve may be dead – but its offspring are thriving. Today, thanks to Messrs Friedman and Phelps, economists talk not of one curve, but two: the short-run Phillips curve and the long-run Phillips curve – and both are, in the jargon, "expectations augmented". The analysis that follows is one which almost all mainstream economists would nowadays accept.

Figure 3 shows a short-run Phillips curve and a long-run curve. Suppose the economy starts at a point such as A, with unemployment of U_1 and an inflation rate of P_1. Next suppose that the government pushes up the inflation rate to P_2. In the short run, unemployment falls, to U_2; the economy moves to point B on the short-run Phillips curve. Gradually, however, expectations adjust, the economy moves back towards equilibrium, and unemployment starts to rise again. The economy moves to point C, on the long-run Phillips curve. Inflation is still P_2 but no unemployment has risen to U_3.

When expectations have adjusted fully and the economy is back in equilibrium, the long-run Phillips curve is actually vertical, as shown in Figure 4. With inflation still at P_2, the economy has moved to point D. Unemployment has returned to U_1, leaving the economy unambiguously worse off: as many people are out of work as before, and the inflation rate is higher.

Great expectations

Is there nothing that the government can do to hold unemployment at U_2 in Figure 3? Yes there is, at least for a while. It could push the inflation rate higher again – moving the economy to a point like B on a new, higher short-run Phillips curve. Another rise in inflation might be enough, as it were, to offset the process by which expectations catch up to the previous rise.

But even this could not go on for long. Inflation would have to keep rising unexpectedly, so that expectations continued to lag behind and the economy was kept out of equilibrium. This means, in the best case, that lower unemployment would be bought at the price of perpetually accelerating inflation. In the worst case, the short-run curve would snap to the vertical, as workers cottoned on to the government's inflationary approach to job-creation. The economy would endure ever-accelerating inflation without even a temporary gain in jobs.

So when economists (and some, but unfortunately not all, politicians) say that there is no trade-off between inflation and unemployment, this is what they mean – or

should mean. In the long run, regardless of the inflation rate, the economy returns to its underlying rate of unemployment – U_1 in Figures 3 and 4.

This underlying rate goes by a confusing variety of names. An accurate, if horribly inelegant, term is the "non-accelerating-inflation rate of unemployment", or NAIRU for short. Why such a messy bit of jargon? The theory encapsulated in Figures 3 and 4 says that at lower rates of unemployment than U_1, inflation tends to rise. (Note the distinction between rising prices and rising inflation). Similarly, at higher rates of unemployment than U_1, inflation tends to fall. At U_1, inflation may be high or low, but it is stable. Hence, NAIRU.

Other names, a bit easier on the tongue, for this special rate of unemployment are "equilibrium unemployment", the "natural rate of unemployment" and "structural unemployment". The trouble is, all of these may mean slightly different things to different economists.

A further word of caution: some of these labels imply that the NAIRU is somehow preordained, beyond the reach of economic policy. That is wrong. The Friedman-Phelps view of unemployment says merely that policies intended to raise inflation will cause no lasting reduction in unemployment. But the NAIRU is itself an economic variable, not an unalterable constant.

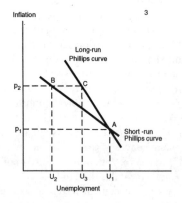 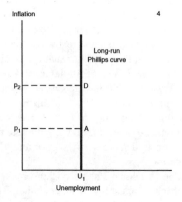

Figures 3 and 4: There is no alternative

Economies with unduly generous unemployment benefits, misguided minimum-wage rules, poor education and training, obstacles to labour mobility (which may in turn be caused by such things as ill-designed pension schemes, disincentives to the supply of rented housing or lack of information for job-seekers) are likely to have a higher NAIRU than they need to.

A gross, but not uncommon, caricature of the Friedman-Phelps approach is to say that nothing can be done about unemployment. Much can be done, on their view – but governments should concentrate on measures to improve the flexibility of the labour market rather than on traditional reflationary cures. The emphasis, in other words, should be on microeconomic not macroeconomic policy.

A different trade-off

However, a big macroeconomic issue remains. It is possible to look at Figures 3 and 4 in another way – and if you do, another sort of trade-off between inflation and unemployment appears. Instead of asking whether the unemployment rate can be permanently reduced by governments accepting a higher rate of inflation (the charts say it cannot), ask how much of a temporary rise in unemployment is necessary to bring down inflation.

Figure 4 shows that, in the long run, inflation can be brought down from P_2 to P_1 with no rise in unemployment. But Figure 3 shows that, in the short run, reducing inflation for P_2 to P_1 would require a temporary rise in unemployment, equivalent to the difference between U_2 and U_1. Suppose Britain's NAIRU is 7%. It might be worth two years of unemployment at 10% (ie, six point-years of "excess" unemployment) to reduce inflation from 15% to 5%. But would it be worth that price to reduce inflation from 5% to 0%?

Clearly, a great deal turns on the relevant parameters. One question is whether any given cut in inflation is harder to achieve when inflation is already low. another is the amount of excess unemployment needed to bring inflation down to any given extent: the ratio between these two things is for obvious reasons called "the sacrifice ratio". Its value will vary from country to country, and according to circumstances.

For instance, between 1980 and 1984, under the influence of tight monetary policy, America's inflation rate fell from more than 10% to just over 3% – that is, by seven percentage points. How much employment had to be sacrificed? In the 1980s America's NAIRU was generally estimated to be about 6%. Adding up, year by year, the amounts by which the unemployment rate exceeded 6% during 1980–84, you get a figure of roughly 11 percentage points. The implied sacrifice-ratio is therefore 11 divided by seven: say 1.5. Every (permanent) fall of one percentage point in inflation requires 1.5 point-years of excess unemployment (eg, one year of unemployment 1.5 percentage points in excess of the NAIRU).

Needless to say, it is not for economists to judge whether this is a price worth paying. That is a political choice. However, economists can point out something else that is extremely important. Like the NAIRU itself, the sacrifice ratio can be influenced by economic policy. As can be seen in Figures 3 and 4, the sacrifice ratio is closely connected to the slope of the short-run Phillips curve. The steeper the curve, the smaller the (temporary) rise in unemployment needed to bring inflation down. What would make the curve steeper? Remembering the importance of expectations in the derivation of the Phillips curves, one answer is an increase in the credibility of government policy.

Suppose a government announced that it would reduce inflation from 10% to 5% over the coming year. If this promise was fully believed by firms and workers, it could be kept without any rise whatever in unemployment – because the conditions for the "equilibrium" shown in Figure 4 would be met. If the government is not believed, some temporary rise in unemployment will be the price of getting inflation down – and the lower the government's credibility, the higher the price will be.

It is not for nothing that economists now regard credibility as one of the most valuable assets an economic policy-maker can possess. The debate begun by Bill Phillips has lasted 36 years; of the economic insights that have emerged so far, this may be the most important. Aptly enough, it is one that Phillips would not have expected.